LANDSCAPES IN THE CITY

MADRID RÍO: GEOGRAPHY, INFRASTRUCTURE, AND PUBLIC SPACE

FRANCISCO BURGOS
GINÉS GARRIDO
FERNANDO PORRAS-ISLA, EDITORS

TURNER

INDEX

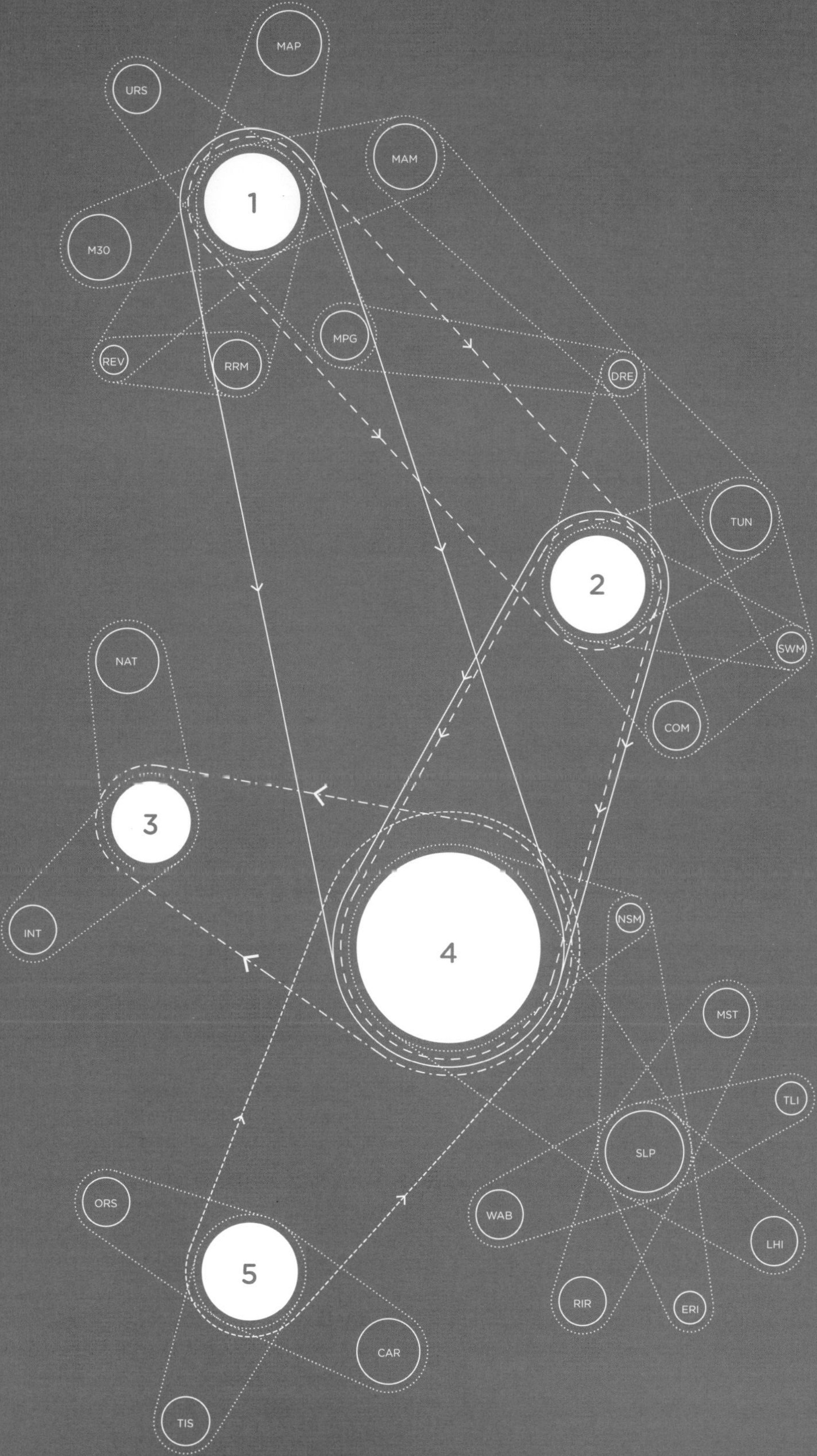

DIAGRAMMATIC INDEX ······ LINK TO CHAPTER/SUBCHAPTER —→ ANTECEDENTS ⟶ ANALYSIS ·-→ MESSAGE - - -→ CORPUS

PREFACE

Scale

If a project conceived for an urban environment affects a surface surpassing the local dimensions of a neighborhood or district, it can be used to generate a new entity capable of modifying relations among the city's component parts. When an action affecting consolidated urban fabric acquires large-scale proportions, its character ceases to be contingent and becomes, instead, a structure that transforms the territory on which it acts. Magnitude is a quality that can single-handedly activate the structural function of an urban element.

Continuity

A strategic operation is instituted as a fundamental structural element for the city when its characteristic principles include the capacity to join innumerable settings through new connections and, in that sense, to establish ties and facilitate itineraries that were previously inexistent. Effective spatial continuity among previously unconnected pieces articulates the morphology of the city as the elements that make this possible become parts of its skeleton.

Erasing the marks

The degree to which any connective structure will take root in the city depends on how close it is to the natural reminiscences that gave rise to its marks, even before the city itself existed. Often, geological features not easily hidden support the silhouette of certain lasting green components, establishing them as parts of an underlying structure. But sometimes, these marks are practically erased because they can easily be replaced by roadways that follow their layout and are thus established over previous natural trajectories, invading them with a constant flow of vehicles.

Closed infrastructures

A powerful communications element, main artery ,or junction generally takes the form of a compact and mono-functional setting. That is the case with major railbeds or highways running through a territory. It is possible to very effectively transit these closed infrastructures, but while their specialized design facilitates linear velocity, it makes them extremely difficult to cross, by minimizing or even annulling lateral transit. Thus, these violent infrastructures act simultaneously as longitudinal connectors and transversal separators.

Revealed traces

The elimination of natural features that mark urban territories to some degree is a phenomenon that has spread to a multitude of cities on all continents. In the 20th century, green areas that had resisted passing time without disappearing were buried under vehicular connecting systems. Now, however, some of the denaturing operations imposed in the recent past are being reversed, so that impenetrable and divisive roadways begin to disappear or are rerouted underground — often at considerable expense — generating new areas of opportunity. Without losing their condition as fundamental and connective infrastructure, these areas take on a new potential that can include a character linked to beneficial environmental values.

The following pages offer an extensive description of just such a process where, between 2004 and 2007, scale, continuity, and respect for natural features made it possible to build a new urban installation over Madrid's underground beltway that is both permeable and open. This new setting, a replica of the recently disappeared infrastructure, recovers its status as a green connection whose construction captures nature. This is an eminently architectural process whose spatial construction takes the form of a constant reaction to the artificial urban context on which it operates. Neither natural nor evocative, the transformation of this landscape is specifically linked to the urban setting, that is, to surroundings profoundly altered — fabricated — by constant human activity.

In this work, the term *landscape* does not refer to the recreation of sight in the presence of nature, nor to the construction of an atmosphere that seeks to rescue it. Here, the word is not intended to remind us of the earliest attempts by German and Dutch painters to reconstruct their own interpretations of territorial analysis on canvas — the early 16th-century *landskip* or *landschaft* — or of those who defend projects dealing with our natural surroundings as a fully relevant discipline. Here, landscape is an operating table, a laboratory capsule, a careful and prolonged observation of the city, an interpretation of its vectors, and therefore, an artificial construct that reunites the fabric of an urban infrastructure. The latter, with one function or another, has always been in the same place but, on the playing field, the primary working element has been vegetation: natural, though imported, materials are employed to generate a huge artifice.

This book is presented as a panorama of visual planes laid out in total continuity with the architectural project and its implementation, like the final link in a single sequence. Its pages successively join back, middle, and foregrounds for the viewer's contemplation. The backgrounds are concentrated toward the beginning to describe the geography and major networks that make it possible to understand the accumulation of physical and temporal events along the Manzanares River's passage through the city of Madrid. The middle grounds occupy the book's central pages, where they appear as infrastructural landscapes belonging to the narrative spun by the river's flow. Finally, the most immediate foregrounds occupy the last pages, where they convey the rules and systems that shape the processes and techniques needed to carry out the work.

This panorama is not selective. Instead, it deliberately includes everything that has actually been done, whether photogenic or not, and without regard for the ultimate success of each as an object. The result is a high-resolution still image, free of arrogance, and that hides nothing. The long view offers an understanding of the project's strategic lines; the close-ups reveal all constituent elements, and their final formal resolution is nowhere near as important as the fact that they belong to a complete syntax. As such, each is only relevant as part of an all-encompassing system, as inseparable components that help to make up the urban installation open to all-inclusive gazes. Thus, this document should become a book-landscape or a landscape-book that represents a constructed proposal, but that also maps data and welcomes an open interpretation of a solid and essentially artificial urban structure built with fragments of nature.

THE EDITORS

MOTHER MADRID
LUIS FERNÁNDEZ-GALIANO

The city of Madrid owes its name and origin to water. Madrid Río project furnishes both recreational uses and a sense of identity. The new Manzanares River Park, which stretches over an underground highway, regenerates the riverside and helps rehabilitate the surrounding popular neighborhoods. It also restores the relationship between the original city center and the fertile valley and farmlands at its feet, recovering views of what has now become a monumental ridge. Moreover, it completes the green corridor that restores the city's relation with its territory. As built, it is a linear park six kilometers long flanked by dense masses of residential buildings, guaranteeing the intensive use that has been manifest ever since it opened. This contrasts with other major parks located on less-accessible and barely visited outskirts, assuring the social usefulness of the undertaking. But Madrid Río is also a symbolic project that reveals the city's relation to its origins and territory, both of which involve water.

Established on a terrace above the Manzanares River, the human settlement that started as a Visigothic *vicus* in the 7th century became a Muslim fortress in the 9th century, taking advantage of its strategic placement between two plateaus as part of the outlying defenses protecting Toledo. Its singularity stemmed from two aspects linked to water: first, it was easy to defend because it was surrounded on three sides by its river and the cliffs generated by two tributaries that later came to be known as Arenal and San Pedro; and second, it had available drinking water in the form of springs and wells, and later through horizontal galleries parallel to the vein of sand permeable to phreatic flows known as *viajes de agua* (water trails). This was important for everyday use and essential in the case of prolonged siege. Water's seminal importance is reflected in the city's name, which philologists derive from the Latin term *matricem,* here meaning mother of water, which led to *matric* in the Andalusian romance language and *magrit* in Andalusian Arabic. So Madrid would be the mother of waters, meaning a place with abundant water. By recovering that element's presence, the Madrid Río project emphasizes both the abruptly defensive topography of the original city center that stood some 60 meters above the Manzanares riverbed, and the city's link to water from the springs and fountains that give birth to its streams, to the meadows alongside the riverbanks that witnessed religious and profane celebrations, or the canals running alongside the river, where a multitude of washerwomen saw to the city's needs.

Water is also the leading element in the city's relations with the surrounding territory. In fact, this linear park is but a fragment of a series of green spaces running through the Manzanares basin from the river's birth in the Guadarrama Mountains to its mouth at the Jarama. By linking the Monte del Pardo with the Casa de Campo and the Campo del Moro, Arganzuela Park and the nature reserves running along the lower end of the river, the project improves access to an environmental corridor dotted with historic gardens while simultaneously drawing the citizenry's attention to Madrid's location in a geographic setting whose principal feature is the river running from the Sierra to the fertile farmlands below. This broader setting also explains the exceptional quality of the water supplied to Madrid's inhabitants by the Canal de Isabel II, a colossal work of hydraulic engineering whose nature hides the origin of the water we drink. In fact, its purity is due to the proximity of mountain springs — something we are only aware of when projects such as Madrid Río draw our attention to this city's relationship with the territory from which it extracts the hydric resources that make it viable.

The Manzanares's diminished flow and prolonged summer state have always been the subject of irony among inhabitants of the city which became home to Spain's royal court and capital under Philip II four-and-a-half centuries ago. From Quevedo's "Manzanares, Manzanares, stream learning to be a river" to Tirso de Molina, who likened it to a university because it was on "vacation in the summer and only ran in the winter," Madrid's river has always been the butt of jokes by those who consider it unworthy of a major city, most of which are located on the coast or along a respectable river capable of providing a transportation route for cargo and passengers. While the city of Madrid lacks these advantages, it can boast of proximity to major nature reserves, from the snowy sierra to the orchards of Aranjuez, that enter the city physically and symbolically through Madrid Río, a metropolitan park that is simultaneously the link that completes this geographic chain of rugged or agreeable places tying the city to the territory that supports it. Our apprentice river is a professor of ecology, and if we have long turned our back to it, using it as a sewer or the shoulder of a highway, the regeneration it has recently undergone rehabilitates it as the geographic basis underlying the city's historical origins.

Nature and history are joined in the sequence of landscapes that make up this project conditioned by its edges and successes, but also inventively imagined as a collection of episodes that offer variety along its length by interpreting its different sections in a pedagogical way. These include what the authors call the Salón de Pinos, a long walk along the narrow right bank marked by the area around two historical bridges – the Renaissance Puente de Segovia, built by Juan de Herrera in 1582. and the baroque Toledo Bridge erected by Pedro de Ribera in 1732. The second area includes the Explanada del Rey, a platform linking the gardens of the Royal Palace with the Casa de Campo and offering exceptional views of the historic bridge. It extends to the recovered Huerta de la Partida, the boulevard of the Avenida de Portugal and the Virgen del Puerto Gardens. Finally, there is the Arganzuela Park, where the river corridor expands to form the project's largest landscaped area which consists of three botanical areas (Mediterranean forest, Atlantic forest, and riverside foliage) and sports areas, along with the vast municipal slaughterhouse complex, which was built a century ago and has now been successfully renovated for cultural uses under the name Matadero Madrid.

Of course the intelligent interpretation of each setting involves shaping the topography and vegetation, as well as a palette of materials for paving, steps, and benches and for the numerous auxiliary structures required for ventilation and emergency exits for the tunnels bearing vehicular traffic beneath the park. Concrete and basalt, and especially granite appear there, and the latter is roughed to form vertical walls that accentuate the naturalistic design of a landscape that is, in fact, eminently artificial in its construction over a major infrastructure with multiple technical and safety requirements. Indeed, its arduous negotiations with the tunnels' engineering has become one of the project's principal merits, as its relationship to the burial of the M-30 ring road goes practically unnoticed in the end result: a large park filled with bicycles and people, where plant life, ponds and singular playgrounds lead us to forget the numerous technical elements present on its surface.

Connections between the two banks are significantly improved by the set of bridges and pedestrian walkways over the river, which also display an agreeable variety of solutions to match its diverse contexts – from the carbon-fiber Almuñécar walkway or the very laconic Princesa one, whose web railings give it structural strength, to the twin bridges across from Matadero, which are constructed with a sheet of warped concrete that bears their suspended slabs, or the singular "Y" bridge, a historicist tribute to 19th century railway trellises. These are complemented by the restored walkways on the existing dams and the remodeling of the Oblique Bridge across the former route of the M-30 ring road. Together, they reinforce the project's social dimension. Madrid Río is a longitudinal corridor that connects the city to its territory, but it is also a transversal element that links privileged areas on the heights of the ridge with popular neighborhoods on the river's right bank, where what was once a defensive barrier had become a clear-cut social divide. With this park, Madrid, the mother of waters, recovers its fluvial geography. At the same time, it expresses a will to integrate its children in a manner we would like to consider part and parcel of the meanings contained in its mythical and uncertain etymology: Mother Madrid.

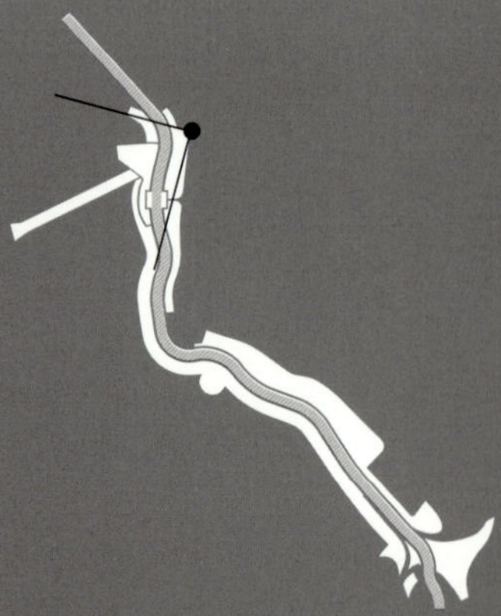

1. LANDSCAPE AND INFRASTRUCTURES

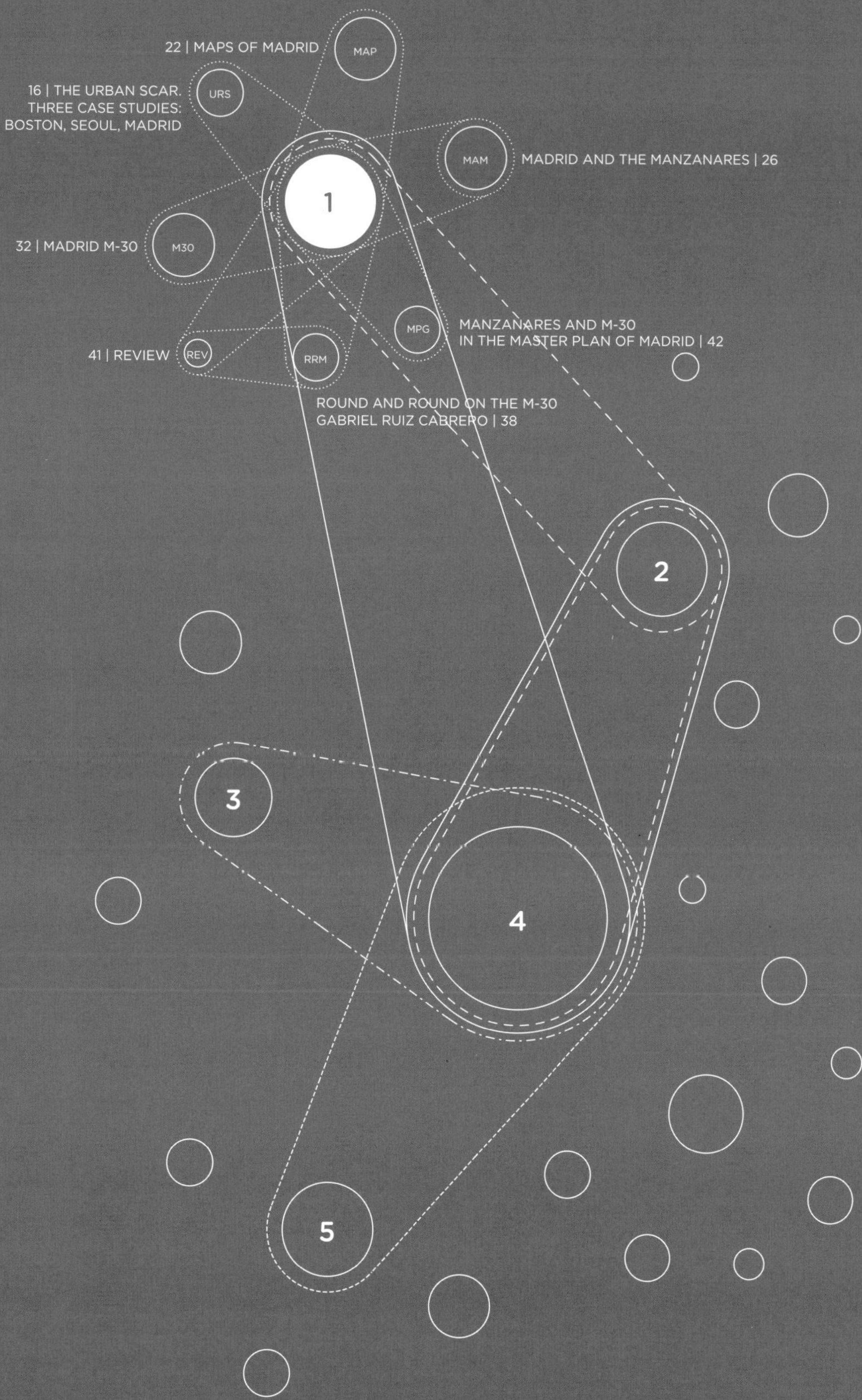

THE URBAN SCAR
THREE CASE STUDIES: BOSTON, SEOUL, MADRID

With the arrival of the 21st century, questions began to arise about the model of mobility predominant in developed countries and exported with little or no reflection to the rest of the world. Gradually, coinciding with other processes linked to the scarcity of resources and climate change, we are beginning to see a mutation in the fundaments of private transportation, at least in the form it has taken until now. This metamorphosis will undoubtedly have a direct effect on the use and collective conception of urban public spaces and empty surfaces from which pedestrians have so often been excluded. The replacement of major asphalted areas with green zones where only sustainable means of transportation are allowed is becoming a reality in some parts of the planet, announcing a new and apparently irreversible dynamic.

The invention of the railway in the 19th century ushered in a revolutionary method of colonizing territories far from urban centers, thanks to the laying of railroads that allowed it to effectively transport considerable loads. But the unidirectional nature of its infrastructure imposed a specific approach to territory and also limited the design of terminals, where the entry and exit of trains is characterized by a minimal capacity for maneuvering and parking. Following the second industrial revolution, in the 20th century, those limitations, along with the discovery of the internal-combustion engine and the low price of petroleum, led to the unstoppable growth of highways, two-dimensional structures that were much cheaper to build. As a result, private transportation grew exponentially.

The paradigms of mobility in place since the Second World War in major North American urban centers rapidly spread to innumerable cities around the world. The golden age of petroleum production and an economy insensitive to the depletion of planetary resources saw the proliferation of infrastructures based on the use of private automobiles as a desirable mode of transportation and a symbol of freedom in evolving Western societies. This phenomenon became an intrinsic part of a new concept of progress in the developed world and led, in both urban and rural settings, to the indiscriminate expansion of a highway system whose design criteria and geometry were based on speed. These roads were often used to impose a new order on urban tissue by building on top of older structures, sometimes using branches of highway to colonize previously vacant interstitial areas or raising them to run above, and duplicate, existing axes.

In urban settings, these public works have had diverse effects, often depending on what kind of city they were installed in and the deeper culture of the societies using them. In the United States, and in a resounding way in many cities on the American continent, the model established in Los Angeles has taken root. There, the automobile can be considered the primary agent for ordering the territory on a metropolitan scale. In emerging Asian cities, the entry of other modes of transportation into city streets presents a compendium of much more rigid variations on that solution, which have had a much greater influence on their urban evolution. One of the most representative examples of this model is the case of mixed infrastructure for local and rapid vehicular traffic as well as interurban and commuter train networks designed by Ove Arup for Bangkok.

Since the turn of the 20th to 21st century, with successive petroleum crises and global concern over the threat of environmental destabilization, it has become clear that the questioning of individual transportation has only just begun. Its scope and progression have yet to be fully grasped. In this context, some cities on the five continents have launched operations to dismantle the decades-old principles that favored the predominant use of private transportation as a determinant agent in the generation of planning models. Three of these cases, in America, Asia, and Europe, respectively, exemplify the manner in which the elimination or burial of infrastructures barely fifty years after their first construction constitute a return to ways of considering nature. In Boston, Seoul, and Madrid, corridors once paved with asphalt have become green systems that articulate large parts of each city.

The privately owned car, as we know it today, is unsustainable as a means of transportation in urban contexts. Its intrinsic drawbacks (wasted time, environmental decay, difficult inclusion in domestic and productive processes, etc.) foreshadow a new transformation for which existing infrastructures are not yet in place. This change will undoubtedly have to include a greater presence of nature in city centers and a new concept of public space as a social

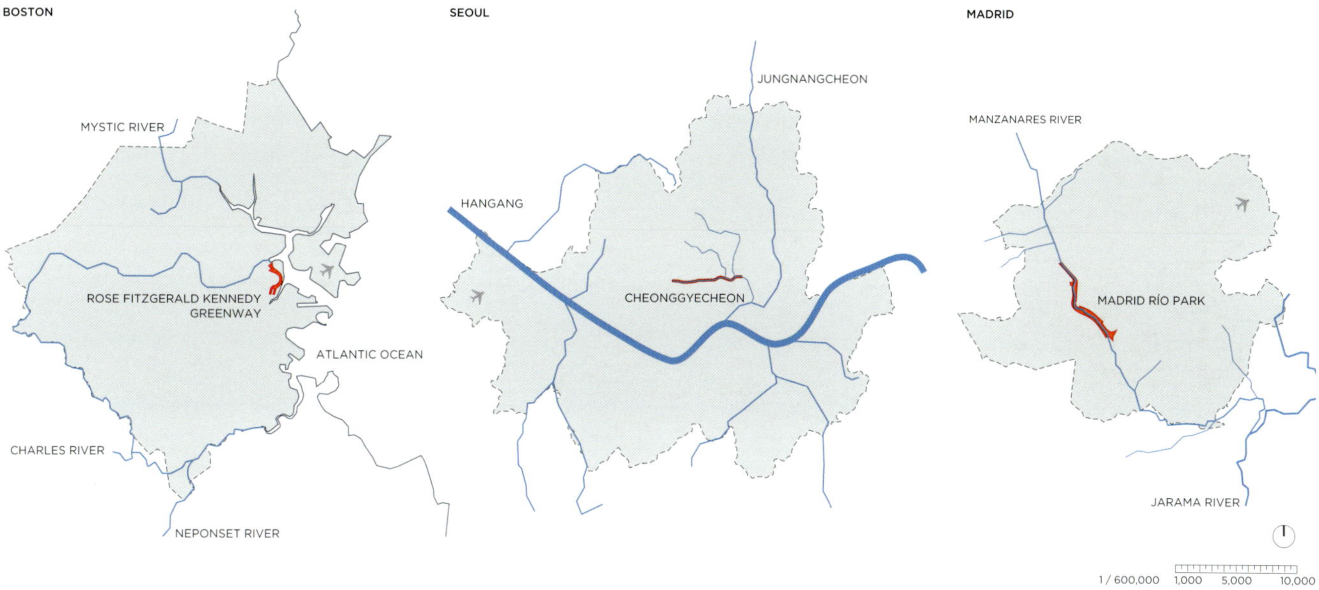

		BOSTON	SEOUL	MADRID
CITY	Surface of the urban conglomerate (approximate)	500 km^2	600 km^2	400 km^2
	Population of the metropolitan area (approximate)	4.5 million	25 million	5 million
URBAN OPERATION	Promoter	Massachusetts Turnpike Authority	Seoul Metropolitan Government	Ayuntamiento de Madrid
	Length of the park	2.40 km	5.80 km	6.70 km
	Length of the tunnels	9.30 km	–	30 km
	Surface of the park	6 ha	37 ha	110 ha
	Surface of the uses	27 ha	3 ha	10 ha
	Total surface	**33 ha**	**40 ha**	**120 ha**
	Periods of planning	1982-91	2002-3	2003-8
	Periods of construction	1991-2008	2003-5	2004-11
	Budget surface works	100 million $	120 million $	500 million $
	Total budget	**22,000 million $**	**380 million $**	**5,000 million $**
	Surface design team	**North End Parks** Crosby, Schlessinger Smallridge LLC Gustafson Guthrie Nichol Ltd **Wharf District Parks** EDAW/AECOM Copley Wolff Design Group **Harbor Islands Pavilion** Utile Design, Inc **Armenian Heritage Park** Tellalian Associates Architects & Planners, LLC **Fort Point Channel Parks + Dewey Square Park** Wolf Landscape Architecture **Chinatown Park** Carol R. Johnson and Associates	**Main Designers** Cheongsuk Engineering Saman Engineering Dongmyung Engineering **Landscape Architects** SeoAhn Total Landscape **ChonGae project** Mikyoung Kim Design	**Architects** Burgos & Garrido Arquitectos Porras La Casta Arquitectos Rubio & Álvarez-Sala Arquitectos with West 8

and environmental catalyst. Deeper geographic aspects that antedate the human presence in each city (hydrography, geology, climate) can now emerge as the constituent elements of major structural forces. Comparing the cases of Boston, Seoul, and Madrid will help us grasp a possible future of this kind.

The Rose Fitzgerald Kennedy Greenway, Boston

The city of Boston (Massachusetts, U.S.A.) lies on the Atlantic coast of North America at the mouth of the Charles and Mystic Rivers. The Rose Fitzgerald Kennedy Greenway is a linear park in this city that now occupies the space made vacant after Interstate I-93, one of the major urban highways running through the city center, was rerouted underground.

In the mid-20th century, vehicular traffic in central Boston was choking the city, especially along the north-south axis. Between 1951 and 1959, the elevated highway known as the Central Artery (the region's key highway) was built between the historic city center and the waterfront. While it was intended to relieve the crowded traffic, it became an important physical barrier separating those two areas of the city. Its layout and construction produced a violent physical and social fracture in Boston's urban fabric and several hundred resident families and small business were displaced to the outskirts. Moreover, from the very start, design errors in this road that received and concentrated both north-south and east-west traffic led to a progressive intensification of vehicular congestion. In 1959, 75,000 vehicles used the highway every day and that number had risen to 190,000 by the 1990s. In light of that progression, those responsible for that city's mobility study predicted 16-hour traffic jams by the year 2010.

To resolve those traffic problems and heal the urban fracture, the Central Artery/Tunnel Project (CA/T) was developed. This megaproject popularly known as the Big Dig was carried out to divert the six-lane elevated Central Artery (I-93) into an eight-to-ten-lane tunnel 5.6 kilometers long. The project also included the construction of the four-lane Ted Williams Tunnel under the port of Boston, which extended the I-90 highway as far as Logan International Airport, as well as the fourteen-lane Leonard P. Zakim Bunker Hill Bridge over the Charles River, and the Rose Fitzgerald Kennedy linear park on the space made available by the rerouting of the I-93 highway.

The project to run the Central Artery underground was developed as part of the Boston Transportation Planning Review in the 1970s and carried out years later. Officially, work on the plans, including the different projects associated with it, began in 1982, after long negotiations between local and federal authorities to determine their respective participation in financing. Work actually began in 1991. After years of political, environmental, and planning difficulties, not to mention the work itself, the highway was rerouted with almost no interruption of vehicular traffic in the area (the old elevated highway continued to function throughout the construction process), despite the difficulties involved in making both the project and its construction compatible with the powerful infrastructures already present in that area (the South Station, with its railway sidings, various subway lines, the city's sewers and storm drains, etc.). The planning and construction of the Big Dig were polemical and controversial because it considerably exceeded both the assigned time and budget. When work began, estimates included a total budget of 5,800 million dollars for the project, and work was supposed to finish in 1998. Reality raised both figures: the project was not completed until 2008, and the final cost climbed to 21,930 million dollars (including interest).

A comparison of traffic and contamination levels before and after the Big Dig show a saving of 62% in daily travel time on the I-93, in connections with Logan International Airport and over the Zakim Bridge, while the filtering of air in the tunnels and greater fluidity in the traffic — flowing traffic generates less gas than stationary vehicles — reduced general levels of carbon monoxide by 12%. Still, a report issued by the Boston Globe in 2008 stated that the phenomenon known as induced demand (greater use produced by the road's increased capacity) effectively led to a reduction of daily travel time on the I-93 but only at the expense of shifting traffic and its ensuing jams to other highways on the outskirts.

Besides improving mobility and environmental quality in central Boston, this project healed the split between neighborhoods long separated by the elevated highway and improved the quality of life throughout the city. The state's environmental legislation obliges the managers of projects of this scope to take action to mitigate negative impact on the area. And these correctional measures have led to an ecological regeneration of the region. Land obtained when the tunnel was excavated has been used to fill and cover various refuse dumps nearby, including the one on Spectacle Island in Boston Bay, which was no longer in use but continued to emit foul odors and allowed contaminants to seep into the marine ecosystem. As part of this project, the island was decontaminated and landscaped, trees were planted, paths and trails laid out, and its beach rehabilitated. Strategies to mitigate the Big Dig's impact also included projects to improve public transportation in the area, such as the introduction of Silver Line busses that link the city center to Logan Airport via a purpose-built tunnel under the port. Other projects of the same sort associated with the enormous Big Dig (the expansion and improvement of subway and streetcar lines) have yet to be completed — some are experiencing prolonged delays, while others have simply been discarded.

The CA/T project created and recovered over 45 parks, plazas, and public spaces for the city, covering a total of more than 120 hectares (including 11 in the city center, 42 on Spectacle Island, and 16 on the banks of the Charles River) and transforming the city. But not all the ground recovered from vehicular traffic through the center has been repurposed as a green zone or as public space. Approximately 25% of that surface has been put to commercial or residential use in low-rise buildings.

The surface area recovered from the I-93 became the Rose Fitzgerald Kennedy Greenway, a linear park consisting

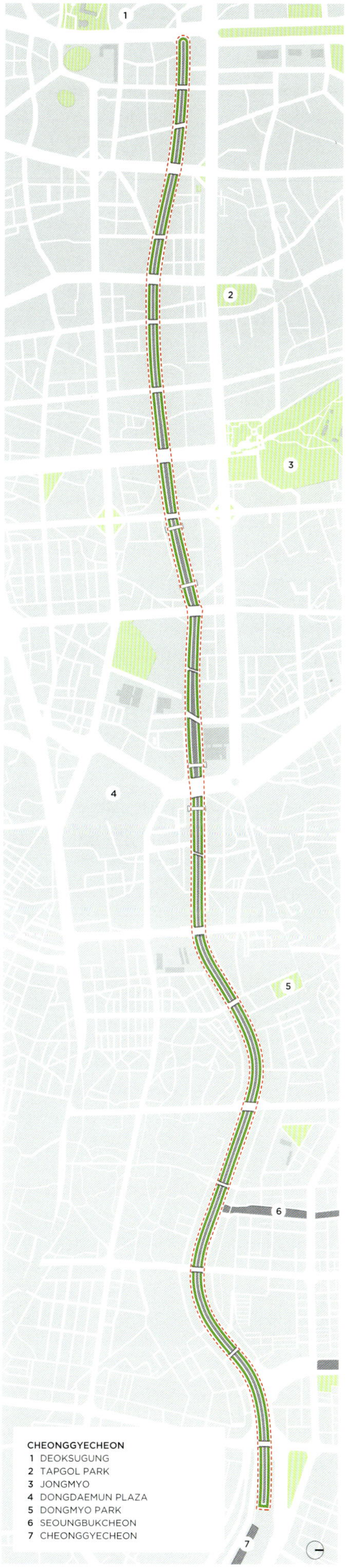

1 / 23,000 20 100 200

of a strip of gardens, boulevards, plazas, fountains, and urban art running two kilometers through residential neighborhoods, the Financial District, and the port. The park opened to the public in October 2008 and covers a total of 6.1 hectares. This expanse of green zones and public spaces is integrated into the city's existing grid and roughly follows the form of its blocks and the continuity of its cross-streets for vehicular traffic. It consists of six parks or groups of different parks and a pavilion, all conceived by different architecture or landscape firms.

In total, some 4 kilometers of sidewalks and roads have been remodeled and the urban furnishings and lighting systems have been totally renovated. The department charged with conserving and maintaining the park organizes a great variety of acts and free public events designed to entice city dwellers and visitors to use this public space. Moreover, it uses ecological methods and organic products to care for it.

Still, the results of the Greenway initiative are limited to the well-intentioned creation of a succession of agreeable parks that unfortunately lack the necessary continuity to empower their complete structural condition. The North American model of individual transit continues to predominate in this city and human-scale public space has not managed to prevail over surfaces dedicated to vehicular traffic. The Rose Fitzgerald Kennedy Park complex is accompanied over its entire length by three lanes of traffic in each direction and is split into fragments by cross-streets of similar width every two-hundred meters or so. Of course, the Big Dig tunnels have reduced high-speed traffic above ground but the green axis has not been able to sufficiently free itself from the aggressive presence of automobiles.

Cheonggyecheon, Seoul

청계천 in the Korean alphabet, is a free public space associated with the Chenonggye Stream that runs 13.7 kilometers from east to west through the center of Seoul (South Korea) to feed into the Jungnangcheon, a tributary of the Han River running east to the Yellow Sea barely 30 kilometers from the city.

Following the Korean War (1950-53), immigration to Seoul was massive and some of the displaced citizens settled illegally on the banks of the Cheonggye in jerry-built housing unconnected to basic sanitation infrastructures that generated high levels of risk and health problems for its inhabitants. In 1958, as a sanitation measure, the stream was covered with concrete and, beginning in 1976, this became the base for a six-kilometer long two-way street. Typically, this consisted of a 50 to 80 meter wide ground-level asphalted platform for cars, called Cheonggye Street, combined with a 16-meter-wide elevated highway called the Cheonggye Highway. The sewer and the original stream were channeled below the surface. A study carried out in 2000 uncovered serious problems of structural stability and degradation in both works, at a time when they were subject to traffic of over 168,000 vehicles per day, with the consequent congestion, contamination, and noise.

At the beginning of the 21st century, the city administration decided to invert its extant urban planning paradigm and put its economic and administrative efforts into recovering the stream and its environment rather than repairing Cheonggye Street and its accompanying highway for long-term use. The overall plan for the recovery of Cheonngyecheon and the economic and social revival of the area began in 2002 and included the restoration of the stream, the demolition of the road and highway, some work to improve the water supply to insure a minimum depth of 40 centimeters in the recovered and intermittent streambed, and a plan to stimulate and improve public transportation and increase pedestrian and bicycle mobility in order to palliate the disappearance of the highway. Twenty-two new crossing points were built to span the stream and bridges and other historical and cultural elements previously present in the area were rebuilt. The urban and landscape design of that setting was guided by concepts of integration, coherence, universal access, the recovery of indigenous biotopes, and safety measures to protect the area from flooding and torrential summer rain, as well as new streets alongside the streambed to handle local traffic and access to adjoining buildings and to the area's multiple stores. Measures were also taken to palliate the inconvenience to citizens, merchants, and businesses caused by the work. All of these actions received significant support from the citizens, making the process a shared one for the city of Seoul, which built a very solid base for its success. Work began in July 2003 and advanced rapidly and unstoppably through the opening of the new urban stream on October 1, 2005.

The entire length of the recuperated streambed is designed to withstand the highest water levels, as calculated from statistics over the last 200 years. This, along with the previous objectives, seeks to avoid the dangerous floods that plagued the city in earlier times. To organize and manage this project's design, including the demolition of existing infrastructures and the construction of new conduits and of the park, the overall area was divided into three smaller parcels that were developed simultaneously by different companies. The final design of the urban space was also divided into three zones so that the streambed could evolve from a more urban character at the eastern end to a more natural one as it reached its mouth on the Jungnangcheon, and from there, the Han River. The total cost of this project reached 380 million dollars (8% over budget), of which approximately 120 million went to the landscaping of the Cheonggyecheon banks.

The process was carefully and constantly overseen and monitored, and some of the information collected is eloquent: while the average speed of vehicular traffic in that district dropped slightly (approximately 12%) due to the elimination of the highway, the number of private vehicles reaching central Seoul dropped by 18%, with a consequent increase (between 6% and 15%) in the use of public transport. As a result, global atmospheric contamination has dropped by 35% and noise contamination by 18%. Thanks to the recovery of the stream as a biological support, the diversity of existing natural species has undergone a total increase of 639%, passing from 98 varieties present in that environment before the reform to 626 following its completion. Birds, fish, amphibians, insects, and small mammals have returned to make their home in this recovered stream where 300 different plant species have also taken root. Moreover, the wind speed along the entire corridor has risen between 2.2% and 7.8% and the heat-island effect has dropped between 3.3° and 5.9°C with respect to temperatures measured on parallel streets nearby. These improvements constitute a new environmental situation that considerably softens the city's extreme summer conditions.

In terms of popular acceptance, the project can be considered a complete success. Estimates put the number of visitors, both local and tourists, at 53,000 per workday along the banks of the Cheonggyecheon, and 125,000 on weekends. As well as the attractive landscape and leisure associated with any park, this one also hosts a multitude of events and cultural activities.

The operation has also been successful in socioeconomic terms, although this is more relative and requires confirmation over a longer term. The Cheonggyecheon urban renewal project acts as a catalyst for the revitalization of central Seoul. The old highway divided the district into two totally separate social and economic zones that the new park has rejoined, and thanks to the cultural and economic reactivation it has generated, the zone has reached a balance that can be extrapolated and applied to the entire city. A rise in real estate prices has been detected and the number of businesses and shops setting up in the zone is increasing, generating a rise in the number of employees that contrasts with the drop in activity in Seoul's city center. Still, these results are easily reversed, generating a process of transformation that would impoverish the neighborhood, displacing its traditional inhabitants and merchants to other more degraded parts of the city. Keeping track of, and adjusting, the delicate and shifting line that separates urban renewal from gentrification (meaning the loss of rich social fabric linked to tradition) will have to be the city authorities' next objective.

MAPS OF MADRID

Silhouettes, lines, and bands
Cartography is a process of intellectual construction, while the map is a concrete, open and autonomous work. Together, they are able to reveal the profound structures that underlie, condition and shape landscape. Sometimes, they do so in an extraordinarily complex way, and others, in a simplified or summary one. The map of the province of Madrid, in central Spain, resembles an iconic and nearly equilateral triangle whose nearly horizontal base slopes gently downward from east to west. The upper vertex of this "summary triangle" coincides with the mountain pass at Somosierra, 1,440 meters high, which leads northward to the Castilian Plateau on the way to France. If we consider this vertex point A and name the other points in a clockwise direction as B and C, we will see that B coincides with the point where the Tagus River (the longest in Spain's geography) touches the province, while "C" marks the mountain known as el Alto del Mirlo (literally: Blackbird's Peak) — 1,770 meters above sea level — in the eastern foothills of the Sierra de Gredos.

Besides its three corners, this triangle has very powerful lines defined by various geographic events. These lines mark families or groups of events that allow us to read the province of Madrid as a weft of bands that have conditioned the colonization of its territory and the transformation of its landscape.

First, we must mention the importance of line A to C, on the left face of the triangle, as it precisely coincides with the crest of the range that includes the Sierra de Somosierra and the Sierra de Guadarrama, groups of mountains pertaining to what is known as the Iberian Peninsula's Central System. Running parallel to this face of the triangle is a band whose width is a practically constant 24 kilometers. Almost all the land in this province whose altitude exceeds 750 meters lies within this area. Thus, the triangular map is divided into two clearly differentiated parts: one within that band, whose geo-morphological characteristics are relatively uniform; and the other, a smaller triangle that covers the rest of the province and is crossed from north to south by the basins of the Guadarrama, Manzanares, Henares, and Jarama Rivers, and from west to east by the Tajuña and the Tagus.

These are the basic lines that structure the diverse elements of Madrid's geography: The Moutain Strip and the Flat Sub-triangle. Together, they make up just two environments: a catchment (mountain) and a distribution area (basin) for precipitation and springs. So, Madrid can be drawn as a triangle ordered by the paths its water takes.

Soil Map
The composition of the province's soils follows the outline of the triangular model described above. The soils that form the Mountain Strip consist primarily of granitic rock (adamellites, granodiorites, granites, and leucogranites), especially in the upper and central parts around El Escorial, and of gneiss and quartzite at the northern end, near the triangle's upper vertex. In the Flat Sub-triangle, two clearly differentiated zones appear, one on each side of the Jarama River. The western side consists predominantly of clay, sands, and silt, while the area southeast and south of the basin consists of a discontinuous surface of gypsum and gypsiferous loams. On the plains, the fluvial marks establish a series of sinuous linear systems of polygenic gravels, sands, and silt that generally do not reach beyond the riverbeds. Such is the case with the Manzanares and Guadarrama Rivers, but in the Jarama, the sandy soil extends beyond the bed to form a powerful line of north-south discontinuity across the territory. Finally, we should mention some insertions of highly impermeable green clays located fundamentally to the northeast and southeast of the Jarama riverbed.

Erosion Map
The band corresponding to the Triangle's A – C side has a concentration of soil highly vulnerable to erosion that is quite precisely limited to the area we have called the Mountain Strip. At the center of that strip, north of the Valmayor Reservoir, an area like a ramified oil stain has been identified. It has excessive seasonal water on the surface with risk of flooding. The Flat Sub-triangle has three clearly differentiated sectors. The first runs alongside the Mountain Strip and is highly vulnerable to erosion. It receives the headlands of the river basins and corresponds to uniform altitudes between 810 and 600 meters. The second, whose main feature is the amorphous shape of the city of Madrid, consists mainly of soil that is moderately

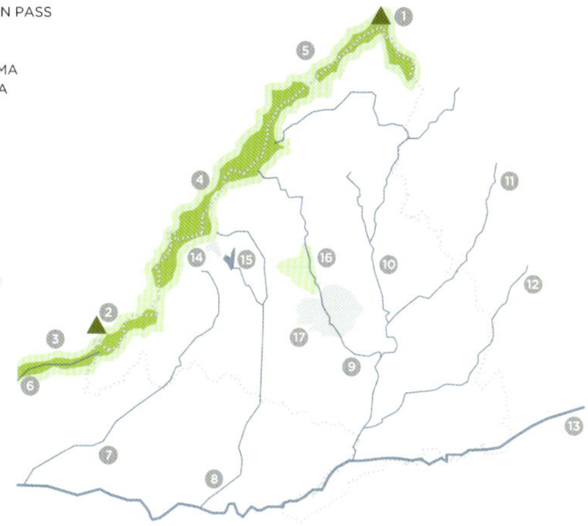

1. SOMOSIERRA MOUNTAIN PASS
2. ALTO DEL MIRLO
3. SIERRA DE GREDOS
4. SIERRA DE GUADARRAMA
5. SIERRA DE SOMOSIERRA
6. TIÉTAR RIVER
7. ALBERCHE RIVER
8. GUADARRAMA RIVER
9. MANZANARES RIVER
10. JARAMA RIVER
11. HENARES RIVER
12. TAJUÑA RIVER
13. TAJO RIVER
14. EL ESCORIAL
15. VALMAYOR RESERVOIR
16. MONTE DE EL PARDO
17. MADRID

vulnerable to erosion, with a scattering of islands subject to greater erosion. The third sector of the Sub-triangle consists of fertile valley lands that are relatively immune to erosion. It coincides with the areas of influence south of the Jarama River and the part of the Tagus River that runs through the province. The most floodable basins, or those that most retain water, are the Manzanares and Jarama, from the point where the former leaves the city of Madrid behind. The headlands of the Jarama, at the northern end of the province, are also an area of influence with excessive seasonal and permanent water.

Vegetation Map
A reading of the distribution of vegetation around Madrid's territory allows us to identify various discontinuous but persistent structures that reveal the appropriateness of distinguishing between Mountain Strip and Flat Sub-triangle in our interpretation of Madrid's physical underpinnings. The former is covered by various large masses of pine forest that reach the highest altitudes of the mountain range. These pine forests coexist mainly with scrub and bush and with some chestnut forests in the triangle's northern vertex. The slopes that mark the transition to the plains are spotted with isolated patches of holm oak, including the vast Monte de El Pardo, at the province's barycenter. Except for the great island representing the city of Madrid, which is somewhat larger than El Pardo, the rest of the lower-altitude soil presents two fundamental components: great expanses of rain-fed crops, which occupy more land than anything else, and irrigated fields running alongside the middle course of the seven rivers already mentioned. We should notice the variety of systems of plant species in the mountains — they are very diverse, interlinked, and sometimes fragmented — as that variety differs greatly from the uniformity of associations of flora on the plains, where most of the land is dedicated to agriculture.

Permeability Map
The outlines of this map are what most clearly reflect the basic lines that form the province's summary triangle. The mountains are marked by a wide band in which soil permeability is low and existing aquifers are very local and fundamentally due to cracking or alteration of the rocks. Running southeast from this band, a large mass coincides with the slope that descends from the mountains to the plains. It can be considered an aquifer of medium permeability with relation to surface porosity and includes the contours of the city of Madrid. This second large area of medium porosity is immediately followed by an alternation of interlinked soils with very different degrees of permeability, running from areas with no aquifers, where green clays are predominant, to high-penetration zones where the soil is fragmented or dissolved, especially between the Jarama and Tajuña basins. Clearly delineated against this area characterized by soils of very diverse permeability levels are a series of aquifers whose considerable permeability is due to the porosity of their substrates, which coincide with the lines that mark the courses of the province's rivers and main streams.

The Geography of Madrid
To draw a map is to construct an open idea that can be partially reconstructed or partially transformed by its reader. Maps are fundamentally elements for action. In reading the six drawings that accompany the present text, we can conclude that this relatively small territory contains highly contrasted situations, from mountain snows that last until the end of the spring to nearly desert lands at the southern end of the region. The territory is defined by two large units or landscape systems: first, the northeastern sierra, and second, the valleys and plains of the Tagus river and its tributaries, to the southeast. Between these two areas lies a transitional zone that is generally called the mountain ramp or piedmont.

The Sierra of Madrid actually consists of three small ranges that are, from northeast to southwest: the Somosierra, the Guadarrama, and the eastern foothills of the Sierra de Gredos. Together, they constitute a mountainous landscape reaching altitudes of over 2,000 meters. In geological terms, the dominant stone in Gredos and Guadarrama is granite, while the Somosierra has an abundance of slates, quartzite, and shale.

Vegetation in this high system varies considerably depending on the altitude. Above 1,800 meters, the slopes are covered by meadowlands grazed by the region's abundant cattle. There are also many species of high-mountain scrub, including mountain boiss and creeping juniper. Some wild pines appear at these altitudes but they are small due to low temperatures and persistent wind. Between 2,100 and 900 meters, the areas of densest growth are primarily wild-pine forests, although there are also some wooded areas of Austrian pine or black pine and, less frequently, ash and birch, which appear in dense patches. Undergrowth consists of ferns, junipers and broom. Below 1,450 meters, the predominant vegetation includes groves of Turkey or Pyrenean oak, while the sunny slopes of the valleys below 900 meters have masses of holm oaks and Phoenicean juniper. At these levels there are also abundant grasslands for predominantly bovine cattle.

The transition between the mountains and the sandy plains to the south takes the form of a mountain ramp or piedmont that extends from the confluence of the Jarama and Lozoya rivers, at the northern end of the province, to the southeast, forming a band parallel to the sierra. These slopes descend from the piedmont at 900 meters to the river valleys at 450 meters.

This is not exactly a landscape unit because its general characteristics fit approximately into the landscapes of the valleys and plains. But this band bears some specific traits that distinguish it as a subunit with a certain degree of autonomy. From a geological standpoint, most of this territory consists of clay layers, sandy clays, and silts. In the grooves worn by the rivers running through them, we find polygenic gravels, sands, and silts.

Vegetation consists of groves of Turkey or Pyrenean oak and holm oaks, Phoenicean juniper, and grazing land for cattle on the lower slopes, with rain-fed crops and areas of brush with a scattering of irrigated crops and small, isolated pine woods of the sort found on the plains and valleys of the Tagus.

The soil of the large plain at the southeast end of the province is made up of sands, gravels, silts, and clays. The slopes that delimit the edges of the basins have areas of clay, gypsum, and carbonates. The substrates that form the upper part of the land between basins contain limestone, loams, and clays.

Vegetation is largely determined by the human presence, as most of the area's surface is farmland. The fertile valleys have intensive irrigated monocultures, mostly cereals, corn, and cabbage, although there are also areas with fruit and vegetable cultures that are more traditional. The flatlands and plains are dedicated to rain-fed crops, especially wheat, olives, and grapes, while the unfarmed lands bear mostly holm, Kermes and Mirbeck's oak, as well as some isolated pinewoods and areas of box and juniper accompanied by herbaceous plants such as thyme, lavender, broom, common dog rose, and some grasses. Riverside vegetation consists of lush masses of willow, black or silver poplar and ash, as well as cane fields on the edges, in still waters or pools.

This main structure constituted by Madrid's land, with all the parameters mentioned above, supports three networks or systems: the hydrographic system, the highway system and a network of population centers. These three systems are diverse in nature and in their manner of structuring the territory, as two are artificial (highways and population centers), while the other is natural (hydrographic). A similar distinction can be drawn between the two linear systems (hydrographic and highway) and the third, which is of extended surfaces (population centers).

The land in the province of Madrid is part of the hydrographic basin of the Tagus River, which crosses the southern part of the region from east to west. Four north-south sub-basins divide the landscape in this geographic setting: the Jarama, the Guadarrama, the Alberche, and the Tiétar, all tributaries of the Tagus. These rivers follow similar paths from their headwaters in the Central System to their mouths at the Tagus, dividing the territory into a clear set of bands or strips.

The most intensely artificial system is the network of highways connecting Madrid with important parts of its distant periphery. This system's radial composition has six main axes: the A-1, which connects with Irún and France; the A-2, leading to Barcelona; the A-3, which reaches Valencia and connects with the Mediterranean costal routes; the A-4, leading to Andalusia and on to Africa; the A-5 to Portugal; and the A-6, which leads to Santiago de Compostela and the Atlantic. This is an extremely simple network, with a central point and six others on the edges of the Iberian Peninsula, but it is complemented by a group of concentric ring roads around the city of Madrid (the M-30, M-40, M-45 and M-50). That double system constitutes a reality that has conditioned, over time, the city's morphology.

Population centers are distributed across the territory, where they depend on the highway system described above. The city of Madrid lies at the center and its most densely populated areas can be found around the ring roads. All together, the capital and its surrounding satellite cities, add up to a total population of over 5 million people. The secondary population centers are clustered along the radial routes, especially the A-2, A-5 and A-6.

In sum, the territory of Madrid is an area with a concentration of numerous large infrastructures, but also visible natural contrasts; a diverse, fragmented, and extremely anthropic landscape.

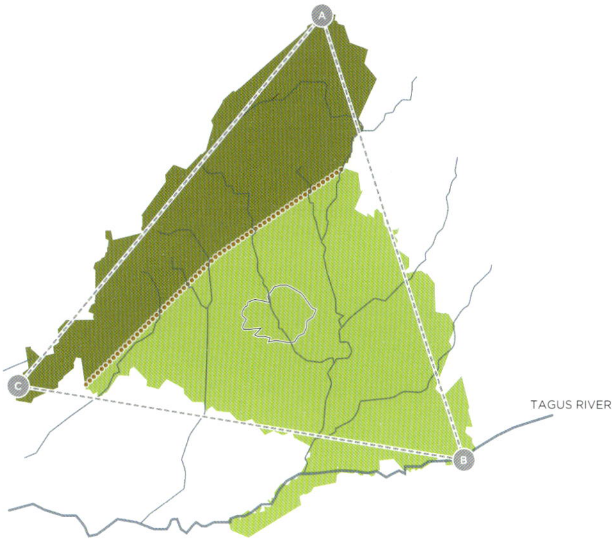

SILHOUETTES, LINES AND STRIPS
- MOUNTAIN STRIP
- FLAT SUB-TRIANGLE

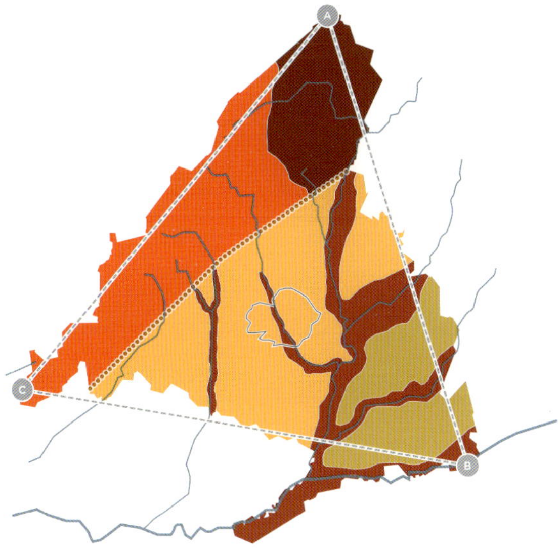

SOILS
- GYPSUMS
- SANDY CLAYS
- GRANITE
- GRAVELS
- GNEISS

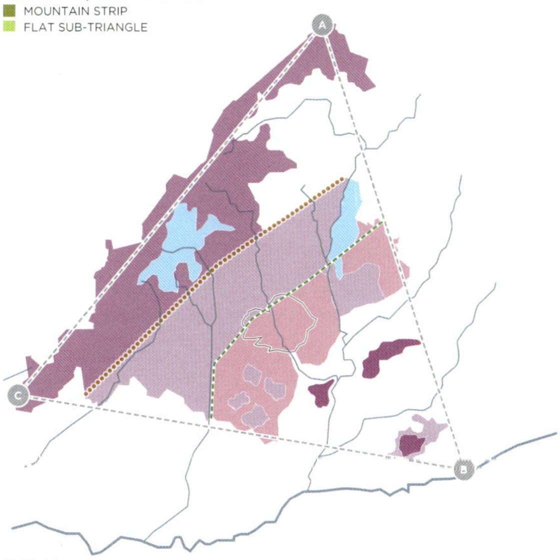

EROSION
- VERY HIGH SUSCEPTIBILITY TO EROSION
- HIGH SUSCEPTIBILITY TO EROSION
- MODERATE SUSCEPTIBILITY TO EROSION
- HIGH SUSCEPTIBILITY TO FLOODING
- EDGE OF PIEDMONT

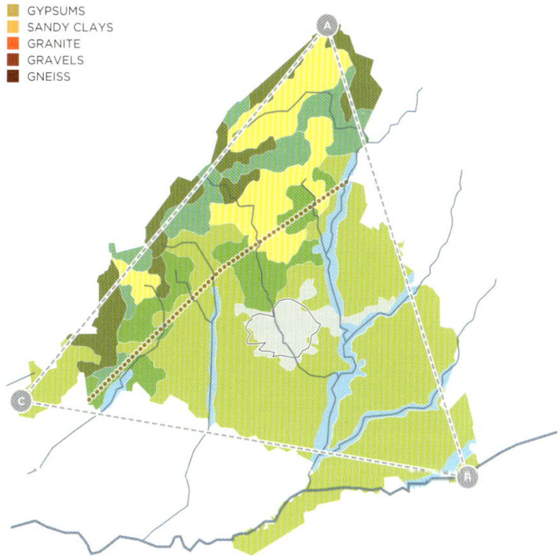

VEGETATION
- PINE WOODS
- BRUSH
- OAK WOODS
- RAINFED AGRICULTURE
- GRAZING LAND
- RIVERSIDES AND IRRIGATED AGRICULTURE

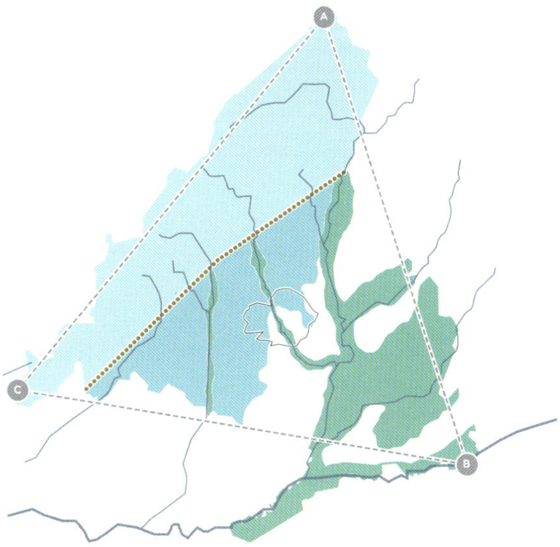

PERMEABILITY
- HIGH PERMEABILITY
- MEDIUM PERMEABILITY
- LOW PERMEABILITY
- DISCONTINUOUS PERMEABILITY

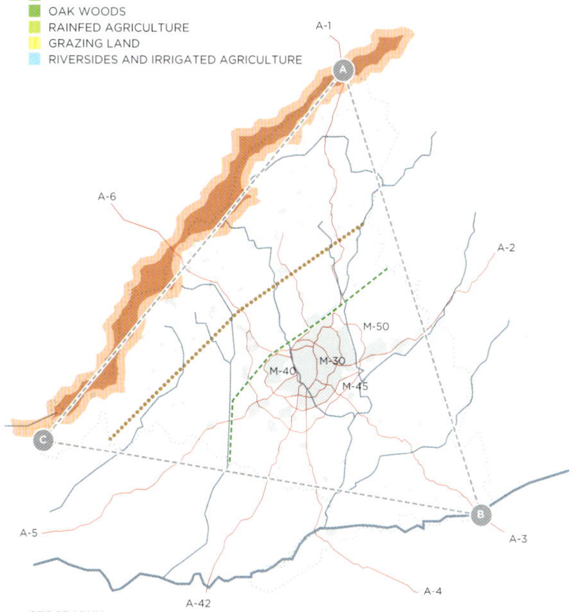

GEOGRAPHY
- BOUNDARY OF THE COMUNIDAD AUTÓNOMA DE MADRID
- MAIN HIGHWAY NETWORK
- AREA OF GREATEST RELIEF
- EDGE OF PIEDMONT

MAPS OF MADRID
- SOMOSIERRA PASS 1440M
- ALTO DEL MIRLO 1770M
- TAGUS RIVER
- HYDROGRAPHIC NETWORK
- SUMMARY TRIANGLE
- EDGE OF MOUNTAIN STRIP

MADRID AND THE MANZANARES

With a length of 190 kilometers, the Jarama River is the longest and most important in the region of Madrid. Its basin constitutes the province's largest surface area and includes those of the Lozoya, Guadalix, and Manzanares rivers, which flow into the Jarama from the right, and the Henares and Tajuña, which feed into it from the left. The most important reservoirs in this basin include Lozoya, El Atazar, Puentes Viejas, Riosequillo, Santillana, and Pedrezuela, which are responsible for the greater part of the entire province's water supply.

The bed of the Manzanares river is 69 kilometers long. It begins at an altitude of 2,250 meters in the Sierra de Guadarrama, descending to 527 meters above sea level where it flows into the Jarama River. Along the way, it receives water from over thirty streams, and north of the city, it feeds the Santillana and El Pardo reservoirs.

The diversity of landscapes and multiple biotopes through which it runs make the Manzanares a singular element with a series of highly contrasting identities, including mountain stream, seasonal gully, man-made canal, urban spillway, and valley wetlands. On its journey from north to south, it flows through all of the environments that make up Madrid's geography, from mountain heights to the lowlands along the Tagus River.

Its upper basin it dotted with the granite masses of La Pedriza, amidst dense pine forests. Further downriver, the landscape loses its vegetation, remaining bare until the Monte de El Pardo, where it flows through forests of holm oak. From there, the banks recover the thick vegetation of linear riversides until reaching the city. Later, it crosses fields of dry, stony gypsum before reaching a fertile basin that feeds orchards and plantations. And finally, it flows into the Jarama.

The river is relatively inaccessible in almost all places. It often marks an uncomfortable interruption in the terrain and goes unrecognized most of the time. Over its course, it coexists with various types of infrastructures, some of which are dedicated to it, including bridges, dams, and reservoirs, while others simply cross or limit it, such as highways, railways, or conduits.

An overall analysis of the Manzanares' basin reveals that the riverbed is not specific to the city. Instead, Madrid is one of many things that have happened to the river. The interaction between the two has evolved over history, but until now, the Manzanares has not stood out as one of the city's attractions. Instead, it has long been something on which the city turned its back.

While the origin of Madrid's name is not completely clear, all authors agree on one thing: its relation to the presence of river or streambeds and other sources of water. Throughout its length, and especially in its urban course, the Manzanares River receives waters from numerous tributaries, many of which have disappeared beneath the city and its infrastructure. But, while these streams may no longer be visible, they have shaped the form and development of the city's urban fabric. Among those that fed into the Manzanares were: the San Pedro, which ran along what is now the Calle de Segovia; the San Bernardino, now occupied by the Calle de la Princesa; and the Leganitos and Embajadores, whose locations are marked by streets of the same name. The city was also crossed by two other larger streams whose presence was fundamental to its present configuration and infrastructures: the Abroñigal and the Fuente Castellana. The first of these began in the north in the area of Chamartin and flowed to the south into the Manzanares near Puente de Vallecas. Its dry bed is now occupied by the eastern sweep of the M-30 ring road. The second marked the axis now occupied by the Paseo de la Castellana, the Paseo de Recoletos and the Paseo del Prado. Beginning at Emilio Castelar Circle, it fed into the Abroñigal close to where the M-30 ring road now crosses the railroad tracks running from Atocha Station. Besides these streams, a water catchment and distribution system was constructed beneath the city by the Arabs in the 10th century and progressively expanded through the 18th century. This infrastructure known as the *water trails* consisted of a group of underground galleries that captured water from its phreatic table and carried it to the city center.

Viewed in section, the river's passage through the city is asymmetrical. On its right bank, to the west, the terrain approaches the river in gently sloping terraces; but its left bank, to the east, is much more abrupt, with escarpments

STREAMS AND RELIEF
GREEN ZONES
A CASA DE CAMPO
B RETIRO PARK
MAIN TOPOGRAPHY

1 ABROÑIGAL STREAM
2 FUENTE CASTELLANA STREAM
3 CANTARRANAS STREAM
4 LEGANITOS STREAM
5 SAN PEDRO STREAM
6 ANTEQUINA STREAM
7 VALDEZA STREAM
8 MEAQUES STREAM
9 MANZANARES RIVER

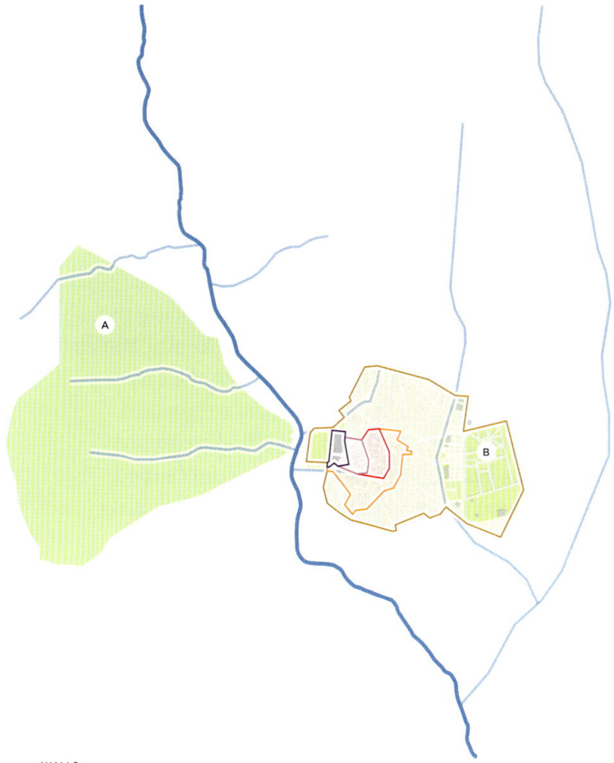

WALLS
GREEN ZONES
A CASA DE CAMPO
B RETIRO PARK

9TH-C. WALL
12TH-C. WALL
14TH-C. WALL
16TH-C. WALL
17TH-C. WALL

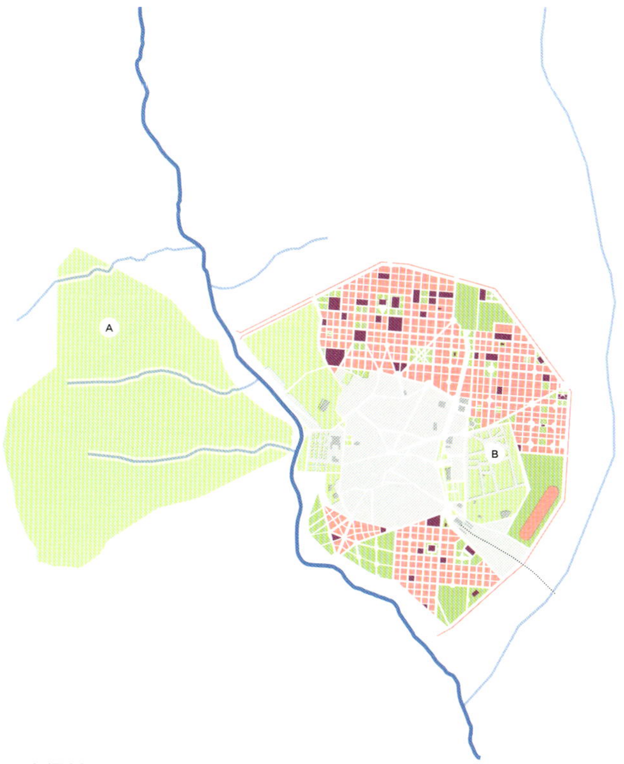

CASTRO PLAN (1860)
GREEN ZONES
A CASA DE CAMPO
B RETIRO PARK

HISTORIC CENTER
CASTRO PLAN URBAN GROWTH
CASTRO PLAN GREEN ZONES
CASTRO PLAN SINGULAR CONSTRUCTION

BIDAGOR PLAN (1941)
GREEN ZONES
A CASA DE CAMPO
B RETIRO PARK

HISTORIC CENTER
CASTRO PLAN
BIDAGOR PLAN URBAN GROWTH
BIDAGOR PLAN GREEN ZONES
BIDAGOR PLAN SINGULAR CONSTRUCTION
URBAN GROWTH AROUND THE RIVER

1 / 125,000 200 1,000 2,000

DIAGRAM OF THE MANZANARES RIVER
ACCIDENTS, EVENTS, AND STRUCTURES

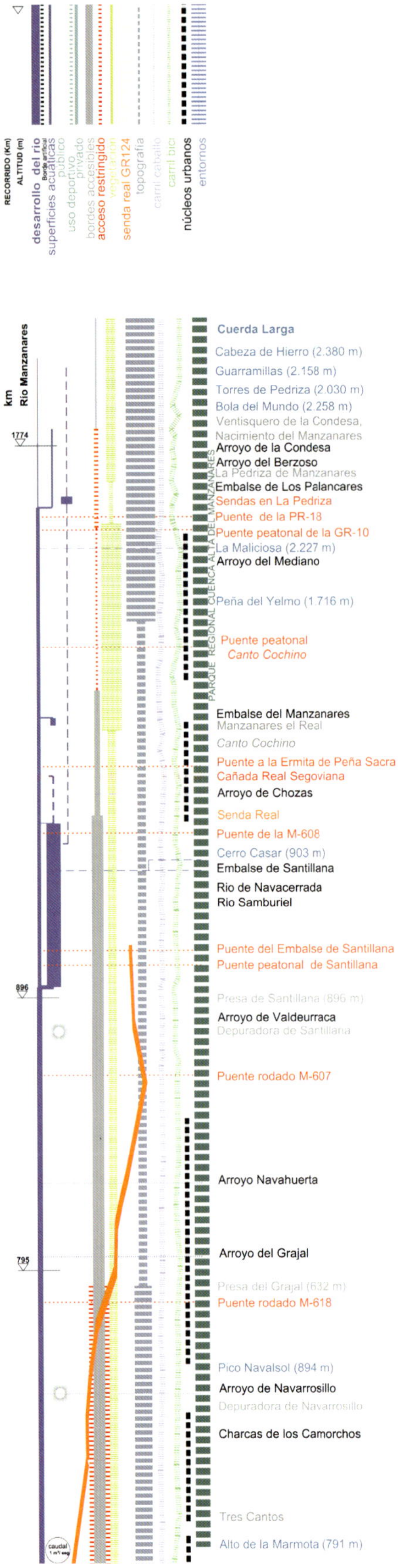

Arroyo del Jaramillo
Puente de la Marmota
Embalse de El Pardo
Monte del Pardo (746 m)
Soto de Viñuelas
Arroyo de Manina
Arroyo Tejada
Granja de Navahermosa (684 m)
Presa del Embalse del Pardo
El Pardo
Puente peatonal + Represa
Arroyo de la Sanguijuela
Palacio de El Pardo
Puente rodado
Arroyo del Convento
Arroyo de la Nava
Encinar de los Reyes
Parque de Valdebebas
Línea Alta Tensión
Ferrocarril Cercanías
Arroyo de Trofa
Complejo Deportivo
Público Somontes
Canal de Isabel II [Canal Oeste]
Puente rodado
Palacio de la Zarzuela
Línea Alta Tensión
Arroyo de la Zarzuela
Ramal de acceso M-40 / M-30 Norte
M-40 Nudo de la Zarzuela
Real Club Puerta de Hierro
Puente del Hipódromo
Arroyo del Fresno
Puente del Arroyo Fresno
Puente rodado
Arroyo de Pozuelo
Ramal de acceso M-30 / N-VI
Autopista A-6
Puente de la M-30
Club de Campo Villa de Madrid
Arroyo de Antequina
Cerro de las Covatillas (642 m)
Cerro de Garabitas (679 m)
Puente de Los Franceses
Carril Bici Anillo Verde Ciclista
Ferrocarril Cercanías
Pasarela peatonal + represa
Puente nuevo rodado + peatonal
Puente nuevo peatonal
Pasarela peatonal
Puente de la Princesa
Pasarela peatonal + represa
Pasarela peatonal
Nuevo Puente del Rey
Pasarela peatonal + represa
Puente de Segovia
Pasarela elevada
Pasarela peatonal + represa
Pasarela elevada
Puente de San Isidro
Pasarela
Pasarela
Pasarela elevada
Pasarela peatonal + represa
Puente de Toledo
Carril Bici Anillo Verde Ciclista
Pasarela elevada
Pasarela elevada
Pasarela
Nuevo Puente peatonal
Puente de Legazpi
Ferrocarril Cercanías Línea C-1 / C-2
caudal 13 m³/ seg
560
532
527
514
Ferrocarril Cercanías Línea C-1 / C-2
Viaducto N-III / M-30 Oeste
Ramal M-30 Oeste
M-30 / Avenida de Andalucía
M-30 Oeste / N-IV Sur
Deportivo *Caja Mágica*
Alto del Espino (650m)
Depuradora de La China
Vertedero de La China
Ferrocarril Cercanías Línea C-1 / C-2 / C-7
Ramal Sur Autopista N-IV
Ramal Norte Autopista N-IV
Ferrocarril AVE
Conexión Oeste M-40 / N-IV
Conexión Este M-40 / N-IV
Cerro del Campillo (671 m)
Canteras del Olivar (615 m)
Línea Alta Tensión
Ferrocarril AVE Madrid-Sevilla
Rivas-Vaciamadrid
Arroyo de La Gavia
Línea Alta Tensión
M-45
Depuradora de la Gavia
[Butarque]
Arganda del Rey
Puente de la Bulera
Laguna de Campillo (Jarama)
Cerro de las Coberteras (650 m)
M-50 Autopista
Gaseoducto
Ferrocarril AVE Madrid-Sevilla
Cañada Real Galiana
Puente Cañada Real Galiana
Rio Jarama
Depuradora Sur
Lagunas de Perales
Cerro de los Ángeles (667 m)
Incineradora + Vertedero de Valdemingomez
Puente peatonal
Puente rodado
Línea Alta Tensión
Arroyo Culebro
Línea Alta Tensión
Depuradora Suroriental
Arroyo de los Migueles
Presa del Rey
Lagunas de El Porcal
Rio Jarama
VEGETACIÓN montaña / prado / ribera
PARQUE REGIONAL CUENCAS BAJAS DEL MANZANARES Y JARAMA

MADRID M-30

In the 1960s and '70s, Madrid experienced a progressive industrial development that resulted in a considerable increase in its population. This process was accompanied by a parallel growth in the use of city center real estate for commercial and office uses to the detriment of its capacity for residential fabric. The combination of these two phenomena shifted industrial activity to the immediate periphery and boosted the density of residential neighborhoods on the city's edge — especially in the area around the Manzanares River.

The 1963 *Plan General para el Área Metropolitana de Madrid* (Master Plan for the Metropolitan Area of Madrid) accepted the elimination of the linear park that accompanied the roadways bordering the river. The planning work of Zuazo and Jansen in 1929, and Bidagor in 1946 proposed a green structure for the banks of the Manzanares and for the so-called Gran Vía del Abroñigal. Nevertheless, the crowding of these building-free zones had already begun with the construction of residential projects spurred mainly by private real-estate agents.

In 1972, the *Plan para la Red Arterial de Madrid* (Plan for the Highway Network of Madrid) was definitively approved, following eight years of studies. This plan defined two systems — one for highways and another for main roads — and each included penetration or radial roads and ring roads or beltways. The plan proposed four concentric ring-roads, which are now known as the boulevards (although their trees were soon removed to permit an expansion of their paved surface), the rounds (conceived exclusively for vehicles), the new M-30 and the future M-40. This plan also specified the routing of a system of radial highways.

With these antecedents, construction began to run the M-30 highway over Manzanares and Abroñigal avenues, adopting the formula of building roads on river or streambeds proposed, in this case, by Bidagor in his 1946 *Plan General de Ordenación* (Master Plan of Urban Zoning) for a new green infrastructure.

On November 16, 1974, work began on the two sectors known as the Manzanares Highway (between the Puente de Segovia and the Puente de Toledo, and the Highway of La Paz (now the western section of the M-30). Together, they constituted the southeastern part of the beltway from Puente de Segovia to the neighborhood known as Parque de las Avenidas.

During the construction of the Manzanares Highway, there was forceful opposition by local residents, because its lanes ran very close to some of the recently constructed residential buildings. It was opened to traffic before pedestrian walkways were built and, during that period, the Manzanares Highway had a series of traffic lights allowing pedestrians to cross at street level.

This highway marked a turning point in the river's history because it involved a specialization of the latter's bank exclusively for rapid transit. Moreover, the density brought about by urban speculation in that area imposed the confinement of the river, whose historic bridges were, by then, wedged among the ramps and lanes of the M-30. As a result, it became practically impossible for pedestrians to cross from one side of the river to the other. The occupation of the areas closest to the river by residential buildings crushed any possible compatibility between the river's role as an infrastructure for vehicular traffic and as a green axis running through the city. The highway's construction simply annulled that aspiration, creating an extraordinary urban conflict in close proximity to the city center.

The beltway was not completed until the 1990s, following a notable modification in its route (which followed Costa Rica and Alberto Alcocer Avenues and crossed the park known as La Dehesa de la Villa). The new route ran further north, along the La Ilustración Avenue (the only part of the beltway still fitted with traffic lights).

Since its inauguration, the M-30 has suffered congestion and delays. The *Plan para la Red Arterial de Madrid* approved in 1972 had specified that the third and fourth beltways (the M-30 and M-40) should be built almost simultaneously. Delays in the construction of the M-40, the beltway running outside Madrid's city center that was not completed until 1996, led to premature crowding of the M-30. By the time the highway network was totally completed, the third beltway was already obsolete. Moreover, the highway constituted a clear barrier between the inner city and the neighborhoods on the other side of the ring created by it.

M-607
A-1
EJE VENTISQUERO DE LA CONDESA
AV. CARDENAL HERRERA ORIA
M-40
M-11
C/ GINZO DE LIMIA
GRAN VÍA DE HORTALEZA
A-6
Pº DE LA CASTELLANA
CARRETERA DE CASTILLA
A-2
AV. DE AMÉRICA
AV. DE SÉNECA
CASA DE CAMPO
CUESTA DE SAN VICENTE
PUERTA DEL SOL
C/ O'DONNELL
RETIRO PARK
M-23
A-5
C/ TOLEDO
AV. DEL MEDITERRÁNEO
AV. CIUDAD DE BARCELONA
A-3
Pº SANTA MARÍA DE LA CABEZA
C/ GENERAL RICARDOS
C/ EMBAJADORES
A-42
AV. DE LA ALBUFERA
AV. DE ANDALUCÍA
A-4
M-30 ABOVE GROUND
MANZANARES RIVER
CONNECTIONS FROM THE M-30
1.ST BELTWAY: LAS RONDAS (THE ROUNDS)
2.ND BELTWAY: LOS BULEVARES (THE BOULEVARDS)
3.RD BELTWAY: M-30 ABOVE GROUND
SECTION COMPLETED IN THE 1970s
SECTION COMPLETED IN THE 1990s
NORTH CLOSURE AS PLANNED IN THE PLAN FOR THE HIGHWAY NETWORK OF MADRID (1972)
SECTION WITH TRAFFIC LIGHTS ON AV. DE LA ILUSTRACIÓN
100 500 1,000

M-30, 1989

M-30, 1989

ESTADIO VICENTE CALDERON

M-30 PUENTE DEL REY

M-30 PUENTE OBLICUO

F. GARCIA

M-30. TOLEDO VIADUCT

M-30. MATADERO

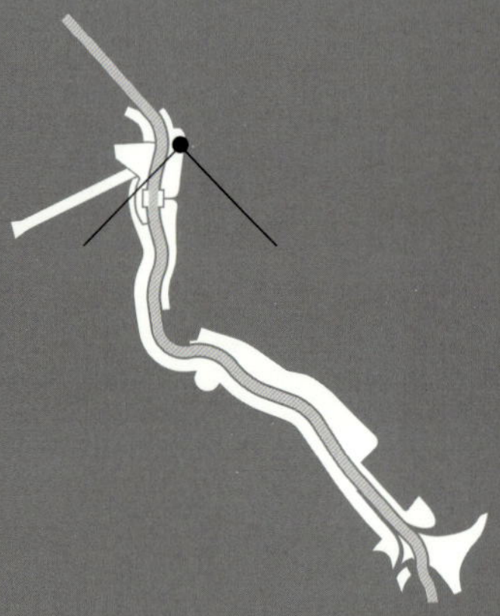

2. MADRID UNDER CONSTRUCTION

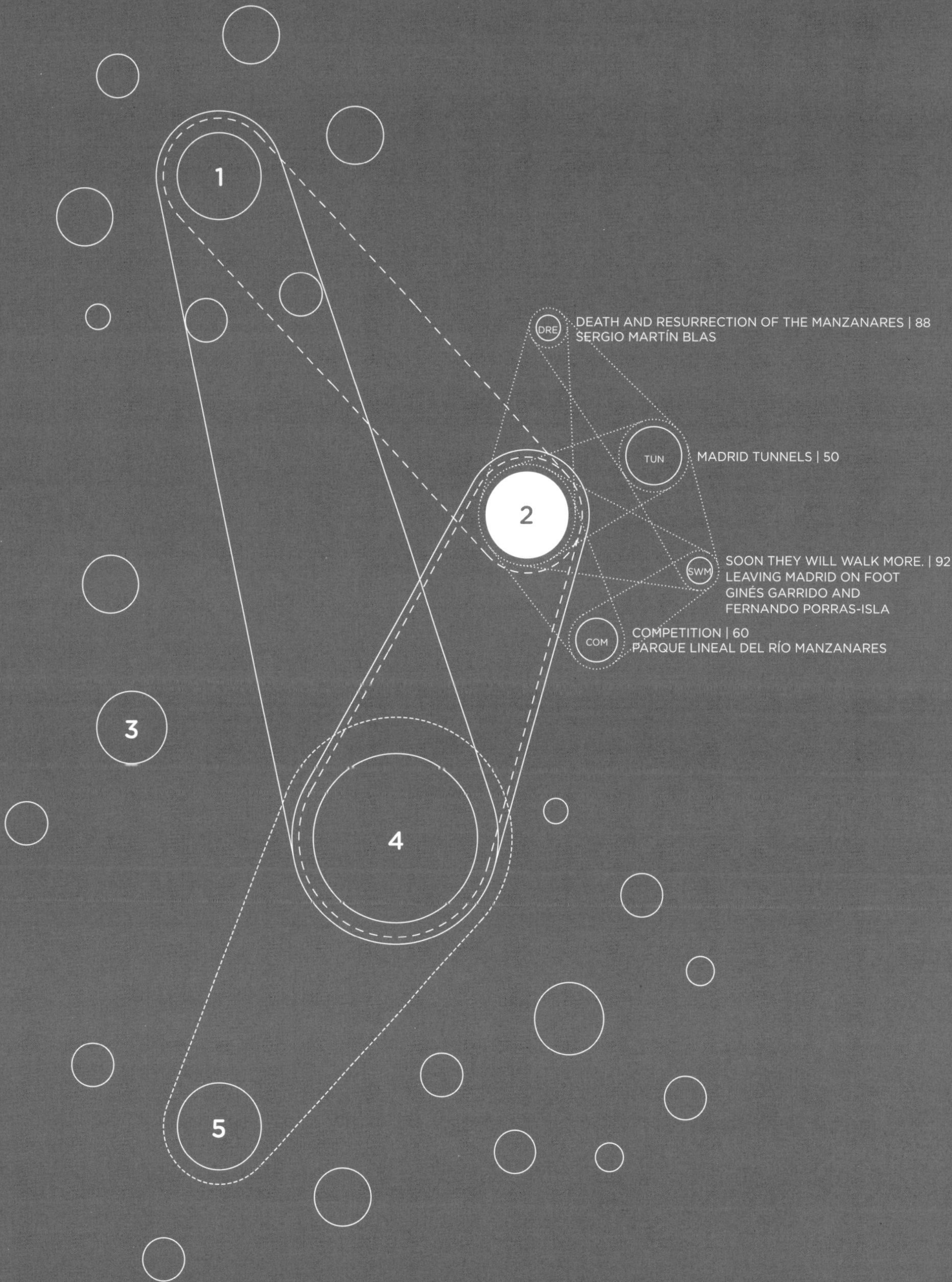

MADRID TUNNELS

In 2003, the Municipal Government of Madrid began renovating the M-30 beltway, which had become obsolete due to the city's growth and an increase of private transportation leading to intense daily traffic jams and a number of accidents that rose on a yearly basis. The central element in this renovation was the burial of six kilometers of highway on both sides of the Manzanares River, where it passes through the capital, and the construction of the southern bypass tunnel, which was excavated to avoid passing through one of its most congested junctions. The major highway changes were accompanied by the renovation of various connections and accesses to the M-30, along with some tunnels within the city. Moreover, the burial of traffic lanes alongside the Manzanares between the Puente de los Franceses and the Nudo Sur (South Junction) also involved reforming storm drains and overflow tanks associated with the river to replace an old system that had become totally insufficient.

The political situation in Spain's capital was momentarily favorable to making the highway reform possible. On one hand, the mayor of Madrid at that moment was clearly willing to undertake a visible and lasting public works project. On the other, he had formerly been president of the Comunidad Autónoma de Madrid, where he had developed strong ties to teams of engineers and construction managers with experience in tunnel building, thanks to work carried out on Madrid's subway system. Both of these factors and the patent obsolescence of the city's infrastructures coincided, at that moment, with a fictitious economic boom to drive the operation.

The municipal corporation took advantage of the final months of 2004, when municipal and national governments belonged to the same political party, to transfer ownership of the M-30 from the Ministry of Development to the Municipality of Madrid. Thus, the beltway acquired the status of a city street, paving the way for administrative measures necessary for the desired construction and eliminating the need for environmental-impact statements that would have made the works impossible to carry out. This cession allowed the municipal government to start work that same year on the Calle 30 Project, which is the name given to the highway and the joint enterprise that manages it.

Work began in 2004 and lasted three years. It soon became a central focus of attention for citizens and press alike. Rather than a gradual project carried out in stages, it was designed to be carried out "all at once" but without interrupting surface traffic. The affected area was soon filled with detours, cranes, provisional roadways, and so on. On any given day, some 4,500 people worked on this project in three consecutive 8-hour shifts. So construction went on around the clock.

The financial design of this operation called for outside funding including bank loans, and also the founding of a mixed-capital enterprise (80% municipal, 20% private) to manage both construction and highway maintenance. Amortization of the acquired debt would be handled by the joint enterprise by drawing on income from the municipal government as payment for the maintenance and exploitation of the highway, thus obtaining a formula for the chronological dilution of payments of debt obligations.

The construction of tunnels along the Manzanares River has been one of the most criticized public works in the history of Madrid. Its high cost (never officially declared but close to 4,000 million euros) and its management with almost no public participation constitute innumerable weak or obscure points. For example, such an investment would have permitted the renovation of over 50,000 dwellings in the city center, or construction of 1,000 kilometers of interurban highway. On the other hand, a priori studies indicate that burying that part of the highway would save 14 million man-hours per year by reducing traffic congestion, and would cut the number of accidents by more than 50%. Many theorists do not consider these benefits sufficient to justify such a huge project.

In any case, the operation has not generated a new model of mobility for Madrid because, notwithstanding improvements in many technical aspects, increased safety, and a reduction of noxious elements such as noise and air pollution, the concept of mobility on underground roads is excessively similar, if not identical, to that existing for surface roads. But the alternatives to the tunnel that were considered — a lower intensity road alongside the Manzanares and rerouting certain traffic to the west of Madrid — would never have completely freed the river. Moreover, it would have negated the possibility of fitting the river with a green infrastructure capable of revealing a new network of free spaces susceptible to long-term development.

M-30 TUNNELS

- MANZANARES RIVER
- CONNECTIONS FROM THE M-30
- M-30 ABOVE GROUND

INTERVENTIONS IN THE DECADE OF 2000

- INTERVENTIONS IN THE M-30 ABOVE GROUND
- M-30 UNDERGROUND
- OTHER INTERVENTIONS UNDERGROUND

CONSTRUCTION OF THE TUNNELS, SURFACE WORK, 2005. PUENTE DE SEGOVIA

GIMNASIO
CIUM

CONSTRUCTION OF THE TUNNELS, SURFACE WORK, 2006. AREA AROUND THE PASEO DE LA VIRGEN DEL PUERTO

CONSTRUCTION OF THE TUNNELS. SURFACE WORK, 2007. TOLEDO BRIDGE - PRAGA BRIDGE

CONSTRUCTION OF THE TUNNELS, UNDERGROUND WORK, 2007

COMPETITION
PARQUE LINEAL DEL RÍO MANZANARES
(MANZANARES RIVER LINEAR PARK)

IDEAS COMPETITION TO SELECT DESIGN AND DEVELOPMENT PROJECTS FOR THE LINEAR PARK ALONG THE MANZANARES RIVER BETWEEN THE NUDO SUR (SOUTH JUNCTION) OF THE M-30 AND THE PUENTE DE LOS FRANCESES

The present competition will take the form of a two-stage juried competition for ideas expressed as draft projects. The first stage will be open to the presentation of ideas based on the competition's objectives and the second will develop those ideas selected by the jury.

That second stage will involve a minimum of six professionals and a maximum of eight selected on the basis of their accredited familiarity and world renown in this subject. Their inclusion will be by invitation, which must then be confirmed.

THE COMPETITION'S PURPOSE

The present competition of ideas has been convoked to obtain urban-planning proposals for a design and urban-development project for the Linear Park of the Manzanares River in the area between the Nudo Sur of the M-30 and the Puente de los Franceses.

The present competition is sponsored by the Municipal Government of Madrid through its Area of Urban Planning, Housing, and Public Works. The organization and coordination of the competition will be carried out by the General Subdirectorate for Urban Development.

COMPETITION OBJECTIVES

Contestants should address the following basic objectives in their development of urban planning proposals:

a) Recovery of the riverbanks, with actions and proposals for:
   - Increasing urban quality, improving the river's surroundings, continuity between the banks.
   - Expansion of the surface of green areas and their connection to the existing network.
   - Interconnection of affected neighborhoods. Connection with the Historic Center.
   - Regeneration of urban fabric.
   - Enhancement of the role of nearby monuments, buildings, and elements of urban value.
   - Enhancement of the role of the landscape. The river as an axis that articulates the surroundings.
   - Treatment of the surface area made available by running the highway underground.

b) Study of the existing public service system with regard to:
   - Treatment of the river and its surroundings as a meeting place that enhances the value of the river's surface.
   - Optimization of the major public service systems of El Matadero (former slaughterhouse) and the Mercado de Frutas (former fruit market).
   - Expansion of the public service system.
   - Utilization of the riverbed for sports and leisure and possible modification of its current course.
   - Creation of footpaths and cycle paths linked with new public services of this type, including the Anillo Verde Ciclista (Green Ring for Cycling) the Senda Real (King's Trail) and so on.
   - Study of the feasibility of moving large containers or possible alternative uses for significant buildings, such as the Center for Hydrographic Studies. Evaluation of the need to modify the location of potentially conflicting service infrastructures.

c) Alternatives to current traffic by:
  - Reorganizing surface traffic, encouraging reduced use of private vehicles, the predominance of public transport and a preponderance of pedestrian use. Possible changes of perimeter roads.
  - Evaluation and treatment of solutions for tunnel entrances and exterior auxiliary elements such as ventilation and emergency exits.
  - Study of negative impact near monuments or green zones and possible alternatives.
  - Opportunity to add new public transit elements inside.

d) Other objectives:
  - Taking advantage of the opportunities this project may offer as complements to, and support of the Olympic project.
  - Articulation of constructed elements and of a new system of free spaces.
  - Concrete conservation and rehabilitation measures linked to the rest of the proposal.

PARTICIPANTS IN THE SECOND STAGE

Contestants invited directly to the competition's second stage must have demonstrated experience in the planning, resolution, and implementation of major urban renewal projects on both an international and national scale.

For that reason, the Contracting Body for participation in the Second Stage of the competition has invited the following professionals, previously selected on the basis of their capacity and world renown in this area: Peter Eisenman, New York; Norman Foster, London; Jacques Herzog and Pierre de Meuron, Basel; Rem Koolhaas, Rotterdam; José Antonio Martínez Lapeña and Elías Torres, Barcelona; Juan Navarro Baldeweg, Madrid; Dominique Perrault, Paris; Kazuyo Sejima and Ryue Nishizawa, Tokyo.

COMPOSITION OF THE JURY

The jury will be composed of the following members, each of whom will have say and vote:
- **President:** The most excellent Mayor and President of the Municipal Government of Madrid or his delegate.
- **Members:** The Councilwoman for Urban Planning, Housing and Public Works or her delegate; the Councilwoman for the Environment and City Services or her delegate; a representative of the Socialist municipal group; five experts of international renown who will be invited by the organizing body.
- **Secretary:** The General Secretary of the Councillorship of Urban Planning, Housing, and City Services of the Municipal Government of Madrid, with say but no vote.

The political representatives may take advice from a specialist in the subject, who will attend jury meetings with say but no vote.

The Councillorship of Urban Planning, Housing, and City Services has invited the following professionals to take part in the Jury: Luis Fernández-Galiano, Kurt Foster, Julio Martínez Calzón, Peter Rowe, Vittorio Magnago Lampugnani, all of whom were chosen on the basis of their international renown.

COMPETITION CALENDAR

- **Competition launching:** March 2005
- **Deadline for the first stage:** July 5, 2005
- **Jury decision for the first stage:** July 15, 2005
- **Deadline for the second stage:** October 28, 2005
- **Public exhibition and final jury decision:** November 28, 2005

Extract of the competition rules.

EXTRACT OF THE COMPETITORS' PROJECT SUMMARIES

JUAN NAVARRO BALDEWEG

Our proposal stipulates five principles for action: First, the establishment of an overall geometry to unify the different parts of the project. Second, shaping the terrain to generate an artificial topography that delimits areas in the open space and adds visibility to different use zones. Third, the implementation of extensive water use. Fourth, the construction of new containers to satisfy social demands and neighborhood activities. Fifth, the reconsideration and articulation of pedestrian, automobile, and bicycle circuits through the new areas, and their connection to the rest of the city.

We should emphasize the intervention intended to join the area below the Royal Palace with the Casa de Campo as one of the most important and delicate enclaves. We enhance the experience of the river through a succession of five large, interconnected, and parallel expanses of water, each twenty meters wide, but of variable length.

In the area currently occupied by Arganzuela Park, three large buildings will be constructed and linked by a hillock running along the entire Yeserías Avenue. The first building will house a large auditorium. The second is a polyhedron with perforations on various sides. It will contain a polyvalent space, a restaurant and a cafeteria and will be able to house popular fiestas. The third building is a large covered area, a sort of urban plaza that will serve as a central meeting area.

HERZOG & DE MEURON

We understand the Manzanares Park as part of a system of natural spaces — specifically, the urban segment of an extensive natural area linking the Sierra de Guadarrama to the north with the Tagus River Valley to the south.

The first proposed intervention is both monumental and modest, straightforward and recognizable to all citizens of Madrid: a promenade covered with flowers that begins at Cathedral Plaza alongside the Royal Palace. This Path of Flowers will run across the Campo del Moro and the river to the Casa de Campo. That Path is a small intervention, but the fact that it can be carried out quickly and its prominent location will make it a symbol and forerunner to the entire operation.

Second, in the center of the park, on the river's tightest bend where Vicente Calderón Stadium now stands, we propose a lake, which we will call "The Mouth." This is the mouth of an enormous reservoir of underground water. The Mouth is a central point for the installation of hotels, spas, restaurants, and other places of interest to tourists that will have a determinant influence on Madrid's global competitiveness with other cities.

Finally, we reactivate some of the existing bridges and propose a new one, which we call The Ark. It will not only be a roadway, but also an outstanding and iconic construction that slows traffic. Built for culture, it will connect the southeastern neighborhoods with the center of Madrid.

DOMINIQUE PERRAULT ARCHITECTURE

As the main object of reflection in this competition, our project proposes an urban recovery materialized in two large areas: the Grand Park (the area between Campo del Moro and Casa de Campo) and the Grand River (between the Vicente Calderón Stadium and the former Fruit Market). Thus, a major longitudinal intervention paralleling the river and a transversal intervention that runs perpendicular to its course.

In essence, the Grand River is a response to something obvious: nowadays, the river does not reflect the scale of a city like Madrid from a cartographic standpoint.

The Grand Park has a fundamental intention: to encourage the recovery of the Casa de Campo and to rediscover it as a place with immense possibilities, not to mention its enormous historical justification, as its original continuity with the city center is now sullied by highways.

We propose removing traffic from the area delimited by two promenades/boulevards that currently exist but are disconnected. Within this area, access would be limited to residents and pedestrians, thus completely freeing the riverbanks.

The proposal also seeks a complete transverse connection of the two banks through the construction of profuse pedestrian walkways across the river and new bridges to continue the streets that abut the banks.

EZQUIAGA ARQUITECTURA, SOCIEDAD Y TERRITORIO

S.O.S. CIUDAD is defined in terms of sustainability through structuring parameters (mobility, social structure, management) and qualifying parameters (water, sound, vegetation).

It is organized to form 3 systems:

- Condensors: elements that function as attractors and aggregators of urban activity: Arganzuela, El Matadero and Market.
- Connectors: elements that overcome the physical, psychological, and environmental barrier of the road and waterways: Madrid Beach, Sports Gardens, Casa de Campo, Aquatic Park, Vicente Calderón Stadium, and Arganzuela.
- Diffusors: elements that change the quality the surroundings and of the physical spaces belonging to the existing city.

KAZUYO SEJIMA + RYUE NISHIZAWA SANAA

The edges of the river adopt a natural shape, freeing themselves of the walls that confine them; the banks become soft topographies allowing a closer and more amenable relationship. New public programs open to the entire city are developed on this surface. A surface that takes the form of an aluminum sheet, stitching all the areas together both horizontally and vertically, unifying the setting and endowing it with an unrepeatable character as an iconic landscape that will be a must-see for any visitor or resident unfamiliar with Madrid's river.

Thus, the setting will acquire its own personality, including pedestrian paths through different thematic areas to create a totally new atmosphere there. Along the pavement, deciduous trees such as white poplars or elms will cast their shade in the summer but allow visitors to enjoy the sun in the winter. The aluminum for this project, which will be used as a sort of deck, can come from recycled material taken from the city itself.

EISENMAN ARCHITECTS + JAMES CORNER FIELD OPERATIONS

Our proposal aspires to create a new form of totally connected and porous urban infrastructure. The project creates a vast fabricated landscape by overlaying a perforated surface that runs the length of the project's area like a new topographical membrane that also extends to the adjacent urban fabric.

This membrane is also an ecological filter consisting of hills and hollows to retain water. It consists of a variety of permeable materials (porous pavement, gravel, different varieties of grass and cane, and synthetic materials), so that its surface functions like a massive water treatment and purification system. The masses of water can grow or shrink over time. They can completely disappear or flood various hollows at the same time. Users can move freely in any direction, lengthwise or laterally, through this new and complex tissue.

MARTÍNEZ LAPEÑA - TORRES ARQUITECTOS

The city will again be able to approach the water. Rescuing the essence and lost spirit of this place. The city will be stitched back together as pedestrians cross the water on eight new footbridges.

Trees will be distributed in bands of jacaranda, rosewood, and horse chestnut that follow the river. Larger existing trees will be allowed to remain in these bands. Prairie grass will play a leading role, filling the gaps between the cobblestones that pave cycling paths and public service accesses.

Vicente Calderon Stadium will leave its mark after it is gone, recalling a place filled with memories and historic, practically sacred emotions. Its grass playing field will be retained and expanded like a Roman *circus maximus* wrapped in acoustic fabric that creates a ring with a diameter of 160 meters and lifts its skirts as though blown by the wind, offering visitors a view inside and beyond, to the river.

BURGOS & GARRIDO, PORRAS LA CASTA, RUBIO & ÁLVAREZ-SALA WITH WEST 8

The river is bigger

We started by thinking that the river is not an element of the city, but the city is actually an event of the river. The proposal must act from a geographical sphere on the understanding that it is going to deal with a biological continuity, a vector which cannot be separated along the lines of the old rural-urban division. The planned interventions on the M-30 motorway are calculated at about 3,000 million Euro. Why not earmark a percentage of these resources for the 50 miles of land through which the river flows? With this money the river could be made accessible in its entirety. Thanks to the river the urban grid could be decompressed, could be naturalized, and could create a continuity of green areas of unimaginable dimensions.The course of the water and its influence area, the biological field generated by the river, offers a sequence of events which many inhabitants of the city do not know and could not even imagine. This active field, the fertile plain of the Manzanares, should be valued from the mountains covered with snow until spring to the plains which seem like remnants of the desert, near its mouth.

Building a landscape

The network of landscapes which links the basin of the river is made up of multiple elements of variable complexity, like the rocky outcrops of La Pedriza, the forest of the Monte de el Pardo or the fertile plain next to the Jarama River. This diverse and intense organism should be offered to the city as a value in which its people can participate, if the new connections reach the same level of continuity as the river itself. The landscape of Madrid will be incorporated into the landscape of the Manzanares River, the city will open up from its own centre towards the natural environment. This centre is understood today as the intersection between the constructed patchwork and the biological field of the river. The edges of this intersection are softened or hardened to create proximity between the water, the riverbank, the old settlement on the right bank and the historical city situated on the left.

A necklace of vegetable pearls

Landscape is brought into the city in an intense way, by means of a necklace of vegetable pearls. The string that joins them is a riverside promenade that accompanies the right-bank of the river in its entirety. Above this common area will arise a green vault composed of fully-grown pine trees, thus suddenly modifying the environment. The 9,000 trees will be selected so that, once planted, they will form a new and patent natural structure. The botanical analyses that have been carried out endorse this reality. Those who have suffered the M-30 for decades will welcome this gift. This vegetable space is an impressive strip capable of integrating the events of the river, the pearls of the necklace, some vegetable, some water and some constructed. To the north, a landscape set is projected which includes the Campo del Moro with its monumental reflection on the other side of the Manzanares in a completely renovated access to the Casa de Campo. In the centre, Arganzuela Park evokes from the contemporary the character of the riverbed. Water becomes present like the mark of furrows that were wet, fragrant paths, diffuse limits. There, the Castilian landscape blends together with the fresh ambience of the river source. To the south, the necklace spreads out over the infrastructures, linking together the city's parks, promising a growth that will breathe nature.

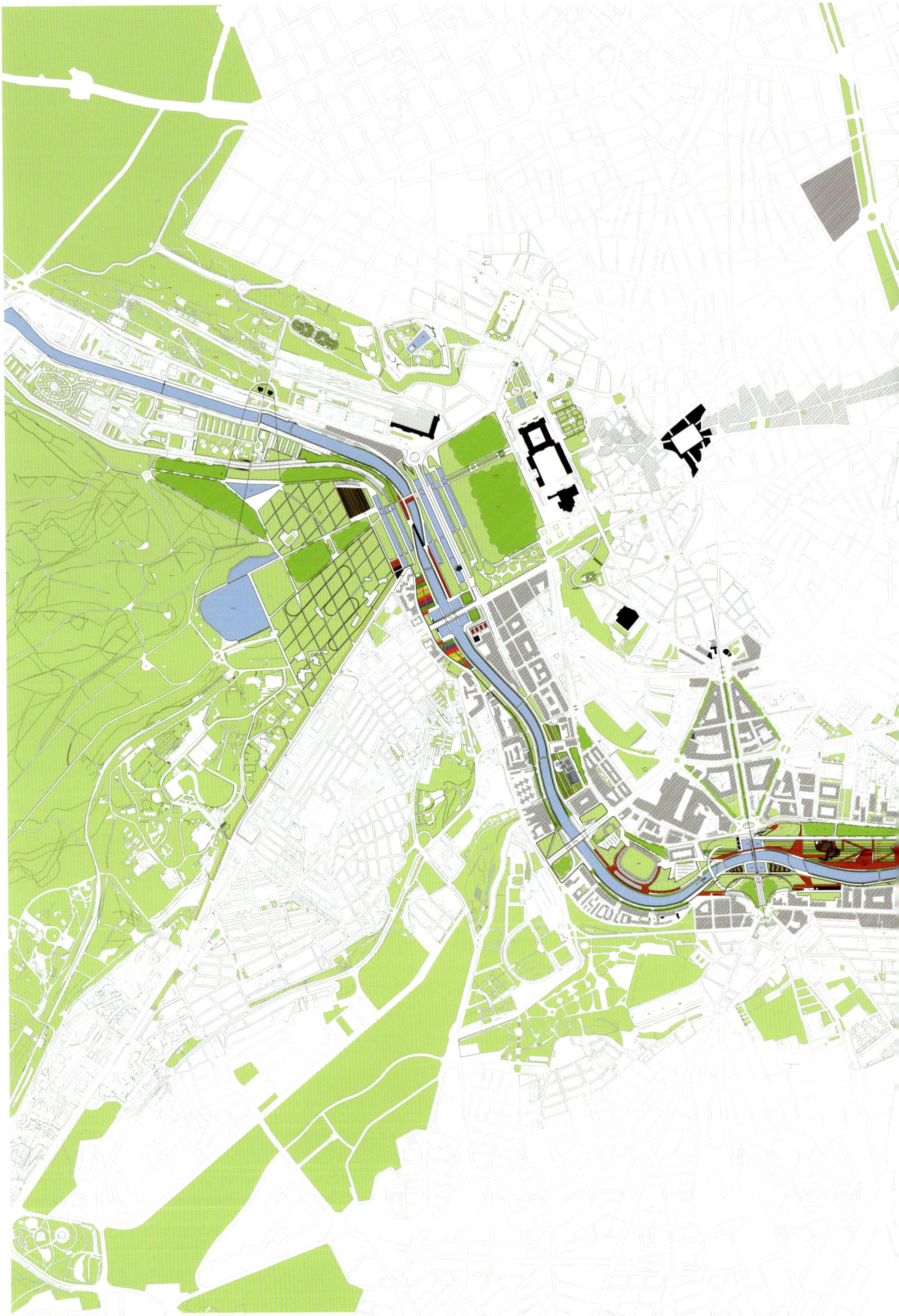

CONCURSO DE IDEAS PARA EL PARQUE LINEAL DEL MANZANARES. OCTUBRE 2005 LEMA: D´ARCY PLANTA DE ORDENACION GENERAL ESCALA 1/5000

CONCURSO DE IDEAS PARA EL PARQUE LINEAL DEL MANZANARES. OCTUBRE 2005 LEMA: D´ARCY PLANTA DE ORDENACION GENERAL . ESCALA 1/5000 2

EL CAMINO DE LAS FLORES
PUENTE DEL REY
LA BOCA
EL ARCA
MONCLOA ARAVACA
COLONIAS DEL MANZANARES
ARGÜELLES
CHAMBERI
ARAPILES
TRAFALGAR
UNIVERSIDAD
ALMAGRO
JUSTICIA
CHUECA
CENTRO
ÓPERA
SOL
CORTES
RETIRO
EMBAJADORES
IMPERIAL
ACACIAS
CHOPERA
ARGANZUELA
PALOS DE MOGUER
LEGAZPI
PUERTA DEL ÁNGEL
LUCERO
LOS CÁRMENES
LATINA
SAN ISIDRO
COMILLAS
OPAÑEL
CARABANCHEL
MOSCARDO
USERA
ALMENDRALES
PRADOLONGO
CALLE DE JARDINES

TRANSFORMACIONES EN CURSO

emprende un inmenso proyecto infraestructural: o de 6 kilómetros de la autopista que circunda la será soterrado, a lo largo del Río Manzanares. La e así ganada será transformada en un parque.

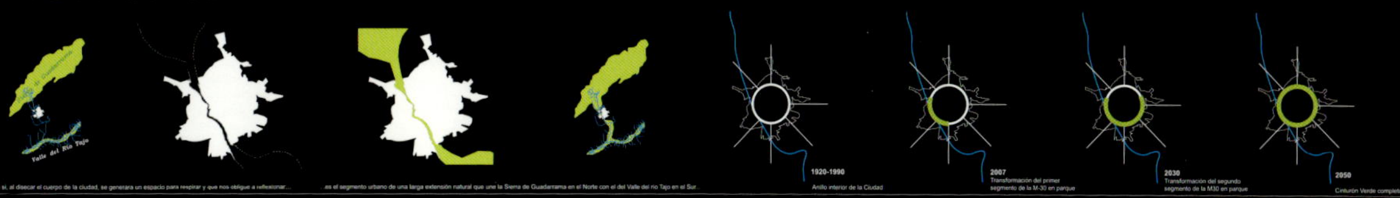

...es como si, al disecar el cuerpo de la ciudad, se generara un espacio para respirar y que nos obligue a reflexionar... ...es el segmento urbano de una larga extensión natural que une la Sierra de Guadarrama en el Norte con el del Valle del río Tajo en el Sur.

Parque emerge: Parque Manzanares

de afirmar que no se asocia Madrid con za. La ciudad no fue fundada a orillas de ningún ificativo, lago importante o a orillas del mar, y se proyectó en el momento de su planificación parque emblemático que formara parte de la d de la ciudad. La "Operación Manzanares" ofrecerá te a la ciudad un espacio natural céntrico. Es , al disecar el cuerpo de la ciudad, se generara cio para respirar y que nos obligue a reflexionar. mos el Parque Manzanares como parte de un sistema de espacios naturales y de recreo: es el segmento de una larga extensión natural que une la Sierra de ama en el Norte con el del Valle del río Tajo en el Sur. formación de este segmento de la autopista M-30 rque podría ser precursora de otras intervenciones, uras generaciones realizarían en sus tramos s, formando así a largo plazo el Cinturón Verde de nscribiéndose en la estructura radial de la ciudad.

unta es entonces: ¿Qué tipo de parque debe e allí? El enlace del nuevo parque con los naturales de las afueras recuerda al Jardín Munich. Pero reproducir un Jardín Ingles tendría sentido como hacerlo con un jardín paisajista o como el *Hyde Park* en Londres o el *Central Park* a York. Pero si nos interesa la forma en que el *Park* revela el subterráneo rocoso de Manhattan. ra semejante, el subterráneo de Madrid –el acuífero *Diétrico de la Fosa del Tajo*- podría inspirar la ón y el carácter del nuevo Parque Manzanares y rio de agua. Como una enorme fortaleza, la ciudad se obre esta bolsa de agua sin llegar a verla. Inclusive, ha dado su nombre a Madrid, proveniente del latín ue describía una densa red de ríos y arroyos en la mayoría de los cuales fueron después canalizados.

ravesaría todo el Parque Manzanares: éste es el mento constante en el curso rítmico y secuencial de esta paisajista que entreteje elementos existentes Parque de la Arganzuela o el antiguo Matadero rvenciones totalmente nuevas. El nuevo carácter del río reemplaza la antigua forma funcionalista rata que tenía desde la segunda mitad del siglo naturaleza artificial del nuevo cauce del río es ática de toda la Operación Manzanares e ilustra bles alteraciones e innumerables transformaciones tramo de río-ciudad ha sufrido desde su origen.

fase del proyecto sobresalen tres intervenciones su escala y su significado tipológico y programático: arela de flores, un lago y un edificio-puente.

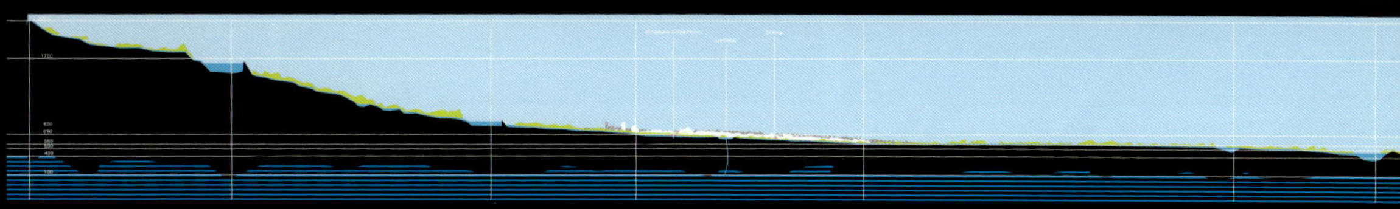

Sección Longitudinal del "Resort"

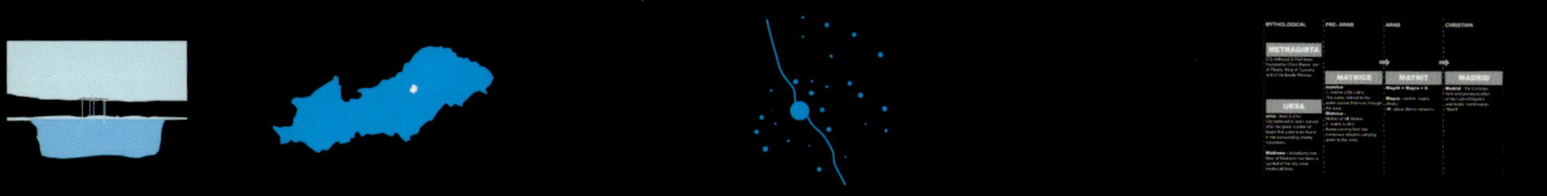

...como una enorme fortaleza, la ciudad se asienta sobre esta bolsa de agua sin llegar a verla... ...una serie de fuentes, las cuales serían alimentadas también por el agua de la Fosa Tectónica del Tajo... ...inclusive, el agua ha dado su nombre a Madrid, proveniente del latín Matrix, que describía una densa red de ríos y arroyos en la región, la mayoría de los cuales fueron después canalizados.

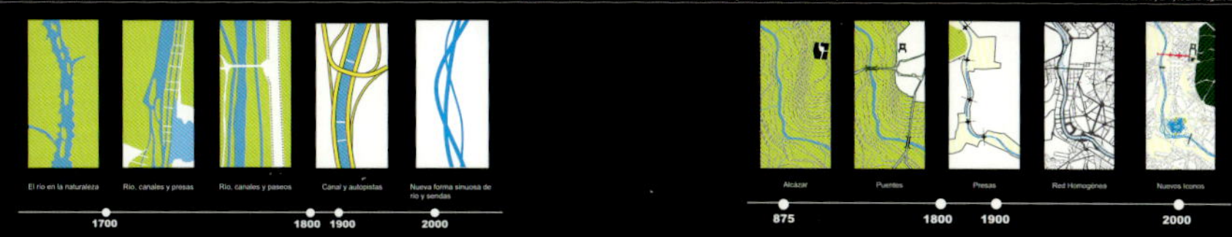

Historia de las Transformaciones del Río y sus Márgenes

Hitos de la Ciudad

Primer Paso: Camino de las Flores

a intervención propuesta es monumental y a la vez sencilla y reconocible para todos los madrileños le de inmediato – incluso tal vez en los próximos na pasarela cubierta de flores. Comienza en la Palacio Real, el sitio de origen de la Ciudad, árabes construyeron el Alcázar. Hoy sigue siendo de visita obligada para el turista y en especial para Español e Iberoamericano, quienes contemplan ma del paisaje español en toda su amplitud a una valla al borde del risco. El Camino de las re esta valla para dar el primer paso por encima o del Moro y el río hasta la Casa de Campo. a Plaza Real con el antiguo coto de caza, el lugar ristas con el sitio de recreo de los madrileños. mino es ciertamente una intervención pero debido a la posibilidad de su rápida n y su prominente situación sería precursor lo de toda la Operación Manzanares.

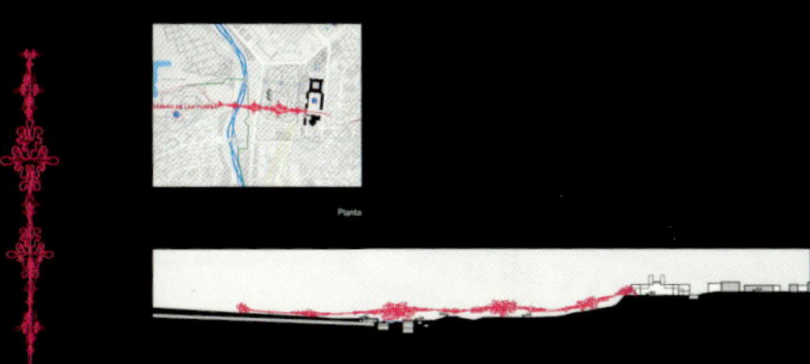

Planta

Sección Longitudinal

Entrada al "Camino de las Flores" desde la Plaza de la Catedral

Lago: La Boca

dio del parque, en el recodo mas pronunciado del cuentra actualmente el Estadio Vicente Calderón, bo ha sido ya decidido. En ese lugar proponemos l cual llamamos "La Boca". Es la desembocadura orme reservorio de agua subterráneo: La Fosa del Río Tajo, que se encuentra a 300 metros udad. La Boca es el centro del "Resort" donde an asentar Hoteles, *Spas*, Restaurantes y s de interés turístico que influyen de manera nte en la competencia global entre ciudades. también el ámbito para alojar asociaciones y clubes a deportes acuáticos, piscinas al aire libre, etc. tradición del Estanque artificial del Retiro -un sitio ueblo va los domingos a remar- y que seguramente iría, junto con las inmediaciones del parque, en uno ares de encuentro preferidos por los madrileños. es también el vacío más grande dentro de los la ciudad donde ambos flancos descienden damente formando el Valle. Aquí se escenifica la vista n Isidro, pasando sobre el río, hasta el Palacio Real y l –la perspectiva pintada por Goya en el siglo XVIII a ciudad consolidada y en lugares específicamente a ambos lados del río, se proyecta una serie de s cuales serían alimentadas también por el agua a Tectónica del Tajo, consiguiendo de esta forma ma del agua sea reintroducido en todo Madrid.

Vista aérea de "La Boca"

...la perspectiva pintada por Goya en el siglo XVIII... ...La Boca se convertiría, junto con las inmediaciones del parque, en uno de los lugares de encuentro preferidos por los madrileños...

Planta

terreno diétrico de la fosa del Tajo

Puente: El Arca

nos algunos de los puentes existentes y proponemos , con el propósito de mejorar significativamente n entre los barrios del oeste desarrollados en s décadas con el Madrid Antiguo al este del río. stos puentes, que llamamos El Arca, sobresale. camente una vía de circulación, sino un edificio e frena el tráfico. Atravesarlo se convierte en toda encia, atractiva para peatones y automovilistas. os este puente porque conectaría la actual calle el paseo cultural de Madrid -los Paseos de la , Recoletos, del Prado- con el Paseo de San Antonio, sideramos el boulevard más importante y con más cial de desarrollo del oeste de la ciudad. El edificio así en la tradición centralista de Madrid Capital, en las calles de salida de la ciudad, monumentos uente de Toledo, o el de Segovia, o emblemáticos tos, como los más recientes al norte de la ciudad. una construcción para la cultura: imaginamos rgaría salas de conciertos para música ánea, teatros alternativos, clubes, espacios te contemporáneo, así como locales culturales s como cines, talleres y puntos de venta de es de moda, publicistas, entre otros. Además, pacios para ir de tiendas, la actividad de ocio ar de nuestro tiempo, la cual es generalmente a la periferia de la ciudad. También se podría endas, que tendrían una vista espectacular y a contribuiría al financiamiento de los espacios El Arca es un icono de la cultura de masas. stá en las cercanías del Matadero -que ya se sformar en un Centro Cultural- y de los barrios que o una gran cantidad de inmigrantes en los últimos es importante, ya que los barrios interraciales ás activos culturalmente en cualquier ciudad.

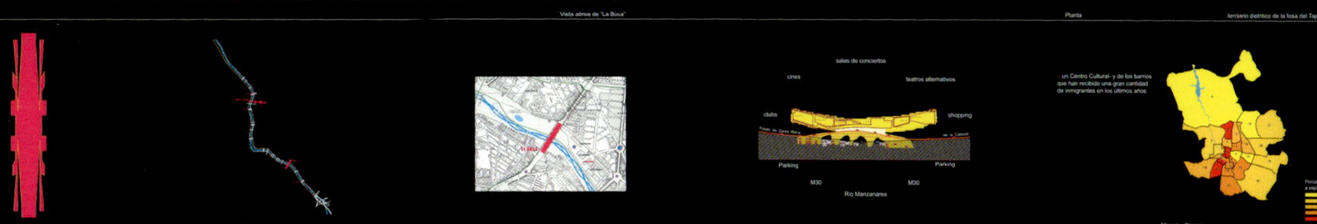

Diagrama del "Arca", las Avenidas y los Puentes

Planta

un Centro Cultural- y de los barrios que han recibido una gran cantidad de inmigrantes en los últimos años.

Minorías Étnicas

Nuevo Distrito

Manzanares, con su lago y sus nuevos os, generaría una revalorización de sus zonas s. Las hileras de edificios y viviendas, que e miran a la autopista, se convertirían en áreas as con vistas panorámicas al parque y al centro d. Los solares ubicados a lo largo del parque an su aprovechamiento, lo que haría posible la ón de nuevas viviendas, especialmente para las e cada vez mas, se mudan bien a la periferia d o fuera de ella. Una parte del valor agregado enos afectados podría ser invertida en la n del parque.
o a la creación urgente y necesaria de espacio generaría así también una densificación rior de la ciudad, ya que al mismo tiempo del parque sería intensamente construido.

os también transformar las calles ubicadas a lo arque y cambiar sus nombres por Avenida Este y este, pensando en *Central Park East and West*. s y estas dos avenidas, generan conjuntamente ctura en forma de escalera sobre el río.

inclusive ir más lejos y constituir un Distrito 22 es", lo cual dotaría a la operación de un peso político endería solamente como un proyecto paisajístico.

"El Arca" vista desde el parque.

Barrios de Madrid: 1. Centro 2. Arganzuela 3. Retiro 4. Salamanca 5. Chamartín 6. Tetuan 7. Chamberí 8. Fuencarral- El Pardo 9. Moncloa Aravaca 10. Latina 11. Carabanchel 12. Usera 13. Puente de Vallecas 14. Moratalaz 15. Ciudad Lineal 16. Hortaleza 17. Villaverde 18. Villa de Vallecas 19. Vicalvaro 20. San Blas 21. Barajas **22. MANZANARES**

a perspectiva cercana podemos constatar que el río se percibe como periférico a la ciudad, relativamente central dentro de sus límites. cambiaría esta percepción, creando una tralidad, dotando a los barrios el oeste de un o y una mejor conexión con el Madrid Antiguo.

ción Manzanares, desde una perspectiva ia, es el proyecto-logo para el Madrid áneo. Obtiene finalmente lo que le escapaba: ubstancial de Naturaleza que se inserta dando forma al río y sus márgenes, dotándoles con de "Resort". Se introducen también nuevos rales y de ocio de forma emblemática, y con la ciudad se convierte en un lugar que atraerá ntes y gente para trabajar y vivir en ella.

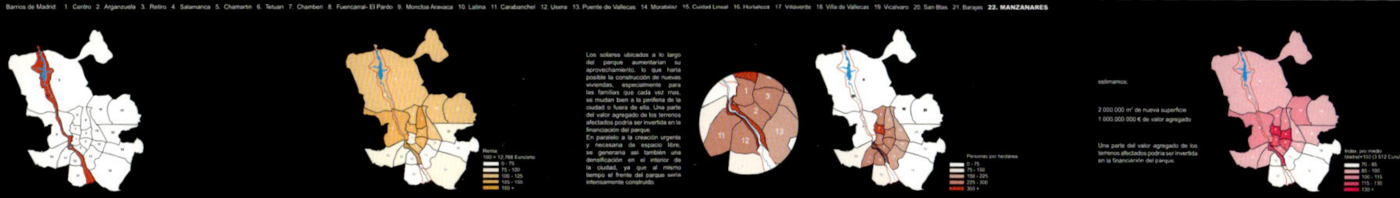

El Distrito Manzanares en el Municipio de Madrid

Distribución de la renta per capita

Los solares ubicados a lo largo del parque aumentarían su aprovechamiento, lo que haría posible la construcción de nuevas viviendas, especialmente para las familias que cada vez mas, se mudan bien a la periferia de la ciudad o fuera de ella. Una parte del valor agregado de los terrenos afectados podría ser invertida en la financiación del parque.
En paralelo a la creación urgente y necesaria de espacio libre, se generaría así también una densificación en el interior de la ciudad, ya que al mismo tiempo el frente del parque sería intensamente construido.

Densidad

estimamos:

2.000.000 m² de nueva superficie
1.000.000.000 € de valor agregado

Una parte del valor agregado de los terrenos afectados podría ser invertida en la financiación del parque.

Precios de la propiedad inmobiliaria

KAZUYO SEJIMA + RYUE NISHIZAWA SANAA

Concurso Internacional para la selección del diseño y proyecto de urbanización del Parque Lineal del Río Manzanares en la zona comprendida entre el Nudo Sur y el Puente de los Franceses

International Competition for the Design of the Linear Park along the Manzanares River

Memoria

El soterramiento de la autovía de circunvalación M-30 permite a la ciudad de Madrid reencontrarse con el Manzanares, cuyas riberas estaban ocupadas por la autovía. El soterramiento permite superar la barrera física y social que suponía la autovía y abre enormes posibilidades de transformación urbana.
La superficie liberada tras el soterramiento deja un terreno desmembrado y desarticulado que exige una actuación coherente y unitaria que vertebre toda el área. Nuestra propuesta se basa en crear a lo largo del río un espacio público nuevo, con un carácter especial y diferente. Un gran espacio de encuentro y disfrute cuya belleza, carácter y atmósfera propios actúen como catalizador de regeneración y revitalización de todo el ámbito.
Este nuevo espacio integra el río en la ciudad mediante operaciones de cambio de forma del río y sus riberas, mediante nuevos programas urbanos y mediante una nueva materialidad. El río y sus riberas adoptan una forma mas natural liberándose de las paredes que lo confinan, las riberas se convierten en topografías suaves que permiten una relación más cercana y amable con el río. Sobre esta nueva superficie se desarrollan nuevos programas públicos abiertos a toda la ciudad que permiten disfrutar del paisaje recuperado, así respondiendo a las necesidades sociales que contribuyen a mejorar la vida de los ciudadanos Madrileños y la mejora ambiental del paisaje. Una superficie cose todas las áreas y unifica el ámbito, un manto de aluminio que dota al área de un carácter irrepetible, un paisaje icónico que será visita obligada para cualquier visitante o residente que no conozca el río de Madrid.

Project brief

The conversion of the M30 freeway into an underground highway allows the city of Madrid to rediscover the Manzanares River, whose banks are currently occupied by the freeway. The underpass allows the city to overcome the physical and social barrier that the freeway supposes, and opens a wide range of possibilities for urban transformation. The liberation of the surface reveals a disjointed and unarticulated terrain that demands a coherent and unifying intervention that structures the area as a whole. Our proposal is based on creating a new public space along the entire length of the river, a space with a special and unique character; a new river of encounter and enjoyment whose beauty, character, and atmosphere act as catalysts for the regeneration and revitalization of the entire site. This new space integrates the river in the city through changes in the contour of the river and its banks, through a new urban program and a new materiality. The river and riverbanks liberate themselves from the canal boundaries that confine it, while the banks are converted into soft topographies that permit a closer and friendlier relationship with the river. Along this new surface, new public programs are developed and opened to the city, allowing the public to enjoy the rehabilitated landscape, thus responding to the social needs that contribute to the improved quality of life of Madrid residents and the betterment of environmental conditions.
One single surface sews together all of the areas and unifies the intervention, a blanket of aluminium that provides the area with a unique character, a singular landscape that will be a sure stop for visitors and residents that are not familiar with the Madrid River.

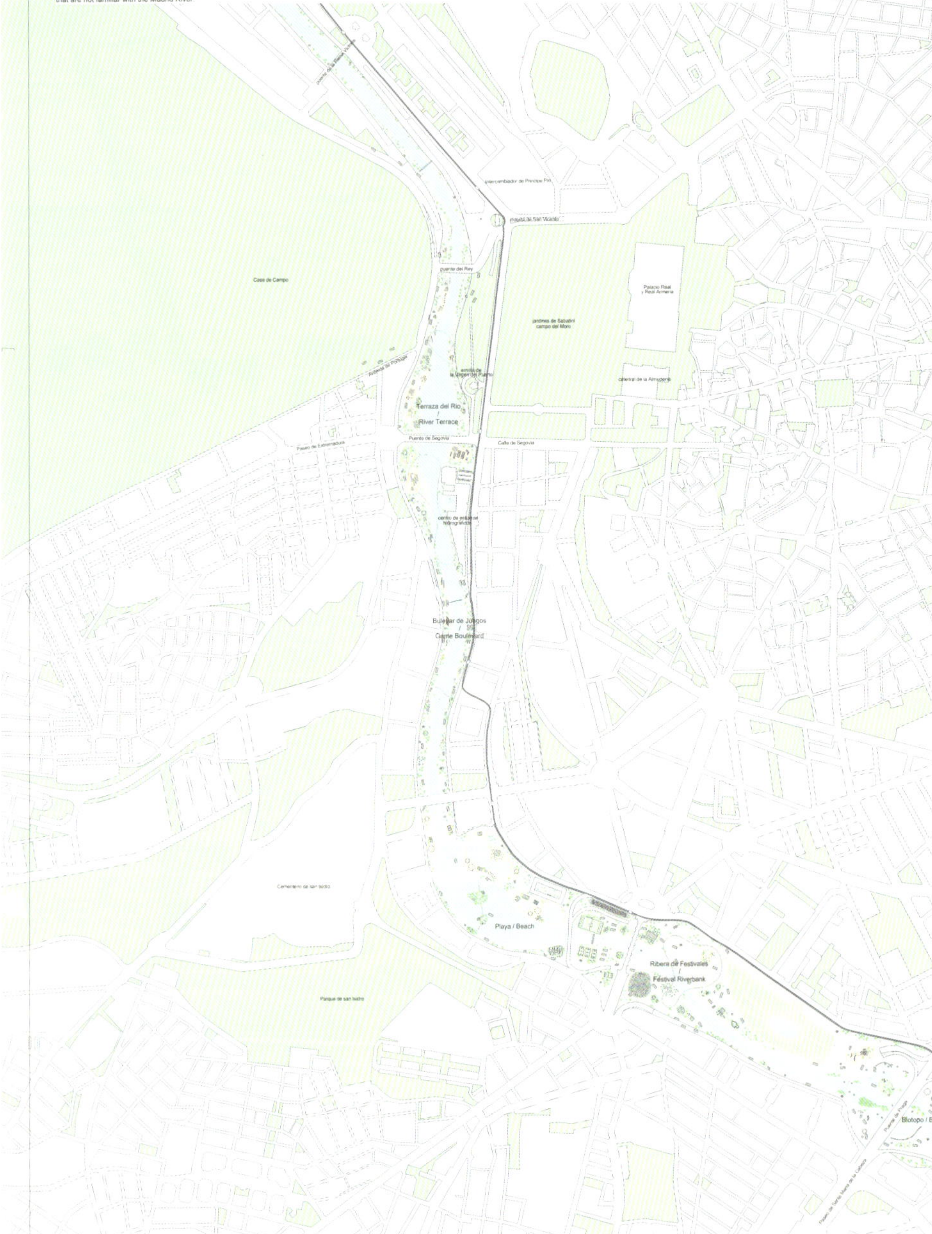

An?isis de Ciudad

Madrid recupera su unidad urbana. La intervención considera el curso del Manzanares como una unidad estructuradora del conjunto urbano, reestableciendo las conexiones del centro histórico con la ciudad global y conectando los barrios a través de una red de espacios verdes y dotaciones.

Esquema de usos existentes y propuestos
El manzanares como nuevo eje atractor social y cultural.

esquema de circulaciones a lo largo del manzanares

Programa
Todo el ámbito de intervención se unifica con un paseo peatonal que atraviesa diferentes áreas temáticas. El ámbito adquiere una personalidad propia al recubrirse el paseo con un material que crea una atmósfera totalmente nueva en el lugar: un pavimento de aluminio. Integrados en el pavimento, árboles de hoja caduca, álamo blanco y álamo temblón, dotan de sombra al paseo en verano y permiten disfrutar del sol durante el invierno.
Dentro del paseo se establece una red de pequeños pabellones (quioscos, cafés, bares de refrescos, puestos de información) y mobiliario urbano (bancos, fuentes, luminarias) que garantizan el confort a lo largo del paseo. Dentro del manto de aluminio, como islas flotando, se distribuyen los nuevos programas culturales, recreativos y de ocio propuestos unidos por rutas peatonales y ciclistas. Estos elementos, junto con los equipamientos preexistentes crean un carácter propio en cada área.

…en izquierda, hacia la zona de la playa artificial. En primer término se ve la zona de piscinas.
…verbank towards the bathing area, with the swimmingpools in foreground.

…n derecha, frente al Parque de la Arganzuela, con el Puente de Toledo al fondo.
…nk, opposite the Arganzuela Park, with the Toledo Bridge in the background.

…n derecha a la altura del Puente de Praga. En primer plano se ve la zona de Biotopo, al fondo, la Ciudad del Arte.
…de riverbank near the Praga Bridge. The Biotope Area and the City of Arts behind, can be seen.

parque río manzanares

Pocas o puede incluso que ninguna propuesta urbana desde 1945 ha creído en la capacidad de la ciudad para generar nuevas formas, nuev estilos de vida y nuevos programas. Históricamente, las utopías han resultado ingenuas, pretenciosas o han ido demasiado lejos, pero independientemente de su ideología, han sido modelos importantes en la formalización de su contexto y de su tiempo. Hoy en día, e esperanza y esa especulación han desaparecido, quizás debido a la complejidad de los proye urbanos actuales, o quizás debido a una aversión a pensar y actuar a lo grande. A pesar de es proyecto Madrid Río Manzanares exige algo nuevo, algo grande, algo que aspire a transforma parte occidental de Madrid en su totalidad.

Partiendo de la audaz iniciativa de soterrar las autovías urbanas, liberando así el río y sus orilla para otras funciones, nuestra propuesta supone sobre todo una reconceptualización del río mismo. El proyecto está diseñado para revitalizar el río como un sistema dinámico, mejorar las infraestructuras cívicas y los espacios para el ocio, y para conectar los dos lados de la ciudad centro histórico y las barriadas periféricas occidentales.

Nuestra propuesta aspira a crear una nueva forma de urbanismo, totalmente conectada y porc El proyecto rompe la linealidad y la separación, disuelve los elementos lineales en un campo abierto y crea un extenso tejido paisajístico. Al reformalizar las relaciones entre sectores urbar históricamente separados, el proyecto permite unificar la ciudad. La principal técnica que se propone para lograr este cometido es la superposición de una superficie agujereada a lo larg del área del proyecto, una membrana topográfica que también se extiende hacia el tejido urba adyacente.

Esta membrana paisajística es también un filtro ecológico, formado topográficamente por coli y cuencas para la retención de agua. Se construye con una variedad de materiales permeable (pavimentos porosos, gravas, distintas variedades de hierbas y cañas, y materiales sintéticos) forma que su superficie funcione como un masivo sistema de tratamiento y purificación de ag Una tipología de 'poros' o aperturas, cubetas y ventilaciones permite la acumulación, filtración flujo del agua del río, la retención del agua de lluvia en cuencas, y el acceso y ventilación de l túneles de las autovías subterráneas. Las masas de agua pueden aumentar y disminuir con el del tiempo, llegar a desaparecer totalmente o inundar varias cuencas a la vez. Estas fluctuacio son el reflejo de mayores procesos climáticos e hidrológicos, al tiempo que transforman periódicamente la forma espacial del parque, siguiendo el flujo y reflujo de las estaciones. A l largo del tiempo, estas masas de agua pueden ser utilizadas para actividades recreativas acu como pescar, remar, usar barcos teledirigidos y otras. A su vez, se transforman en fuentes, surtidores, vaporizadores o cascadas. El ritmo y el espectáculo del agua sugieren la conversió Manzanares en un parque hidrológico activo, el equivalente contemporáneo de la Villa Lante c jardines del Tívoli.

Los usuarios podrán moverse libremente en cualquier dirección, longitudinal y transversalmen través de este nuevo tejido paisajístico. Se definen senderos especiales para bicicletas y pea dejando áreas para campos de deportes, recreación activa, jardines de exposición, actividade acuáticas, exhibiciones botánicas y áreas para representaciones, activando un espectáculo d riqueza y diversidad para el parque urbano del Madrid del siglo XXI.

Una cubierta de árboles de varias densidades dotará a la superficie topográfica con texturas sombras y diversidad espacial. Esta cubierta, compuesta de una variedad de especies autóct en diferentes plantaciones ortogonales, se cultiva siguiendo modernas técnicas silviculturales cuidado y transplante hasta la madurez de los árboles.

Etapas:
Consideramos la implementación por etapas como una necesidad y proponemos que este n paisaje se construya en etapas coherentes y flexibles:
Una primera fase a lo largo del sector meridional: desde el Nudo Sur y el Parque Lineal hasta Puente de Praga. Esto permitirá la prolongación del parque existente hacia el tejido urbano, a vez que se aprovechan los servicios del Mercado de la Fruta, el área del renovado Matadero y inmediato desarrollo de los terrenos adyacentes.
La segunda fase conlleva la construcción restante del parque hasta el Puente de los Frances el norte. La tercera fase extendería el parque hacia el este, para permitir superficies más anch para la práctica de deportes y recreo, y sería definida por una nueva fachada urbana continua largo del límite oriental. Este paisaje ampliado permitiría traer los puentes y monumentos histó así como los tres nuevos edificios institucionales situados en el parque, a un primer plano par ser percibidos como objetos icónicos. El lado occidental se densificaría con proyectos de rel variados, con el requisito de que dichos edificios respeten la orientación perpendicular al par para asegurar la permeabilidad y conectividad, especialmente con conexiones a los principale corredores de espacios verdes.

Esta propuesta cumple y supera todas las demandas planteadas por los objetivos del espóns
- ofrece importantes mejoras ambientales de vanguardia mediante la filtración y el tratamie del agua, la reforestación extensiva, paisajes sostenibles de bajo mantenimiento y la conectiv las zonas verdes adyacentes;
- aporta nuevos e importantes espacios libres para la ciudad a escala metropolitana, con e y extensos servicios recreativos, incluyendo deportes y espectáculos cívicos;
- optimiza la conectividad a lo ancho de la ciudad, con máximas conexiones y continuidad longitudinal como transversalmente;
- realza los puentes históricos y los monumentos de la ciudad, ofreciendo una nueva visib y percepción icónicas ;
- permite la construcción en fases coherentes, literalmente creciendo de sí misma en fase sucesivas;
- prepara las condiciones ideales para el desarrollo del área construida y el desarrollo económico a ambos lados del río (tanto en el relleno a pequeña escala como en la gran esca
- es flexible y adaptable en términos de organización específica por fases, programación e implementación.

Few if any urban proposals since 1945 have believed in the future capacity of the city to generate new forms, new lifestyles and new programs. Utopias may have historically proven naïve, over-reaching or grandiose, but whatever their ideology, they have been si models in shaping their time and context. Today, such hope and speculation has all but disappeared – perhaps because of the complexity projects today, or perhaps because of an aversion to thinking and acting big. And yet, the Manzanares River project demands something n something big, something that aspires to transform the entire western section of Madrid.

Beginning with the bold initiative to sink the urban motorways underground, thus freeing the river and its edges to serve other functions, ou is first and foremost a rethinking of the river itself. The project is designed to revitalize the river as a dynamic system, to improve civic infras and social amenity, and to connect the two sides of the city: the historical center with the peripheral neighborhoods to the west.

We applaud the bold and audacious move to sink the roadways along the Manzanares River and create a new linear park along the riverba is a generous gift to the people of the Madrid, a significant improvement in civic infrastructure and a strong gesture toward connecting the of the City: the historical center with the peripheral neighborhoods to the west.

How can we take these bold urban initiatives to the next level? How may the river be given a unique presence, beyond that of a deep and drainage channel? How can barriers and impediments to connectivity and flow across the City be removed and remade? How might we a fully interconnected and porous form of urbanism?

Our proposal aims to create a new, fully inter-connected and porous form of urbanism. The project breaks down linearity and separation, c linear elements into an open field, and creates extensive landscape tissue tying the city together by re-figuring relationships between histor separated sectors of the City. The primary technique for achieving this is the overlay of a perforated surface across the length of the projec graphic membrane that also extends into the adjacent city fabric.

Importantly, this landscape membrane is also an ecological filter – topographically shaped into "hills and hollows" to work with water retent constructed from a variety of permeable materials (porous paving, gravels, grasses, reeds and synthetics), the surface functions as a massi management and cleansing device. A typology of "pores" – or openings, sinks and vents – allow river water to pool, filter and flood, rainwa retained in basins, and air and access to be provided to the roadway tunnels below. Water bodies may rise and fall over time, sometimes d ing altogether, and flooding into multiple basins at the other extreme. This interactivity reflects larger climatic and hydrological processes a periodically transforming the spatial form of the park, as with the ebb-and-flow of the seasons. In turn, these water bodies may be used for fishing, paddle boating, toy sail boating and other activities, as well as at times becoming fountain, bubble, spray, waterfall or white-water d The pulse and spectacle of water suggests that the Manzanares might become a dynamic hydrological park, the contemporary equivalent t Lante or Tivoli Gardens.

People can move freely and in any direction – both longitudinal and transversal - across this new landscape architectural fabric. Special bi walking paths are defined, and areas for sports fields, active recreation, display gardens, distinct water features, botanical exhibits, perform and other park amenities activate a rich and diverse spectacle of urban park life for the 21st century Madrid.

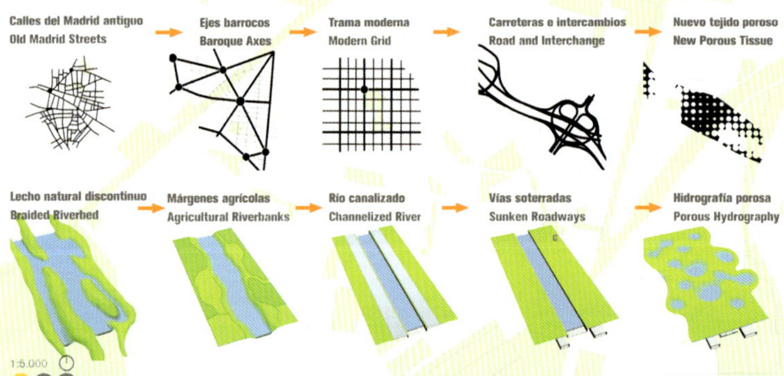

1:5.000

parque río manzanares

parque acuático
water park

parque deportivo
sports park

la playa
the beach

PROPUESTA GENERAL DE INTERVENCIÓN E:1/5000

MEMORIA

Las nuevas riberas del Manzanares acompañarán al cordón de agua y relacionarán la secuencia de parques y áreas ajardinadas desde el Puente de los Franceses hasta el Nudo Sur de la M30: Puerta de Hierro, Ciudad Universitaria, La Casa de Campo, el Campo del Moro, la Cuña Verde de la Latina, Parque de San Isidro, Parque de Tierno Galván y en el Nudo Sur el Parque del Río Manzanares.
El Manzanares, ajeno al crecimiento histórico de Madrid, nunca alimentó su urbanidad callejera, aunque es parte de su geografía original y fue lugar de esparcimiento, juegos y meriendas; fue maltratado y se le desconsideró; así se le adosó la M30 que se apropió de sus riberas y la ciudad terminó asumiendo su presencia residual e ignorando su cauce. (El gran río-vaguada urbano de Madrid es el Paseo de La Castellana- Recoletos –El Prado).
Al desaparecer de la vista la M30, la ciudad respirará tranquila, más silenciosa, podrá comunicarse entre riberas y volverá a ver a su río como la guía de un largo y ondulante parque verde que irá descubriendo mientras recorre su curso.
La ciudad podrá volver a acercarse al agua, completarse y restañar sus heridas, porque volverá a verse a sí misma saneada. Se asomará de nuevo a contemplarlo y hacer de sus márgenes placer. Se adecentarán fachadas obsoletas, se edificaran solares, se sustituirán edificios. Se hará presente con las nuevas edificaciones. Unas fachadas casi continuas en ambas riberas que se mirarán unas a otras a través del río. Se coserá la ciudad al pasar andando sobre el agua por ocho nuevos puentes de viandantes.
El agua, el verde y las edificaciones que se alejaran y acercarán al agua en sinuosas cintas de fachadas- a lo largo de las riberas formarán un conjunto continuo.

a/ El paso del río por el Puente del Rey desde el Campo del Moro para llegar a la Casa de Campo será bajo la Avda. Virgen del Puerto: amplio, con taludes y techo iluminados con pavés.

b/ En el Puente de Segovia el cauce del Manzanares recuperará la anchura natural, bajo los arcos de sus ojos se podrá volverá a pasear.

c/ Al desaparecer y trasladarse, el estadio Vicente Calderón dejará una huella, una memoria de un lugar de recuerdos, de emociones históricas, casi sagrado. Se hará permanecer su terreno de juego de césped que se extenderá por cuatro como un "circo máximo romano".
Esta hondonada de césped se envolverá con una tela acústica, en forma de aro de 160 m. de diámetro, que levantará sus faldones, como movidos por un vendaval, para poder ver su interior y desde de allí ver el río. Su estructura podría soportar publicidad y datos de actividades urbanas. El césped que se dirige al río es cubierta de una edificación de servicios y pequeños comercios.
Este lugar se acompaña de nuevas edificaciones, con aparcamientos subterráneos y con dos puentes peatonales que cruzan el río.
La geometría del aro se traza sobre el futuro soterramiento del lazo elevado de la M30, que ahora permanece pendiente del traslado del Vicente Calderón a las "peinetas".

d/ También en el Puente de Toledo volverá a exhibir sus ojos, se podrá volver a pasear por ellos. Junto al puente se construirán aparcamientos subterráneos en las salidas de la M30.

e/ Las nuevas edificaciones que completarán los espacios intersticiales entre edificios actuales, serán manzanas que se alinearán con las calles y cuyos interiores serán zonas libres ajardinadas y abiertos hacia las aceras exteriores en las esquinas.
De la misma forma los nuevos edificios en los terrenos de la Fabrica Mahou, serán oficinas, servicios y equipamientos públicos, con aires de manzanas vecinas, pero versátiles en sus profundidades edificables y de interiores de "barrio de Salamanca" revisitado. Más respetuosa con la ciudad en el exterior –alineaciones- más diversa en su interior.

f/ Entre el recordatorio del Vicente Calderón y el antiguo matadero se situará la mayor área de esparcimiento público. Un área abierta con edificaciones para actividades deportivas y de entretenimiento: pista de atletismo, piscinas abiertas, y otros centros deportivos y gimnasios que potencien el uso lúdico deportivo de la intervención. Se propone la rehabilitación de la fuente oval, convertida en "playa manzanares".
Gradas y pasarelas cubiertas elevadas unen con sombrajos fijos las pequeñas edificaciones.
Desde el Paseo de Yeserías se accede a nivel a la pasarela elevada. La cubierta puede ser soporte para paneles fotovoltaicos.
El matadero extendería sus futuros usos hacia esta área de esparcimiento. En su interior sus edificios albergarán actividades lúdicas, educativas- centro de artes y oficios, extensión universitaria - y entretenimiento.
Complejidad de actividades urbanas y ligadas a esta nueva "pax river".

g/ Las manzanas se completarán en el frente del río. La ciudad edificada se hará reconocer como fachada del parque verde lineal.
Al llegar al Nudo Sur, el río se cruza por el puente del tren procedente de Atocha y que pasa bajo la Avenida del Planetario; Aquí cuatro fachadas curvas- arcos-, reconocen este vacío de autopista, que algo tienen de otros edificios curvos de la M30 que acompañaran a la forma del nudo; puentes elevados y enlaces tentáculo.

h/ Los árboles se distribuirán en franjas que seguirán al río.
Bandas de jacarandas, tipuanas y castaños de Indias.
Intercalados entre estas franjas aparecerán los arboles de mejor porte que existen y que puedan permanecer.
El césped de pradera será protagonista y se difuminará en los intersticios entre los adoquines, que formaran caminos, recorridos de bicicletas y pasos de servicios públicos.
Las fuentes aparecerán entre juntas de los mismos adoquines esmaltamos, brotando como reventones, convirtiéndose en polvo de agua y refrescando el tórrido verano madrileño.
Habrá bancos prefabricados de hormigón con respaldo y sin respaldo, con o sin apoyabrazos.

i/Las ventilaciones gigantes de la M30, ovaladas, rectangulares o de la forma final con la que crucen las losas de cubierta, emergerán en todo su volumen hasta una altura de
10 m. convirtiéndose por la noche en las lámparas del paisaje del parque del río.
Lámparas que se construirán con paneles prefabricados de pavés circular y que en su parte superior los huecos son mayores para poder instalar focos y lanzar la luz mas lejos.
Intercaladas en las zonas donde las ventilaciones luminosas no alcancen con su luz se colocarán lamparas de la misma, altura de diámetro 1,5m y de características similares.
También las ventilaciones serán, donde sea necesario, soporte de graderías, de cubiertas de sombra y servicios de asistencia: kioscos para bicicletas, chiringuitos de río, etc..
Las barandillas del río y puentes peatonales tendrán luz en su interior irradiada por pavés circulares . De noche el río se verá como una franja luminosa de dos bandas que se duplicarán en el agua.
Bajo los puentes también la luz iluminará la oscuridad de sus tableros.

j/ La Avenida de Portugal se hará caminando...
El soterramiento de la Av. de Portugal deja entrar al manto del parque de la Casa de Campo desapareciendo la barrera que el trafico que producía hasta el momento. Se propone el acercamiento de la casa de campo como si un líquido se filtrara por las calles que llegan de forma perpendicular a la avenida.
Convirtiendo así la avenida en un pasaje peatonal con estructura de bulevar, que acompaña lateralmente a la casa de campo hasta dar entrada al Campo del Moro. Las fachadas de las edificaciones recuperan oxígeno y respiran entonces los aromas verdes de la Casa de Campo. Las ventilaciones seguirán teniendo protagonismo respaldando las necesidades de la nueva rambla; kioscos, chiringuitos, y pequeñas dotaciones apoyarán la propuesta del nuevo vial.

Rescatar la esencia , el espíritu perdido de este lugar .
Hacer emerger la presencia histórica del río con nuevos elementos y edificaciones emparentados con los que existen y existieron, con ademanes parecidos.
Renovar rescatando un nuevo río verde y urbano, optimista y refrescante, un lugar ahora tangencial para que pase a ser central para los ciudadanos de mañana de la Villa y Corte.

Merienda a la orilla del Manzanares, Francisco de Goya, 1776

Baile a la orilla del Manzanares, Francisco de Goya, 1777

A la orilla del Manzanares, Ferdinand Hodler, 1879

PROPUESTA EN PLANTA SOTERRAMIENTO M_30 E:1/5000

PROPUESTA GENERAL DE INTERVENCIÓN E:1/5000

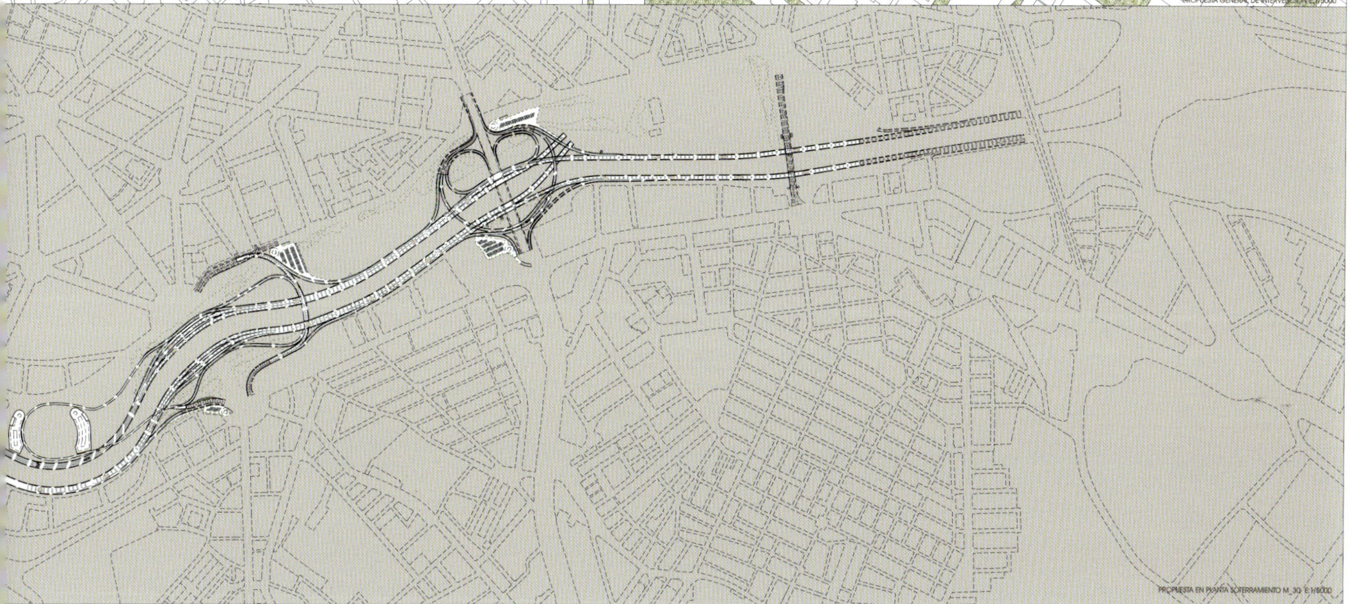

PROPUESTA EN PLANTA SOTERRAMIENTO M_30 E:1/5000

BURGOS & GARRIDO, PORRAS LA CASTA, RUBIO & ÁLVAREZ-SALA, CON WEST 8

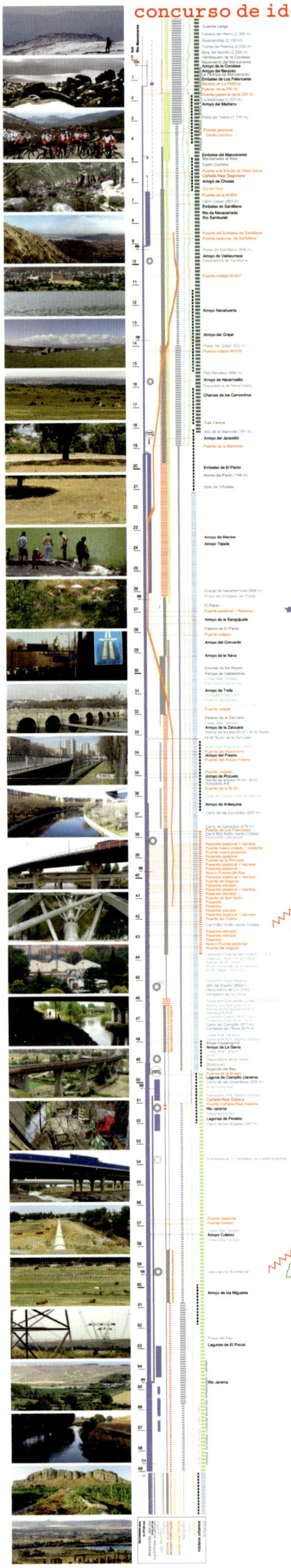

concurso de ideas parque lineal del manzanares

m-río

El río es más grande

Enfrentarse al problema que se nos presenta puede abordarse por el camino erróneo, pensando que el río es un accidente de la ciudad.
Nada más lejos de la realidad, la ciudad es uno de los eventos propios del río.
La propuesta debe responder a esta dimensión y actuar desde una esfera geográfica, entendiendo que se va a negociar con un continuo biológico, un vector que no se puede segregar según el viejo binomio rural-urbano.
Las intervenciones previstas sobre la M-30 se cifran en unos 6.000 M €
¿Por qué no destinar un porcentaje de estos recursos a los 69 km de territorio que recorre el Manzanares?
Con ellos se podrá materializar la tarea de volver accesible el río en toda su longitud.
Accesibilidad gradual, accesibilidad controlada, accesibilidad ordenada.
A través del río el tejido urbano podrá descomprimirse, naturalizarse y alcanzar una continuidad de áreas verdes que cobraría dimensiones no imaginadas.
Tomemos esta verdadera oportunidad para hacer de la ciudad un lugar memorable.
Madrid se ruborizará de verde cuando conozca de verdad a su río.
El curso del agua y su área de influencia, el campo biológico que el río genera, presenta una secuencia de acontecimientos que muchos de los habitantes de la ciudad no conocen ni pueden intuir. Este campo activo, la vega del Manzanares, deberá valorarse del Norte al Sur, desde la sierra con nieves que pueden persistir en abril, hasta las llanuras que parecerían retazos del desierto, cerca de su desembocadura.
Es indispensable considerar toda esta unidad como objeto de estudio y ámbito de la propuesta.
Cualquier otra delimitación se antoja falta de vista, casi ciega ante una realidad prometedora.

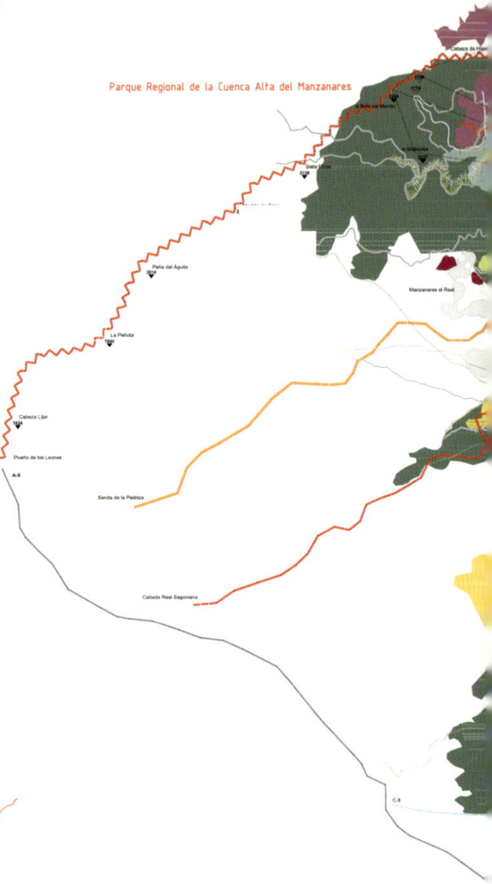

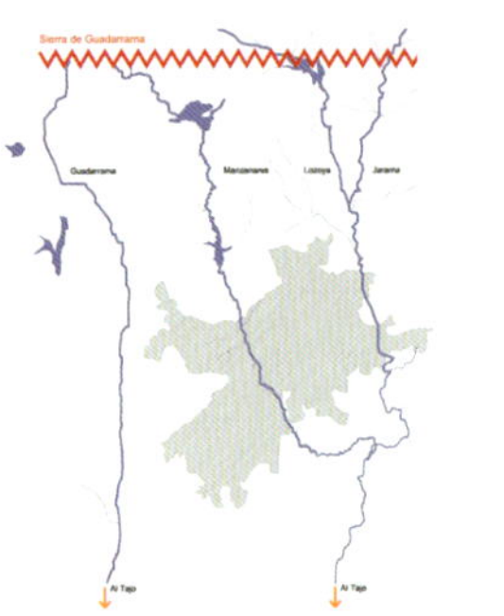

El territorio es la figura, no el fondo

Es necesario recuperar para la ciudad la estructura territorial y geográfica sobre la que se asienta.
Tres ríos, Guadarrama, Manzanares y Jarama, discurren Norte-Sur de la sierra al Tajo.

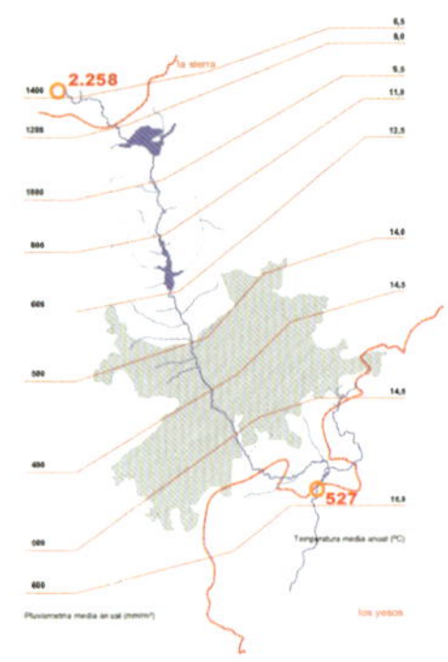

Del Cabo Norte a Tarifa

Un ciclista puede recorrer desde la desembocadura del río Manzanares, a 527 m de altitud, hasta su nacimiento a 2.258 m los mismos biotopos que encontraría en un viaje entre las estepas áridas del Sur de España y las tundras heladas del Norte de Noruega sólo recorriendo los 69 km del cauce del río.

Parque Lineal del Manzanares

Madrid tapón

La ciudad de Madrid no ha sido capaz, hasta ahora, de dar continuidad a los ámbitos naturales Norte y Sur.
Hoy es imprescindible enlazar el Parque Natural de la Cuenca Alta del Manzanares con el Parque Natural del Sureste.

Invertir en rescatar el río

Sólo tiene sentido la inversión en el río cuando ésta lo recupera en su totalidad.
El río es una unidad geográfica completa y con sentido que Madrid ha maltratado y que ahora podemos volver a descubrir.
Restaurar la estructura vegetal en determinados lugares puede servir para activar áreas mucho mayores.

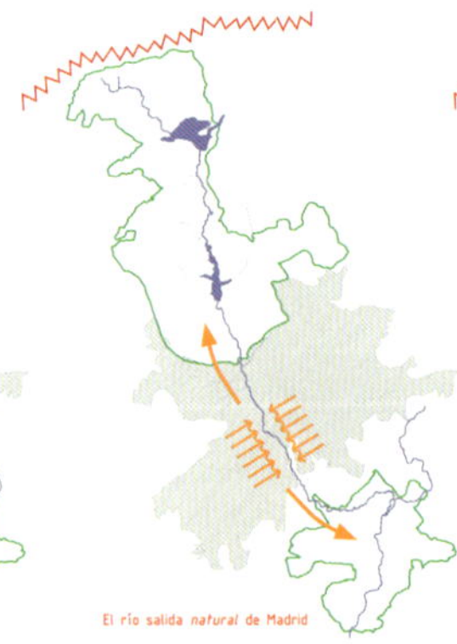

El río salida *natural* de Madrid

Se podrá salir a pie o en bicicleta desde el centro de Madrid hacia la sierra de Guadarrama o a las Vegas del Jarama.
El río es la puerta de Madrid.

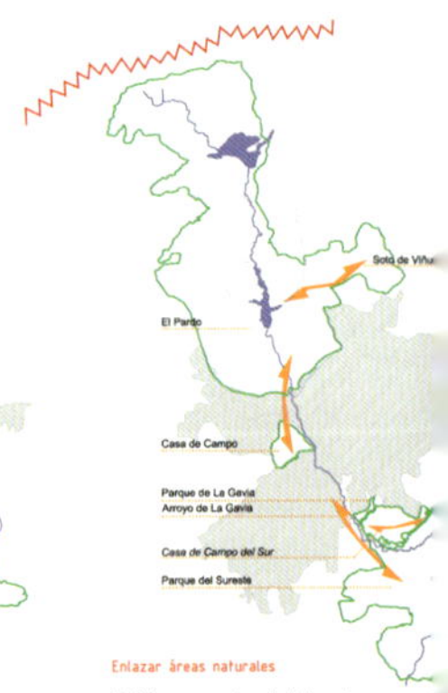

Enlazar áreas naturales

El río Manzanares puede ser el vehículo con el que recompone[r la] estructura de un territorio fragmentado, desgarrado y destruido [por el] abandono y las infraestructuras.
Es obligado enlazar el Soto de Viñuelas con el Norte del Monte [de El Pardo] recuperando una continuidad natural perdida.
Igualmente la Casa de Campo con el Monte de El Pardo y en e[l Sur el] Arroyo de la Gavia con el Parque del Sureste.

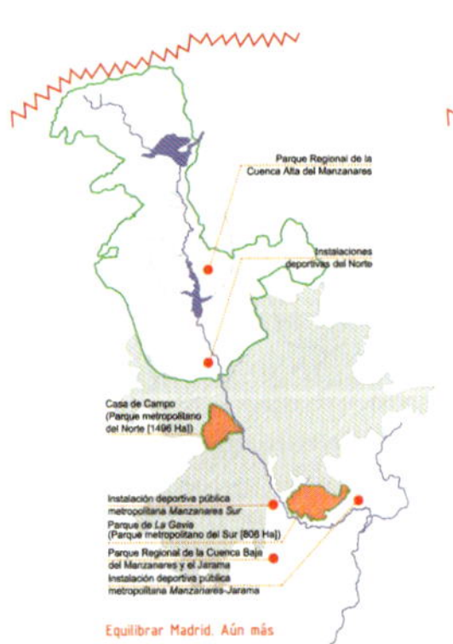

Equilibrar Madrid. Aún más

Madrid ha materializado en sus infraestructuras, equipamientos y desarrollo urbano una situación injusta y desequilibrada entre el Norte, más favorecido, y el Sur.
El río ahora es una demostración más de esta situación.
Intervenir en el río es equilibrar Madrid.

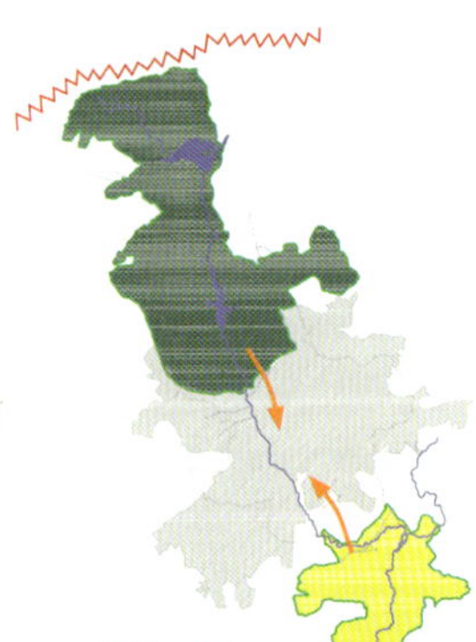

Del Norte y del Sur

Proponemos construir un nuevo paisaje en el interior de la ciudad que tome su carácter de los bosques saludables y frescos del Norte, pero también de la dureza áspera del Sur. Los verdes del Norte y los ocres del Sur.
Ambos se encuentran en Madrid.

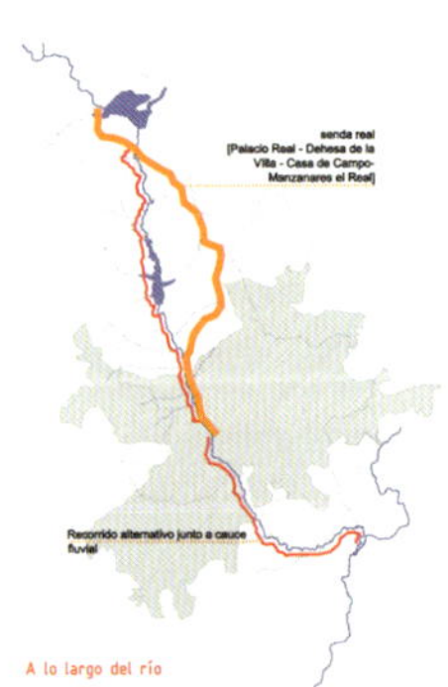

A lo largo del río

El río ha sido el soporte vertebrador de los cotos de caza reales. El camino que el Rey podía hacer desde el Palacio Real hasta el Palacio de El Pardo y el Castillo de Manzanares el Real se conservará, mejorará y será verdaderamente transitable.
Una senda a lo largo del río, desde su nacimiento hasta su desembocadura, articulará éste con la red, aún sin explotar, de cañadas y vías pecuarias existentes.

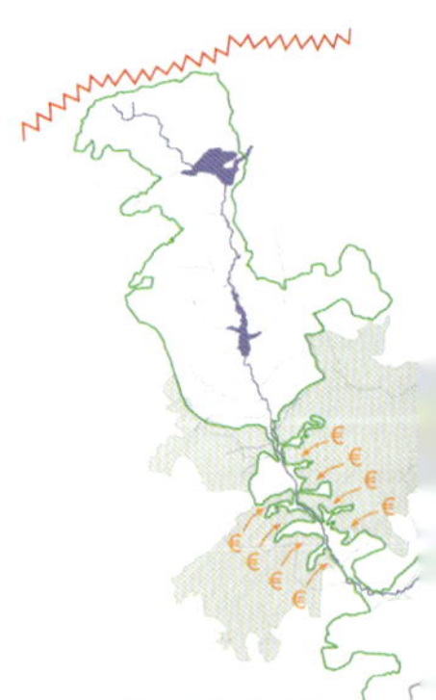

El Río conquistará la ciudad

Aunque su caudal es casi ridículo, hasta secarse durant[e …,] confiar en su fuerza y persistencia.
Transformará la ciudad colocándolo en el centro, y la ciu[dad devolverá al] río la inversión realizada.
Seguro, confiamos en él.

1

El río cruza Madrid.
Empleemos su estructura hidrológica para mantenerlo vivo.
El río vertebrará la ciudad de Madrid.
Su lecho es el origen de las formas de los parques que se proponen.

El paisaje castellano, mediterráneo, continental, que encontramos en el entorno de la ciudad es un patrimonio valioso, característico y con enorme energía plástica. Tiene la dureza y la sequedad de Madrid domesticado, civilizado y urbanizado, está en el origen de este proyecto.

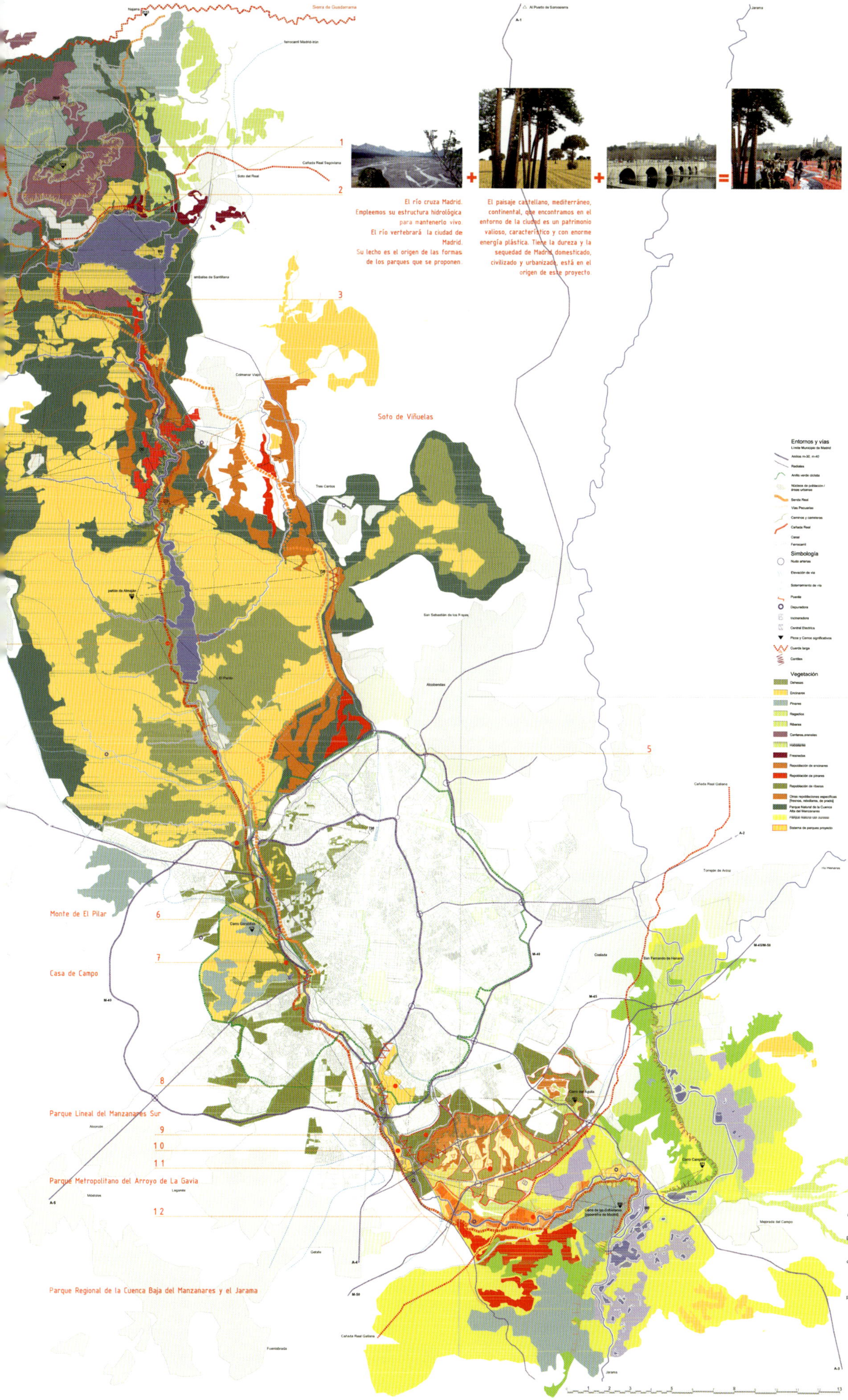

1
Acondicionar las sendas existentes

La red de cañadas y cordeles es un patrimonio casi sin explotar. Acondicionarlas, señalizarlas, equiparlas, de modo que sea posible recorrer nuestro territorio sin interrupciones es un anhelo. Conoceremos mejor nuestro país si lo recorremos a pie.

2
Parque natural de la Pedriza. Nacimiento del Manzanares

La presión a la que está sometido el Parque Natural de la Pedriza disminuirá cuando éste no sea más que una parte de un conjunto accesible.
En cualquier caso limitar de construciones indeseables y controlar aún más, si es necesario, su acceso es inevitable.

3
Repoblar el Sur del Embalse de Santillana

Se arbolará con vegetación autóctona las lomas al Sur del Embalse de Santillana.
Los bosques de El Pardo tendrán continuidad con los nuevos con el río como estructura vertebral.
La senda que discurre al borde del río tendrá un carácter suave y poco construido.

4
El Monte de El Pardo tendrá un acceso restringido a los ciudadanos

El acceso estará controlado y sólo será posible hacerlo a pie, en bicicleta o a caballo, estableciendo un límite de acuerdo con el equilibrio natural existente.

5
Playas en Madrid

Aún es posible pensar en bañarse en el río.
Entre el Embalse de El Pardo y la Depuradora de Viveros el agua está limpia y podemos acondicionar y mejorar áreas para baño, equipándolas y relacionándolas con el Bosque de El Pardo.

6
Se sale de Madrid por el río

Estableceremos una continuidad total del río para introducir el medio natural en la ciudad.
Madrid así tendrá una puerta al exterior en el centro.
Enlazar el Monte de El Pardo con la Casa de Campo sobre el nudo de Puerta de Hierro y el del Puente de los Franceses es imprescindible.
Los nudos de las infraestructuras parecen obstáculos insalvables para los peatones y ciclistas. Intervenir en ellos para domesticarlos y para que con otros sistemas de transportes se puedan cruzar debe ser un objetivo de las obras en la *´calle M-30´*.

7
La Casa de Campo fue un fragmento del bosque de El Pardo

Recuperar la continuidad perdida entre los bosques cercanos a Madrid, generando un sistema continuo de áreas verdes, es el objetivo fundamental de esta propuesta.

8
Terrain vague entre el Abroñigal y el Manzanares

Entre Entrevías, al Este el río, y la playa de vías de los accesos ferroviarios a Atocha, San Fermín y el Parque Sur, queda un *terrain vague* que es imprescindible acabar.
De modo natural está herida abierta en la ciudad le pertenece al río.
Nuevos usos lucrativos y cierta continuidad verde con el río lo ordenarán.

9
El espacio público es la estructura de la ciudad

Limpiar de construcciones ruinosas y de asentamientos humanos inaceptables en un país moderno y rico es una obligación.
También lo es enlazar las distintas intervenciones verdes.
El *Parque del Arroyo de La Gavia* no puede quedar aislado del *Parque Lineal del Manzanares Sur*, es una prolongación natural de él.

10
El entorno del río debe ser el lugar de usos híbridos recreativos y deportivos

El espacio entre la carretera M-45, la N-IV y el río será el borde de Vicálvaro al río.
Lo acondicionaremos para usos deportivos de baja intensidad, con piscinas y nuevos usos acuáticos.
Este área deportiva enlazará el interior de la ciudad con el *Parque Natural del Sureste*.
Albergará aparcamientos en superficie y se construirán puentes sobre el río que enlazarán el nuevo *Parque del Arroyo de la Gavia* con la vega del Manzanares.

11
Los paisajes transformados del Sur de Vallecas también son valiosos

El verde también es ocre, amarillo y blanquecino.
La ciudad debe apropiarse del paisaje del Sur y explotarlo como un valor sin descubrir.
Arbolar, limpiar, tratar algunos caminos que recuperaran las sendas y cañadas existentes transformaría este territorio en una ´Casa de Campo Sur´.
Además es imprescindible acometer la difícil tarea de liberar de construcciones y restaurar la Cañada Real y realojar a la población marginal que vive allí.
El encuentro entre el Manzanares y el Jarama es un lugar especialmente señalado.
Entre el río, la N-III y las lomas que trepan hacia Valdemingómez se construirá una instalación deportiva de escala metropolitana con vocación acuática y con un paisaje construido que diluya su presencia entre los bosques de la ribera del río.

12
Vega del Manzanares Sur

Se arbolará, se restituirá la vegetación de las riberas y se mantendrán los usos agrícolas junto a nuevos usos recreativos.
La naturaleza en cierto modo urbanizada permitirá paseos, sombra y el contacto con el fluir del agua a escasos kilómetros del centro de Madrid.

concurso de ideas parque lineal del manzanares

m - r i o

Fabricando un paisaje

La red de paisajes que enlaza la cuenca del río está constituida por múltiples eventos de complejidad variable, algunos sobrecogedores como las afloraciones rocosas de *La Pedriza*, la densa dehesa de *El Monte de El Pardo* o la vega fértil en las proximidades del Jarama.
Este organismo diverso e intenso debe ser ofrecido a la ciudad como valor del que ésta podrá participar si las conexiones vehiculares adquieren el mismo grado de continuidad que el propio río.
El paisaje de Madrid quedará incorporado al paisaje del Manzanares, la ciudad se abrirá desde su centro hacia el medio natural. Centro que se entiende hoy como la intersección entre tejido construido y el campo biológico del río. Los bordes de ésta intersección se ablandan o endurecen para crear relaciones de proximidad entre el agua, la ribera, el antiguo arrabal de la margen derecha y la ciudad histórica situada en la izquierda.
No se trata de proponer el tratamiento del borde de un canal sino de trabajar sobre un perfil en el que se implica lo natural, lo artificial, lo amplio y lo constreñido, donde lo importante no es tanto el transcurso de la hebra de agua como la ancha zona húmeda que esta produce.

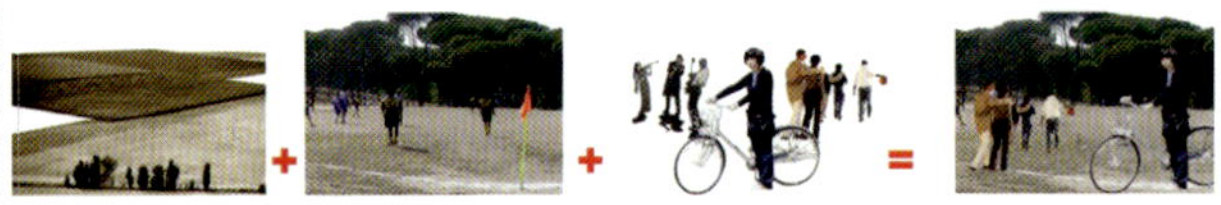

La Casa de Campo se reencuentra con el río

El actual deterioro de la Casa de Campo es manifiesto en muchos lugares. Sin embargo, importantes acontecimientos históricos han ocurrido en ella desde 1553, cuando la corona española la compró a la Familia Vargas, y desde 1931, cuando se abrió definitivamente a los ciudadanos.

La Casa de Campo necesita un sustrato cultural que la soporte como parque urbano.
Por un lado, es necesario domesticarla, pero también, naturalizarla. Domesticarla valorando las trazas que tiene y construyendo con ellas lugares espectáculares que la geografía nos regala.
Haciéndola más salvaje con el cuidado de su masa forestal.

Debemos aceptar que está siendo usada en capas de diversas intensidades y, así, se materializará desde la recuperación de los *Jardines de El Reservado* y las *Praderas de El Corregidor* hasta las plantaciones de arbolado en riberas y montes.

Una nueva Casa de Campo

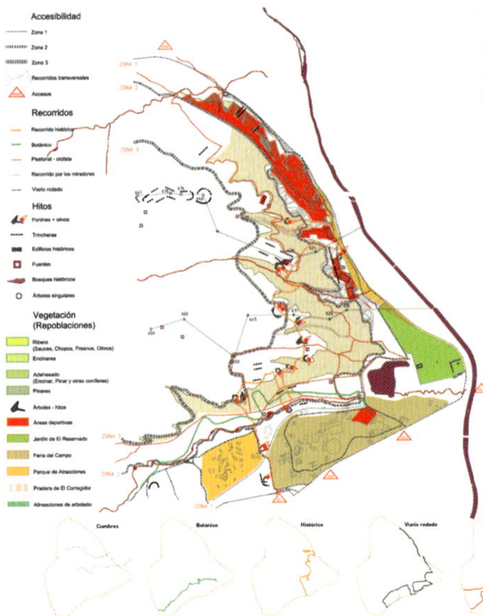

Accesibilidad y recorridos

La *Casa de Campo* está sometida a un proceso de presión antrópica insostenible.

Graduar la intensidad de uso sobre ella es una decisión pendiente. Se establecerán áreas diferenciadas de uso intensivo, medio y restringido que hagan compatible disfrute ciudadano y conservación.
Además, la *Casa de Campo* necesita de un soporte cultural que articule sus usos y su territorio.
Este soporte existe. Las huellas que la historia ha dejado en ella.
Las batallas fraticidas que se produjeron entre 1936 y 1939 podrían articular el paisaje.
Aquellas batallas y escaramuzas se produjeron señalando los lugares más protegidos, los más escarpados, los más visibles o los que dominaban mejor el entorno.
Así la estrategia bélica, como la arquitectura, podrían considerarse disciplinas de la geografía.

Estra tegia vegetal

Las plantaciones propuestas recuperan bosques de encinas, fresnos o pinos, que han sufrido cierto deterioro.
Completan, enriquecen y hacen más diverso el bosque existente.
Una segunda plantación consiste en alineaciones que señalan paseos y los construyen.
Otras, con un criterio más formal, envuelven y construyen algunos espacios que recuerdan los acontecimientos históricos ocurridos.

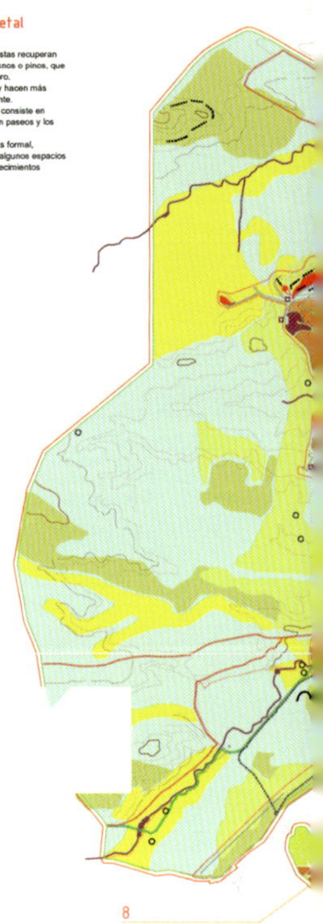

Parque Lineal del Manzanares

Continuidad longitudinal + heterogeneidad

La orilla Oeste establece la imprescindeble unidad que le aporta la energía y claridad al proyecto. Un salón de pinos. El hilo.

La orilla Este es una sucesión de espacios que establecen los vínculos con el pasado, con la ciudad y con el río. Un rosario de parques con una referencia común, ocupar el lecho del río y de él extraer sus formas.

Transversal y visual

Ambas orillas has estado segregadas por la M-30.
Ahora se vincularán. Pero los vínculos no deben ser del mismo tipo a lo largo del río.

Al Norte, entre el *Jardín del Moro* y el *Jardín de El Reservado*, un conjunto de franjas con distintos tratamientos, masas de árboles frutales, jardines acuáticos configuran una tierra de nadie ornamental, que se sitúa a los pies del Palacio Real.
Más al *Sur*, masas de árboles protegen los bordes de los puentes de Segovia y Toledo y más al Sur aún, sobre el *Parque de Arganzuela* se establecen dos niveles de puentes peatonales y rodados, de modo que en su conjunto establecen la necesaria continuidad entre ambas orillas.

Corredores verdes

De Norte a Sur en la orilla Oeste del río se plantaría una doble hilera de pinos piñoneros que forman un paseo vegetal de intensidad inusual.
Este hilo verde liga el conjunto de espacios abiertos que están a lo largo del río, pero también con otros corredores verdes que desde el río trepan hacia el centro de Madrid.

El parque que enlaza dentro de la ciu[...] de la *Virgen del Puerto*, el *Campo de*[...] *de Campo*, al Norte, con el *Parque d*[...] al Sur, está fundado sobre dos condi[...]

La primera, consecuencia de la estra[...] establece la máxima continuidad con[...] Por ello el margen Oeste del río se re[...] longitudinalmente con un *Salón* de e[...] paisajística y urbana homogénea.
Un gran paseo, arbolado con pinos p[...] darán carácter y sombra al mismo.
Desde él nos asomamos al río y a la[...]

La segunda, manteniendo la interpre[...] que hemos hecho del río, recuerda l[...] lecho del río y con él se ocupan los e[...] M-30 ha liberado.

Un jardín castellano sobre el lec[...]

Nuevo Parque Metropolitano del Arroyo de La Gavia

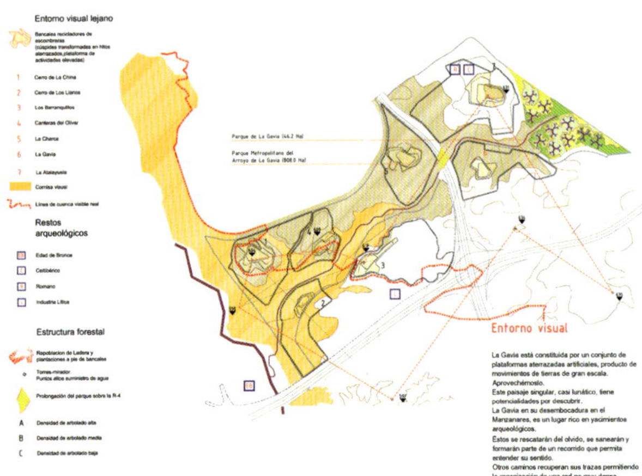

Entorno visual

La Gavia está constituida por un conjunto de plataformas aterrazadas artificiales, producto de movimientos de tierras de gran escala.
Aprovechémoslo.
Este paisaje singular, casi lunático, tiene potencialidades por descubrir.
La Gavia en su desembocadura en el Manzanares, es un lugar rico en yacimientos arqueológicos.
Estos se rescatarán del olvido, se sanearán y formarán parte de un recorrido que permita entender su sentido.
Otros caminos recuperan sus trazas permitiendo la organización de una red no muy densa.

Estructura forestal

Aprovechando esta topografía artificial, la vegetación va fijándose al terreno, sobre sus laderas.
Al mismo tiempo se establece un calendario de actuaciones vegetales que permitan asentar especies apropiadas para hábitats más exigentes. Siempre poniendo en valor lugares con vistas singulares o riberas.

El Sur también es valioso, o m[...]

Los paisajes secos y yesíferos[...] sido maltratados por las infrae[...] depredadora del hombre.
Si consideramos el Río Manza[...] estructura capaz de dar sentid[...] Madrid, descubrimos un gran v[...] de Vallecas y el río Manzanare[...] de La Gavia.
Una oportunidad de equipar la[...] escala metropolitana cuyo car[...] nos reconcilia con nuestro pai[...]

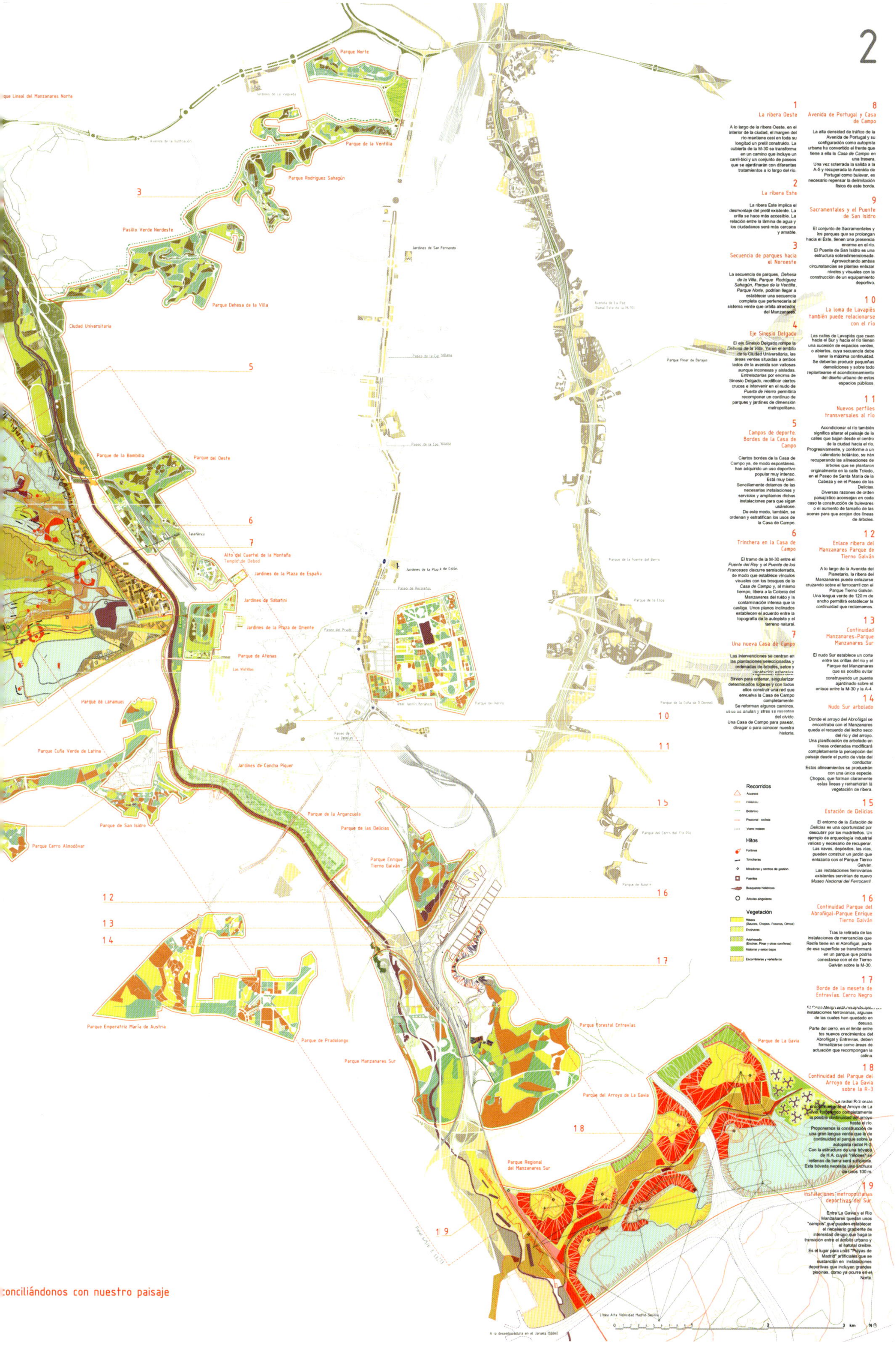

1
La ribera Oeste

A lo largo de la ribera Oeste, en el interior de la ciudad, el margen del río mantiene casi en toda su longitud un pretil construido. La cubierta de la M-30 se transforma en un camino que incluye un carril-bici y un conjunto de paseos que se ajardinarán con diferentes tratamientos a lo largo del río.

2
La ribera Este

La ribera Este implica el desmontaje del pretil existente. La orilla se hace más accesible. La relación entre la lámina de agua y los ciudadanos será más cercana y amable.

3
Secuencia de parques hacia el Noroeste

La secuencia de parques, *Dehesa de la Villa*, *Parque Rodríguez Sahagún*, *Parque de la Ventilla*, *Parque Norte*, podrían llegar a establecer una secuencia completa que pertenecería al sistema verde que orbita alrededor del Manzanares.

4
Eje Sinesio Delgado

El eje Sinesio Delgado rompe la *Dehesa de la Villa*. Ya en el ámbito de la Ciudad Universitaria, las áreas verdes situadas a ambos lados de la avenida son valiosas aunque inconexas y aisladas. Entrelazarlas por encima de Sinesio Delgado, modificar ciertos cruces e intervenir en el nudo de *Puerta de Hierro* permitiría recomponer un continuo de parques y jardines de dimensión metropolitana.

5
Campos de deporte. Bordes de la Casa de Campo

Ciertos bordes de la Casa de Campo ya, de modo espontáneo, han adquirido un uso deportivo popular muy intenso.
Está muy bien.
Sencillamente dotamos de las necesarias instalaciones y servicios y ampliamos dichas instalaciones para que sigan usándose.
De este modo, también, se ordenan y estratifican los usos de la Casa de Campo.

6
Trinchera en la Casa de Campo

El tramo de la M-30 entre el *Puente del Rey* y el *Puente de los Franceses* discurre semisoterrada, de modo que establece vínculos visuales con los bosques de la *Casa de Campo* y, al mismo tiempo, libera a la Colonia del Manzanares del ruido y la contaminación intensa que la castiga. Unos planos inclinados establecen el acuerdo entre la topografía de la autopista y el terreno natural.

7
Una nueva Casa de Campo

Las intervenciones se centran en las plantaciones seleccionadas y ordenadas de árboles, setos y vegetación extensiva.
Sirven para ordenar, singularizar determinados lugares y con todos ellos construir una red que envuelva la Casa de Campo completamente.
Se reforman algunos caminos, otros se anulan y otros se rescatan del olvido.
Una Casa de Campo para pasear, divagar o para conocer nuestra historia.

Recorridos

- Accesos
- Histórico
- Botánico
- Peatonal - ciclista
- Viario rodado

Hitos

- Fortines
- Trincheras
- Miradores y centros de gestión
- Fuentes
- Bosquetes históricos
- Árboles singulares

Vegetación

- Ribera (Sauces, Chopos, Fresnos, Olmos)
- Encinares
- Adehesado (Encinar, Pinar y otras coníferas)
- Matorral y setos bajos
- Escombreras y vertederos

8
Avenida de Portugal y Casa de Campo

La alta densidad de tráfico de la Avenida de Portugal y su configuración como autopista urbana ha convertido el frente que tiene a ella la *Casa de Campo* en una trasera.
Una vez soterrada la salida a la A-5 y recuperada la Avenida de Portugal como bulevar, es necesario repensar la delimitación física de este borde.

9
Sacramentales y el Puente de San Isidro

El conjunto de Sacramentales y los parques que se prolongan hacia el Este, tienen una presencia enorme en el río.
El Puente de San Isidro es una estructura sobredimensionada.
Aprovechando ambas circunstancias se plantea enlazar niveles y visuales con la construcción de un equipamiento deportivo.

10
La loma de Lavapiés también puede relacionarse con el río

Las calles de Lavapiés que caen hacia el Sur y hacia el río tienen una sucesión de espacios verdes, o abiertos, cuya secuencia debe tener la máxima continuidad.
Se deberían producir pequeñas demoliciones y sobre todo replantearse el acondicionamiento del diseño urbano de estos espacios públicos.

11
Nuevos perfiles transversales al río

Acondicionar el río también significa alterar el paisaje de la calles que bajan desde el centro de la ciudad hacia el río.
Progresivamente, y conforme a un calendario botánico, se irán recuperando las alineaciones de árboles que se plantaron originalmente en la calle Toledo, en el Paseo de Santa María de la Cabeza y en el Paseo de las Delicias.
Diversas razones de orden paisajístico aconsejan en cada caso la construcción de bulevares o el aumento de tamaño de las aceras para que acojan dos líneas de árboles.

12
Enlace ribera del Manzanares Parque de Tierno Galván

A lo largo de la Avenida del Planetario, la ribera del Manzanares puede enlazarse cruzando sobre el ferrocarril con el Parque Tierno Galván.
Una lengua verde de 120 m de ancho permitirá establecer la continuidad que reclamamos.

13
Continuidad Manzanares-Parque Manzanares Sur

El nudo Sur establece un corte entre las orillas del río y el Parque del Manzanares que es posible evitar construyendo un puente ajardinado sobre el enlace entre la M-30 y la A-4.

14
Nudo Sur arbolado

Donde el arroyo del Abroñigal se encontraba con el Manzanares queda el recuerdo del lecho seco del río y del arroyo.
Una planificación de arbolado en líneas ordenadas modificará completamente la percepción del paisaje desde el punto de vista del conductor.
Estos alineamientos se producirán con una única especie.
Chopos, que forman claramente estas líneas y rememorán la vegetación de ribera.

15
Estación de Delicias

El entorno de la *Estación de Delicias* es una oportunidad por descubrir por los madrileños. Un ejemplo de arqueología industrial valioso y necesario de recuperar.
Las naves, depósitos, las vías, pueden construir un jardín que enlazaría con el Parque Tierno Galván.
Las instalaciones ferroviarias existentes servirían de nuevo *Museo Nacional del Ferrocarril*.

16
Continuidad Parque del Abroñigal-Parque Enrique Tierno Galván

Tras la retirada de las instalaciones de mercancías que Renfe tiene en el Abroñigal, parte de esa superficie se transformará en un parque que podría conectarse con el de Tierno Galván sobre la M-30.

17
Borde de la meseta de Entrevías. Cerro Negro

El Cerro Negro está rodeado [illegible] instalaciones ferroviarias, algunas de las cuales han quedado en desuso.
Parte del cerro, en el límite entre los nuevos crecimientos del Abroñigal y Entrevías, deben formalizarse como áreas de actuación que recompongan la colina.

18
Continuidad del Parque del Arroyo de La Gavia sobre la R-3

La radial R-3 cruza dramáticamente el Arroyo de La Gavia, rompiendo completamente la posible continuidad del arroyo hasta el río.
Proponemos la construcción de una gran lengua verde que le de continuidad al parque sobre la autopista radial R-3.
Con la estructura de una bóveda de H.A. cuyos "riñones" se rellenan de tierra será suficiente.
Esta bóveda necesita una anchura de unos 100 m.

19
Instalaciones metropolitanas deportivas del Sur

Entre La Gavia y el Río Manzanares quedan unos "campos" que pueden establecer el necesario gradiente de intensidad de uso que haga la transición entre el ámbito urbano y el natural creíble.
Es el lugar para unas "Playas de Madrid" artificiales que se sustancian en instalaciones deportivas que incluyen grandes piscinas, como ya ocurre en el Norte.

concurso de ideas parque lineal del manzanares

m-rio

Una nueva sustancia, el Centro del S XXI

La reacción química de dos elementos puede dar lugar a una tercera sustancia de naturaleza distinta, mucho más valiosa que una simple adición de dos sumandos. En el laboratorio, esta interacción puede catalizarse o acelerarse con uno u otro aditivo. Desde esta óptica científica interpretamos en la macro escala el significado de la oportunidad que se presenta para Madrid. Entendemos el soterramiento de la M-30 como elemento catalizador de la operación. Las dos sustancias actuantes se identifican respectivamente con la naturaleza que el lecho del río transporta y con el tejido sólido de la ciudad consolidada. El resultado de esta combinación cobra una entidad absolutamente diferente, que con toda probabilidad no se podrá encontrar en otras ciudades desarrolladas. Siendo capaces de transportar las claves geobiológicas del lecho del río a esta franja urbana, se generará una nueva unidad central que, a partir de la liberación del espacio que hoy ocupa la M-30, comenzará a tomar una intensa calidad ambiental. La incorporación de nuevos usos colectivos a lo largo de este espacio, la generación de elementos naturales y la inmediata mejora y revalorización de los barrios de carácter doméstico del entorno, producen una pieza única, en constante desarrollo e irreconocible en el medio plazo. Si en el S. XIX , la colonización del arroyo Castellana dio lugar a la que es hoy la avenida más noble de la ciudad, no dudamos en ambicionar y en creer firmemente que aquélla va a ser superada en el S.XXI, cuando el Manzanares reaparezca como centro urbano.

Madrid-río Centro 2005

Ya hemos expresado el convencimiento de que la ciudad es un accidente más del río Manzanares y no al revés. Pero también tenemos la certeza de que el soterramiento de la autopista no produce exclusivamente una mejora del tráfico y una extensa red lineal de parques para la ciudad. La operación Calle-30 , entre el Puente de los Franceses y el Nudo Sur, tiene consecuencias que superan ampliamente estas aspiraciones. Se redescubre un nuevo centro de Madrid, cuando su tejido se superpone al lecho del río. Como en una reacción química, la comunión de estos dos elementos genera una tercera "sustancia" diferente. Se trata de una nueva estructura urbana, un centro del S.XXI, con una enorme capacidad de progresión.
Aplicando una perspectiva suficientemente enfocada hacia el futuro, nos percatamos de estar ante un área que se regenerá por si misma, cambiando su actual carácter, ennobleciendo velozmente su condición, concibiendo sucesivas oportunidades para todos los agentes que interactúan en la ciudad. La propuesta acentúa la potencialidad de los mágenes del río para redescubrir cada fragmento del tejido urbano. Las posibilidades de conectividad longitudinal y tranversal así como las formas plurimodales de movilidad, han sido tratadas en el proyecto como materiales esenciales para consolidar la estrategia que genera todas y cada una las piezas que, ligadas entre si por la macroestructura geográfica que el río representa, constituyen un elemento global, un rosario de oportunidades que es una oportunidad en si mismo.

Transporte público

La propuesta contiene una línea bidireccional de tranvía. Esta infraestructura liga los barrios longitudinalmente y tiene además una importante componente panorámica ligada al recreo o al turismo, dado el intenso recorrido que explota todas las posibilidades paisajísticas de los hitos históricos de su itinerario. La instalación del tranvía, por ortra parte, reducirá de forma apreciable la carga de líneas de autobuses existente.

Movilidad plurimodal

Los circuitos de movilidad limpia, hoy día inexistentes en los bordes del río, compondrán una red que lo supera como barrera y por el contrario, lo potencia como estructura vehicular. En la margen derecha se ha diseñado un sistema de senderos bajo la arboleda lineal, continuo en toda su longitud. En la margen izquierda, penetrando y ligando el sistema de parques, se plantean corredores para ciclistas y patinadores que, además de enlazar los distintos barrios, son infraestructuras para el ocio.

Conectividad entre barrios

La mejora en la red de puentes, el tratamiento selectivo que aloja el tráfico rápido enterrado y la propuesta de una red lenta local, configura el sistema que mejora radicalmente la accesibilidad de los barrios. Se ha proyectado una malla que acompaña al río en toda su longitud y se desarrolla de forma que los puentes no interrumpen su recorrido. Las nuevas intervenciones propuestas cosen grietas urbanas y abren accesos entre las microestucturas de la ciudad.

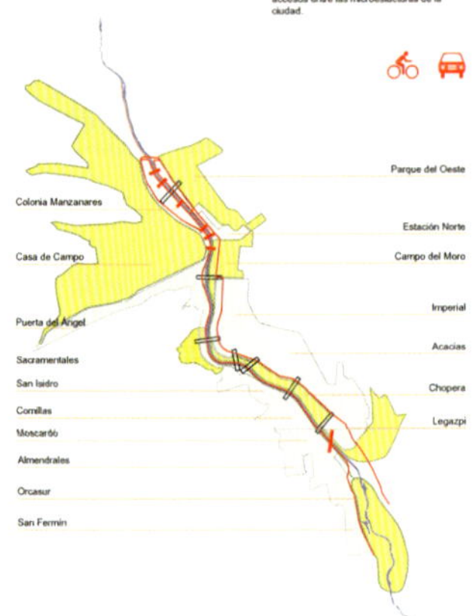

Potencial de usos colectivos

La doble condición Central-Lineal de la estructura que resulta de la interacción del río y la ciudad, permite una sucesión altamente conectada de espacios para la colectividad. Se trata de un eje en el que convivirán importantes dotaciones que aportan un intenso carácter institucional al centro urbano pero que se imbrican de lleno con la ciudad doméstica y viva.

Madrid-río Sur 2005

La apertura de un camino hacia el Sur no es sólo la obtención de un recorrido que acompaña el transcurso del Manzanares, sino que tiene un efecto estructurante de gran escala urbana. Actualmente, las áreas destinadas a usos y tráfico ferroviario ocupan dos bolsas donde el tejido urbano se ha degradado a pesar de su posición estratégica y suponen sendas barreras que hacen impenetrables las conexiones y aislan los diferentes barrios destinándolos a vivir de espaldas a la ciudad sin poder ser regenerados.
Las conexiones rodadas existentes no superan estas barreras. La calle Antonio López se desvía sin enlazar el sistema básico de movilidad que los barrios necesitan. Las vías rápidas crean nuevos límites que dificultan tanto un crecimiento que supere los modos caducos del *zonning* como la comprensión de las zonas verdes como elementos de un sistema de rango superior. Las áreas residenciales son, en el campo de juego actual, islas inconexas incapaces de oxigenarse.

Ferrocarril

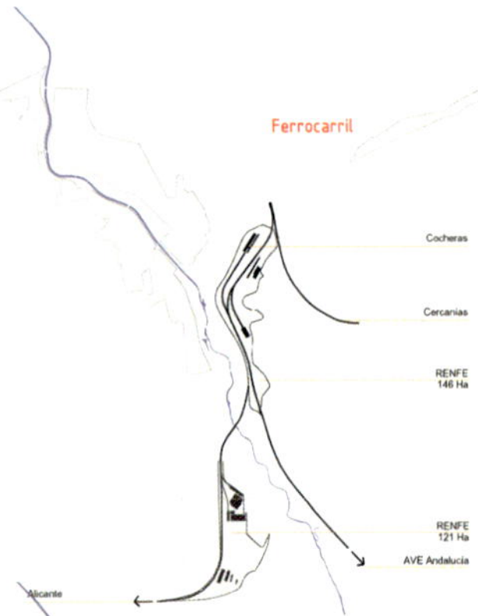

Tráfico rodado

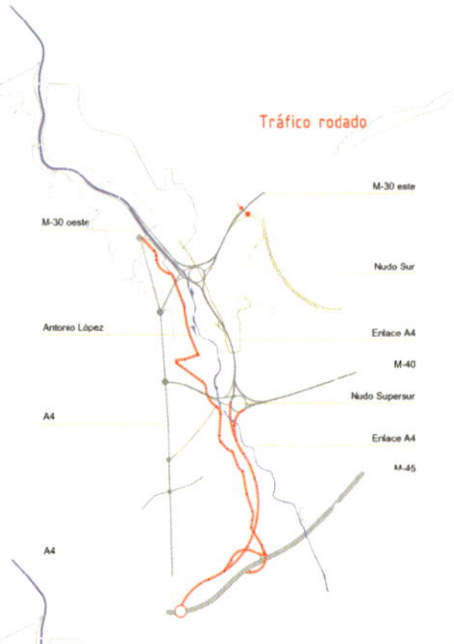

Sistema verde

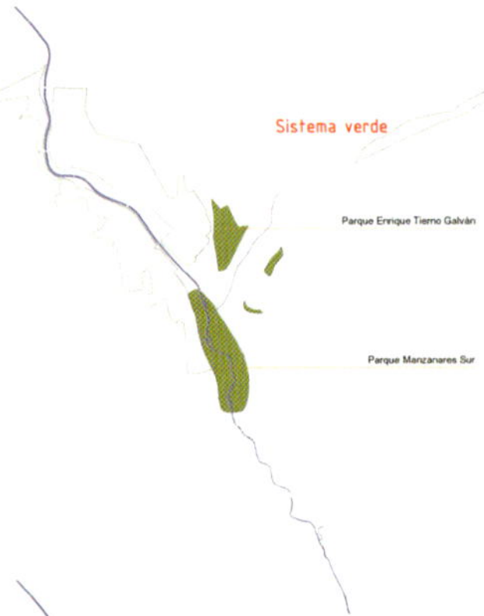

Desarrollo urbano

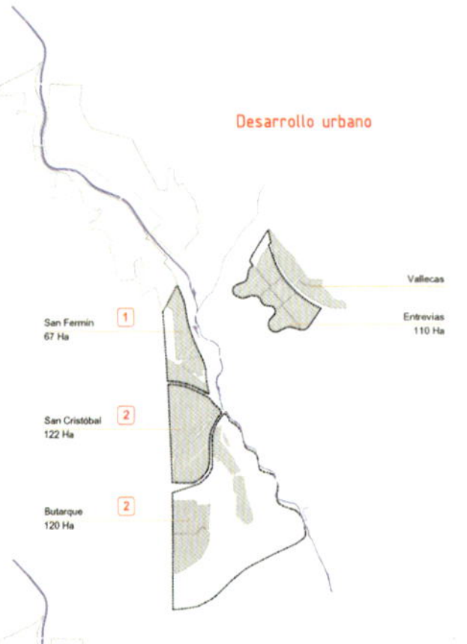

Madrid-río Sur 2020

El traslado a medio plazo de las instalaciones ferroviarias y la propuesta de conexiones que encarna el proyecto, generará un **"Nuevo Sur de oportunidades"**. Junto a la prolongación de Antonio López y la accesibilidad del río hasta su desembocadura, se consigue la conexión del sistema de movilidad, la continuidad del tejido de los barrios y el enlace de las zonas verdes a lo largo de la ribera. El diseño de los nuevos barrios potenciará los valores de interconexión entre lo existente y lo nuevo, lo vacío y lo lleno, lo público y lo privado, alejándose del sistema de zonificación que atiende sólo a las siluetas que las redes circulatorias producen. La desaparicición de la estación de contenedores está prevista en los programas de Renfe. Sin embargo la línea del Ave se mantendrá en su posición de salida desde Atocha. De este modo el "Área Abroñigal" verá minimizada la presencia de la red ferroviaria, que queda reducida a la línea del AVE, por lo que allí se genera un importante nodo de crecimiento con una proximidad al centro de Madrid que lo destaca como un notabilísimo "suelo estratégico" cuyas posibilidades se presentan en la propuesta.

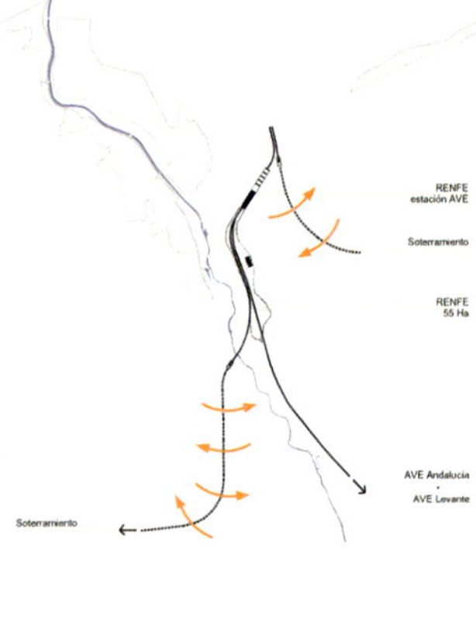

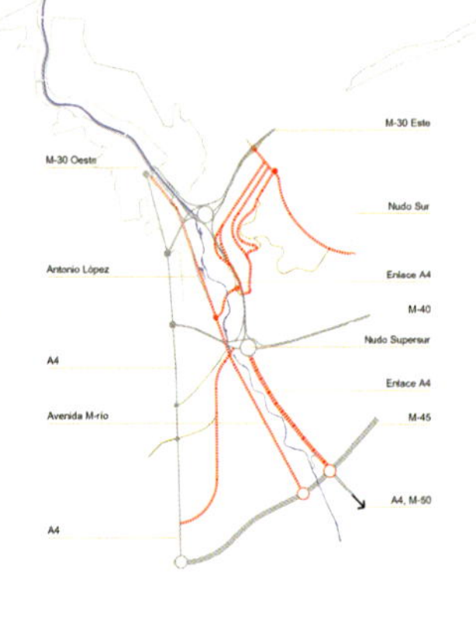

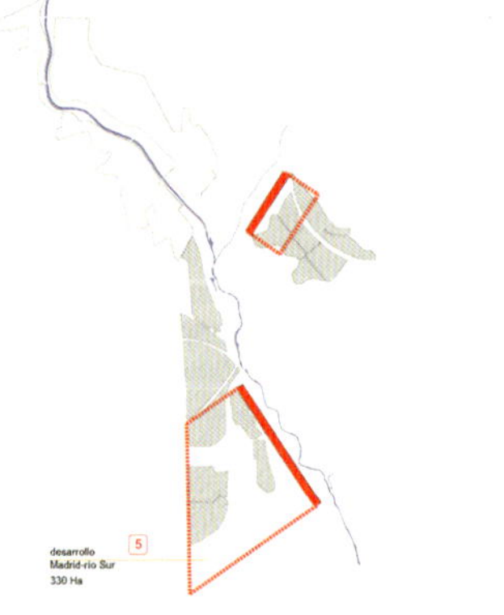

3

1
El río y la M-40

La senda que discurre a la vera del río es continua. Debe cruzar el nudo de la M-40 con la carretera de El Pardo. Para ello, es necesario liberar parte del terreno actualmente ocupado por el club *El Tejar de Somontes*

2
Instalaciones ecuestres

El camino que hemos trazado desde Madrid hasta la sierra puede recorrerse a caballo. Una instalación aneja al hipódromo puede ser un lugar adecuado para el inicio de la senda ecuestre.

3
Conexiones generales metropolitanas

El parque deportivo *Puerta de Hierro* necesita de la construcción de algunos puentes peatonales que enlazarán la orilla izquierda con su derecha. El río formará parte del paisaje del parque deportivo.

4
Viveros de la Villa

La orilla izquierda del Manzanares en su tramo comprendido entre el nudo *Puerta de Hierro* y el *Puente de los Franceses* está ocupada por diversas instalaciones, entre ellas el *Instituto Municipal de Acústica* y los Viveros de la Villa. Estas instalaciones impiden el acceso al río, por lo que es necesario replantear su ocupación de las márgenes para permitir pasos transversales y longitudinales.

5
Puente de los Franceses

Se modifica el actual viario sobre el río junto al *Puente de los Franceses* que impide la salida a pie desde Madrid hacia el norte. La M-30 cruza el río soterrada y el viaducto de entrada hacia el *Parque del Oeste* y la Avenida de Valladolid se elevan para dejar paso a cota cero. El nudo se completa con un puente de tráfico local y tranvía para cerrar el anillo de Marqués de Monistrol y la Avenida de Valladolid.

6
Aparcamientos disuasorios

Es necesario graduar el acceso rodado a la almendra central. La restricción al tráfico privado a algunas áreas del centro es un anhelo razonable a medio plazo. La M-30 será un anillo de distribución de tráfico dotado de aparcamientos disuasorios. Aquí proponemos tres en el tramo oeste: bajo los futuros bulevares de la Avenida de Portugal, Santa María de la Cabeza y la Av. de Andalucía.

7
El paisaje del *Puente de Toledo*

Se modifica la estructura del nudo del *Puente de Toledo* para soterrar su lazo norte. Los nuevos puentes, de dirección única, desligan completamente los tráficos locales y metropolitanos y establecen con el puente histórico un diálogo ambicioso.

8
Tráfico transversal *Puente de Praga*

El *Puente de Praga* soporta una intensidad de tráfico en el límite de lo aceptable para la ciudad. El soterramiento previsto reducirá en parte su carga de tráfico. Su agresiva presencia se mejora mediante la construcción de unas pistas deportivas sobreelevadas.

9
Santa María de la Cabeza

Está previsto la incorporación soterrada desde la M-30 hacia Santa María de la Cabeza, no así en el sentido inverso. Proponemos soterrar también la incorporación hacia la M-30 sur desde Santa María de la Cabeza arriba. De este modo se liberará superficie para los peatones y será posible mejorar su paso sobre la c. Antonio López.

10
El tejido residencial sur se enlaza con el centro

El barrio de *San Fermín* y más al sur *El Espinillo* y *Villaverde* encuentran su salida natural y conexión con el centro de la ciudad através de la calle Antonio López que cruza con una sección generosa bajo el Ferrocarril y sobre la M-30.

11
Traslado de las instalaciones ferroviarias

Las instalaciones ferroviarias del Abroñigal pueden trasladarse a la periferia de la ciudad. Ordenar y limitar estas instalaciones permitirá ganar áreas para mejorar los accesos ferroviarios a Madrid y construir la estación del AVE Madrid- Barcelona. Sobre este área se construirán grandes puentes verdes que liberarán de su "encierro" a Entrevías, conectándolo con el *Parque de Tierno Galván*.

12
Tejido urbano El Abroñigal.

Sobre el área liberada se proyecta un polo de centralidad con la construcción de diversos edificios terciarios para el trabasjo y el comercio, así como un barrio residencial que ordena el borde del poblado de Entrevías.

13
Trazado del Tranvía

El tranvía que recorre de norte a sur, por ambas márgenes el río, es un instrumento de cohesión ciudadana norte-sur, que intensifica el caracter lineal del río y resuelve problemas de movilidad y congestión empleando un modelo de transporte sostenible.

14
Nuevo Sur de oprtunidades

La deslocalización de las instalaciones y vias de Renfe al oeste del río y el soterramiento de las infraestructuras viarias genera nuevos espacios para el crecimiento ordenado de la ciudad.

15
Instalaciones deportivas Super Sur

En el límite del crecimiento de la ciudad los espacios libres se enriquecen con un sistema de instalaciones deportivas vinculadas al río y al parque regional del Manzanares.

Área Abroñigal

Dentro del "Nuevo Sur de Oportunidades" se propone el desarrollo del "Area Abroñigal" que surge con una extremada claridad una vez que se produzca el traslado de la estación de contenedores y las cocheras y talleres de Renfe. Solo quedará activa la línea férrea del tren de Alta Velocidad. Se desvela de este modo la pertinencia de las siguientes operaciones:
Soterramiento de la vía férrea en la Avenida de Entrevías. Recuperación de dicha avenida como elemento de relación de la ciudad para el tráfico peatonal y rodado.
Acercamiento efectivo de la Asamblea de Madrid al centro de la ciudad.
Regeneración del Poblado de Entrevías y barrios adyacentes. Mejora de su conectividad a través de la Avenida de Méndez Álvaro.
Nueva continuidad verde del Parque Tierno Galván hacia el Sur, suturando el vacío que separa la zona del centro urbano.
Mejora de las comunicaciones rodadas hacia la M-30 y M-40.
Restauración de la cornisa Verde de la Ronda Sur de Entrevías como parque local integrado en el sistema de espacios verdes ligado al río.
Oportunidad de desarrollo con usos mixtos con la proyección de una nueva estación del Ave complementaria de la de Atocha.

Usos Previstos:

Ferroviario. Estación AVE	75.000 m2c
Terciario Oficinas	180.000 m2c
Terciario Comercial	66.000 m2c
Residencial	145.000 m2c

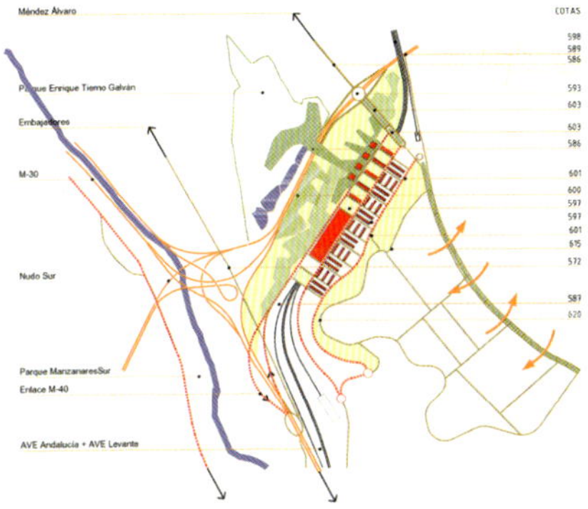

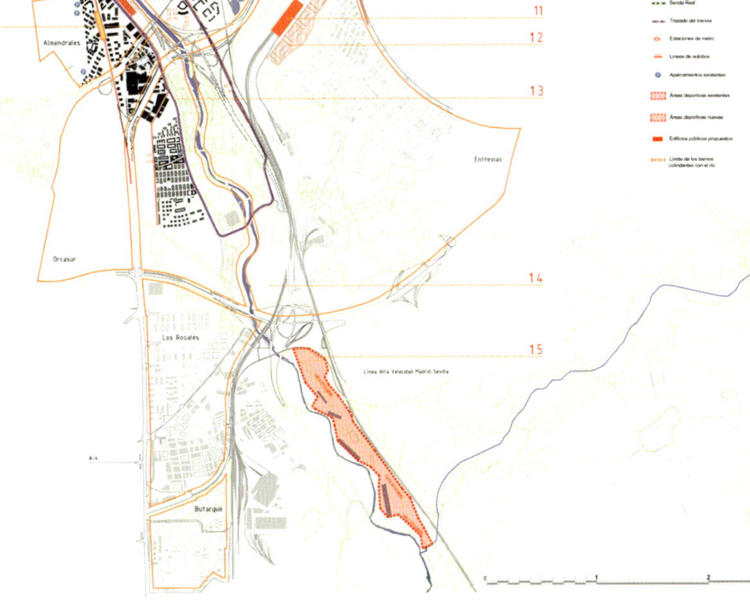

DEATH AND RESURRECTION OF THE MANZANARES

SERGIO MARTÍN BLAS

In 1864, when Casiano de Prado published his *Descripción Física y Geológica de la Provincia de Madrid* (Physical and Geological Description of the Province of Madrid), the Manzanares River had barely changed since it was drawn by Antonio de las Viñas or painted by Joli and Goya. Flowing through Madrid in its natural bed, it was flanked by farmlands, trees, and wild bushes, and used as the capital's laundry and sewer.

In his book, Casiano described how the watercourse descended from its high, clean source in the granite and gneiss mountains, turning into swampy, seasonally voluble wetlands when it reached the soft sand-and-clay terrain below. Erosion had created numerous hills and ravines that built up just before the Manzanares crossed the line separating sandy lands from the gypsum, loam, and limestone plains of La Mancha. Somewhat further south, the river turned southeast and there, on its right bank, a ridge or natural theater was formed. From precisely there, it was still possible to make out the horizontal skyline of Madrid, a former Muslim lookout built where the Manzanares natural heights could serve as its western border, just as it appeared to Goya.

For Casiano, the river explained why the city was founded there, where the region's different landscapes meet, generating extraordinary variety. But its "natural" state was incompatible with a great metropolis. The river had to be transformed into a modern infrastructure — a drain and sewer for a growing population that required its channeling and the addition of water from the nearby Lozoya River. Without that, Madrid would never equal the splendor of Europe's great capitals. When Casiano died in 1866 he had no idea that the Manzanares and its banks were about to begin a long and difficult process of transformation. Over the course of almost a century and a half, the river's existence as a natural stream surrounded by greenery faded progressively from the memory and imagination, eclipsed by its role as urban infrastructure.

The first important step in this process came with the city's disorderly growth towards the river, which was accelerated by the construction of a railway bypass on the left bank in 1851 and the demolition of Philip IV's enclosure in 1868, following approval of the *Ensanche* (literally, expansion) laid out by Castro in 1860. Pío Baroja's 1904 work, *La Busca,* describes that peculiar section of Madrid's outskirts along the Manzanares, where the walls and chimneys of factories and warehouses serviced by the railway coexisted with cramped houses, shanties, landfills, rubble heaps, and farms, generating a fragmented landscape that was a backdrop for the scenes of exploitation and poverty played out by Madrid's marginal and working classes. The Manzanares, especially towards the south, had become the capital city's dump, a home to urchins, vagabonds, ragmen, and prostitutes. Its waters were permanently black, witness to an alarming deterioration of public health conditions that called for urgent action.

The channeling and decontamination of the river where it passed through the city could definitely not be put off any longer. And yet, this and many of Madrid's other pressing needs received the same age-old response: "Come back tomorrow." After an exasperating succession of contests and frustrated proposals, the first effective step was taken in 1914, when the river's soft, changing path was replaced with an imperturbably hard and geometric course that has barely changed since. Designed by engineer Eduardo Fungairiño, this project channeled the river into a canal of constant width, with decontamination facilities and a space for roadways on its banks. Thus, the opportunity to appreciate the riverbanks' valuable role in ordering and limiting growth in that area was postponed in favor of the urgent public works to which the river was subjected.

Work to channel the river ended in 1925 and that same year, municipal architect Gustavo Fernández Balbuena presented an urban-development project for its banks. He was the first to propose an overall conception of the river as a large metropolitan park linked to the city's need for hygiene and improved traffic flow. That park was supposed to provide a basis for modern transit infrastructures, organized industry, and workers' housing. As a large park-road much like the American *parkways*, it implicitly assumed some of the objectives associated with modernity: specialized transit, improved public health, recreation, and *social redemption* of the masses through a *return to nature*. Nature, infrastructure, and city were integrated for the first (and possibly, the only) time in a unified concept of landscape specifically linked to the river's presence.

The sun sank into eventide,
And 'tween dark clouds it sought to hide
So not to see the snarl below

Fray Diego González,
"Llanto de Delio y profecía del Manzanares", 1783

The ideas put forth by Balbuena perfectly matched efforts to control metropolitan growth that started in 1926 with plans adopted from international urban culture. The *Plan de Extensión* (Expansion Master Plan) of 1926, Zuazo and Jansen's plan for the 1929 contest, and the *Plan de la Oficina Técnica Municipal* (Master Plan of the City Council's Technical Office) from 1931 all emphasized the same thing, though with different nuances: the river's value as a large linear park and transit corridor. Ideally, the Manzanares would become part of a relatively narrow "green belt" to ease urban congestion, home to the first beltway, and a connection between leisure areas in El Pardo and El Jarama on a regional scale.

However, as we well know, reality bypassed the theoretical evolution of urban planning. Only fragments of modernity budded in this area, including Gutiérrez Soto's *Piscina de la Isla* (Island Swimming Pool – 1931) or Ferrero Llusiá's *Mercado de Frutas y Verduras* (Fruit and Vegetable Market) at Legazpi (1935), as the riverbanks continued to suffer the disorderly growth of Madrid's outskirts. This contradiction between planning efforts and reality only worsened in the post-war years.

Beginning in 1941, the Manzanares was the object of opposing hypotheses. One was set out in the Bidagor Plan, in which the park-road defined before the Spanish Civil War (1936-39) as an antidote to metropolitan congestion took on new meaning as a source of leisure and recreation for the masses. According to this plan's rhetoric, the Manzanares should recover its role as a "green pedestal" on which to display the symbols of the new state as part of the capital's representative façade, a fundamental element in its hierarchical separation from the periphery and a key to the restoration of "traditional" urban order. The latter was based, in turn, on a natural order: the river as a connection between the region's two large landscape systems (and by an absurd extension, the entire peninsula's): the mountains and woods to the northwest and the landscape of La Mancha, to the southeast. Thus, Madrid was cast as the center, the sum of all at the point of equilibrium that confirmed its role as capital.

The other hypothesis was put forth by the Ministry of Public Works and was a specific plan for the Manzanares directed by engineer Carlos Mendoza, former president of Madrid's subway system. Here, the urgent need to channel the riverbed following wartime destruction served as an excuse to divide the entire riverside area into lots zoned for construction, completely cancelling the linear park foreseen by Bidagor and the urban planners. Approval of the Mendoza or MOP Plan in 1943 brought out something present in the new regime since the beginning: the contradiction between an official discourse that assumed control of urban development in defense of the common weal, and the reality of a city in the hands of the real-estate business's personal interests and expectations, frequently supported by major public works.

Carlos Mendoza's plan set the premises for the effective long-term transformation of the river: reform and urban renewal in exchange for extraordinary private exploitation. Once again, the classic mechanisms of speculation were applied with total indifference to the singularity of the place. And yet, the plan's contents did not exactly, or immediately, coincide with reality. In the mid-1950s it was still possible to enjoy the view of Madrid's skyline from natural surroundings at the *Pradera de San Isidro* (San Isidro Meadows) where construction of several blocks of residential real estate was planned. That was the last time the edge of the river appeared as a large empty space capable of stimulating the image of a landscape closely linked to the city's memory. The following year, urban planning fired its last salvo with the Perpiñá Project, which addressed the stretch of riverside between the Puente de Segovia and the Puente de Toledo. This plan discarded the clumsy blocks of housing stipulated by the Ministry of Public Works in favor of a more pertinent modern garden city with tall apartment buildings perpendicular to the river. But that alternative was never carried out, either.

The definitive transformation of the Manzanares began in earnest with the beginning of *Desarrollismo* (literally, development-ism) in the late nineteen fifties. The Mendoza Plan was supposed to guide the process but reality introduced two significant changes. First, the uniform blocks of four-story buildings topped with gracious spires and slate roofs were abandoned in favor of greater exploitation. The result was a continuous barrier of construction, including imposing and massive buildings at specific "strategic" locations. Second, the charming riverside road that appeared in the nineteen-forties plan became the M-30 urban highway, which

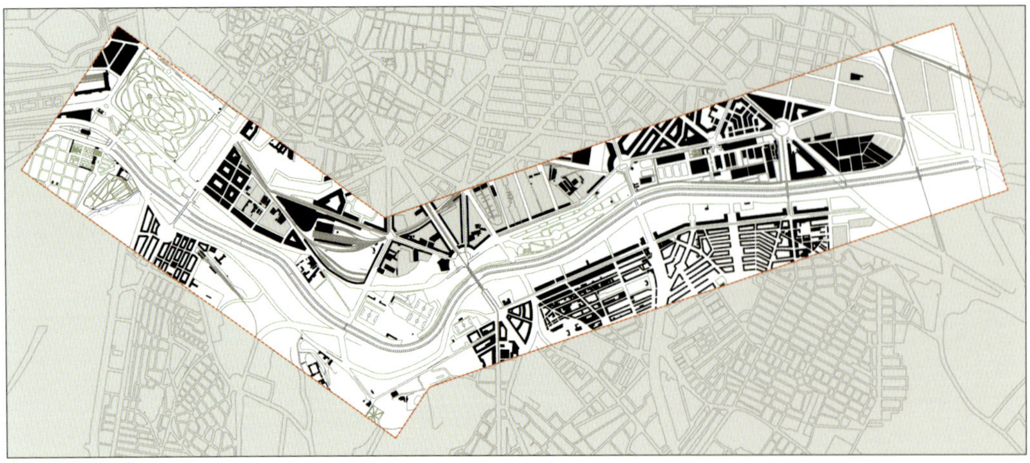

BIDAGOR

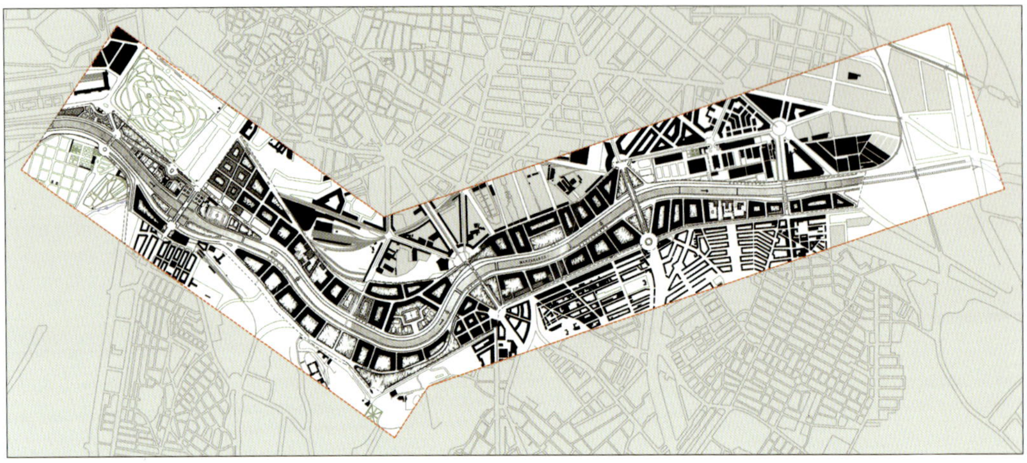

MENDOZA

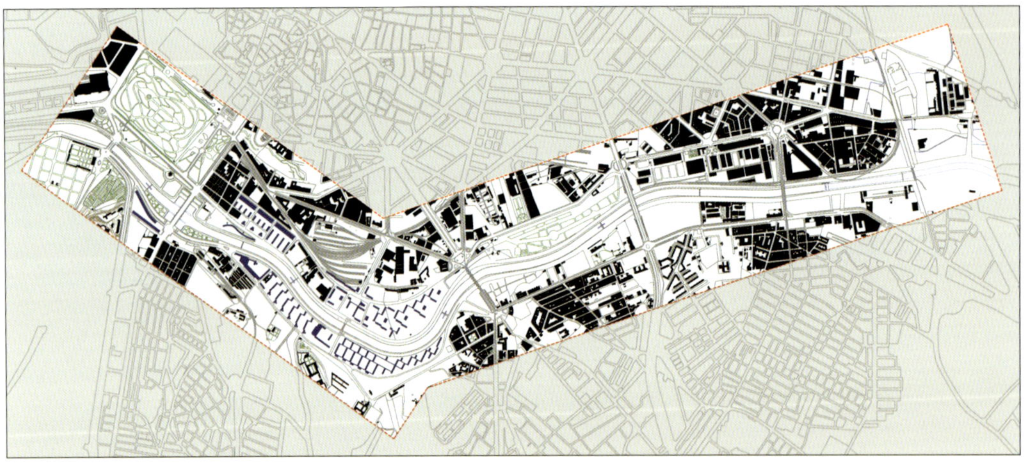

PERPIÑÁ

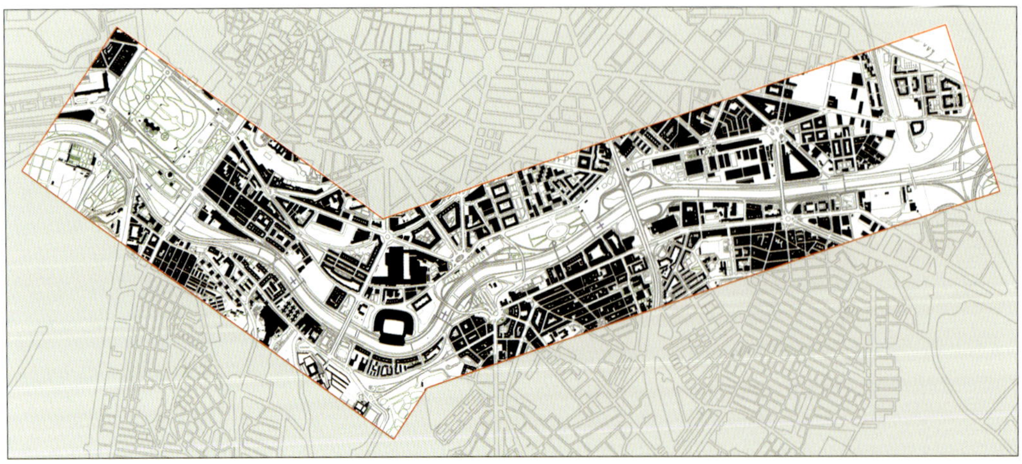

2000

barely fit the narrow space left between the buildings and the river itself. The inauguration of the M-30 West in 1974 not only clarified the primacy of sector-oriented policies; it also constituted a disproportionate expansion of the river's historical and natural role as a place for infrastructure.

As was to be expected, the eighties' spirit of reparation based on an illusory "end of growth," wasted no time in renewing the promise of a "green" Manzanares. And this time, it was accompanied by a curious combination of meanings and connotations. First, there was a call to restore the area's historical value, which was once again identified with the presence of nature. Thus, Madrid as center and summary of the region's landscape, or the Manzanares as the natural connection between the mountains and La Mancha, reemerged as undisputable arguments that echoed Bidagor's earlier geographical determinism. Second, the river was associated for the very first time with the recently addressed "environmental question," the need to *recover* a supposed ecological balance lost to the excesses of *Desarrollismo*, as represented by the polluted state of the river's water and, most of all, the harmful presence of the M-30.

The solutions seemed obvious. With the exception of Juan Navarro's eloquent project from 1981, which postulated the Manzanares' fragmented and disjointed condition as a reason for developing a new sense of the city; the projects from that period returned in more or less banal ways to the idea of a green corridor, which was by then accepted as a "belt" because construction had left it so narrow. These plans employed a curiously therapeutic vocabulary, with references to the need to *cure, stitch, fill voids,* or *heal fractures* produced by the major infrastructures around the river. The highway was supposed to disappear from the riverside, which would thus recover its "original" identity as a recreational area. But reality took a different course. At the end of the eighties, the M-30 not only continued to occupy the bank of the Manzanares; it had become part of a policy of territorial infrastructures that was determinant in late-20th-century urban expansion. From then on, the M-30's permanence was dissociated from the image of a green Manzanares laid out in a restorative and environmental manner. The highway's existence had virtually disappeared from all discourse.

From that viewpoint, the current large urban project for the Manzanares can be seen as the simple materialization of that dissociation. Between 2004 and 2007, the M-30 highway was expanded and hidden underground so Madrid Río's large linear park could be constructed above it. This embodied a gesture of fundamental importance: regaining ground level for pedestrians signifies a democratization of public space simply by placing it in the dominant position that it deserves. But, beyond its clear and well-known benefits, what is the new Manzanares's significance for the 21st-century city?

On one hand, the operation seems to reflect the frequent reduction of the concept of "landscape" to "nature," with a consubstantial acceptance of some of the restorative premises from the eighties. In that sense, the fact that the large metropolitan infrastructure has not been included in the place's image seems rather anachronistic — recalling what Koolhaas called "well-intentioned urban planning," with all its faults and ambiguities. It may be possible to call for a greater complexity in the concept of contemporary urban landscape without hypocrisy — to call for a landscape that includes major metropolitan (infra)structures, even if it does so with a certain degree of rawness.

On the other, and at the opposite end of the spectrum, the river's most recent transformation cannot be dissociated from 21st-century urban culture and politics. History will very probably convert this episode into an emblematic example of a period dominated by the illusion of unlimited growth, much like the megastructural visions of the sixties. But it may also be cast as a representation of the postindustrial era's own paradoxes: the image of a huge mechanized infrastructure linked to an environmental nightmare is simply replaced by the promise of a new "digital" environmentalism, that is, a clean, bodiless, and liberating technology that offers reconciliation with a nature that is actually being produced synthetically. And it is precisely where this synthetic condition appears most clearly, as in Ken Smith's well-known garden for MoMA, that truly contemporary landscape emerges. The dry tree trunks surrounding its playgrounds, the emergency exits, ventilation grills, and piles of rubble transformed into recreational hillocks are where the new Madrid Río attains its greatest relevance and intensity.

Finally, beyond its cultural implications, the Manzanares must be viewed from a historical perspective that allows it to be understood as a manifestation of the contemporary relation between image and structure. In other words, between discourse that fosters consensus based on environmental improvement and social redemption through a "return to nature," and the hidden reality of an urban model based on the indiscriminate consumption of land and resources in the interest of further growth and development. The linear park that covers the new M-30 thus emerges as a very effective rhetorical argument that includes received ideas about redressing natural and social imbalances, varying landscapes and their connections on a regional scale, references to the river as the city's origin, or the need to recover its "original state" as a "recreational component." In the pastoral and domesticated nature of the new Madrid Río, the metropolitan congregation is able to play and forget, if only for a moment, the anxieties of daily life. Under the surface, the structural reality is something else entirely. There, the determinant factors are a desire for the increased productivity brought by a larger highway. A highway built with the greatest investment as an autonomous model of mobility and infrastructures based on the primacy of private transportation and a vision of continuous territorial growth. The promise of a "green" Manzanares is thus finally satisfied, thanks to an extraordinary simulacrum, an unmistakable sign of our times. The contradiction between discourse and reality remains, but it goes unseen.

SOON THEY WILL WALK MORE. LEAVING MADRID ON FOOT

GINÉS GARRIDO AND FERNANDO PORRAS-ISLA

Walking, two different ways

A plethora of texts on the act of walking, strolling, or rambling, with or without any particular purpose, have occupied the philosophers and artists of modernity in an intense corpus of reflections and conclusions. Tracing a precise path through the bibliography that draws on these arguments put forth by contemporary thought is an attractive and straightforward task, although undoubtedly a lengthy one, as well. The references jostle and multiply like milestones along a dazzling path.

Like part of a continuous progression, each step contributes to an active, complex, and very sophisticated manifestation — a first approach to sizing up a place, establishing a consistent narrative, and determining a continuum that links physical and mental. Dozens of centuries of human life have refined this subtle and infallible art in which, with every step, the head, joints, limbs, senses, heart, and breathing share decisions and organize the dynamics of moving forward.

But let us pause to address this question in specific ways that, while hardly unprecedented, are certainly consubstantial with the task of creating a landscape, piece by piece. That is the job we carried out when constructing the green infrastructure that politicians, citizens, or even, we, ourselves, spontaneously decided to call Madrid Río.

We should point out the fundamental distinction between the only two manners of walking present in our civilization at this time. First, walking as an everyday act, an instrumental, though sometimes leisurely, means of occupying space that begins when we abandon our horizontal state of rest. This archaic, founding, biological, and ecological activity is linked to our consciousness as an evolved species. We could even call it an obligatory and inexorable act that therefore lies beyond our cognitive will. And yet, in another, very different way, walking could be presented as an activity that triggers a pattern of behavior beyond the purely physical — one loaded with meanings that can only be grasped by cultures and societies posterior to the industrial revolution. In this approach, the walker draws the territory, and that is when the latter emerges, free of any discourse or connotations. Walking, when one does so with no specific purpose, when it is not tied to our nomadic origins, becomes a manifesto, resistance, or provocation. In this case, it will not be the same to walk alone, in company, or as part of a crowd, carrying weight or free of any load, with or without a specific direction. But it will always be an activity closer to the projection of the future than to the legitimate inheritance of past origins.

Marking the gates facilitates transit

When we confront the city with its territory, we are immediately pitting opposing terms against each other. Empty or full, traveled or unexplored, artificial or natural. But this dialectic also awakens the middle ground, the blurred edges and interstices — semi-colonized places, or those crossed by isolated, if deeply implanted, lines of infrastructure that imbue them with the fragility of something about to change.

Until the end of the Renaissance, cities sought to diminish their vulnerability. In a manner that seems ingenuous from a spatial standpoint, they established barriers between outside and inside, between what merited defense above all other considerations, and what could be invaded, reconnoitered, or trampled by other peoples. This border was first drawn, then walked, before it finally took substance as a defensive wall. Once limit became infrastructure, it had to combat its own existence, reproducing itself concentrically in successive enclosures until it finally disappeared under the pressure of a population whose growth within the walls was mirrored by the waning risk of possible invasion from without. Those walls' fiscal uses, in which controlled entry allowed the registering and taxation of merchandise, gave way to more modern methods that no longer depended on the capacity to enclose the city, and from then on, continuous and opaque urban containment no longer made any sense at all.

With the disappearance of physical limits, a new system of peripheral settlement began, and this consolidated a true permeability between inside and out, urban and rural, solid and ephemeral. Paradoxically, over the course of the 20th century, cities freed themselves of their cloistered medieval condition only to close themselves in another sense — this time with barriers that are simultaneously connections. Bypasses, beltways, and infrastructural links serving the automobile are the new walls that keep the population from even considering the possibility of walking out of, or into, the city like creatures that tread the earth. Today, city dwellers seem to have agreed to accept the idea that they cannot escape on foot from the setting where they live their daily lives.

The gates of today's city are no longer linked to a physical continuum that connects them to population centers. They are virtual or distant gates, new connections that require structures totally unrelated to our condition as bipeds: airports, supply lines, digital networks, computer bases, or financial centers whose characteristic virtue is generally their immediacy. Madrid is a medium-sized city by Western standards and its importance as the nation's capital city owes much more to its central location than to its historical dimension. Like almost all cities of its size, it has enough connections to make it part of any contemporary network that supports concentrated human activity in an urban setting. And yet, it still has natural gates through which it is possible to distinguish inside from outside in an essential manner. This is feasible despite the fact that its solid borders have been blurred by constant urban sprawl, leading to a metropolitan area – including surrounding dormitory communities – almost completely covered by buildings and domesticated open spaces of varying density and scale.

Exceptionally, some of Madrid's gates echo geographic features that relate the center of the Iberian Peninsula with its borders facing Europe or the coast: three concrete points of communication situated several dozen kilometers from this capital. Two are mountain passes leading north to Galicia (the Puerto de Guadarrama) and France (the Puerto de Somosierra), respectively, while the third is the passage across the Tagus River at Aranjuez, which connects with the south on the way to Andalusia. And each makes its existence known within the city limits, though sometimes in nearly imperceptible ways. They bear no direct relation with the former gates of the five successive walls that enclosed Madrid since Arab times, but they have left deeper marks as lines of penetration, that is, ancient trails which have now become highways of the first order connecting Madrid with the mountain passes to the north and across the Tagus River to the south. These main roads run parallel to the Manzanares River and its tributary, the Arroyo Abroñigal, which flow from the northwest and northeast, respectively, and meet where the Manzanares's bed coincides with the beginning of the road southwards, forming an indelible "Y" that has been present to a greater or lesser degree in all of the city's overall urban plans.

Unquestionably, these roads follow the banks of the rivers that have guided their paths across Castile, and the city itself has, in turn, taken its shape from the roads. So, Madrid's status as political capital is almost exclusively due to its geometric position as the center point, origin, and destination of the main routes linking the peninsula's diverse territories.

City, roads, and rivers accumulate energy where they meet or intersect, and we can interpret these spaces as gates: specific places leading from inside to outside or vice versa. In the past, these points explained transit between natural and artificial settings, entry and exit. The ring infrastructures installed around Madrid in the second half of the 20th century paid little heed to the special nature of these gateways, occupying them as they did all other parts of the territory. Moreover, they used the lines defined by Madrid's rivers as easily appropriated bases for the fastest highways, built in direct and raw contact with the adjoining city. Nevertheless, the persistence of the former riverbeds' geological conditions has made it possible to rediscover their presence as opportunities for strollers. The river has emerged as a fundamental agent that allows us to recognize inside and out, and thus, to determine the surroundings where direct contact between the two is possible.

Implementing continuity, a structural action

In 2007, during the final phase of work to run the M-30 underground, the Manzanares was almost totally, if temporarily, dry. This allowed heavy trucks to cross its bed, where they were loaded with the remains of the surface highway. The wound opened in the city's fabric did not uncover organic tissue; it revealed raw spaces, arid wastelands of refuse, rubble, and demolition. This was a rough, dry scar, a scrap of desert whose high temperatures were due not only to the persistent sun, but also to running motors, recently spread asphalt, and setting concrete.

At that point, when the waterline had literally disappeared, we undertook an action whose main purpose was to ratify that the

FERNANDO PORRAS-ISLA. MADRID GATES, AFTER *BALD MARSCHIEREN MEHR*, PAUL KLEE, 1934

riverbed was the only accessible passageway for establishing effective contact between the city and the outlying territory. That was not the activity's only objective, as its main promoter, catalan painter and poet Perejaume, decided to carry three 18th-century drawings along the entire path on his shoulders. These academic drawings were of two left feet and one right foot and belonged to the library at the university's School of Fine Arts, north of the city. We therefore decided to cross Madrid, starting from the School and continuing until we had exited the city to the south, leaving it behind.

We chose the Manzanares' riverbed, which was then a linear battlefield, as the basis for our journey. This action sought to question concepts such as the resonance between the feet represented on paper and the limbs of those carrying them along a precise path, the multiple authorship of the action, the city's nature as a collective and incommensurable work, and the quality of the Academy as a generator of accepted models and strategies. But over and above all these ideas, we perceived the value of continuity through the trench running the length of the river, which could be returned to the city as an essentially open public asset.

The project to regenerate the spaces that appeared after the highway was rerouted underground was then being conceived, and it combined the extreme complexity of creating an efficient green space over the structure of an underground highway with the straightforward need for a continuous element whose condition, scale, and accessibility would make it one of the most important structures in the city. Moreover, for the first time, this structure would be conceived for pedestrians, an area to be crossed on foot without the interference of automobiles.

Measuring and appropriating, step by step

This new structure could then combine the possibilities of crossing the city from north to south and recreating its dimension as an organic setting favorable to the social transformation and reflexive creation of strollers. On a more primitive level, it could also return to the city the features of an itinerary capable of connecting walkers with settings that still symbolize the rural, promising a sort of superior protection embodied by the outline of the mountains always visible in the distance.

The construction of a continuous public space around a river, which we are fortunate enough to have in Madrid, and of new links and connections to span it, expands and extends the structural dimension of these collective surroundings. So it is now possible to act upon it with critical or creative criteria, understanding the public dimensions of this urban undertaking in all their complexity. To make it one's own with the sole act of measuring it, mentally taking it in and defining its expanse as we move across it without any other purpose than retracing the itineraries we have walked before. To recover something snatched away from pedestrians decades ago by the automobile: the chance to enjoy safe and reliable surroundings. To return a lost dimension to a city that had progressively reduced the space allotted to walking, thus forgetting its origins: the path along which it was born and the river it approached.

Now, the green park living over the tunnels has three overlapping speeds: hidden underground, a velocity only available to humans in the form of motor vehicles; on the surface, and intimately linked to the ground, the vertical growth of living plants, imperceptibly slow, yet constant; and between the fastest and slowest, the variable speeds of walking humans — those who, from the very first day, have intensely and permanently taken possession of the wound now healed. These speeds will change over time. Someday, the tunnels may lose all meaning as roadways and when the underground highway disappears, the current conception of the area's plant life will also have to be changed or questioned. Moreover, the occupation of the river's banks, its plazas, streets, and avenues should be increased without intermediate elements. So walking bodies will be able to acquire an aware confidence based on the cultural traits, both classic and contemporary, of our human condition.

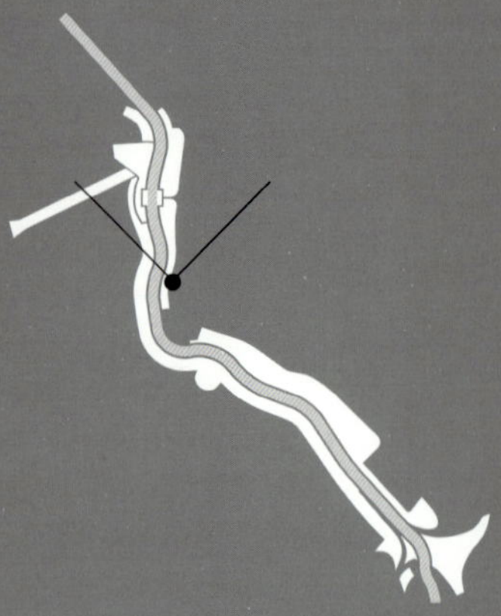

3. PRESS COVERAGE

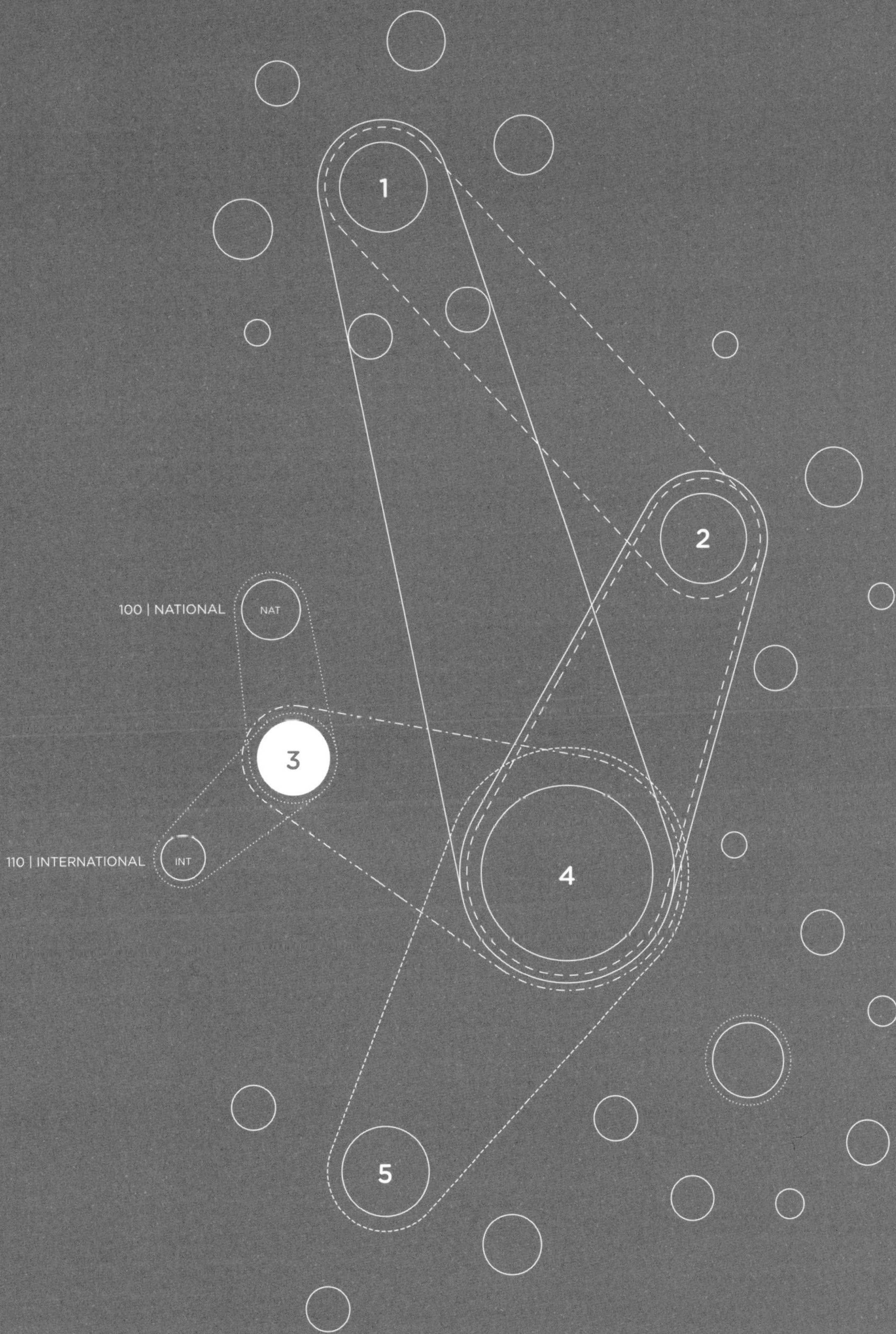

s derribadas

xplicó que para ac-
n poblado hay que
iso de las chabolas
Un trabajador social
enso y estudia cada
casos", indica. Para
los poblados crez-
s se beneficien de los
stablece un sistema
por la policía muni-

a destacó la dificul-
entra el Consistorio
sos. "En Plata y Cas-
ente que se niega a
as chabolas". En ese
ntamiento pide una
l para desalojar las
s.

los vecinos, "el 98%
na", según De Gra-
beneficiarse del plan
unicipal deben cum-
de requisitos: esco-
los niños, empadro-
egistro en documen-

adas que les entrega
ento son de alquiler.
udiando una posibi-
e una vez transcurri-
puedan adquirir las
recisa.

a informó de que el
o ha renovado el
la Fundación Secre-
no mediante el cual
yo social a las fami-

EL PAÍS (MADRID) JULY 11, 2006.
THE ARTICLE DESCRIBES A CATALAN COUPLE LOST AMONG THE PUBLIC WORKS ON THE M-30 UNTIL A PAIR OF MADRILENIANS HELP THEM FIND THEIR WAY OUT BY CAR.

PP, que insistían en que se estaba cumpliendo la ley".

De Rossa celebró que la concejal de Urbanismo le dijera estar presta "a un acuerdo

ciones". Luego ha-
brá que ver si lo hac
considerar urgente
declaración de Pi
nez".

Fernando García y María Escobar. / SUSANNA PÉREZ

. Ha-
Hay que
te esa
Martí-

que no hay nada que objetar a los planes de modernización y desarrollo del alcalde, siempre y cuando se ajusten a la ley.

M-30, que están pendientes de la prolongación del paseo de la Castellana, y al hacerlo evalúa los efectos acumulados por la reforma de la vía”.

¿Dónde está la autovía de Barcelona?

Una pareja guía con su coche a través de las obras a un matrimonio catalán

ANA ALFAGEME, **Madrid**
Una buena idea, un trayecto accidentado y un final feliz. Fernando García y María Escobar regresaban el jueves de Extremadura, de celebrar con un viaje en coche sus 40 años de matrimonio. Pero de vuelta a casa, a Villafranca del Penedès, en Barcelona, el maestro jubilado, de 64 años, y su esposa, de 62, ama de casa, se enredaron en las señales amarillas de la M-30 levantada sin encontrar la indicación de la autovía de Barcelona. Hasta que una pareja de madrileños tomó su propio coche y les guió hasta su destino.

El jueves Fernando y María, tras 20 minutos de dar vueltas, detuvieron su coche en un parque. María estaba tan agobiada que ni se bajó. Después de un rato, pasó una pareja con una niña de la mano, a la que le preguntó Fernando, también concejal de Villafranca por CiU. Venían del pediatra. “La mujer le reprochaba a él que nos iba a mandar para otro sitio”, recuerda el hombre, por teléfono, “él la tranquilizaba, pero al final nos dijeron: ‘¿Sabe qué?, véngase detrás de nuestro coche y les sacaremos de Madrid. Y no se asusten cuando entremos en la M-30, que pasarán los camiones casi rozándoles”. Así fue. Los catalanes siguieron el coche gris de los madrileños entre el polvo y los tráileres, hasta que éstos, 10 minutos después, señalaron el desvío. María les mandó un beso. Fernando se quedó con la pena de no tener su teléfono.

Ayer, desde Barcelona, María llamó a la alcaldía de Madrid. Les pidió que, por favor, señalizaran mejor la M-30.

NATIONAL

Over the years, work to run the M-30 highway underground, and subsequently to condition and develop the riverbanks made available by the construction of those tunnels, took on a social dimension that was covered by communications media from the very start. Week by week, the print media constructed a journalistic history that soon resembled a serial fable.

During the period when work was going on, events considered worthy of note by the print media's editorial directors were covered primarily by Madrid's press or by local editions of the national press. References to that work appeared in the national and international press at the two high points of the process: the completion of the tunnels and the definitive opening of Madrid Río.

This sustained coverage of an urban transformation project by the print media calls for its consideration as a factor that made a certain degree of noise in Madrid's social and political forum. Therefore, we have included three lists here that cover 120 news items from the three most widely distributed newspapers in the city: *El País* (national circulation of 473,407 copies in July 2011, according to the OJD*), *El Mundo* (national circulation of 383,713 copies in July 2011, according to the OJD) and *ABC* (national circulation of 326,584 copies in July 2011, according to the OJD). These lists were drawn up by consulting online editions of each newspaper. In the case of *El País* and *ABC*, paper and digital editions are very similar, although the internet editions are more rapidly updated and contain some news that printed editions do not have time to include due to their lesser immediacy. The virtual and print editions of *El Mundo*, however, are completely separate. While they frequently include the same news, it is presented with different headlines, texts, and images.

These three lists, which contain only the title and publication date of the news, offer readers the opportunity to form an oriented opinion of the work carried out. Moreover, it is possible to identify the position each of the three newspapers took with regard to the project. Ideologically, *El País* was opposed to the work; *El Mundo* was opposed to the figure of the Mayor and his team, while *ABC* sought to maintain greater objectivity but nevertheless revealed a position close to that of the municipal government.

The number of times certain words or concepts appear in each of the lists of headlines has also been tracked, and it reveals how the news focused mainly on Madrid, the M-30, the mayor, or the tunnels, and almost never (or never) on architects, engineers, legal problems, or landscape.

KEY WORD	EL PAÍS	EL MUNDO	ABC
MADRID	26	21	14
M-30	51	82	51
GALLARDÓN / MAYOR	14	18	14
TUNNEL	12	9	16
MADRID RÍO	15	12	6
PROJECT	3	3	4
ARCHITECTURE / ARCHITECT	2	0	1
ILLEGALITY / ILLEGAL	0	1	0
ENGINEERING/ENGINEER	0	0	0
LANDSCAPE	0	0	0

We have also reproduced eight complete news articles from the three national newspapers mentioned above. The graphic reproduction of the newspaper pages in which these articles appear is intended, here, to reflect how these communications media narrated the most relevant aspects of the process. The news is sometimes unconventional and not always direct, reflecting the spectrum of interests awakened by the operation. Moreover, it is often tangential to the work itself and its various phases.

*OJD: Spanish Office of Justification of the Diffusion.

SELECTION: 120 HEADLINES FROM *ABC*

04/29/2005 Partner wanted for managing the M-30
05/09/2005 Work begins on the monumental project to bury the M-30
05/15/2005 University professors and architects call the M-30 project "absurd".
06/04/2005 Work to run the M-30 under the Manzanares River leaves it dry.
06/09/2005 The world's largest tunneling machine will come to Spain in July to dig the southern M-30.
08/03/2005 Public works mean gridlock for Madrid, even in August
08/04/2005 M-30 construction sparks huge traffic jams
08/07/2005 A bird's eye view of the M-30: fences, cranes, narrowing, and winding lanes.
10/10/2005 City Hall dismantles the contemporary-design footbridge near the Puente de Segovia.
10/18/2005 Madrid, the only city in the world with twelve tunneling machines working at the same time.
11/09/2005 The Manzanares triples its flow with water drawn from 34 kilometers of storm drains.
11/12/2005 Children want the city to have a beach on the Manzanares
11/19/2005 Children's stuff for the Manzanares

01/02/2006 Gallardón writes a letter apologizing for work on the M-30
01/25/2006 A court recognizes the M-30 as a city street so work there does not require an environmental impact statement
02/22/2006 The Southern Bypass's second tunneling machine will begin digging the M-30 in March
03/08/2006 Rome's mayor praises the burial of the M-30 and says he's "envious"
03/28/2006 The M-30's financing receives a European prize for its "innovative structure"
04/05/2006 The European Commision brings suit against Spain for an infraction in the M-30 case
04/07/2006 68% of local residents believe M-30 improvements will outweigh the inconveniences
06/27/2006 Gallardón promises impact statements for the three M-30 projects yet to begin
06/27/2006 Eurodeputies conclude that M-30 work violates norms
06/27/2006 "I just want them to let me sleep"
05/07/2006 Ecologists in Action denounce worsening air quality due to M-30 work
07/17/2006 Gallardón says work will be finished before the end of the year
07/18/2006 "Dulcinea" completes one of the M-30 tunnels in just seven months
08/11/2006 The RACE reports that the M-30 is the most dangerous European highway under construction
08/29/2006 "Dulcinea" and "Tizona" are ahead of schedule on the M-30's Southern Bypass
09/13/2006 Eurodeputies that visited the M-30 seek compensation for local residents
10/30/2006 Rajoy, Gallardón, and Aguirre at the M-30 construction site
10/31/2006 Digging for the M-30's Southern Bypass complete
11/04/2006 City Hall considering a project to bury the A-6 where it enters the capital
11/25/2006 Gallardón will inaugurate the first length of M-30 tunnel in December
11/12/2006 City Hall will hold concerts over the M-30 during the San Isidro Celebrations
12/13/2006 The first underground section of the M-30 will open on the 20th, marking 4 months of inaugurations
12/21/2006 The first M-30 tunnel to open already allows access to 20,000 cars

---

01/07/2007 Underground routing work will end on March 30
01/07/2007 The M-30 improvements raise the value of apartments near the Manzanares by 20%
01/09/2007 Two out of three Madrid residents believe M-30 improvements will outweigh the inconveniences
01/14/2007 40 year-old cherry trees and 9 meter pines shape the park over the M-30 tunnels
01/17/2007 The land excavated from the M-30 would fill twenty Santiago Bernabéu Stadiums.
01/31/2007 The M-30 enters its final round with the opening of a two-kilometer tunnel beneath the Manzanares
01/31/2007 "We can finally see light at the end of the tunnel"
09/02/2007 An open letter to the councilwoman for the environment
12/02/2007 The Manzanares is sick
02/12/2007 Objective: "making Madrid beautiful"
03/04/2007 Stage
03/09/2007 The Avenida de Portugal will become a boulevard without cars, with 1,400 trees and a cycle path
03/09/2007 Study says M-30 works will reduce accidents by 400 in 2007
03/24/2007 The M-30's southern arc already has the longest urban tunnel in Europe: 7.5 kilometers
03/30/2007 Gallardón inaugurates the M-30's exterior tunnel accompanied by the president of Chile
03/31/2007 With the tunnel's inauguration, cars are gone from the Manzanares
03/31/2007 The entire M-30 in 43' 15"
04/03/2007 The Manzanares River will have grass "beaches" and sections with rowboats
04/21/2007 The bypass's southern tunnel brings up the rear of the work
04/21/2007 The M-30 enters the final round with two tunnels linking Embajadores to the A-4
04/25/2007 The final M-30 tunnel will open just four days before the campaign begins
04/27/2007 A leak causes an enormous waterfall in a new M-30 tunnel
05/05/2007 A grand landscaped boulevard eliminates 100,000 vehicles a day from the Avenida de Portugal
05/06/2007 Last night, the Manzanares inaugurated its over 10,000 "fireflies"
05/07/2007 The M-30's final work, the southern Bypass, opens tomorrow
05/08/2007 Juan Bravo: "we have never even considered a toll for the M-30"
05/09/2007 Gallardón completes M-30 work with the longest urban tunnel in the world
05/09/2007 The opening of the longest urban tunnel in the world marks the end of M-30 construction
05/09/2007 Ruiz-Gallardón, mission accomplished
05/13/2007 Madrid beseiged, the challenge of leaving on foot
05/20/2007 Gallardón proposes a large riverside park with a beach, fishing, sports centers, and culture
06/06/2007 The new M-30 has increased the value of nearby apartments by 24% since 2003
06/22/2007 Manuel Melis, the technological mind behind the M-30 and Metrosur resigns
07/12/2007 The "new" Manzanares already has 648 pines and will have a wharf, rowboads, and a beach
09/18/2007 The "new" M-30 reduces traffic by 6% in the Capital's central hub
12/05/2007 The mayor visits the M-30 tunnels with a delegation from the United States
12/14/2007 Objective: saving the Casa de Campo's grottoes

01/24/2008 Madrid's residents can express their opinon of the project between February and April
01/24/2008 Beach, wharf, cycle path, and footbridges will make the Manzanares Madrid's center
02/19/2008 Work begins to transform the Manzanares River
02/19/2008 Work on the wharf and beach will not begin until 2009
04/04/2008 The M-30's "oblique bridge" will be saved from destruction and become a footbridge
04/25/2008 17.5 million euros for six new footbridges
05/04/2008 Mayors who change Europe
07/26/2008 EU says environmental impact statements will be required for future M-30 work
08/17/2008 The underground waterways
09/18/2008 Flooding on the M-30, "a series of misfortunes"
09/20/2008 Melis
10/03/2008 Bravo
12/20/2008 Zapatero pays "Madrid Río"
12/27/2008 City Hall will pay for work on the Zapatero Fund projects in 30 days
12/28/2008 Two large operations will transform the capital at a cost of 12,000 million
12/30/2008 Calle 30

01/23/2009 The Puerta del Rey will be repaired, three years after it was damaged by a truck
04/16/2009 Fighting about the Puerta del Rey
07/04/2009 The crisis will not stop the new Manzanares
07/06/2009 El Matadero dressed in green
07/09/2009 Another 66 million for the Manzanares park and "beach"
10/08/2009 Flooding, traffic interruptions, and complaining neighbors following last night's storm
10/09/2009 A storm drain caused the flooding on the Avenida del Manzanares
10/14/2009 Madrid residents will visit the river in two months
11/21/2009 Indigents evicted from the banks of the Manzanares
11/12/2009 Gallardón inaugurates the new puente del Rey and a new section of Madrid Río
12/12/2009 A stage across from the Palace
12/28/2009 Madrid Río, pays Zapatero

01/16/2010 A carpet of pines on the river
02/05/2010 The monument, buried by the remodling of the M-30
05/11/2010 The Manzanares, more of a river than ever before
05/18/2010 The Mapocho River reformation copies that of the Manzanares
06/25/2010 Seoul will build its own "M-30"
10/15/2010 Madrid will have a beach in April 2011
11/11/2010 Arganzuela, a park multiplied by three

02/09/2011 Work on the river will end on April 15
02/11/2011 Ecologists want Gallardón and Botella jailed
03/17/2011 Double judicial findings against the licensing ordinance and the M-30
03/23/2011 The Delegate criticises a public work the minute after she inaugurates it
04/03/2011 The new Madrid's surgeons
04/04/2011 Once again, Madrid has a river
04/13/2011 Merce and Paco's cave-house under the Puente de Toledo
04/16/2011 Madrid Río opens to the public today
07/05/2011 Madrid Río opens a café-bar with one-euro deck chairs by the beach
07/12/2011 The "Times" says Boston's "Dig Big" is "small change" compared to Madrid Río
07/22/2011 The beach gets its outdoor café
07/22/2011 An elevator to the viaduct makes for easy access

SELECTION: 120 HEADLINES FROM *EL MUNDO*

05/02/2004	The PSOE reveals that M-30 construction will be exempt from environmental impact statements
02/13/2004	The opposition calls Ruiz-Gallardón's electoral promise to reform the M-30 a "fraud"
02/18/2004	The PSOE reveals that Gallardón wants to start work on the M-30 by hiding its impact
02/19/2004	20% of the company that will reform the M-30 will be private and it will have 70 million in social capital
02/29/2004	The Government hands over the M-30 to Gallardón and grants him 53 million to manage the construction
02/20/2004	The New M-30 will be constructed and managed by a trading company created by City Hall
09/20/2004	Fierce criticism of the M-30 reform

04/13/2005	City Hall says it will not dismantle the Arganzuela greenhouse during M-30 construction work
04/24/2005	Legazpi residents occupy the Tierno Galván Park in opposition to M-30 construction
05/24/2005	The impact of M-30 construction denounced in the European Parliament
06/16/2005	Ecologists denounce tree killing on the M-30
07/28/2005	Dragados, Ferrovial and API join the business group that will manage M-30 construction
08/04/2005	Madrid, the eternal suffering of construction work in the capital
08/13/2005	City Hall denies using potable water for M-30 construction
08/13/2005	M-30 construction causes more traffic cuts in the capital
09/27/2005	The PSOE reveals that M-30 construction work will "kill" Tierno Galván Park
10/14/2005	Residents affected by M-30 construction will demonstrate today
11/03/2005	Gallardón promises that M-30 construction will bring in 254,000 new trees by 2007
11/04/2005	City Hall and La Riviera deny that M-30 construction will cause cancellation of the Paul Weller concert
11/16/2005	Environmental Protection will verify presumed irregularities in M-30 construction
11/18/2005	Children request a riverside beach at the "municipal plenary meeting"
11/24/2005	Sabanés asks the EU to intervene in the "disastrous" M-30 construction
11/25/2005	The European Parliament delays its decision to send a delegation to the M-30 construction until January
11/29/2005	The Castellana's underground ring and the M-30 construction are the capital's greatest "horrors"
11/30/2005	Calderón Stadium in danger following the selection of Ginés Garrido's plan to recover the Manzanares
12/02/2005	IU accuses the mayor of improvising the M-30 construction and warns of damage to the Puente de Toledo
12/07/2005	Madrid's City Hall seeks permission from the Comunidad de Madrid to work on the Puente de Toledo
12/14/2005	Taxi drivers denounce the loss of 14 million passengers a year due to M-30 construction
12/23/2005	The regional government still unclear about M-30 construction at the Puente de Toledo

01/13/2006	The Guardia Civil discovers irregularities in M-30 construction
01/18/2006	Plataforma de la M-30 requests greater oversight after Confederación Hidrográfica del Tajo halts work in one section
01/20/2006	Environmental Protection gives the green light to construction of the M-30's Puente de Praga section
01/23/2006	Judges to hear Ecologists in Action's appeal against M-30's underground routing
01/25/2006	Court rules that M-30 does not require environmental impact statement
01/26/2006	City Hall will send a technician rather than a politician to explain the M-30 reform in Brussels
01/26/2006	A delegation of the European Parliment will analyze M-30 construction on site beginning in March
02/17/2006	Almudena Grandes and Leo Bassi will support Sunday's event by the "Platform against the M-30"
02/19/2006	Five hundred citizens denounce Gallardón's "lies" about the M-30 construction project
02/20/2006	Gallardón says opponents of the M-30 modernization have "grown old before their time"
02/20/2006	On Wednesday, Sabanés will denounce in Brussels that M-30 construction flauts European directives
02/21/2006	In March, the Tizona tunneling machine will begin the "final section" of the M-30 construction
02/22/2006	Brussels hears City Hall and the opposition but sets no date to visit the M-30
02/22/2006	M-30 construction debated at the European Parliament
02/22/2006	Judges disallow IU efforts to appeal the entire M-30 reform project
02/23/2006	Warning that M-30 construction is provoking an increase in the number of cockroaches, rats and mice in the area
04/05/2006	Bruselas reprimands Spain for failure to carry out an environmental impact study of M-30 construction
04/06/2006	Cobo says "no environmental impact statment would have imposed more conditions" on M-30 construction
04/06/2006	The PSOE asks City Hall to issue an environmental impact statement on M-30 construction
04/06/2006	Narbona asks Gallardón to halt M-30 construction and Urban Planning says it obeys all current legal requirements
04/12/2006	Brussels calls for Madrid to issue an environmental impact statement on M-30 construction
04/20/2006	The Prosecutors' Office expresses "concern" about the contaminating effects of M-30 reform works
04/25/2006	A delegation of the European Parliament will visit M-30 construction in June
04/26/2006	The Minister of the Environment initiates three more investigations of City Hall for M-30 construction
06/26/2006	European deputies examining M-30 construction begin their visit by meeting with experts
06/27/2006	During Brussels' visit, Gallardón announces he will inform them of the M-30's environmental impact
06/27/2006	Urban Planning councilwoman says it is the Commission's job to straighten out M-30 disagreements
06/27/2006	European deputies call meeting with the Comunidad (de Madrid) "a waste of time"
06/28/2006	European deputies conclude that M-30 construction violates EU environmental norms
07/10/2006	M-30 construction should have had an environmental impact statement
08/03/2006	Ecologists denounce the disappearance of the Manzanares' historic orchards
09/14/2006	The European deputies that visited the M-30 construction seek indemnities for local residents
09/28/2006	Councilwoman Martínez says M-30 construction will be finished in six months
09/28/2006	M-30 construction cost overrun reaches 355 million euros
10/25/2006	Visiting the insides of the new M-30 with Gallardón
10/31/2006	"Tizona" finishes digging the M-30's southern bypass
11/20/2006	Neighbors believe the M-30 chimneys will increase mortality levels
11/28/2006	M-30 construction generates contamination ten times higher than normal
12/08/2006	M-30 tunnels will begin opening in two weeks

01/10/2007	64% of Madrid residents believe M-30 construction will be worthwhile
01/11/2007	Mayor considers legal conflict over M-30 construction resolved
01/12/2007	The PSOE and the CECU accuse the mayor of opening an unsafe tunnel in the M-30
01/17/2007	The PSOE denounces illegal dumping of M-30 rubble
01/22/2007	M-30 construction work a tourist attraction
01/02/2007	IU denounces the inauguration of another M-30 tunnel without functioning emergency exits
02/06/2007	Within the year, the Manzanares River will have "bathing" quality water
03/09/2007	The Avenida de Portugal will become a "green corridor" with 1,400 trees and a cycling path
03/12/2007	City Hall accused of hiding M-30 pollution data
03/29/2007	The recovery of the Manzanares
03/30/2007	With the new M-30 tunnel, the Manzanares bids farewell to cars
04/28/2007	Rubalcaba: "Gallardón is the only person in Spain who doesn't want it to rain"
05/08/2007	Ruiz-Gallardón announces the end of the M-30 reforms after three and a half years of construction
05/11/2007	The RAE scolds City Hall for using by-pass rather than *baipás*
07/05/2007	The mayor disdains archeology
07/19/2007	An à la carte exit from the M-30
09/18/2007	Renaissance grottoes used as storage areas for M-30 construction

04/07/2008	None of the M-30 emergency tunnels is prepared for the handicapped
04/22/2008	Arganzuela residents protest against the Manzanares beach
04/30/2008	EU lawyer believes M-30 construction may have breached norms
07/25/2008	Brussels rules that works like the M-30 must be subject to environmental impact studies
09/18/2008	Calvo admits that a Madrid Río wall was one of the causes of M-30 flooding
09/18/2008	The PSOE accuses the mayor of hiding information about the M-30 tunnel flood
09/25/2008	Martínez denies that a Madrid Río wall was involved in M-30 tunnel flood
09/26/2008	Cobo boasts that the M-30 is finished now that public works have been halted due to the crisis
10/22/2008	The Madrid Rio Park open for reforms
10/28/2008	A Madrid court annuls approval of M-30 construction in the Manzanares
10/12/2008	Local residents want the 554 million for equipment rather than grand projects
12/19/2008	City Hall receives 554 million and will create almost 9,000 jobs

01/05/2009	...while the tunnels' emergency exits are blocked
08/10/2009	Flooding was not due to the M-30 but to a storm drain
12/22/2009	Money from the State Fund for Madrid Rio and the Conde Duque

01/10/2010	Urban renewal will come to the Manzanares neighborhoods
01/26/2010	This is the plan to rehabilitate the area around the Manzanares River
03/02/2010	The Madrid Río Platform warns of the Manzanares railings
04/01/2010	Few refuse bins and absence of containers in Madrid Río
06/06/2010	The Puente de Segovia ponds are fenced off but people continue to bathe in them
06/25/2010	Gallardón shows the M-30 tunnels to the Mayor of Seoul, South Korea
07/29/2010	City Hall will spend 12.5 million euros a year in Madrid Río upkeep
09/08/2010	Madrid exports its model of urban transformation
10/06/2010	Ecologists in Action denounce the extermination of trees along the Manzanares River
10/27/2010	Madrid Río already shows some damage
10/28/2010	Dangerous damage to Madrid Río

01/29/2011	Madrid Río as presented by the project's director
03/09/2011	The death of Austin T. Bice reawakens concerns about Madrid Río's safety
03/17/2011	Madrid Río construction absorbs 1,000 square meters of the Casa de Campo's nursery
03/23/2011	Lissavetzky and City Hall quarrel over the inauguration of Madrid Río
03/28/2011	IU denounces that the Manzanares River has "a desolate appearance"
04/06/2011	Madrid Río chokes on its cafés
05/17/2011	Twelve proposals to "polish" Madrid Río
06/06/2011	The first protest in Madrid Río will be on bicycles and to request a high school
06/27/2011	Ecologists in Action denounce the death of trees in Madrid Río

SELECTION: 120 HEADLINES FROM *EL PAÍS*

09/04/2005 City Hall admits it did not know how to explain the project's benefits
09/25/2005 A sea of cars floods the river
10/04/2005 "What do we do with the Manzanares River?"
10/17/2005 RICARDO AROCA / Dean of architects: "We have managed to mitigate the impact of the M-30 construction"
10/23/2005 ALBERTO RUIZ-GALLARDÓN / Mayor of Madrid "The construction has only reduced traffic speed by one kilometer per hour"
10/24/2005 CARLOS HERNÁNDEZ PEZZI President of the Superior Council of Architects: "The M-30 transformation is a very difficult project"
10/25/2005 IU affirms that the M-30 construction violates environmental regulations
11/04/2005 M-30 construction forces The Jam's ex-leader to cancel his Madrid recital
11/11/2005 "Dulcinea's" inaugural journey
11/12/2005 A school contest advocates building a beach on the Manzanares
11/25/2005 The European Parliament will require information on the M-30 construction
11/29/2005 The project that won the river contest plans to replace the Calderón with a lake
12/01/2005 M-30 construction uncovers a paleolithic hunters' village
12/05/2005 Life amidst the M-30 construction
12/13/2005 The Socialists call the M-30 the most dangerous road in Europe due to remodeling work
12/24/2005 Gallardón thanks citizens for their patience

01/21/2006 The Hydrographic Confederation revokes the halting of M-30 construction
01/25/2006 A sentence exempts the M-30 construction from an environmental impact statement
01/28/2006 A thousand local residents demonstrate against the M-30 construction
01/28/2006 The PSOE denounces cost overruns of 4,382 millon for M-30 construction
01/29/2006 I invite you to the M-30, JESÚS RUIZ MANTILLA
02/10/2006 The opposition denounces the cutting of 20,000 trees during M-30 construction
02/11/2006 City Hall says it has cut 13,800 trees and planted 38,000
02/14/2006 Local residents tormented by dust from South M-30 construction
02/22/2006 The second M-30 tunneling machine will begin digging in March
02/28/2006 At the heart of "Dulcinea"
03/08/2006 The PSOE denounces that tons of rubble from the M-30 is stored on urban lots
03/27/2006 The harvest of three years' work
04/12/2006 Avenida de Portugal residents protest against the M-30 tunnel
04/27/2006 Environmental Protection reprimands the municipality for damaging the river during M-30 construction
05/02/2006 A stable by Juan de Villanueva discovered in the M-30
05/24/2006 The Comunidad (de Madrid) obliges City Hall to exhibit the bridges discovered on the M-30
06/13/2006 The tunnel under the Avenida de Protugal is completed four months ahead of schedule
06/18/2006 A motorbike in the livingroom
06/20/2006 M-30 construction destroys the protected remains of a 16th-century bridge
06/26/2006 Chimneys to ventilate the tunnels
06/27/2006 Two European deputies in a state of shock
07/11/2006 The European deputies that visited the M-30 ask Gallardón to compensate local residents
07/12/2006 Gallardón announces work to "make the city beautiful" if reelected mayor of Madrid
09/14/2006 The European Parliament's report on M-30 construction requests indemnization for local residents
09/27/2006 A study says the new M-30 will save 13 million hours in traffic jams
09/29/2006 The M-30 will cost 355 million more
10/22/2006 It will take five years to build the green M-30
10/25/2006 A broken dike floods a tunnel in the M-30 construction
10/28/2006 The first two M-30 tunnels along the river will open between December and January
10/31/2006 Gallardón turns a visit to the M-30 into a party activity with Rajoy
11/22/2006 Sebastián: "The work will never end with Gallardón"
11/22/2006 M-30: much more than a highway. Peter Rowe.
11/24/2006 Healing the M-30's scars
12/09/2006 Work to be done on the M-30 CARMELO ENCINAS
12/21/2006 Cars inaugurate the first M-30 tunnel by the river after a year and a half of construction

---

01/05/2007 The new M-30 tunnel's emergency exits are blocked
01/23/2007 Basurama posts its critical trip through the M-30 on Internet
02/01/2007 The PSOE demands closure of a branch of the M-30 opened without emergency exits
02/09/2007 A new M-30 tunnel floods just hours after Gallardón inaugurates it
03/02/2007 The longest tunnel has evacuation problems
03/24/2007 Europe's longest tunnel suffers from congestion after its inauguration
04/06/2007 From small residential street to M-30 exit
04/27/2007 Leaks in the M-30 and more water in Ventisquero de la Condesa
05/06/2007 Seeing the light (not much) on the Manzanares
05/08/2007 The M-30, is (finally) finished
05/14/2007 M-30, a great achievement and a great debt
06/11/2007 A less than perfect work
06/12/2007 The new M-30 also sleeps
07/06/2007 Dry trees after the elections
07/30/2007 City Hall contracts the sale of the Calderón with Atlético
08/09/2007 Opening a window closed for 33 years
09/22/2007 An M-30 for Buenos Aires
11/23/2007 Gallardón delays environmental impact statement for the M-30

01/24/2008 Beaches, boats, and bikes on the Manzanares
02/06/2008 El Matadero construction: delays and failures
02/17/2008 The Río Project drowns local residents
02/17/2008 The unending construction of the Manzanares
03/26/2008 From South Junction to the Puente del Rey by wheelchair
09/12/2008 "The M-30 may have been made too quickly"
09/17/2008 M-30 creator blames flood on Urban Planning bungle.
09/17/2008 Calvo admits Madrid Río construction caused M-30 tunnel flood
09/18/2008 City Hall admits it pierced M-30 tunnel
09/18/2008 An open letter from the "father" of the M-30
09/19/2008 Gallardón: Melis did not warn that Madrid Río would cause problems, says Gallardón
09/25/2008 Urban Planning accuses the "father" of the M-30 of not knowing the work
12/10/2008 What would you do with 554 million?

03/03/2009 The Casa de Campo loses its gate
05/01/2009 Gallardón promises to finish almost all of Madrid Río this year
08/03/2009 Madrid Río won't shape up
08/16/2009 The long-dreamed Manzanares beach
12/12/2009 Madrid discovers its river
12/13/2009 The first walk around Puente del Rey without cranes

---

01/09/2010 The riverside washes its face
01/16/2010 Another notch in the Manzanares reform
05/18/2010 The Manzanares "exported" to Chile
06/04/2010 Bathing in the prohibited "swimming pools"
07/18/2010 Madrid's seafront promenade
07/18/2010 The Manzanares changes its look. The World Cup celebration gives Madrid Río a new face
07/20/2010 Madrid Río will have to wait a year to open its kiosks
07/30/2010 50 million for Madrid Río's upkeep
08/23/2010 Paddleball courts, tennis, and a cycling circuit are Madrid Río's sports facilities
08/25/2010 Sportiing footbridges for El Matadero
09/07/2010 Madrid, the tenth best city in which to live
10/08/2010 Towards a city with three centers
10/15/2010 Here, there will be a beach (sort of).
11/03/2010 The mayor seeks ecological alms

02/04/2011 Just 10 weeks to Madrid Río's completion
02/17/2011 New contest to adjudicate four kiosks in Madrid Río
03/15/2011 Matadero begins to fill in its ditches
03/18/2011 Madrid Río grows larger
03/22/2011 Madrid Río adds the Salón de Pinos and the Virgen del Puerto Gardens
03/24/2011 Inauguration at Madrid Río... Again
04/10/2011 Madrid inaugurates its river
04/15/2011 Kisses in Madrid Río
04/17/2011 The end of a liquid nightmare
05/09/2011 Rajoy kicks off with a Madrid Río rally
06/13/2011 Madrid Río won't open its kiosks until the fall
06/13/2011 Cyclists and pedestrians quarrel
06/16/2011 "The city is no longer split in two"
06/24/2011 Gallardón will cut expenses by 500 million in 2012 if he does not refinance the debt
07/05/2011 Madrid and Andorra build bridges
07/06/2011 One-euro deck chairs at Madrid Río
07/19/2011 Catfish and carp are biting at Madrid Río
07/22/2011 Everything but sand and seawater

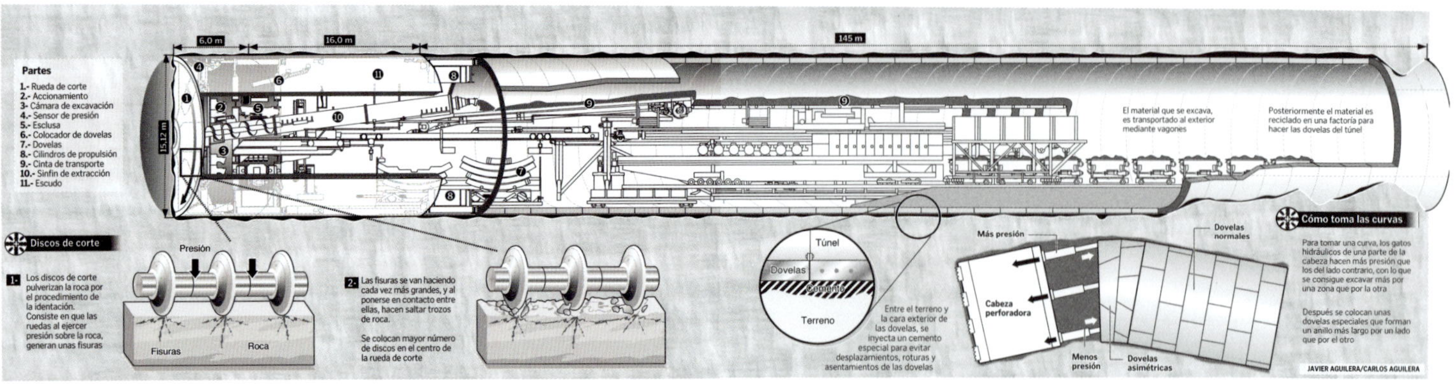

Madrid, la única ciudad del mundo con doce tuneladoras trabajando a la vez en sus obras

Sólo Taipei (Taiwán) se ha aproximado a este récord, con ocho máquinas en marcha al mismo tiempo

• Aguirre puso ayer en marcha «Excavolina», la décima tuneladora de la ampliación de Metro, que se encargará de llevar la línea 11 hasta el PAU de Carabanchel Alto

JOSÉ M. CAMARERO

MADRID. Ninguna ciudad, no ya de Europa, sino ni siquiera del mundo, había acometido unas obras públicas en su subsuelo tan importantes como las que se están llevando a cabo en la Comunidad de Madrid, que ya cuenta con 12 tuneladoras, repartidas entre las 10 que se encargan de ampliar la red de Metro; la que soterrará el tramo de la M-30 desde Conde de Casal a Santa María de la Cabeza —a falta de otra que horade el trayecto contrario—; y la que desde hace algunos meses construye un nuevo «túnel de la risa» para conectar Atocha con Chamartín.

La única ciudad que se había aproximado a este récord, según los datos que maneja la consejería de Infraestructuras, fue la taiwanesa de Taipei, en la que trabajaron, a la vez, hasta 8 máquinas de este tipo para construir su red de Metro. En Europa, sólo Oporto ha utilizado en los últimos meses una tuneladora, mientras que en Polonia se está construyendo un tren urbano, pero en superficie. Eso sí, es China el país con más tuneladoras en activo del mundo en todo su territorio.

La presidenta, ayer, tras poner en marcha la tuneladora «Excavolina» SIGEFREDO

Este sistema para construir túneles tiene varias ventajas: sólo afectan a los ciudadanos en los espacios urbanos por donde se introducen al subsuelo y pueden excavar a un ritmo de 500 metros mensuales. Y aunque la población podría asustarse ante 12 tuneladoras trabajando a la vez, desde la Comunidad recuerdan que existe un Centro de Control de Obra y Auscultación que se encarga de detectar cualquier anomalía y de paralizar la perforación de los túneles, en casos de peligro.

Ampliación de la línea 11

Esta acumulación de tuneladoras la culminó ayer la presidenta de la Comunidad, Esperanza Aguirre, con la puesta en marcha de «Excavolina», la gran máquina que se encargará de construir el túnel para ampliar la línea 11 de Metro, entre Pan Bendito y el PAU de Carabanchel Alto. Es la última de las diez que, desde ayer, la empresa pública Mintra —encargada de la ampliación del suburbano— utilizará para ampliar en 90 kilómetros las líneas 1, 3, 4, 5, 7 y 10, además de la 11.

Será, aproximadamente, a finales del próximo año cuando estas máquinas acaben sus trabajos, aunque habrá que esperar hasta la primavera de 2007 para que las estaciones estén completadas y los trenes dispuestos a entrar en marcha.

Aguirre explicó, junto a la consejera de Infraestructuras, María Dolores de Cospedal, ayer, en el PAU de Carabanchel —desde donde partirá «Excavolina» hasta llegar a la estación de Pan Bendito— que este plan de ampliación «es el más grande nunca realizado y un paso más» en obras públicas «que será muy apreciado por los vecinos en los próximos años».

De hecho, el compromiso de la Comunidad era el de crear 60,2 nuevos kilómetros de Metro, aunque se llegará a los 90, por ajustes como el de la propia línea 11 . «Aunque en un principio sólo estaban proyectadas dos estaciones más, decidimos ampliarla hasta el PAU porque está ya con un 60% de ocupación en sus casas», recordó Aguirre. Así, más de 50.000 personas se verán beneficiadas con esta nueva infraestructura, que les permitirá conectar con la línea 6 en Plaza Elíptica. Un barrio el de Carabanchel que ve así cumplida una de sus «demandas históricas», tal y como recordó la propia presidenta.

La ampliación de esta línea supondrá una inversión de 172,3 millones de euros para los 2,7 kilómetros que se prevén construir. Unos trabajos que ya están muy «adelantados», según la Comunidad, porque tanto las estaciones de Avenida de los Poblados como la de Avenida de Carabanchel Alto están ejecutadas a un 15 y un 60%, respectivamente.

La presidenta quiso destacar, tras poner en marcha «Excavolina», que, tras todas estas obras, tendremos más de 350 estaciones en toda la red de Metro, cuando hace ocho años eran 100, lo que implicará «una de las mejores redes del mundo, tras unos trabajos realizados de la manera más rápida, cómoda eficiente y ecológica posible».

Diez máquinas con personalidad

Carpetana. Ya ha completado el túnel de ampliación de la línea 1 al PAU de Vallecas y ahora trabaja para la extensión de la línea 5 hasta la Alameda.
Verne. Es la encargada de la unión de las líneas 1 y 4 de Metro en Chamartín.
Guster y Adelantada. Se encuentran trabajando en las obras de ampliación de la línea 3 hasta Villaverde.
Rompearenas y Mascastiza. Son las que avanzan a buen ritmo para la ampliación de la línea 7 hasta Coslada y San Fernando.
Chotis, Metromachine y Madriladora. Para la construcción del Metronorte se precisan de estas tres tuneladoras que unirán Madrid con Alcobendas y San Sebastián de los Reyes.
Algunas de ellas también ha sido utilizadas para los trabajos del «túnel de la risa», además de «Excavolina», puesta en marcha ayer en la línea 11.

Fin de las ocupaciones viales en Nochevieja

A pesar de que el trabajo con estas tuneladoras apenas afecta a los ciudadanos en las calles, sí que se han tenido que producir algunos cortes parciales de las vías urbanas madrileñas en los últimos meses, sobre todo para excavar pozos de ventilación, ascensores para mejorar la movilidad, y salidas y entradas de estas grandes máquinas de perforación.

Sin embargo, fuentes de la Comunidad de Madrid han asegurado a ABC que se comprometen ante los ciudadanos a que el próximo 31 de diciembre, el día de Nochevieja, todas las calles, carreteras o espacios urbanos como parques afectadas por la ampliación del Metro vuelvan a su estado original.

Entre ellas, se encuentran la calle Princesa, con la ocupación parcial de carriles por las obras de la línea 3 y las consiguientes desviaciones del tráfico por Hilarión Eslava hasta Moncloa; o la glorieta de Embajadores, donde se llevan a cabo obras para la remodelación de la línea 3 y 5 del Metro.

También existe una ocupación parcial de las calles en torno al puente de Ventas, por la ampliación de la línea 2 a La Elipa.

Un compromiso de la Comunidad que aliviará, en parte, la situación de muchos barrios madrileños plagados de estas y otras muchas obras.

Fomento promete al Ayuntamiento que no cortará Sol en Navidad

Propone cerrar seis meses la carrera de San Jerónimo o dejar un solo carril en ese periodo

• El Ayuntamiento ha recibido el plan de las dos opciones y las está estudiando; después, tomará una decisión sobre este tema, que ha estado lleno de polémica

ABC

MADRID. El Ministerio de Fomento propuso ayer al Ayuntamiento de la capital cerrar durante seis meses la carrera de San Jerónimo, desviando el tráfico por fuera de la Puerta del Sol, o bien dejar un solo carril en ese periodo, de manera que se mantengan totalmente funcionales todos los movimientos de la plaza en las tres próximas Navidades.

Así lo comunicaron a Efe fuentes próximas a la negociación que mantienen ambas Administraciones para alcanzar un acuerdo que permita hacer las obras del llamado segundo «túnel de la risa» y la estación de Cercanías de Sol-Gran Vía, conservando a la vez el tráfico en superficie y garantizando la seguridad de los viandantes.

Según las mismas fuentes, en la reunión mantenida ayer por responsables de ambas instituciones públicas, el ministerio que dirige Magdalena Álvarez aseguró que las obras se pueden hacer manteniendo los movimientos ahora existentes en la plaza las tres próximas Navidades; esta situación no cambiaría el resto del tiempo que duren las obras, salvo en el movimiento desde la Calle Mayor a la carrera de San Jerónimo. En estas últimas vías, Fomento ha planteado dos alternativas: seis meses de ocupación total de la carrera de San Jerónimo, desviando el tráfico por otras calles, o dejar un solo carril para ese movimiento durante ese mismo periodo.

No hay confirmación oficial

Desde el Ministerio rehusaron confirmar que éstas sean las propuestas que quedaron ayer encima de la mesa, ya que no van a divulgarlas: «Esperamos que el Ayuntamiento haga buen uso de ellas, las estudie y se pronuncie», dijeron. Asimismo, fuentes municipales explicaron que el Ayuntamiento «va a estudiar las dos propuestas de Fomento, y, en función de esos estudios, se tomará una decisión».

A la reunión de ayer asistieron el subdirector de Construcción de Ferrocarriles, Antonio Gutiérrez, y, por parte del Ayuntamiento, el director general de Movilidad, Javier Conde.

La presidenta regional realizó el mensaje de Navidad ante el Nacimiento de la Real Casa de Correos COMUNIDAD

Aguirre fija como primer deseo en 2006 «un Madrid donde reine la libertad»

En su mensaje navideño, pide generosidad para resolver los problemas

• «Los políticos —dijo— debemos buscar siempre soluciones a los problemas de los ciudadanos y nunca utilizar la representación para crearles problemas»

ABC

MADRID. La presidenta de la Comunidad de Madrid, Esperanza Aguirre, expresó su deseo de que esta autonomía sea en 2006 un lugar «en el que reine la libertad», donde «todos impulsemos el progreso y cultivemos la solidaridad con los que nos necesitan» y donde los problemas se resuelvan con generosidad. En su mensaje de Navidad y de Año Nuevo, Esperanza Aguirre dijo que su principal deseo para el nuevo ejercicio es que «las oportunidades de prosperar» lleguen a todos los madrileños que, según dijo, «formamos una especie de familia» donde «es mucho más lo que nos une que lo que nos separa». Una «familia» en la que, según la presidenta, «como es lógico no faltan los problemas» y su solución pasa, apuntó, porque todos ejerzan «la generosidad», comenzando por «los que ostentamos la representación política».

«Los políticos debemos buscar siempre soluciones a los problemas de los ciudadanos y nunca utilizar la representación que esos mismos ciudadanos nos han otorgado para crearles problemas», añadió la presidenta en su mensaje. «Deseo además —prosiguió— que la libertad continúe en el centro de nuestra vida política social y cultural» y que sea la base sobre la que construir el progreso de la región.

La dirigente autonómica se mostró decidida en este año a «defender la libertad, empezando por la de opinar y de informar», que, agregó, «es el primer deber de todos los que queremos que la nuestra sea una democracia viva y profunda».

Hizo también un llamamiento a la solidaridad de los madrileños con los colectivos más necesitados y tuvo un recuerdo especial para las personas mayores, enfermos, discapacitados, desempleados e inmigrantes, de quienes dijo «nos ayudan a crecer» y hacen que Madrid sea «más grande y más rico». La presidenta se comprometió a otorgarles cada vez más ayuda, «porque prestarles ese apoyo es una cuestión de estricta justicia».

A todos ellos, y a quienes «tienen problemas para aprovechar las oportunidades de la Comunidad», Aguirre les dedicó «palabras de especial afecto». Y deseó que en 2006 «seamos capaces de utilizar nuestra libertad de la manera más creativa y solidaria posible».

Gallardón escribe una carta donde pide perdón por las obras de la M-30

• El regidor informa a los madrileños que residen en la zona del Manzanares del proyecto Madrid Río y destaca los beneficios que supondrá para sus vecinos

ABC

MADRID. El alcalde de Madrid, Alberto Ruiz-Gallardón, ha enviado una carta a los madrileños afectados por las obras de la M-30 de la zona del río Manzanares, en la que pide disculpas por las molestias que les están ocasionando, aunque destaca los importantes beneficios que supondrán estas obras. En su misiva, fechada el 29 de diciembre de 2005, el alcalde informa a los vecinos sobre el proyecto Madrid Río, que supondrá el soterramiento de seis kilómetros de la M-30, la recuperación de 500.000 metros cuadrados de espacios para zonas verdes y la modernización de la red de saneamiento del Manzanares.

La carta de Gallardón va acompañada de un amplio folleto sobre el Proyecto Madrid Río de la empresa municipal Madrid Calle 30, que recoge todos los detalles de la obra para recuperar y hacer más accesible el río madrileño.

Segun el alcalde, la M-30 ha ido acumulando numerosas reformas pendientes, siendo uno de los tramos más obsoletos el que discurre junto al río Manzanares. Por ello, asegura que las obras que se están llevando a cabo comportarán «importantes beneficios medioambientales para toda la ciudad y contribuirán de forma directa a mejorar la calidad de vida de más de 320.000 personas que residen en los doce barrios por los que discurre el proyecto Madrid Río».

Reducir la contaminación del aire

Asegura que gracias al soterramiento de la M-30 se reducirá la contaminación acústica y atmosférica, y que también mejorará con las obras la calidad del agua del Manzanares y la accesibilidad al río. Además, a juicio del alcalde, la ciudad ganará en zonas verdes y se mejorará también el paisaje urbano de una zona muy deteriorada, recuperándose puentes históricos.

«Somos conscientes —dijo— de que la realización de cualquier obra, y máxime de la trascendencia de ésta, siempre supone inconvenientes y estamos haciendo todo lo que está a nuestro alcance para aminorarlos. Le pedimos disculpas por las molestias que podamos ocasionarle y le agradecemos el esfuerzo solidario que está realizando, convencidos de que los beneficios que el proyecto Madrid Río traerá a los vecinos de la zona y a toda la ciudad compensarán el esfuerzo realizado», concluye en su carta el alcalde madrileño.

La apertura del túnel urbano más largo del mundo pone fin a las obras de la M-30

Este subterráneo del by-pass sur ha costado 551,9 millones y tiene accesos en el Calderón y Marqués de Vadillo

LA «NUEVA» M-30

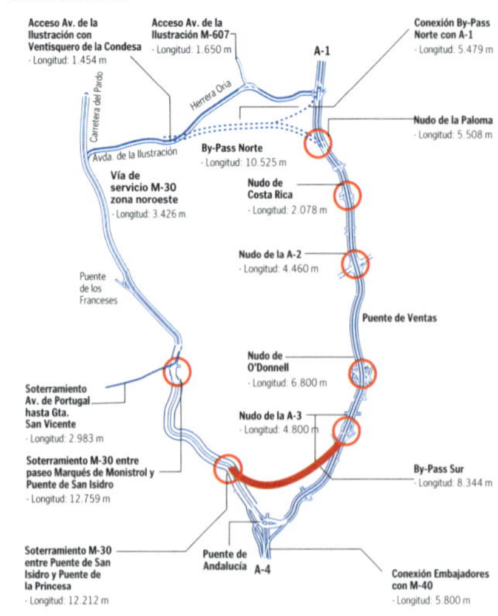

Apertura del túnel sur del by-pass

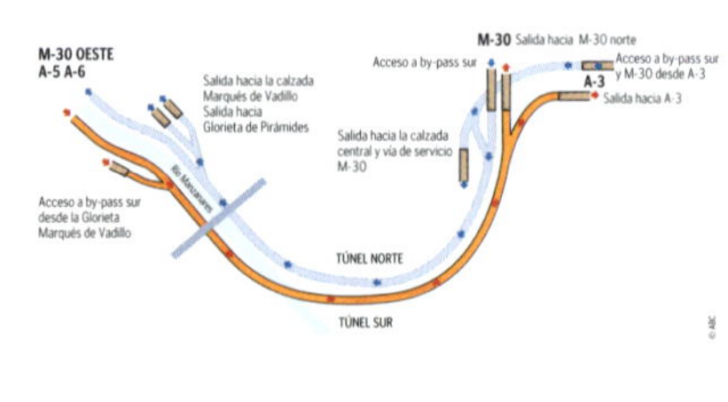

MERCEDES CONTRERAS

MADRID. «Se nos ve contentos, porque lo estamos», dijo ayer el alcalde, Alberto Ruiz-Gallardón, en la inauguración del túnel sur del by-pass sur. No era para menos porque con la apertura al tráfico de este túnel se daban prácticamente por finalizadas las obras de soterramiento de la M-30, lo que le llevó a calificar la jornada como «día para la historia». El Ayuntamiento ha invertido para su reforma 3.508 millones de euros y ha necesitado casi tres años para completarla. Ahora, quedan otros cuatro años para completar el ajardinamiento sobre los túneles.

Durante los últimos tres años, la autovía de circunvalación de Madrid se ha visto envuelta en una gigantesca obra continua, en la que han llegado a trabajar hasta 5.300 operarios simultáneamente, y que ha supuesto una inversión de 3.500 millones de euros, pagadera en 30 años y que le supone al Ayuntamiento haber situado su deuda en 6.000 millones. El proyecto, según destaca el Consistorio, recupera el río, sienta las bases para un parque de un millón de m2, reduce la accidentalidad en más del 50%, elimina 35.000 toneladas de gases de efecto invernadero este año y permite la peatonalización de muchas zonas.

Dos accesos

El nuevo subterráneo, que se abrió ayer, comienza junto a Santa María de la Cabeza y finaliza en el entorno de la avenida del Mediterráneo y la conexión con la carretera de Valencia. Ahora, este by-pass, unido al tramo procedente de la avenida de Portugal, se ha convertido, con sus 12 kilómetros, en el túnel urbano más largo del mundo. Su gemelo es el más largo de Europa si se accede desde la A-3 y se llega hasta el Vicente Calderón.

El túnel, en el que se han invertido 551,9 millones, tiene dos accesos: el primero, por el sistema de subterráneos del río a la altura del estadio Vicente Calderón, mediante un tramo soterrado de 1,6 kilómetros y el segundo, a través del ramal de Marqués de Vadillo.

Igual que su gemelo en dirección este-oeste, que se abrió al tráfico el 23 de marzo, ha sido construido con tuneladora. «Tizona», con sus 15,2 metros de diámetro, excavó los 3,6 kilómetros de túnel que pasa bajo el Parque de Tierno Galván. En total, la obra ha durado 30 meses. El nuevo tramo, como el resto de los túneles realizados, cuenta con los más avanzados sistemas de seguridad, «vigilados» desde el Centro de Control de Túneles de Calle 30. Se han instalado 92 cámaras, 21 paneles de mensaje y 374 altavoces, al tiempo que se han construido 19 salidas de emergencia y conexiones con el túnel gemelo, junto a una calzada inferior para vehículos de emergencia.

Las previsiones de tráfico de este by-pass que ahorra 1,5 kilómetros de recorrido cifran en 80.000 vehículos diarios su uso, ya que este arco sur de la M-30 suelen utilizarlo 260.000 coches. El Ayuntamiento espe-

La reforma del paseo del Prado no implicará talar árboles «de gran porte»

El alcalde de Madrid aseguró ayer que la remodelación del paseo del Prado no supondrá la tala de ningún árbol «de gran porte», aunque reconoció que «en determinadas operaciones urbanísticas es necesario podar algunos». Así lo indicó Ruiz-Gallardón en el Colegio de Arquitectos, ante un auditorio de unas 80 personas, una de las cuales se levantó cuando el alcalde pronunció estas palabras y exclamó que el eje Prado-Recoletos «es la fisonomía de Madrid», poniendo como ejemplo que «los Campos Elíseos (en París) no se han tocado nunca». El candidato del PP respondió que «si alguien se asoma a la Cuesta del Moyano», donde «antes había coches y ahora hay árboles», comprobará cuál es «el lenguaje que va a hablar el eje Prado-Recoletos».

IU: «Hacer ahora declaración de impacto no les libera de la responsabilidad de lo hecho»

(Viene de la página anterior)

su juicio, el Gobierno Central no tiene necesidad de cambiar ninguna ley: ya traspuso en su momento «y correctamente» las normas medioambientales comunitarias.

Inés Sabanés, promotora de la denuncia que ha traído a Madrid a los eurodiputados, aseguraba que lo de ayer era «la crónica de una situación anunciada»: las prometidas DIA para las obras sin iniciar es justamente lo que solicitaba IU desde hace tiempo. «No podían decir otra cosa con los inspectores aquí; pero es absolutamente insuficiente y no les libera de la responsabilidad de lo hecho hasta ahora».

Visita de obra

Los eurodiputados y sus acompañantes visitaron, junto a los técnicos municipales, las obras en Príncipe Pío —sin prensa cerca— y después acudieron a la planta 17 de un bloque de viviendas al final de la calle Antonio López, justo en el «epicentro» de las obras. Y desde allí vieron y vivieron lo que la vecina que reside en esa casa aguanta desde hace más de un año: obras, polvo, ruido y muchas molestias. A la salida, no evitaban comentarios sobre el «impacto ambiental» de los trabajos que habían visto.

Despacho de la ministra

La siguiente parada en su viaje —sin comer, aunque eran más de las cinco de la tarde— fue el despacho de la ministra de Medio Ambiente, Cristina Narbona. La ministra tampoco recibió con mucha alegría la noticia de los tres estudios de impacto futuros: lamentó que se hiciera este anuncio «cuando una parte muy importante de la obra está prácticamente hecha».

Con los vecinos

El último encuentro de una apretadísima agenda que seguro que los eurodiputados no olvidarán fue con las asociaciones de vecinos afectados. A éstos se les pidió intervenciones de no más de un minuto para dar cuenta de los problemas producidos en sus vidas por las obras. El rosario fue casi interminable: patrimonio cultural perdido, despilfarro de agua potable, el polvo siempre presente, la pérdida de árboles, el ruido, los cambios en sus hábitos a que les han obligado los trabajos... Hoy, la delegación oficial continuará la visita. Hay reuniones previstas con representantes del Gobierno regional y con los diputados autonómicos. En el plazo aproximado de un mes, redactarán un informe.

A medio comer, con un calor de infarto y tras más de seis horas de reuniones, a los eurodiputados les esperaba aún el impacto de **ver las «tripas» de la M-30 desde un piso 17**

«Yo sólo pido que me dejen dormir»

TEXTO: **SARA MEDIALDEA** FOTOGRAFÍAS: **JAIME GARCÍA**

Tras las explicaciones técnicas, las objeciones legales y las artimañas políticas de unos y otros, los eurodiputados se enfrentaron a la —siempre más dura— realidad: contemplar a sus pies, desde una altura de más de 45 metros, el meollo de las obras de la M-30 para enterrar las calzadas a su paso por el río Manzanares, entre el puente de Praga y el de Toledo. **Paula Fernández** les abrió las puertas de su casa —con mucho sentimiento de su perro, aterrorizado ante tal invasión— para que pasaran ellos y los más de 40 periodistas que les siguieron durante todo el día, y vieran lo que ella ve, y escucha, jornada tras jornada y hora tras hora, sin tregua. «Yo no soy política, y respeto todas las opiniones; sólo pido que me dejen dormir», repetía.

«Hoy estamos muy tranquilos», aseguraba; «a diario cuento más de treinta máquinas trabajando. Y lo peor es que no paran ni por la noche. Desde hace un año tomo pastillas para dormir». Su caso no es único, aunque reconoce que en su mismo bloque hay vecinos que están a favor de las obras. «Yo sólo sé que antes veía coches, pero también árboles, algunos eran ya enormes cuando yo llegué aquí hace 32 años. En el futuro, no sé qué veré: tal vez unos palitos finos de esos que plantan ahora».

La tortilla de Trini

Los eurodiputados llegaban al borde de la extenuación: su jornada se inició a las diez de la mañana, llevaban cuatro reuniones y más de siete horas en pie, y lo único que habían comido eran unos pinchos de tortilla y empanada que les ofreció la concejal socialista, **Trinidad Jiménez**, cuando les visitaron en el edificio de los grupos de oposición, a ellos y a **Inés Sabanés** y su equipo.

Su primer recorrido por las obras tuvo ciertas dificultades para arrancar: había «sugerencias» para cambiar la ruta prevista, y los responsables municipales insistían en que también se vieran las partes del proyecto terminadas, no sólo las que estaban a medio hacer. Con el autobús que les trasladaba lleno a rebosar —hubo quien se quedó fuera y tuvo que seguirles en coche particular—, finalmente hubo dos paradas.

La primera fue en Príncipe Pío, con muchas más dificultades para la prensa de las que hubo cuando el Ayuntamiento enseñó las obras al alcalde socialista de Lyón, sin ir más lejos. La segunda parada fue en la Torre de Praga, piso 17. A 45 metros sobre lo que parece, a primera vista, el caos, pero que en el futuro será una zona ajardinada y peatonal que sustituya a los carriles de circulación que ahora atraviesan 250.000 vehículos al día.

«La idea loca del alcalde»

Los eurodiputados alucinaron: el socialista **Proinsias de Rossa** aseguraba: «No soy abogado, pero creo que en Irlanda habríamos tomado algún tipo de medida medioambiental en una obra de estas dimensiones». Su colega la danesa **Margrete Auken**, de Los Verdes, iba más allá: «Esta idea loca del alcalde de enterrar los coches y agruparlos no va a suponer que haya menos tráfico, sino más».

Ambos coincidían en que lo que estaban viendo no podían imaginarlo cuando contemplaron el vídeo sobre el proyecto M-30 que proyectaron las autoridades locales.

Los periodistas seguían al autobús de los eurodiputados como auténticos «paparazzi» tras una folklórica; tanta atención sin duda sorprendió a los políticos europeos. Pero lo mejor estaba por venir.

De hecho, había una tercera parada prevista en su ruta por la gincana madrileña: las futuras salidas de humos de la calle Antracita, tan cerca de las viviendas que los vecinos están alarmados. El retraso acumulado en una agenda imposible de cumplir impidió realizar esta visita, y el microbús marchó rumbo al Ministerio de Medio Ambiente, donde les recibió la titular, **Cristina Narbona**, con la que cambiaron impresiones sobre las normativas europeas y su transposición en la legislación española, y la adecuación del proyecto madrileño a las leyes actuales.

17:30 h. Los eurodiputados, tras ver las obras desde el piso 17 de la Torre de Praga

12.00 h. El alcalde Ruiz-Gallardón recibe a los dos eurodiputados

16.00h. Los diputados europeos contemplan los trabajos en Príncipe Pío.

EXAMEN A LA M-30 ■ LA COMISIÓN EUROPEA VISITA LAS OBRAS

Al vídeo de 20 minutos realizado por el PP sobre la autovía se opone otro de 9 minutos hecho por ecologistas

Ratas «como conejos»

No obstante, la jornada no había terminado: en la nave de terneras del antiguo Matadero de Legazpi les esperaban más de doscientos vecinos que, a partir de las 7:30 y durante más de 90 minutos, estuvieron pormenorizándoles, en intervenciones cortas pero intensas, todos los problemas con que se enfrentan a causa de los trabajos. Sin excluir las ratas «negras y grandes como conejos» que según dicen se ven ahora por portales y jardines, a consecuencia de la tierra removida en torno al cauce del río.

Proisias de Rossas se ganó la ovación del personal cuando afirmó que el Parlamento Europeo, aunque parece algo muy lejano, no lo es en realidad, y allí estaba él y su colega, agotados y seguramente hambrientos, pero al pie del cañón.

El último capítulo del día fue la «guerra de los vídeos»: el Gobierno local les pasó de mañana uno de más de 20 minutos de duración, en el que se explica pormenorizadamente qué se va a hacer en la M-30, las causas de las obras y las consecuencias beneficiosas que tendrán los cambios para el tráfico en la ciudad.

Por la tarde, los grupos ecologistas, vecinales y políticos que plantearon la demanda ante la Comisión de Peticiones de la Unión Europea sacaron a relucir el «otro» vídeo, uno elaborado por ellos y mucho más breve, de nueve minutos de duración, en el que dan su versión de la vida en la zona desde que existe el proyecto M-30.

La visita de los eurodiputados continúa hoy, aunque algo más relajada. A primera hora, encuentro en la consejería de Medio Ambiente del Gobierno regional con la directora general de Calidad y Evaluación Ambiental de la Comunidad de Madrid, **María Jesús Villamediana**.

Desde allí, se desplazarán hasta la Asamblea de Madrid —en Vallecas— para mantener un encuentro con los grupos parlamentarios regionales. Finalizarán oficialmente su visita tras mantener un encuentro con la prensa local en la Oficina del Parlamento Europeo.

A partir de ese momento, se abre un plazo de aproximadamente un mes en la que los eurodiputados elaborarán un informe que elevarán a la Comisión de Peticiones, que además valorará la respuesta dada por las autoridades madrileñas a la carta de emplazamiento que les enviaron desde Europa.

La nueva M-30 revaloriza un 24% el precio de los pisos en la zona desde 2003

as últimas infraestructuras permitirán que el sector «resista» el actual parón inmobiliario

IGUEL OLIVER

ADRID. El mercado inmobiario será uno de los grandes eneficiados por las obras de eforma de la M-30 a la altura el río Manzanares. Un estuo de la consultora Aguirre ewman revela que el entorno e la obra, que ocupa parte de s distritos de Arganzuela y sera, «resistirá mejor» el enriamiento de precios que afeca este mercado desde hace nos meses.

La mejora de las infraescucturas en este ámbito (entre Nudo Sur y el Puente de Pra) ayudará a revitalizar la zo, que es una de las que aporta ayor número de nuevas prorociones dentro de la almena central.

El estudio de Aguirre Newan revela que el precio medio e suelo finalista para uso resiencial se sitúa en este momen por encima de los 2.200 euros metro cuadrado, lo que supoe casi el 60 por ciento del valor nal de una vivienda en la zoa (3.676,5 euros). Por lo que especta a la revalorización el mercado residencial, los das de la consultora apuntan ue el barrio de Arganzuela ha ncarecido sus precios un 24 or ciento desde 2003 —año en que se dio a conocer el proecto de soterramiento de la -30— hasta mediados del año asado.

El inventario de suelo realiado por la consultora en la zoa arroja un total de 300.000 meos cuadrados. Este volumen e suelo vacante puede llegar a ansformarse en 83.000 meos cuadrados de superficie dificable para uso residencial que a su vez puede dar lugar desarrollo de unas 900 viendas en un futuro próxio— y 110.000 metros para uso rciario.

Además, las actuaciones del antiguo Matadero de Madrid y del Mercado de Frutas y Verduras aportarán otros 100.000 metros cuadrados para equipamientos sociales.

Inversión: 1.628 millones

Las inversiones públicas para mejorar las infraestructuras en el área objeto del estudio de la consultora inmobiliaria —133 hectáreas entre el Puente de Praga y el Nudo Sur de la antigua M-30 que la atravesaba formando un eje de 1,5 kilómetros— ascenderán, cuando acaben las actuaciones, a 1.628 millones de euros.

Tres grandes proyectos públicos afectan a esta área: Calle 30, en concreto Madrid Río (720 millones de euros); la conexión del paseo de Santa María de la Cabeza con la A-3 (742 millones de euros); el proyecto Matadero (11 millones de euros), que supondrá la recuperación de una parcela de 150.000 metros cuadrados; y la remodelación del Mercado de Frutas y Verduras (22 millones de euros), donde está previsto trasladar la Concejalía de Urbanismo del Ayuntamiento de Madrid y desarrollar una torre para oficinas de más de 30.000 metros cuadrados.

Además, la ampliación de la línea 3 de Metro, con 9 kilómetros y siete nuevas estaciones entre Legazpi y Villaverde Alto, mejorará las comunicaciones en el transporte público.

El estudio ha localizado en la zona 43 solares vacantes y 14 promociones, de las cuales cuatro no están aún a la venta, dos están destinadas a alquiler y ocho se encuentran en venta.

Existen cinco sectores urbanísticos en desarrollo dentro del área analizada, que suponen 63.000 metros cuadrados de superficie total, de los cuales 14.000 metros cuadrados son de superficie sin desarrollar.

La edificabilidad sin materializar de estos cinco sectores alcanza los 26.500 metros cuadrados, lo que permite calcular que en esa zona se puedan construir unas 264 nuevas viviendas.

Un estudio detecta 43 fincas vacantes junto al río Manzanares, donde podrían construirse unas 900 viviendas

PRECIOS DEL SUELO EN EL ENTORNO DE LA NUEVA M-30

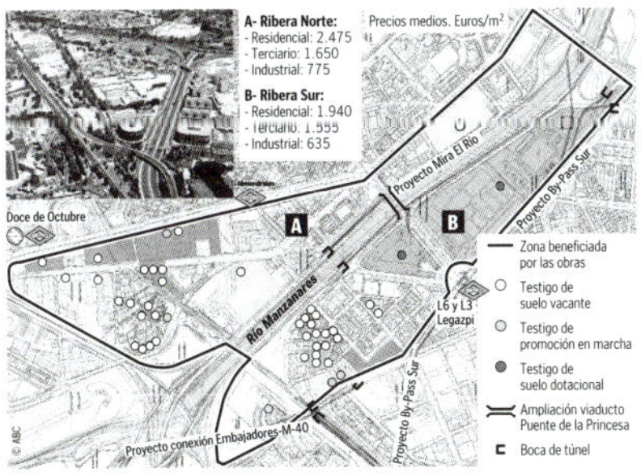

Indemnizan a una paciente con 36.000 euros por extirparle el pecho sin avisar

ABC

MADRID. El Tribunal Superior de Justicia de Madrid condenó ayer al Servicio Madrileño de Salud (Sermas) a pagar una indemnización de 36.000 euros a una paciente a la que se le realizó una mastectomía, sin previo aviso en 1999.

A la paciente, M. T. G., le detectaron un nódulo en el pecho derecho sugestivo de fibroadenoma, el tumor benigno más común de la mama. Una vez fue diagnosticada, la enferma firmó la hoja de consentimiento para la extirpación del nódulo, una intervención que le realizarían en el Hospital Puerta del Hierro. Con anterioridad a la operación, fue informada de que consistiría en la extirpación del fibroadenoma y de que, en caso de que fuera maligno, le realizarían una cirugía conservadora.

Según asegura el abogado de la paciente, Álvaro Sardinero, ni ésta ni su familia tuvieron constancia en ningún momento de la posibilidad de que se realizase una mastectomía —extirpación del pecho—, a pesar de que ésta era necesaria y ni siquiera se pidió consentimiento a los familiares durante la operación.

El abogado de la paciente aclaró que su clienta está satisfecha con la sentencia y que la indemnización no se solicitó por la realización de la mastectomía, que era necesaria, sino por «el daño moral que se le ocasionó, al no haber tenido tiempo para asimilarlo». Además, la sentencia indica que la falta de información pudo afectar negativamente a la evolución de la enferma, ya que «una situación estresante como la que puede padecerse tras despertarse de una operación con la mama sorpresivamente extirpada disminuye el sistema inmunológico de la paciente con la consiguiente afectación a la evolución de su patología».

El «puente oblicuo», en su estado actual (izquierda) y una recreación que muestra cómo quedará tras la reforma (derecha) AYUNTAMIENTO

El «puente oblicuo» de la M-30 se salva del derribo para convertirse en peatonal

Las obras, que comenzarán de inmediato, durarán seis meses — Aprobadas 110 viviendas en las cocheras de Bravo Murillo

SARA MEDIALDEA

MADRID. El «puente oblicuo» del paseo de la Virgen del Puerto, que se salvó «in extremis» de la demolición durante las obras de enterramiento de la M-30, se convertirá ahora en una pasarela peatonal y ciclista. Las obras, anunció ayer el alcalde de la ciudad, Alberto Ruiz-Gallardón, van a comenzar de inmediato, y supondrán, de hecho, una de las primeras actuaciones de la «nueva» M-30 tras la desaparición bajo tierra de seis kilómetros de la autovía.

El «puente oblicuo» cruza el tercer cinturón a la altura del paseo de la Virgen del Puerto. Antes era utilizado para el paso de vehículos, pero desde la reforma de la autovía, perdió este uso. En seis meses —el tiempo que durarán las obras—, sus 125 metros de longitud se habrán convertido en pasarela ciclista y peatonal.

El presupuesto para esta actuación ronda los 1,5 millones de euros. La superficie del puente queda dividida en dos franjas longitudinales iguales. En una se colocará una jardinera de ocho metros de ancho, con pradera y pinos. La otra franja acogerá la acera peatonal y el carril ciclista.

El alcalde destacó cómo este puente se salvó de la demolición por voluntad de los arquitectos que han diseñado la recuperación de la superficie ganada al río. El equipo de Garrido Colmenero consideró que debía mantenerse este puente, aunque transformando su uso. De este modo, le llegó la «amnistía», y en breve formará parte de esas once nuevas pasarelas que, junto con la 12 actuales, permitirán que más de un millón de residentes de los seis distritos que rodean a la actuación Madrid Río lo utilicen para cruzar.

Por otra parte, la junta de gobierno municipal aprobó ayer el plan que convertirá las antiguas cocheras de Bravo Murillo en zona de viviendas, espacios deportivos y parque.

Cocheras de Bravo Murillo

Las cocheras, que ocupan 8.600 metros cuadrados entre las calles de Bravo Murillo, Doctor Santero, Garellano y Almansa —junto a la glorieta de Cuatro Caminos—, albergaron incluso buena parte de la flota de tranvías que circularon por Madrid.

Aunque el proyecto ya había sido presentado hace más de un año —cuando se falló el concurso para su desarrollo, que ganó el equipo de arquitectos FAM—, ahora es cuando realmente se pone en marcha, con la aprobación del plan parcial de reforma interior que permitirá que las obras se inicien «de forma inmediata», indicó el regidor.

De hecho, según sus cálculos, las 110 viviendas protegidas que se construirán en este ámbito «deberían estar terminadas en un plazo de 24 meses».

Además, también habrá allí 2.500 metros cuadrados de nuevas zonas verdes, y 900 destinados a actividades deportivas al aire libre, además de 1.400 metros para un equipamiento dotacional y 1.500 a viales de conexión.

Debajo del nuevo jardín que se va a construir, se está contemplando la posibilidad —si hay demanda suficiente— de construir un aparcamiento para residentes.

Madrid, entre las 15 ciudades del mundo con pabellón propio en Shanghai 2010

S. M.

MADRID. Sólo 15 ciudades del mundo, entre ellas Madrid, contarán con un pabellón propio en la Exposición Universal de Shanghai 2010. La capital española ha sido elegida entre más de 188 candidatas para participar de forma singular en este evento, que reunirá a 192 participantes de 172 países y espera recibir más de 70 millones de visitantes.

Según datos de la Oficina de Coordinación de la Expo de Shanghai, recogidos por Efe, Madrid quedó la primera en la categoría de «construcciones habitables». En Europa, sólo la acompañan París, Londres, Hamburgo y Milán.

Casa de bambú y «bioárbol»

Todas ellas, y las demás hasta las 15 señaladas, compondrán la «ciudad simulada», a la que Madrid contribuirá con dos proyectos: la Casa de Bambú —una reproducción a tamaño real del edificio de viviendas protegidas de la EMV en Carabanchel, diseñado por el arquitecto Alejandro Zaera— y un árbol del Bulevar Bioclimático del Ensanche de Vallecas, diseño de Belinda Tato, José Luis Vallejo y Diego García-Setién.

Aunque España tendrá su propio pabellón, otro grupo de 40 ciudades —entre ellas Barcelona, Santiago de Compostela y Bilbao — dispondrán de un espacio compartido para explicar y exhibir algunos de sus proyectos urbanos emblemáticos, Madrid contará con su espacio propio para estos proyectos singulares.

Las obras del Prado-Recoletos en Atocha empezarán en diciembre

S. M./C. F.

MADRID. Entre «diciembre y enero» habrán comenzado las obras de remodelación del eje Prado-Recoletos en la zona de Atocha. El cálculo es del alcalde de Madrid, Alberto Ruiz-Gallardón, quien reiteró ayer que «toda la normativa» valida la decisión municipal de echar a andar con este proyecto en las zonas que «únicamente dependen normativamente del Plan General de Ordenación Urbana en vigor».

El Gobierno regional indicó hace sólo unos días que el Ayuntamiento precisaría de una serie de permisos autonómicos para llevar a cabo esta reforma, que afecta a zonas declaradas en su día bién de interés cultural.

Intervención

Ruiz-Gallardón indicó que «en todos los casos en que sea necesaria la intervención de otras administraciones, éstas se producirán». Pero el resto de actuaciones —entre las que se van a llevar a cabo en Atocha y en la plaza de las Cortes— se regirán por lo recogido en el actual Plan de Urbanismo, «en el que ya intervino en su día la Comunidad de Madrid» y que, recordó, está en vigor. Por eso, insistió, «ejecutaremos el proyecto cumpliendo estrictamente la ley, y dentro de la normativa vigente».

Una vez que estén redactados y adjudicados los proyectos para Atocha y Las Cortes, las obras en ambos puntos podrían iniciarse «entre diciembre y enero», precisó el regidor.

Sin embargo, el vicepresidente primero y portavoz del Gobierno regional, Ignacio González, tiene algunas reticencias con respecto a este planteamiento. Asegura que el proyecto «tal y como se conoce hoy, es integral y, por lo tanto, debe tener un tratamiento integral». Ahora bien, según el vicepresidente, si el Ayuntamiento «quiere presentar un proyecto distinto (al actual), esto es, troceado», el Gobierno regional no tiene inconveniente en estudiarlo.

No obstante recordó que, cuando exista «algún tipo de protección» del patrimonio histórico, artístico o arqueológico, «es preferible contar con una autorización de la Dirección General de Patrimonio».

El alcalde asegura que el proyecto se ajusta en todo a la ley, pero la Comunidad mantiene reticencias

Turnos de 24 horas para acabar la M-30

Ayuntamiento. Los técnicos prevén trabajar de forma ininterrumpida en zonas donde no se moleste por la noche a los vecinos, como el río. Un estudio de la Politécnica prevé que la reforma ahorre 708 millones de horas de viaje, lo que se traduce en 3.915 millones de euros: el coste inicial de toda la obra

FERNANDO MAS

Los técnicos no están nada contentos con los 14 meses que se han llevado los trámites previos —alguno dilatado por desavenencias e intereses políticos— necesarios para iniciar la reforma de la M-30. Ya tiene en marcha el alcalde, Alberto Ruiz-Gallardón, su gran obra para Madrid. Su promesa electoral incluía un plazo de entrega: mayo de 2007.

Si entonces no ha concluido, el guirigay de tráfico en la ciudad será histórico. El río empantanado, el norte colapsado... Pese a que el periodo de ejecución de los proyectos oeste y norte es de tres años, pese a que quedan menos de 36 meses para la fecha límite, pese a que ninguna de las dos obras se haya adjudicado, desde el Ayuntamiento se insiste en que la reforma se acabará en el tiempo prometido.

¿Cómo? Los técnicos se guardan una carta en la manga: los turnos de 24 horas, el trabajo ininterrumpido en algunos puntos de la obra.

La primera vez que en Madrid se utilizó este sistema fue durante la construcción del paso inferior de Cristo Rey, infraestructura impulsada por el alcalde Agustín Rodríguez-Sahagún, que acudía por sorpresa a cualquier hora del día a supervisar la obra. El que fuera alcalde de la capital a final de la década de los 80 y principios de los 90, impulsó este método de trabajo con el fin de ganar tiempo y evitar molestias a los vecinos.

El alcalde de Madrid y la concejala de Urbanismo, Pilar Martínez, observan el Manzanares el día que presentaron la reforma de este tramo de la M-30. / EL MUNDO

Cuando se plantean todas estas variables a los máximos responsables de la reforma de la M-30 (premura de tiempo, reducción de molestias...), éstos aclaran literalmente: «Cuando haga falta y no moleste, *sí* se trabajará en tres turnos».

—¿Y junto al río?

—Casi con total seguridad. Sí.

Y a continuación dan la explicación pertinente: «Tienen un poquito más de coste, pero al final se sale ganando. El metro cuadrado de pantalla —el sistema que se utiliza para hacer los túneles a cielo abierto, sin tuneladoras— es más caro si se hace por la noche, pero si tenemos en cuenta que se acorta el tiempo de ejecución de la obra, se reducen los gastos generales, con lo que se compensa el gasto extra».

Lo normal es trabajar en un turno de ocho horas, que en ocasiones se puede prolongar ligeramente. Si hace falta se movilizan dos turnos. En un caso excepcional, tres. Será el caso para acelerar las tareas de reforma en aquellos puntos donde se arranque con retraso.

Como las críticas a esta obra no concluirán con su inicio, el Ayuntamiento prevé empezar a destapar informes que avalan sus bondades. Uno de ellos ha sido elaborado por la Universidad Politécnica. La *Evaluación Socio-Económica y Ambiental del Programa de Mejoras de la M-30 de Madrid* explica, entre otras cuestiones, que los conductores se ahorrarán 708 millones de horas de viaje —en 37 años— gracias al nuevo trazado de la autovía. Eso se traduce, dice literalmente la página 67 de ese informe, «en 3.915 millones de euros». Agrega que este «es el beneficio fundamental, que justifica por sí sólo el programa de mejora». Lógico, si se conoce que la inversión inicial para esta obra, excluyendo el IVA, es inferior a esa cantidad. Otro cantar será el coste definitivo, con los intereses que se pagarán, a partir de su conclusión, durante 35 años. Todo un *peaje en la sombra* que se cargará a los bolsillos de los contribuyentes vía impuestos, según la oposición.

En 2007, cuando se abra al tráfico, el ahorro al día en la zona Este —la más beneficiada de la M-30— será de 19.995 horas al día. El ahorro se eleva a 43.256 horas en este punto en el año 2037.

Pero quizá donde más hincapié hacen los técnicos es en la seguridad vial. Los beneficios globales por la reducción de accidentes se cifran en 770 millones de euros a lo «largo de la vida útil del proyecto», que elude decir cuál es. La zona sur es la más beneficiada por los cam-

CIFRAS PARA JUSTIFICAR LA REFORMA

708/3.915. El estudio de la Universidad Politécnica *Evaluación Socio-Económica y Ambiental del Programa de Mejoras de la M-30* prevé que el ahorro de horas de viaje en 30 años, de 2007 a 2037, será de 708 millones. Eso, traducido a dinero, equivale a 3.915 millones de euros. Casualmente, 300 millones de la inversión inicial (sin IVA) prevista para reformar toda la calle. El sector Este es el que sale mejor parado, en este capítulo, por la remodelación, seguido del oeste (transcurre junto al río). En el primer caso, el ahorro será en 2037 de 43.256 horas al día, y en el segundo, de 30.741 ese mismo año. En el tramo donde se ahorran menos horas es en el Sur, con 2.905 en 2007, 4.055 en 2012 y 10.449 en 2037. Dentro de 33 años, en el norte se ahorrarán 21.701 horas al día.

64.000. Si todo sale como está previsto, uno de los mayores beneficios de la reforma de la M-30, siempre según el mismo estudio al que ha tenido acceso M2, corresponderá con la disminución de la contaminación. El tráfico más fluido —es lo que se pretende— ayudará a reducir las emisiones de dióxido de carbono. En 2007, cuando en teoría estará en marcha la nueva M-30, las emisiones de CO_2 se reducirán 35.000 toneladas al año, cantidad que se elevará a las 64.800 toneladas en 2037. Estas reducciones suponen un ahorro anual que varía entre los 5,5 y los 10,1 millones de euros. Dice el informe que con el incremento de la velocidad lo hacen también los óxidos de nitrógeno, aunque queda compensado este aumento con la disminución considerable de los óxidos de azufre y compuestos orgánicos volátiles.

259. El beneficio, en millones de euros, para los vecinos por la supresión del *efecto barrera* en las zonas en túnel. La población directamente afectada por las mejoras de los túneles es de 270.000 personas, a los que, dice el estudio, habrá que sumar los que visiten la zona. Un ejemplo claro es la prolongación del subterráneo de Santa María de la Cabeza. En las zonas de túnel se recuerda que se realizarán 18 millones de viajes correspondientes a 10 líneas de la EMT. Como es lógico, no se refiere a los pasos inferiores de la M-30, sino a los que se están construyendo en el interior para evacuar el tráfico al exterior de la ciudad. Las inversiones en la obra, dice el informe en su página 71, «producirán un efecto claro de generación de rentas y puestos de trabajo que pueden estimarse en 125.000».

71,66. Se ha analizado, incluso, el número de árboles que ganará la ciudad con la reforma de la M-30. Si hoy hay 35,25 por cada hectárea, en el futuro, una vez soterrada parte de la autovía, se llegará a 71,66. La distancia media entre las zonas verdes pasará de 353 metros a 205, mientras que los metros cuadrados de zona verde por habitante se incrementará de 1,98 a 2,4. Uno de los datos más llamativos es que se incrementará el número de usuarios potenciales de estos espacios naturales. Si hoy se estima que rondan los 489, en 2007 se triplicarán y llegarán a los 1.573. También mejora la calidad del río. Este informe reconoce que la dilución de las aguas es hoy de 1:1, cuando llegará, tras la reforma de todos los saneamientos y colectores, a 1:10 una vez concluida la obra.

Medio Ambiente. Los agentes del Seprona encuentran presuntas irregularidades durante una inspección de los trabajos que se realizan entre Legazpi y Santa María de la Cabeza

La Guardia Civil contra las obras de la M-30

Obras de la reforma de la M-30, la semana pasada, ocupando el cauce del río a la altura del puente de Praga. / CARLOS MIRALLES

LUIS F. DURÁN

Las faraónicas obras de la M-30 se han encontrado con una nueva pega. Los agentes del Seprona denunciaron los trabajos que realiza para el Ayuntamiento de Madrid la empresa FCC (Fomento de Construcciones y Contratas) en el tramo comprendido entre el puente de Praga (Santa María de la Cabeza) y el puente de Legazpi, según fuentes de Interior.

En una inspección realizada el pasado mes de noviembre comprobaron que existía una posible ocupación ilegal del cauce del río, a la altura del Puente de Praga. También apreciaron una presunta irregularidad por parte de la constructora al verificar que se había montado una tubería a lo largo de 800 metros del río. Los agentes del Seprona exigieron a los encargados los permisos correspondientes de la Confederación Hidrográfica del Tajo. Sin embargo, los empleados no pudieron presentar ninguna de las autorizaciones exigidas, según dijeron fuentes del Ministerio del Interior.

Como consecuencia de estos hechos, los agentes del Seprona denunciaron los hechos a la Confederación Hidrográfica del Tajo, dependiente del Ministerio de Medio Ambiente, que todavía no se ha pronunciado a este respecto. Dicha denuncia tampoco ha afectado al desarrollo de las obras.

El Ayuntamiento de Madrid aseguró ayer que las obras de la M-30 que afectan al río Manzanares cumplen con todos los requisitos establecidos por la Confederación. Agregaron que la entidad hidrográfica tiene un control exhaustivo de la marcha de los trabajos, ya que todas las semanas el comisario de la Confederación Hidrográfica del Tajo inspecciona las obras.

El portavoz municipal confirmó que los agentes acudieron a inspeccionar las obras. No obstante, añadió, sólo levantaron acta de la visita ya que se le entregaron todos los permisos correspondientes. «No nos consta que denunciaran las obras y tampoco la Confederación ha comunicado la existencia de alguna traba», añadieron desde el Ayuntamiento de Madrid.

Sin embargo, el informe del Seprona pone en entredicho la «extracción de agua del margen derecho del río procedente de la salida de bombeo de la línea 3 del Metro». Ese agua que se saca del suburbano es utilizada para las obras, extremo que cuestiona el Seprona. Los agentes añaden que el agua del metro es trasladada luego hasta una planta depuradora mediante una tubería termosellada, de 800 metros de longitud, que se ha colocado en el margen izquierdo del río.

Asimismo, la Guardia Civil no encontró el permiso para que FCC asentará una planta de lodos bentonímicos que se emplea en la confección de los pilares de las nuevas intraestructuras.

De acuerdo con el informe de los agentes, el tramo en obras inspeccionado puede vulnerar el Real Decreto 849/1986 sobre dominio público hidráulico. Los agentes consideran que sólo la falta de los permisos correspondientes puede suponer una san-

Lotería Nacional — SORTEO DEL JUEVES — SORTEO 3 / 06

SORTEO DEL DÍA 12 DE ENERO DE 2006

Seis series de 100.000 billetes cada una

Lista acumulada de las cantidades que han correspondido a cada una de las seis series de los números premiados, clasificados por su cifra final

Estos premios podrán cobrarse hasta el día 12 de abril de 2006, INCLUSIVE

0 Números	Euros/Billete	1 Números	Euros/Billete	2 Números	Euros/Billete	3 Números	Euros/Billete	4 Números	Euros/Billete
67500	300	67501	300	67502	300	67503	330	67504	330
67510	300	67511	300	67512	300	67513	330	67514	330
67520	300	67521	300	67522	300	67523	330	67524	330
67530	300	67531	300	67532	300	67533	390	67534	330
67540	300	67541	300	67542	300	67543	330	67544	330
67550	300	67551	300	67552	300	67553	330	67554	330
67560	300	67561	300	67562	300	67563	330	67564	330
67570	300	67571	300	67572	300	67573	330	67574	330
67580	300	67581	300	67582	300	67583	330	67584	330
67590	300	67591	300	67592	300	67593	330	67594	480
71300	300	71301	300	71302	300	71303	330	71304	330
71310	300	71311	300	71312	300	71313	330	71314	330
71320	300	71321	300	71322	300	71323	330	71324	330
71330	300	71331	300	71332	300	71333	390	71334	330
71340	300	71341	300	71342	300	71343	330	71344	330
71350	300	71351	300	71352	300	71353	330	71354	330
71360	300	71361	300	71362	300	71363	330	71364	330
71370	300	71371	300	71372	300	71373	330	71374	330
71380	300	71381	300	71382	300	71383	330	71384	330
71390	300	71391	300	71392	300	71393	8.130	**71394**	**300.000**
		Terminaciones		**Terminaciones**		**Terminaciones**		**Terminaciones**	
		711	150	962	150	1683	780	1394	1.230
						953	180	1624	780
						33	90	394	480
						3	30	94	180
								4	30

5 Números	Euros/Billete	6 Números	Euros/Billete	7 Números	Euros/Billete	8 Números	Euros/Billete	9 Números	Euros/Billete
67505	360	67506	300	67507	300	67508	300	67509	330
67515	300	67516	300	67517	300	67518	300	67519	330
67525	300	67526	300	67527	300	67528	300	67529	330
67535	300	67536	360	67537	300	67538	300	67539	330
67545	300	67546	300	67547	300	67548	300	67549	330
67555	300	67556	300	67557	300	67558	300	67559	330
67565	300	67566	300	67567	4.665	**67568**	**60.000**	67569	4.695
67575	300	67576	300	67577	300	67578	300	67579	330
67585	300	67586	300	67587	300	67588	300	67589	330
67595	300	67596	300	67597	300	67598	300	67599	330
71305	360	71306	300	71307	300	71308	300	71309	330
71315	300	71316	300	71317	300	71318	300	71319	330
71325	300	71326	300	71327	300	71328	450	71329	330
71335	300	71336	360	71337	300	71338	300	71339	330
71345	300	71346	300	71347	300	71348	300	71349	330
71355	300	71356	300	71357	300	71358	300	71359	330
71365	300	71366	300	71367	300	71368	300	71369	330
71375	300	71376	300	71377	300	71378	300	71379	330
71385	300	71386	300	71387	300	71388	300	71389	330
71395	8.100	71396	300	71397	300	71398	300	71399	330
Terminaciones		**Terminaciones**		**Terminaciones**		**Terminaciones**		**Terminaciones**	
8605	810	6796	750	067	150	328	150	9	30
405	210	496	150			908	150		
775	150	656	150						
855	150	36	60						
05	60								

ESTE SORTEO ADJUDICA 2.127.000 DÉCIMOS PREMIADOS POR UN IMPORTE TOTAL DE 12.600.000 EUROS

PREMIO ESPECIAL 1.170.000 € Núm. 71394 PRIMER PREMIO	FRACCIÓN	SERIE	PREMIO ACUMULADO
	5.ª	3.ª	1.200.000 €

A la izquierda, Leo Bassi, realizando malabares. A la derecha, uno de los manifestantes disfrazado de 'Faraón Ruiz-Gallardón'. / JAVI MARTÍNEZ

Sátira y charangas contra las obras

M-30. Un millar de vecinos se manifestó ayer en el Puente de Toledo reclamando a 'Ruiz-Vallardón' el cese de las talas y de las obras del tercer cinturón, apoyados por Leo Bassi

LUIS F. DURAN

Eligieron el mismo epicentro de las obras de reforma de la M-30. Desde el estruendo del Puente de Toledo, cerca de mil personas, convocadas por la plataforma *M-30 no más coches*, reclamaron ayer al mediodía «no más talas, no más obras y no más mentiras». Durante más de 90 minutos bailaron y cantaron por la salvación del río Manzanares y por la protección de los parques. Fue un acto festivo que, además, contó con la animación de Leo Bassi —bufón, se llamó él— y de un cómico disfrazado de Faraón que imitaba al alcalde *Ruiz-Vallardón*, que corearon los manifestantes.

La plataforma ecologista *M-30 no más coches* repartió ente los asistentes un tríptico titulado «M-30, no más mentiras», en el cual se denuncian «19 engaños» del alcalde. En el folleto, donde se puede ver una fotografía de Ruiz-Gallardón con la nariz larga de Pinocho, se describen las contradicciones del Ayuntamiento. A cada promesa del regidor sobre la M-30, sigue una explicación de que se trata de una mentira.

Por ejemplo, dice el folleto: «Vamos a ampliar zonas verdes». A lo que la plataforma contesta: «Los datos cantan, en lo que va de legislatura se han destruido 80 hectáreas de parques, muchos de ellos históricos». Asimismo, el tríptico delataba el coste de la obra de la M-30 que se «se estimaba en torno a los 1.700 millones y ya vamos por los 5.000».

Por el escenario colocado para el acto pasaron los portavoces de todos los barrios afectados por las obras, para «escuchar la voz que Ruiz-Gallardón, niega a los vecinos», según Paco Segura, portavoz de la Plataforma. Roberto Tornamira, del Nudo Super Sur, denunció «que Gallardón destroza un parque, un parque que en su día fue una escombrera y que Tierno Galván convirtió en zona verde, con una chimenea que cada año emitirá tres toneladas de partículas contaminantes y cancerígenas». Maribel, de Puente de Praga, acusó a Gallardón de mentir ya que «va a poner enfrente de nuestras casas los grandes pozos de ventilación de los túneles de la M-30». Amelia, de la Asociación la Flor del Barrio del Pilar, lamentó el «afán del alcalde por poner las carreteras entre las casas cuando en los pueblos más remotos sacan las carreteras fuera».

También hubo fandangos y bailes por un Madrid más sano, con la música del grupo Samba da Rúa, y una particular versión de los versos de Jorge Manrique, titulada *Coplas por la muerte de tu parque*. Mucha sátira y charanga. «Vecinos, viandantes, escuchad con atención; los árboles de mis parques nos los taló Gallardón (El Faraón). No han entrado en La Zarzuela, otros parques han tocado; M-30, Montijo, Arganzuela, este tío está pirado».

En apoyo a los vecinos acudieron el portavoz adjunto del PSOE en el Ayuntamiento de Madrid, Óscar Iglesias, y la portavoz municipal de IU, Inés Sabanés. Ella dijo que la obra no sólo tendrá efectos durante su ejecución, sino también cuando estén terminadas «por la tala de 42.000 árboles». Iglesias anunció que pedirán un estudio sanitario ya que «las obras están afectando a la salud de las personas».

También estuvieron presentes los portavoces de Urbanismo y Medio Ambiente de los grupos municipales, Félix Arias y Concha Denche, respectivamente, así como el eurodiputado socialista Carlos Carnero, quien dijo a Efe que el próximo miércoles se reunirá la Comisión de peticiones del Parlamento Europeo. En esta comisión se determinarán la fecha y la composición de la delegación que viajará a Madrid para evaluar estas obras, aunque Carnero lamentó el «poco valor» de Ruiz-Gallardón por no acudir a Bruselas «a escuchar las cuatro verdades sobre la M-30».

El artista Leo Bassi, se proclamó «creyente» en el medio ambiente y aseguró «no ser tan ateo como pensaba porque tengo un dios que es la naturaleza». Luego se subió sobre una furgoneta e hizo malabares.

En contra de esta obra y «a favor de la vida en Madrid», justificó su presencia en esta concentración la escritora Almudena Grandes, que cerró el acto reivindicando el derecho a vivir en una ciudad habitable y no en un lugar que en estos momentos «soporta cotas de desamor épicas y legendarias». Grandes definió como «filosóficamente intolerable» el soterramiento de la M-30.

EL ALCALDE REPLICA A LOS VECINOS

El alcalde de Madrid, Alberto Ruiz-Gallardón, considera que el futuro «se gana apostando por la modernización y no quedándote quieto» e insistió en que actitudes «conservadoras» ante obras o proyectos pueden acabar «anclándote en el pasado». Con estas declaraciones a Efe, pronunciadas en Lalín (Pontevedra), contestaba a las protestas de los vecinos, políticos de la oposición y ecologistas que ayer al mediodía se manifestaron en el Puente de Toledo contra los daños causados por la reforma de la M-30.

Durante la protesta, los convocantes acusaron al Gobierno municipal, del PP, de mentir y de endeudar a los madrileños 35 años con esta obra.

Sin embargo, subrayó Gallardón, las actitudes «conservadoras, en el sentido sociológico del término», probablemente no generan incomodidades. Y añadió: «Esas actitudes pusilánimes al final te acaban anclando en el pasado. Si quieres ganar el futuro, lo que hay que hacer es hacer». «A los políticos se les elige en sus puestos no para dejar las cosas como están, sino para intentar mejorar; ésa es la forma que tenemos de devolver a los ciudadanos la confianza que nos han dado con sus votos», zanjó.

BREVES

La región activa el Plan de Inclemencias Invernales por nieve

La Dirección General de Protección Ciudadana de la Comunidad de Madrid, a través del teléfono de emergencias 112, activó anoche el Nivel 0 de Preemergencia del Plan de Inclemencias Invernales, debido a las precipitaciones en forma de nieve y granizo que comenzaron a caer ayer tarde en la sierra. La previsión del Instituto Nacional de Meteorología anuncia para hoy nevadas por encima de los 800 metros, que podrían generar una capa de más de 10 centímetros de nieve, así como fuertes rachas de viento en la zona de la sierra madrileña. EFE

Un joven herido grave en un accidente de tráfico por granizo

Un joven de 28 años resultó ayer herido muy grave en el kilómetro 10 de la avenida de Andalucía, después de que perdiera el control del vehículo que conducía por una calzada en la que había granizo y barro, según informaron fuentes de Emergencias Madrid. El accidente tuvo lugar sobre las 20.30 horas, cuando el conductor perdió el control del vehículo, chocó y dio varias vueltas de campana. P. HERRAIZ

El PSOE denuncia los gastos de propaganda de Esperanza Aguirre

El PSOE denunció ayer el «excesivo y desproporcionado» gasto destinado por la Comunidad de Madrid a propaganda en 2006, cuya cantidad asciende a 137 millones de euros. Aseguró que esta cifra significa una partida casi 10 veces superior a lo que se invierte en la reducción de la lista de espera diagnóstica y 800 veces más que el dinero aportado para la atención de las víctimas de terrorismo. EP

Faunia toma medidas contra la gripe aviar

El director técnico de Faunia, Agustín López Goya, afirmó que se han tomado «medidas» en colaboración con el Ministerio de Agricultura, Pesca y Alimentación para «prevenir» un posible foco de gripe aviar en los parques y zoológicos de España. «Ya se han tomado medidas preventivas, del tipo vacunas y control sanitario de los animales», reiteró López. EP

Los embalses se sitúan al 39,2%

A pesar de la lluvia registrada el fin de semana, la sequía continúa en toda la región. Las reservas de agua en los embalses madrileños se sitúan al 39,2%, lo que supone 370 millones de metros cúbicos, con un mínimo del 4%. EP

Inauguración del túnel exterior de la M-30 hasta el Nudo Sur

El túnel abierto hoy tiene una longitud total de 9.952 metros. De ellos, 5.973 corresponden al tronco central y 3.978 a los ramales de acceso y salida.

Seguridad vial

· **132 cámaras** conectadas al Centro de Control de Madrid Calle 30 velarán por la seguridad. Cualquier incidencia será atendida inmediatamente.

· Todas las entradas y salidas cuentan con **carril propio** para disminuir el riesgo que suponen las incorporaciones para el tráfico.

Sección del túnel

El tronco central mantiene en todo su recorrido al menos tres carriles, si bien a lo largo de su trazado hay tramos con mayor número de carriles, en función de los accesos y salidas.

FUENTE: Ayuntamiento de Madrid. ChMS / EL MUNDO

Dos carriles más bajo el Manzanares

Ayuntamiento. Hasta ahora, sólo se podía circular bajo tierra del Nudo Sur a Marqués de Monistrol. Hoy se pone en funcionamiento parcialmente el subterráneo en el otro sentido

C. SERNA

Los túneles del Manzanares, uno de los proyectos de la M-30 que más peligros traía consigo en su ejecución por la proximidad del acuífero, han llegado a su fin bajo tierra, a falta de pulir algunos detalles y de iniciar las obras de recuperación de la superficie. Hoy se abre la calzada exterior del anillo, es decir, casi seis kilómetros de tronco central más cuatro de conexiones, desde Marqués de Monistrol hasta el Nudo Sur.

Con esta inauguración se eliminan definitivamente los coches de la superficie del río Manzanares, aunque su apertura contará, en principio, con sólo dos carriles. Durante las fiestas de Semana Santa, se derribará un muro de obra que posibilitará el uso de los cuatro carriles.

También se pondrán hoy mismo en funcionamiento la mayoría de las conexiones del subterráneo pero quedarán aún sin uso el ramal a la carretera de Toledo, el acceso a la glorieta de Pirámides, la conexión con Santa María de la Cabeza y del Puente de Praga, hacia la avenida del Manzanares, en dirección glorieta de Cádiz.

Esta infraestructura será utilizada por más de 107.000 vehículos de los que, según los estudios de movilidad, 70.000 vendrán del *by-pass* Sur, ya que este subterráneo estará conectado con el túnel sur cuando entre en funcionamiento el próximo mes de abril.

En todo este tramo, se han eliminado las entradas en trenza y cada conexión dispondrá de un carril único para incorporarse. Además, el subterráneo contará con 132 cámaras de vigilancia para su seguridad.

Semana Santa

El 40% de los madrileños se irá de viaje

C. SERNA

Cada vez son más los madrileños que deciden pasar sus vacaciones de Semana Santa fuera de la ciudad. Si el año pasado, fue el 32,5% de los habitantes de la capital quienes hicieron la maleta, este año, los dispuestos a aprovechar el tradicional puente para dejar Madrid será más del 40%, según el barómetro municipal que realiza el Ayuntamiento de Madrid.

El destino preferido para la mayoría de los madrileños es otra comunidad autónoma (el turismo nacional lo elegirá el 31,8%). Sólo un 2,6% de los viajeros se quedará en la Comunidad de Madrid pero en otra localidad, mientras que un 5,8% ya tiene pensado un destino internacional para estos días. Eso sí, el barómetro municipal indica que hay un 55% de los madrileños que tiene claro que no va a dejar su casa durante las fiestas, ocho puntos menos que en 2006.

Lo más jóvenes y los estudiantes son el viajero típico para pasar la Semana Santa en otra comunidad autónoma. En el otro lado, los que no se moverán, se encuentran los jubilados, que en su mayoría no han planificado ningún viaje, y las amas de casa.

Lo que sí queda claro en la encuesta es que para estas vacaciones, los madrileños prefieren planear su viaje por su cuenta (un 91% del total) y sólo un 7% acudirá a una agencia de viajes. De ahí que, casi el 87% de los que viajan a otra región lo haga con su propio vehículo y que los que han elegido un destino extranjero hayan comprado sus vacaciones por Internet (un 65%) y el resto en una agencia de viajes.

M2

EL MUNDO/LA REVISTA DIARIA DE MADRID
SÁBADO 31 DE MARZO DE 2007

Metro
Aguirre amplía «la puerta Norte de Madrid» y prolonga la Línea 1 con la nueva estación de Chamartín /3

Teatro Real
Sylvie Guillem, musa de los grandes coreógrafos, presenta el espectáculo 'Push' /10

Un río sin coches

...sta general de la zona del río Manzanares y la M-30 a la altura de Príncipe Pío tomada ayer al mediodía: los coches ya circulan en el interior del nuevo túnel de casi 6 kilómetros. / CARLOS MIRALLES

...allardón habla de «día histórico» al inaugurar el túnel entre Marqués de Monistrol y el Nudo Sur que soterra la M-30 /16-17

Rebelión china en Usera
La Asociación de Comerciantes Chinos asegura que hay más casos de abusos policiales y prepara nuevas denuncias /2

LA M-30 EN LOS AÑOS 90. El 30 de junio de 1992, el río Manzanares se veía así, como una mancha en un paisaje lleno de coches y pasarelas. La M-30 se convertía en una barrera entre vecinos de un mismo barrio. LARRY MANGINO

Urbanismo. El alcalde inaugura los seis kilómetros de soterramiento de la M-30 desde Marqués de Monistrol al Nudo Sur, eliminando así los coches de la ribera del río Manzanares

Gallardón junto a Ricardo Lagos y a ocho alcaldes. / JOSÉ HUESCA / EFE

Gallardón dice saber «gestionar la utopía»

CARMEN SERNA

En el estómago del alcalde vivía ayer una colonia de mariposas. No es la primera vez que visita un tramo de la M-30 terminado pero para la puesta en funcionamiento del túnel desde Marqués de Monistrol al Nudo Sur, iba acompañado de ocho alcaldes de distintas partes del mundo, del ex presidente chileno, Ricardo Lagos, y del secretario general de la OCDE, Ángel Gurría. Una oportunidad perfecta para *sacar barriga* de «un día histórico que muchos pensaban que no iba a llegar y que ha llegado para quedarse». Todo un lema que el regidor repite en cada tramo inaugurado.

Lo que enseñó a los distintos alcaldes, entre los que se encontraban el de Lisboa, Milán, Montevideo, Singapur, Sarajevo o Abu Dhabi, es la diferencia entre un río Manzanares sin coches y otro, el de hace años, lleno de tráfico (como se observa en las dos fotografías). Eso sí, para ello utilizó una pantalla gigante y un vídeo promocional que ayudó a que los regidores se hicieran una idea de lo que se ha cambiado en dos años, después de 32 años viendo pasar los coches por las ventanas de estos vecinos.

Y eso que faraónica ya había sido la entrada del alcalde. El himno de la alegría se escuchó justo en el momento en que la comitiva internacional pisaba el túnel mientras el escudo del Ayuntamiento de Ma-

«ES UNA OBRA FANTÁSTICA»

El alcalde de Lisboa, Antonio Carmona, aseguró ayer tras visitar el túnel de la M-30 que se trataba de «una obra fantástica» y que «va a mejorar la calidad de vida de muchos ciudadanos y la calidad ambiental». Según el regidor de la capital del país luso, «es obligatorio en una ciudad que crece, que se adapten las infraestructuras».

Sin embargo, Carmona quitó importancia al tamaño del subterráneo y aseguró que estaba «acostumbrado» a ver obras de este tipo.

Como puntos fuertes del proyecto, el alcalde lisboeta apuntó la «señalización, mucha ventilación y una de las zonas más modernas». Además, aseguró que «lo más importante es la seguridad».

EL TÚNEL EN CIFRAS

6 Km. El subterráneo en sí tiene casi seis kilómetros de distancia entre Marqués de Monistrol y el Nudo Sur. Además, hay que añadirle otros cuatro kilómetros de ramales que darán acceso a toda la ribera del río.

132 cámaras. El tráfico estará vigilado por 132 visores que están conectados con el centro de control de pantallas.

9 ramales sin abrir. De las 16 conexiones que tiene este túnel, sólo están operativas ahora siete. El resto (desde Pirámides hasta la glorieta de Cádiz) se irán poniendo en marcha conforme se acaben los trabajos.

...id, proyectado en el techo, se ...ezclaba con saludos de bienveni... en los idiomas de los invitados. ...espués, hasta tres responsables ...el proyecto explicaron cosas co... «la recuperación de los cinco ...entes de la capital» o «la mejora ... la calidad del aire que supone la ...ra» o «el gran parque que se for...ará hasta Getafe gracias al sote...amiento».

...ágrimas

...plausos, sonrisas, orgullo en cada ...esto y lágrimas de emoción en los ...os de Ruiz-Gallardón. Y el mismo ...scurso (casi literal) que el que ha ...cho el alcalde en otras grandes ...auguraciones como el *by-pass* ...r o la otra dirección de este mis...o túnel.

«Muchos dijeron que era una ...opía y dijimos que sí, que era una ...opía, pero que éramos capaces ... gestionarla», arengó el alcalde ...radeciendo el trabajo a las em...esas, a su Gobierno y a los veci...os afectados por las obras duran... 22 meses. «No hay ninguna meta ...e esta ciudad se proponga y la ...ordemos juntos, que no poda...os realizarla», añadió.

Casi una a una mencionó las ca...es que más problemas han sufri... con los trabajos de la M-30 pero ...eguró que, en total, el túnel del ...udo Sur, de casi seis kilómetros ... longitud, beneficiará a un mi...ón de personas entre viajeros y ...ecinos. Directamente, a los ...7.000 vehículos que transitan ...ariamente por esta zona.

En total, el Ayuntamiento ha in...ertido 522 millones de euros para ...iminar los vehículos de este lado ...el Manzanares, casi 50 millones ...r kilómetro soterrado, con el ob...tivo de liberar al río y a las zonas ...erdes que hay a su vera del humo ... los coches.

Sin embargo, los que no se sal...ron ayer de alguna retención ...eron los usuarios de este túnel ...e sólo han podido utilizar dos de ...s cuatro carriles y la mitad de las ...nexiones de las que dispone. ...demás, la salida de la M-30 con la ...rretera de Toledo aún no está ...erativa.

Los carriles estarán abiertos a la ...elta de las vacaciones, según las ...evisiones municipales, y las cone...ones se irán poniendo en funcio...amiento conforme terminen las ...oras que se retomaron ayer al ter...inar la apertura del túnel a las ...10 horas.

Vea el vídeo 'El Manzanares sin coches' en: www.elmundo.es/

TRES TRAMOS Y ...UCHAS CONEXIONES

...asta el 11 de mayo, fecha límite ...e se dio el alcalde de Madrid, Al...erto Ruiz-Gallardón, para inaugu...r todos los tramos de la M-30 (an...s del inicio de campaña), le que...an al regidor cortar varias cintas: ...ncretamente tres tramos gran...es y varias conexiones de los tú...eles ya operativos que se irán po...endo en marcha sin hacer un ac... de inauguración.

Los tramos que están todavía en ...oras son el túnel sur del *by-pass* ...ur, la unión de la M-30 con Sor ...ngela de la Cruz (en el distrito de ...etuán) y la conexión de Embaja...ores con la M-40. Durante los días ...e quedan también se irán po...iendo en funcionamiento los ra...ales que ahora están cerrados.

CARLOS MIRALLES

LA M-30, AYER. Los últimos coches que circularon junto al río cruzaron la M-30 ayer hacia la una del mediodía. Después, se abrió el túnel que va desde Marqués de Monistrol hasta el Nudo Sur y se liberó la ribera del Manzanares, que tendrá que esperar para su recuperación total a la próxima legislatura.

>PRECAMPAÑA / La 'batalla' por Madrid

Ayuntamiento. Gallardón visita las obras del Manzanares tres veces en 12 días y aún lo hará una vez más antes de que lo prohíba la Junta Electoral Central. El candidato socialista a la Alcaldía acudirá hoy para poner en valor el dinero del Plan E

Todos al río a 'pescar' votos

JAIME G. TRECEÑO

Llega la primavera y el olor electoral está en el aire. Quienes mejor lo saben son todos aquellos que se la juegan en las urnas, esencialmente, los candidatos y sus colaboradores. Uno de *caladeros estrella* de la precampaña está siendo Madrid Río, una de las dos obras de relumbrón del alcalde de Madrid, Alberto Ruiz-Gallardón (la otra es la reforma del Eje Prado-Recoletos), para esta legislatura.

De ello, puede dar buena fe el propio alcalde, la delegada del Gobierno en Madrid, Amparo Valcarce, y el secretario de Estado para el Deporte y candidato del PSOE a la Alcaldía de la capital, Jaime Lissavetzky. PP, PSOE e IU juegan con la idea de que pasado mañana el Consejo de Ministros apruebe el decreto de convocatoria de las elecciones autonómicas y municipales de mayo. Y es que, a partir

> La delegada del Gobierno aguardó a que se marchara el alcalde para criticarlo

del próximo martes 29 ningún cargo público podría cortar la cinta de infraestructura alguna que hubiese proyectado, ya que sería a partir de entonces cuando entra en vigor.

Sea por ello o no, lo cierto es que el alcalde de la capital ya ha visitado tres veces en 12 días las obras de reforma de las riberas del Manzanares (entorno de Matadero, día 9; parque de Arganzuela, día 18 y zona norte del Salón de Pinos, ayer). Pero no será la última. El regidor regresará por última vez al río, seguramente mañana, para hacerse la última foto antes de la elecciones, esta vez junto al uno de los símbolos de Madrid Río, el puente del arquitecto Dominique Perrault. Se trata de una infraestructura con un peculiar diseño en tubo que se encuentra junto al Puente de Toledo. Perrault fue el diseñador de otra obra emblemática cercana, la Caja Mágica, situada en la Cuña del Manzanares.

Pero el alcalde no estará sólo en esa tarea de *mostrar* a los madrileños lo bien que ha quedado el entorno del río. La delegada del Gobierno, como ya hiciera en otras ocasiones anteriores, también acudió ayer junto Ruiz-Gallardón a la apertura de la zona norte del Salón de Pinos. Y es que, Valcarce da la cara en representación del Ejecutivo, ya que las obras se han ejecutado con cargo a los fondos estatales del Plan E.

Para dejar claro, quien ha proyectado, ejecutado y financiado la infraestructura, el alcalde se encargó de recordar que el Estado ha aportado sólo el 6% del coste total de las obras de soterramiento de la M-30 y de recuperación de las obras de las riberas, «que no es poco», dijo.

Después del paseo por los nuevos caminos de la remozada orilla del Manzanares, la delegada del Gobierno se *despojó* de sus ropajes institucionales y, una vez que se había ya marchado el alcalde, le hizo un traje. «Estas obras han sido muchísimo más caras porque se ha querido hacer en unos plazos que no era los que necesitaba la obra, sino las urgencias electorales del alcalde de Madrid», dijo, según informa Europa Press.

Y es que, Valcarce también *número dos* de la lista del PSOE a la Asamblea, parece haber hecho buenas las críticas de los *populares* que le reprochaban e incluso han exigido su dimisión, por utilizar el puesto institucional para hacer campaña.

El candidato socialista a la Alcaldía acudirá hoy a las orillas del río para poner en valor la inversión realizada por el Estado a través del Plan E en el remozado Manzanares. Desde la Administración General del Estado se han aportado 120 millones de euros a Madrid Río entre 2009 y 2010.

La delegada del Gobierno, Amparo Valcarce, junto a Ruiz-Gallardón y a su edil de Urbanismo, Pilar Martínez. / B. RIVAS

Manzanares

Botella invita al PSOE a contar animales

J. G. T.

La delegada de Medio Ambiente, Ana Botella, invitó ayer el portavoz socialista del ramo, Pedro Santín, a contar por sí mismo las especies y animales que habitan en el Manzanares. La concejala daba contestación así a la pregunta formulada por el concejal socialista en relación «a las medidas adoptadas por el Área de Medio Ambiente, en su caso, para la reintroducción, [illegible] fauna en el tramo urbano del río Manzanares».

La delegada de Medio Ambiente llegó incluso a invitar al edil socialista a pedir a Martinsa –la empresa encarga del mantenimiento del Manzanares– «un buzo» para comprobar por sí mismo los datos que se estaban ofreciendo, ya que la edil puso en cuestión la verosimilitud de las cifras que se estaban aportando.

Especialmente, llamativo fueron las referencias que hizo en torno a la existencia o no de la gaviota reidora. Respecto a la salud ambiental del río dijo que «está mejor que nunca gracias al PP». Botella señaló que hay entre 8.000 y 10.000 tipos de peces y entre 300 y 500 aves.

'Varapalo' por la M-30. El Tribunal Superior de Justicia de Madrid ha vuelto a *tumbar*, a través de dos sentencias, tramos del nudo Sur y Norte de la M-30. El motivo esgrimido por el tribunal es el mismo que empleó la pasada semana con otra sentencia similar.

El Ayuntamiento eludió realizar Evaluación de Impacto Ambiental, para no retardar los proyectos que se sacaron a concurso. La efectividad de la sentencia es igual que la de la semana pasada, ninguna. El candidato del PSOE a la Alcaldía, Jaime Lissavetzky, se comprometió a hacer la evaluación si es alcalde.

ELMUNDO.es
▶ Vídeo: Vea a Botella en la Comisión de Medio Ambiente

Las obras de la M-30, vistas desde el subsuelo

Dos obreros avanzan hacia la cola de la tuneladora *Dulcinea* por el tramo ya perforado. *Dulcinea* ha excavado 800 metros desde el pasado noviembre. / RICARDO GUTIÉRREZ

En el corazón de 'Dulcinea'

Las mayores tuneladoras del mundo excavan el subterráneo que servirá de atajo al nudo sur de la M-30

VERA GUTIÉRREZ CALVO, **Madrid**

La gigantesca obra de la M-30 —que implica la construcción de más de 15 kilómetros de túneles en todo el anillo de circunvalación— tiene una musa, y está en el mar. Se llama *teredo navalis*: un molusco con forma de gusano que destruye los barcos de madera con su letal capacidad tuneladora. Con el caparazón, que es como una mandíbula, va haciendo un agujero en el barco, y mientras se come la madera segrega una baba que endurece y sostiene las paredes.

Ese diminuto gusano es el origen de una tecnología que ha alcanzado cotas increíbles de sofisticación, pero que, en esencia, se reduce a eso: avanzar comiéndose la tierra y, al mismo tiempo, ir apuntalando las paredes. El *teredo navalis* es, según cuentan los ingenieros del Ayuntamiento, el antecedente y la inspiración de las tuneladoras. De la que excavó el primer túnel bajo el río Támesis, en Londres, en el siglo XIX y también, hoy, de las dos más grandes y modernas del mundo, *Dulcinea* y *Tizona*. Dos monstruosas lombrices de hormigón y metal que horadan el subsuelo madrileño para construir uno de los subterráneos más complejos y caros (740 millones) de la M-30: el doble túnel del nudo sur.

Dulcinea es la que primero echó a andar, hace ya tres meses, y su misión es excavar el túnel norte: 4,2 kilómetros —3,6 se harán con tuneladora— desde la conexión de la M-30 con la autovía de Valencia, al este, hasta los jardines del viejo matadero de Legazpi, al oeste. En paralelo —pero avanzando en sentido contrario— trabajará desde marzo la tuneladora Tizona, encargada del túnel sur.

Serán, con tres carriles cada uno y un diámetro de 15 metros, "los túneles más grandes construidos nunca con tuneladora". "La madre de todos los túneles", sentencia Joaquín Torres, jefe de obra. Pero también "los más seguros del mundo", según ha prometido el alcalde, Alberto Ruiz-Gallardón. Con ellos pretende el Ayuntamiento aliviar la congestión del nudo sur —250.000 conductores pasan por ahí cada día—, construyendo un atajo subterráneo que enlace los ejes este y oeste de la M-30. Los grupos de oposición (PSOE e IU) replican que, lejos de reducir el número de coches, la obra duplicará la capacidad del nudo sur.

Dulcinea ha excavado ya 800 metros de túnel, y se encuentra justo bajo el haz de vías férreas de la zona de Méndez Álvaro. El corazón de la máquina, casi tan insondable como el de la dama cervantina que le da nombre, late en estos momentos a 40 metros de profundidad. Para llegar a él hay que descender al gigantesco pozo de ataque —excavado a lo largo de todo un año cerca de la plaza del Conde de Casal— y caminar después por el tramo de túnel ya construido.

Por fin, al fondo, se divisa la cola de la tuneladora, que en total mide 150 metros de largo, 35 de alto y tiene un diámetro de 13,4 metros. La más grande del mundo, con su gemela Tizona. Una mole como un edificio de cuatro plantas, abierta por detrás y envuelta en el ensordecedor ruido de los motores hidráulicos que dan vida al monstruo. Hasta aquí llega el frío

Pasa a la **página 32**

El doble túnel de la M-30 Sur

La tuneladora *Dulcinea* comenzó la excavación el 13 de noviembre y había construido hasta el viernes pasado 778 metros de túnel.
La *Tizona* arrancará en el mes de marzo.

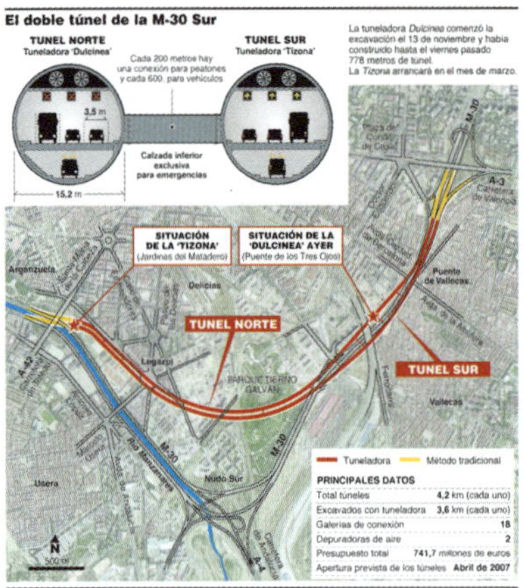

PRINCIPALES DATOS	
Total túneles	4,2 km (cada uno)
Excavados con tuneladora	3,6 km (cada uno)
Galerías de conexión	18
Depuradoras de aire	2
Presupuesto total	741,7 millones de euros
Apertura prevista de los túneles	Abril de 2007

Fuente: Ayuntamiento de Madrid. — G. HERMOSO

De izquierda a derecha, David Lowe, secretario del Parlamento Europeo, la eurodiputada verde danesa Margrete Auken, el eurodiputado socialista Carlos Carnero y la portavoz municipal de IU, Inés Sabanés, observan las obras de la M-30 desde la terraza de una vecina de la calle de Antonio López. / LUIS MAGÁN

Dos eurodiputados en estado de choque

Los parlamentarios enviados por Estrasburgo muestran sus dudas ante la obra de la M-30

V. G. C., **Madrid**

"I'm shocked". Así, impresionada, sobresaltada, "más que sorprendida" se declaró la eurodiputada danesa Margrete Auken (verde) mientras, con ojos abiertos como platos, observaba las obras de la M-30 desde la terraza de una vecina, en el piso 17 de la Torre de Praga, junto al Manzanares. Auken y el irlandés Proinsias de Rossa visitaron ayer las obras enviados por el Parlamento Europeo en respuesta a una petición de IU, Ecologistas en Acción y la plataforma vecinal Afectados Nudo Sur.

De Rossa, socialista, sugirió que la obra debería haber sido sometida a un estudio ambiental previo. Auken, del grupo Los Verdes, auguró que el soterramiento de la M-30 atraerá más coches al incrementar el número de carriles. El informe que elaboren estos eurodiputados a su vuelta a Estrasburgo no será vinculante ni tiene que ver con el expediente abierto a España por la Comisión Europea por las obras de la M-30, según explicó un portavoz de la Oficina del Parlamento Europeo en Madrid.

"Las declaraciones de los eurodiputados, con todo respeto, ni nos preocupan ni nos sorprenden. Su juicio es político, lo traían de antemano", afirmaron fuentes del gobierno municipal. El grupo popular europeo no mandó a ningún representante. La concejal madrileña de Urbanismo, Pilar Martínez, apuntó: "Creo que han considerado que esta misión estaba politizada".

La jornada de Auken y De Rossa comenzó con una reunión en la Oficina del Parlamento Europeo a la que asistieron varios expertos designados por los peticionarios (IU, Ecologistas en Acción y Afectados Nudo Sur): dos urbanistas, un bioquímico, un ingeniero de caminos, una física del Consejo Superior de Investigaciones Científicas (CSIC) y un arquitecto. A la salida, los dos eurodiputados declararon que el asunto era "tan serio" como creían, y los expertos se mostraron unánimemente preocupados por las consecuencias de las obras en la calidad del aire, la seguridad vial y la movilidad urbana.

A toda prisa llegaron Auken y De Rossa al Ayuntamiento de Madrid, donde les esperaban el alcalde, Alberto Ruiz-Gallardón; la concejal de Urbanismo y el equipo técnico que dirige las obras. Estuvieron dos horas: se les puso el DVD sobre la M-30 que el Ayuntamiento ha buzoneado por todo Madrid y se les explicó que, según el gobierno municipal, la obra cumple escrupulosamente la ley. Después se reunieron con PSOE e IU, y otra vez a la carrera se montaron en un autocar para recorrer las obras y ver con sus propios ojos lo que unos habían pintado como la mejor obra de ingeniería acometida nunca, y los otros, como la mayor catástrofe perpetrada jamás. La visita fue de lo más clarificadora, según dijeron después Auken y De Rossa. Los grupos peticionarios habían pedido a Paula Fernández, vecina del piso 17 de la Torre de Praga, en la calle de Antonio López, que dejara subir a su terraza a la comitiva. Ella accedió y abrió su casa a De Rossa, Auken, tres eurodiputados que los acompañaban a título particular —el socialista Carlos Carnero, el *verde* David Hammerstein y Willy Meyer, de IU— y una veintena de periodistas.

"¡Pero esto es impresionante, no había visto algo así en mi vida!", exclamó la danesa oteando el paisaje de grúas. Después añadió: "En mi opinión, aumentar el número de carriles atraerá más tráfico, aunque vaya bajo tierra". "Yo no soy abogado, y no puedo dictaminar si esto es una calle o una autovía [de eso depende la obligatoriedad de pasar estudio ambiental], pero si este proyecto se hubiera hecho en Irlanda, lo hubiéramos sometido a la más estricta legislación ambiental", subrayó De Rossa.

No les dio tiempo a hablar con Paula Fernández, que se desahogaba con los periodistas: "Por favor, sólo pido que me dejen dormir. ¡Que paren las máquinas por la noche! Llevo meses tomando pastillas, no puedo ni sacar a pasear a la perra, ¡hablo sola con la televisión y le digo palabrotas cuando dan algo de las obras! Mi hijo se pone música en las orejas hasta que consigue dormirse... Yo nunca le agradeceré esta obra a Gallardón".

Catarsis en Legazpi

R. FRAGUAS, **Madrid**

Hasta 27 vecinos del Nudo Sur, afectados por las obras de la M-30, dieron ayer salida de viva voz a sus tribulaciones y pesares. Fue por la tarde, en el matadero de Legazpi, donde se habían congregado hasta 400 personas más. Argumentaron con pasión y con razones. Trataban así de persuadir a los parlamentarios europeos presentes de lo que, en su mayoría, consideran una agresión a sus vidas cotidianas, por perturbar sus recuerdos y amenazar su futuro. Se sienten atrapados en un Madrid hoy para ellos invivible, polvoriento y ruidoso, al que ya no reconocen: no se les permite pasear, ni el descanso ni el sueño; no se sienten seguros encima del crepitar de las tuneladoras; temen que sus hijos no puedan volver a respirar con normalidad. Y ello por obras de una escala insólita, que arrasan árboles y memoria convirtiendo sus vidas en una dolorosa llaga. Los parlamentarios trasladarán sus quejas a la Comisión de Peticiones y al Parlamento Europeo. Pero antes se conmovieron al ver latir en la pasión razonada de los vecinos su confianza en la democracia de los ciudadanos que Europa, ayer, para todos encarnaba.

Gallardón anuncia ahora el estudio ambiental de las obras pospuestas

V. G. C., **Madrid**

La concejal de Urbanismo, Pilar Martínez, anunció ayer, tras reunirse con los eurodiputados, que el Ayuntamiento realizará una declaración de impacto ambiental para las tres obras de la M-30 aún no iniciadas: los dos túneles del *bypass* norte y un tercer túnel que unirá aquéllos con la A-1. Esas obras no van a realizarse en este mandato sino, en todo caso, en el siguiente (2007-2011), porque dependen de que se ponga en marcha la Operación Chamartín.

"No estamos obligados a nada, hemos cumplido la ley desde el primer día. Pero para mostrar nuestra buena fe vamos a proponerle esta solución a la Comisión Europea", dijo Martínez. La Comisión abrió expediente a España el pasado abril porque considera que la M-30 es una carretera (no una vía urbana) y que su reforma debió pasar hace dos años un estudio ambiental. El Ayuntamiento replica que la ley española dice lo contrario, y que todo el conflicto viene por una "mala trasposición" de la normativa europea a la española.

En paralelo a la declaración de impacto de los proyectos del norte, el Ayuntamiento hará —"y someterá a información pública", aseguró la concejal— un estudio para ver si las obras ya terminadas han tenido algún "efecto negativo". En ese caso, se corregirán "con medidas complementarias", a posteriori.

"Esto es una rectificación del Ayuntamiento. Lamento que llegue cuando casi toda la obra está hecha", afirmó la ministra de Medio Ambiente, Cristina Narbona, que también recibió ayer a la delegación europea. "Hacer ese estudio ambiental no sirve de nada, la obra no es un proyecto por partes", señaló la socialista Trinidad Jiménez. Inés Sabanés, de IU, declaró: "Es una rectificación, pero es insuficiente".

Reservas de agua

En millones de metros cúbicos

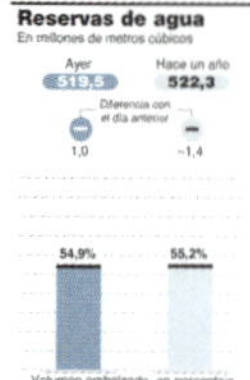

Fuente: Canal de Isabel II

Las nuevas infraestructuras

Inundación en el nuevo túnel de salida de Madrid hacia la A-5. / CLAUDIO ÁLVAREZ

Un nuevo túnel de la M-30 se inunda horas después de ser inaugurado por Gallardón

El subterráneo, de 2,3 kilómetros, permite salir desde la glorieta de San Vicente hasta la A-5

VERA GUTIÉRREZ CALVO / JAIME G. TRECEÑO, **Madrid**

Ha costado 133 millones de euros, pero no soportó la lluvia caída durante toda la mañana y se inundó. El nuevo túnel de la M-30, que permite salir directamente desde la cuesta de San Vicente hasta la autovía de Extremadura (A-5), fue inaugurado a media mañana por el alcalde, Alberto Ruiz-Gallardón, y horas después tuvo que ser parcialmente cortado al inundarse un tramo de unos 20 metros —el subterráneo tiene 2,3 kilómetros— bajo el río. "Es normal, muchos túneles de Madrid se han inundado alguna vez en un día de lluvia", alegó un portavoz municipal.

El acto de inauguración, en el que Alberto Ruiz-Gallardón estuvo acompañado por siete de sus ocho concejales de Gobierno y todos los altos cargos de Urbanismo, terminó sobre las 12.30. Dos horas más tarde, los conductores que atravesaban el túnel pudieron ver ya la balsa de agua que se formaba sobre la calzada, en el tramo que, poco después de la boca de entrada, pasa bajo el río.

Los tres carriles que tiene el subterráneo en ese tramo —uno de ellos, no abierto aún al tráfico— habían quedado reducidos a uno, y por él avanzaban en fila los asombrados conductores. Los otros dos carriles estaban anegados, y los operarios habían delimitado la zona con balizas de obra. Una hora después, las balizas flotaban por la calzada. Un portavoz de Urbanismo explicó que a las cuatro de la tarde habían empezado los trabajos para achicar el agua y que hora y media después todo estaba solucionado, y el tráfico, restablecido.

"Han sido 10 centímetros de agua en uno de los dos carriles, y lo han resuelto los propios trabajadores de la obra. Los bomberos han acudido, pero no ha sido necesaria su intervención", afirmó el portavoz municipal, que quiso restar importancia al incidente: "En días de lluvia esto es normal, ha ocurrido en otros túneles. Además, en este caso es más fácil que suceda porque el techo del subterráneo aún no está ajardinado", señaló.

Los grupos de oposición no fueron tan condescendientes. Inés Sabanés, portavoz de IU, habló de "bochornoso espectáculo". "Que a las pocas horas de inaugurarse se haya producido ya una inundación es una vergüenza que esta ciudad no se merece, y menos por las prisas electorales de su alcalde. Habrá que preguntarle si esto forma parte de esa vanguardia europea a la que tanto apela y si es el ejemplo que deben seguir otras ciudades", protestó.

El socialista Óscar Iglesias arremetió contra el alcalde por convertir el túnel en "una piscina" y sus accesos en "pistas de patinaje" sólo por su empeño en "inaugurar las obras". "La lluvia ha puesto en evidencia las deficiencias de las obras", sentenció.

Por la mañana, Ruiz-Gallardón había subrayado que los túneles se están abriendo "en el momento en el que son aptos para la circulación de vehículos", para acabar ya con los desvíos que los conductores llevan dos años soportando. En el nudo de conexión M-30-Avenida de Portugal, por ejemplo, ya han sido inaugurados dos ramales distintos —la salida a la A-5 desde la M-30 Norte y la de ayer, desde la cuesta de San Vicente— y quedan otros dos: el ramal que desde la misma cuesta de San Vicente conduce a la M-30 Sur y el que enlaza el túnel Vicente Calderón-Marqués de Monistrol, desde el sur, con la A-5.

Cuando todos los ramales del nudo estén en funcionamiento, por ahí pasarán bajo tierra 65.000 coches que ahora circulan en superficie, según el alcalde. De ellos, unos 30.000 vehículos —incluidos 1.900 autobuses públicos con 90.000 pasajeros— utilizarán, cada día, el subterráneo abierto ayer.

De izquierda a derecha, Alberto Ruiz-Gallardón, las concejales Pilar Martínez y Ana Botella y el vicealcalde Manuel Cobo, durante la inauguración. / EFE

El alcalde se hará la foto dos veces

V. G. C., **Madrid**

El túnel que ayer fue abierto al tráfico "está por terminar". Lo dijo uno de los técnicos responsables de la obra, y lo aclaró: el subterráneo es "perfectamente apto para circular", pero ni todas las salidas de emergencia están acabadas —tiene 15, y algunas están siendo usadas para transportar material para el carril aún en obras— ni el aspecto es el de un túnel nuevo y reluciente: faltan remates, cubrimientos de luces y de canalizaciones, algún revestimiento...

"Esto es inevitable. La oposición critica que los túneles se abran sin estar perfectamente terminados, pero es que no puede ser de otra manera: hay que ir abriendo tramos para meter por ahí los coches y poder así terminar los ramales que faltan, ahora ocupados por desvíos en superficie. Eso es lo que tiene que hacer una obra como ésta, en plena M-30, sin cortar el tráfico. Lo importante es que lo que se vaya abriendo sea seguro y útil, y lo es", explica Manuel Arnaiz, director general de Infraestructuras.

Arnaiz y el propio alcalde, Alberto Ruiz-Gallardón, subrayaron que "la seguridad está garantizada" a pesar de que varias salidas de emergencia no están operativas: "Si pasara algo, se podría salir a la calle corriendo por el carril en obras", alegó el director general de Infraestructuras.

Así que el túnel se abre sin que la foto sea perfecta, pero eso no es problema. Ruiz-Gallardón quiso dejar claro en su discurso que la inauguración fetén aún está por llegar: "Esto no es una inauguración, es una puesta en funcionamiento. Dentro de unos meses, cuando todas las obras estén terminadas y en uso, sí procederemos a la inauguración completa de todas y cada una", anunció. Es decir, que el alcalde se hace la foto dos veces con cada túnel: una el día que los pone en servicio y otra el día en que, oficialmente, los inaugure.

Un carril en obras

El subterráneo inaugurado ayer soterra todo el tráfico que, desde el centro de Madrid, enlaza con la A-5 para dirigirse al oeste de la región y de la Península. Su trazado de 2,3 kilómetros parte del antiguo túnel de la cuesta de San Vicente, cruza el cauce del río, discurre bajo la avenida de Portugal y vuelve a salir a superficie en el Alto de Extremadura. En el primer tramo tiene tres carriles, pero sólo se han abierto dos: el tercero, aún en obras, enlazará dentro de un mes con el intercambiador de transportes de Príncipe Pío y la M-30 sur.

En el segundo tramo, bajo la avenida de Portugal, los dos carriles se transforman en cuatro al sumar el tráfico proveniente de Marqués de Monistrol (M-30 norte). El túnel paralelo, en sentido entrada a Madrid desde la A-5, aún se está terminando. Las obras han durado 21 meses.

Ruiz-Gallardón destacó que el subterráneo implica también recuperar para el peatón el puente del Rey, construido en 1816 para entrar en la Casa de Campo y usado desde hace décadas como *carretera* por los coches.

Elecciones 27M

M-30, se acabó (por fin)

La colosal reforma del cinturón de la ciudad culmina hoy, dos días antes del inicio de la campaña electoral

La obra estrella del alcalde Gallardón ha costado 3.508 millones. El presupuesto inicial era un tercio más bajo

4.500 personas han trabajado a diario durante tres años para construir 55 kilómetros de túneles. Nueve han muerto

J. SÉRVULO GONZÁLEZ, **Madrid**

Durante casi tres años, miles de madrileños han evitado circular por la M-30. La principal vía de circunvalación de la ciudad estaba invadida por grúas, máquinas y un verdadero ejército compuesto por más de 4.500 obreros. Además, en su interior se guardaba el arma definitiva: las dos tuneladoras más grandes del mundo, según los responsables municipales, bautizadas como *Tizona* y *Dulcinea*. Dos monstruos metálicos que han horadado las entrañas de la capital.

Pero ahora los conductores ya pueden recorrer toda la M-30 sin temor a las máquinas, los cambios continuos de trazado y los peligrosos carriles retorcidos por las obras. El Ayuntamiento de Madrid estrena hoy, dos días antes del comienzo de la campaña electoral, el tramo que pone punto final al proyecto estrella del alcalde, Alberto Ruiz-Gallardón: el túnel sur del *bypass* sur, un atajo que permite atravesar el sur de la ciudad bajo tierra entre el Vicente Calderón y la carretera de Valencia (A-3). Sólo este subterráneo, que mide 5,9 kilómetros, ha costado 622 millones de euros.

Cuando hoy el alcalde inaugure el túnel, podrá respirar tranquilo. Al menos, de momento, porque los nuevos subterráneos ya han sufrido algún problema: tres inundaciones provocadas por roturas de colectores que discurren paralelos al Manzanares.

El proyecto de soterramiento de la M-30 está construido sobre una montaña de cifras mareantes. Sólo su coste asciende a 3.508 millones de euros (IVA incluido), según los responsables municipales. El presupuesto inicial era de 2.500 millones.

A mediados de 2004, la primera máquina desordenó el tráfico en la principal vía de circunvalación, que recorrían más de 300.000 vehículos diarios, desde entonces las empresas concesionarias de la obra —17 constructoras entre las que están las de mayor volumen de España— han reformado 20 tramos. Y han horadado bajo la antigua M-30 más de 25 kilómetros de túneles y casi otros 30 en vías de acceso, nudos, salidas y ramales de conexión con otras vías. El plan municipal, calificado como la infraestructura pública más cara de Europa, tiene ocho túneles que conectan varios distritos.

Algunos de los tramos más complejos han sido los dos túneles que se extienden junto al Manzanares. Este tramo, el más largo con casi ocho kilómetros, posibilita que el río se olvide de los coches. Junto a él habrá un gran parque. Aunque han tenido que ser talados 20.000 árboles.

Construir la serpiente subterránea ha costado la vida de nueve trabajadores, según el sindicato CC OO, y se han producido más de mil accidentes laborales. La gran obra ha tenido un fuerte rechazo vecinal y ha llegado a Bruselas por carecer (al no catalogarla el Ayuntamiento como autovía) de declaración de impacto medioambiental.

La reforma de la M-30 y otros grandes viales

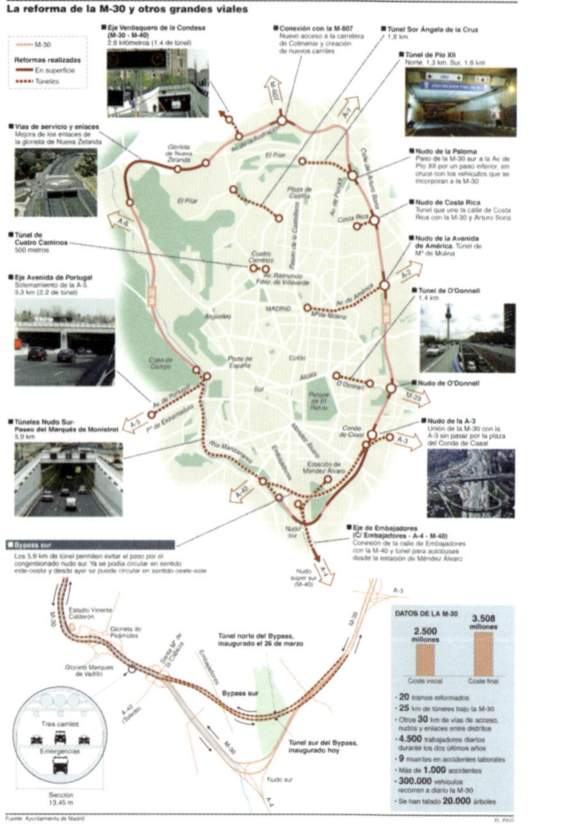

Fuente: Ayuntamiento de Madrid. — EL PAÍS

"Pido al alcalde que rehaga el proyecto"

Melis afirma que la obra de ajardinamiento seguirá causando daños al túnel de la M-30

VIENE DE LA PRIMERA PÁGINA

La inundación, según el ingeniero autor de la reforma de la M-30, Manuel Melis —que hoy imparte clases como catedrático de Ferrocarriles de la Universidad Politécnica—, no tuvo nada que ver con la capacidad de los colectores que discurren paralelos al túnel: "Están perfectamente diseñados y construidos y son capaces de llevar mucha más agua de la exigida por la Confederación [Hidrográfica del Tajo]", asegura. Lo que ocurrió, sostiene Melis, es lo siguiente:

Para montar un paseo ajardinado sobre el tramo de carretera soterrado, Urbanismo lleva semanas elevando la cota del suelo junto al cauce del río, entre el puente de Segovia y el de San Isidro. ¿Cómo? Construyendo, "sin ningún cálculo hidráulico previo ni nada", un murete de unos dos metros de altura. El día de la granizada, el agua que no pudo ser contenida por el estanque de tormentas de San Rufo llegó a ese punto y, en lugar de saltar al cauce del río —como ha ocurrido otras veces—, se quedó embalsada contra el murete, que hizo de presa. Ésa fue la primera "insensatez" que llevó a lo que Melis califica de "gran desastre".

La segunda se habría producido unos metros más abajo, junto al puente de San Isidro: los obreros que estaban colocando los cimientos de una de las pasarelas de diseño que van a construirse sobre el río perforaron hace días una de las losetas de hormigón que cubren el techo de la M-30 soterrada. No llegaron a horadar el túnel —y de hecho los conductores ni lo notaron— pero sí destrozaron parte del hormigón protector, una capa más superficial que impermeabilizaba el subterráneo.

"En lugar de estudiar el proyecto y hablar con quienes hicimos el túnel, rompieron el techo, la capa de compresión de la losa, y quitaron las tierras de encima", protesta Melis.

> Un muro construido junto al río hizo de presa y embalsó el agua de la lluvia

> La instalación de una pasarela habría perforado por error el túnel

Y volvemos al día de la granizada: el agua embalsada por el murete se fue acumulando, corrió en forma de riada hacia el sur y acabó colándose por la loseta agujereada. Todo según la versión del ingeniero.

Eso, por sí solo, no habría bastado probablemente para inundar el túnel: el problema es que tampoco funcionaron después las bombas de achique con las que cuenta el subterráneo y los bomberos tuvieron que evacuar el agua manualmente. Para ese fallo Melis no encuentra explicación, aunque cree que las máquinas de obra pudieron romper "el cable de alimentación de las compuertas del tanque y de la alimentación del pozo de bombeo, con lo que las bombas no pudieron sacar el agua".

El Ayuntamiento y el propio alcalde ya han reconocido que hubo un fallo eléctrico —aún sin causa conocida— que convirtió en inservibles las bombas. El pasado jueves, el vicealcalde Manuel Cobo aseguró: "En el 99% de la vía no hubo problemas, sólo pasó en un colector en concreto, y ésa es la causa que hay que analizar porque tenemos muchísimo interés en saber qué pasó para que no vuelva a ocurrir".

El proyecto Madrid Río, que pretende convertir en un gigantesco jardín urbano el solar al que dio lugar el soterramiento de la M-30, está presupuestado en 863 millones de euros e incluye 11 pasarelas de diseño que cruzarán el río de orilla a orilla. También un "bosque de pinos" en uno de los márgenes del Manzanares, una idea que ya fue muy criticada por Melis antes de dejar el Ayuntamiento y que ahora vuelve a descalificar en su escrito. "Las raíces [de los pinos] son muy dañinas, pueden destrozar la losa del túnel", afirma.

El ingeniero —que no entra a explicar las razones de las otras inundaciones ocurridas en la M-30 desde que se estrenó— comandó, antes de esa obra, la otra gran infraestructura del gobierno de Ruiz-Gallardón: la extensión de la red de metro, con 100 kilómetros nuevos en los ocho años que duró su mandato al frente de la Comunidad.

Manuel Melis no quiere polemizar ahora con el alcalde, a quien dice admirar más que a nadie, pero sí le pide que reconduzca el proyecto Madrid Río. "Le pido que mande a los arquitectos demoler inmediatamente todos esos muros del jardín, y que los diseñadores se ajusten a las cotas necesarias sin recargar las losas. Le pido que mande reestudiar urgentemente todo ese proyecto por alguien que entienda lo que hay debajo, quitando inmediatamente los puntos bajos donde el agua se va a embalsar sin salida sobre el techo del túnel. Le pido de nuevo que mande quitar esos pinos de encima de las losas de techo, y que ordene poner otras especies con raíces menos peligrosas", concluye.

Tres claves para explicar la inundación de la M-30

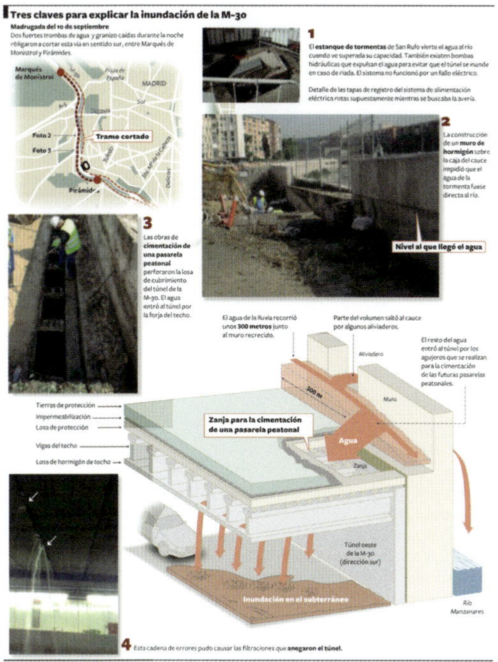

Fuente: elaboración propia. NACHO CATALÁN / EL PAÍS

MANUEL MELIS Catedrático de Ferrocarriles y Geotecnia

Comandó la obra de ingeniería más gigantesca (y la más cara) acometida por un ayuntamiento. Ahora advierte a Ruiz-Gallardón de lo que, a su juicio, no se está haciendo bien tras su marcha

Carta abierta del 'padre' de la M-30

En los últimos 13 años he recibido muchos elogios, demasiados, y sin duda todos inmerecidos, por parte del Excmo. Sr. Alcalde, con ocasión de las enormes infraestructuras que he tenido el honor de hacer bajo su dirección. Por ello, cuando aparecen en la opinión pública dudas sobre la calidad de las obras de soterramiento de la M-30 o sobre precipitación en su construcción me parece mi obligación tratar de explicarlo a los madrileños, que ya iban muchos días de silencio. No pudo ser así en otras ocasiones, como cuando la inundación del Nudo de Valencia, ya que desde el Ayuntamiento yo no podía explicar que después de un año no se tenía aún el permiso para conectar el enorme nuevo colector de alivio de los Abroñigales porque cruzaba bajo unas determinadas vías. Pero hoy, desde la Universidad, creo que no hay inconveniente en hablar con la claridad que la Universidad exige. Aunque me duele bastante eso de "*excusatio non petita*" de ayer. Encima de que intento explicar las cosas... Hay que ver qué importuno es quien lo dijo.

> "Aparecen en la opinión pública dudas sobre la calidad de la obra de la M-30. Es mi obligación explicarlo"

> "Las obras no se hicieron deprisa: el Canal de la Mancha se construyó en 36 meses, el Empire State en 13"

Los túneles de la M-30 son una de las más impresionantes infraestructuras hechas nunca en el mundo. La primera máquina sólo pudo entrar en el río en julio de 2005, y toda la obra se puso en servicio en 22 meses. Pero esto no es un plazo corto sino el plazo normal: los 150 kilómetros de túneles del Canal de la Mancha se hicieron en 36 meses escasos; el Empire State, en 13 meses; los 11 kilómetros y 14 estaciones de la línea 1 del metro de París se construyeron en 1899 por Fulgence Bienvenue en 18 meses; la línea Cuatro Caminos-Sol de nuestro metro la hicieron Otamendi, Mendoza y González Echarte en 26 meses; el enorme anillo de Metrosur, con sus 42 kilómetros y sus 34 estaciones e intercambiadores, se abrió en 34 meses; y nuestro Hotel Palace en 18 meses.

Las obras de la M-30 no se han hecho deprisa, se han hecho como se deben hacer. Lo que ocurre es que ya creemos en España que son normales los lánguidos plazos de otras infraestructuras y nadie protesta. Sólo bajo el mandato de Gallardón se volvió a recuperar la forma correcta de hacer las infraestructuras, y quien le copia las hace bien. Los madrileños deben estar tranquilos porque el proyecto de soterramiento de la M-30 está hecho por las mejores ingenierías consultoras de España, y las obras por las cuatro mejores constructoras de España, es decir, de Europa o del mundo.

Melis visita con el alcalde, en 2004, el tramo en el que iba a ser soterrada la M-30. / ULY MARTÍN

> "Lo que no se puede es, para poner un jardín encima, hacer enormes agujeros en los túneles"

> "Tras mi familia, Gallardón es la persona a la que más quiero; pero creo que no le han contado algunas cosas"

Lo que no se puede hacer y es muy reprobable es, tras terminar las obras y para poner un jardín encima, hacer enormes agujeros en el techo de los túneles por donde circulan los coches. Cualquier gota de agua que caiga del cielo entra naturalmente en el túnel. Y si, además, se han puesto por motivos estéticos unos muros muy altos en los bordes de las calzadas, el agua no puede ir al cauce, se embalsa; y lo que entra en el túnel por esos agujeros ya no son unas gotas, es lo que ha sido.

Aunque ya no trabajo con él y me jubilo enseguida, debo decir que, tras mi familia, creo que es Ruiz-Gallardón la persona a la que más quiero y admiro; y espero no se moleste conmigo por estas líneas, pero me parece que no le habían contado algunas cosas. Le pido que mande tapar esos agujeros del techo del túnel y ordene buscar otras formas de cimentar esas pasarelas de diseño. Le pido que mande a los arquitectos demoler inmediatamente esos muros del jardín, y que los diseñadores se ajusten a las cotas necesarias sin recargar las losas. Le pido que mande reestudiar urgentemente todo ese proyecto del jardín por alguien que entienda lo que hay debajo, quitando los puntos donde el agua se va a embalsar sin salida sobre el túnel. Le pido de nuevo que mande quitar esos pinos de encima de las losas y ordene poner otras especies con raíces menos peligrosas. Y le pido que haga todo esto aunque no quieran algunos de sus subalternos, que veo que no quieren pero ya vemos lo que pasa. Si les hubiéramos hecho caso a ellos aún estaríamos realizando la unión de las líneas 8 y 10 en Gregorio Marañón y el metro al aeropuerto.

Termino. El 29 de junio de 2007 me fui del Ayuntamiento porque cuando me hizo ir a su despacho [el concejal de Hacienda] Juan Bravo lo que me ofreció si seguía allí me hubiera parecido bien cuando acabé la carrera hace 40 años y estaba trabajando en el Cargadero de Aaiún. Así que me volví a la Cátedra como hubiera hecho cualquiera. Por eso no sé con exactitud por qué las bombas tardaron 16 horas en vaciar el agua, que lo hubieran hecho en cinco minutos porque son enormes y magníficas y muy caras.

Los minibuses nuevos irán por el Fuencarral peatonal

P. A., **Madrid**

La segunda línea de minibuses públicos previstos para recorrer el centro de Madrid (M2) discurre desde ayer entre la calle de Sevilla y Argüelles. Los pequeños autobuses, que circulan por el casco histórico, podrán entrar por el tramo de la calle de Fuencarral que el Ayuntamiento de Madrid planea hacer peatonal con una remodelación en 2009.

Los minibuses de color azul y blanco, conocidos como *Gulliver*, incluyen 25 plazas, 18 sentadas y 17 de pie. El interior dispone de una zona trazada para las sillas de ruedas y una rampa de acceso a discapacitados. Los viajes en la nueva línea, que funciona de ocho de la mañana a nueve de la noche, cuestan un euro igual que el resto. Los abonos de transporte público son válidos para este sistema.

El nuevo recorrido de los *Gulliver* se suma al que empezó a operar en febrero entre la plaza de Embajadores y la glorieta de Sevilla. El tamaño reducido de los vehículos, cinco metros de largo por tres de ancho, le permite adentrarse en barrios de difícil acceso, como Malasaña o Conde Duque, tomar curvas impensables para un autobús normal o meterse en túneles vetados al transporte público anterior, como el de Jacinto Benavente.

La velocidad máxima que pueden alcanzar estos vehículos reducidos son 30 kilómetros por hora. El nuevo itinerario parte de la parada situada en la intersección de la calle de Alcalá con Sevilla. Después enlaza la Puerta del Sol, se adentra por Gran Vía, recorre Fuencarral y también los bulevares, según una nota del Ayuntamiento de Madrid. Estos autobuses funcionan con un motor de baterías eléctricas con 12 horas de autonomía que no emite gases contaminantes.

Finaliza el proyecto Madrid Río

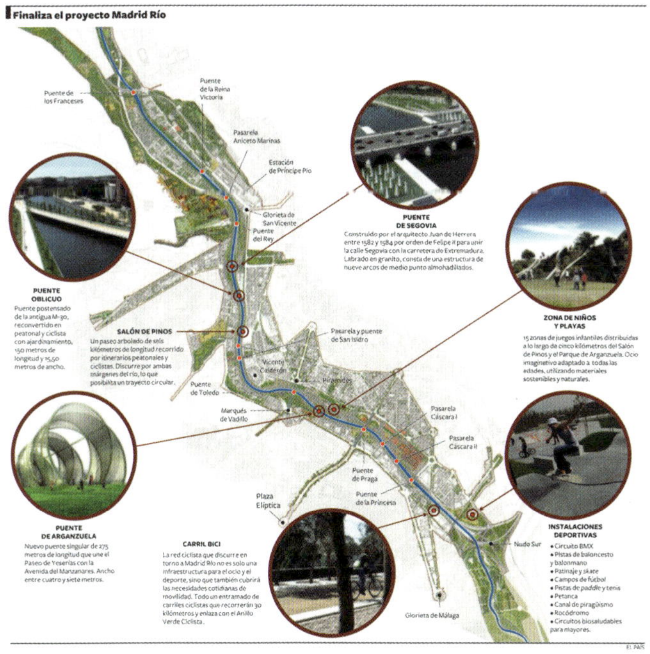

EL PAÍS

Madrid estrena río

El viernes abre sus puertas la última fase del megaproyecto de Gallardón

MARÍA JOSÉ DÍAZ DE TUESTA
VÍCTOR LÓPEZ, **Madrid**

El 15 de abril. Esa es la fecha para que se abra al público el parque de la Arganzuela, el último tramo que queda para completar otro de los planes estrella del alcalde Alberto Ruiz-Gallardón. El soterramiento de la M-30, dos legislaturas, una deuda multimillonaria que los madrileños van a tener que pagar durante décadas e innumerables críticas de la oposición y asociaciones de vecinos, pero Gallardón tiene lo que tantas veces ha señalado: un proyecto que da un nuevo sentido a la ciudad, que vuelca su mirada hacia un río, el Manzanares, que ha sido objeto de chanza durante siglos por parte de locales y visitantes (ya Góngora hacía sangre con su caudal: "¿Cómo has menguado y has crecido? / ¿Cómo ayer te vi en pena y hoy en gloria? / Bebióme un asno ayer, y hoy me ha meado", decía el poeta en un soneto). Una transformación que, asegura Pilar Martínez, la concejal de Urbanismo, "vertebra la ciudad y la hace más sostenible".

En 2004 empezó la transformación de toda la zona con la construcción de los túneles de la M-30, que ha generado una polémica política, social (y judicial) como pocas. Las cifras del proyecto, como no podía ser menos con Gallardón (que, mal que le pese, será recordado como el alcalde faraón), marean. Una intervención a lo largo de casi ocho kilómetros, una superficie de 1.200.000 metros cuadrados justo en el centro de la ciudad, la rehabilitación o construcción de 32 puentes y pasarelas, más de 33.000 árboles plantados y 429 nuevas hectáreas de zonas verdes. Y mucho espacio para caminar, montar en bici, ir con los niños, hacer deporte, tomar el sol o darse algún remojón en verano.

Todo eso, a disposición de los madrileños a partir del viernes, poco más de un mes antes para las elecciones municipales y autonómicas. Un reclamo electoral de envergadura que el PP no quiere desperdiciar, y del que el PSOE no se olvida. El candidato socialista a la alcaldía, Jaime Lissavetzky, ha reiterado estos días que Madrid Río también se ha construido con los fondos que el Gobierno de Zapatero ha aportado a la capital.

PASA A LA PÁGINA 2

El PP presenta la lista más aguirrista para la Asamblea

Diputados del PP cuentan que en las últimas semanas muchos cargos del partido se acercaban a Esperanza Aguirre para pedirle un hueco en la lista regional. Aseguran que la presidenta les decía a todos que sí. Ayer se conoció la composición de la candidatura del PP para la Asamblea. La lista más aguirrista y con más peso del municipalismo está integrada en su mayoría por cargos del Gobierno regional y por regidores, exalcaldes y candidatos locales del PP.

PÁGINA 5

Fin de una pesadilla líquida

Las obras de Madrid Río han tardado ocho años y han costado más de 400 millones

DANIEL BORASTEROS
Madrid

Las obras han durado ocho años. Pero no siempre al mismo ritmo. Hace menos de 500 días, las ratas correteaban por los alrededores del puente de Praga y los empleados municipales vertían un líquido verde indescifrable para los vecinos. En casi toda la margen derecha del río Manzanares, que ayer puso el rótulo de fin a los trabajos, había callejones cortados, baches ondulados, basura acumulada y la vista de un barrizal anudado por una alambrada en el que yacían inmóviles las grúas. "¡Qué hagan algo, aunque sea provisional!", clamaban los vecinos que se diseminan en los seis kilómetros que hay entre los puentes de Praga y de los Franceses.

Ya lo han hecho. Más de 400 millones después, más del doble de lo presupuestado, y dos elecciones mediante, la tarea ha concluido. Donde antes había una especie de manglar por el que patinaban en fila india los coches ahora hay más de 20.000 árboles. En las mismas zonas donde las charcas devolvían los malos olores de los años ochenta hay ahora una especie de estanques con chorros de agua saltarines. En las zonas donde los vecinos, como la octogenaria Carmen, se lamentaban de que no había ninguna pasarela para cruzar a "la civilización" ahora hay dos puentes nuevos que se iluminan y parecen túneles del viento.

> La zona cuenta con más de 20.000 árboles y diferentes zonas de ocio

> Algunos colectivos han visto cómo se aceptaban sus reivindicaciones

Los afectados vieron primero cómo las grúas tomaban posiciones bajo sus ventanas. Años de vibraciones y siestas interrumpidas. Meses de tortura y veranos con las ventanas cerradas. Después llegó la calma. Pero las calles se habían convertido en un territorio peligroso, un alocado laberinto lleno de agujeros e irregularidades por el reinado de la maquinaria pesada. Después de muchas protestas y algunas sospechas, la dinámica electoral, con su capacidad motora, ha hecho brotar las promesas en forma de árboles y cascadas. De carriles bici y hasta una playa urbana.

Las calles de ese lado del río, una sucesión de edificios habitados por funcionarios de distintos Ministerios, se han revalorizado muchísimo. "Hemos aguantado muchas molestias, ruido y hasta situaciones peligrosas, como que no pudieran entrar las ambulancias, pero ha merecido la pena", concede Rafael, de 42 años y vecino de la ribera. Casi todos los comercios de esa parte de la vía han cerrado a lo largo de estos años. Casi ninguno consiguió sobrevivir al encajonamiento que conllevaron los trabajos. Pero la pesadilla ha terminado. Ahora hay hasta playa y circuito de *skate*.

Un espacio de 1.210.000 metros cuadrados que desde el pasado viernes está sobreimpreso en dos dimensiones en unos mapas que servirán para no perderse en esta superficie con 17 parques infantiles y numerosas zonas deportivas y de ocio. La información está dividida en seis apartados: ocio, deporte, miradores, "nuevos iconos", conjunto histórico y espacios verdes.

Algunas de las asociaciones vecinales más críticas con el proyecto y, sobre todo, con su proceso, han visto cómo se incluía en el plan final algunas de sus reivindicaciones. Las alegaciones se hicieron en abril de 2008, hace tres años. En ese periodo, las obras permanecieron en punto muerto, "porque los avances se están dando en los despachos", según se justificó en su momento el Consistorio. En la reanudación de los trabajos, como no se ha cansado de repetir el candidato socialista Jaime Lissavetzky, influyó la inyección económica del Plan E gubernamental, que finalmente ha supuesto un 6% del presupuesto global.

DE LA PIQUETA A LA VEREDA. Las obras de soterramiento de la M-30 convirtieron en 2006 la zona sur de esta vía en una zona llena de grúas, de piquetas, de obreros y de entradas y de salidas a la calzada que asemejaban a un rally urbano. Cinco años después, el terreno ganado al asfalto, que ahora transcurre por los túneles, se ha convertido en un conjunto de veredas, de parques y de zonas de ocio. / REPORTAJE FOTOGRÁFICO DE KIKE PARA

INTERNATIONAL

International

Once work on Madrid Río was completed, the project began to appear in the foreign press. European newspapers such as *Il Corrirere della Sera, Die Welt* or U.S. dailies such as *The Wall Street Journal* or *The New York Times* published reports on the park.

南方周末 *(Nanfang zhoumo)*

Country China
Headline 马德里：城市改造风雨兼程
"Madeli: Chengshi gaizao fengyu jiancheng"
[Madrid: the vicissitudes of rapid urban transformation]
Date of publication July 8, 2010
Author / agency 孟登科
Meng Dengke
Number of words / characters 1,406 Chinese characters
Link www.infzm.com/content/47285

The Wall Street Journal

Country United States
Headline "Architect Ginés Garrido Walks Around Madrid"
[El arquitecto Ginés Garrido se pasea por Madrid]
Date of publication April 8, 2011
Author / agency Pablo Domínguez
Number of words / characters 734 words
Link http://online.wsj.com/article/SB10001424052748703806304576236373318065778.html?KEYWORDS=madrid+rio

Iltalehti

Country Finland
Headline "Madrid sai keinotekoisia hiekkarantoja"
[Madrid receives artificial beaches]
Date of publication April 15, 2011
Author / agency STT-AFP
Number of words / characters 94 words
Link http://www.iltalehti.fi/matkajutut/2011041513557986_ma.shtml

The Independent

Country United Kingdom
Headline "Sizzling, landlocked Madrid gets cool new 'beach'"
Date of publication April 16, 2011
Author / agency AFP
Number of words / characters 656 words
Link www.independent.co.uk/travel/news-and-advice/sizzling-landlocked-madrid-gets-cool-new-beach-2268805.html?origin=internalSearch

Reforma

Country Mexico
Headline "Pasea por la ribera del Manzanares"
[Strolling the Banks of the Manzanares]
Date of publication May 8, 2011
Author / agency Carlos Rubio
Number of words / characters 1,434 words
Link Link unavailable

Clarín

Country Argentina
Headline "'La joya del río' reluce en Madrid"
["The River's Jewel" Glitters in Madrid]
Date of publication May 31, 2011
Author / agency Daniel Moya
Number of words / characters 982 words
Link www.clarin.com/arquitectura/titulo_0_490750923.html
(link inoperative at the time this document was published)

Le Figaro

Country France
Headline "Vivre Madrid"
[Living Madrid]
Date of publication October 29/30 2011
Author / agency Unidentified
Number of words / characters 2,900 words dedicated to Madrid Río, approx.
Link Link unavailable (see: www.ananance.com/editorial/_news_lefigaro.htm)

Madrid Río in *Le Figaro*

In its weekend supplement, *Le Figaro Partner*, the Paris daily, *Le Figaro*, published a ten-page insert on current events in the city of Madrid. Pages 1, 3, and 5, which are more-or-less half the insert's content (the rest are publicity pages), feature a four-section report on the Madrid Río project with photographs by Ana Nance. The first section serves as a front page and presentation to the reader, describing the city's attractions, including the new environmental quality offered by the Manzanares River project as well as its effect on lifestyles in the city's southwestern neighborhoods. The second, *Madrid Río Reinvents the Concept of Strolling,* offers a very succinct three-column description of the phenomenon of a new park in the middle of the city. A separate section on that same page — a single, double-width column — discusses the contribution to cultural activity constituted by the newly rehabilitated former municipal slaughterhouse. Finally, the newspaper publishes an interview with Daniel Canogar concerning his ornamentation of the twin concrete bridges constructed over the river. The interview is illustrated with a large-format photograph showing the mosaics created by that artist. The report bears no byline, which would seem to indicate that it is totally based on an official press release by Madrid's municipal government.

Le Monde

Country France
Headline "Madrid réconciliée avec le rio Manzanares"
[Madrid Reconciled with the Manzanares River]
Date of publication December 14, 2011
Author / agency F.E.
Number of words / characters 218 words
Link www.lemonde.fr/cgi-bin/ACHATS/acheter.cgi?offre=ARCHIVES&type_item=ART_ARCH_30J&objet_id=1178037&xtmc=madrid_rio&xtcr=3

The New York Times

Country United States
Headline "In Madrid's Heart, Park Blooms Where a Freeway Once Blighted"
Date of publication December 26, 2011 (online edition)
December 27, 2011 (print edition)
Author / agency Michael Kimmelman
Number of words / characters 1,415 words
Link www.nytimes.com/2011/12/27/arts/design/in-madrid-even-maybe-the-bronx-parks-replace-freeways.html?pagewanted=all&_r=1&

Madrid Río in *The New York Times*

In early December 2011, the architecture critic and regular New York Times writer, Michael Kimmelman, visited Madrid. He had organized his trip for the exclusive purpose of visiting the new parks on the banks of the Manzanares River in order to publish an article with his impressions.

His airplane landed on December 7 and he spent the next day calmly reconnoitering the area. At midmorning, he met Pilar Martínez the municipality's top urban planning official at a bar near the park, alongside the Puente de Segovia. On a later walk, he was accompanied by three people, including Ginés Garrido, team director, to whom she asked numerous questions. He also briefly interviewed a few passers by. Less than three weeks later, he published the report listed above on the front page of that prestigious newspaper. The municipal government celebrated this event and immediately publicized it through social networks and on its webpage.

The article is divided into various parts. It begins with a somewhat literary description of his walk. Then, it puts the park in context, comparing it to other ambitious projects carried out in cities around the world, including the author's own, New York. Through literal quotes of comments by some neighbors, Kimmelman again focuses the text on the city of Madrid to describe the previous conditions of the spaces alongside the river, including, of course, the highway built there in the seventies, whose rerouting underground made the new park possible. He positively values the results, the organization of the competition and the results, which he characterizes as "discreet and practical," eschewing the spectacular, and thus, "more American than European." He also supplies a few figures, including the official budget and the number of trees planted.

The article ends with a reflection on the possibility of exporting certain efficient practices to the United States, and with praise of the eminently public character of these spaces that did not need any commercial interest to justify their construction. Millennium Park in Chicago is mentioned as an example. The last few lines contain an undisguised criticism of the "oversized footbridge" constructed to cross the park, a work by Dominique Perrault underwritten by the municipal government, which was "evidently nervous about leaving the project without a new architectural landmark... "

The Sydney Morning Herald

Country Australia
Headline "Roads going underground"
Date of publication January 20, 2012
Author / agency Michael Kimmelman
Number of words / characters 844 words
Link http://smh.domain.com.au/neighbourhoods/roads-going-underground-20120120-1q96o.html

Diario Libre

Country Puerto Rico
Headline "Madrid Río. Esta obra pública madrileña ha recuperado la ribera y las aguas del río Manzanares"
[Madrid Río. This Public Work in Madrid has Recovered the Banks and Waters of the Manzanares River]
Date of publication January 27, 2012
Author / agency Erick Dorrejo
Number of words / characters 231 words
Link www.diariolibre.com/espacios/2012/01/27/i321856_madrid-rio.html

Die Welt

Country Germany
Headline "In Madrid ist ein Park der Superlative entstanden"
[A Superlative Park is Born in Madrid]
Date of publication April 5, 2012
Author / agency Simon P. Balzert
Number of words / characters 1,018 words
Link www.welt.de/reise/staedtereisen/article106157967/In-Madrid-ist-ein-Park-der-Superlative-entstanden.html

Madrid Río in *Die Welt*

This Hamburg-based newspaper covered the project in an extensive report by its Madrid correspondent, Simon P. Balzert. That article mentions the newness of the large park over recently dug tunnels in the city center. The text begins with a brief reference to the Manzanares River's recent past, when it was hidden by a highway and forgotten by Madrid's inhabitants. It then briefly mentions the work of rerouting the M-30 underground, which freed the space now occupied by the new park. To construct his narrative, the author quotes several citizens and then, to give the reader an idea of the enormity of the project, he offers data such as the number of trees planted or of streetlamps and benches installed in the park. On one hand, he emphasizes how well the project was carried out, its singular new bridges, and the manner in which historical monuments have been given their rightful place thanks to the project. On the other, he mentions how fully it has been accepted by the citizenry that has received this large-scale operation along with the increased value of the real estate in its area of influence. The report is rounded out with numerous photographs that concentrate especially on the bathing area in Arganzuela Park, which is popularly known as the Playa de Manzanares.

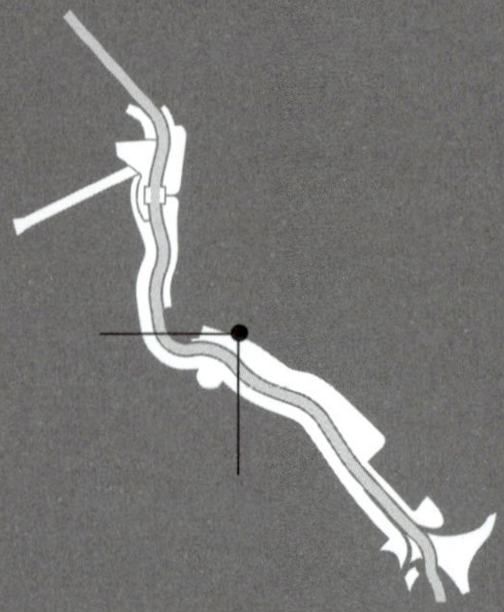

4. SIX LANDSCAPES OF MADRID

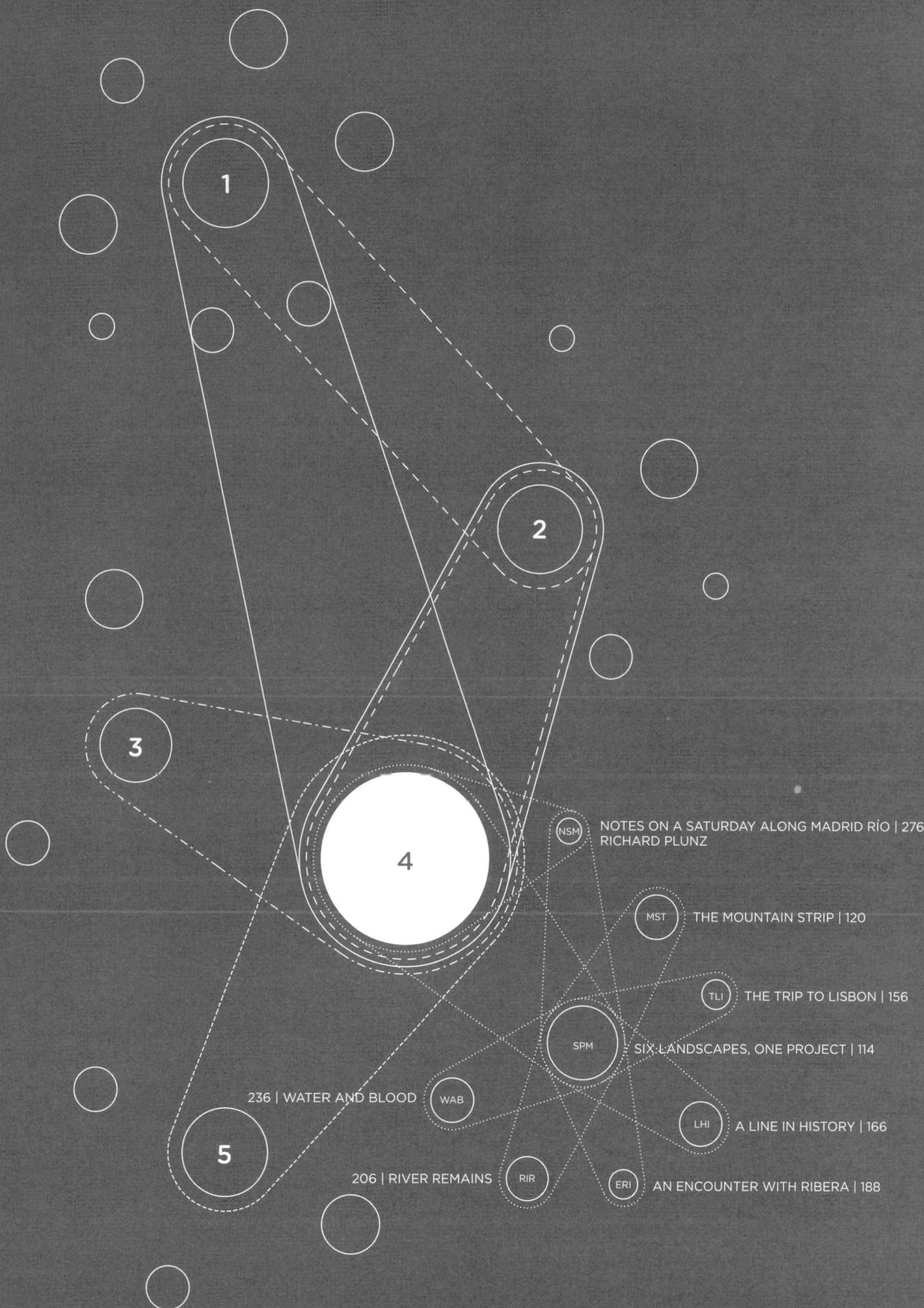

SIX LANDSCAPES, ONE PROJECT

In early 2004, the city of Madrid looked on as, day by day, an enormous and violent wound opened alongside the scrawny river that crosses it. A wound over six kilometers long appeared as preparations were made to run the western section of the M-30 beltway underground. While construction was under way, the 200,000 vehicles that use that section on a daily basis were provisionally rerouted along the devastated riverbanks and even through a part of the river's bed, which had been drained for the occasion. The wound began to stabilize in April 2007 when the tunnels opened to traffic and motor vehicles definitively disappeared from the riverbanks, eagerly occupying their new lair underground. The mark left after their departure had the same surface area as El Retiro, the city's most important historic park, and it was as long as the longest of Madrid's major traffic axes, the Paseo de la Castellana, between Plaza de Castilla and Atocha Train Station.

The significance of this space recovered for the citizenry considerably surpasses the ineluctable, immediate, and direct operation carried out to landscape its naked soil. At the very least, a conscious regeneration of the entire length of that empty space had to include the following: reestablishing links among formerly isolated neighborhoods; bringing them closer to the city center, insuring access on the part of the most socially disadvantaged citizens to the improved quality of life brought by this new environment; actively implementing official and unofficial initiatives for the use of public space as a medium for personal and social relations; globally reconsidering means of transportation in light of the new availability of spaces where non-contaminating vehicles can be used; applying specific treatment to the urban landscape by constructing new surroundings for urban architecture; restoring settings in which to insert elements with historic value and heritage; implementing predominantly collective uses; establishing new itineraries and connections both along the park and across it, with the river as their nexus, origin, and destination. All of these predictable consequences were among the proposal's initial objectives and together they define a part of the city in which the river has become a new and central urban element as well as a gateway to connect the constructed city (which is actually just another aspect of the Manzanares River's middle course) with its outer territories, that is, those settings that still retain a natural character rooted in the river basin.

Therefore, the challenge of returning riverside lands to Madrid after years of vehicular subjugation becomes a question of suturing the city's wound, of bringing unity to its new fabric. But it also becomes a question of infrastructures, where the construction of a new environmental axis not only fosters collective use but also helps us rediscover a way to connect physical and human geography, joining the most preserved medium with the most artificial and modified space.

The common strategy underlying these goals to generate a global project addresses two very different but complementary aspects. First, making it possible for the new structure to respond to urban needs and deficiencies, and even to foresee those yet to appear. And second, casting the entire project in a legible language capable of bringing coherence to the recovered space, imbuing it with a specific quality, a distinctive character based on the definition of each setting in terms of its structural, constructive, and formal resources. The underlying arguments needed to articulate this coherence have been discovered among the multiple data offered by the territory itself, and these data come from both the natural environment and the landscape transformed by humanity.

There are therefore referential elements that have become parameters or figurative resources to unify the solutions contained in the project, and many of them come from analyses of the river basin's varied environments. First, there is the granite substratum that is the Sierra's main geological component. This is the stone most widely used in multiple ways in this project, from the raw boulders scattered around the park to the industrially cut stones used for horizontal paving or vertical facing, as well as the gravel used in all the soil areas. Second, the groups of vegetation that have been installed in an associative manner, appearing just as they do naturally in the river basin. So, the largest plant areas always coexist with tree-bearing surfaces to form symbiotic groups analogous to those appearing naturally along the banks of the Manzanares. Moreover, the materials and sediments carried along by flood waters, such as raw driftwood and river stones, are also present in this park, where they serve as useful elements for play and physical exercise. Other less direct or less-tangible references subject to varying degrees of interpretation have also served to define a unifying language.

HUERTA DE LA PARTIDA
AVENIDA DE PORTUGAL
PUENTE DE SEGOVIA GARDENS
SALÓN DE PINOS
PUENTE DE SAN ISIDRO GARDENS
PUENTE DE TOLEDO GARDENS
PUENTE DE PRAGA GARDENS
SALÓN DE PINOS
VIRGEN DEL PUERTO GARDENS
ARGANZUELA PARK
NUDO SUR
K.P. 2.00
K.P. 3.00
K.P. 4.00
K.P. 5.00
K.P. 6.00
K.P. 7.00
K.P. 8.00
1
2
3
4
5
6
7
8
9
10
THE PARK AND THE CITY
MANZANARES RIVER
CITY PARKS
1 CASA DE CAMPO
2 OESTE PARK
3 CAMPO DEL MORO
4 CUÑA VERDE OF LA LATINA PARK
5 SAN ISIDRO PARK
6 RETIRO PARK
7 SUR PARK
8 PRADOLONGO PARK
9 TIERNO GALVÁN PARK
10 MANZANARES SUR LINEAR PARK
GREEN ZONES
MADRID RÍO PARK
SALÓN DE PINOS
K.P. KILOMETER POINT OF THE MADRID RÍO PARK
1/23,000 20 100 200

For example, elements linked to the place's history, the evolution of preexisting aspects or even the setting's previous infrastructure offer information that can be included in the project as conceptual stimuli.

Beginning with these varied arguments drawn from a nearly automatic analysis of the context in which we are working, we find six different elements that correspond to six different urban situations and also to six groups of references that inspire the reality of the six Madrid landscapes that constitute a single project. These six landscapes include both natural and artificial values resulting from the appropriation, interpretation, adaptation, and transformation of previous data to formulate specific proposals. And, as part of a unified intervention based on a single shared language, these six landscapes constitute a uniform materialization and a series of technical resources that are repeated but that take on a specific character on each occasion as they dialog with the city's diverse circumstances. These six landscapes respond to six ways of contemplating sometimes-distant territories that do not always coincide with the place where the materials are actually installed. For example, the *Mountain Strip* comes from the mountains north of the city; the *Trip to Lisbon* includes visual memories and material images from a voyage to the Atlantic; *A Line in History* is based on the lines that link Madrid's historical center to green areas historically inaccessible to pedestrians; *An Encounter with Ribera* is built around Toledo Bridge, which was designed by that baroque architect from Madrid; *River Remains* is based on recovered elements used to build Arganzuela Park, and sixth and last, *Water and Blood* includes the former municipal slaughterhouse as a key element to round out this group.

Spatial continuity among these six settings depends on the river, but also on the itineraries laid out to connect the city with exterior spaces to the north and south. Those itineraries are completely longitudinal, producing uninterrupted paths for pedestrians or cyclists throughout the river's urban course. The transition from one landscape to the next is always natural and almost imperceptible because the connecting structures do not change along the way and the mechanisms that relate them to each other are overlapping and interconnected. We should not forget that, underneath them all, an extremely artificial element — the tunnel — runs continuously along both banks. Moreover, that buried infrastructure imposes the same necessities on all six settings, all of which must use the same approach and resources to integrate elements that emerge to service the underground highway's installations (ventilation chambers, chimneys, technical rooms, emergency exits, control posts, drains, etc.).

In sum, the project calls for a global approach to multiple and complex questions derived fundamentally from its size and nature as a major urban element inserted in the very center of the city. An urban element that is ancient in terms of infrastructures, historical heritage, edges, and primary connections, yet new in terms of uses, landscaping, images, and secondary connections.

The six landscapes must be understood as a compact group that offers a unified response to the presence of a powerful infrastructure beneath it, built with an extraordinary plentitude of means and procedures that would be impossible in today's climate of global economic crisis. The project makes sense by presenting a manner of responding to that infrastructure, demonstrating that natural material is the most efficient for integrating it, recuperating the environment's capacity to regenerate and interconnect itself, and drawing on renewable resources, such as water, which have been wasted in this city for centuries.

EMERGENCY AND EVACUATION

- SURFACE ROUTE WITH LIVE LOAD OF 1,500 KG/M²
- SURFACE ROUTE WITH LIVE LOAD OF 400 KG/M²
- TUNNEL EMERGENCY EXITS
- AREAS WITH SPECIAL LIVE LOAD OF UP TO 1,500 KG/M²
- MANZANARES RIVER
- MADRID RÍO AREA

TYPES OF TUNNEL SLABS

- SLAB WITH LIVE LOAD OF 2 T/M² + 400 KG/M²
- SLAB WITH LIVE LOAD OF 3 T/M² + 400 KG/M²
- BEAMS WITH LIVE LOAD OF 2 T/M² + 400 KG/M² SOIL HEIGHT
- BEAMS WITH LIVE LOAD OF 3 T/M² + 400 KG/M²
- SPECIAL SPILLWAY SLAB
- SLAB NDER RIVER WITH LIVE LOAD OF 2 T/M² + 6 M WATER ABOVE
- MANZANARES RIVER
- MADRID RÍO AREA

1/23,000 20 100 200

LEISURE ROUTES+ROAD CONNECTIONS

- PEDESTRIAN AND CYCLE ITINERARIES
- PEDESTRIAN ITINERARIES
- ACCOMPANIMENT PEDESTRIAN ITINERARIES
- PEDESTRIAN AND CYCLE CONNECTIONS
  1 MANZANARES NORTE LINEAR PARK
  2 CASA DE CAMPO
  3 MANZANARES SUR LINEAR PARK
- TRANSVERSE PEDESTRIAN CONNECTIONS
  4 TOWARDS PRINCESA-GRAN VÍA SHOPPING DISTRICT
  5 P.º DE EXTREMADURA
  6 TOWARDS CITY CENTER SHOPPING DISTRICT
  7 P.º ERMITA DEL SANTO
  8 TOWARDS LA LATINA SHOPPING DISTRICT
  9 TOWARDS CARABANCHEL
  10 TOWARDS CASTELLANA / P.º DEL PRADO CULTURAL DISTRICT
  11 TOWARDS PAU CARABANCHEL
  12 TOWARDS P.º DELICIAS SHOPPING DISTRICT
  13 TOWARDS CIUDAD DE LOS ÁNGELES AND VILLAVERDE
  14 ENRIQUE TIERNO GALVÁN PARK
- CULTURAL / SPORTING POINTS OF INTEREST
  15 PADDLEBALL COURTS
  16 ERMITA VIRGEN DEL PUERTO
  17 SPORTS COURTS
  18 VICENTE CALDERÓN STADIUM
  19 SPORTS COURTS
  20 BEACH
  21 SOCCER FIELD
  22 PADDLEBALL COURT
  23 SKATE PARK
  24 MANZANARES RIVER INTERPRETATION CENTER
  25 MATADERO
  26 SPORTS COURTS
  27 BMX COURSE
- MANZANARES RIVER
- MADRID RÍO AREA

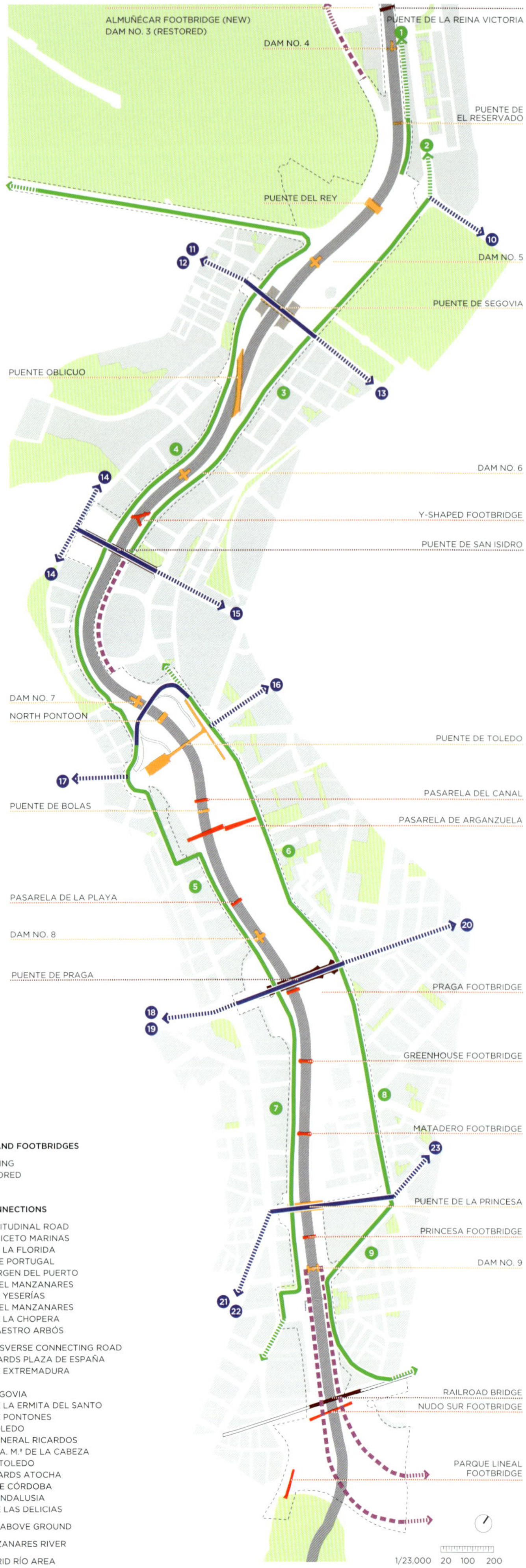

BRIDGES AND FOOTBRIDGES

- EXISTING
- RESTORED
- NEW

ROAD CONNECTIONS

- LONGITUDINAL ROAD
  1 C/ ANICETO MARINAS
  2 P.º DE LA FLORIDA
  3 AV. DE PORTUGAL
  4 P.º VIRGEN DEL PUERTO
  5 AV. DEL MANZANARES
  6 P.º DE YESERÍAS
  7 AV. DEL MANZANARES
  8 P.º DE LA CHOPERA
  9 C/ MAESTRO ARBÓS
- TRANSVERSE CONNECTING ROAD
  10 TOWARDS PLAZA DE ESPAÑA
  11 P.º DE EXTREMADURA
  12 A-5
  13 C/ SEGOVIA
  14 P.º DE LA ERMITA DEL SANTO
  15 P.º DE PONTONES
  16 C/ TOLEDO
  17 C/ GENERAL RICARDOS
  18 P.º STA. M.ª DE LA CABEZA
  19 A-42 TOLEDO
  20 TOWARDS ATOCHA
  21 AV. DE CÓRDOBA
  22 A-4 ANDALUSIA
  23 P.º DE LAS DELICIAS
- M-30 ABOVE GROUND
- MANZANARES RIVER
- MADRID RÍO AREA

PLANT FAMILIES
PINES
MEDITERRANEAN FOREST
DECIDUOUS SLOPE
ATLANTIC FOREST
RIVERSIDE FOREST
FRUIT TREES
BUSHES
ORNAMENTAL PLANTS: HEDGES AND FLOWERS
PLANE TREES
CHERRY TREES
GROUND COVER AND AROMATIC PLANTS
EXISTING TREES
MANZANARES RIVER
MADRID RÍO AREA

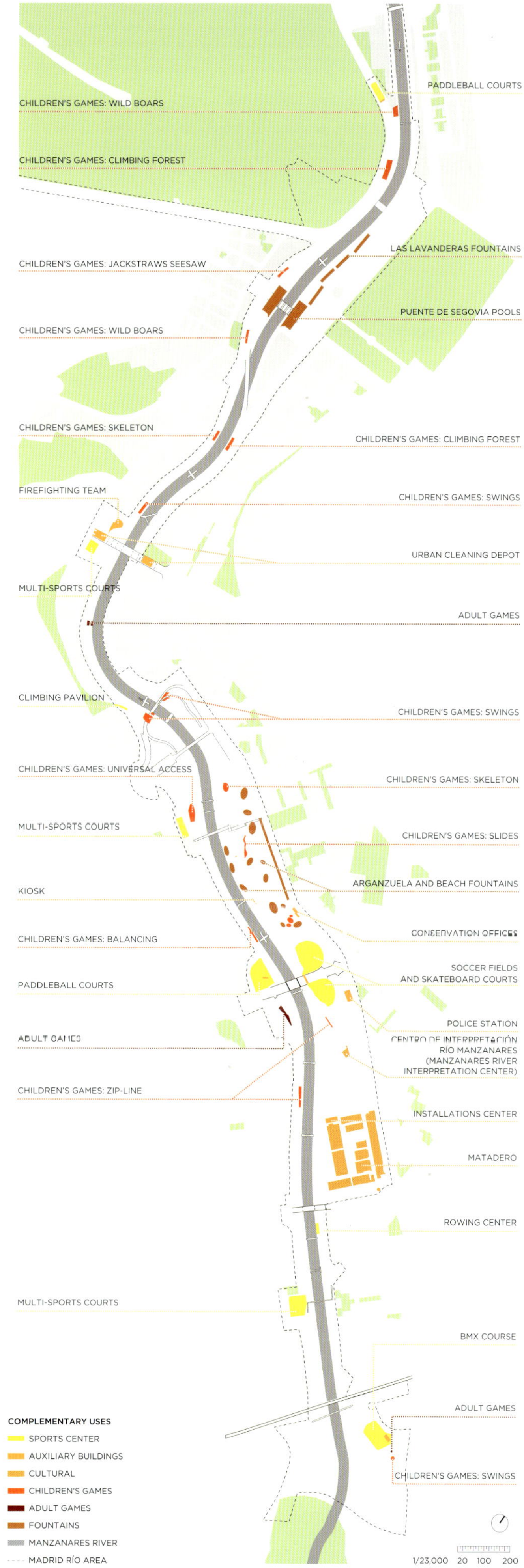
PADDLEBALL COURTS
CHILDREN'S GAMES: WILD BOARS
CHILDREN'S GAMES: CLIMBING FOREST
LAS LAVANDERAS FOUNTAINS
CHILDREN'S GAMES: JACKSTRAWS SEESAW
PUENTE DE SEGOVIA POOLS
CHILDREN'S GAMES: WILD BOARS
CHILDREN'S GAMES: SKELETON
CHILDREN'S GAMES: CLIMBING FOREST
FIREFIGHTING TEAM
CHILDREN'S GAMES: SWINGS
URBAN CLEANING DEPOT
MULTI-SPORTS COURTS
ADULT GAMES
CLIMBING PAVILION
CHILDREN'S GAMES: SWINGS
CHILDREN'S GAMES: UNIVERSAL ACCESS
CHILDREN'S GAMES: SKELETON
MULTI-SPORTS COURTS
CHILDREN'S GAMES: SLIDES
ARGANZUELA AND BEACH FOUNTAINS
KIOSK
CONSERVATION OFFICES
CHILDREN'S GAMES: BALANCING
SOCCER FIELDS
AND SKATEBOARD COURTS
PADDLEBALL COURTS
POLICE STATION
ADULT GAMES
CENTRO DE INTERPRETACIÓN
RÍO MANZANARES
(MANZANARES RIVER
INTERPRETATION CENTER)
CHILDREN'S GAMES: ZIP-LINE
INSTALLATIONS CENTER
MATADERO
ROWING CENTER
MULTI-SPORTS COURTS
BMX COURSE
ADULT GAMES
CHILDREN'S GAMES: SWINGS
COMPLEMENTARY USES
SPORTS CENTER
AUXILIARY BUILDINGS
CULTURAL
CHILDREN'S GAMES
ADULT GAMES
FOUNTAINS
MANZANARES RIVER
MADRID RÍO AREA
1/23,000 20 100 200

HOTEL
HOTEL

MST
THE MOUNTAIN STRIP

Starting point
The nature of the Manzanares River as a thread running through the city from north to south foregrounds the importance of its banks as places where it is possible to link spaces outside Madrid with the inner city itself. As is immediately apparent, the riverbed's linear and persistent condition offers the possibility of inclusion as an element that adds continuity to any urban operation based on it. Thus, the river's dual identity as, on one hand, a connecting element or gateway to areas outside and inside the city and, on the other, as a line on which to establish a spatial continuum, allows us to determine the starting points for a first landscape.

The riverside works as a line, a way in and a way out, but also as a linking axis running the length of the city. The riverbanks become an area open to the nearby landscape, a home for materials and elements contained in the Sierra de Guadarrama, which is omnipresent on the city's horizon. So, a bit of the Sierra can make its way down to the city, crossing it by way of a new green structure that expresses the geographical essence of the nearby north through its primordial elements: vegetation, stone, and water.

The place
The city, a complex artifact, has approached the river in different ways over its history. Until the 20th century, the Manzanares was a distant element, and most of all, a lateral interruption of Madrid. The first buildings kept their distance until its banks were channeled and its floodwaters controlled. Then, beginning in 1950, the compact urban fabric that had always kept its distance on the river's eastern flank crossed it to rapidly develop the barren lands to the west. New, densely built neighborhoods sprang up quickly there and their growth generated two façades that reflect the city's manner of expanding over the years. The east bank, where growth was slow, has retained an open area of some width that serves as a filter between the river and the buildings. But on the west bank, the buildings are much closer to the water, leaving only a narrow space free of construction. That is the bank chosen by the Madrid Río project to bear a reconstruction of the mountain strip that descends from the territories north of Madrid, which also serves as a large green structure connecting different parts of the proposal.

When work to recover the riverbanks began, this narrow band had already been totally transformed by the rerouting of the highway. What occupied the space in a constant and repetitive manner were the technical installations associated with that infrastructure. The tunnels running over six kilometers along this bank also emerge from time to time, belying their supposed invisibility. So the new natural structure had to take root on an artificial base, a building lying down, buried at times and visible at others. There were innumerable technical quarters, emergency exits, and access openings for automobiles, making this a terrain filled with irregularities with which the Guadarrama landscape had to negotiate.

Concepts and character of the proposal
Those were the starting conditions for laying out the Salón de Pinos, which was the name given to the mountain strip expected to coexist with the underground highway. The word "hall" was chosen in reference to linear public spaces like promenades that used to be called "salones" in Spanish places to meet, to see and be seen. Conceptually, the construction of this space is extremely straightforward. It consists of two main autonomous elements that are permanently intertwined over the length of the river's course. First, a strip of trees with the density of a forest, which has been planted in the most radical possible way, wherever there are even minimum conditions for plants to survive. And second, a paved strip that insures the most comfortable access to the entire length of the area. These two units run through the city on the tunnels' back, adjusting their surface to existing streets at times, and not, at others, and adapting their topography to the jutting irregularities of the river's bank and channel. As such, they occupy the full six kilometers of the Manzanares's left bank, that is, the western riverside. The clarity of this solution gives it a character in which constant repetition of details, the rather rough texture of its vegetation, and other accompanying elements generate a unity with a very specific appearance.

Like the other landscapes in this park, the Salón de Pinos has its own singular character, which could be qualified as sober, silent, and tough. And this is not so much the result of specific building solutions applied to given preconditions

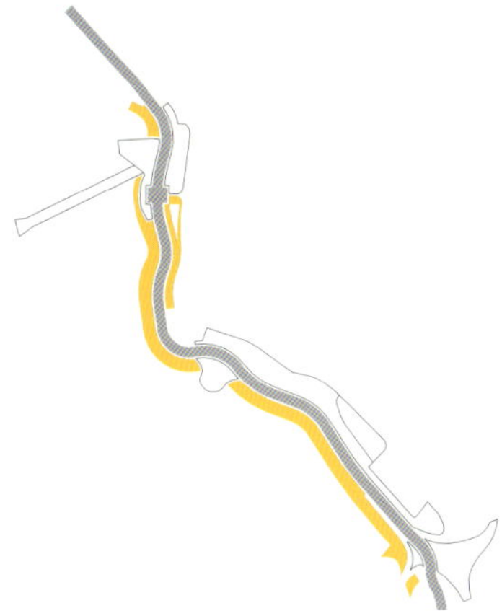

(the riverbank, accesses, relations to adjacent streets, intersections with other urban elements) as to a willingness to bring new forms and languages into the existing city.

Description of the landscape

The Salón de Pinos has become a dynamic axis whose main activities are walking, cycling, and other non-contaminating ways of moving through the shade of pines that should rapidly grow quite large. In section, this area can be viewed as a group of parallel strips running along the riverside from its inner edge, which abuts the river's containment wall and serves as a protective apron against floodwaters, to its outer edge, which consists of slopes planted with aromatic bushes and ramps leading to the city's renovated streets. The uniformity of this solution allows an immediate and specific reading of the space, and the latter's relation with its users and occupants is constant throughout the diverse districts through which it runs. Those districts vary in their degree of affluence on a scale that descends from north to south. In that sense, the Salón allows a social permeability previously unknown in this part of the city, as north-south movements mix with those in the opposite direction, leading to a new, mixed and socially open way of occupying the street. The promenade thus manages to interweave the city's dense fabric, which is drawn to the river for the first time in a way that does not vary over its six-kilometer extension. Where it coincides with the large roadways, it responds by generating new contexts for collective activity, including sports and leisure.

The topography of this continuous landscape is shaped in response to three different problems. First, it must guarantee a return period of 500 years in calculating protection against flooding caused by the river overflowing its banks. That solution has led to the systematic elevation of the river's channel or walls, which is the determining factor in the height of the skirt that serves as the promenade's edge. Second, it must resolve the problem of precisely adjusting the new mountain strip so that it fits properly over a rigid structure that sometimes emerges and sometimes runs deeper, thus transmitting its own volumetric problems to the city's new base level. Third, it must respond to the need to establish longitudinal ties (with the streets that accompany the Salón de Pinos), transversal ones (with the main connections that cross the river, including new and existing pedestrian walkways) and links with other landscape units that are part of the overall park. The demands of this topographical conciliation produce a situation in relief that is almost automatic, as it furnishes the only unified contours capable of responding to such diverse questions.

Technical solutions

The specificity of the substratum underlying this landscape calls for a brief description of the solution adopted in the extremely artificial operation of growing a living layer over the top of a reinforced-concrete tunnel. Shaping a landscape of natural elements — trees, bushes, and stones — over the rigid caisson called for a unique and specific installation.

Six basic operations were combined to make up a layer whose thickness varies between eighty centimeters and three meters. Beginning at the level of the structural slab and ending at surface level, these operations were: first, laying continuous waterproofing in the form of sheets protected by a coat of mortar of consistent thickness; second, draining rainwater with a slight incline and a filter layer of natural gravel of compensated diameters properly protected against settling; third, lightening the load on slabs with very limited load-bearing capacity made up of sheets of expanded polystyrene; fourth, creating a base to anchor the trees, using a steel mesh that is not fixed to the structure but reinforced by the weight of the soil; fifth, laying a natural substratum of earth with two different layers — a mineral layer that allows roots to take hold and receive oxygen, and an organic layer that allows the trees to receive nutrients — and sixth, planting vegetation with a stabilization system that uses biodegradable cables laid in connection with the deep mesh.

This stratified package has been fitted with automatic irrigation set to function in two different stages. The initial stage lasts two years and involves watering only around the undeveloped roots. The second is slower. It will begin three years after planting so that the feeding and growth of the root system occurs in a horizontal direction to generate a thick and interwoven mesh of tree roots in the first ninety centimeters below the surface.

KILOMETER POINT (K.P.) 3.70 OF THE MADRID RÍO PARK

Materials and elements

The landscape of the mountain strip is constructed with materials that combine to generate concrete elements or societies belonging exclusively to that landscape and responsible for its identity. The main elements that coexist in the Salón are, forest, path, soil, edges, and games.
The forest is a single element consisting mostly of plant species associated with woodlands.

The wooded areas combine three species of pine planted according to a slightly modified grid of 3.6 x 3.6 meters, which is the proper layout for repopulating the countryside. Of the three species of conifers planted in this area, 12,209 are *Pinus halepensis* (aleppo pine), 4,023 are *Pinus pinea* (stone pine) and 172 are *Pinus pinaster* (maritime pine). A series of wooden stakes complement the underground anchoring and can be distinguished by color and inclination according to their distance from the river and the slope of the soil where they stand. The bushes planted massively on the slopes consists of low-maintenance aromatic plants that need little water: *Lavandula spp.* (lavender), *Rosmarinus officinalis* (rosemary), *Santolina chamaecyparissus* (lavender cotton or Santolina) and *Salvia Officinalis* (sage). The choice of trees was deliberately carried out in lumber production fields with climates analogous to Madrid's. Besides the healthiness and strength of each tree, attention was given to their irregular shape, with abundant curves, twists, and exceptions. In that sense, the natural character of the forest is accentuated and influences the urban atmosphere. The green structure is completed with the punctual placement of large discarded granite boulders brought from mountain quarries, which appear like witnesses to an ancient watercourse.

The path runs through the woods like a loose ribbon. In fact, it is a length of semi-rigid draining pavement bordered by a granite strip that gently lifts it above ground level. The winding layout of this path effectively expresses the continuity of itineraries along the entire length of the river's course through the city. The strength of its layout and its clear presence on the horizontal plain are complemented by the pattern established by series of vertical elements for illumination, which are at regular distances and equipped with a number of lights that varies according to the condition and width of the spaces to be lit.

The surface not occupied by the path has a soft, fragmented texture of decomposed granite. It includes systems to aerate and water the plants as well as lighting units that color the tops of the trees. This clean surface can be shaped to fit the sometimes-eventful topography that includes the variable geometry of the tunnel roofing. Its non-urban character constitutes a twisting inorganic layer bearing trees in a manner analogous to nature.

The edges of the Salón de Pinos allow smooth transitions at different levels through curbing, copings, benches, ramps, stairs, walls, and protection. All of these elements are entirely of granite, the only kind of stone present in all of this project's landscapes. The multiple nature of the problems to be resolved has led to a systematic catalog of model solutions

that are repeated as need be. Each element is adapted to each particular case without losing the characteristics that make it part of a preconfigured system.

Games appear in small playgrounds that form a coherent, uniform, and articulated group throughout the landscape. Their form and the way they have been installed generate a strong contrast between the apparent naturalness of each group and the profound artificiality of its construction. Each playground constitutes a small setting that differs from the rest of the woodlands that make up the mountain strip. A randomly distributed group of robinia trunks with dramatically irregular shapes create a space for the playground elements themselves, which are also built from practically unprocessed and irregularly shaped trunks. The use of wood as a basic material allows children to identify and establish relations with the natural surroundings, experiencing sensations with all their senses and understanding the mechanisms that distinguish risk from danger.

Landscape and city

This landscape took shape as a powerful idea with an undeniably unified character that made it a determining element thanks to its capacity to articulate the park's free space, paths, and roadways and consolidated building. At the same time, it provides an axis for continuous soft mobility that was immediately adopted by residents of both local neighborhoods and those much farther from the river.

DIAGRAM OF THE SALON DE PINOS

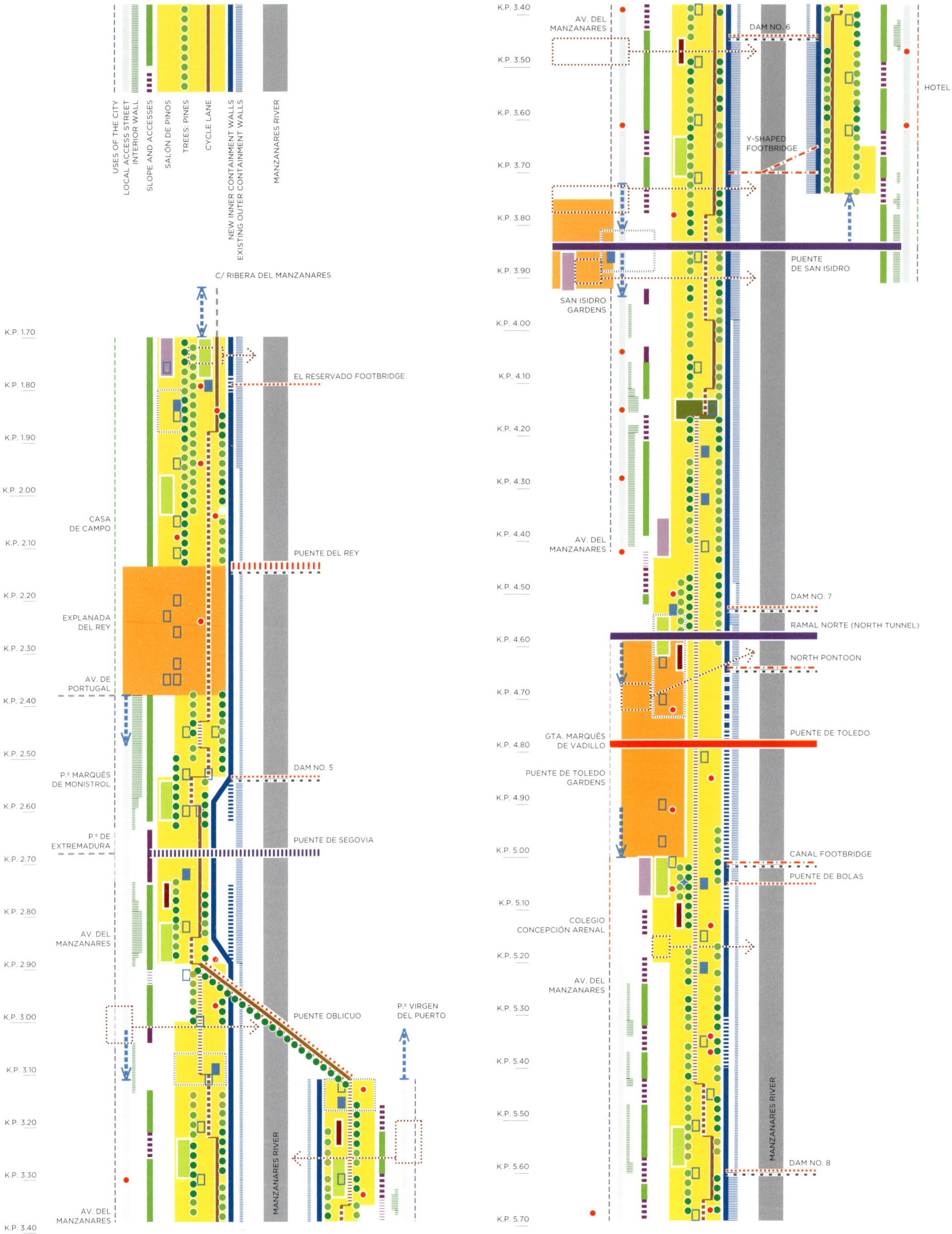

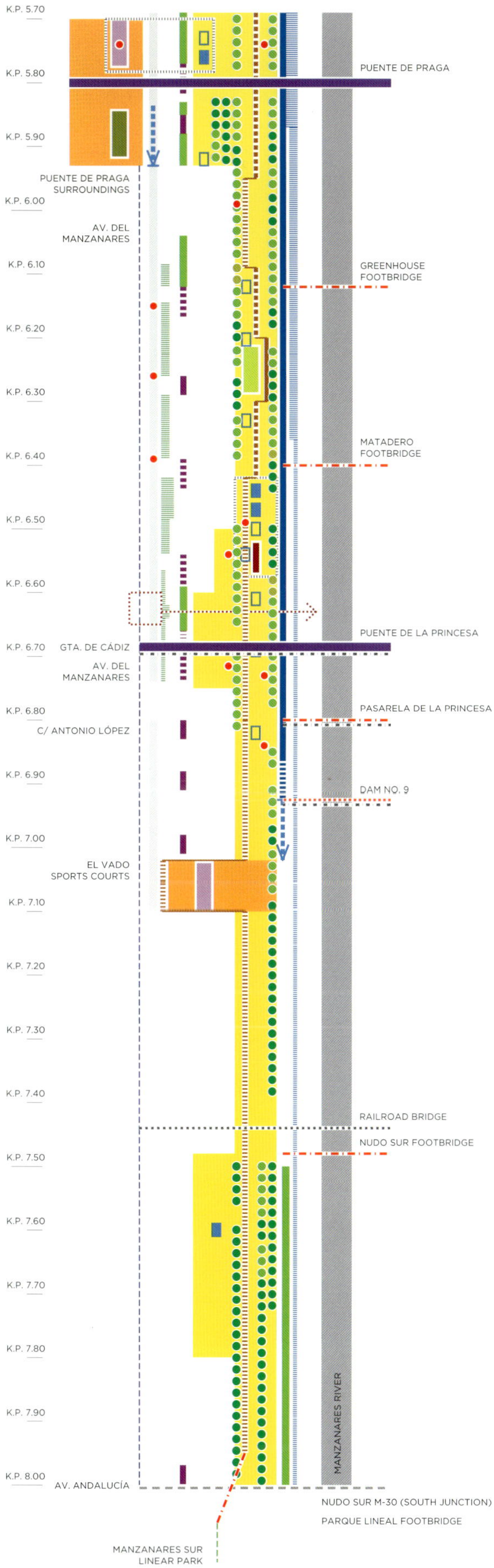

BORDERING THE RIVER

- EXISTING OUTER CONTAINMENT WALLS: <1 M WIDE
- EXISTING OUTER CONTAINMENT WALLS: 1-2 M WIDE
- EXISTING OUTER CONTAINMENT WALLS: >2 M WIDE
- NEW INNER CONTAINMENT WALLS: MASSIVE
- NEW INNER CONTAINMENT WALLS: RAILING
- NEW INNER CONTAINMENT WALLS: STEP

SALÓN DE PINOS DIMENSIONS

- <25 M WIDE
- 25-30 M WIDE
- >30 M WIDE
- AREAS OF INTERFERENCE

POSITION OF CYCLE LANES

- <5 M FROM OUTER CONTAINMENT WALLS
- 5-10 M FROM OUTER CONTAINMENT WALLS
- >10 M FROM OUTER CONTAINMENT WALLS

BORDERING THE CITY

- LOCAL ACCESS ROADS
- INNER WALL TO STREET: <1 M HIGH
- INNER WALL TO STREET: 1-2 M HIGH
- INNER WALL TO STREET: >2 M HIGH
- SLOPE

ENTRANCES FROM THE CITY

- LEVEL
- RAMP
- STAIRS

CITY USES

- RESIDENTIAL
- EQUIPMENT
- PUBLIC SPACE
- GREEN ZONES

BRIDGES AND FOOTBRIDGES

- RESTORED FOOTBRIDGES AND PEDESTRIAN DAMS AT GROUND LEVEL
- RESTORED BRIDGES FOR PEDESTRIAN AT GROUND LEVEL
- RESTORED BRIDGES FOR PEDESTRIAN ABOVE GROUND LEVEL
- NEW FOOTBRIDGES AT GROUND LEVEL
- VEHICULAR TRAFFIC BRIDGES AT GROUND LEVEL
- VEHICULAR TRAFFIC BRIDGES ABOVE GROUND LEVEL
- RAILROAD BRIDGE ABOVE GROUND LEVEL
- INSTALLATIONS WALKWAY

TREES

- *PINUS PINEA* (STONE PINE)
- *PINUS HALEPENSIS* (ALEPPO PINE)
- *PINUS PINASTER* (MARITIME PINE)

USES OF THE SALÓN DE PINOS

- CHILDREN'S GAMES
- ADULT GAMES
- SPORTS
- KIOSKS

TECHNICAL AND SERVICE ELEMENTS

- EMERGENCY EXITS
- ELEVATED VENTILATION TOWERS
- FLUSH VENTILATION GRILLS
- STORM WATER TANK
- SPILLWAYS
- TECHNICAL ROOMS
- TUNNEL EXIT
- TUNNEL ENTRANCE

K.P. 6.50

SALÓN DE PINOS AT AVENIDA DEL MANZANARES

PLAN. K.P. 3.20 - K.P. 3.35

SECTION TYPE s1

1/750 0 1 2 3 4 5 10

SALÓN DE PINOS AT NUDO SUR (SOUTH JUNCTION)

PLAN. K.P. 7.50 - K.P. 7.65

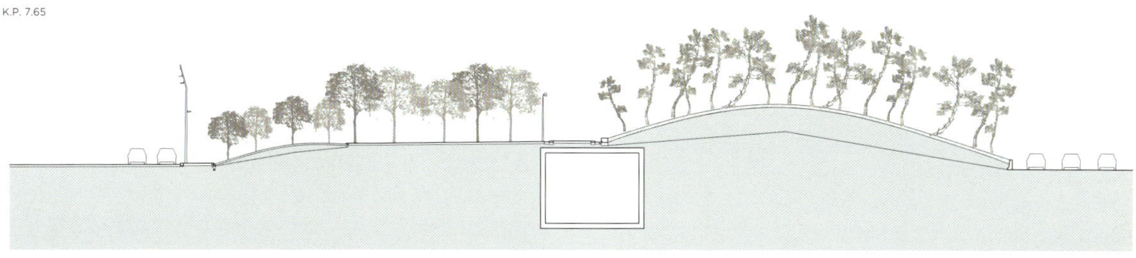

SECTION TYPE s1

1/750 0 1 2 3 4 5 10

K.P. 760

SENDA CICLABLE
Prioridad
Peatonal

CHILDREN'S GAMES

Structure White locust and oak tree trunks (climbing woods)
Slides, rings, and metal pieces of stainless steel
Nets of natural rope with galvanized steel cores
Completion date 2010

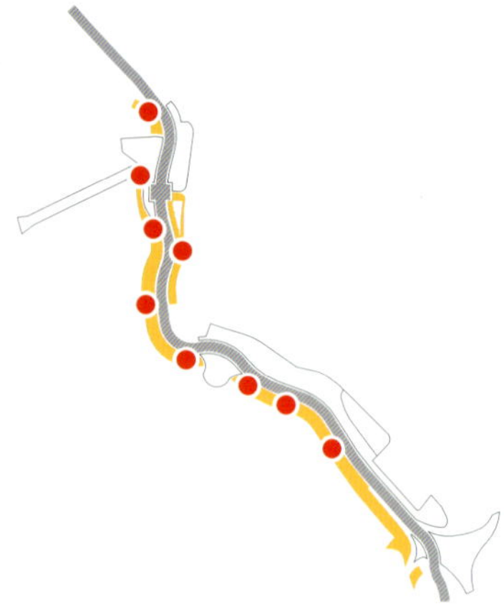

Architects* Burgos & Garrido, Porras La Casta, Rubio & Álvarez-Sala
with West 8
* COMPLETE CREDITS OF THE MADRID RÍO PROJECT APPEAR ON PAGE 327, EXCEPT THE ONES SPECIFICALLY MENTIONED ON THEIR OWN DATA SHEETS.

K.P. 1.75 - K.P. 2.00 - K.P. 2.60 - K.P. 2.85 - K.P. 3.25 - K.P. 3.65 - K.P. 4.60 - K.P. 5.05 - K.P. 5.55 - K.P. 6.25

WILD BOAR. SWINGS. SPIDERWEB. CURVE TRACK. MARBLES TABLE AND SEESAWS

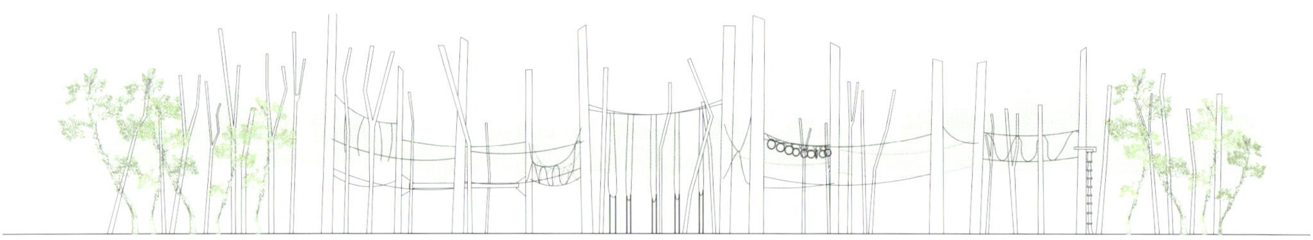

CLIMBING WOODS

HAMMOCKS. BALANCING BLOCKS AND JACKSTRAWS SEESAW

R.P. 285

DAMS

Length on axis 42 m
Length between supports 16.50 m
Deck width 3.80 m
Structure Metal beams with wooden deck over restored original structure
Date of construction existing structure 1955
Date of completion 2010

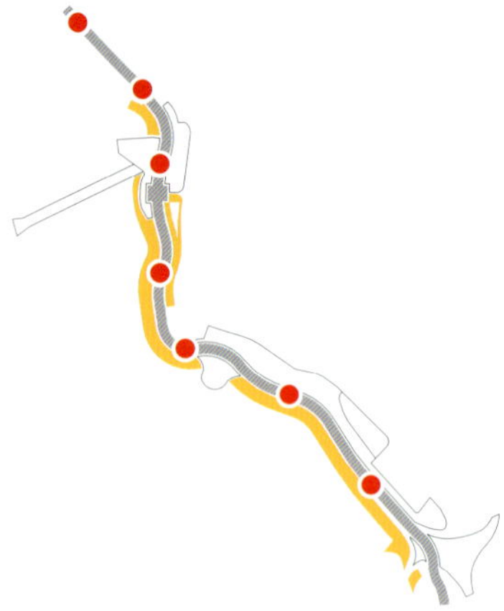

K.P. 0.31 - K.P. 1.50 - K.P. 2.45 - K.P. 3.44 - K.P. 4.52 - K.P. 5.60 - K.P. 6.92

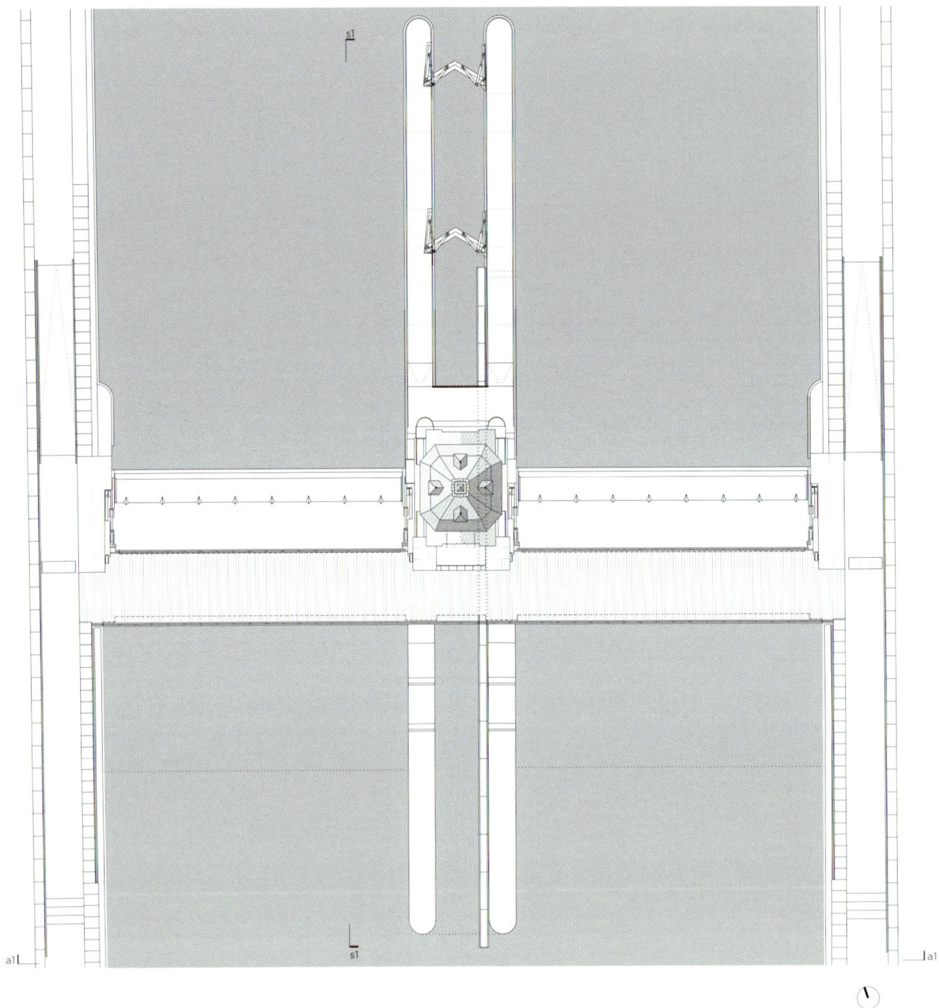

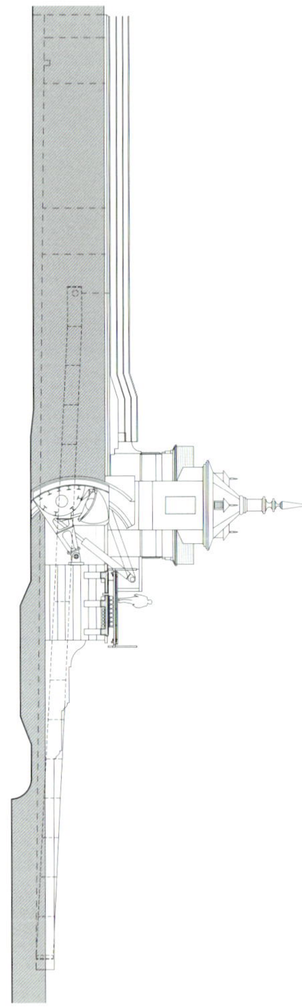

SECTION s1

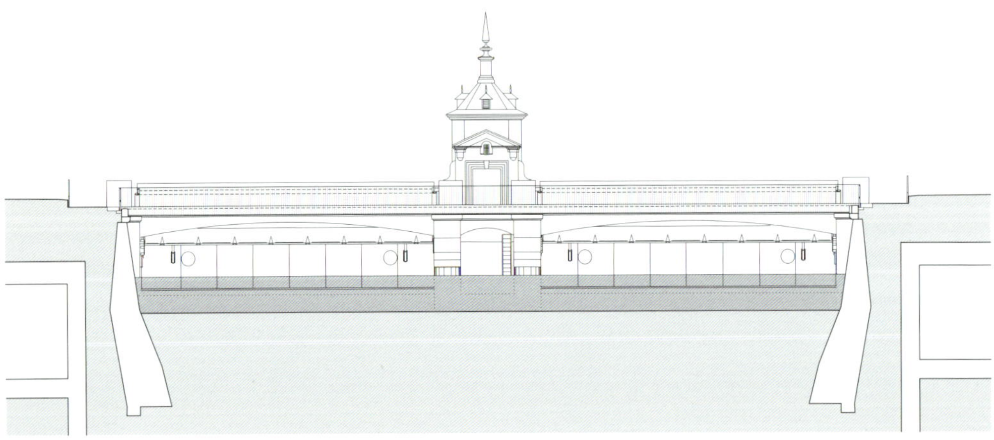

ELEVATION a1

1/400 0 1 2 3 4 5 10

R.P. 3.44

ALMUÑÉCAR FOOTBRIDGE

Length on axis 47.50 m
Length between supports 40 m
Deck width 4 m
Structure Carbon-fiber box girder ballasted with pieces of prefabricated concrete
Date of completion 2011

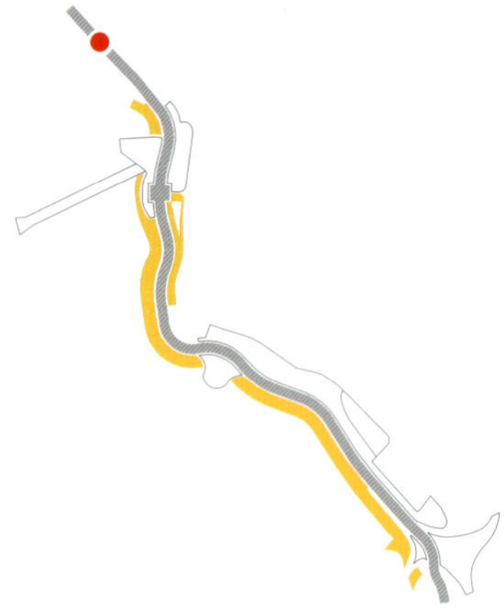

K.P. 0.88

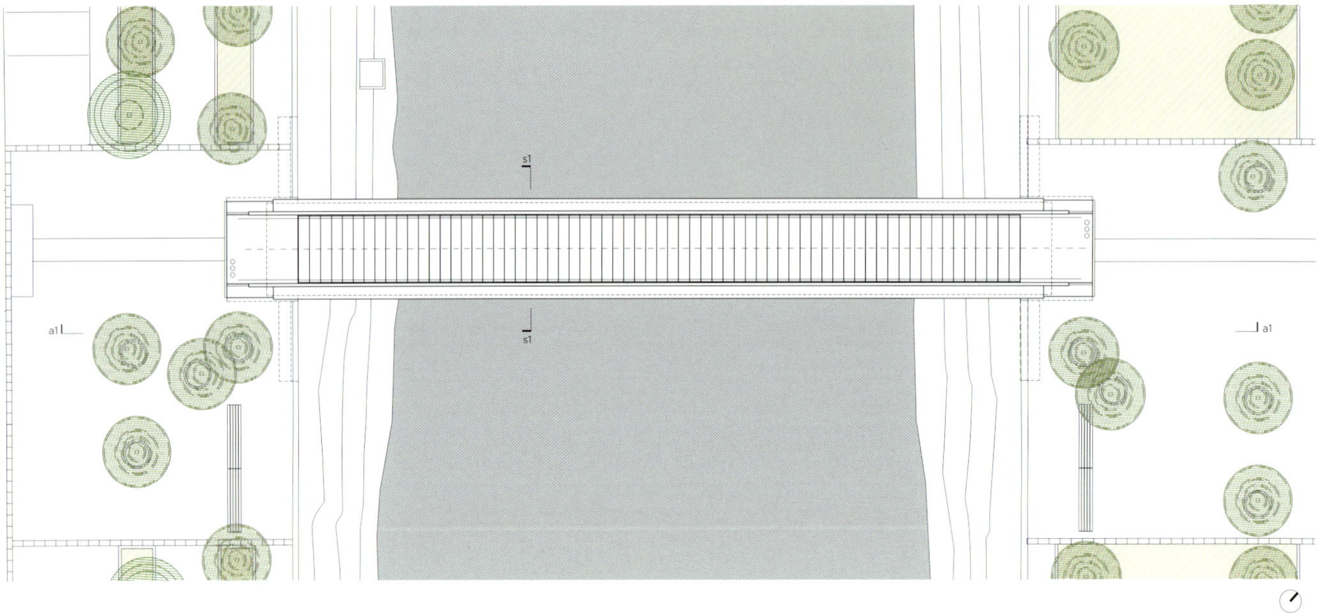

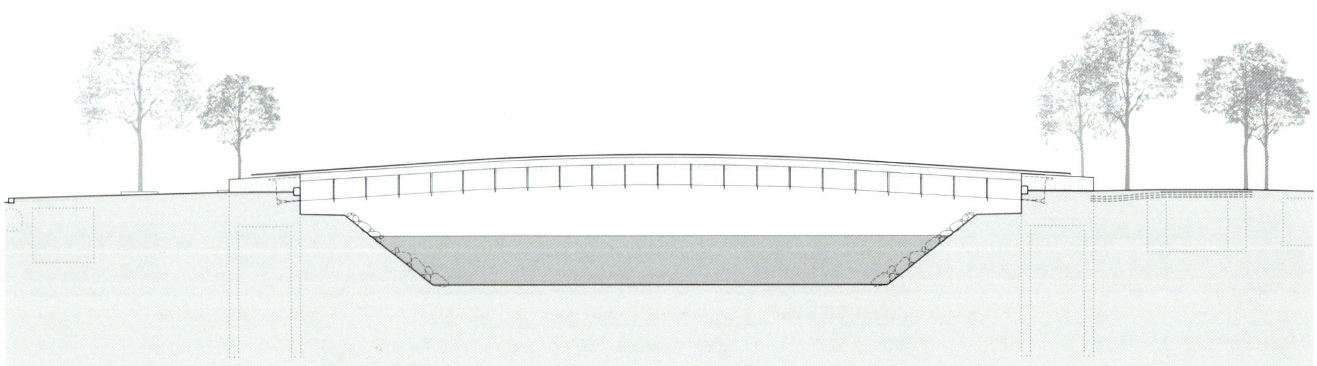

ELEVATION a1

1/400 0 1 2 3 4 5 10

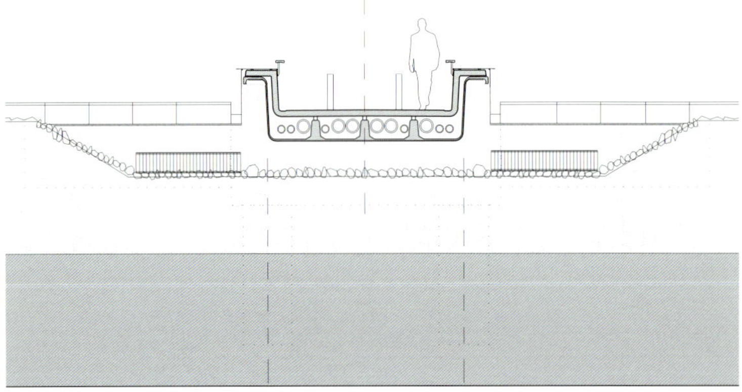

SECTION s1

1/150 0 1 2 3 4 5 10

R.P. 0.88

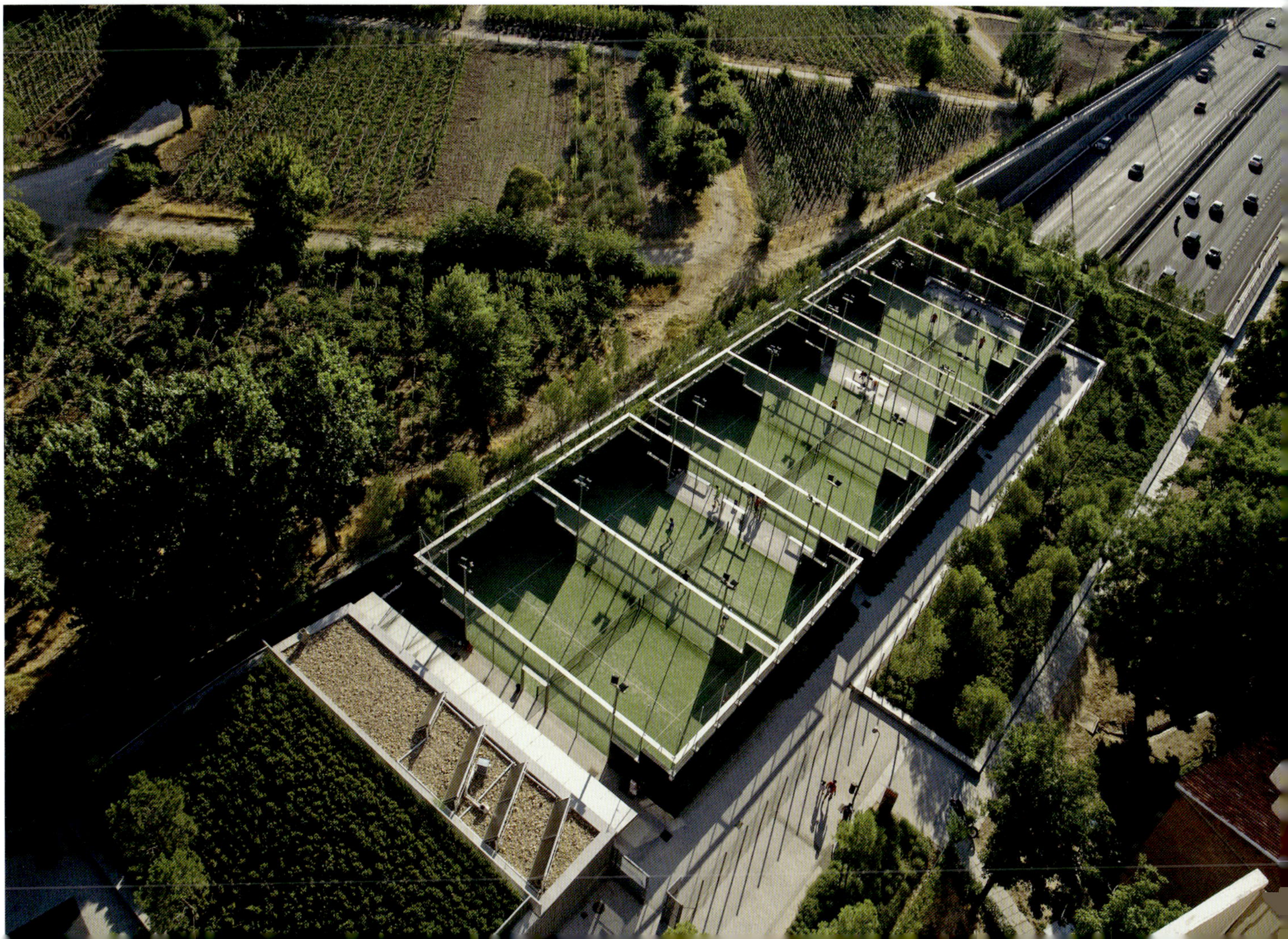

R.P. 1.09 (DATASHEET ON THE NEXT PAGE)

PADDLEBALL COURTS SALÓN DE PINOS

Effective surface area dressing rooms 95.80 m^2
Constructed surface area dressing rooms 116.15 m^2
Floor dimensions 5.55 x 20.85 m
Height above ground level 3.16 m
Date of completion 2011
Uses 01. Paddleball court / 02. Reception / 03. Men's dressing room / 04. Women's dressing room / 05. Handicapped dressing room

K.P. 1.69

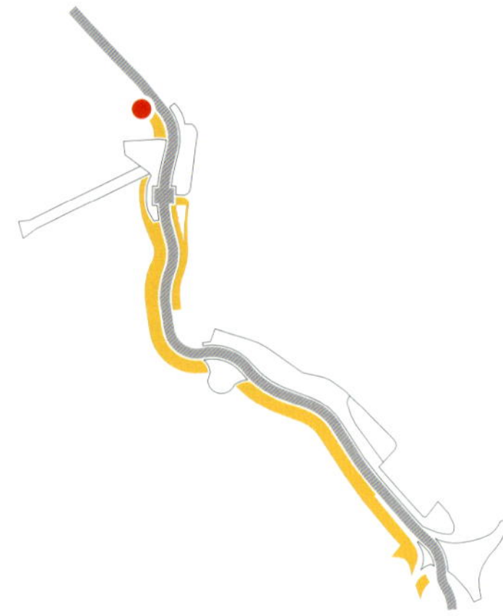

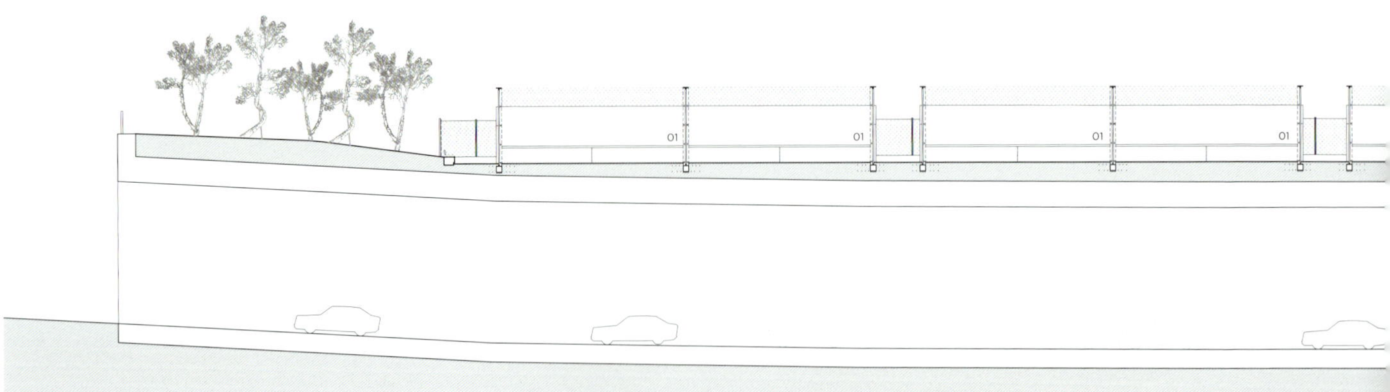

SECTION s1

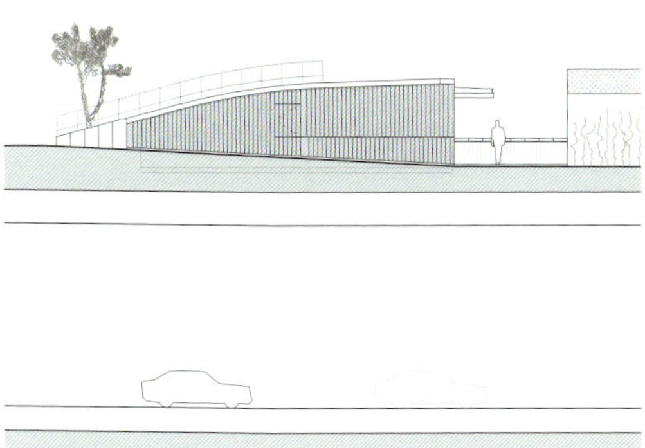

ELEVATION DRESSING ROOM a1

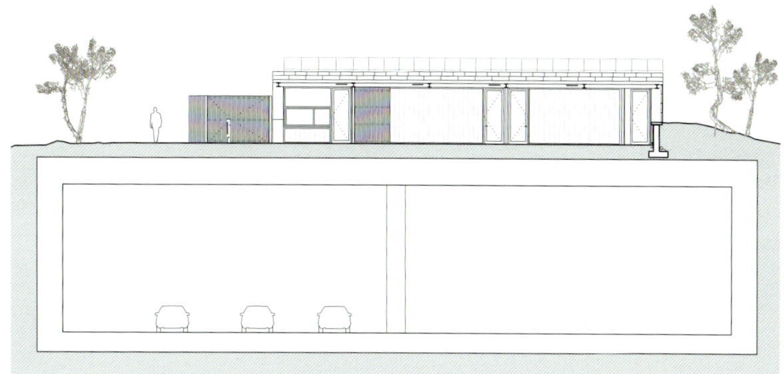

ELEVATION DRESSING ROOM a2

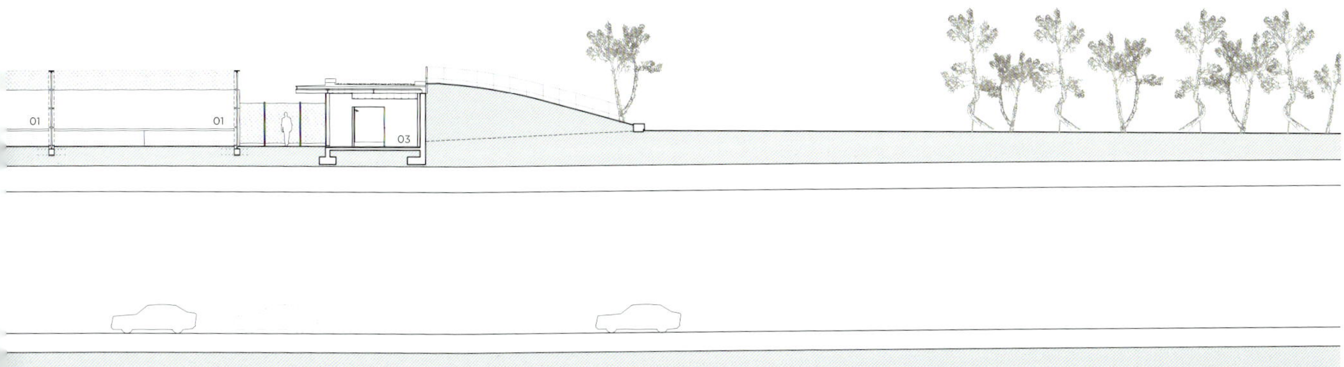

1/400 0 1 2 3 4 5 10

PUENTE OBLICUO RESTORATION

Length on axis 145 m
Length between supports 25 m
Deck width 16 m
Structure Pre-stressed and lightened concrete slabs resting on bracing beams. Concrete deck
Project engineer of the original bridge Carlos Fernández Casado
Date of construction of existing structure 1976
Date of completion 2008

K.P. 3.01

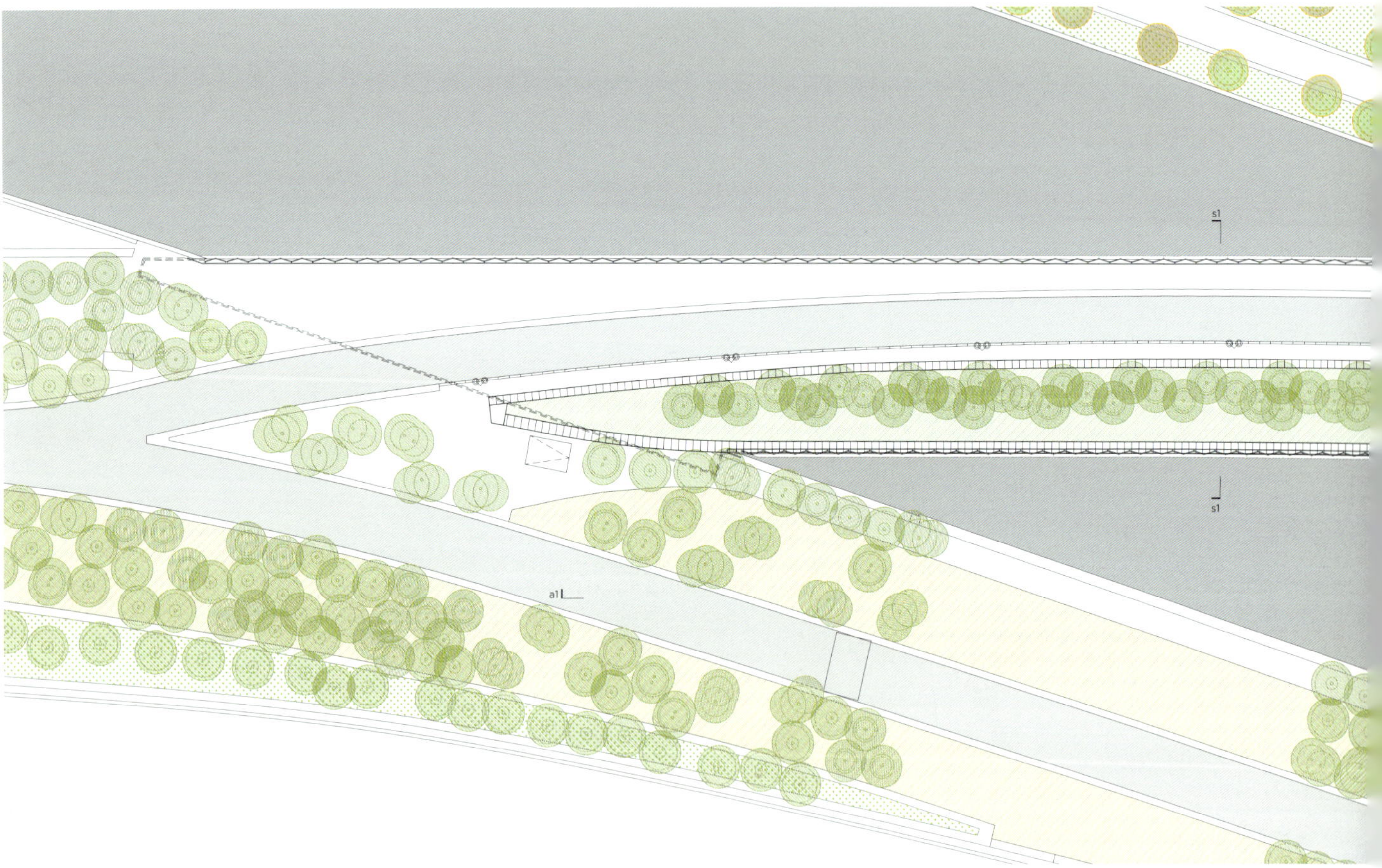

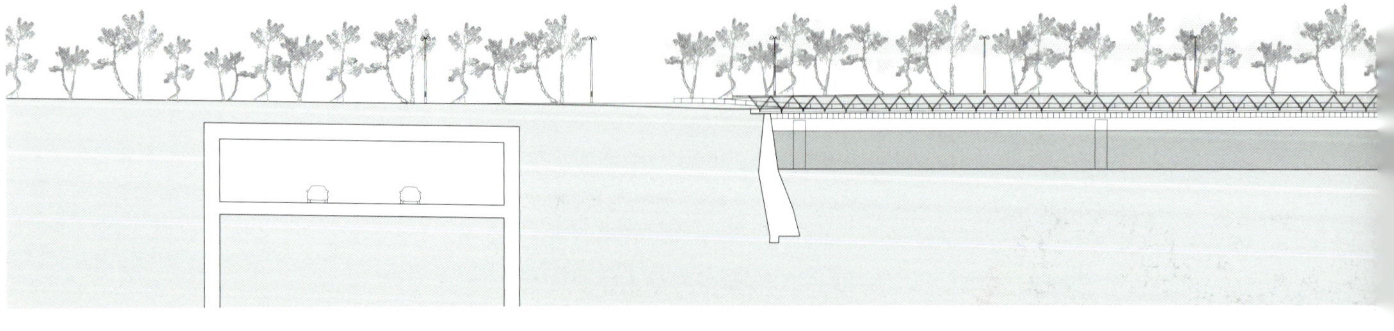

ELEVATION a1

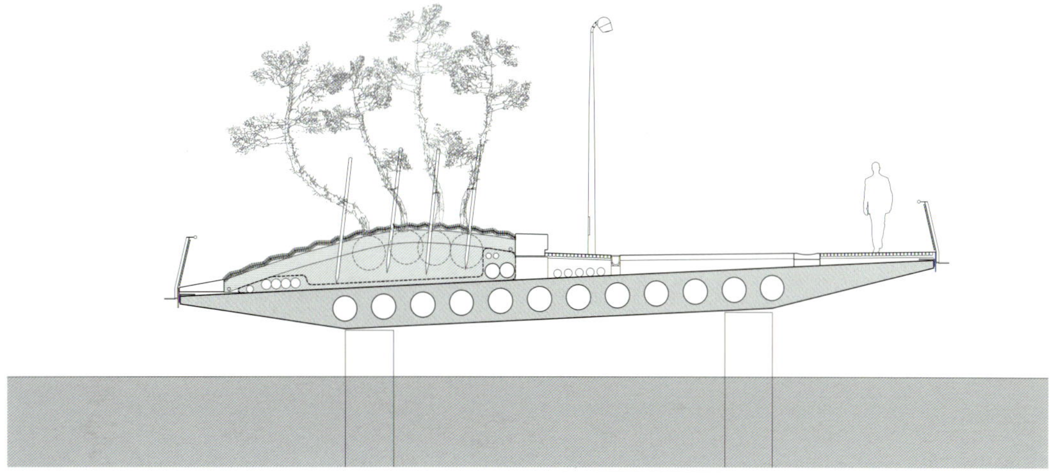

SECTION s1 1/150

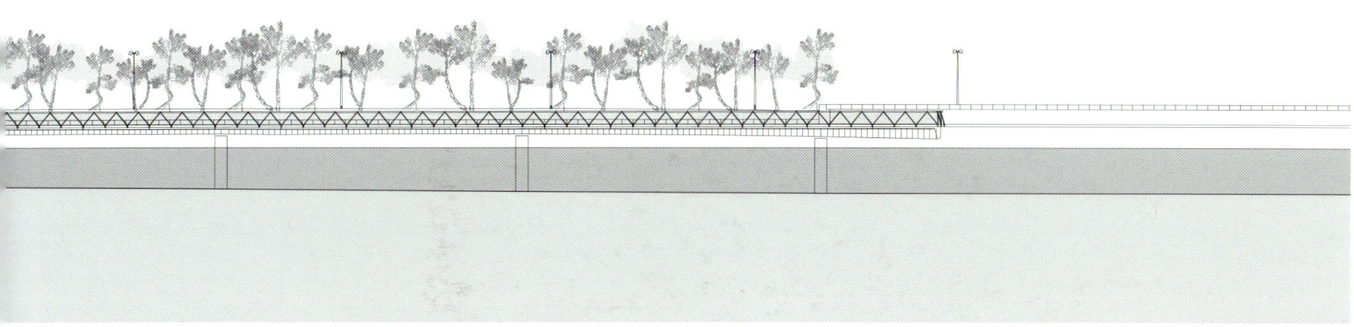

1/600

Y-SHAPED FOOTBRIDGE (PRINCIPADO DE ANDORRA WALKWAY)

Length on axis West and northeast sections: 69 m / southeast section: 35 m
Length between supports 63.35 m
Deck width 3.50 - 7.00 m
Free height 2.20 - 4.50 m
Structure Metal structure of lattice beams with wooden deck over metal substructure
Date of completion 2008

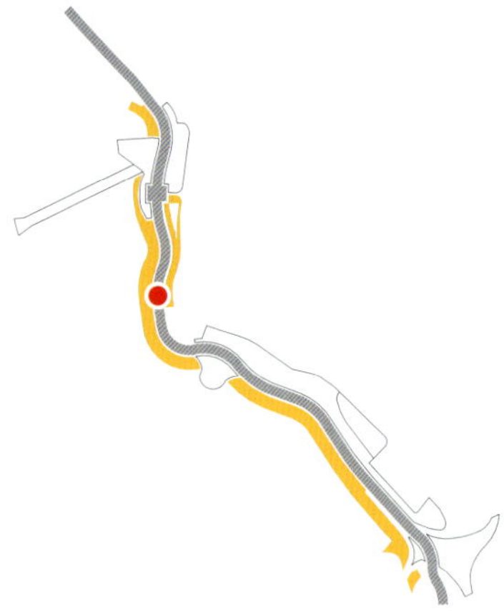

K.P. 3.70

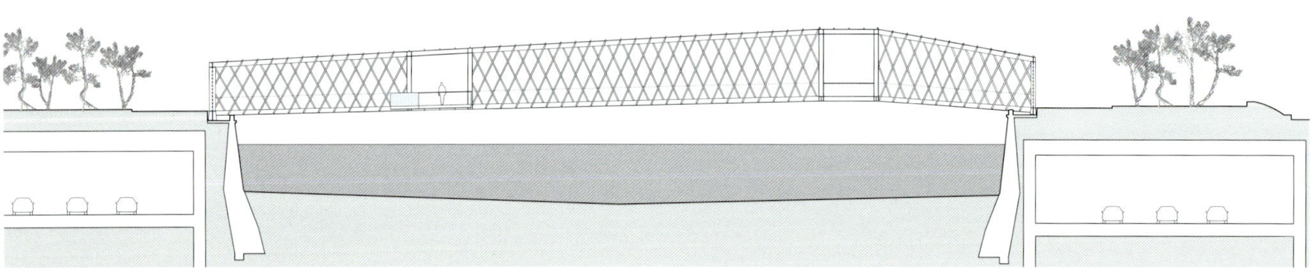

ELEVATION a1

K.P. 3.75

K.P. 3.70

CLIMBING PAVILION

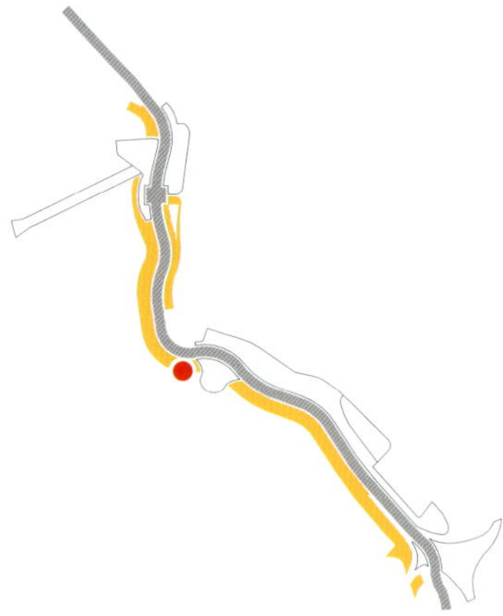

Effective surface area 480.33 m^2
Constructed surface area 627.28 m^2
Floor dimensions 7.00 - 8.50 x 53.45 m
Height above ground level 6.15 - 7.80 m
Date of completion 2010
Uses 01. Covered climbing area / 02. Reception / 03. Storage / 04. Toilet for handicapped / 05. Office / 06. Dressing rooms

K.P. 4.45

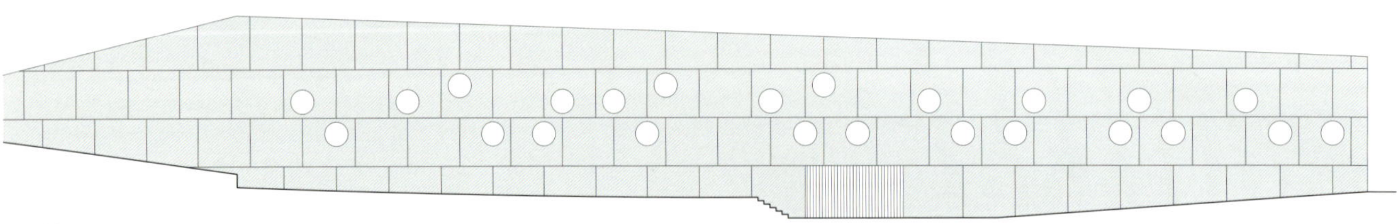

ELEVATION a1

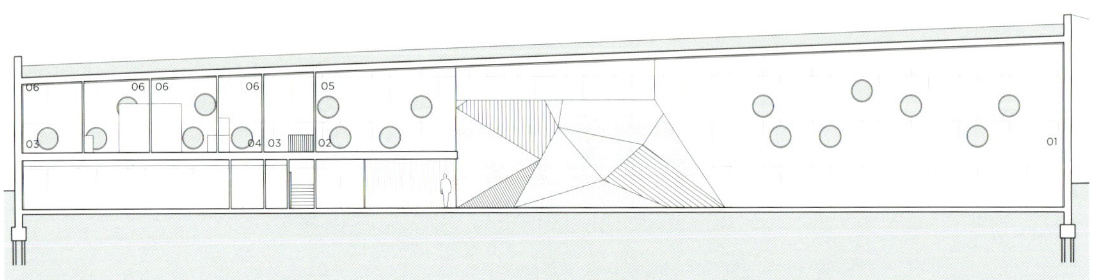

SECTION s1

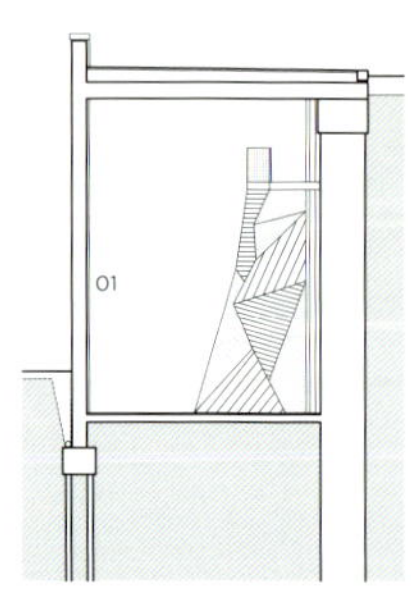

SECTION s2

1/400 0 1 2 3 4 5 10

K.P. 4.45

K.P. 3.78 (DATASHEET ON THE NEXT PAGE)

PRINCESA FOOTBRIDGE

Length on axis 45.60 m
Length between supports 41.12 m
Deck width 4.50 m
Structure Metal beams with exterior vertical stiffeners and wooden deck
Date of completion 2010

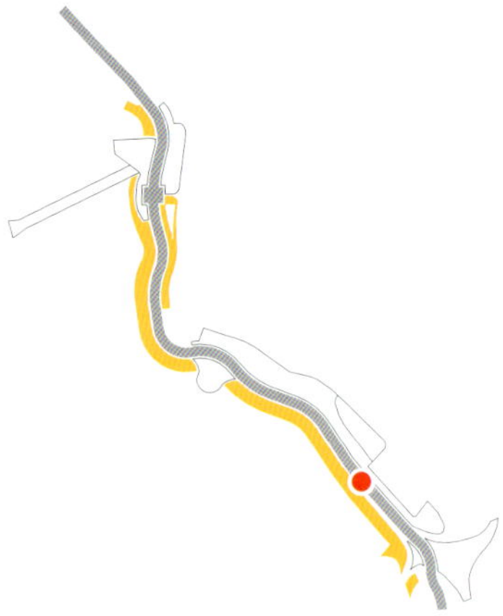

K.P. 6.80

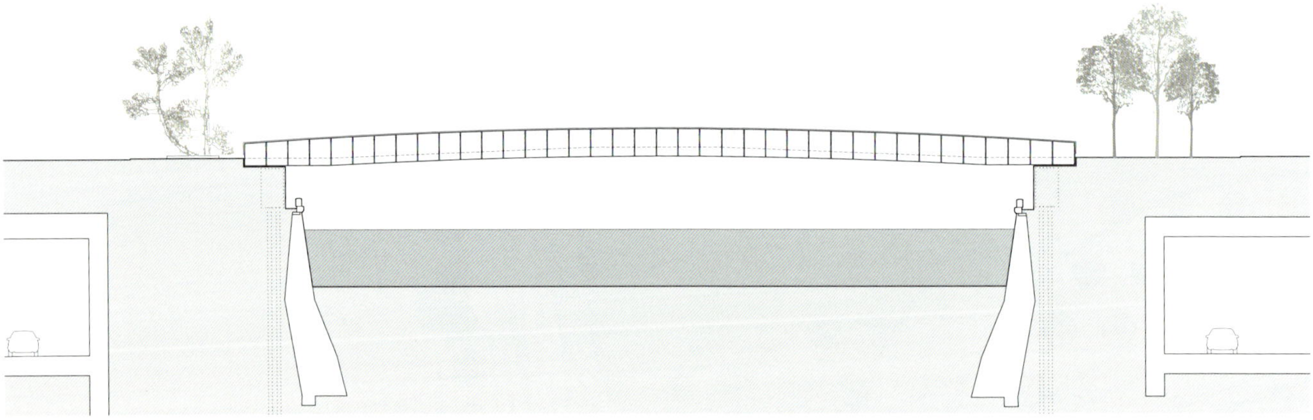

ELEVATION a1

1/400 0 1 2 3 4 5 10

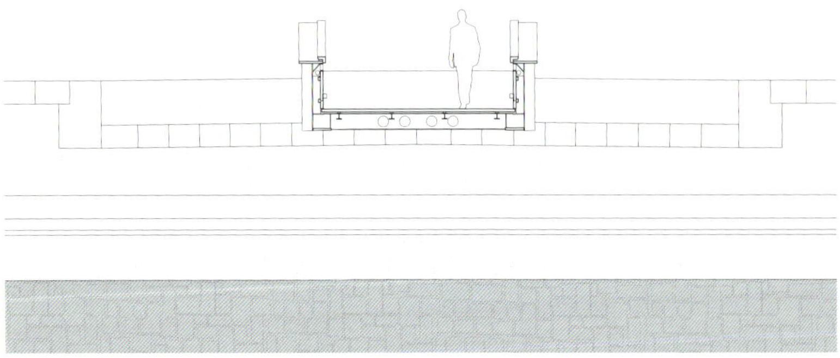

SECTION s1

1/150 0 1 2 3 4 5 10

TLI

THE TRIP TO LISBON

Starting point
Due to its central position on the Iberian Peninsula, the city of Madrid has had a historical need to make radial connections. Of these, the roads heading northeast (to Segovia), west (to Lisbon), and southwest (to Toledo) all required crossing the river. Yet, despite close ties between the kingdoms of Spain and Portugal, Madrid did not originally establish a direct connection with the western side of the Iberian Peninsula. On the other hand, its links to Segovia and Toledo were established at almost the same time that the city was reinforced as a population center regained from the Muslims. Two bridges were built over the river and named after the cities to which their respective roads led: Toledo and Segovia. But the direct route to the Atlantic did not have its own exit from the city until the 20th century.

This new access road was named Avenida de Portugal (Portugal Avenue) and its connection with the city center was achieved by enlarging the stone structure of the Puente del Rey (the King's Bridge) to bear motor vehicles. This had not happened sooner because building such a route involved occupying part of the Casa de Campo, a game park that belonged to the King of Spain until 1931. The new road ran straight across the royal park, cutting off a section that was immediately sold and became a densely populated residential section of the city. Traffic along the Avenida de Portugal grew constantly and by the end of the 20th century it had reached over 100,000 vehicles a day, consolidating the avenue's status as a definitive barrier between the large park and the city.

As a six-lane highway, the Avenida de Portugal was an inviolable border, and the progressive occupation of the Puente del Rey by motor vehicles — by 1960, only automobiles were allowed to use it — further exacerbated the avenue's character as a separation. The city's largest park, the Casa de Campo, is almost directly adjacent to the river, but the avenue isolated it from the city center and made it unreachable by pedestrians and cyclists. The avenue impeded access from the district of La Latina to the southwest, where the urban fabric is densest and the population most numerous, and that barrier ran somewhat less than two kilometers from the edge of the river near the Puente del Rey to its confluence with the Paseo de Extremadura (the Extremadura Promenade). There, it became the A-5 highway, which connects with Lisbon in almost a straight line. Thus, the highway constituted the physical edge of the large park, stripping it of any connection along its southwest side that would allow the neighborhoods in that area even a minimal access. The avenue and its prolongation closed off the park in an impenetrable way.

The place
As part of the major public works to bury the highway that formerly bordered the river, vehicular traffic on the Avenida de Portugal was also rerouted through a tunnel, freeing an area almost two kilometers long and 45 meters wide. This area offered a new opportunity to recover the Casa de Campo's connection to populous southwestern neighborhoods and its considerable slope made it possible to build two different underground levels, with residential parking on the upper level and the length of tunnel connected to the rest of the underground system on the lower one. The construction of a double underground structure affected what could be done above-ground, because the higher ground level there was studded with large gas-evacuation chimneys and entryways to the parking area, including stairs and elevators for pedestrians and entry and exit ramps for vehicles.

Inside the park, the spaces closest to its border with the Avenida de Portugal have been subject to intermittent construction since 1950. Beginning in that decade, a series of buildings were constructed for the Agricultural Fair, a showcase for livestock and crops from various regions and provinces of Spain. By the time work began to run the avenue's six lanes underground, the surviving fair pavilions were mostly restaurants accessible only by car.

The two sides of the area freed by this operation are extraordinarily different from each other. The southeastern side consists of dense urban fabric with apartment buildings and small streets, while the northeastern side is parkland with a scattering of isolated pavilions, each with its own small parking lot. On that side, the number of buildings shrinks in direct relation to the proximity of the river while vegetation occupies an increasing amount of park space and becomes denser.

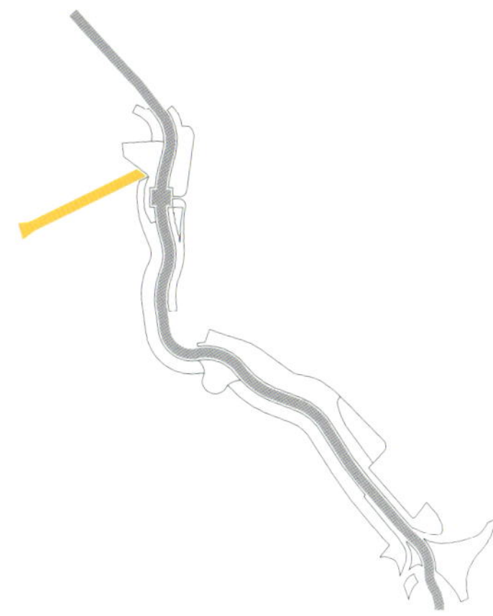

Concepts and character of the proposal
The preliminary approach to the project established that the new treatment for this area should make it possible to walk from the city to the park. It also had to resolve the modulated connection between the densely constructed urban fabric and the vast park as a buffer zone with its own intrinsic interest. Finally, because of its slope, attention had to be paid to its visibility from the city's historical center. So it became important to formalize it as a highly exposed urban object with its own characteristics. These operations had to be compatible with local vehicular traffic above ground, allowing certain movement over the avenue and not impeding vehicular access to restaurants in the nearest part of the park.

Moreover, the proposal assigned greater importance to the characterization of the avenue as a recognizable and, to a degree, narrative and selective landscape. The story underlying the conception of the new boulevard is constructed with materials that could be found on an imaginary trip between Madrid and Lisbon, and they provide the visual references that make up the project's basic lines. While the complexity of the new situation calls for many elements to resolve the problems involved (local traffic, neighborhood density, access to parking, and to restaurants in the park, etc.), the proposed landscape narrative is based exclusively on three essential and complementary units: wooded areas, paving, and the treatment of volumes that emerge above ground. These were the minimum elements employed in an effort to create a new landscape capable of retaining its identity despite being alongside a major park, able to function as a buffer zone that would soften the effects of pedestrian and vehicular movement, and to provide lateral access to the Casa de Campo for the first time.

Description of the landscape
Describing the Avenida de Portugal is as simple as succinctly recounting a trip from Madrid to Lisbon, or at least, recalling some of the most memorable objects and textures seen in different parts of the journey. Three characteristic elements were enough to build a lasting memory. First, to represent the path that separates the point of departure from the destination, we imagined the visual strength of the Jerte valley. Its cherry orchards, the valley's only crop, constitute an enormously powerful landscape, especially when flowering, because of the almost infinite repetition of fruit trees. The image chosen to evoke Lisbon, a reference to the texture of its pavement, called for the development of a graphic system defined by small stone elements used to build it. These small stones, none larger than 10 x 10 centimeters, make the surface vibrant in a characteristic and unmistakable way. Finally, Portuguese ceramics were chosen as the ideal material for covering the largest elements that stick up above ground level. The varied shades of blue that constitute its main color were considered appropriate for dotting the group wherever necessary.

So that was the way to construct a landscape meant to be reconnoitered, with a central footpath dominated by elements from the imaginary journey. Connections with existing construction on both sides were handled in two different ways: contact with the city was established with tree-lined sidewalks that include ventilation shafts and access to underground parking, and the side adjacent to the park bears a cycling path and four new entries to the Casa de Campo.

But this recovered space in which mobility becomes the defining characteristic cannot be fully understood without viewing it from a distance. Its constant slope of nearly 5% gives it the appearance of a vertical plain when viewed from the historic city center, and its seasonal transformations make it a new and recognizable visual experience for the city's residents and, as such, a part of Madrid's imagery.

Technical solutions
Two very concrete technical questions are treated as critical and fundamental aspects of this project. First, the manner of guaranteeing with absolute certainty the correct installation and optimal growth of the wooded areas — in this case, some rather fragile trees — and second, the correct construction of the walking surfaces, so that rainwater is efficiently evacuated from an area whose longitudinal slope is considerable.

The installation of wooded areas called for the construction of biological islands — independent enclosures individually connected to primary drainage systems over the slab that

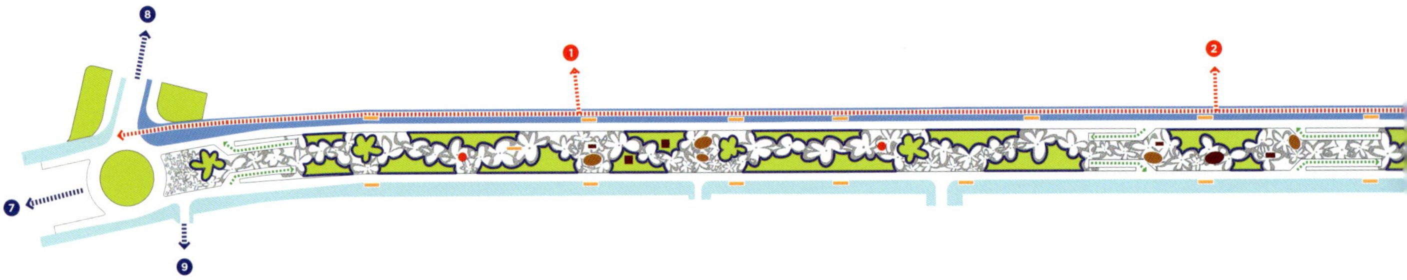

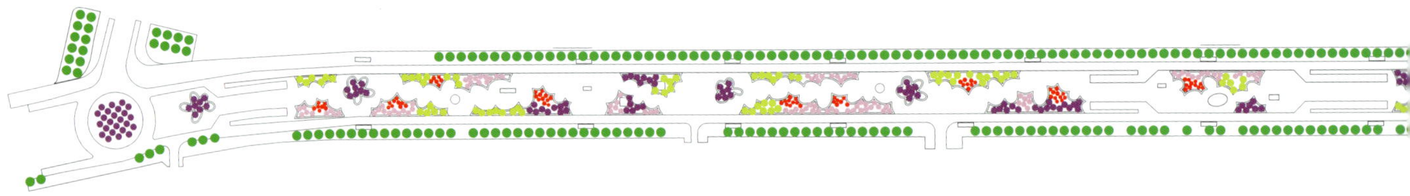

serves as the parking area's roof. Each of these islands has its own multilayered system for selectively filtering rainwater, maintaining humidity, and rationalizing the watering system. The location of each island required calculating the weight of soil, the planned weight of the trees after they reached full size, and where they could be installed on the slab, as not all parts of the slab could bear the same weight. Surface drainage was resolved using specific software to define a subtle topography that would take into account accessibility, interruptions caused by the physical edges of the biological islands, above-ground service elements pertaining to the subterranean installations and the location of the best drainage points. A graphic system defined by two types of stone was installed over this sensitive topography. The size of each stone was defined by maximum visible dimensions of 10 x 10 centimeters, and the computer-aided placement system insured a perfectly continuous surface that nonetheless followed the underlying contours well enough to make the initial conditions compatible with ideal drainage performance.

Materials and elements

The Avenida de Portugal has a practically constant section throughout its length. Its asymmetrical nature responds very differently to its two borders: the dense city to the southeast and the historical park to the northwest. The avenue can be understood as a series of six longitudinal strips that make up that section and run parallel to each other from the river to the mouth of the tunnels.

In order from south to north, the first strip is the rebuilt sidewalk that gives access to all of the buildings on the urban side. This sidewalk is paved with small-format granite elements that resolve all encounters with cross streets and blend with the underground parking area's pedestrian exits. This sidewalk is lined with plane trees in individual tree wells. It is lit by high streetlights that diversify the light, distinguishing between pedestrian zones and the street. This strip is designed for maximum accessibility and includes parking spaces for vehicles associated with nearby housing. The second strip is a conventional asphalted roadway for motor vehicles whose only particularity is its useful width, which allows limited mobility and impedes irregular parking.

The third strip defines the avenue's character and makes it a boulevard. It is actually a tree-lined promenade consisting mainly of biological islands and patterned pavement. The islands are irregular elements whose edges are 45 centimeters above the walking surface. That edge is made with pieces of prefabricated concrete whose ergonomic shape allows them to be used as benches or seats. The placement of each island is complemented by patterns in the pavement so that its outer edge responds to a dialog of empty and full patterns in negative and positive. The islands bear over 700 cherry trees from four different species: *Prunus Avium, Prunus Avium Plena, Prunus Yedoensis,* and *Prunus Watererii.* This insures consecutive flowering throughout spring, as naked treetops turn white and finally green, forming a changing cloud over the course of March and April. The continuous pavement is also a substantial element in this space. Its configuration with small-format elements brought from northern Portugal was installed by craftsmen from that country. Computer-aided design was used to generate a large figurative pattern on the walkway, although its huge scale appears abstract to those actually walking on it. That pattern's motif is, in fact, a series of variations on the simplified figure of a cherry blossom, thus establishing a coherent narrative line for the boulevard's formal elements. The relation between the surface and the benches, which also constitute the edges of the islands, lies

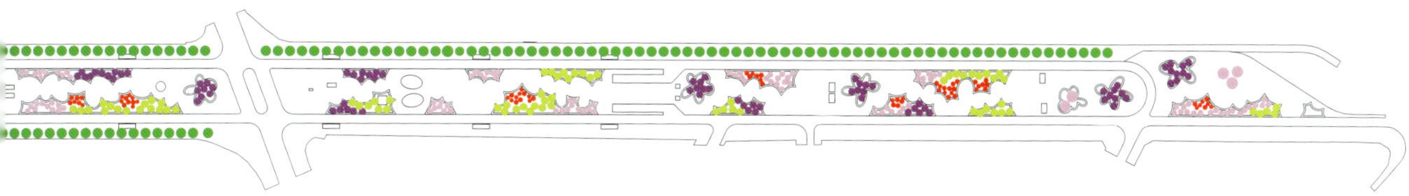

in the blossoms of the trees planted there. This pattern helps position the vertical lighting elements, which are distributed to light the promenade's rest areas. The boulevard is dotted with some of the most important installations servicing the infrastructure below ground, especially a series of large gas-evacuation chimneys that are over 2.5 meters high, and the elevators leading to the underground parking. These elements are integrated as high points that partially block the view. Their cylindrical shape and Portuguese ceramic covering, which reproduces the pavement patterns in shades of blue, turns them into agreeable if rather mysterious elements that reflect the changing light over the course of each day.

Still moving north, the following strip again responds to local vehicular movement and has the same characteristics as its counterpart on the urban side. It is followed by a strip containing a cycle path and a sidewalk with its own line of plane trees. The sixth and final strip marks the border with the Casa de Campo, where four new entrances enhance the mutual permeability of park and city that was lost almost a century ago. These new entries have been opened in the wall constructed during the 1950s, using metal gates that obey the same graphic criteria as the avenue's pavement.

Landscape and city

It is now possible to walk, cycle, or skate the entire length of the Avenida de Portugal, a former urban-access highway with six lanes occupied by over 100,000 motor vehicles each day. Crosswise, it is a buffer zone linking a district that grew along the avenue and always suffered from the latter's condition as a highway. Now, local residents have direct access to the huge Casa de Campo Park they could always see from their windows. And they can do so in a natural manner, in quiet surroundings filled with cherry trees where they can sit on benches that wind around tree-studded islands. This is a sloping boulevard and its irregularities occupy a plain that rises to the point of nearly vertical visibility. It has thus become a recognizable and ever-changing element of the city, a landscape of its own that stands out alongside the green expanse of the Casa de Campo.

K.P. 2.40

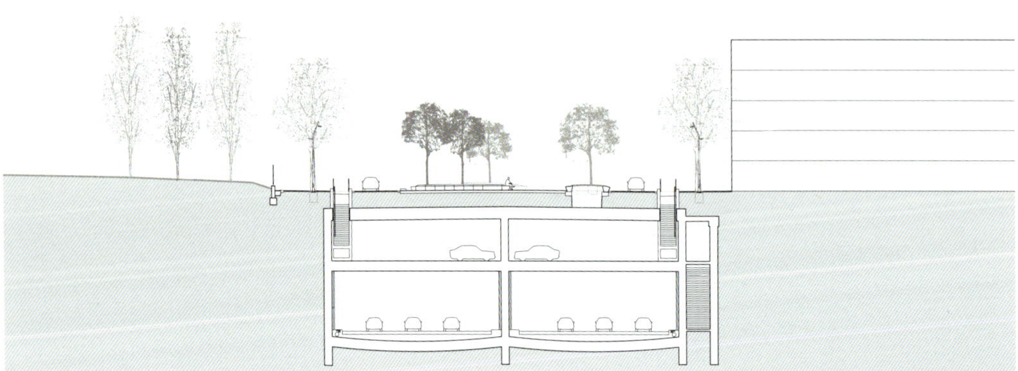

SECTION TYPE

1/750 0 1 2 3 4 5 10

LHI

LHI

A LINE IN HISTORY

Starting point
The city of Madrid began on a promontory sixty meters above the river. That is where the Arabs built the first fortified defenses that were replaced by the Alcázar, the walled palace of the Hapsburg dynasty. The city began to grow around that compound, expanding away from the river. Its growth surpassed the capacity of five consecutive city walls until the last, known as Philip IV's enclosure, was demolished in the mid-19th century.

Between the 16th century and the first third of the 20th, the kings of Spain owned and enjoyed an enclosed and wooded game park of over 1,700 hectares directly across the river. Known as the Casa de Campo, this game park was practically joined to the royal castle for centuries, with the river as the only separation. But in the late 20th century, powerful highways dissolved this connection in an apparently irreversible way.

The Madrid Río project has made it possible to recover the links that crossed the river and connected the city's original center with the vast royal game park, which is now publically owned and constitutes the largest and most valuable green space inside the city limits. These references to the past are the conceptual material that has provided the main basis for the reworking of those surroundings.

The place
The context that frames this landscape is informed by a multiplicity of historical events. The evolution of this part of the city has left marks that are still visible in many of its spaces, although the construction of the M-30 highway and the application of mobility models to serve private transportation in the 20th century weakened some of its internal links to the point of disappearance. Both this infrastructure and the Manzanares River fragmented the continuum formed by the diverse pieces that run in an uninterrupted fashion from the former Alcázar Palace to the Casa de Campo.

These pieces form a descending sequence that relates them to each other in a natural manner, and that relation is clearly perceptibly in the different heights that allow them to be seen, one above another, like parts of a panorama. They run from east to west, perpendicular to the river.

The highest, at an altitude of 640 meters above sea level, is the Royal Palace, a baroque building constructed over the remains of the Alcázar, the Habsburg's former palace. The wooded slope of the Campo del Moro extends from the foot of this building downwards towards the river without actually reaching it. This historic garden was reconceived in the second half of the 19th century and currently retains two different layouts that coexist despite belonging to two opposing concepts of landscape. On one side, a longitudinal strip of grass connects the highest part of the garden with the lowest. Its neoclassical layout is marked by the absence of trees and the presence of two historic fountains. On the other, the rest of the garden is densely wooded, with winding paths that give the space a natural appearance resembling that of a forest. The western edge of the Campo del Moro is bordered by the Paseo de la Virgen del Puerto, a road elevated over a slope at an altitude of 590 meters above sea level. This elevation is an artificial operation that corresponds to the area's urban development in the late 18th century. One of its purposes at that time was to protect the royal garden from the river's floodwaters. Another gentle slope runs from this street down to the Manzanares, and it was at the base of this embankment (at 590 meters above sea level) that Pedro de Ribera built the hermitage known as Ermita de la Virgen del Puerto, completed in 1718.

This slope running from the Paseo de la Virgen del Puerto to the river has been gradually colonized by the city. Because of its low altitude, it suffered successive floods that impeded its use for centuries. But a series of canals were dug there in the early 20th century for use by Madrid's washerwomen, workers of humble origin who made their living as laundresses for almost all the city. Each had her own reserved area, both for washing and for hanging laundry to dry under the sun. So the space was usually filled with hundreds of articles of clothing hanging from flimsy clotheslines. This activity occupied the space as far as the Puente de Segovia, which became the main structure over the river following its construction in 1584 and the principle connection between the city and the outlying road system.

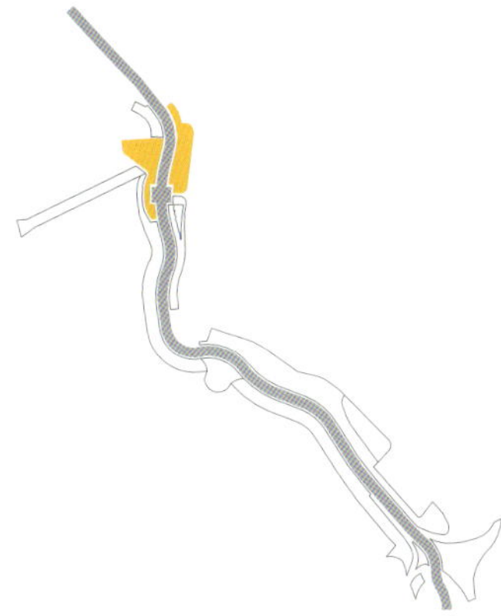

The river's opposite bank is home to the Casa de Campo, mentioned above. This compound was enclosed on all sides by a stone-and-brick wall, one of whose main gates opened onto another bridge over the river. First built of wood, this bridge was replaced by a stone structure in 1828, when it became known as the Puente del Rey. Several very important historical elements lie within the Casa de Campo in close proximity to the bridge, including a mansion belonging to the Vargas family, the original owners of this hunting preserve. There are also two gardens planted with renaissance-style geometric layouts, known as El Reservado Grande and El Reservado Chico, as well as the Huerta de la Partida, an orchard intended to produce fruit for the king's employees.

Concept and character of the proposal

The project for this area must address each of these pieces, individually and as a group, in a setting that takes on a new meaning following the burial of the M-30. It must interconnect them in a way that emphasizes the importance of the new unit they form together. As a unit, they now provide a new and direct link between the city center and the Casa de Campo at a point where pedestrian access had been impossible for several decades.

The proposal addresses five elements. On the left bank, these are: the slope that begins at the elevated road and includes the area around the Ermita de la Virgen del Puerto; the flat lands between this slope and the river; and the Puente del Rey, which leads to a platform on the right bank in front of the Casa de Campo. Also on the right bank are the Huerta de la Partida and the gardened areas around the abutments of the Puente de Segovia.

These operations have a sober, monumental character that makes the area a setting or background for the historic elements already present there. At the same time, the setting interrelates those elements, generating a new and open urban entity, a sort of porous nucleus at the heart of the historical city.

The work occupies both banks of the river, drawing on three elements that span it in order to establish the necessary links between them. From north to south, these are: the Puente del Rey, Dam number 6 and the Puente de Segovia. Each is significantly different than the others. The first is a pedestrian bridge of considerable width that serves as the threshold between the slope on the left bank and the open spaces – the esplanade and the Casa de Campo – on the right bank. Thanks to its width, it works as a public space – practically a plaza over the river. Just 300 meters further south, Dam number 6 has been rehabilitated as a pedestrian walkway between the river's banks, as well as a structure for connecting urban installations. Moreover, on the right bank, it allows access to the area closest to water level, near the Puente de Segovia. Finally, the latter allows motor vehicles to cross the river and connects the city center with the Paseo de Extremadura, Madrid's main highway to the west.

The operation includes treating topography as a conceptual mechanism of the first order, clearly differentiating it in each area. First, the slope adjoining the Campo del Moro is proposed as a single inclined plane in the flat area along the river, and it is specifically shaped to allow an open space around the Ermita de la Virgen del Puerto. At the foot of this slope, the project calls for a flat area with a minimum inclination that runs to the straight line of the riverbank. The other side consists of a platform between the riverbank and the Casa de Campo. Its surface is shaped with a topography whose gentle curves allow an almost natural integration of all the tunnels' technical elements without permitting them to obstruct the space's continuity. Finally, the project stipulates a new topography in the Huerta de la Partida, which becomes a single inclined plane with a practically imperceptible slope that rises as it draws away from the river. This redesigned topography is one of the project's means of action and it provides a new way to articulate the spaces that converge on the river.

Description of the landscape

Unity, based primarily on the importance of providing connections between the two sides of the river; and the diversity of the parts that make up the whole like links in a chain – each characterized by its own peculiarities – overlap to form a new point of attraction. The latter's intensity is reinforced by the layout of multiple itineraries that connect the Principe Pío transit exchange – one of the city's most important – with the Salón de Pinos, which functions as

K.P. 2.30

the project's principal axis. This point becomes the main access to the park from the historical part of the city through the Glorieta de San Vicente and its landscape consists of a succession of five settings that, while significantly different from each other, are totally linked.

First, the slope of Virgen del Puerto constitutes a longitudinal strip that abuts the existing roadway of the same name and the Glorieta de San Vicente. The green strip consists of various elements resembling a plane stretched between that street and the flatlands along the river. That plane contains various elements: a series of footpaths that converge at specific points of the immediate landscape, such as the Puente del Rey, the Hermitage or the gate of the Casa de Campo, a grassy surface referenced to the smooth slope that descends from the Royal Place to the edge of the Campo del Moro; and finally, overlapping that lawn, a strip of trees planted in a dense, regular grid with species that can be found in the most natural part of the Campo del Moro [*Cercis siliquastrum* (Judas tree), *Acer freemanii* (Freeman maple), *Quercus rubra* (northern red oak), *Aesculus hippocastanum* (horse chestnut), *Tilia platyphyllos* (linden), *Cupressus sempervirens* (cypress), *Cedrus deodara* (cedar), *Ginkgo biloba* (ginkgo), *Pittosporum tobira nanum* (Japanese pittosporum 'nanum')]. That way, as time passes, the textures on the two sides of the street will even out, as if the vegetation had managed to cross the barrier. At the south end, the green strip is cut to embrace a stairway leading to the Ermita de la Virgen del Puerto and to generate a clear area around it. The resulting space includes a generous rock surface bearing horizontal gardens on each side of the temple. This resolves the hermitage's previous situation, in which, despite its architectural value, it was practically buried and inaccessible.

Second, at the foot of the slope, the almost flat surface that accompanies the riverside promenade uses diverse materials to trace its contained composition. On a neutral base, four rectangular blocks are laid out according to the axes of the area's main urban elements: the Puente de Segovia, the hermitage, Dam number 6, and the Puente del Rey. These blocks consist of orthogonal rows of plane trees on grass prairies. Each block includes a pedestrian walkway and a linear fountain of carved granite whose longitudinal waters recall the canals used by washerwomen on a daily basis until the early 20th century.

Third, the group consisting of the Puente del Rey, which is treated like a plaza over the river, and the esplanade to which it leads, and which separates the river from the Casa de Campo on the left bank. That space is constructed over the mark of the buried tunnels and has become a free and open setting that serves as an immense balcony from which to overlook the river and enjoy the atmosphere crowned by the Royal Palace on the heights of Madrid. The esplanade consists of an ample expanse of granite and limestone whose gently rolling topography reflects the need to adapt to the installations imposed by the underground highway. This carpet of stone chips bears a huge design of flower petals that continues in the nearby Avenida de Portugal, and it is crossed by a trail set a few centimeters higher that insures the continuity of pedestrian and cycle movement along the entire riverside.

Fourth, the two spaces generated by the area's second historic bridge, the Puente de Segovia, contain gardens conceived as reserves for riverside woodlands trees [*Populus alba* (white poplar), *Populus tremula* (aspen), *Populus canescens*

(grey poplar)]. They are modulated by broken lines, forming successive terraces that lead down to the water's surface, which grows wider at this point, generating a mirrored surface that reflects the bridge. It also bears two monumental fountains and two fields of water lilies.

Finally, the Huerta de la Partida (the Partida Orchards) has been completely recovered. This area was especially affected by the construction of the underground highway, which buried it under a fifteen-meter-high pile of unusable soil and rubble. That same refuse was used to bring a new topography to the orchard, which now slopes gently upwards, away from the river. Its uniform surface has been planted with various species of fruit trees [*Prunus domestica* (plum), *Pyrus domestica* (pear), *Punica granatum* (pomegranate), *Olea europea* (olive), *Morus alba* (mulberry), *Juglans regia* (walnut), *Malus domestica* (apple), *Corylus colurna* (hazel), *Ficus carica* (fig), *Prunus dulcis* (almond)], on a regular grid that reproduces the modules of popular crops.

Materials and elements

The basic materials in the landscape are repeated successively, but they are applied in a different way each time. Thus, the entire area enjoys a unity based on the use of a very soft surface, essentially a meadow, as the base for various species of trees planted in regular grids. This pattern is applied to the inclined slope, the flat land along the river, the area around the Puente de Segovia and the Huerta de la Partida. Pedestrian and cycle paths define and bring out the different geometry of each green platform, which is triangular on the slope, rectangular on the riverside, broken around the Puente de Segovia and trapezoidal on the Huerta de la Partida. The following tree species are planted in a regular manner on these diverse geometries: the same species as in the Campo del Moro on the slope; plane trees on the riverside, in the same place they had previously been; around the Puente de Segovia, poplar trees, which do well near water; and of course, fruit trees on the orchard. The paths are accentuated with lighting that always emphasizes the linear character of the itineraries, either in wells (on the slope and in the Huerta de la Partida) or with fixtures hidden in the pavement (around the Puente de Segovia). In this predominately green context of grassy horizontal, sloped, or terraced surfaces, a different space stands out: the esplanade in front of the Casa de Campo, which is paved with granite and limestone so that it can function as an open area for the celebration of public events. As a space for activities that may require an outdoor stage, it needs to be hard and accessible, and this also allows crowds to walk near the river and to contemplate the elevated landscape of the historical city.

Landscape and city

Opening the Campo del Moro and the Casa de Campo to the city through the actions contemplated in this project has generated an unprecedented situation for Madrid. The multiple flows that were previously cut off by vehicular traffic can now reach a green oxygen-producing area of over 1,700 hectares. The historic, consolidated, and dense city center is smoothly linked to a natural space filled with thousands of trees. The transition between city and park is carried out using pieces sensitive to the past — subtle and sober elements that bring monumentality to the feet of the city above it.

YEAR 1870. WALLS, CHANNELS, BRIDGES, AND INFRASTRUCTURES

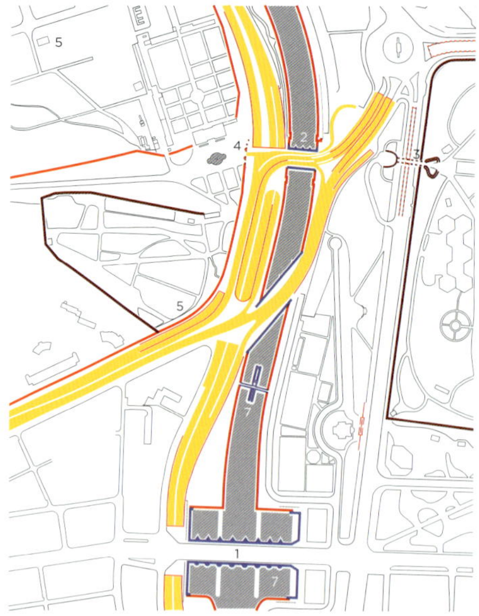

YEAR 2000. WALLS, CHANNELS, BRIDGES, AND INFRASTRUCTURES

YEAR 1870. CONSTRUCTION

YEAR 2000. CONSTRUCTION

YEAR 1870. PLANTING

YEAR 2000. PLANTING

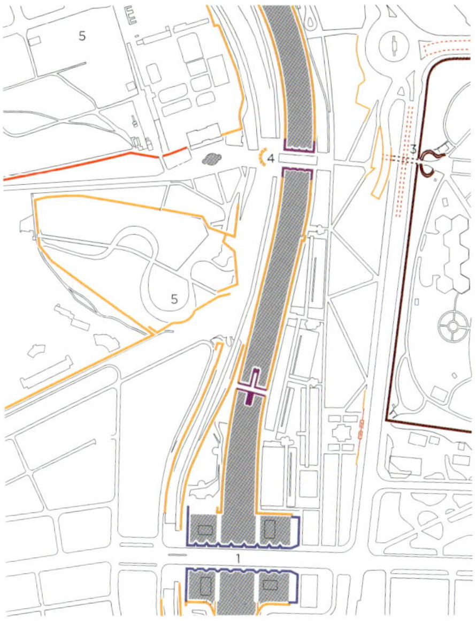

YEAR 2011. WALLS, CHANNELS, BRIDGES, AND INFRASTRUCTURES

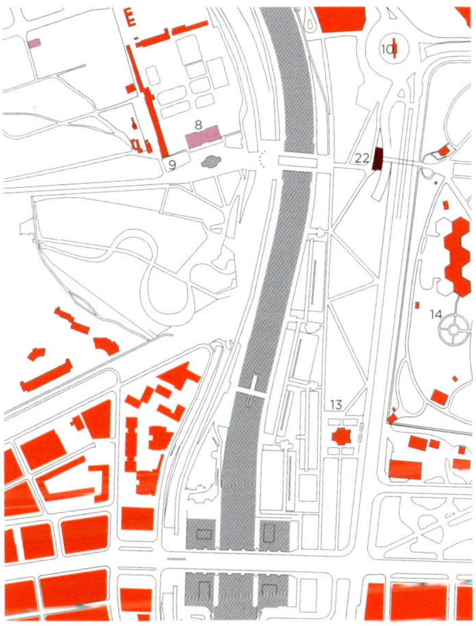

YEAR 2011. CONSTRUCTION

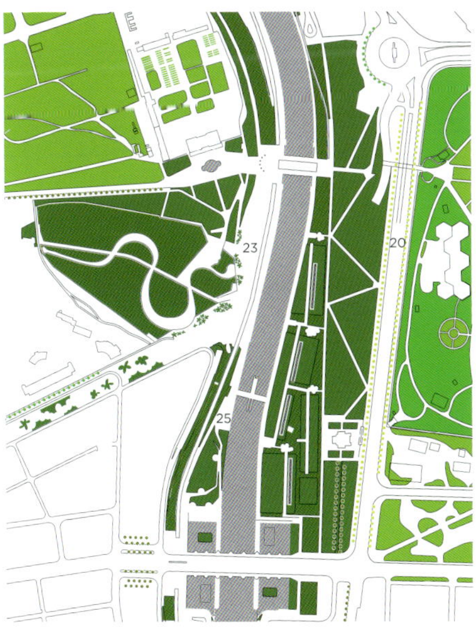

YEAR 2011. PLANTING

HISTORICAL EVOLUTION OF THE AREA AROUND PUENTE DEL REY - PUENTE DE SEGOVIA

1 **Puente de Segovia**
Designed in 1584 by Juan de Herrera
Widened in 1943

2 **Puente del Rey**
Designed in 1828 by Isidro González Velázquez
Widened in 1935 for vehicular traffic
Converted to pedestrian use in 2010

3 **Bonaparte Tunnel**
Designed in 1811 by Juan de Villanueva
Reformed in 1891 by Enrique Repullés

4 **Puerta del Rey**
Designed in 1811 by Juan de Villanueva
Moved and modified in 1935 to provide vehicular access to the Casa de Campo
Dismantled and moved again in 2010

5 **Gates and fence of the Casa de Campo**
Laid out by Juan de Villanueva in 1811
Modified in 1935 to adapt them to vehicular traffic
Reconstructed in 2010

6 **Camino de Aravaca Jetty**
Built in 1750

7 **Second channeling of Manzanares River**
Carried out between 1943 and 1955, includes construction of river containment walls, dams and fluvial ponds under the Puente de Segovia
Rehabilitated in 2010

8 **Casa de Vargas**
Built in 1519 by the Vargas family
Acquired by Philip II in 1560
Reformed in 1773 by Francesco Sabatini

9 **Mannerist grottoes**
Built in 1560
Partially destroyed in 1930
Partially restored in 2008

10 **Puerta de San Vicente**
Designed in 1772 by Francesco Sabatini
Dismantled in 1890
Replica from 1995

11 **Washerwomen's shelter**
Built in 1871
Demolished in 1946

12 **Washhouses**
Designed in 1811 by Juan de Villanueva

13 **Ermita de la Virgen del Puerto (Virgen del Puerto Hermitage)**
Designed in 1718 by Pedro de Ribera
Destroyed during the civil war and rebuilt in 1945
Restored in 2011

14 **Carriage Museum**
Designed in 1960 by Ramón Andrade

15 **M-30**
Built in 1979
Rerouted underground in 2007

16 **Reservado Grande and Reservado Chico Gardens**
Planted in 1560
Converted to municipal nurseries in 1935

17 **Huerta de la Partida**
Planted in 1560
Destroyed in 1936 and recovered in 2009

18 **Puente de Segovia wooded rotunda**
Designed by Juan de Villanueva in 1810

19 **Campo del Moro**
Planted in 1891 by Ramón Oliva

20 **Virgen del Puerto elevated walkway**
Built in 1772 by Francesco Sabatini

21 **Virgen del Puerto Woods**
Planted in the 18th century
Cut down and converted to sports installations in 1965
Rehabilitated as gardens in 2011

22 **Bonaparte Pavilion**
Built in 2011 at the Bonaparte Tunnel's exit

23 **Explanada del Rey**
Built in 2010

24 **Puente de Segovia Low Gardens**
Built in 2010

25 **Salón de Pinos**
Built between 2009 and 2011

1 / 11,000 20 100 200

AREA AROUND PUENTE DEL REY

BONAPARTE - HUERTA DE LA PARTIDA AXIS - K.P. 2.10 TO K.P. 2.40

SECTION s1 - s2 - s3

BONAPARTE TUNNEL AND PAVILION

1/1,500 2 4 6 8 10 20

K.P. 2.60

AREA AROUND PUENTE DE SEGOVIA

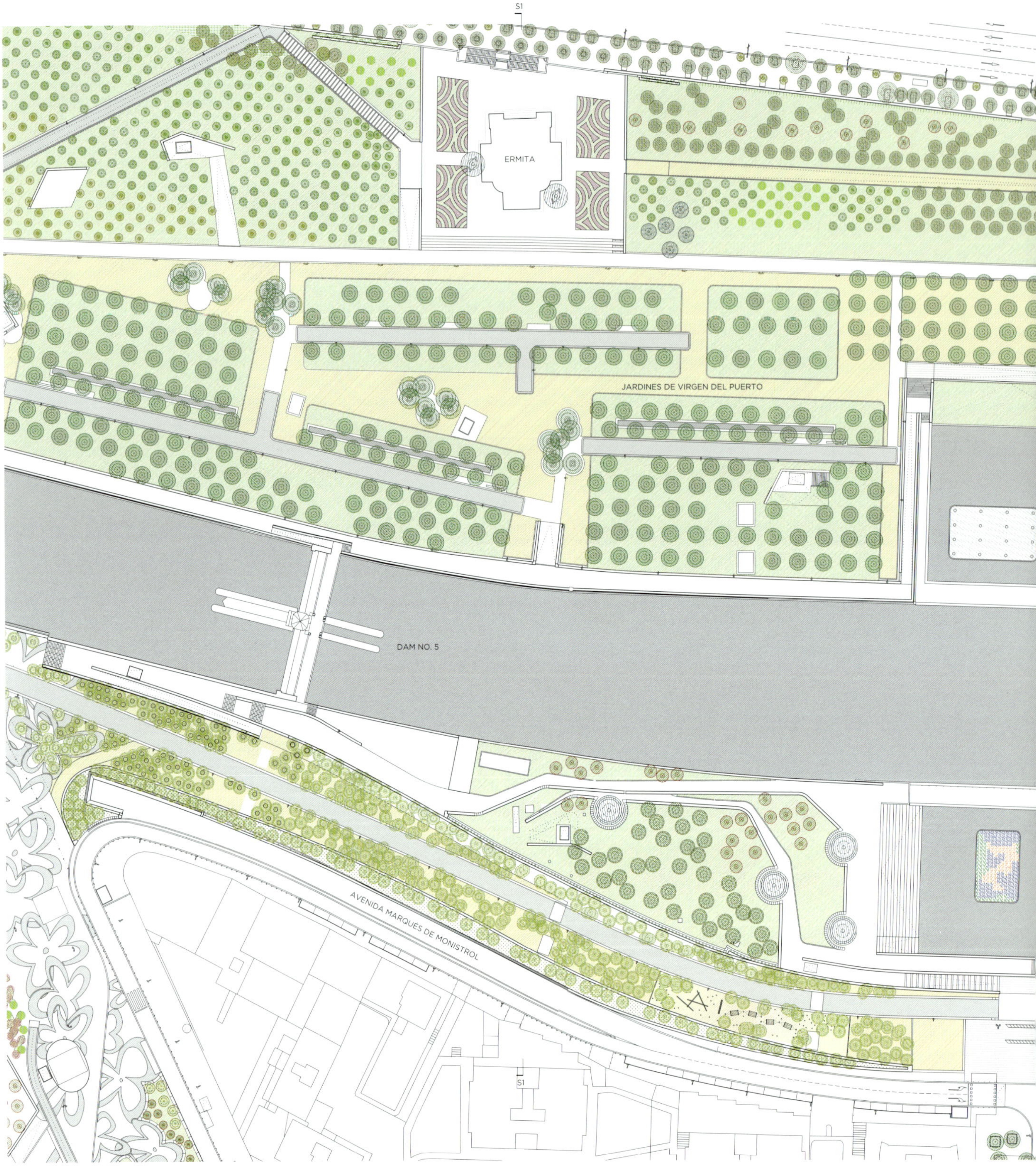

ERMITA VIRGEN DEL PUERTO – PUENTE DE SEGOVIA LOW GARDENS – K.P. 2.40 TO K.P. 3.00

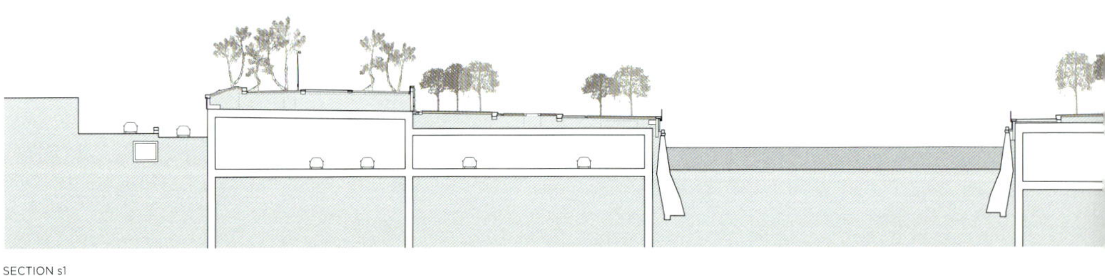

SECTION s1

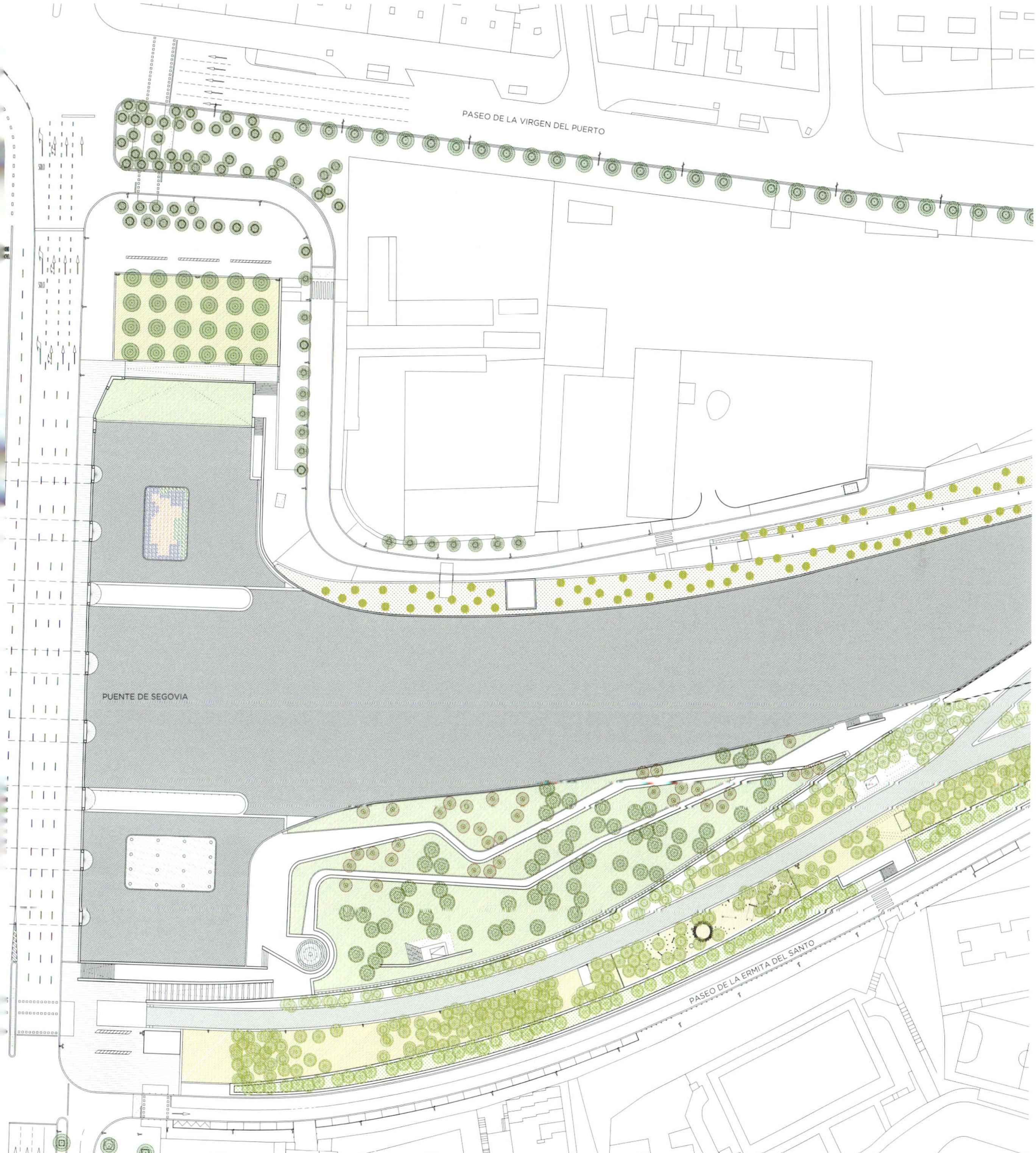

1/1,500 2 4 6 8 10 20

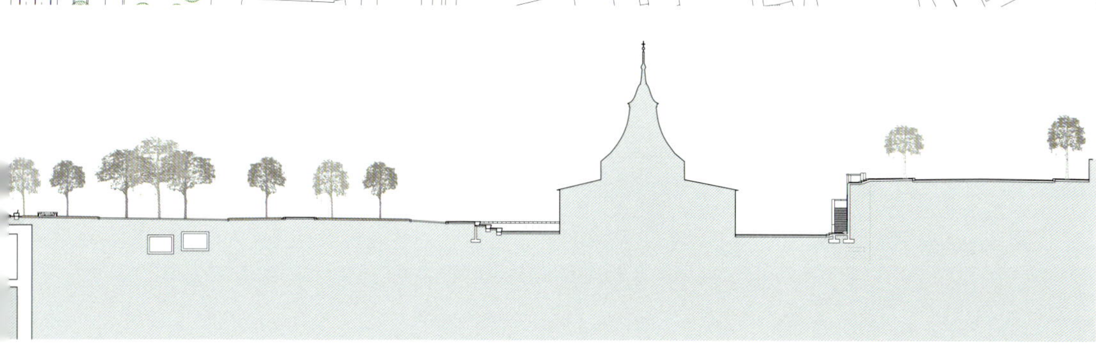

1/1,000 1 2 3 4 5 10

BONAPARTE PAVILION

Effective surface area 313.98 m^2
Constructed surface area 416.21 m^2
Floor dimensions 11.46 / 13.91 x 25.27 m
Height above ground level 3.50 m
Height below ground level 3.75 m
Date of construction Bonaparte Tunnel: 1811 / Pavilion: 2011
Uses 01. M-30 Emergency exit / 02. Entrance / 03. Bonaparte tunnel / 04. Campo del Moro / 05. M-30 Tunnel / 06. P.º Virgen del Puerto / 07. Tunnel P.º Virgen del Puerto - P.º del Rey / 08. L6 Subway tunnel

K.P. 2.12

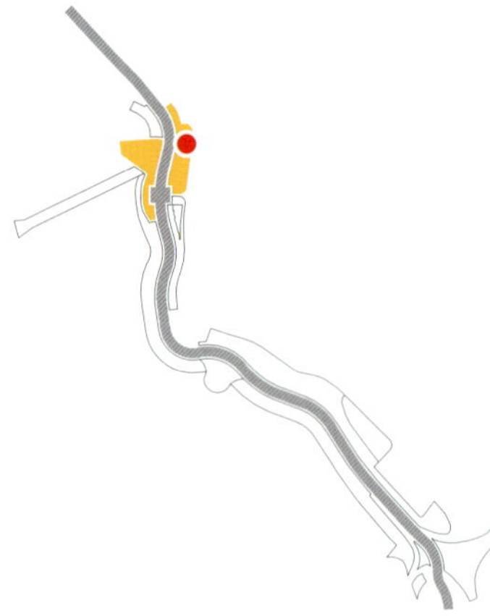

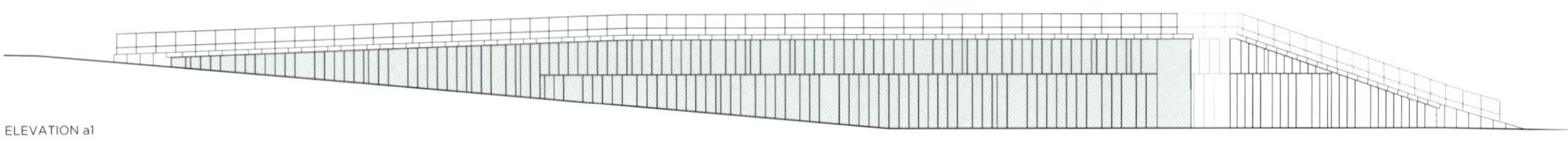

ELEVATION a1

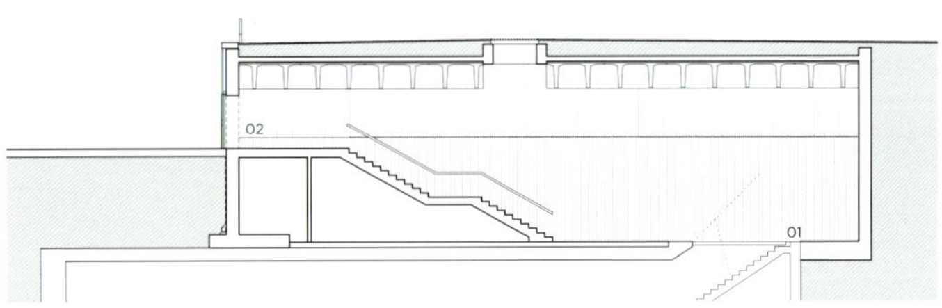

SECTION s1

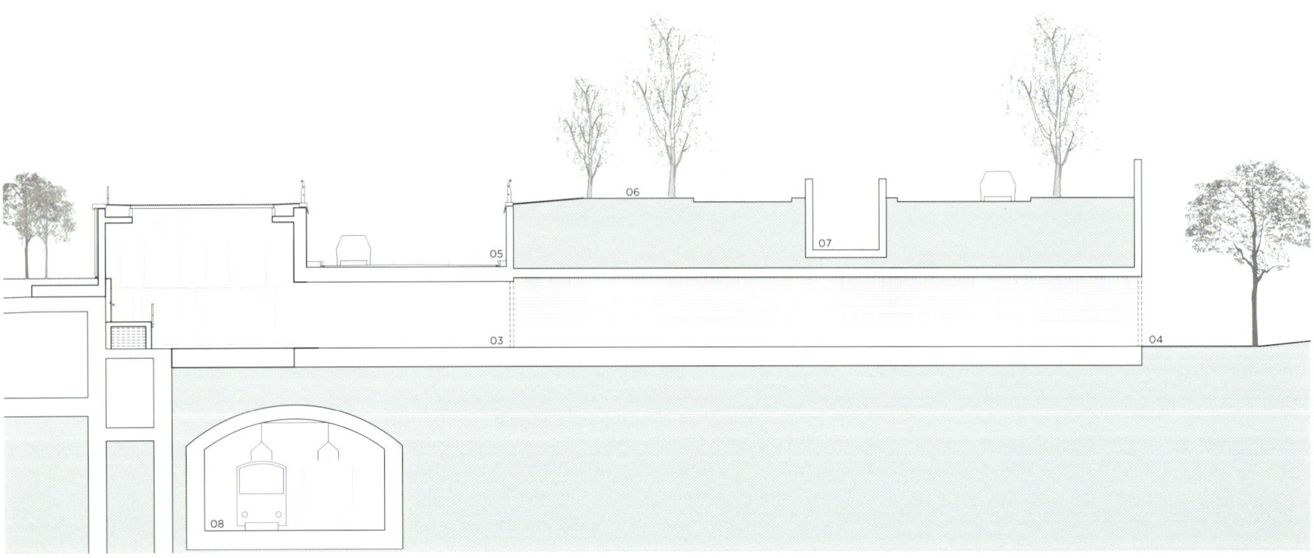

SECTION s2

1/400 1 2 3 4 5 10

K.P. 2.13

K.P. 2.12 (DATASHEET ON THE NEXT PAGE)

LAS LAVANDERAS FOUNTAINS

Length 60.30 m / 53.10 m
Width 2.70 m
Depth of basin 0.38 - 1.04 m
Date of completion 2011

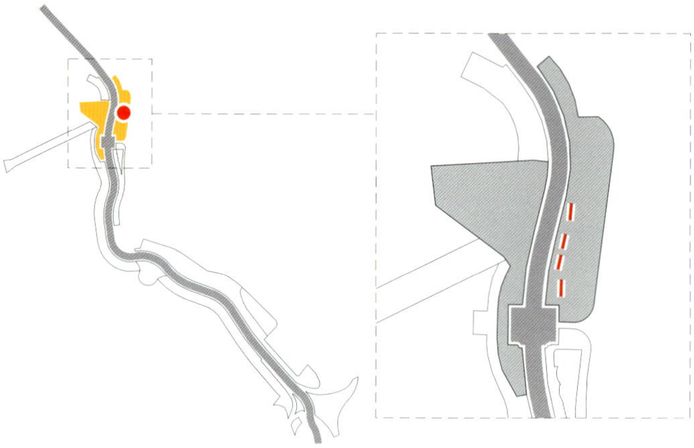

K.P. 2.30 - K.P. 2.40 - K.P. 2.45 - K.P. 2.55

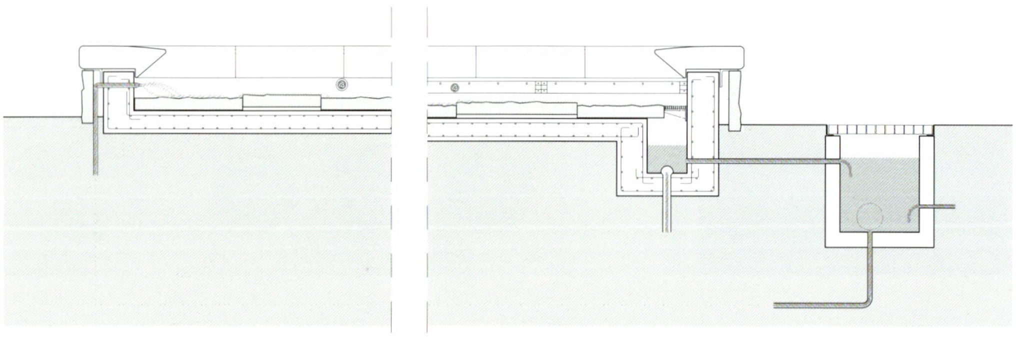

SECTION s1

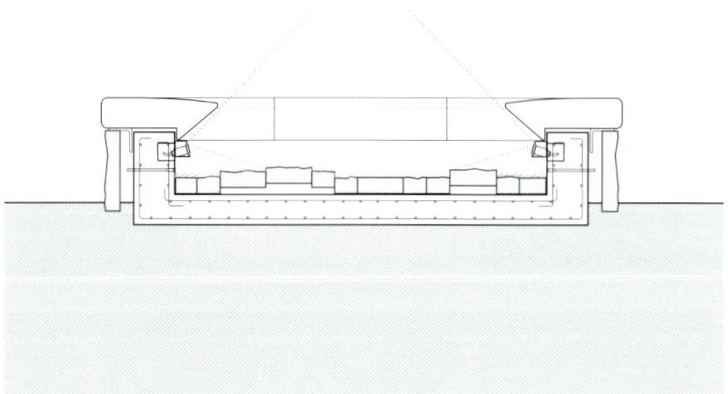

SECTION s2

1/50 0,1 0,3 0,5 1

R.P. 2.30

R.P. 2.08 (DATASHEET ON THE NEXT PAGE)

PUENTE DE SEGOVIA, POOLS, AND FOUNTAINS

Length on axis 155 m
Length between supports 15-18 m
Deck width 31 m
Design of the original bridge Juan de Herrera
Date of construction of existing structure 1584
Date of completion 2010

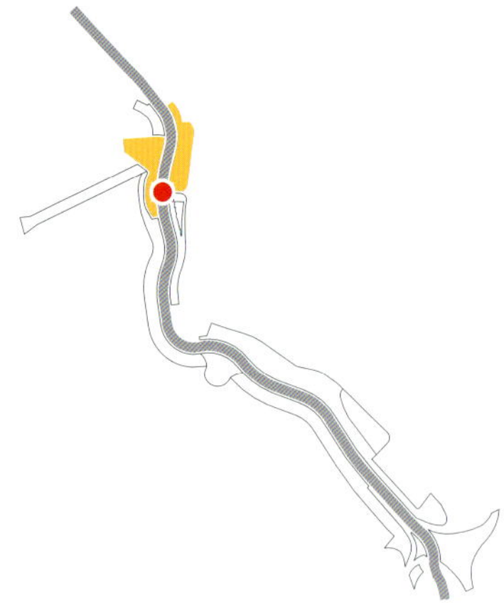

K.P. 2.68

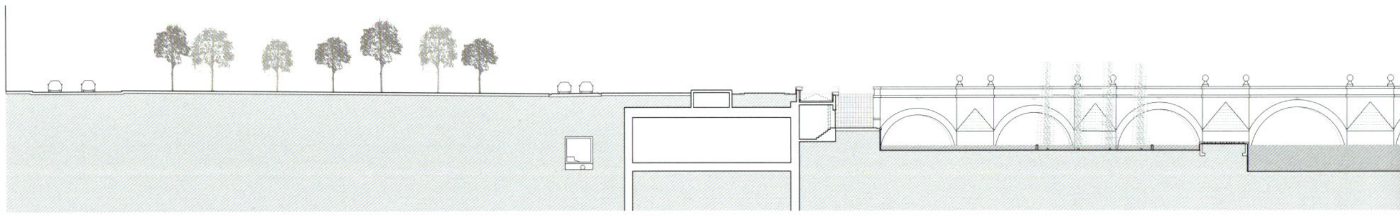

ELEVATION a1

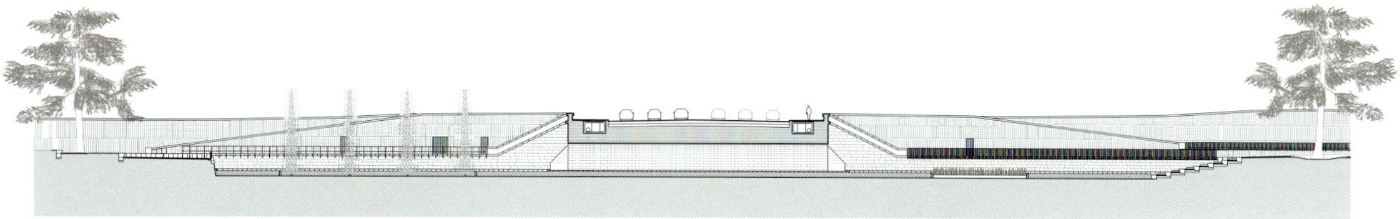

SECTION s1

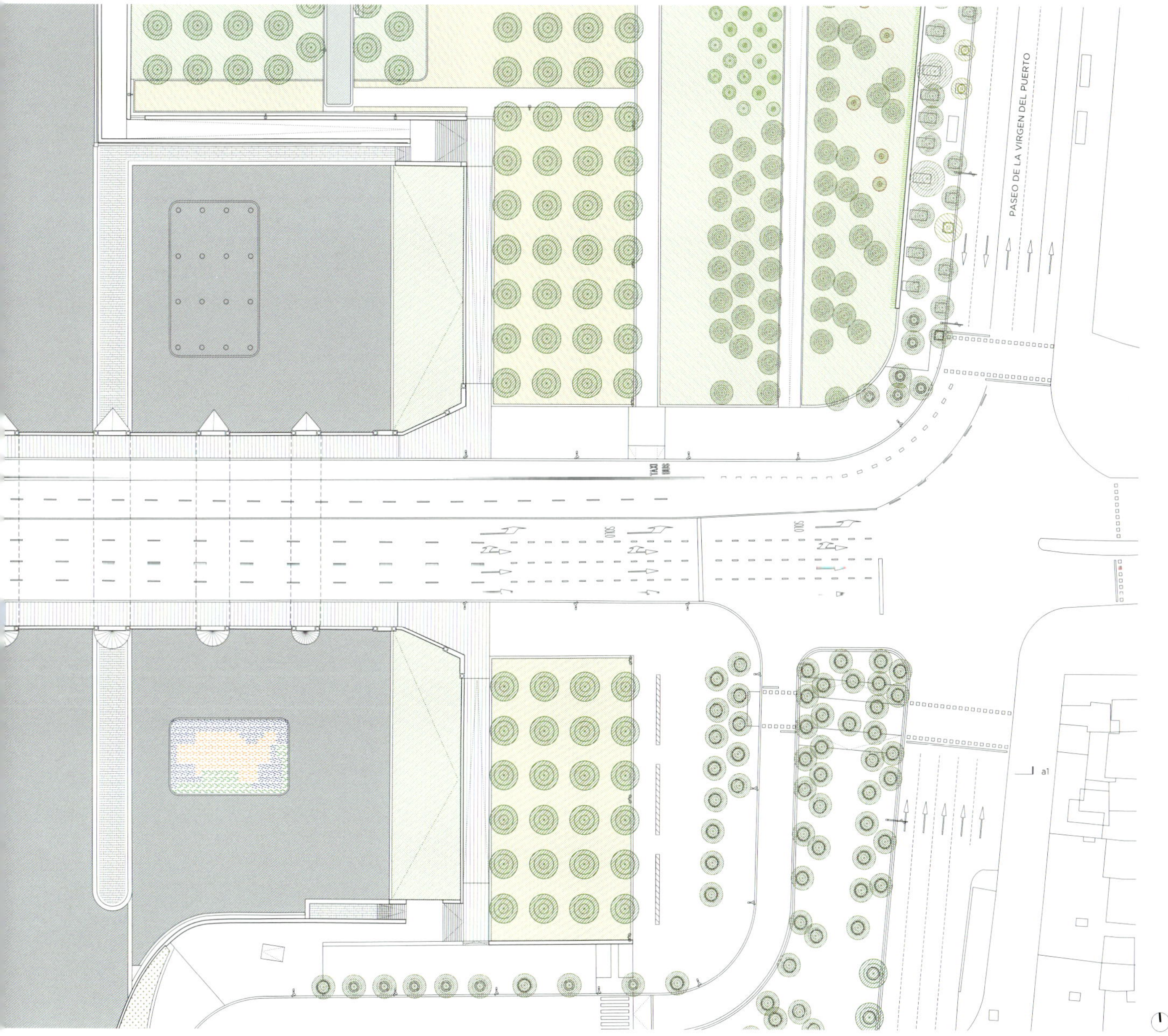

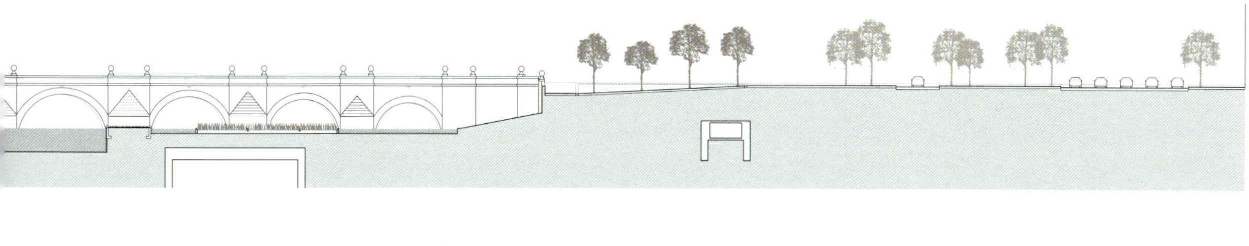

1/1,000 12345 10

ERI

ERI

AN ENCOUNTER WITH RIBERA

Starting point

Until the 18th century, Madrid expanded in an almost spontaneous way, without paying even partial attention to plans or zoning systems. Most of the city center grew more or less concentrically in a disorderly manner for centuries. The first construction projects to include geometric layouts, compositional axes, or zoning based on a general underlying idea were carried out around the Manzanares River when the Bourbon dynasty took the Spanish throne. Of these, some of the most remarkable occurred around the Puente de Toledo, which linked the city center with one of the most important cities on the Peninsula, 72 kilometers southeast of Madrid.

Toledo was founded during the Roman occupation of Iberia and became a leading population center during the second century B.C.E. It was the imperial capital and home to outstanding institutions before the court settled permanently in Madrid. Therefore, from the time the modern capital began to take shape, the connection between these two cities has been one of the virtual axes structuring Madrid's urban fabric.

In that same sense, from the moment the city began to expand beyond the successive Christian walls built around the Hapsburg's Alcazar palace, there has always been a means of crossing the Manzanares nearby. Like many of the other bridges built over the river, the Puente de Toledo was repeatedly washed away by floodwaters, and it wasn't until 1718 that it adopted a form solid enough to survive as we know it today. The construction of this extraordinarily important urban work took place at a moment of particular political opportunity for Madrid, when Philip V, the first Bourbon king of Spain and a Frenchman by birth, took the Spanish throne during the war of succession. The Bourbons were much more ambitious and cosmopolitan than the Hapsburgs in matters related to the city's public spaces, and their public works reflected both the first king's French origins and the Italian influence he received from his second wife, Isabel of Farnesio, which is visible in a series of works carried out along the Manzanares. The first of these was the new Royal Palace and the last, the Puente de Toledo. These works were supervised by the city's mayor and chief magistrate, Francisco Antonio de Salcedo y Aguirre, Marquis of Vadillo, who appointed Pedro de Ribera chief director of works and fountains and commissioned him to design the bridge. It was completed in 1730 and opened that same year. Today, it is the only historical bridge in Madrid that has never been widened.

During the reign of Charles III of Bourbon, a trident of plane-tree-lined avenues was built to link the former gate of one of the walls with the river, effectively joining the city and its new bridge. This itinerary outside the city walls was conceived as a group of wide, French-style tree-lined roads that constituted a baroque approach to the riverside landscape that drew on those carried out 200 years earlier in Aranjuez and in Versailles in the late 17th century.

As the city's growth accelerated towards the end of the 19th century, the mid-16th century wall blocking its expansion was demolished and the land around the bridge filled with a disorderly group of industries and outlying neighborhoods that did not, however, affect the roads. As a result, the latter served as an overriding structure that regulated them. In the 20th century, when the city began its definitive growth towards the river, the housing in this area grew gradually denser but the mark of the boulevards, including a wide avenue connecting the bridge and the Puerta de Toledo (Toledo Gate) remained as vestiges of the baroque conception of a possible urban plan that never came to pass.

In the 20th century, the construction of the M-30 highway included routing vehicular traffic under the bridge and constructing two viaducts that wrapped around it, hiding it and minimizing its scale. This was the greatest aggression that monument had ever suffered, and after the M-30 was rerouted underground, the opportunity arose to work on the area around the bridge, on the river's right bank. This made it possible to recover the stylistic tradition of its designer, Pedro de Ribera, with a project that highlights the architecture of his Baroque creation.

The place

The Puente de Toledo stands at the geometric center of the six Madrid landscapes, in an extremely sensitive position

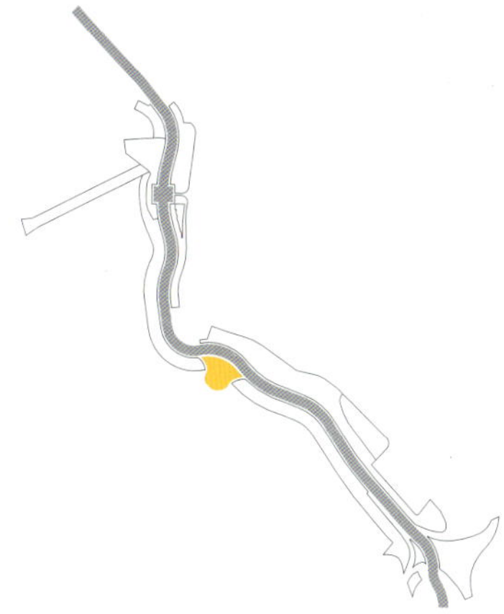

where the Manzanares River changes direction with a bend of almost 120 degrees. The bridge's area of influence, on the river's right bank, is increased where it separates from the buildings, as there is still an important open space that formerly contained one of the city's most important open laundries. That space, which was later crossed by the M-30 highway that irreverently ran under the arches of the 18th-century bridge, was always a residual area. Despite its considerable size, it did not fit into the city as a usable space. In recent decades, the former open-air laundry was replaced by a series of deplorable shacks housing highway services and maintenance vehicles.

Furthermore, the singularity of this area is reinforced by its special circumstances as a juncture of infrastructures on an urban scale. That is where the most important electric, gas, and potable water lines cross the river, along with two subway lines that run under its bed. There is also a new storm water tank built to improve the drainage of rainwater. Two of the most important junctions of the underground tunnel have been built beneath this area, allowing multiple changes of direction, not to mention a length of the former highway, which is the only elevated passage that was not eliminated when the rest was rerouted underground.

So the Puente de Toledo and its immediate surroundings play an exceptional role as central elements in the project carried out there, not only because of the bridge's importance, but also because of the river's bend, the empty space around its abutments, and the group of service and transit arteries serving the city.

Concept and character of the proposal

The landscape installed in this empty area bearing such complex infrastructures has to reflect two objectives. First, potentiating the presence of the Baroque bridge and its importance as a singular element in urban surroundings. Second, completely integrating all of the elements that cross the area and that have made it unusable until now as a civic space; that is, the major conduits for electricity, water, and gas, some of which remained above ground when the highway was rerouted, as well as the road junctions, the storm water tank, and so on.

Both needs were approached by conceiving and shaping a new topography adapted to include all existing infrastructures while simultaneously allowing the creation of an accessible space. This surface links the riverbank with the dense city through paths and trails that connect the bank with Marqués de Vadillo Plaza, a spatial prelude to the consolidated residential fabric. Over this softened artificial topography crossed by pedestrian and cycle paths that respond to the highway infrastructure running underneath, a pattern of vegetation articulates a figurative language around the monument. That language constitutes a sign of identity legible from the dominant position of the bridge's walkway.

The French and Italian tradition of garden spaces over which a new geometry is established with plants has some important forerunners in Madrid and its surroundings, including the geometric hedges in the gardens of El Escorial, the landscaping of the Royal Seats at La Granja and Aranjuez, the Maze at the Dutchess of Osuna's El Capricho Park, the gardens at Oriente Plaza, and different versions of geometric gardening that were never actually carried out in the Campo del Moro at the foot of the Royal Palace. These local references reveal the suitability for this space of a green pattern with a contemporary design that would nonetheless remain close to Madrid's tradition of filling large open areas with linear structures of plants. Such a design should bring a solemn and specific character to the atmosphere around the bridge.

Description of the landscape

The structural elements in this setting are: the bridge that dominates the space, the recovered and newly accessible river, the city as an opaque background and the new surface that joins them, shaped to serve as the operation's main support. The bridge has a determinant effect on the proposal, due to both its image as a stone object pierced by nine archways and its height with regard to the city, that is, the distance between the base of its pilings, which rest on dry ground, and the surface of its deck. In that sense, the riverbank has to achieve a smooth connection with the deck by ascending gently until it reaches the level of the plaza where the city begins. The difference of altitude is 4.5 meters.

GEOMETRIC GARDENS IN MADRID

FLOWERBEDS IN ARANJUEZ'S LA ISLA GARDENS (16TH CENTURY)

FRIARS' GARDEN AT THE MONASTERY OF EL ESCORIAL (16TH CENTURY)

FLOWERBED AT THE RETIRO PARK (18TH CENTURY)

MAZE IN THE GARDENS AT LA GRANJA DE SAN ILDEFONSO (18TH CENTURY)

FLOWERBED IN THE GARDENS AT LA GRANJA DE SAN ILDEFONSO (18TH CENTURY)

The solution applied here is a graphic design whose most important lines are established by plant silhouettes that stand 1.2 meters high. A secondary part uses plants of lesser height to create a play of positive and negative. This large-scale pattern establishes a hierarchy that defines various itineraries and disappears gradually as it approaches the river, allowing clear passage to the cycling path. The layout of the hedges widens to generate rest areas and narrows to define paths or connections. Towards the north and south, where it abuts with the Salón de Pinos, the space becomes less accessible and more wooded, with masses of bushes and trees planted in a dense framework. The cycle path mentioned above establishes the continuity linking this space with the wooded structure of the Salón de Pinos and it also separates the strip that runs along the bank north of the bridge, leading to terracing that unfolds before its stone arches and cutwaters.

Technical solutions

This area's most important technical aspects concern multiple infrastructures and easements that have to run underground but above the level of the highway tunnels. The combination and compatibility of multiple conduits and the limitation of maximum allowable loads on the tunnel slabs result in a complex stratum that could, itself, be considered an invisible landscape. The abundance of networks running through this setting, from the most superficial (electricity) through the deepest (subway tunnels) reduces the amount of space available for draining an intensely planted surface. As a result, a process of arthroscopy has been used to run storm drains between conduits of very diverse scales and diameters, and to connect them with areas of porous terrain or with extant collectors.

Materials and elements

The construction of the space around the Puente de Toledo could be described as a succession of elements at increasing distances from ground level. First, we should mention the materials that make up the new topography, or starting point. These can be divided into those that can be walked on and those that cannot. The former are made fundamentally of granite, which paves the walk along the river and the main paths linking the garden with the open spaces, plazas, and streets of the nearby urban fabric; and decomposed granite, which is used to finish secondary paths. The latter also employ two materials: earth extended as a substratum to feed the vegetation; and further back, crushed recycled brick, whose intense color helps define the pattern. These materials are separated according to their uses by granite borders whose layout follows the geometry of the overall surface pattern.

The outlines of the pattern are also reinforced by the lines of wooden benches that stand 45 centimeters above ground and are grouped in the most static rest areas. On the terrace 60 centimeters above the starting point are three complementary plant areas: first, those delimited by a red flower known as *Rosa spp.* (Sevillian rosebush), whose patches of monochrome red are part of the linear pattern; second, the spongy texture of *Lavandula spp.* (lavender), which is used to soften the appearance of the mouth of the tunnel running through the garden's northern sector; and finally, *Hypericum calycinum* (St. John's wort), a ground cover planted on the slopes near the garden's urban edge. Visually, these three components become especially important in late spring as all blossom at the same time, generating a combination of red roses, violet lavender, and yellow St. John's wort.

FLOWERBEDS IN THE ORIENTE GARDENS
(19TH CENTURY)

MAZE IN THE GARDEN AT
EL CAPRICHO (19TH CENTURY)

FLOWERBEDS IN THE GARDENS
AT PUENTE DE TOLEDO (21ST CENTURY)

1 / 2,000 10 20 50

Four types of bushes appear 1.2 meters above the level of the walkway: *Ligustrum japonica* (Japanese privet), *Viburnum tinus* (laurestine), *Buxus sempervirens* (box), and *Laurus nobilis* (bay laurel). Together, they form the large figurative pattern visible near the bridge. Each species has been cultivated in hedges whose lines zigzag to generate silhouettes that form recognizable closed shapes like a sort of huge tattoo on the earthen skin that bears the pilings of the Baroque bridge.

The trees planted among the hedges appear at 3.6 meters above the walkway. These are mainly *Albizia julibrissin* (Persian silk tree), *Liriodendron tulipifera* (tulip tree), *Populus simonii* (Chinese poplar), *Pinus pinea* (stone pine), and *Pinus halepensis* (Aleppo pine). Each of these species is placed according to its size, type of leaf, and shape. Thus, the first two are planted singly while the poplars and pines are laid out in groups.

Landscape and city

Landscaping the area around Puente de Toledo responds to certain important questions that had gone unaddressed in the city of Madrid since that bridge was constructed in the 18th century. Integrating the spaces near the riverbank and establishing continuity between the bridge's deck, its abutments and the surrounding area has generated a definitive dialog between the ancient structure and the nearby urban space. The bridge acquires a new role as a viewpoint from which to contemplate the garden below, whose design appears like an inlaid pattern of plant life. The riverside promenades offer pedestrians the unprecedented experience of walking beneath the bridge's stone arches thanks to their capacity to provide efficient and unfettered access to the spaces running along the river from north to south.

The presence of the monument designed by Pedro de Ribera and the intense concentration of low vegetation compatible with the extraordinary complexity of the infrastructures present just below the surface offer a new, powerful, and sophisticated image that emphasizes this area's eternal leading role as a central space in Madrid.

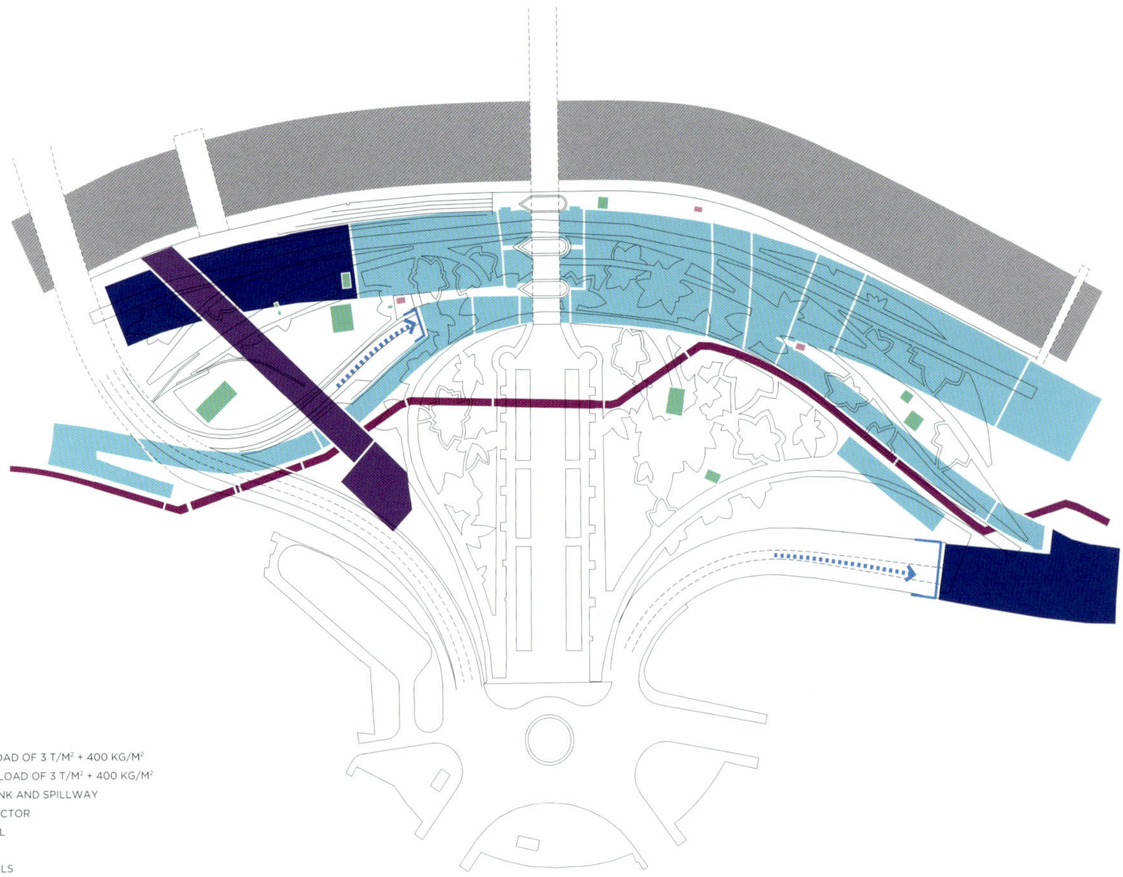

SLABS

- SLAB WITH LIVE LOAD OF 3 T/M² + 400 KG/M²
- BEAMS WITH LIVE LOAD OF 3 T/M² + 400 KG/M²
- STORM WATER TANK AND SPILLWAY
- RIVERBANK COLLECTOR
- VENTILATION GRILL
- EMERGENCY EXIT
- ACCESS TO TUNNELS

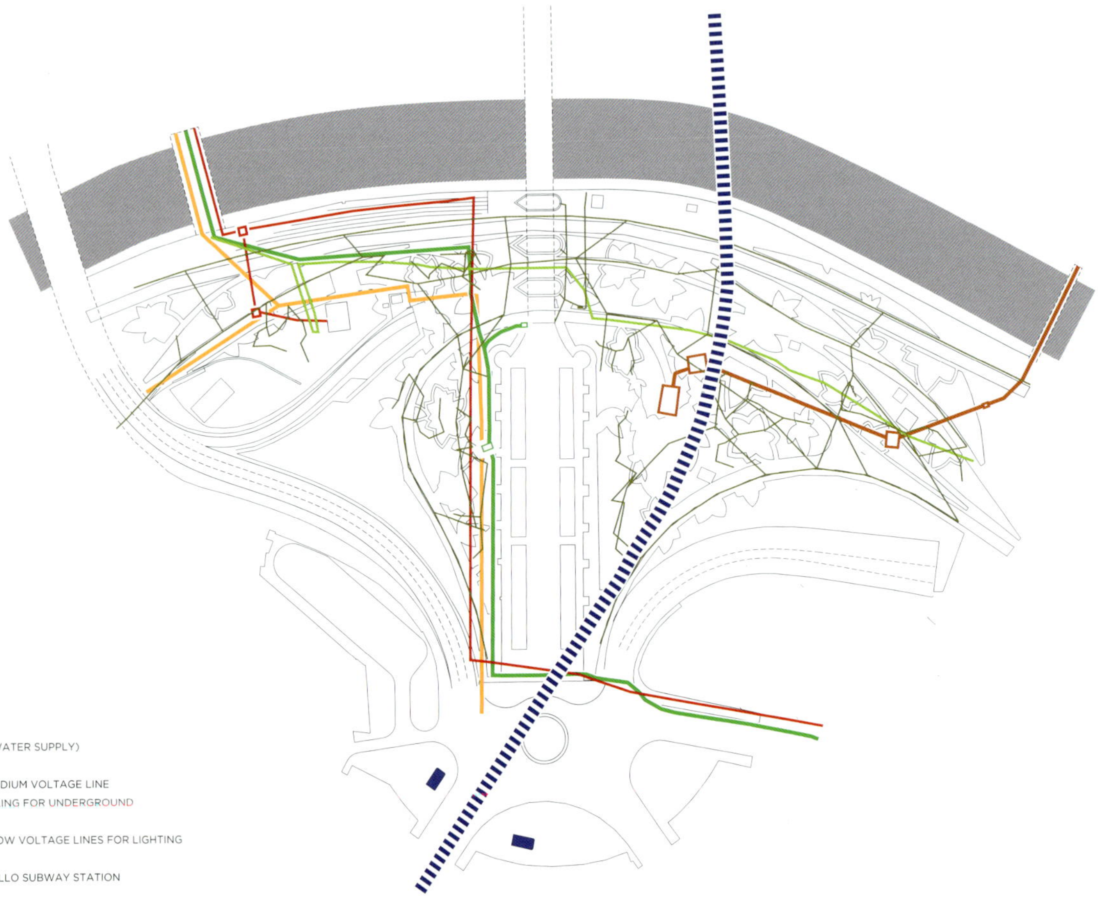

INSTALLATIONS

- NATURAL GAS
- CANAL ISABEL II (WATER SUPPLY)
- OPTICAL FIBER
- UNDERGROUND MEDIUM VOLTAGE LINE
- RESERVE CHANNELING FOR UNDERGROUND MEDIUM VOLTAGE
- CHANNELING OF LOW VOLTAGE LINES FOR LIGHTING
- SUBWAY LINE 5
- MARQUÉS DE VADILLO SUBWAY STATION

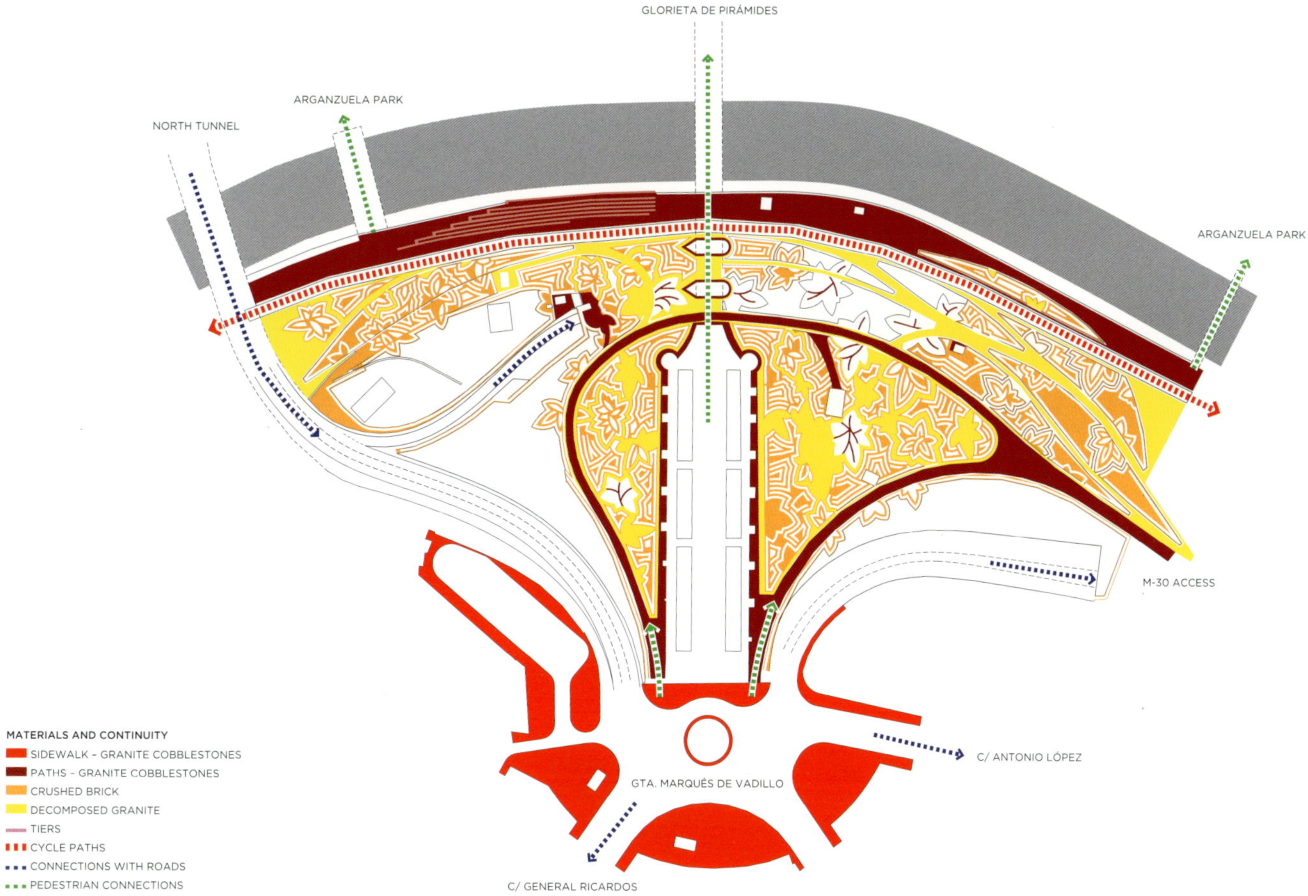
GLORIETA DE PIRÁMIDES
ARGANZUELA PARK
NORTH TUNNEL
ARGANZUELA PARK
M-30 ACCESS
C/ ANTONIO LÓPEZ
GTA. MARQUÉS DE VADILLO
C/ GENERAL RICARDOS
MATERIALS AND CONTINUITY
SIDEWALK – GRANITE COBBLESTONES
PATHS – GRANITE COBBLESTONES
CRUSHED BRICK
DECOMPOSED GRANITE
TIERS
CYCLE PATHS
CONNECTIONS WITH ROADS
PEDESTRIAN CONNECTIONS

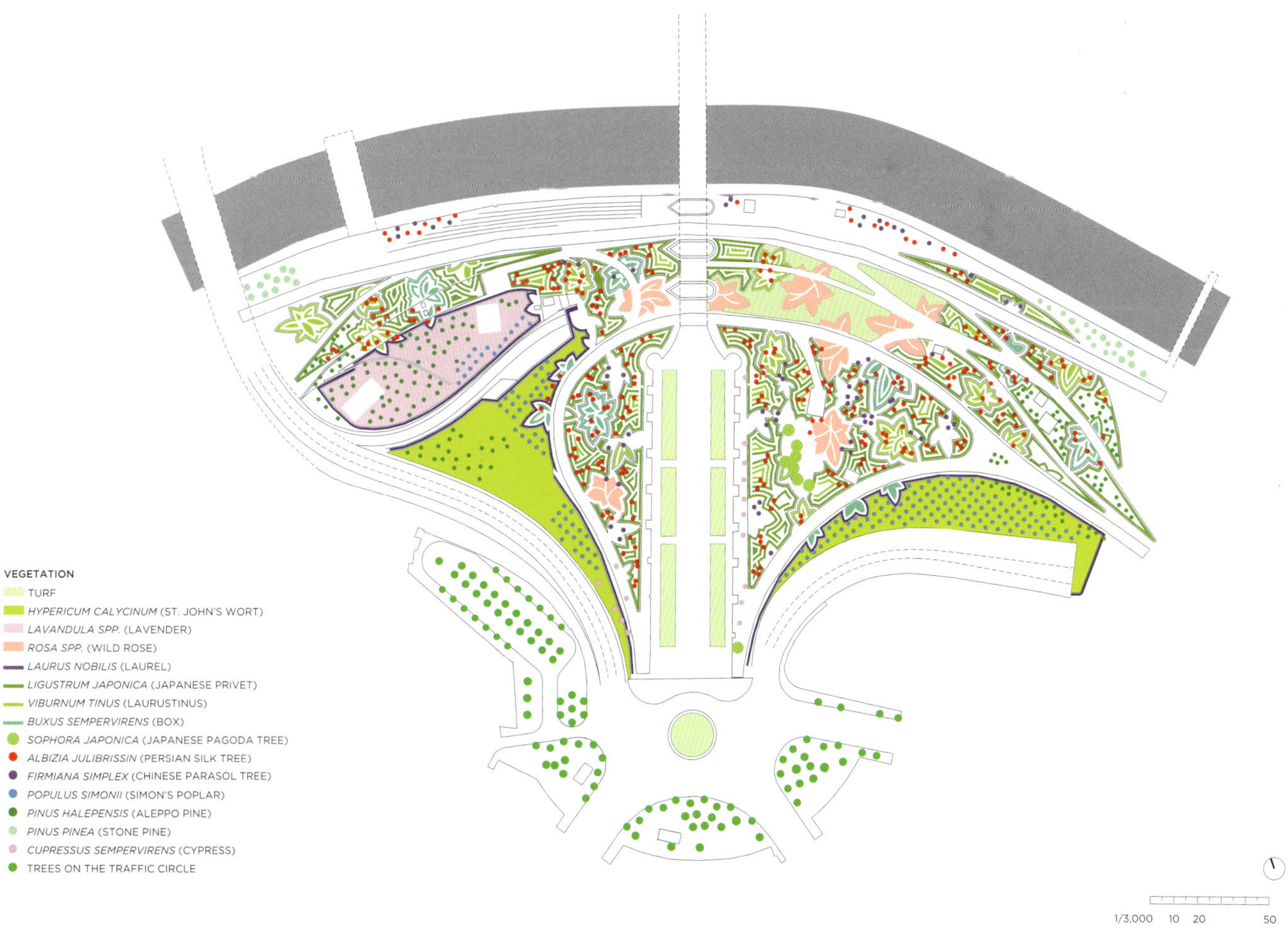
VEGETATION
TURF
HYPERICUM CALYCINUM (ST. JOHN'S WORT)
LAVANDULA SPP. (LAVENDER)
ROSA SPP. (WILD ROSE)
LAURUS NOBILIS (LAUREL)
LIGUSTRUM JAPONICA (JAPANESE PRIVET)
VIBURNUM TINUS (LAURUSTINUS)
BUXUS SEMPERVIRENS (BOX)
SOPHORA JAPONICA (JAPANESE PAGODA TREE)
ALBIZIA JULIBRISSIN (PERSIAN SILK TREE)
FIRMIANA SIMPLEX (CHINESE PARASOL TREE)
POPULUS SIMONII (SIMON'S POPLAR)
PINUS HALEPENSIS (ALEPPO PINE)
PINUS PINEA (STONE PINE)
CUPRESSUS SEMPERVIRENS (CYPRESS)
TREES ON THE TRAFFIC CIRCLE
1/3,000 10 20 50

K.P. 3.90

AREA AROUND PUENTE DE TOLEDO

PLAN. K.P. 4.60 - K.P. 4.90

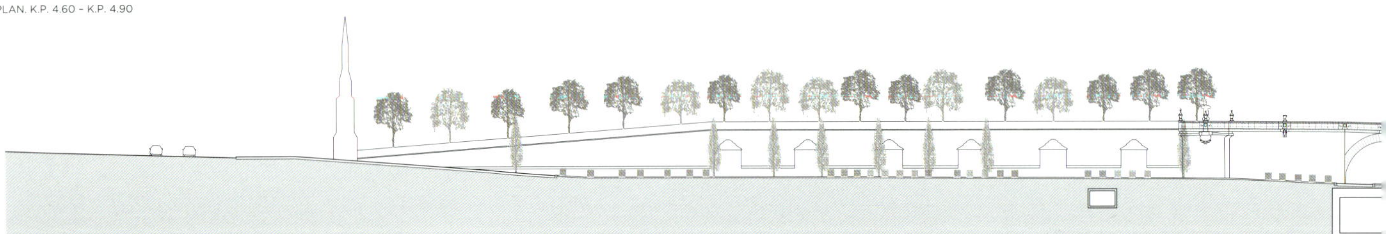

ELEVATION a1

P.º DE LOS MELANCÓLICOS
P.º IMPERIAL
GTA. DE PIRÁMIDES
C/ TOLEDO
PUENTE DE TOLEDO
a1
P.º DE LAS ACACIAS
P.º DE YESERÍAS
1/1,500 2 4 6 8 10 20

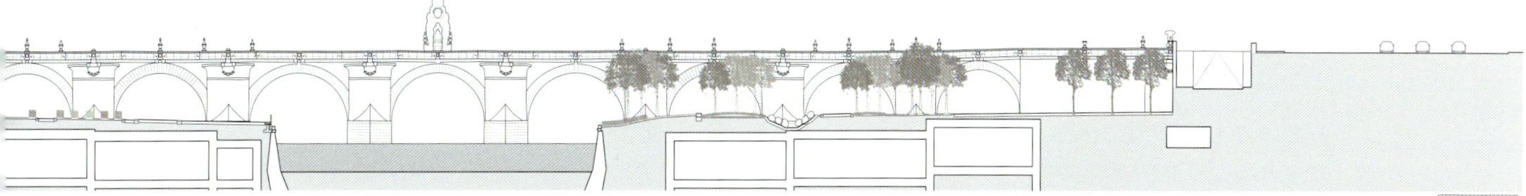
1/1,000 1 5 10

K.P. 4.80

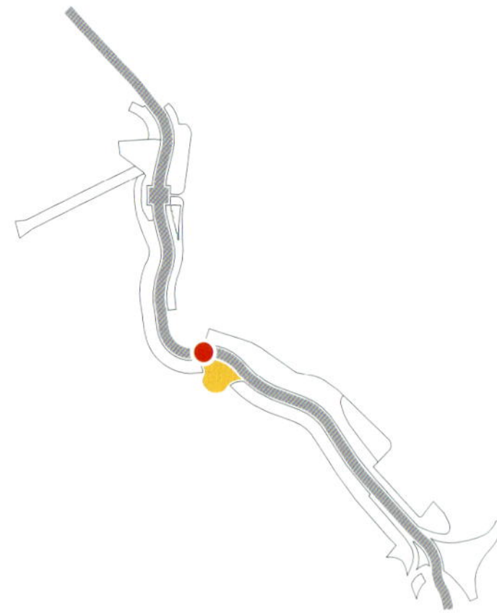

NORTH PONTOON

Length on axis 41 m
Length between supports 13.75 m
Deck width 12.20 m
Structure Prefabricated concrete beams on existing pilings and concrete slab
Date of construction of existing structure 1965
Date of completion 2008

K.P. 4.64

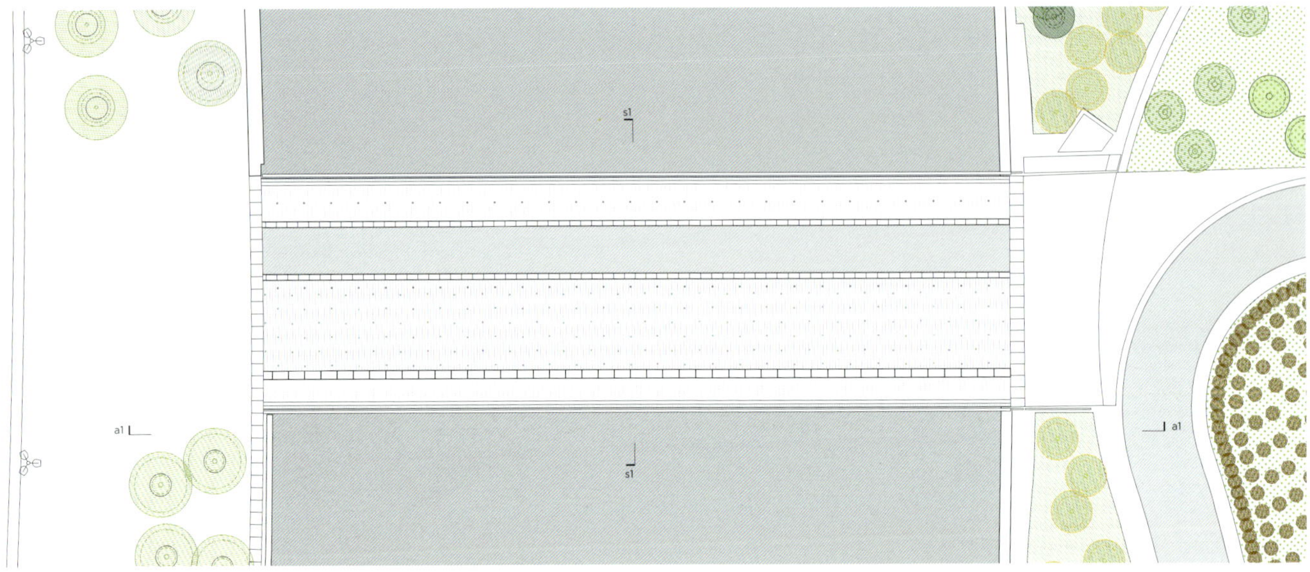

PLAN

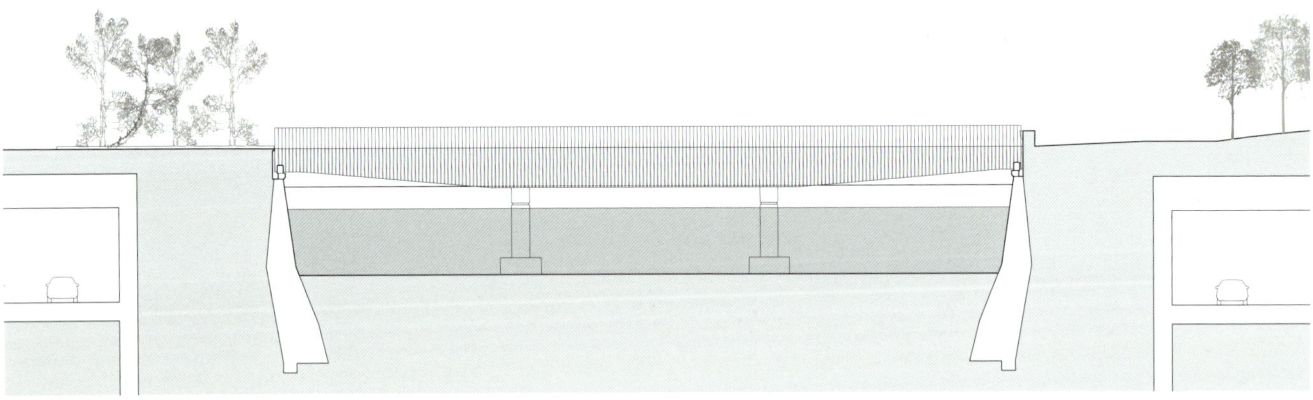

ELEVATION a1

1/400 1 2 3 4 5 10

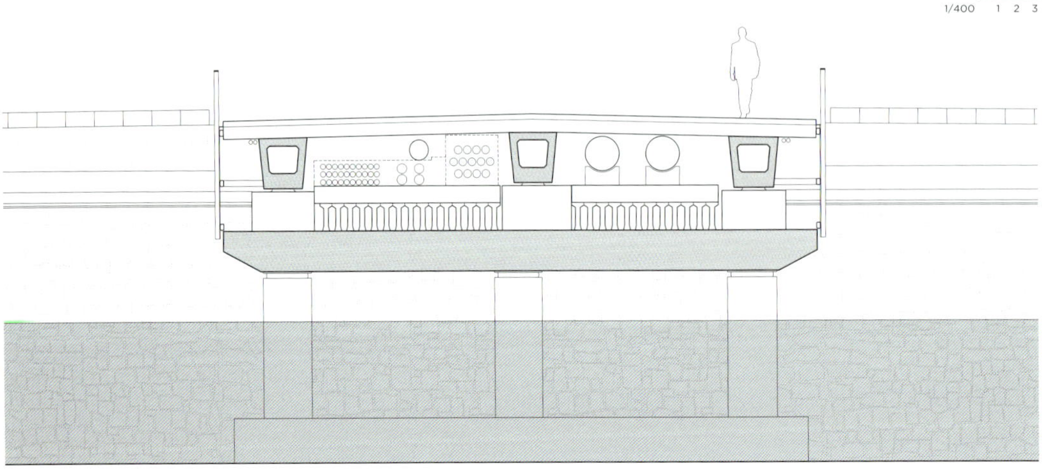

SECTION s1

1/150 1 2 3 4 5 10

K.P. 4.64

K.P. 5.01 (DATASHEET ON THE NEXT PAGE)

CANAL FOOTBRIDGE

Length on axis 43.34 m
Length between supports 45 m
Deck width 3.44 m / 4.13 m
Structure Metal beams to bear existing conduit and wooden deck
Date of completion 2008

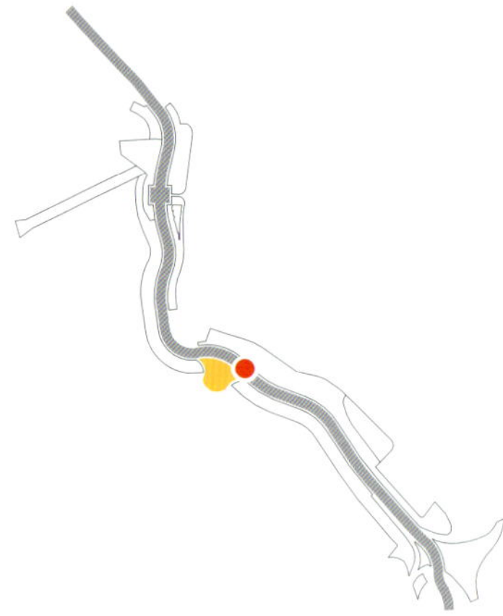

K.P. 5.01

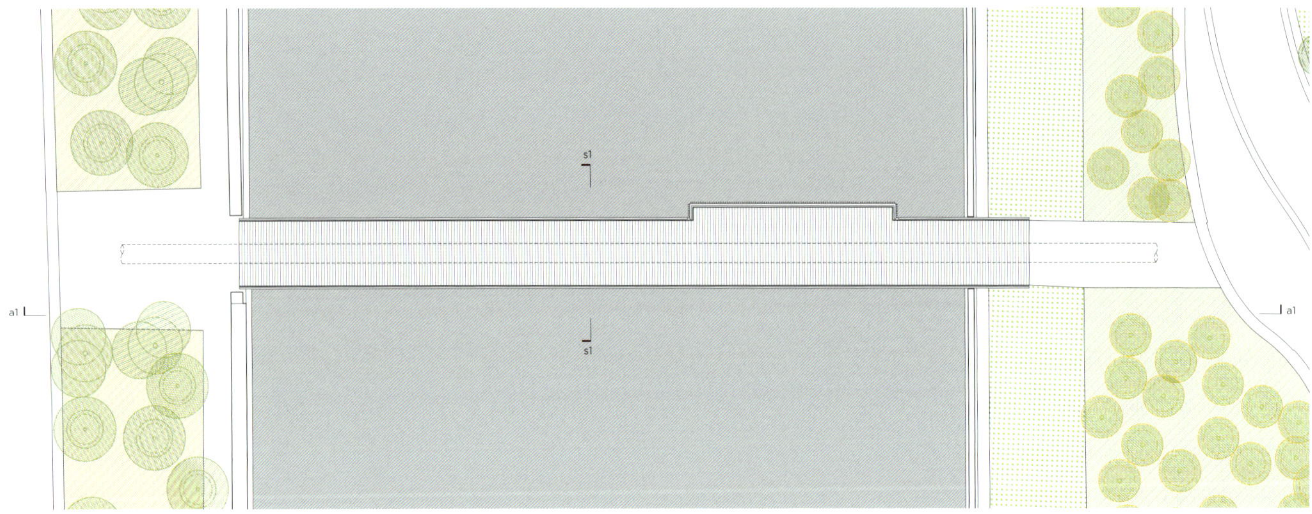

PLAN

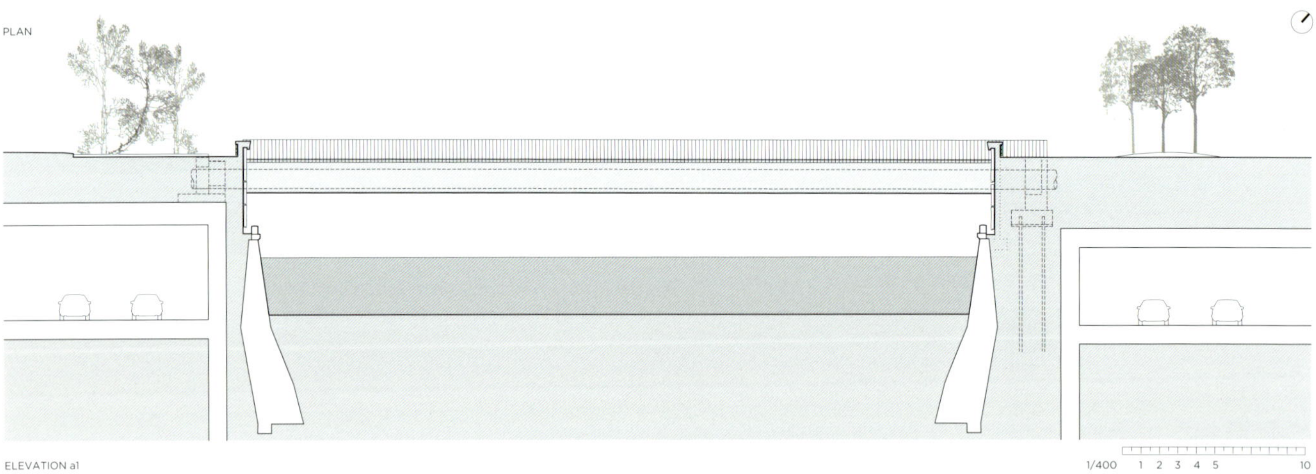

ELEVATION a1

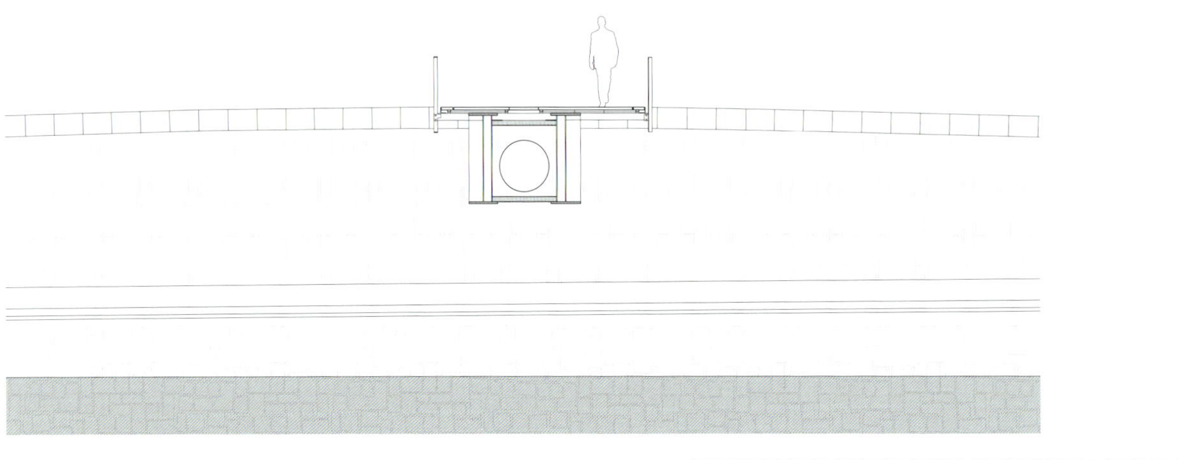

SECTION s1

PUENTE DE BOLAS

Length on axis 40.83 m
Length between supports Central span 26 m / Lateral spans 6.50 m
Deck width 4 m
Structure Metal beams to shape conduit passages and wooden deck over original structure
Date of construction of existing structure 1955
Date of completion 2008

K.P. 5.05

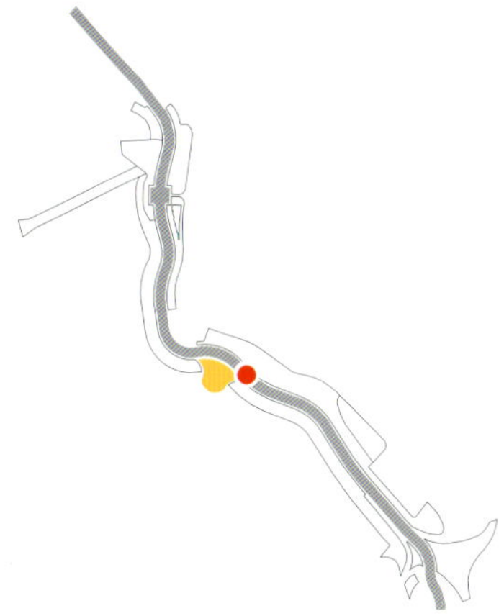

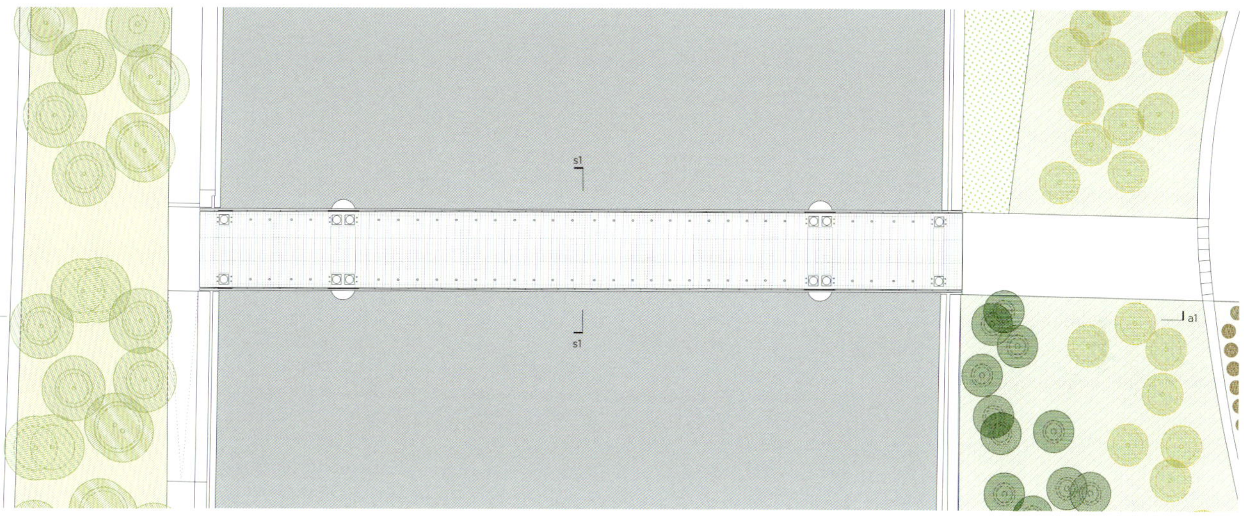

PLAN

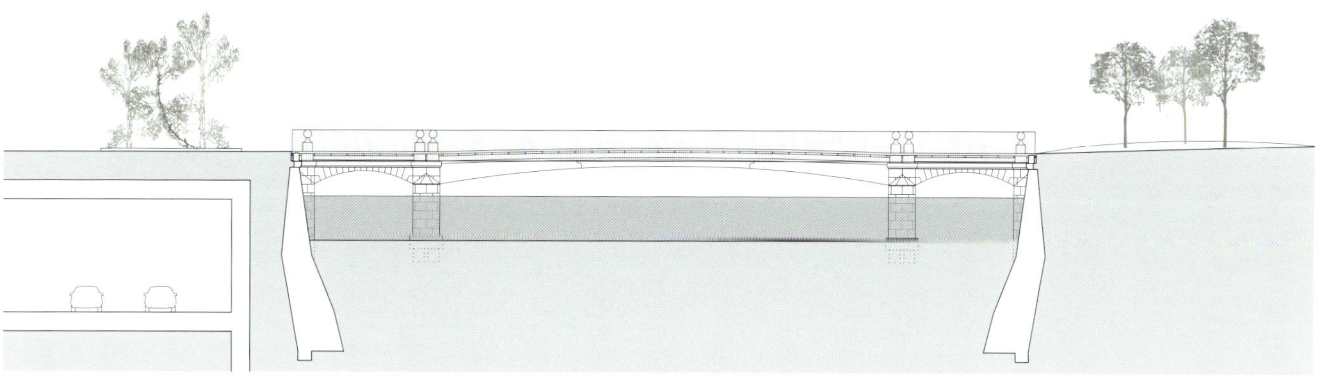

ELEVATION a1

1/400 1 2 3 4 5 10

SECTION s1

1/150 1 2 3 4 5 10

RIR

RIR
RIVER REMAINS

Starting point
The city separates from the Manzanares River along its left bank, south of the Puente de Toledo (Toledo Bridge). That separation creates a free space 2,200 meters long , with an average width of 150 meters, running northwest to southeast. Its long sides are almost parallel and adjoin the channeled river, on one side and, on the other, the urban axis where the Paseo de Yeserías and and Paseo de La Chopera meet. Running along these streets, away from the river, are a series of city blocks densely filled with apartment buildings, generating a totally consolidated urban fabric.

This is an area of almost 30 hectares bordering a considerable expanse of the river. Its northwestern edge, near Vicente Calderón Stadium, is clearly defined by nearby urban construction that closes off the free space right up to the riverbank. Its southeastern edge, though, is frayed like a thread running along the riverside and ending in a complex highway intersection known as nudo Sur (South Junction).

This enclave has its own importance in the projected work on the left bank for two fundamental reasons: first, because of its size, which justifies a unified and characteristic proposal that differs from the other landscapes in this ordered group; and second, because it is located in a very dense part of the city, where there are hardly any empty spaces available to the numerous population for leisure, and because its location involves intense contact with construction on both sides—with the city, and also with the river.

A part of this setting has been occupied by Arganzuela Park since the nineteen sixties and about a third of that park's trees have survived both the original construction of the M-30 highway and the later work to run it underground.

The idea underlying the proposal reflects the impermanence of rivers in the central Iberian Peninsula, where their flow varies greatly depending on the time of year and the duration of winter rains. These rivers appear and disappear, flowing abundantly during the spring and then almost completely drying up in the summer. The new Arganzuela Park is designed to reflect the idea of a riverbed whose wet periods leave behind various elements visible after it dries: sediments transported by the water, vegetation that proliferates in wet ground, and various spaces that emerge where linear marks intersect.

The place
Historically, the wooded meadows of Arganzuela were an open municipal space on the river's edge. Cattle grazed freely there until industry and railway lines occupied it in the second half of the 19th century. These uses emerged successively as a result of the availability of two transportation infrastructures that coexisted there until the beginning of the 20th century. First: railway lines linking the stations known as Príncipe Pío, Imperial, and Delicias; and second, the Real Canal del Manzanares (Royal Manzanares Canal), which was built to allow the transportation of raw materials from the south of the region, especially gypsum extracted from the barren lands further downstream.

While the city grew, industrial installations were gradually replaced by residential buildings but the wooded meadows were never occupied. Instead, from the beginning of the 20th century, they were subjected to different gardening projects that culminated in the construction of a park in the 1960s. That park was always separated from the river by a roadway that soon abandoned its local character to become one of the lanes of the M-30 highway. The latter, and the river itself, made the green zone practically inaccessible from the south or west, making it an almost unused neighborhood park.

Tunnel construction at the beginning of the 21st century had two opposing effects on the area: first, the disappearance of automobiles made it possible to expand the area available for the park, almost tripling the original 10.5 hectares. Second, the tunnel work itself totally devastated the land (except for the wooded area farthest from the river). Its public ownership and distance from residential construction led it to be used as an area for storage and logistics, activities that are extremely aggressive to the ground.

After the M-30 was rerouted, Arganzuela emerged as a place suitable for a complete overhaul, given that the persistent memory of that space as a green area openly conflicted with its appearance at that time, which resembled nothing so much as a battlefield.

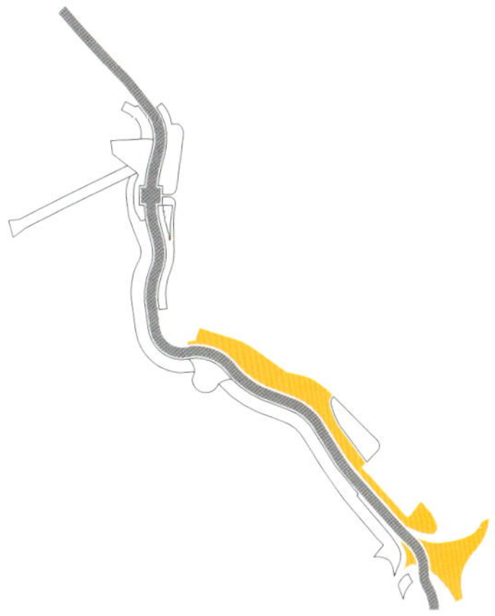

Concept and character of the proposal
The idea of building a park with the remains of the riverbed as figurative material provided the basis for its design, including its general structural layout and the different parts that respond to the space's functional needs. The project is adapted to the particular conditions of the setting, including its dimensions, proportions and position. Its lengthy shape offers considerable contact with the city, as well as very open access to the river. As a result, neighborhoods that previously could not reach it or had only very limited contact, now have much wider access, thanks to the construction of entryways from the city and walkways over the river. But that long, narrow shape also affects the internal organization of the green space, due to the difficulty of distributing its uses.

Once the land was freed, its easy access suggested very intense use and an eminently urban character as an installation that would serve a very numerous population. At the same time, its recovered status as a riverside park supported the decision to propose solutions that would emulate nature. This double character as a highly frequented urban park and as a riverside park underlies the global conception of the space and fits well with the objective of configuring a territory influenced by the coming and going of water over its surface.

Thus, longitudinal lines, urban activities, access, water, and plant life became the tools for creating a new green organism that makes sense for the city.

Description of the landscape
The park acquires its own identity, which differs from the other parks belonging to this overall project because of its size, because its contact with the city makes it highly accessible, and because it is adjacent to Puente de Toledo, the center point of the entire urban renewal operation.

The possibility of working on a setting whose only preexisting identity was as a wooded pasture that had survived previous construction work, allows an intervention in which topography and vegetation are used to radically modify the space, changing its scale and adding a texture previously unknown in the city. The project proposes shaping the surface as the main argument on which all other decisions depend. The topography, designed to integrate the multiple installations generated by the tunnels, is also what explains the principal elements that make up the landscape: paths, playgrounds, spaces for water, auxiliary installations, and rest areas.

The first element stemming from the topographical reshaping is the network of paths running through the park. In response to the latter's proportions, these paths run from northwest to southeast, leading to each part of the park, to the city accesses, and to the bridges and walkways. These paths follow three different itineraries and differ according to the relief on which they rest. The widest and flattest path has a variable width that maintains a relatively constant level throughout its length. Designed for rapid and direct movement, it is a broad promenade that allows access to all of the main activity areas. The second path adapts to a more varied topography, and its constant width runs through less open areas, making it more suitable for slower meandering. The third trail is lower than the overall ground level, a deep groove that offers shifting views of the surrounding vegetation. In that sense, it resembles a branch of the Manzanares that is dry at the moment but maintains its wetlands, giving life to wilder nature along its edges and generating a strip of intense green on the landscaped space.

These three lines interweave, cross, and overlap each other, generating settings of different sizes characterized by groups of plants, fountains, activity spaces, and rest areas. One of the itineraries is extended to bring continuity to the park along the Manzanares' left edge until it connects with the green areas and land outside the park at the city's southern end.

Besides its use for outdoor leisure and rest, strolling, skating, or cycling; the park hosts three types of activities: those related to sports, play, and water. The first require defined spaces with specific dimensions, and the park includes various *bocce* pitches, a soccer field, a skate park, and a rowing center associated with the river. The playgrounds follow the guidelines developed for the Salón de Pinos and are based on three elements: a large structure for climbing, an artificial hill with eight slides running down its slope, and a long zip line. Activities associated with water allow different degrees of

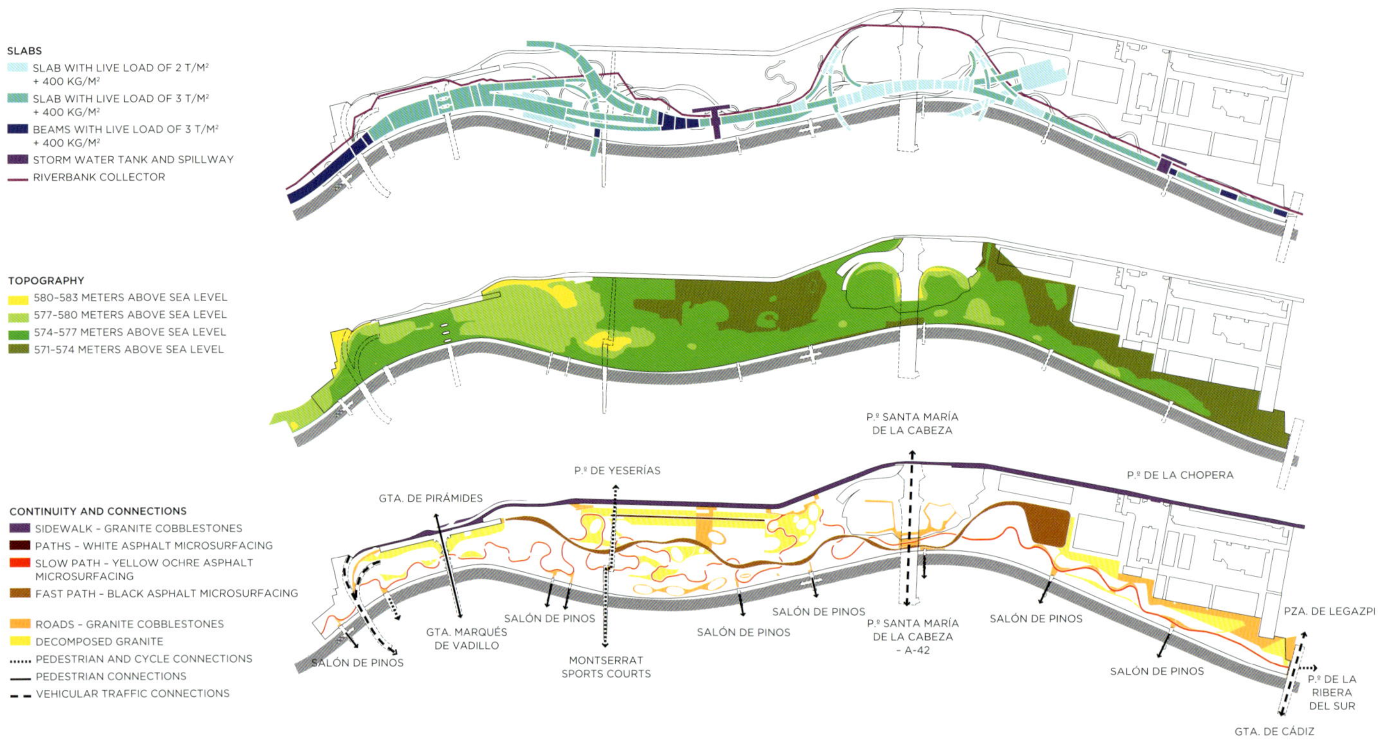

contact: from the contemplation of its nearly immobile flow in the vertical fern fountain to total interaction in the group of three ovals that constitute a sort of river beach for cooling off; as well as the sights and sounds of the waterspouts that make up a constellation of ten ornamental fountains.

The park also includes a series of bridges and pedestrian walkways that connect it to neighborhoods to the southwest, providing intense access. Two of these walkways are conceived as twin pavilions. Their domed structure makes crossing the bridge a spatial experience further enhanced by a photo-mosaic by artist Daniel Canogar that lines the inside of the domes.

Technical solutions

Arganzuela Park's considerable size encompasses two circumstances that differ considerably from a technical standpoint. On one hand, over a third of the park's surface has tunnels running underneath, and on the other, the park includes those tunnels' main service installations. In some cases, these are large, semi-interred buildings that have to be integrated into the park as hard points. The technical solution applied here is the same as in the Salón de Pinos, where drainage, protection of tunnel slabs and the installation of a substratum needed by plants generate a complex set of layers with diverse behavior and functions. Of course, the part of the land not occupied by tunnels allows a natural placement of plant life and inert elements, and the topographical design takes these circumstances into consideration in its response to land areas with different degrees of resistance. Each reconstructed level has been analyzed in terms of the substratum that bears it, and remodeling has been carried out both with mineral materials extracted during the tunneling and with lighter synthetic materials able to generate considerable volume while transmitting very little weight.

Materials and elements

The park's organization is based on a dialog among the paths and the settings generated by their crossing, curves and openings. The two types of paths are marked with analogous materials, using granite for the edging and asphalt microsurfacing of two different colors to indicate their different uses. The third trail, which is conceived like a dry riverbed, is edged by granite boulders from the mountains north of Madrid. Its bed is covered with river stones extracted from the Manzanares River's gravel pits. The elements at these three lines' meeting points (bridges, crosspieces, transition pieces, and so on) offer a hierarchical reading of each path.

The islands generated by the paths' linear movement serve as differentiated areas for planting interrelated species to form groups of flora that are appropriate for the region's geography. Four groups of plants appear independently throughout the park, defining a diverse and dense texture closer to wild growth than to gardens. They belong to the following categories: Atlantic forest, with *Aesculus hippocastanum* (chestnut), *Celtis australis* (hackberry), *Liquidambar styraciflua* (red gum), *Liriondendron tulipifera* (tulip tree), and *Tilia platyphyllos* (linden); Mediterranean forest, which includes *Arbutus unedo* (strawberry tree), *Quercus cerris* (oak), *Quercus ilex* (holm oak), and *Quercus suber* (cork oak); riverside forest, with *Ginkgo biloba* (ginkgo) and *Populus nigra* (black poplar); dry-river vegetation, including *Acer palmatum* (Japanese maple), *Acer freemanii* (Freeman maple), *Acer saccharinum* (silver maple), *Fraxinus angustifolia*

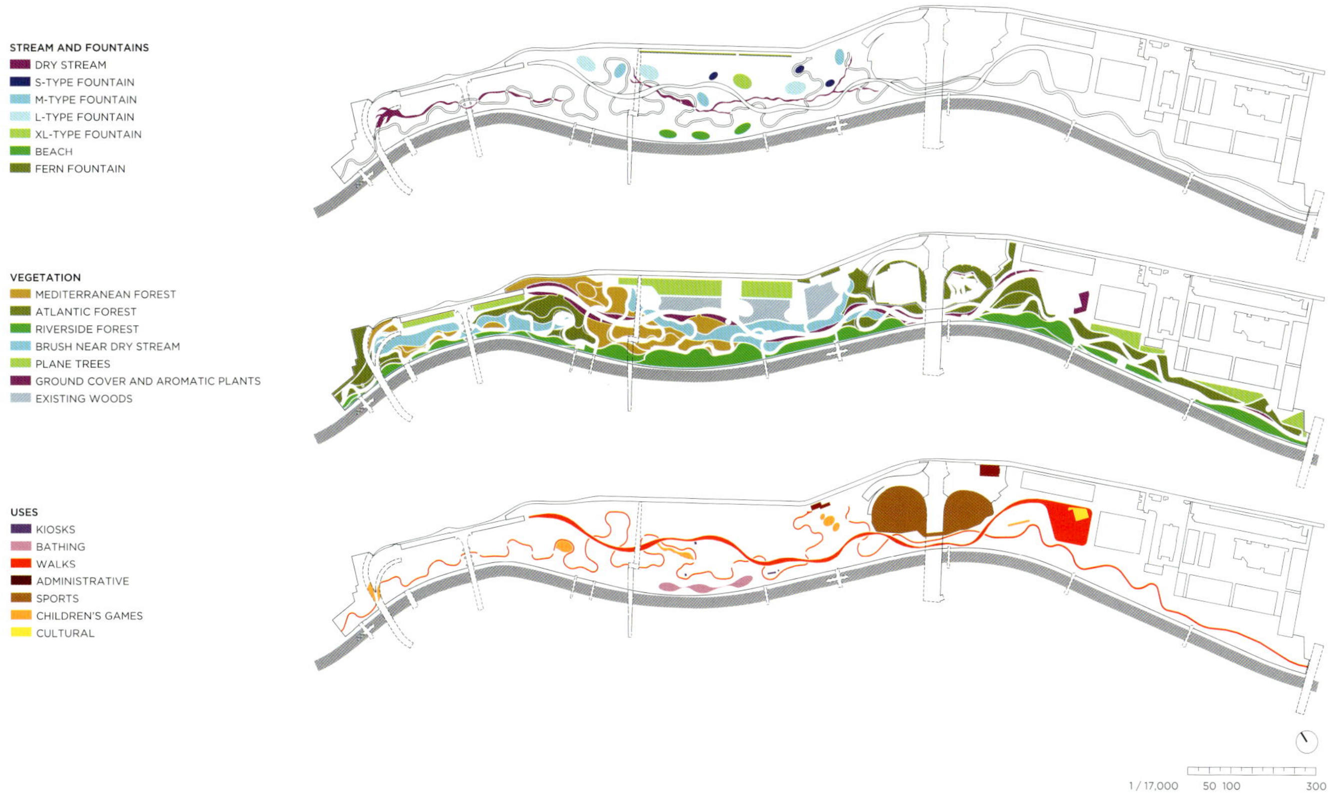

(narrow-leaved ash), and *Pterocarya fraxinifolia* (Caucasian wingnut). The shapes generated by the paths are lined with avenue trees such as *Melia azedarach* (white cedar), *Catalpa bignonioides* (catalpa), and *Prunus yedoensis* (Yoshino cherry).

This organic pattern of plants also provides the base for a constellation of ten ellipses of different sizes, each bearing an ornamental fountain with its own play of water. The most important and largest fountain marks the widest entrance to the park from the dense city. The other nine fulfill three different functions according to the water's scale, lighting, and movement, which constitute a variety of visual and sound experiences. Each fountain has its own small and enclosed setting, with a sloped green back sprinkled with *ficus caricai* (fig), *Punica granatum* (pomegranate), and *Malus domestica* (apple). The system of ornamental fountains is joined by a triple platform of clean-water spouts that invites users to interact with its unpredictable succession of flat sheets of water, clouds of mist, or a play of different-sized jets.

Paths, vegetation, and fountains form a permanent base on which activities occur in a mobile, changing way. The sports installations and playgrounds form a family of objects that almost disappear among the wavy shapes of the park that order and structure them like the bends in a millenary river.

Landscape and city

Arganzuela Park has become a leisure area for the city. Leaving its local dimension and neighborhood scale behind, it has become a structural element in Madrid's network of green spaces. Its double condition as an urban park and a riverside park is accentuated by its construction as a branch of a natural riverbed in which water appears and disappears, generating exuberant associations of plants. Its topography, the structure of its itineraries, the density of its plant areas, and the constant presence of water make this space intensely natural, an organic setting where social activities and visitors from near and far can easily find a place. As a landscape of form and figure, its meaning is constantly defined by the changing interaction between the two.

CHILDREN'S GAMES

Structure White locustwood tree trunks. Slides, stainless-steel rings, and metal pieces. Natural cord nets with galavanized steel cores
Date of completion 2011

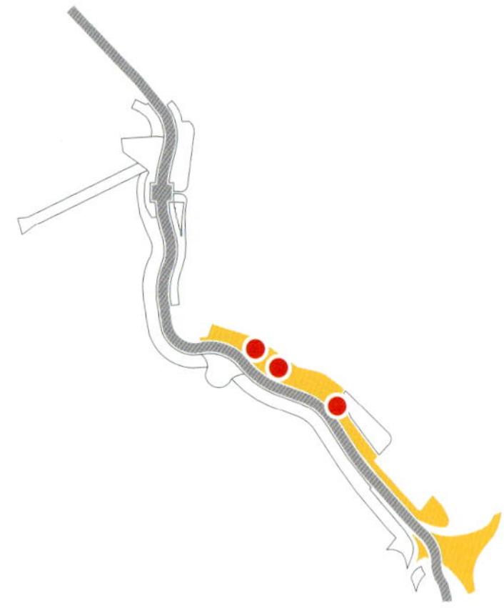

K.P. 4.95 - K.P. 5.20 - K.P. 5.95

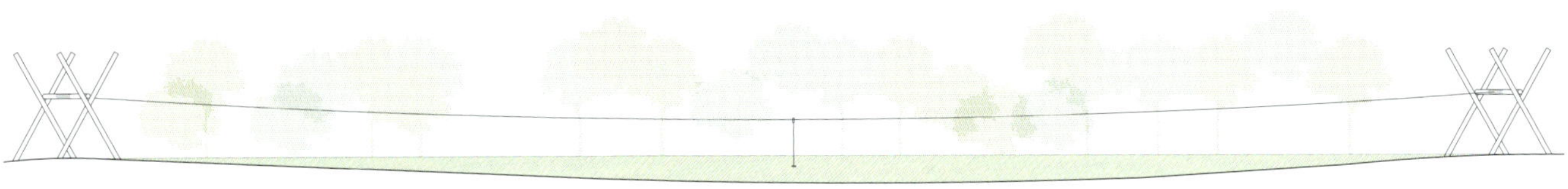

ZIP LINE

SKELETON

SLIDES

K.P. 4.95

K.P. 5.20

(DATASHEET ON THE PREVIOUS PAGES)

K.P. 5.80 (DATASHEET ON THE NEXT PAGE)

ARGANZUELA FOUNTAINS

Date of completion 2011

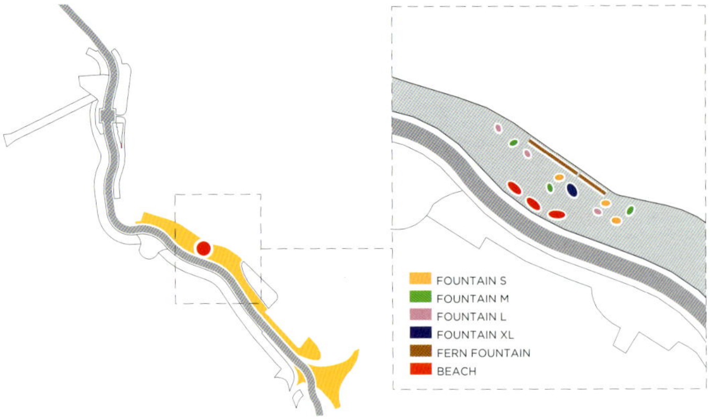

K.P. 5.00 - K.P. 5.63

S-TYPE FOUNTAIN

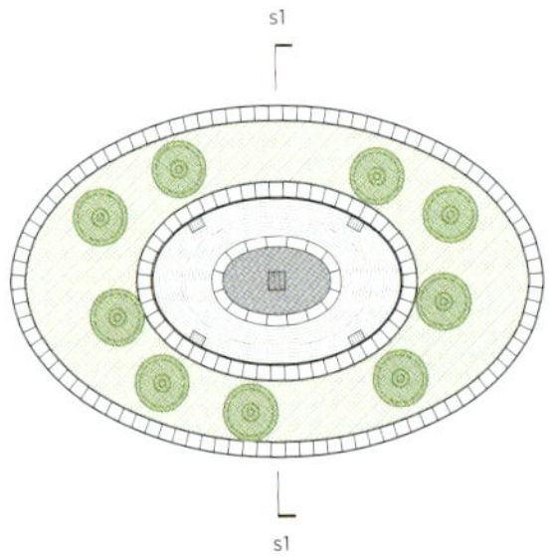

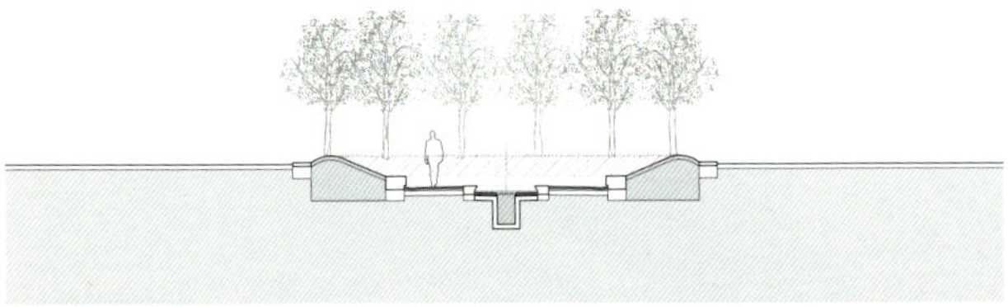

SECTION s1

M-TYPE FOUNTAIN

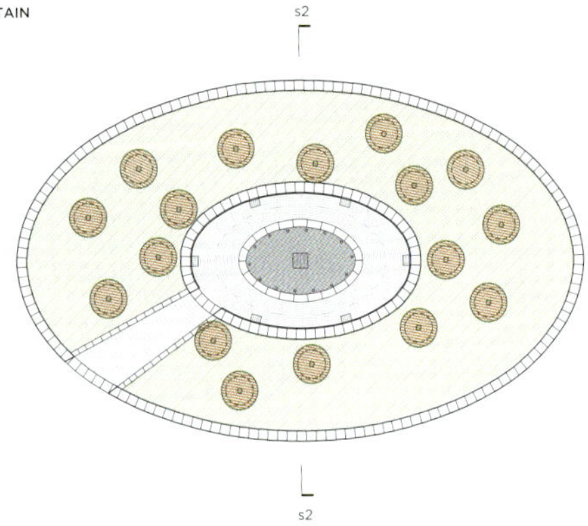

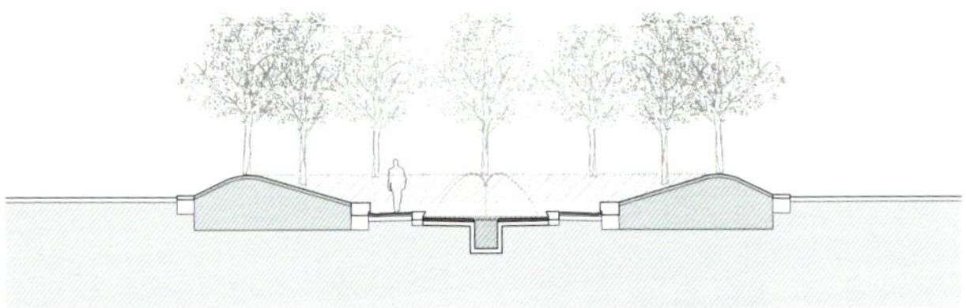

SECTION s2

L-TYPE FOUNTAIN

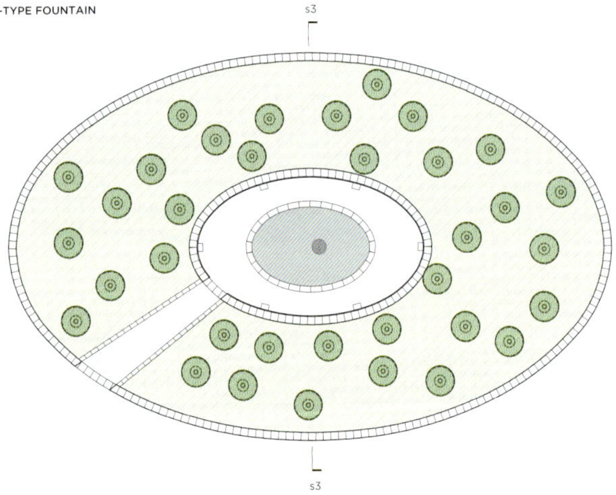

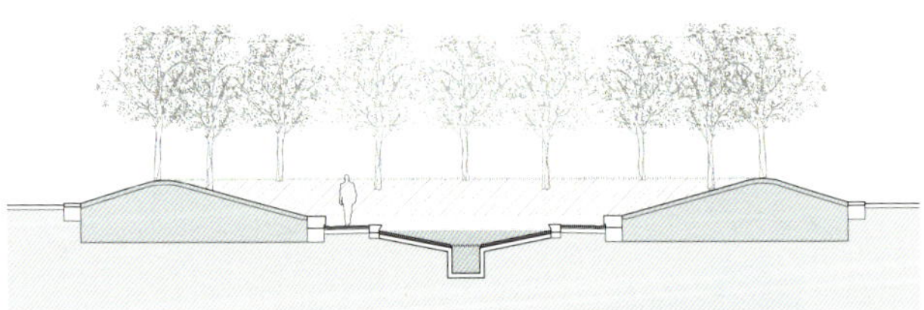

SECTION s3

1/600 1 2 3 4 5 10

1/400 1 2 3 4 5 10

FERN FOUNTAIN

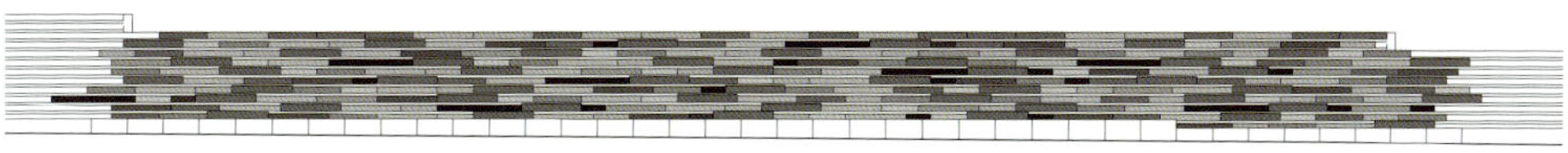

SYSTEM OF STONE PIECES ELEVATION

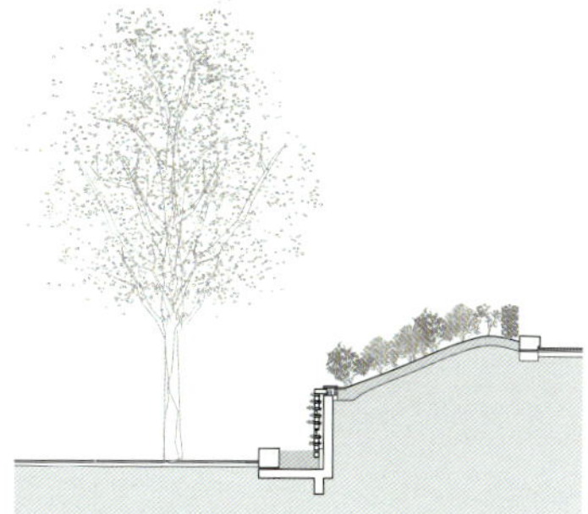

SECTION s4

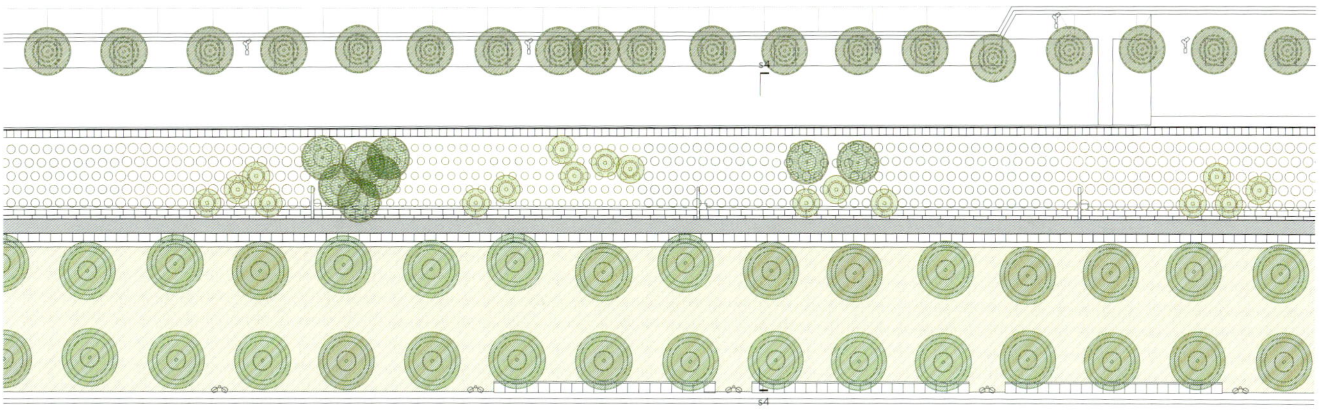

1/600 1 2 3 4 5 10

XL-TYPE FOUNTAIN

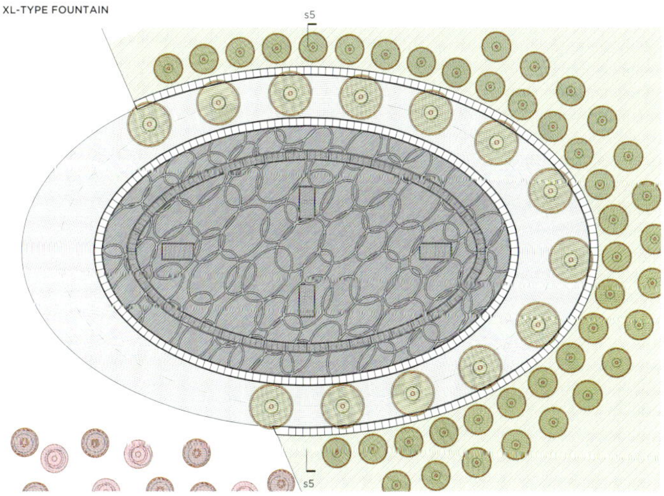

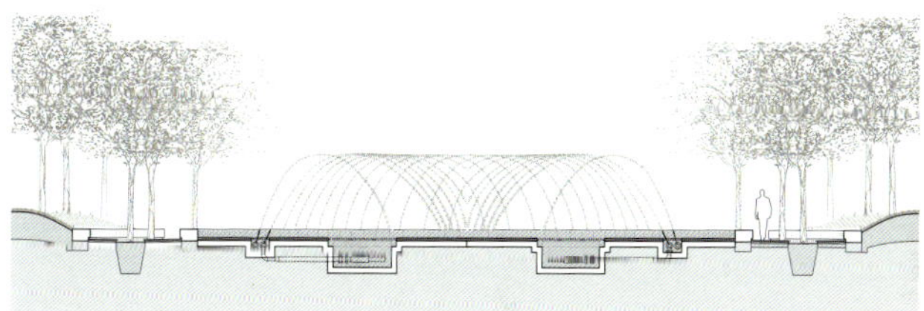

SECTION s5

BEACH (THIRD MODUL)

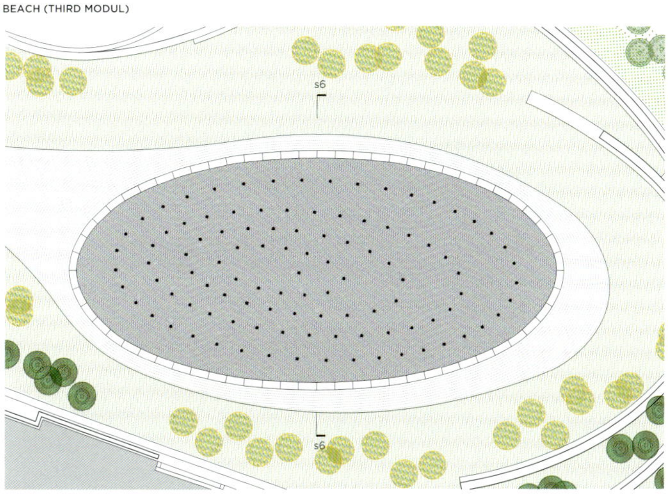

1/600 1 2 3 4 5 10

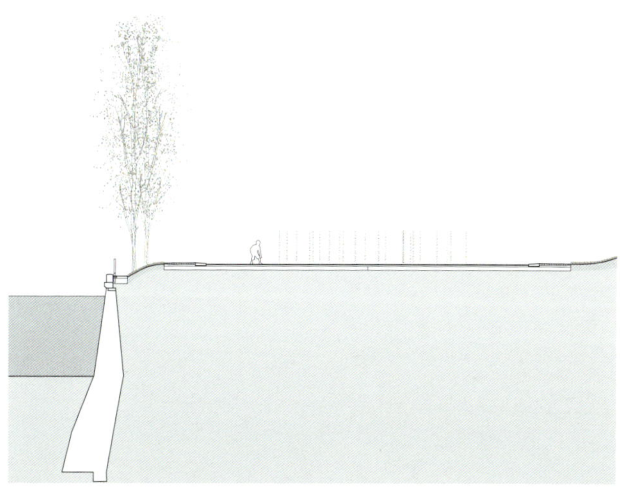

SECTION s6

1/400 1 2 3 4 5 10

K.P. 5.10 - K.P. 5.50

MADRID RÍO PARK CONSERVATION OFFICES

Effective surface area 330 m^2
Constructed surface area 405.33 m^2
Floor dimensions 14.35 x 42.11 m
Height above ground level 4.56 m
Uses 01. Lobby / 02. Reception and administration / 03. Office / 04. Pantry / 05. Toilets / 06. Garage / 07. Meeting room / 08. Patio-Garden / 09. Archives

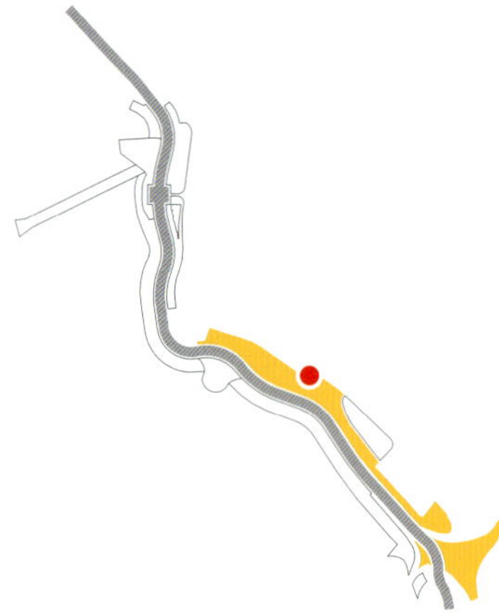

K.P. 5.60

PLAN

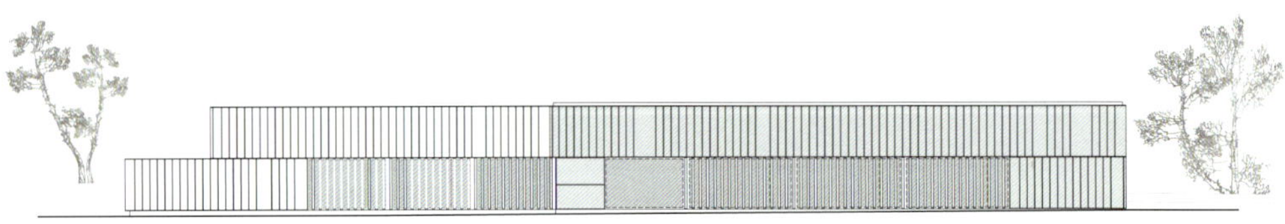

ELEVATION a1

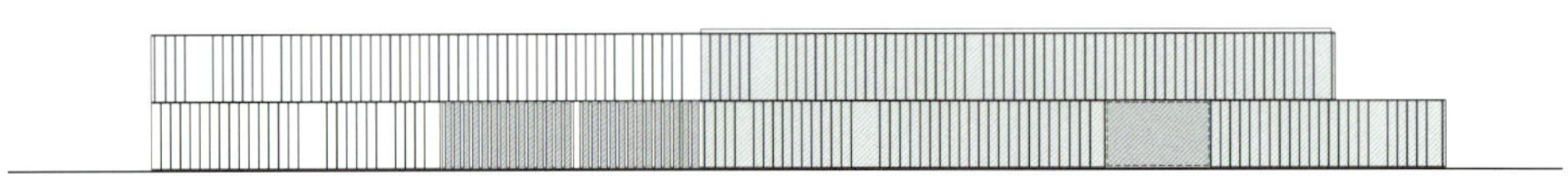

ELEVATION a2

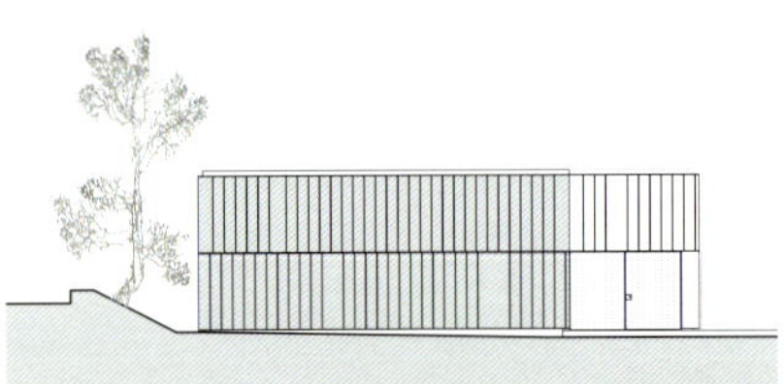

ELEVATION a3

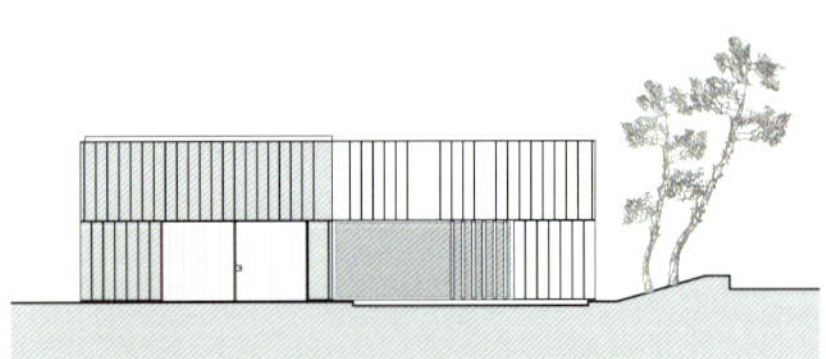

ELEVATION a4

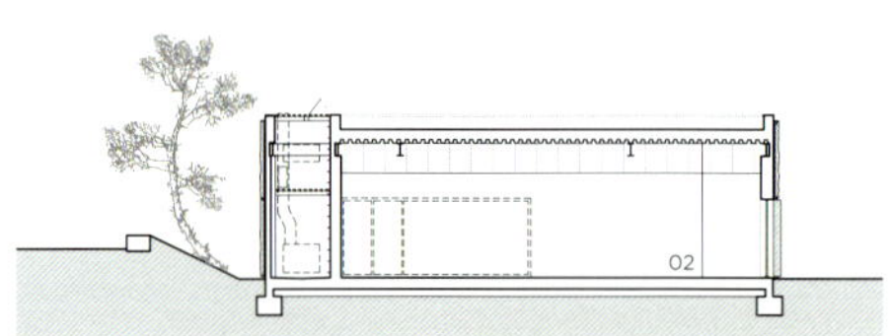

SECTION s1

1/400 1 2 3 4 5 10

K.P. 5.60

MATADERO AND GREENHOUSE FOOTBRIDGES

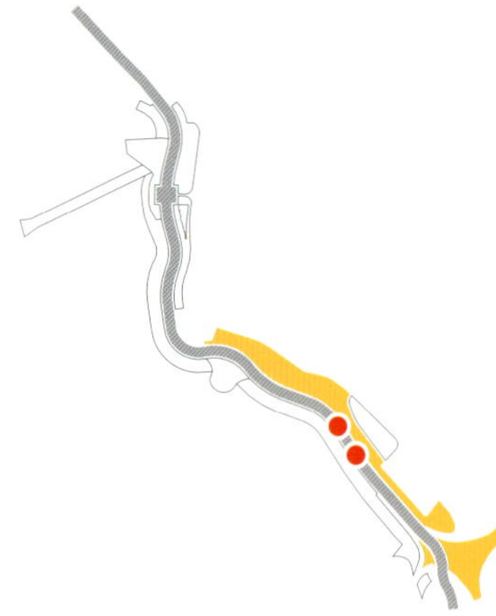

Length on axis 49.08 m
Length between supports 43.46 m
Deck width 4.20 m - 7.48 m
Free height 4.23 m - 7.57 m
Structure Double-curved reinforced concrete sheet from which the metal deck structure is suspended
Artist of the dome's mosaic Daniel Canogar
Date of completion 2010

K.P. 6.12 - K.P. 6.40

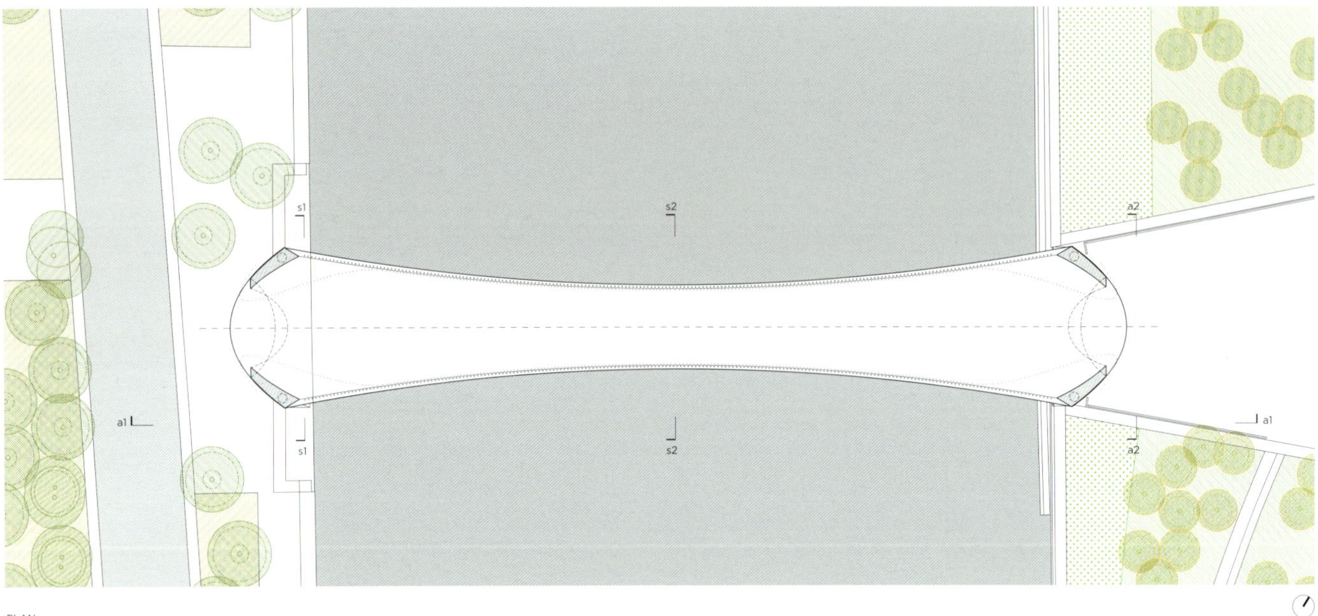

PLAN

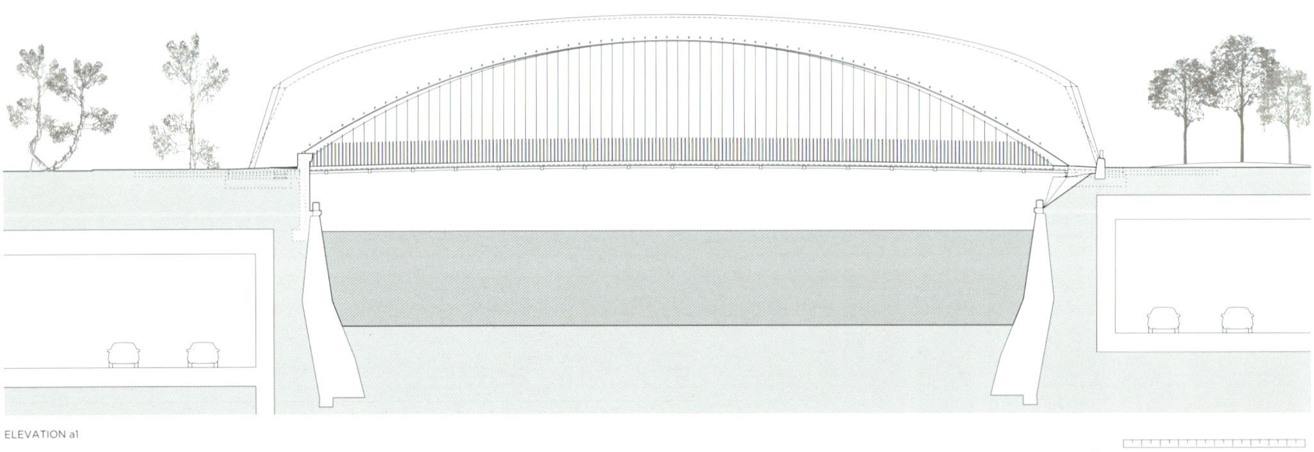

ELEVATION a1

MOSAIC

ROWING CENTER

Effective surface area 367.29 m^2
Constructed surface area 440.08 m^2
Floor dimensions 10.26 x 42.87 m
Height above-ground level 4.62 m
Uses 01. Kayak storage area / 02. Offices / 03. Dressing rooms / 04. Shelter / 05. Installations room / 06. M-30 emergency exit

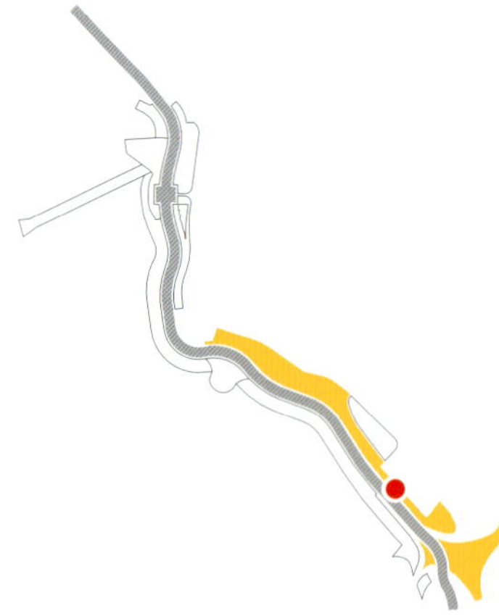

K.P. 6.76

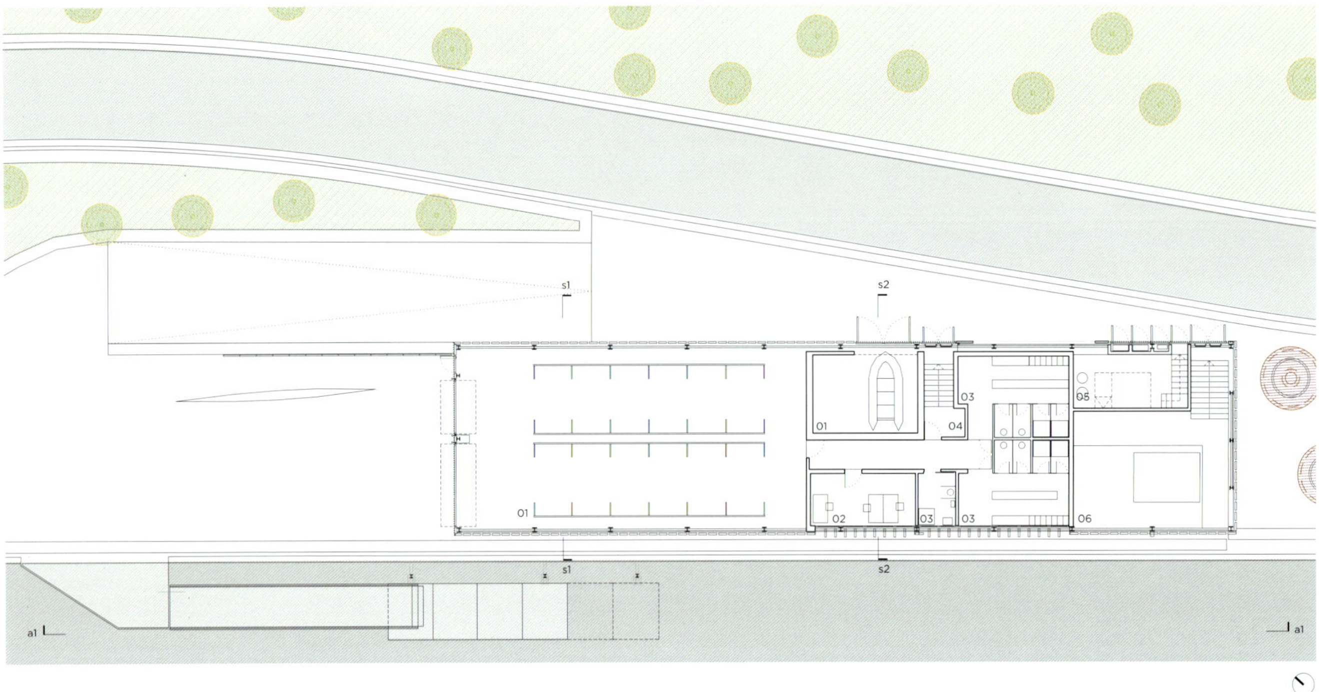

PLAN

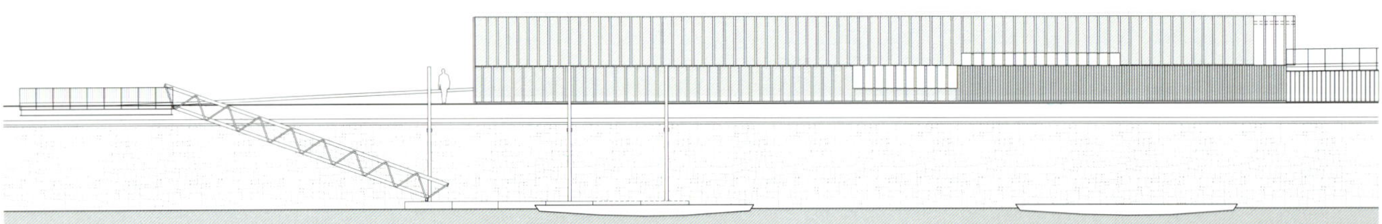

ELEVATION a1

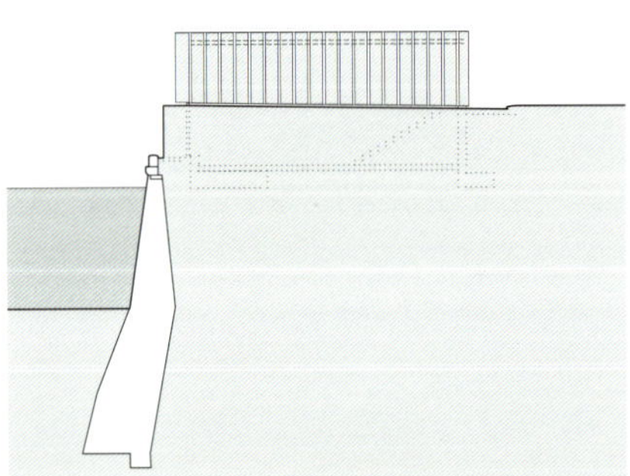

ELEVATION

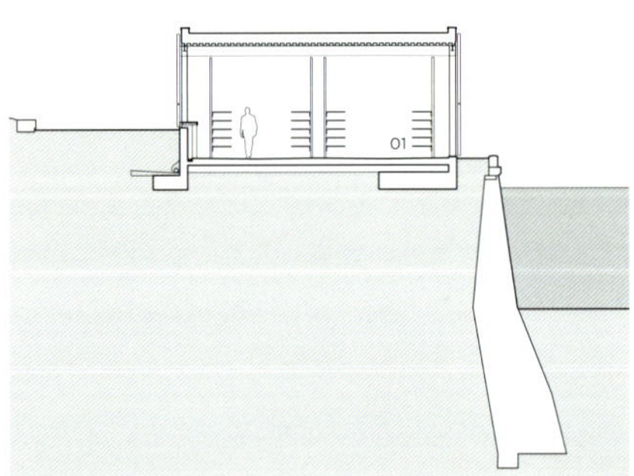

SECTION s1

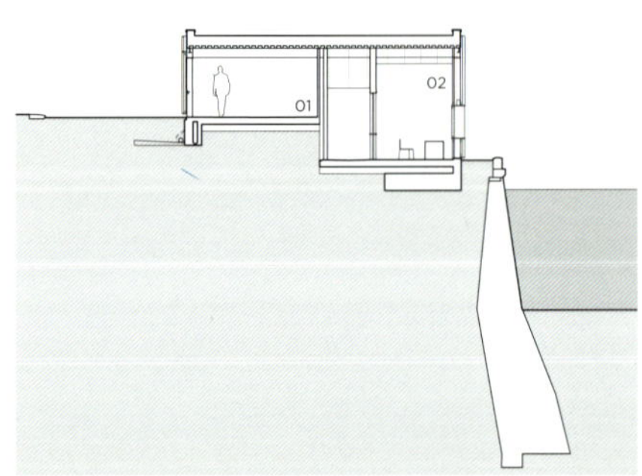

SECTION s2

1/400 1 2 3 4 5 10

NAVE
16

K.P. 6.25

EVOLUTION OF THE USES OF MATADERO

OUTLINE OF MATADERO'S USES - 1914

SLAUGHTER

- BOVINE KILLING FLOORS
- CALF KILLING FLOORS
- SHEEP KILLING FLOORS
- PIG KILLING FLOORS
- GUTTING SHOP
- ANIMAL BY-PRODUCTS AND HIDE DRYING
- COLD-STORAGE ROOMS

CATTLE MARKET

- ENTRANCE FOR WILD CATTLE
- ENTRANCE FOR DOMESTIC CATTLE
- STABLES FOR BEEF CATTLE
- EXHIBITION AND SALE
- CORRALS FOR BEEF CATTLE
- CALF STABLES AND EXHIBITION
- SHEEP STABLES AND EXHIBITION
- PIG STABLES AND EXHIBITION
- CALF CORRALS
- SHEEP CORRALS
- PIGPENS

MARKET FOR DRAUGHT ANIMALS

- TESTING FIELD
- CATTLE EXHIBITION AND SALE
- CATTLE STABLES

GENERAL SERVICES

- ADMINISTRATION

OTHER USES

- HEALTH SECTION
- TRACKS AND SPURS

OUTLINE OF EL MATAERO'S USES - 2012

- NAVES 13/14 - CASA DEL LECTOR (LIBRARY)
- NAVE 17C - CENTRAL DE DISEÑO (DESIGN EXHIBITION HALL)
- NAVE 17C - INTERMEDIAE (SOCIAL AND DIGITAL LABORATORY)
- NAVES 10/11/12 - TEATRO ESPAÑOL (THEATRE)
- NAVE 8
- NAVE 9
- NAVE 17C - LOBBY
- NAVE 17C - INTERMEDIAE (SOCIAL AND DIGITAL LABORATORY)
- CENTRO CULTURAL DEL DISTRITO (DISTRICT'S CULTURAL CENTER)
- NAVE DE DANZA (DANCE SCHOOL)
- GREENHOUSE
- SPECIES REPOSITORY
- CENTRO DE INTERPRETACIÓN DEL RÍO (MANZANARES RIVER INTERPRETATION CENTER)
- NAVE DE TERNERAS - DANCE HALL
- NAVE 16 - EXHIBITION HALL
- NAVE 15 - MUSIC ACADEMY
- INSTALLATIONS CENTER
- NAVES 17D / 17E / 17F - CINETECA (CINEMA)
- JUNTA MUNICIPAL DE ARGANZUELA (MUNICIPAL BOARD OF ARGANZUELA)

1 / 6,000 10 50 100

MATADERO ON THE PASEO DEL ARTE

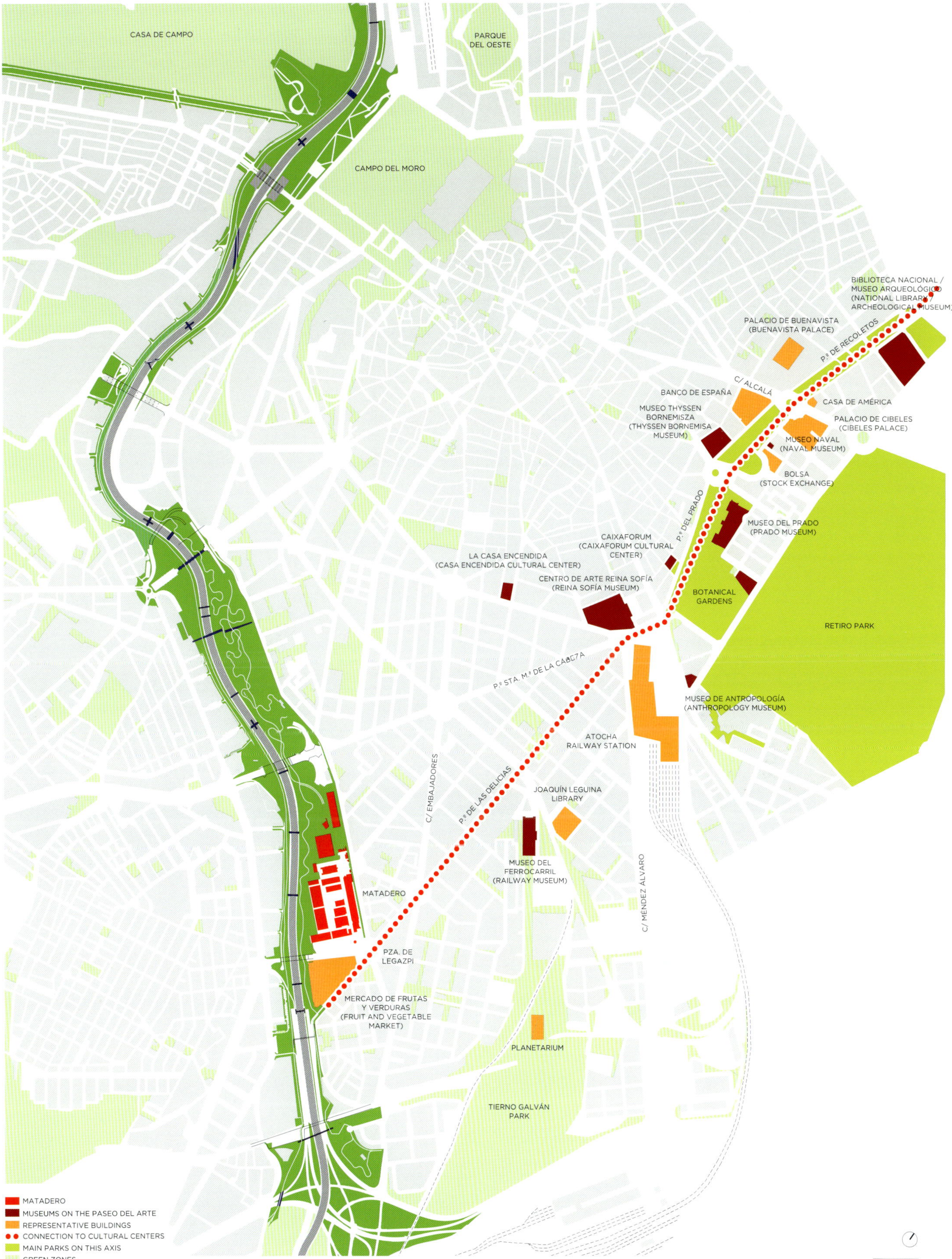

orthogonal lines underlying the placement of the buildings and, in that sense, their placement is somewhat rigid, but their mobility makes it possible to remove or install them at any time, thus favoring flexibilty.

The open part has some lines finished in granite that add continuity to the spaces inside the complex. The main street continues northwards, following an alignment of *Platanus x hispanica* (plane trees). Granite benches and *Koelreuteria paniculata* (goldenrain trees) are aligned perpendicular to the river to form rows leading to the park, so the outlines of the former corral dividers are now occupied by benches and trees that blend into the curved lines of new paths.

Landscape and city
Over its history, the city of Madrid has been home to various slaughterhouses, always within its walls. In the early 20th century, it became necessary to close them, mainly because of the difficulty of bringing animals directly into the city for slaughter. Instead, a central slaughterhouse was designed to work like a functioning city. The clever treatment and architectural quality of the structures housing stables, storage areas, refrigeration units, killing floors, and so on has permitted them to be completely repurposed, both inside and out, to generate a very significant complex linked to art production. This complex is presented as a unified whole thanks to the fact that its architecture can be taken in at a glance. The possibility of including it as the park's main cultural infrastructure has only multiplied its presence by making it accessible from the other side of the river and improving its accessibility to the streets linking it to the city. It is no longer a slaughterhouse from which the city must protect itself, but instead, a more accessible complex available to all citizens and park visitors.

K.P. 6.45

a new relation among them, and their location on smooth, unified surface makes each a singular object imbued with a new vitality.

Technical solutions

In this setting, the most complex issue to be solved with technical means is the implementation of service installations, both in the open spaces and in the buildings. The decision to completely hide all cables or conduits and to thus recover the clean silhouette of each building resting on an unbroken surface called for an underground system of technological connections. This, in turn, led to the decision to centralize the most important installations, which had two very significant consequences. First, the construction of a building exclusively designed to house all of the main systems for generating and supplying utilities. Two thirds of that building are underground, where heat and air conditioning are generated for all of the rehabilitated spaces. This building also handles closed-circuit surveillance and security for the complex. Second, beginning at the building's lowest levels, a series of underground galleries has been constructed, each with a section of 3 x 3 meters. These connect the central installations to all of the other buildings through supply conduits. The galleries have been constructed underneath the vacant spaces and lead to the basements of each of the rehabilitated buildings.

Bellido's plazas, generated according to the separation of the buildings to configure sizeable open spaces, also had to be equipped so that they could be used for art events and performances that require electricity, drinking water, restrooms, and so on. Therefore, the main open spaces have connections inserted in the pavement near the underground galleries. This also optimizes the paths of the supply conduits to those connections. The registers, grills, and covers pertaining to this buried infrastructure generate a second order of patterns in the texture of the architectural support plans, which take on the character of functioning artifacts.

Materials and elements

As mentioned above, to explain the main elements that define this territory, we must begin by differentiating the enclosed and limited space, which can be locked, from the open part that consists fundamentally of the different areas connected to the Arganzuela Park. The enclosed part is the largest, consisting almost exclusively of two main elements: the buildings and the surface on which they rest. The former are complex and diverse, while the latter is unadorned and unifying. The spaces it occupies are finished with two dominant materials; granite cobblestones for the streets and small rest areas, and concrete with granite aggregates for the large central plaza. For the first two, massive use was made of the former slaughterhouse's original pavement (irregular granite cobblestones of 12 x 21 x 9 centimeters, easily recoverable and reusable). The decision to give the leading role to the buildings, rather than to their surroundings, explains the total absence of vegetation in the inner enclosure. Moreover, to emphasize the buildings' nocturnal presence, and as a reference to the blood spilled inside them, they are lit in red by light sources built into the pavement. The elements used to close the area (doors for trucks or pedestrians, grillwork, etc.) are integrated into the proposal with a sober, abstract language in keeping with the industrial spirit that still characterizes the complex. These elements follow the

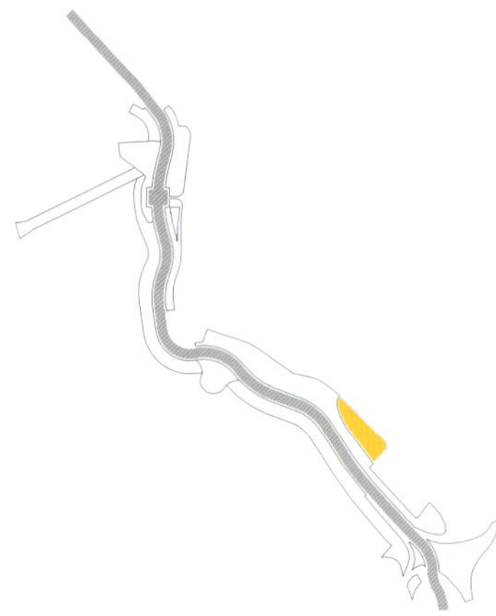

with a secondary geometric order that drew on the layout of the buildings themselves. The complex underwent various changes over the course of the 20th century but its spirit and atmosphere have remained intact and have even increased in intensity as the open areas have been reinterpreted as emergent spaces free of the compartmentalization that defined them as corrals.

Concepts and character of the proposal

The intervention in this setting had to bring out the great value of the preexisting elements by making them a part of the new park. To do so called for solutions based on a dialog between the edges of the former slaughterhouse and the river itself (and therefore concentrates on the direct links between this small city and the riverside area). It also had to include a clear idea of how the open spaces between the early 20th-century buildings would be used. Some of these are interstitial areas between pavilions, but others are large surrounding lots that have been recovered by demolishing old buildings that were in poor condition and of little value.

The intervention's double mission consists of a group of permeable and mobile barriers that delimit the area inside and outside the slaughterhouse. The outer edges of these barriers absorb and expand using vegetation that grows ever denser as it approaches the river. This generates a series of spaces for rest or transit that gradually become a part of the green-zone activities. Within the complex itself, the intervention serves mainly to configure a neutral platform from which each building emerges, and thus concentrates especially on the paved surfaces. This treatment seeks to emphasize the importance of each building and to bring out the nature and position of the empty spaces within the hierarchy established by those buildings. The result is a successful coexistence of the soft character of elements belonging to the park that run from the edge of the Matadero complex down to the river, and the hard character of the actions carried out within that complex, and of its points of contact with the city.

Description of the landscape

The main change in the area was the establishment of a solid surface on which the buildings stand like parts of a still life. This surface became the main landscape element, covering the entire enclosure and extending beyond its borders wherever there are buildings. As such, it functions as a clean base on which to unify diverse elements with different functions. Its only two materials, concrete and granite, share a uniform color scheme. This base seeks to bring out the metaphysical character of the overall group, establishing it as a place outside time, where ancient buildings slowly awaken from their deep sleep. The sections and textures of the pavement help define uses for the open spaces: street, plaza, field for activities or events, loading and unloading zone. These various parcels of land are part of a continuous surface but their uses depend on their relation to building entrances or to the enclosure's main pathways (rapid or slow, light or heavy, exclusive or public). The pavement varies from 6 x 6 centimeter granite cobblestones to continuous slabs of reinforced concrete measuring 4.5 x 31.5 meters. The choice depends on the nature, frequency, and weight of the traffic each area has to bear. Thus the surface designed to support the buildings is a unified element whose uses are marked by different materials that order it like a carpet of different textures. These variations draw on the orthogonal axes and follow the layout established by the distribution of the buildings, which in its day rationalized the movement of cattle.

The buildings' new uses are the result of architectural renovation, and each was the object of a specific project by a specific architect. These projects reflect the new uses, so each indoor area is different, as each architect adapts the preexisting building for functions related to the promotion, fostering, and display of artistic activity. A library, a cinema, theaters, and studios for recording music, for graphic design and multimedia, as well as exhibition rooms, listening spaces, and all the general services needed to keep the complex working combine to form a municipal institution called Matadero Madrid that serves as the main cultural infrastructure in support of the city's contemporary creators. Despite its diversity of uses, the different architects responsible for its buildings and the resulting variety of languages inside them, the outer volumes and the buildings' shells have not been modified, so the uniformity of the original complex has been maintained as a unifying element. In sum, the progressive rehabilitation of all the buildings generates

WAB

WATER AND BLOOD

Starting point

The overall project carried out along the riverside occupies spaces that became vacant when the highway was rerouted underground. It only included pre-existing buildings on one occasion, when it made them an inseparable part of its proposal. The fact that the restoration of the city's former slaughterhouse complex was completed in the same timeframe as the landscaping made this inclusion fully possible. The municipal slaughterhouse consists of twelve buildings of various sizes, all constructed between 1915 and 1925, but those installations continued to expand and, by the time the complex stopped functioning in the 1970s, in included over 40 buildings. It closed definitively in 1996 and from then until 2006, it was unused, outside the circuit of municipal installations.

The starting point for the proposal was the great strength of the existing buildings, which are open to new uses without losing the character or identity they bring to the entire area. So the proposal approaches these buildings as mutually complementary objects capable of generating a specific public space.

Their layout in the urban territory, the wealth of empty spaces among them, and their proximity to the river makes them an element that can conserve its autonomy while simultaneously functioning as part of the riverside park. The project combines a post-industrial language based on the orthogonal order of early 20th-century buildings with the organic layout of a new design for the free areas.

The place

Construction of the slaughterhouse and municipal cattle market began in 1915, on public land 730 meters along the riverbank. That zone marked the city's southern edge, with a scattering of industries, warehouses, and low-quality housing among vacant lots, some of which were still used as grazing land. The terrain was crossed by the railway lines running parallel to the river between Príncipe Pío Station to the north, and Delicias to the south. One of the river's most important bridges also stood in this area — the 19thcentury Puente de la Princesa de Asturias (Princess of Asturias Bridge).

The slaughterhouse was designed by municipal architect Luis Bellido. After a rigorous study of successful complexes of this type throughout Europe, he opted for the German model, with independent and complementary pavilions for the slaughterhouse and cattle market. Each pavilion was assigned a specific use related to both the type of activity to be carried out there and the size and species of animal to be processed within. The installation was organized to function like an ambitious and complex industrial city characterized by its extreme order and laid out on the terrain in a clear, straightforward manner reflected in its unyielding orthogonal geometry. Some long but shallow buildings were aligned to enclose the urban space and the rest were inserted with greater autonomy as freestanding structures of considerable width whose main axes run perpendicular to the river.

The nearby railway lines favored running track within the complex for heavy transportation. This was complemented by a small-scale installation that ran directly into the pavilions themselves. The specialized buildings included refrigeration units, ovens, storage areas, and other technological installations necessary to make Bellido's planned industrial micro-city a reality. From an architectural standpoint, the complex was designed to offer a unified image, despite the diversity of its constituent buildings, each with its own specific proportions. This unified character was achieved through the expressive language of each building, based on the construction materials, the treatment of sections using roofs that allow the sunlight to enter from above, and forceful orthogonal floor plans. The outer walls were adorned with a controlled formal wealth that contrasts with the austere floor plans and layout. That expressive wealth was based on a combination of three materials (granite, limestone, and brick) that accentuates the architect's desire to include elements and languages rooted in Madrid by reinterpreting certain neo-Mudejar and picturesque components. These stylistic elements, along with the advanced use of reinforced concrete and steel structures to generate large spans with few supports, generated architecture whose extraordinary interest is further reinforced by the relation among the buildings and their interaction with the surrounding open spaces. The latter, some of which are quite large, were used as temporary livestock stables and were compartmentalized

WAB

K.P. 6.35

MATADERO

PLANTA. K.P. 5.95 - K.P. 6.60

CURRENT USES

1. NAVE DE DANZA (DANCE SCHOOL)
2. CENTRO CULTURAL DEL DISTRITO (DISTRICT'S CULTURAL CENTER)
3. CENTRO DE INTERPRETACIÓN DEL RÍO (MANZANARES RIVER INTERPRETATION CENTER)
4. GREENHOUSE
5. JUNTA MUNICIPAL DE ARGANZUELA (MUNICIPAL BOARD OF ARGANZUELA)
6. NAVE DE TERNERAS - DANCE HALL
7. NAVES 13/14 - CASA DEL LECTOR (LIBRARY)
8. NAVE 17C - INTERMEDIAE (SOCIAL AND DIGITAL LABORATORY)
9. NAVE 17C - LOBBY
10. NAVE 17C - EXHIBITION HALL
11. NAVE 17C - CENTRAL DE DISEÑO (DESIGN EXHIBITION HALL)
12. NAVES 17D / 17E / 17F - CINETECA (CINEMA)
13. NAVE 12 - THEATER CAFÉ
14. NAVES 10 / 11 - TEATRO ESPAÑOL (THEATER)
15. INSTALLATIONS
16. NAVE 15 - MUSIC ACADEMY
17. NAVE 16 - EXHIBITION HALL
18. NAVE 8
19. NAVE 9
20. SPECIES REPOSITORY
21. MATADERO PLAZA

MATERIALS AND TEXTURES

DOUBLE LAYER OF CONCRETE PAVING 15 CM + 15 CM

GRANITE COBBLESTONE, 2x15x6 CM, SHEARED ON ALL SIDES AND BUSHHAMMERED ON THE VISIBLE SIDE

GRANITE COBBLESTONE, 15x15 CM, SAWED ON ALL SIDES AND FLAMED ON THE VISIBLE SIDE. THICKNESSES OF 6 OR 9 CM

GRANITE SLABS 15x30-90x9 CM, SAWED ON ALL SIDES AND FLAMED ON THE VISIBLE SIDE

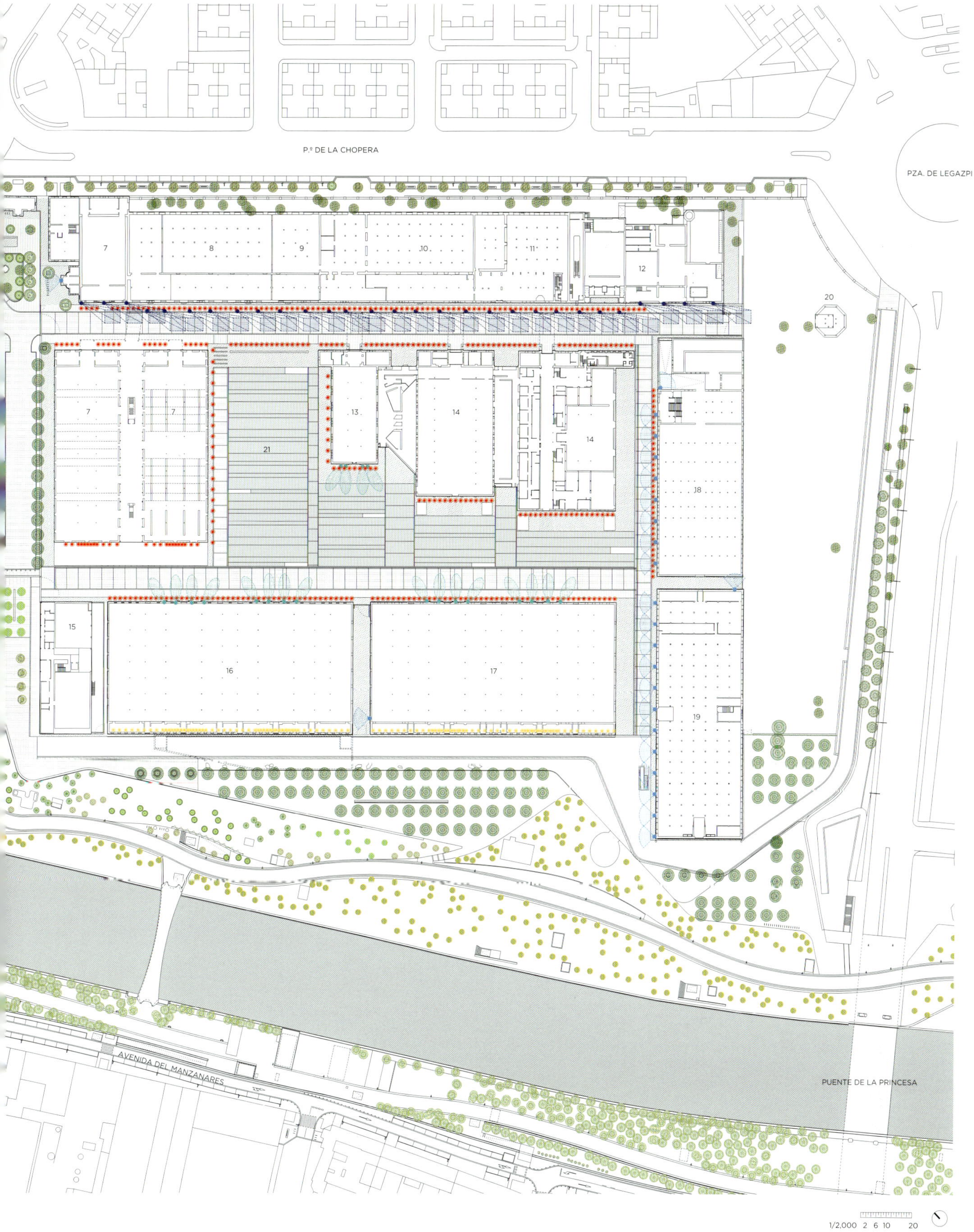

GRANITE COBBLESTONE, 9x9x9 CM, SAWED OR SHEARED ON ALL SIDES AND FLAMED ON THE VISIBLE SIDE

GRANITE COBBLESTONE, 6x6x6 CM, SHEARED ON ALL SIDES AND FLAMED OR SHEARED ON THE VISIBLE SIDE

HYDRAULIC TILE

OUTLINE OF LIGHTS

WHITE-LIGHT PROJECTOR ON PORTICO – LIGHTING OF CALLE A (A STREET)

WHITE-LIGHT PROJECTOR ON CORNICE – LIGHTING OF STREETS

WHITE-LIGHT PROJECTOR ON CORNICE – LIGHTING OF PLAZA

RED LED SET INTO PAVEMENT – ORNAMENTAL LIGHTING OF NAVES

RED LED ON CORNICE – ORNAMENTAL LIGHTING OF NAVES

NAVES 13 AND 14 - CASA DEL LECTOR (LIBRARY)

Constructed surface area 7,000 m²
Architects Ensamble Studio [Antón García-Abril]
Engineering Prainsa, Úrculo Ingenieros
Date of completion 2012

K.P. 6.38

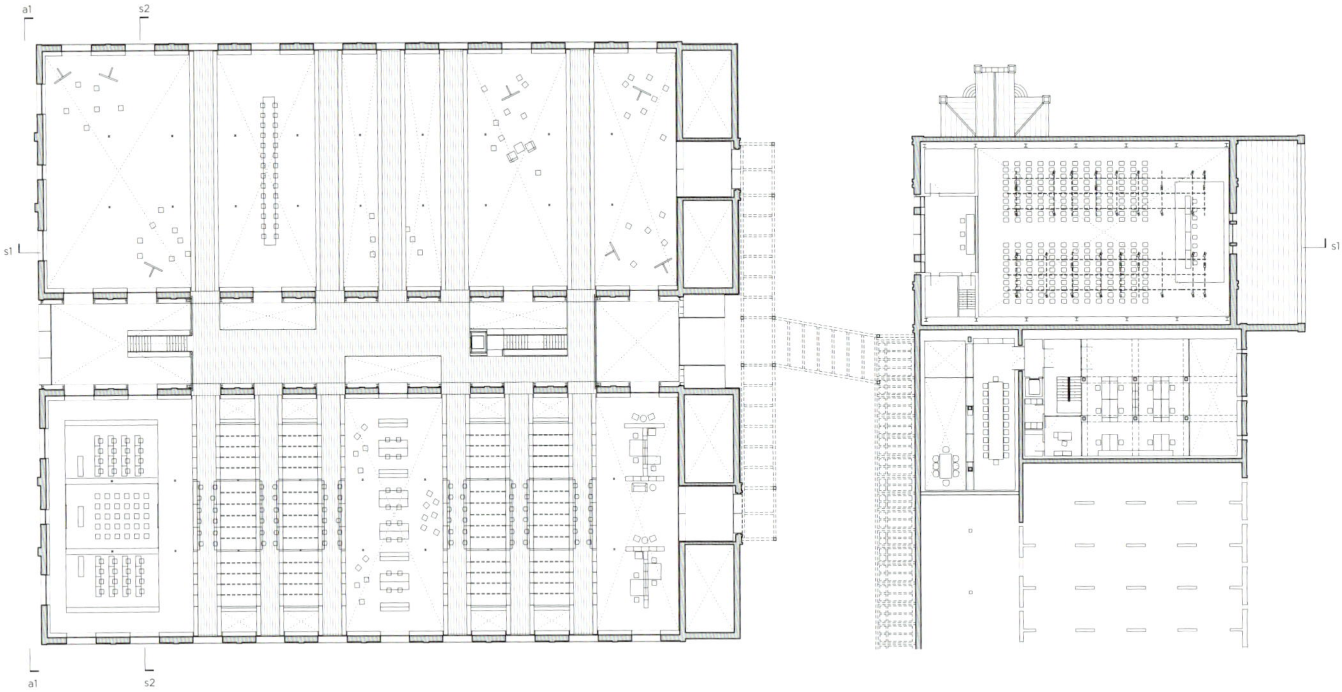

TOP FLOOR

ELEVATION a1

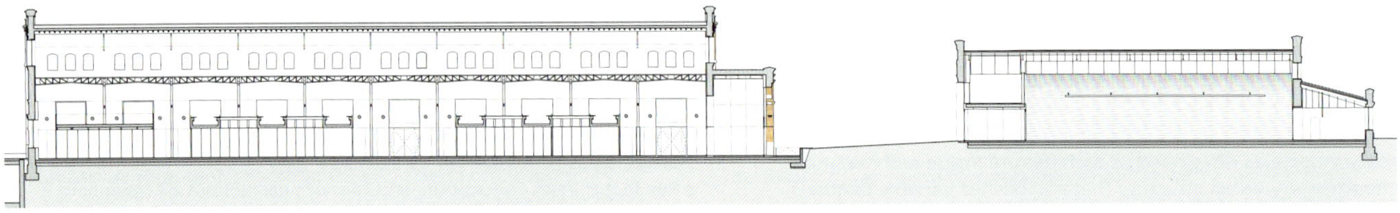

SECTION s1

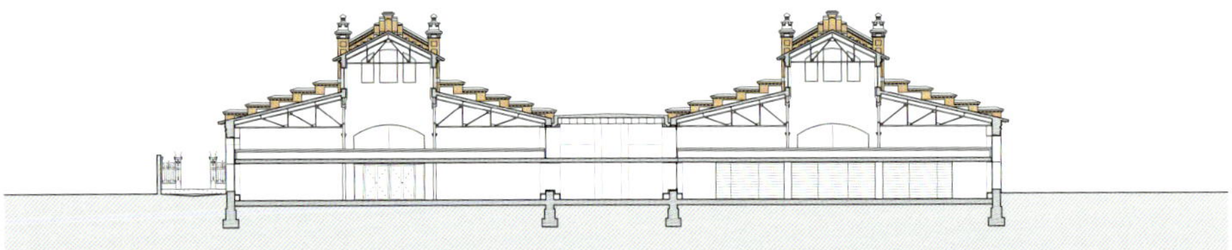

SECTION s2

1/750 1 2 3 4 5 10

NAVE 17c - INTERMEDIAE (SOCIAL AND DIGITAL LABORATORY)

Affected surface 6,000 m²
Architects Arturo Franco, Fabrice van Teslaar
Date of completion 2006

K.P. 6.44

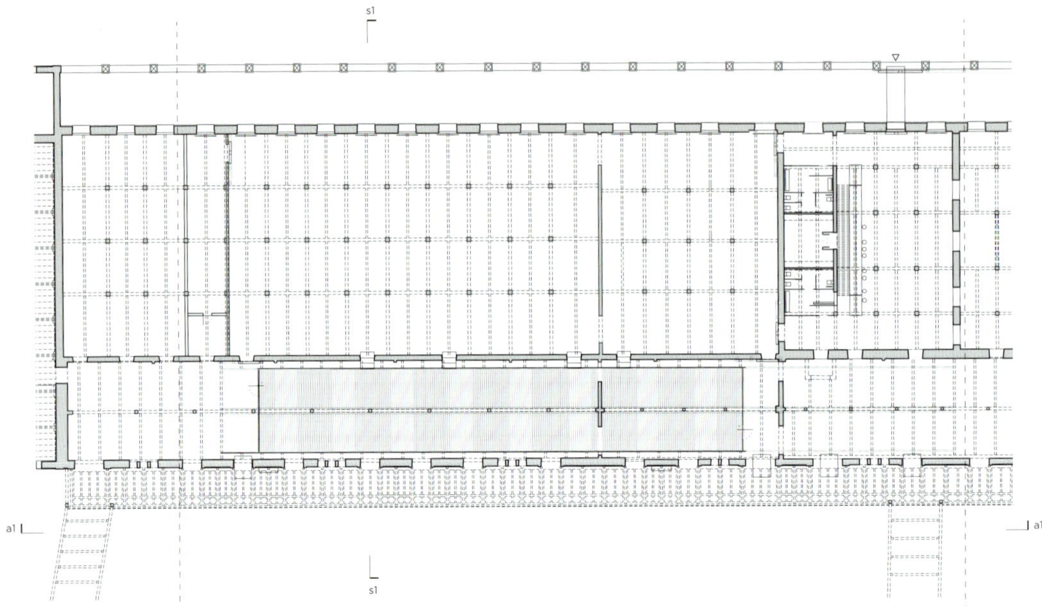

GROUND FLOOR

ELEVATION a1

SECTION s1

1/750 1 2 3 4 5 10

K.P. b.44

NAVE 17c - CENTRAL DE DISEÑO (DESIGN EXHIBITION HALL)

Affected surface 1,650 m²
Architects Md15 Arquitectos
[José Antonio García Roldán]
Date of completion 2007

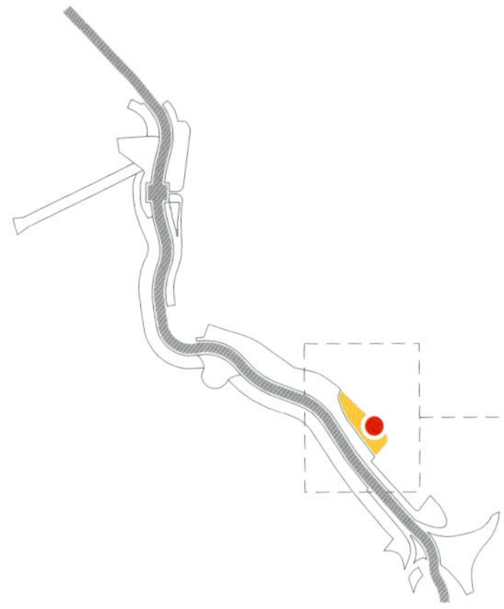

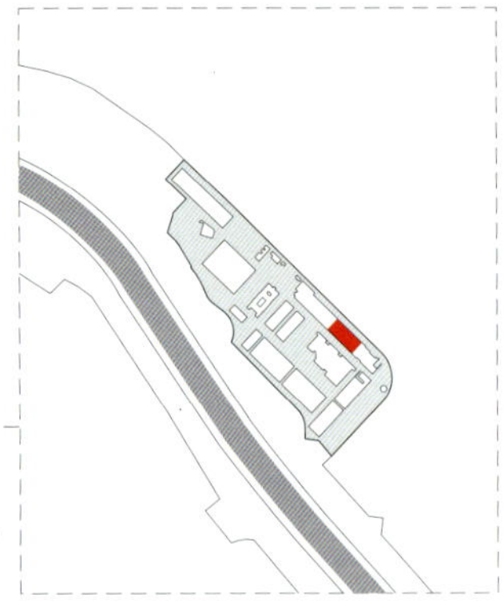

K.P. 6.47

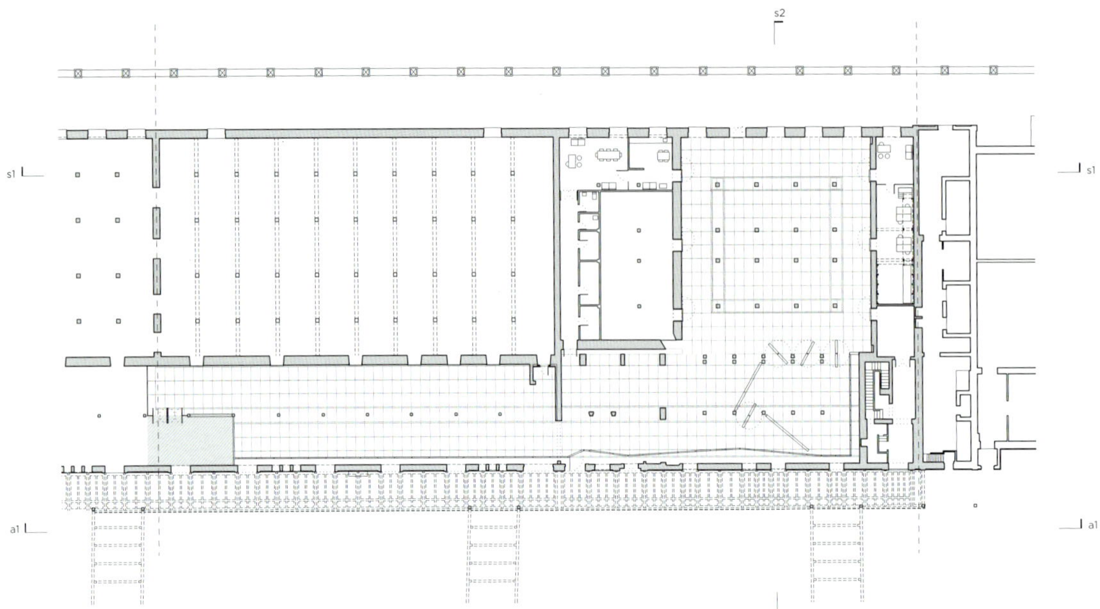

GROUND FLOOR

ELEVATION a1

SECTION s1

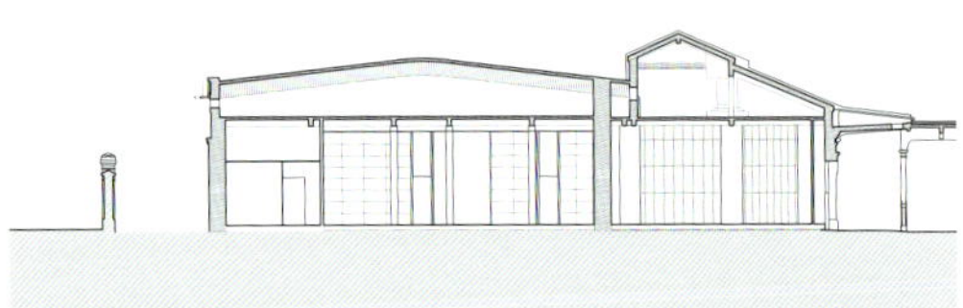

SECTION s2

K.P. 6.47

NAVES 17d / 17e / 17f - CINETECA (CINEMA)

Constructed surface area 2,688 m²
Architects ch+qs arquitectos
[José M.ª de Churtichaga,
Cayetana de la Quadra-Salcedo]
Engineering Úrculo Ingenieros
Date of completion 2011

K.P. 6.65

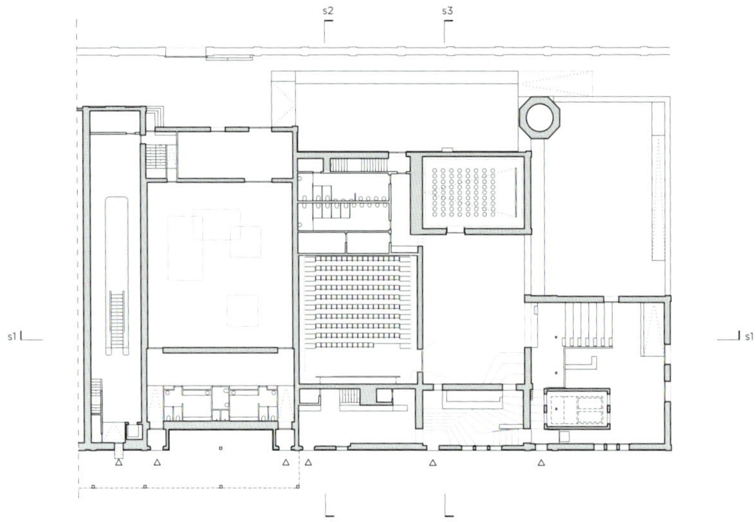

GROUND FLOOR

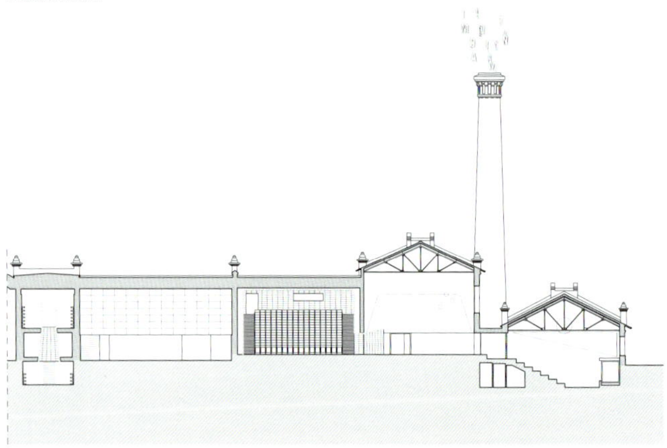

SECTION s1

SECTION s2

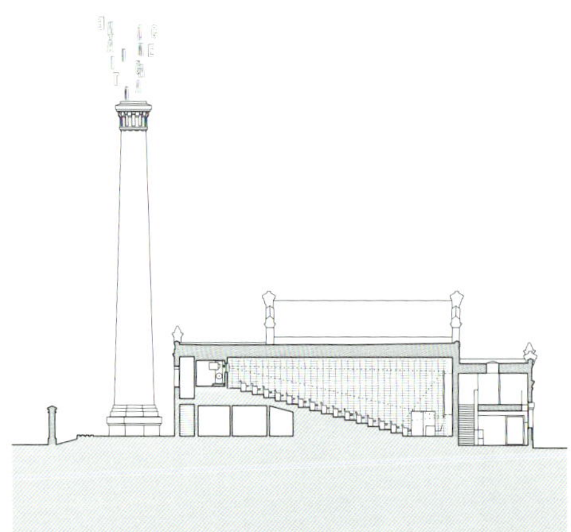

SECTION s3

1/750 1 2 3 4 5 10

SALA

D10 D08 D06 D04 D02 D01 D03 D05 D07
C08 C06 C04 C02 C01 C03 C05

SPECIES REPOSITORY

Constructed surface area 330 m^2
Architects Langarita Navarro
[María Langarita, Víctor Navarro]
Date of completion 2011

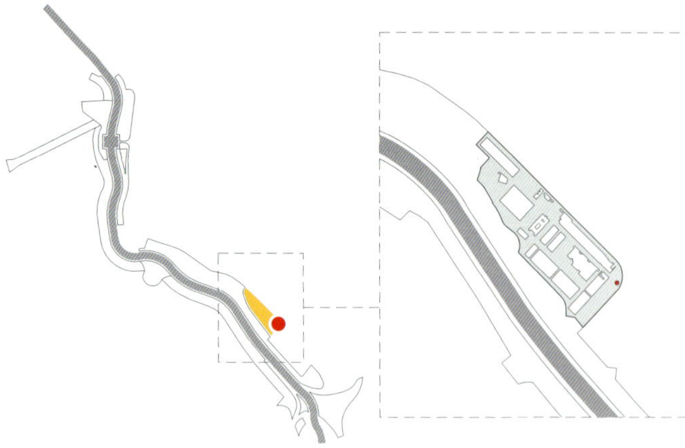

K.P. 6.64

ELEVATION a1

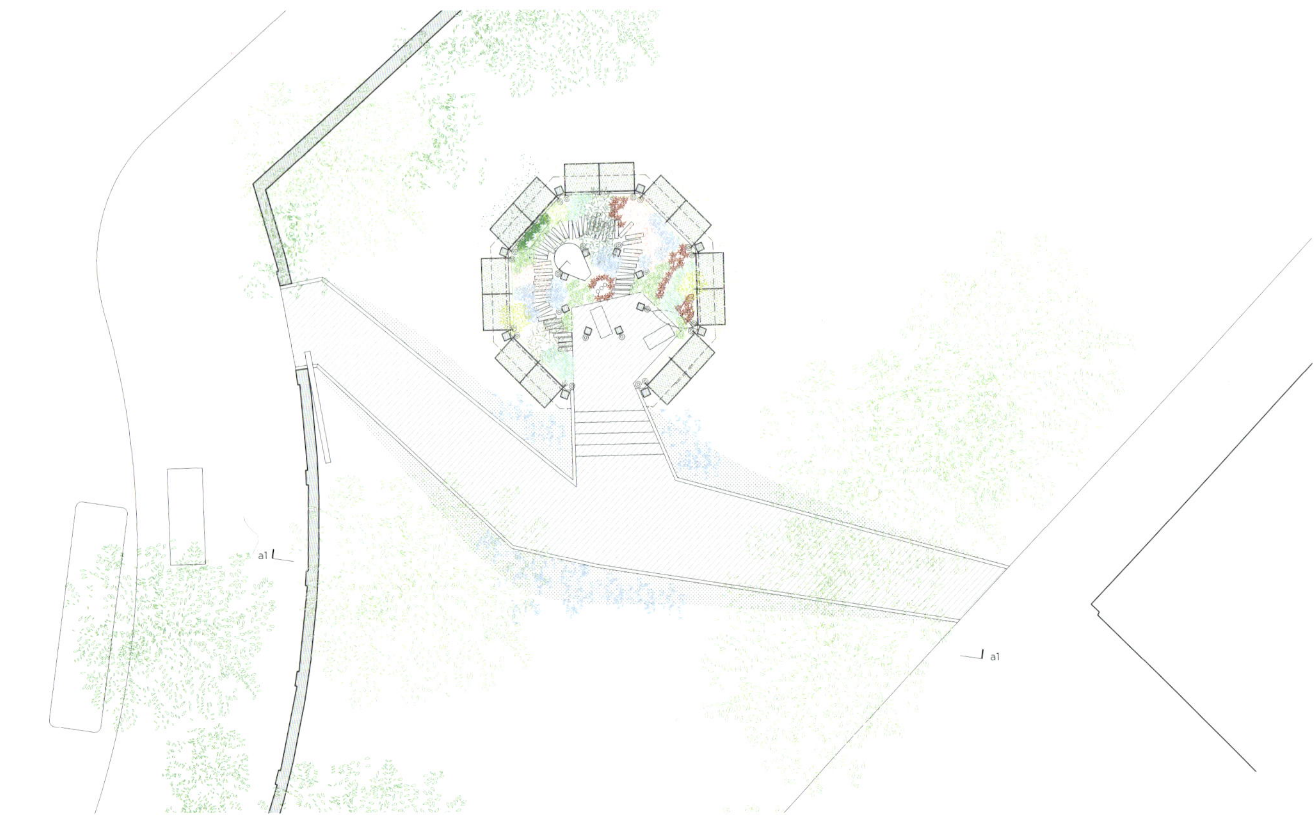

FLOOR PLAN

1/400 1 2 3 4 5 10

K.P. 6.04

NAVES 8 / 9 - OFFICES

Affected surface
20,891.85 m^2
Architects
Arturo Franco, Juan Arregui
Engineering
Mecanismo
Date of completion
2011

K.P. 6.60

NAVE 8b - OFFICES

Affected surface
1,000 m^2
Architects
Arturo Franco
Engineering
Mecanismo
Date of completion
2009

K.P. 6.60

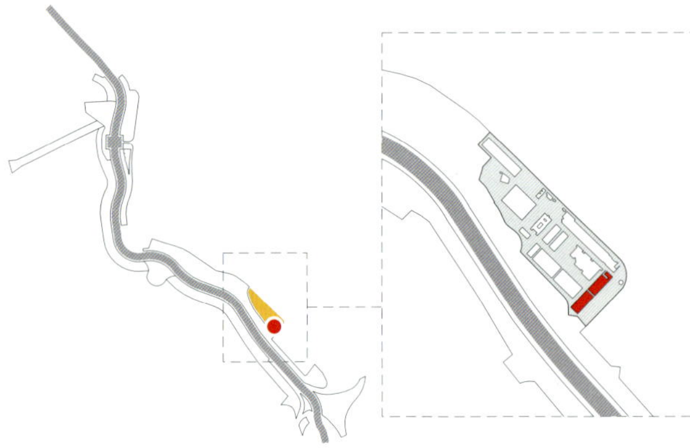

FLOOR PLAN

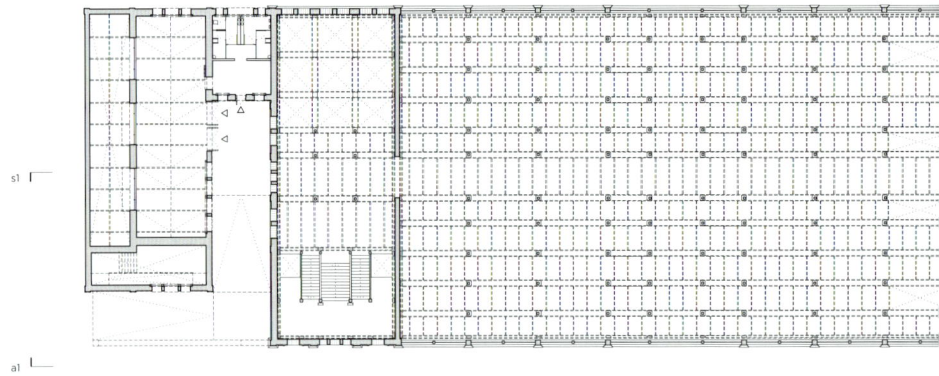

NAVE 8B - SECOND FLOOR

NAVE 8 - FOURTH FLOOR

ELEVATION a1

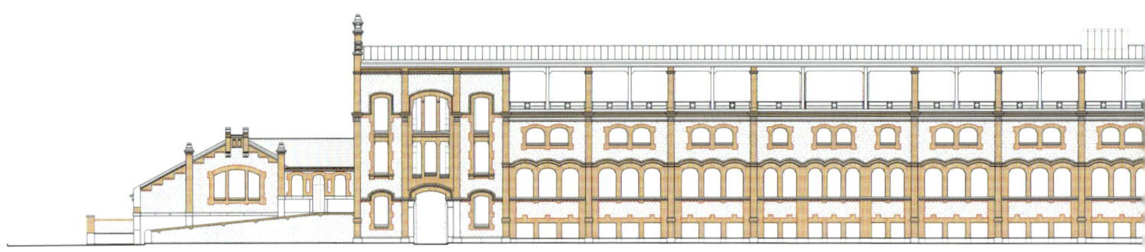

NAVE 8B

NAVE 8

SECTION s1

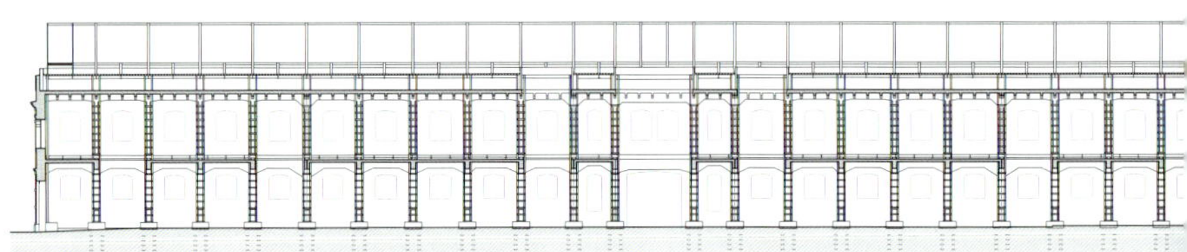

NAVE 8B

NAVE 8

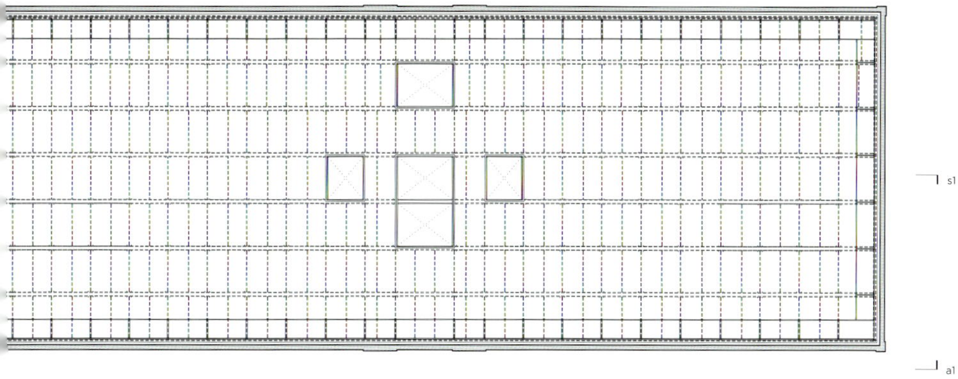

NAVE 9 – THIRD FLOOR

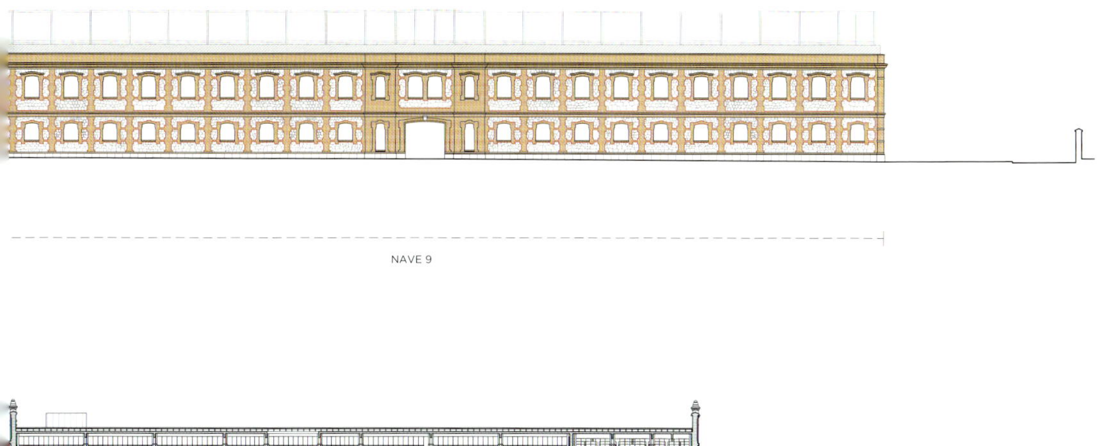

NAVE 9

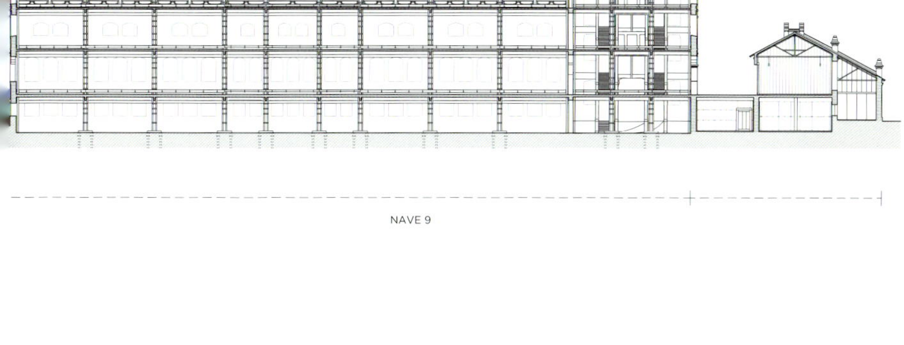

NAVE 9

EMERGENCIA

NAVES 10 / 11 / 12 - TEATRO ESPAÑOL (THEATER)

Constructed surface area 7,423 m^2
Architects Emilio Esteras (1st phase),
Justo Benito (2nd phase)
Performing Arts Advisor Francisco Fontanals (1st phase)
Quantity surveyor Ramón Suso
Engineering BCP Ingenieros, JG Ingenieros
Date of completion 2011

K.P. 6.47

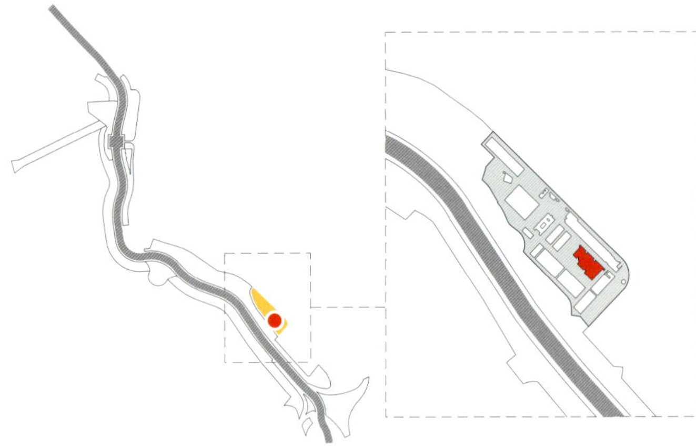

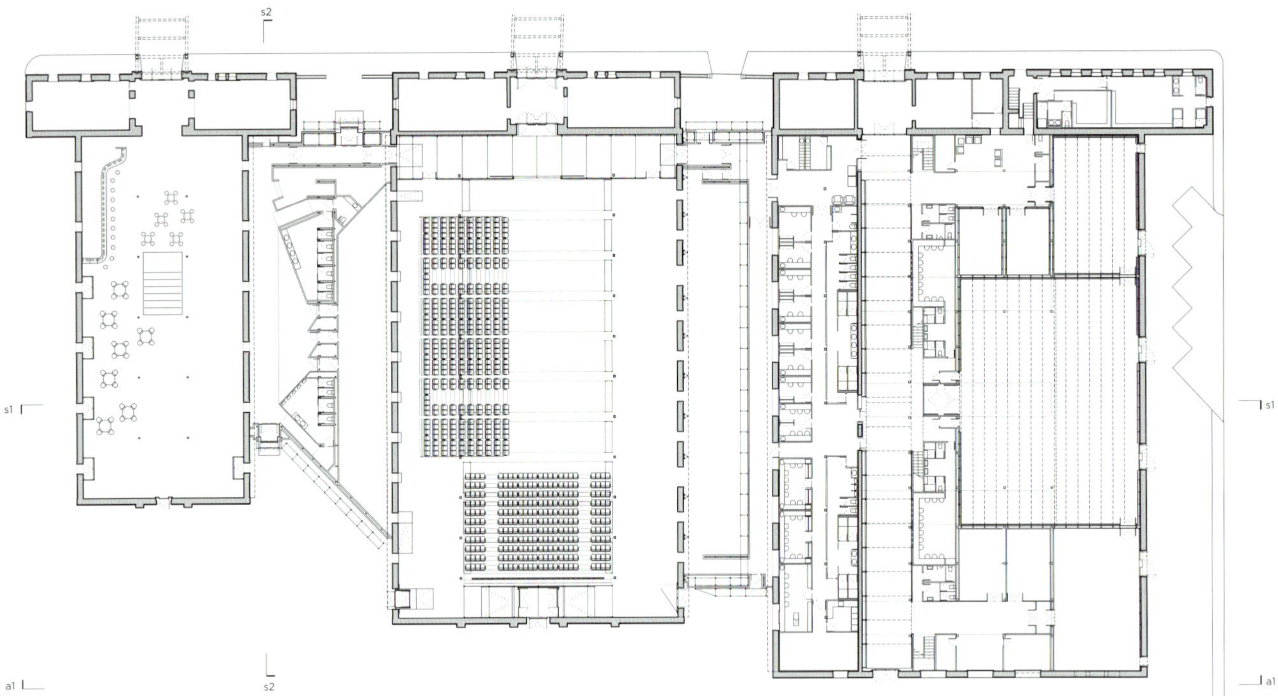

FLOOR PLAN

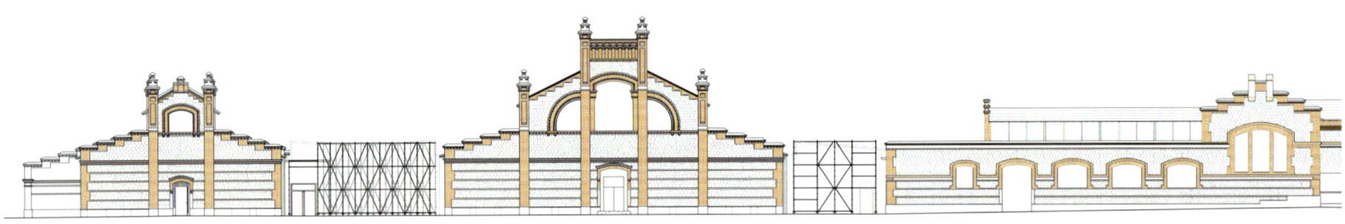

ELEVATION a1

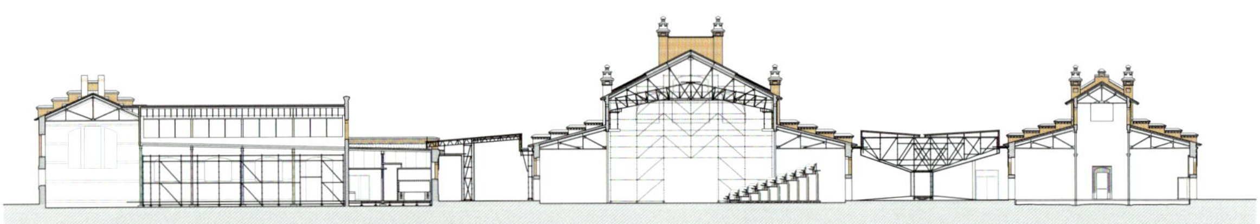

SECTION s1

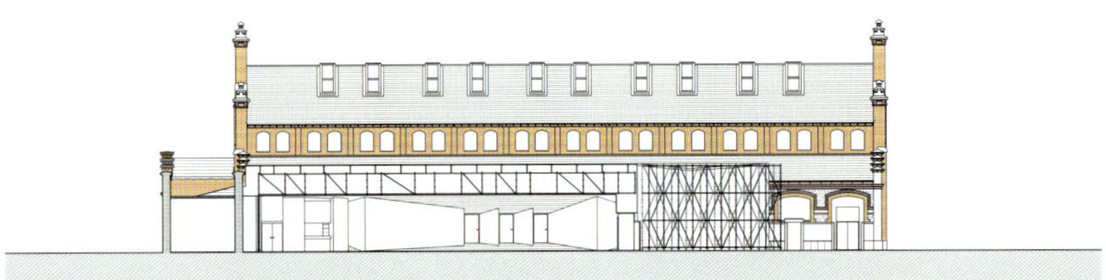

SECTION s2

1/750 1 2 3 4 5 10

NAVE 15 - MUSIC ACADEMY

Constructed surface area 4,750 m²
Architects Langarita Navarro
[María Langarita, Víctor Navarro]
Engineering Mecanismo, Imar Sanmartí Acousthink, Arquiges, Cuatro50, Úrculo Ingenieros
Date of completion 2011

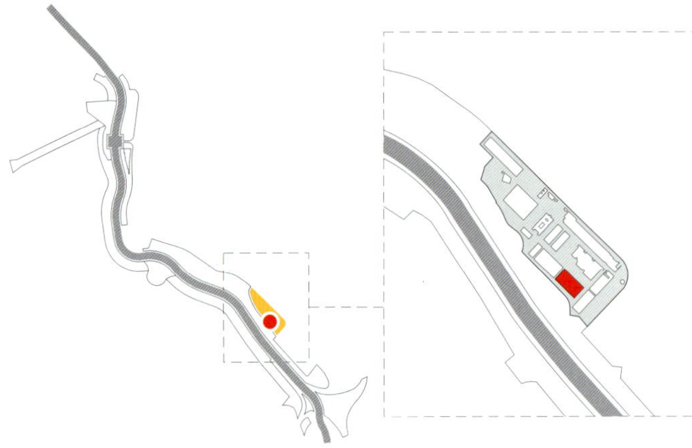

K.P. 6.50

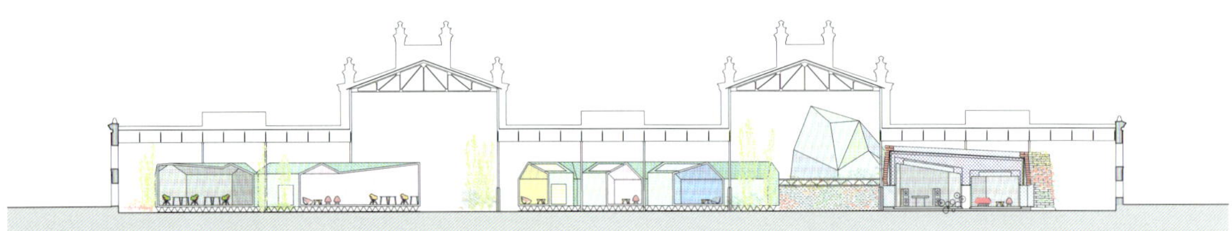

SECTION s1

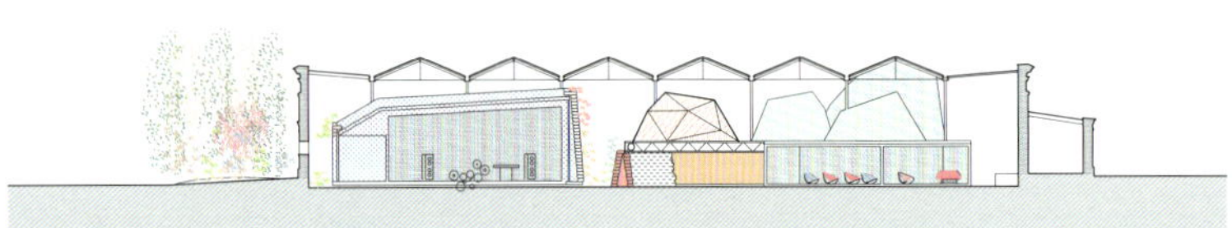

SECTION s2

1/750 1 2 3 4 5 10

2
4
5

NAVE 16 - EXHIBITION HALL

Constructed surface area 5,913.58 m^2
Architects ICA Arquitectura
[Iñaki Carnicero, Alejandro Virseda, Ignacio Vila]
Engineering JG Ingenieros, Mecanismo
Date of completion 2011

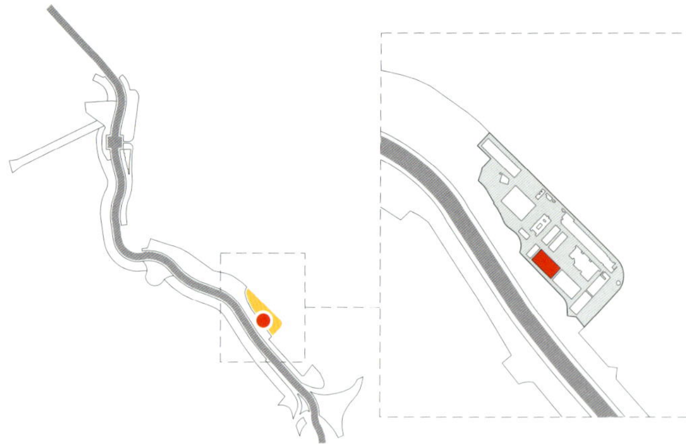

K.P. 6.44

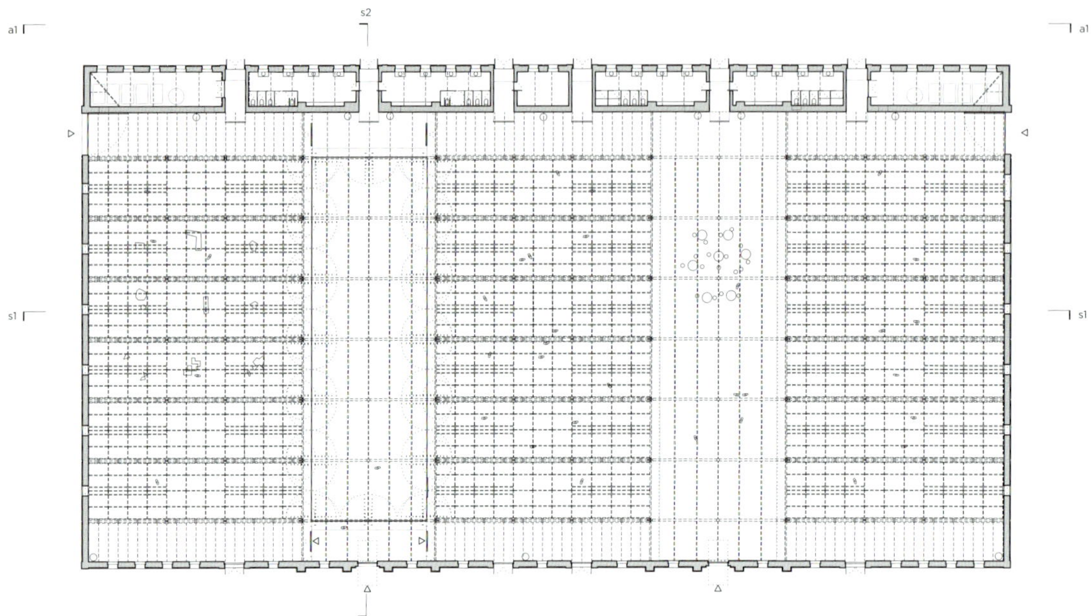

FLOOR PLAN

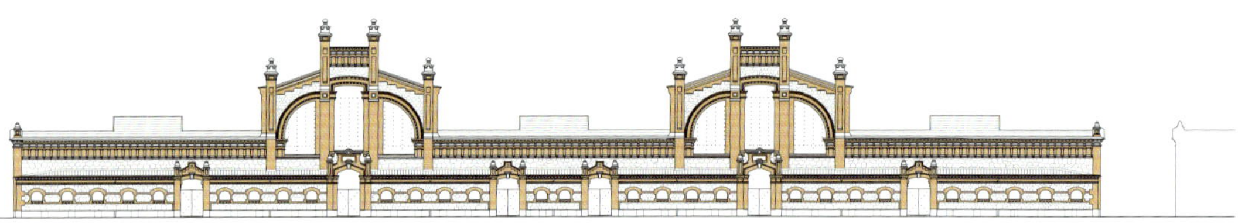

ELEVATION a1

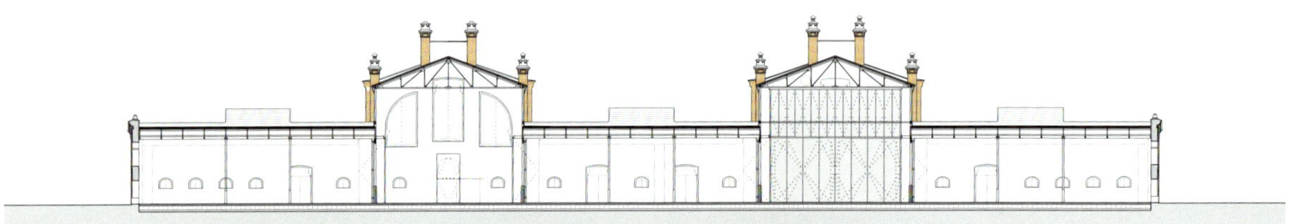

SECTION s1

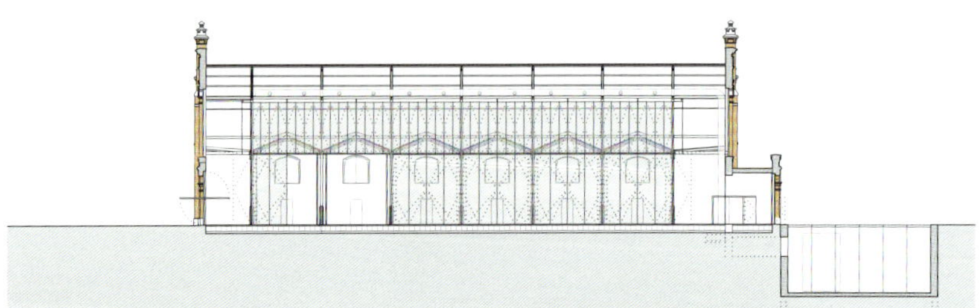

SECTION s2

1/750 1 2 3 4 5 10

INSTALLATIONS CENTER

Effective surface area 3,026.26 m²
Constructed surface area 3,401.60 m²
Floor dimensions 20 x 50 m
Height above ground level 6.85 m
Height below ground level 7.80 m
Date of completion 2012

K.P. 6.35

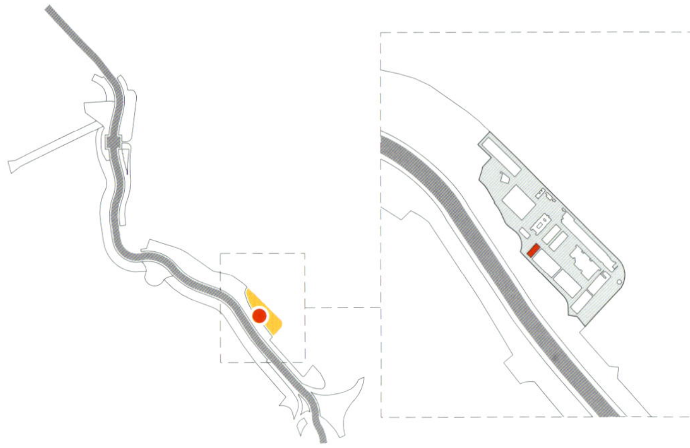

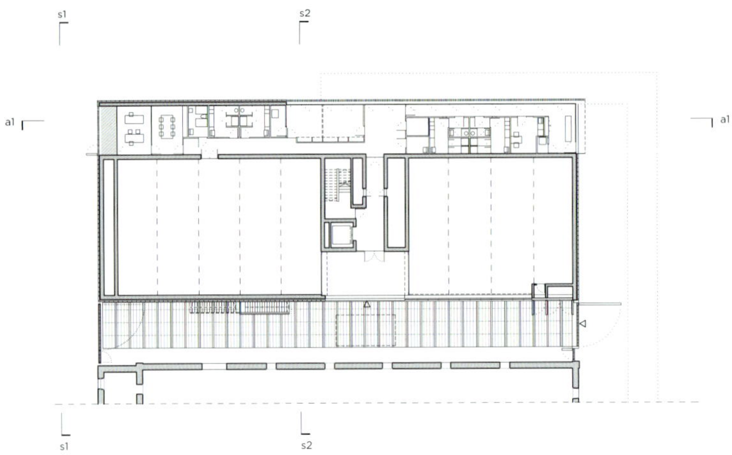

FLOOR PLAN

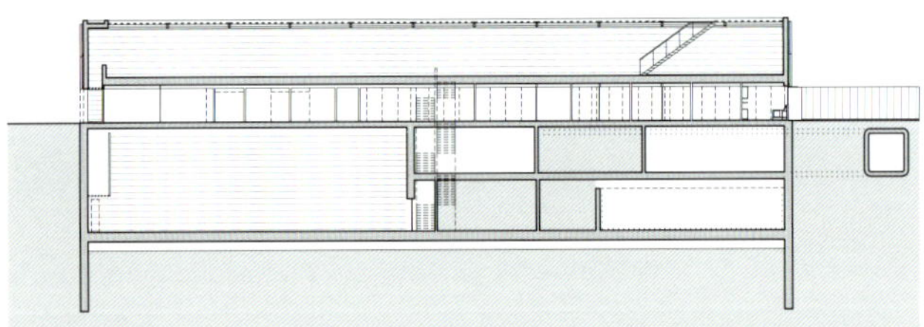

SECTION s1

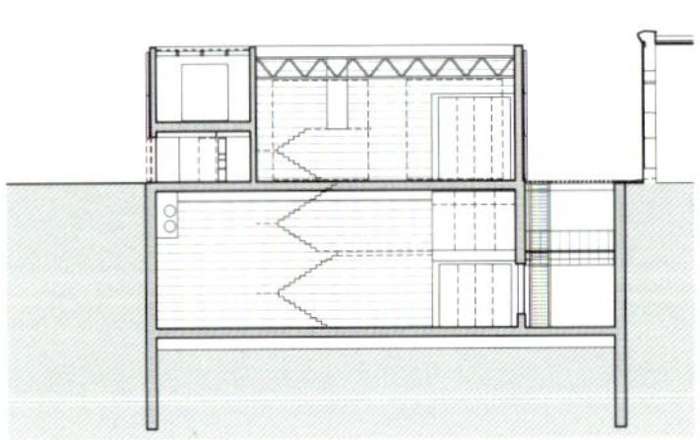

SECTION s2

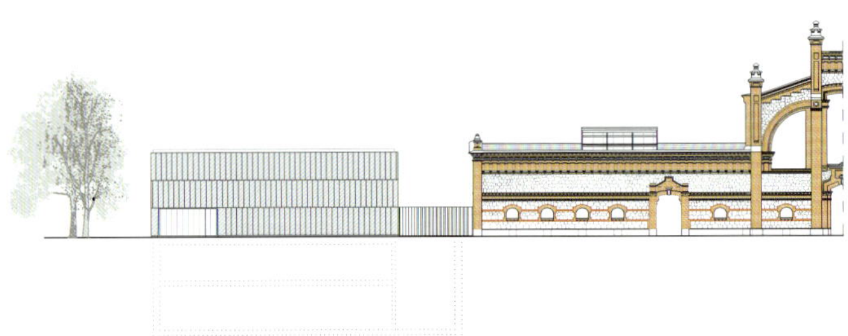

ELEVATION a1 TOWARDS MATADERO / ARGANZUELA PARK

1/750 1 2 3 4 5 10

CENTRO DE INTERPRETACIÓN DEL RÍO (MANZANARES RIVER INTERPRETATION CENTER)

Effective surface area 624 m^2
Constructed surface area 704.45 m^2
Floor dimensions 24 x 29.5 m
Height above ground level 4.40 m
Date of completion 2011

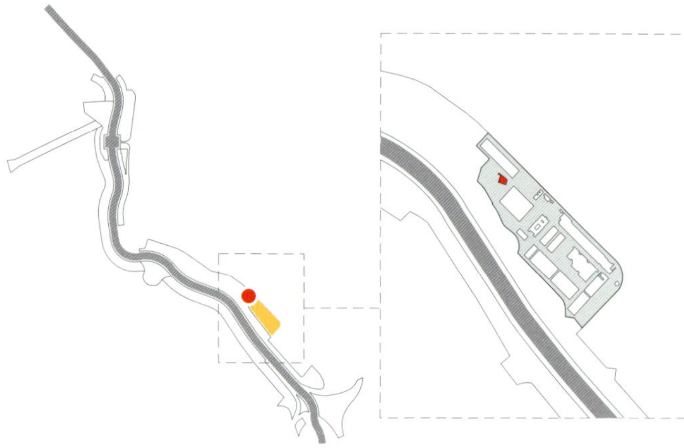

K.P. 6.09

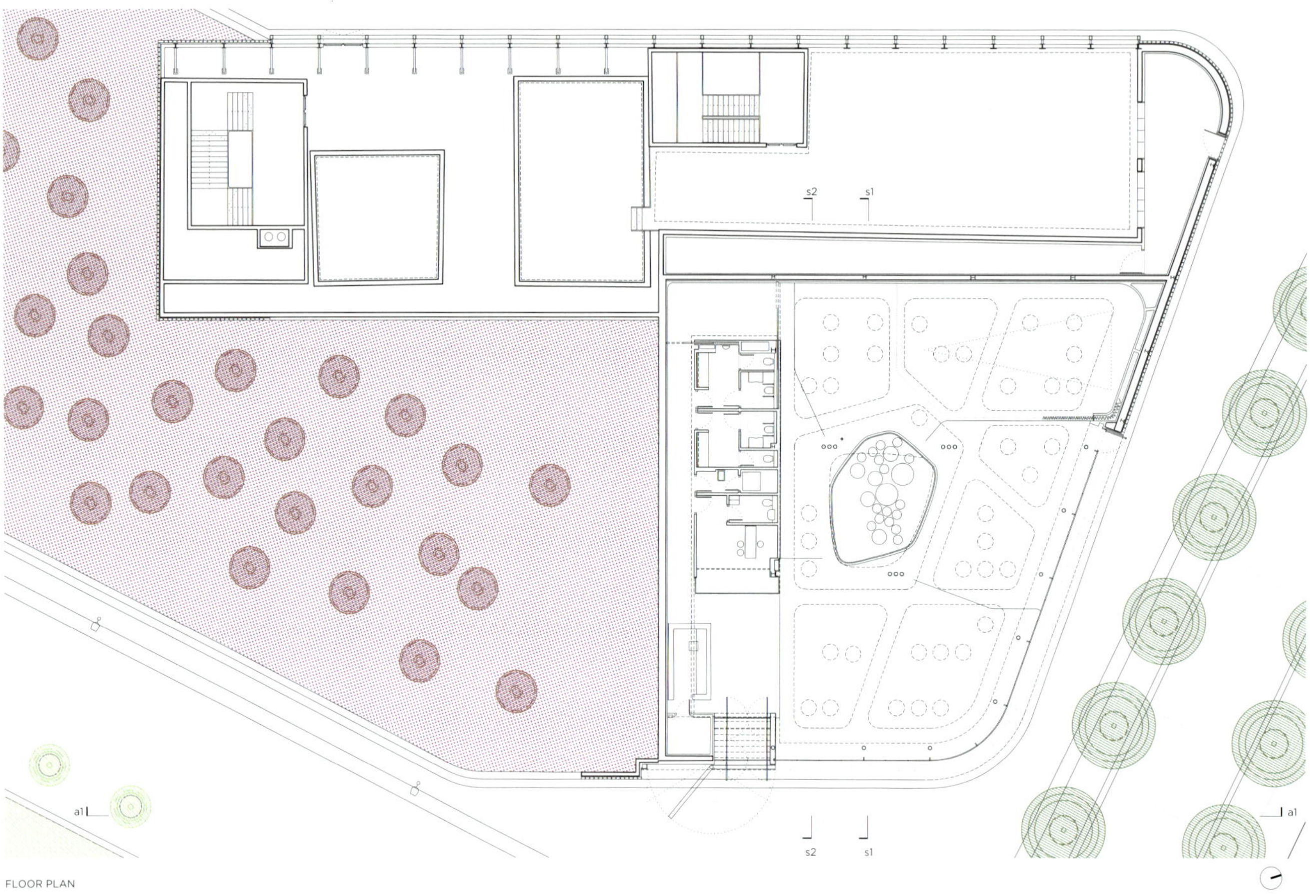

FLOOR PLAN

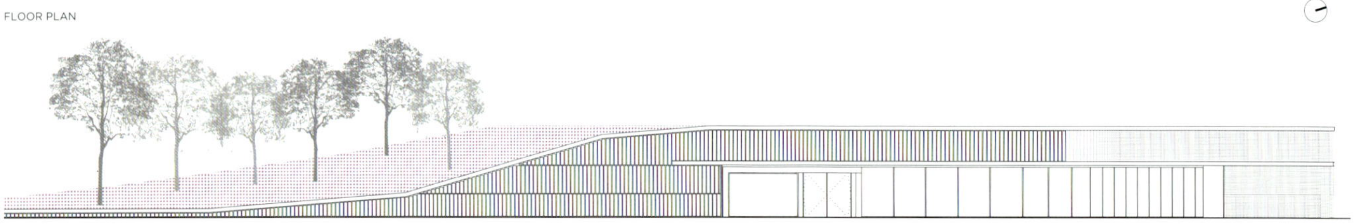

ELEVATION a1

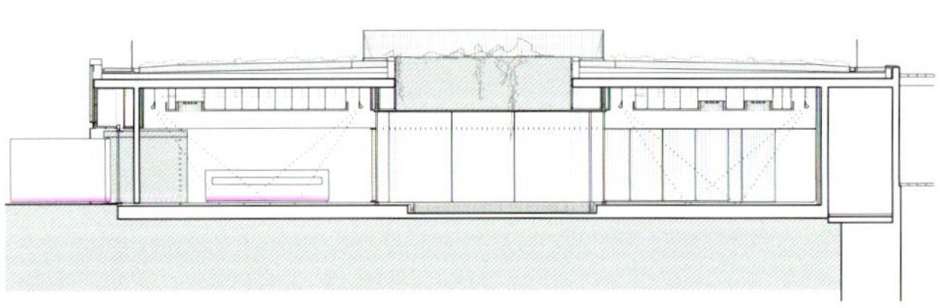

SECTION s1

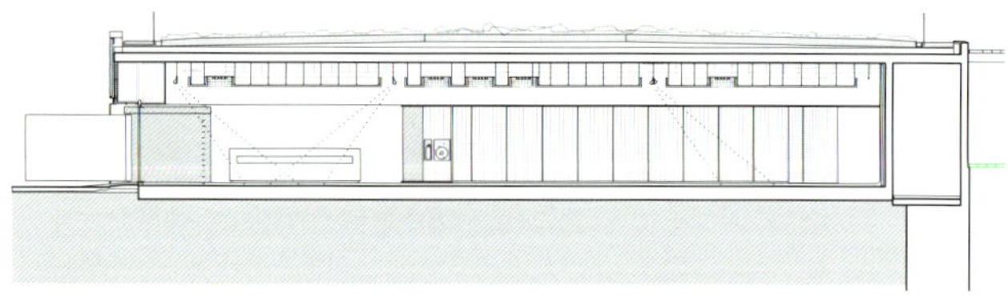

SECTION s2

1/400 1 2 3 4 5 10

NOTES ON A SATURDAY ALONG MADRID RÍO

RICHARD PLUNZ

As a classic urban design exercise the immense impact of Madrid Río on the city will remain in perpetuity. One could hardly ask for more. But there is more. I felt a little like my fellow Manhattanite, Washington Irving, who in 1828 famously traveled to Grenada to see the Alhambra. I am not so sure that the Madrid Río makes Madrid a Grenada of the 21st century, but it did evoke that sensibility at first sight. Surely the Cheonggyecheon in Seoul is another prominent "restoration" precedent, but its ultimate impact on the city as a whole is far more limited. Although Boston's "Big Dig" cost several times more than Madrid Río, it is proving far less effective as a contribution to the social fabric of that city. As both urban design and metropolitan strategy, Madrid Río is extremely interesting. It is first and foremost about social fabric. As urban catalyst it succeeds to cut across social class lines in contrast to that other new generation park that I know well; the "High Line" in Manhattan, which is a successful real estate operation but too dominated by the enormous private investment in luxury housing along its path.

My visit to the park started at the Cuesta San Vicente and my first intuition was that the Madrid Río strategy was likely to be more socially inclusive in contrast to present practice in New York, where public space initiatives necessarily involve substantial private investment and return. When I asked I was quickly put on notice that Madrid Río was public investment for the public good before all else; and that in fact the bordering real estate along the river edge comprises a large proportion of moderate income and social housing; such that any question of subsidizing luxury was moot. Quickly this became obvious. Madrid Río has reversed the social polarity of the city. Overnight the back doors of the city have become the front doors. And the amenity of a six kilometer-long park in place of high-speed roads and an open sewer, already appears to be encouraging fabric regeneration and robust economic activity.

We began our itinerary with a visit to a bicycle rental shop on Calle Aniceto Marinas and they were surely doing well on Saturday morning. As we set out there already was plenty of competition from other cyclists; and then from an admixture of scores of people of seemingly of all sorts doing all kinds of things. The city descended on Madrid Río in an affirmation that "urban design" can still absolutely change the behavior of an entire city.

By midday the city had enveloped its new park with such intensity that one could not help but wonder: how dysfunctional could Madrid have been before? Apparently pretty dysfunctional; and not without its share of mis-guided planning adventures, some rather prominent on the skyline. Fortunately the banality of the Cuatro Torres is not visible from the Huerta de la Partida viewpoint, although the towers of the Plaza de España are present as a reminder of major unresolved planning issues facing the city. But the orchard holds its own; with its subtle reference to another Madrid; of Carlos III and of the expansive 18th-century urban scape; and to the earlier global ambitions of the melding with Italy and the Kingdom of the Two Sicilies. In some ways it reminded me of Caserta; but all the more impressive for the underworld presence of the automobile. It is a traffic junction as orchard for the 21st century.

Fundamentally, the design of Madrid Río represents a didactic tool that addresses its urban context and herein lies a huge opportunity that is not yet exploited. It is a learning machine. History in diverse layers is written all over the park design as a stitching device. Perhaps the reinvention of the ancient orchard and the Casa de Campo being its most literal. But there is also the Puente de Toledo Gardens at the Baroque bridge where the Baroque influences the new planting, and the paths for pedestrians were designed following traces of the road underground in a hybridization between Baroque and high speed geometries. In Arganzuela Park there are the circulation geometries that reflect the historical traces of the Manzanares River within this former flood plain. There are also archeological traces here. The stones of the historical fountain once on the site are incorporated into the cladding of a retaining wall.

The significance of the above layers remains oblivious to the park user. The public would be well served to have a clear understanding of the architects' didacticism; of the representations of the historical layering; of the pre-automobile ecology of the riverbed as an essential component of the park in accomplishing both spatial and cultural stitching. Included should be the dimension related to flora and fauna. What will be the ecological succession that this project has launched? Which are the fish now feeding at the base of the restored dam just below the Puente de Toledo? What should we understand of the whole restored hydraulic infrastructure? The functioning of the seven dams has been a crucial component of the overall work, and of themselves of great public interest.

Cities everywhere are essentially cultural objects expressing diverse layers of development. The richness of Madrid in this sense is well expressed in the park. Having made this enormous public investment, the city should better capitalize on what it offers in creating public awareness as to what Madrid Río was before, is now, and can be in the future.

With or without didactics, however, the public is seizing the opportunity to be there. The strength of the whole ensemble is that it is being used no matter what. The most expressive use belongs to the children. Returning upstream from the Matadero, the slide tubes at the playground in Arganzuela already had plenty of takers by mid-morning, including adults. Further up, to the north the undercroft of the highway bridge, painted with Calderesque patterns and with suspended children's swings, was crowded by midday and testament to care in social retrofitting. That bridge, a traffic necessity becomes no less a public space amenity, including acoustics that, with its echoes, heighten the presence of the Manzanares River. Then there are the new twin new pedestrian bridges, the overturned "boats" with their mosaics by Daniel Canogar — not just crossings but rooms with their own micro-climates. Places to stay and savor what heightened comfort the river can offer.

It is hard to predict what will be the evolution of the Madrid Río intervention after fifty years, or even in ten years. Surely there will be big future development moves along the path. The Matadero stockyards have yet to mature as a cultural destination. Perhaps the largest question has to do with the future of the huge area of the Vicente Calderón stadium. Undoubtedly this will entail a "public-private" real estate operation and with the decline of public funds one can only hope that the inevitable private influx will prove as effective and wise as the Madrid Río outcome. But the spine of the park will be omnipresent for all to see, as evidence of the level of intervention that represents the city's substantial capabilities; and hopefully to be further exploited in the coming period. It is an important lesson for us all; and especially for Madrid. Hard to do Madrid Río justice in just a few words.

K.P. 2.40

K.P. 2.70

K.P. 4.80

K.P. 5.20

K.P. 5.20

K.P. 5.80

K.P. 6.70

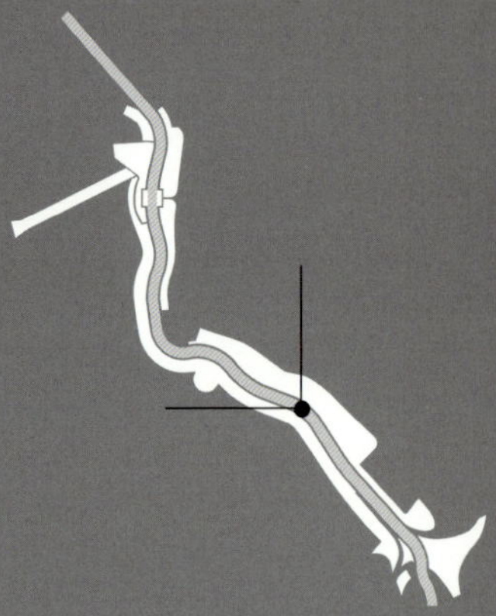

5. SYSTEMS, CATALOGS, AND RULES

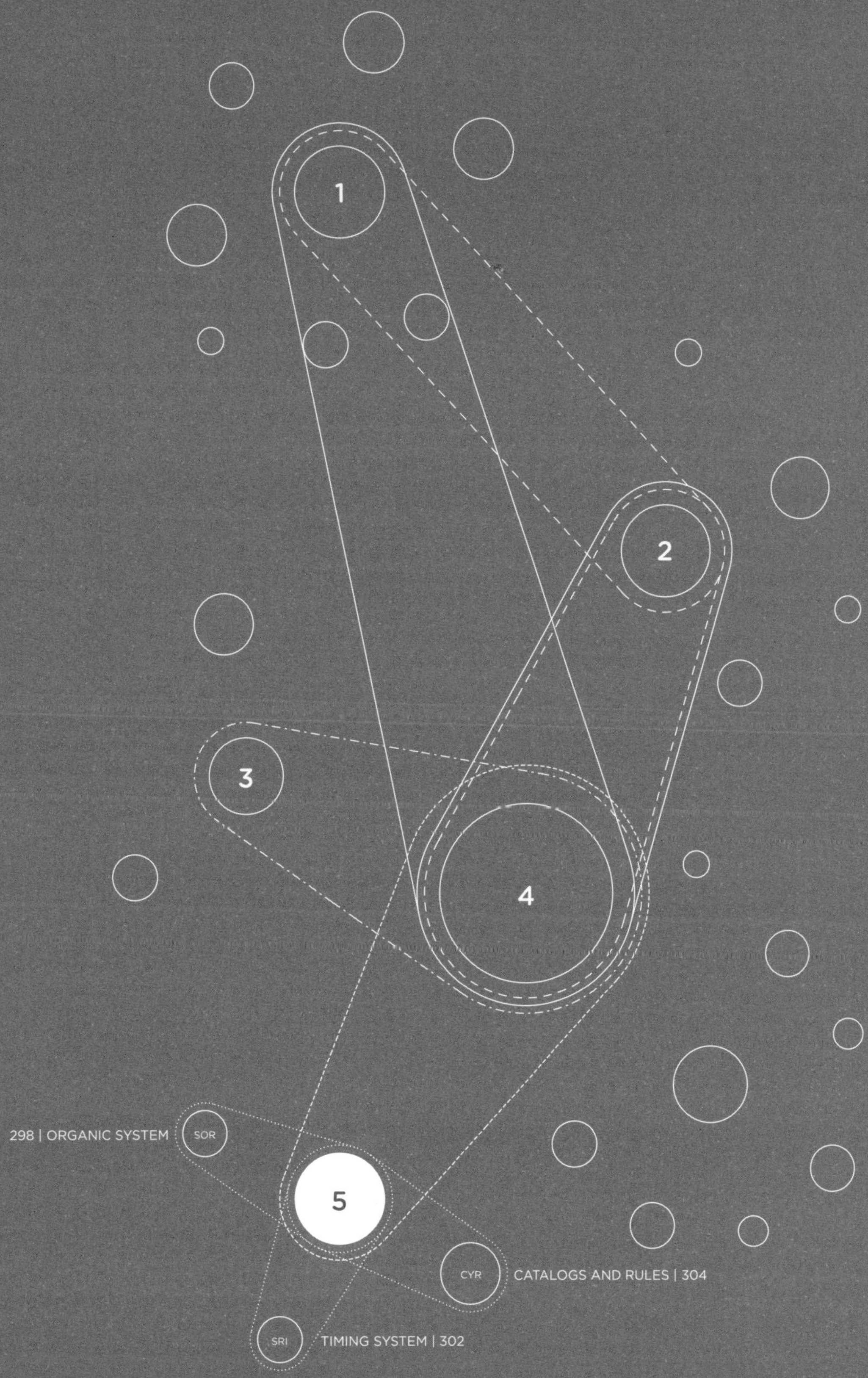

ORGANIC SYSTEM

The construction of the M-30 tunnels followed organizational models tested by the government of the Community of Madrid when expanding its subway lines between 1996 and 2002. The works' similarities permitted co-participation in management processes whose direction was entrusted to a small and tightly knit organization of senior officials very close to the mayor and a small number of leading construction firms (the country's most important ones) that carried out the work and whose highly experienced specialists in the field of civil engineering employed their resources to address problems arising as the construction progressed. Following this model, with the participation of seven companies to build seven sections, the tunnels were completed in little less than four years (between 2004 and 2007). Construction costs, which reached over 3,900 million euros, were financed through bank credits drawn by a mixed-capital company (Madrid Calle30) founded with 80% municipal participation. This also guaranteed the constant advance of the digging without economic tension. At that time, the world financial crisis had yet to begin.

The execution of 150 hectares of park over the tunnels followed a different organization system. The political power embodied by the figure of the mayor provided its only sustenance. The existence of a single design team chosen for all of the projects through a juried contest, and the fragmentation of the actual work among over 90 different sectors handled by 49 different construction companies called for a specific structure. A new General Office was set up with two managements departments (economic-judicial management and technical management) by the municipal government, and both answered to the Urban Planning Council. These new organisms took control of the project and handled municipal coordination of the construction work. Thus, with political guidelines specifying only that deadlines be met, three executive teams began work. Two had their own structures and hierarchy (the municipal technical team and the independent design team), while the third consisted simply of all the different construction companies and followed the guidelines laid by the other two.

The municipal team consisted almost exclusively of city-government employees (engineers, architects, lawyers, experts, administrative personnel, etc.) drawn from either the municipal organization responsible for tunnel construction or other existing departments. In total, 51 people were brought into the process over time. This structure was not definitively consolidated until the beginning of the second term of office in which work was going on, that is, the last trimester of 2007. Eight supervisory companies were contracted, along with four companies specialized in job safety coordination.

The independent design team chosen through an international competition consisted exclusively of architects and landscape architects. In total, 90 people belonged to the team, but the maximum number of specialists present at any given time was 27. This core team was aided by outside consultants whose first job was to test the true load-bearing capacity of the tunnel structures in order to plant the greatest possible number of trees over them. A fundamental part of that consulting consisted of analyzing existing installations and maintaining urban services during the construction. In that sense, forestry and botanical advice was crucial as each plant had to be selected beforehand and duly treated in order to survive its radical change of habitat. In total, the design team contracted 15 companies to advise them in 9 different fields.

Both the municipal personnel and the design team had to begin, first, by including requests by the citizenry, by District Councils — the construction affected six districts with a total population of approximately 1,110,000 inhabitants — and by all Government Departments related to public space, from firefighters and emergency medical services to those handling maintenance of lighting and pavement, as well as those responsible for mobility, historical heritage, and waste management. Second, the two teams, each from its own area of responsibility — works management and urban design, respectively — directed the different construction companies charged with carrying out the specified proposals on schedule and within budget. The total cost of this work reached 420 million Euros.

ORGANIC SYSTEM TABLE

ACTIONS	AGENTS	RESPONSIBILITIES
MANAGEMENT	MAYOR'S OFFICE	Political decisionmaking Strategic decisionmaking
	DEPARTMENT OF TOWN PLANNING AND HOUSING (URBAN PLANNING COUNCIL)	Political supervision Management facilitation
	DEPARTMENT OF ECONOMICS, REVENUE, AND PUBLIC ADMINISTRATION	Administrative decisions on financial resources Intervention and fiscalization of spending Partial financing of public works (municipal budget)
	DEPARTMENT OF THE ENVIRONMENT	Management of park maintenance
	GENERAL COORDINATION OF SPECIFIC PROJECTS	General administrative management: - Adjudications and contracts - Citizen participation - Public information General economic management: - Construction contracts - Assistance contracts General time management: - Tactical implementation Management of municipal technicians: - Control of project documentation - Technical and economic control of construction
	PRESS OFFICE	Management of communication with the media
	OTHER GOVERNMENT DEPARTMENTS	Identification and requests for necessities (mobility, green property, urban furnishings, lighting, water, local police, firefighters, tunnels, historical heritage, promotion of tourism, creation and culture, cleaning and maintenance)
	DISTRICT COMMITTEES	Identification and requests for district necessities (Usera, Arganzuela, Carabanchel, Latina, Centro, Moncloa)
	GENERAL ADMINISTRATION OF THE STATE	Partial financing of public works: - State fund for local investment (Fondo Estatal de Inversión Local, FEIL) - State fund for local employment and sustainability (Fondo Estatal para el Empleo y la Sostenibilidad Local, FEESL)
	EUROPEAN UNION	Partial financing of public works: - European fund for regional development (Fondo Europeo de Desarrollo Regional, FEDER)
DESIGN	DESIGN TEAM	Design decisions Design development Inclusion of outside requirements (Government departments, district committees, citizen participation) Drawing up projects for tendering Drawing up construction documents Generating images for the press Definition and selection of materials, vegetation and trees Construction oversight
	GENERAL ENGINEERING	Participation in the drawing up of projects for tendering Participation in the drawing up of construction documents Calculation of urban installations Ordinary structural calculations
	SPECIFIC ENGINEERING	Technical design, calculations, and testing of special structures
	OUTSIDE TECHNICAL ADVISORS	Participation in the design of lighting and ornamental fountains
	OUTSIDE ENVIRONMENTAL ADVISORS	Participation in evironmental, botanical, forestry, and river biology evaluations
	OUTSIDE DESIGN ADVISORS	Graphic design, art, computer graphics, models
WORK	CONSTRUCTION COMPANIES	Tendering of bids Execution of construction work
	OUTSIDE TECHNICAL ASSITANCE	Technical control of work Job health and safety Work measurements Aid to municipal technicians
	SUPPLIERS	Supply of construction materials
PARK USE	CITIZENRY	Opinion and enjoyment
	PARK MAINTENANCE CONCESSION	Park maintenance

ORGANIC SYSTEM

PROJECT ACTIONS

GST MANAGEMENT

DIS DESIGN

OBR CONSTRUCTION WORK

PRQ PARK USE

PROCESS ACTIONS

ALC MAYOR'S OFFICE
AGU DEPARTMENT OF TOWN PLANNING AND HOUSING (URBAN PLANNING COUNCIL)
AGE DEPARTMENT OF ECONOMICS, REVENUE, AND PUBLIC ADMINISTRATION
AGM DEPARTMENT OF THE ENVIRONMENT
CPS GENERAL COORDINATION OF SPECIFIC PROJECTS

OPR PRESS OFFICE
OAG OTHER GOVERNMENT DEPARTMENTS
JDD DISTRICT COMMITTEES
EST GENERAL ADMINISTRATION OF THE STATE
EUR EUROPEAN UNION
EDI DESIGN TEAM
IGG GENERAL ENGINEERING
IGE SPECIFIC ENGINEERING

CTE OUTSIDE TECHNICAL ADVISORS
CME OUTSIDE ENVIRONMENTAL ADVISORS
CDE OUTSIDE DESIGN ADVISORS
ECO CONSTRUCTION COMPANIES
ATE OUTSIDE TECHNICAL ASSISTANCE
SUM SUPPLIERS
CIU CITIZENRY
MAN PARK MAINTENANCE CONCESSION

AGENTS PARTICIPATING IN EACH ACTION

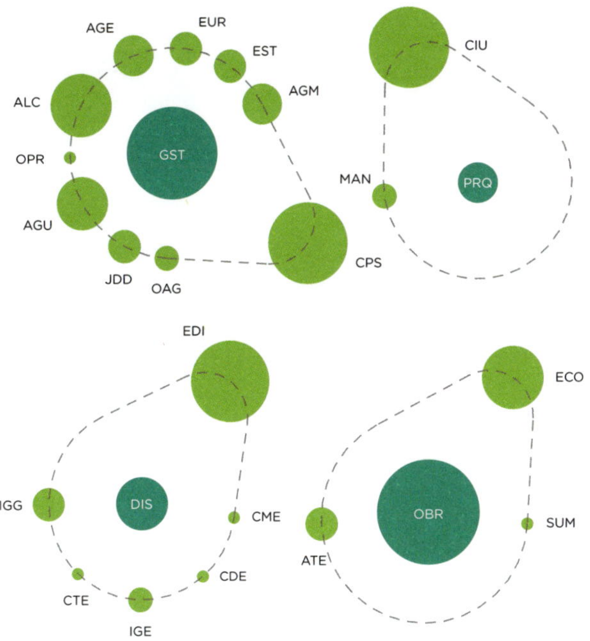

RELATIONS BETWEEN ACTIONS AND OUTSIDE AGENTS

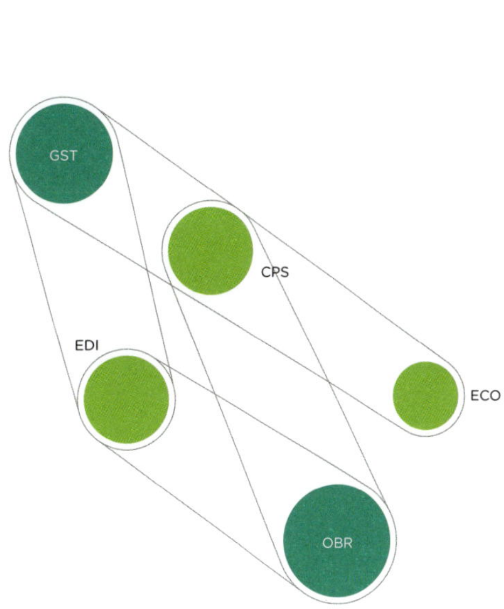

RELATIONS AMONG ACTIONS

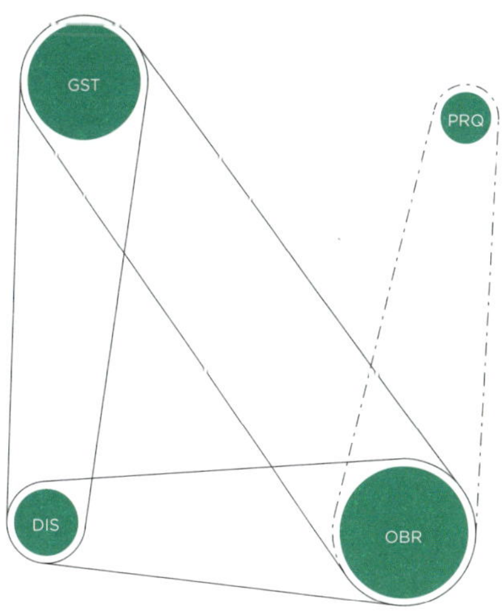

RELATIONS AMONG AGENTS

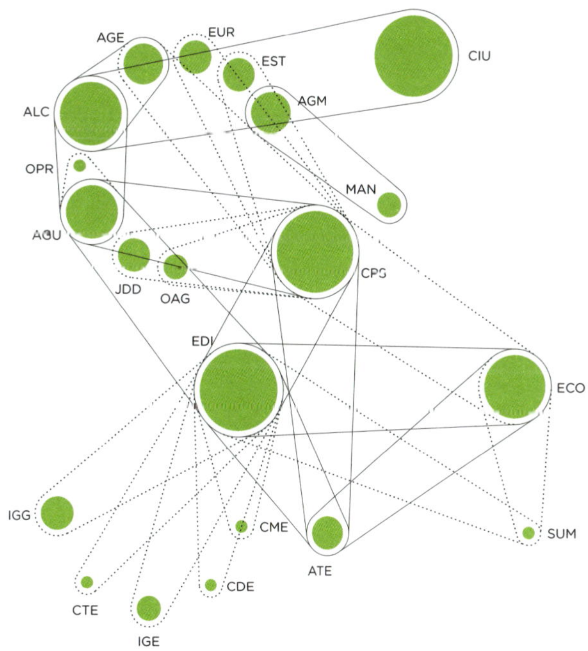

- ACTIONS
- AGENTS
- LINK BETWEEN ACTIONS AND AGENTS
- MAIN AGENT ASSOCIATED WITH EACH ACTION
- RELATION BETWEEN ACTIONS AND OUTSIDE AGENTS

RELATIONS AMONG ACTIONS

- IMMEDIATE RELATION
- DELAYED RELATION

RELATIONS AMONG AGENTS

- PERMANENT RELATION
- INTERMITTENT RELATION

TIMING SYSTEM

The implementation of this project required understanding and accepting various forms of time management, as time was the main axis of what began as an undefined, complex, and changing process.

The first, clearest, and most unequivocal approach was dictated by the rhythms of municipal politics. When the results of the International Competition were announced, the end of the electoral period (from 2003 to 2007) was exactly a year-and-a-half away. If the mayor who had promoted this operation was reelected he would have at least four more years to lead it, making a total of five-and-a-half years to complete work over the tunnels. So once the winning proposal was chosen, there were eighteen months in which to develop the general technical documents needed to define a global idea of the project, and also to materialize at least a visible part of the project that would allow expectant voters to appreciate what the grand park could become. Thus, charmed with the results, they would reelect the same municipal government that had made it possible.

If the reelection was successful — polls indicated this was very likely — there would then be a four-year window for completing the work needed to heal the wound opened by tunnel construction, which had begun in early 2004, almost two years before the contest results were announced. Therefore, the calendar for surface work was divided into two periods: the first from 2006 to 2007, and the second from 2007 to 2011. The greatest work intensity coincided with the end of the first period, when the citizens' votes were at stake.

Another form of time management grew out of the training of working-team personnel and the consolidation of their intellectual and technical discourse. The first works were intended to form the earliest images that would give the project social visibility. They were defined while all of the competition ideas were being brought into focus with unified parameters based on a precise but progressive knowledge of the problems emerging from the construction of the tunnels and the particular circumstances of the neighborhoods adjacent to the river, including their urban conditions and hidden infrastructures. A stable, inner team of young architects was needed, and they had to be involved with this project, with clearly defined responsibilities that would allow them to reliably control the 150-hectare area under development. Moreover, this period running from early 2006 through the end of 2008 saw the drawing up of the necessary agreements between the architects responsible for the project and all the advisors and consultants outside the design team. Little by little, they began to receive work, some of which was enormously urgent for the development of plans and calculations — especially tasks related to the future survival of vegetation planted over concrete slabs. Municipal elections were held in the middle of this period and both the mayor and the councilwoman responsible for this work were reelected. In early 2008, the human team, the thematic conception and the compendium of technical resources designed for the project had taken shape and were very stable. This allowed the architects' work to move forward, so, while only four projects were produced for 13.4 hectares between 2006 and 2007; 75 projects were drawn up for 125.4 hectares between 2008 and 2011.

Third, and in a much less systematic fashion, the timing of the operation was subject to relations among the different public works contracted, their modes of financing and the rate at which economic resources had to be invested. This was unquestionably and rigidly conditioned by the political calendar but it had a certain degree of autonomy as well due to the fact that half of the park construction costs were assumed by City Hall and the other by the National Government's employment stimulus plans, whose contribution was divided to fund projects with budgets under five million euros each. That is why the initial number of projects, which were conceived as autonomous documents needed to landscape complete sections of the city, passed from 24 to 93. The rate at which three quarters of these documents were drawn up — *a priori,* they only defined an area of action and an amount to be spent, thus permitting the adjudication of independent contracts to construction companies — accelerated exponentially in the final three years, and projects subject to this system were literally being defined as they were built. Much of what was drawn up on Tuesday was constructed the following Wednesday. That way, the process became a sum of *micro-times* adapted to the overriding objective of meeting the completion deadline in the *macro-time* of four years, which was how long the municipal government would be in office.

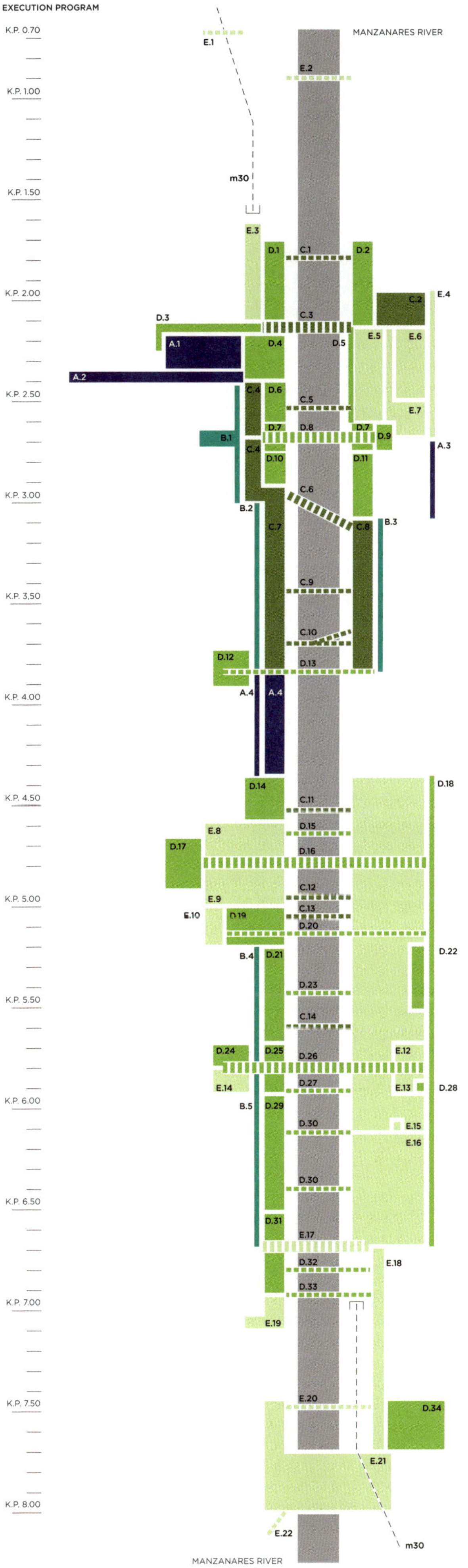

YEAR		PROJECT	TENDER BUDGET SURFACE	AREA / LENGTH
2007 ELECTIONS 2007	A.1	HUERTA DE LA PARTIDA	3,092,929 €	3.94 HA
	A.2	AVENIDA DE PORTUGAL	14,776,883 €	7.21 HA
	A.3	VIRGEN DEL PUERTO SIDEWALK	2,842,815 €	0.43 HA
	A.4	SALÓN DE PINOS. PUENTE DE SAN ISIDRO - PUENTE DE TOLEDO	3,100,000 €	1.80 HA
2008	B.1	SIDEWALKS AND ROADWAYS. AV. PORTUGAL - PUENTE DE SEGOVIA	1,633,498 €	3.94 HA
	B.2	SIDEWALKS AND ROADWAYS. PUENTE DE SEGOVIA - PUENTE SAN ISIDRO	5,765,389 €	7.21 HA
	B.3	SIDEWALKS AND ROADWAYS. ESTUDIOS HIDROGRÁFICOS - PUENTE SAN ISIDRO	3,527,003 €	0.43 HA
	B.4	SIDEWALKS AND ROADWAYS. PUENTE TOLEDO - PUENTE PRAGA	2,648,438 €	1.80 HA
	B.5	SIDEWALKS AND ROADWAYS. PUENTE DE PRAGA - PUENTE DE LA PRINCESA	2,648,438 €	1.80 HA
2009	C.1	RESTORATION OF ANICETO MARINAS HISTORIC FOOTBRIDGE	601,000 €	40 M
	C.2	ANICETO MARINAS SLOPE	1,919,941 €	1.70 HA
	C.3	REMODELING OF PUENTE DEL REY	2,497,915 €	0.60 HA
	C.4	SALÓN DE PINOS. AV. DE PORTUGAL - PUENTE DE SEGOVIA	6,912,095 €	1.44 HA
	C.5	REHABILITATION OF DAM 5	350,624 €	40 M
	C.6	REHABILITATION OF PUENTE OBLICUO	1,400,000 €	55 M
	C.7	SALÓN DE PINOS. PUENTE DE SEGOVIA - PUENTE DE SAN ISIDRO	11,219,224 €	2.22 HA
	C.8	SALÓN DE PINOS. ESTUDIOS HIDROGRÁFICOS - PUENTE SAN ISIDRO	8,357,645 €	1.75 HA
	C.9	REHABILITATION OF DAM 6	350,624 €	40 M
	C.10	FOOTBRIDGE BETWEEN PUENTE SEGOVIA AND PUENTE SAN ISIDRO	2,150,000 €	106 M
	C.11	REHABILITATION OF DAM 7	660,000 €	40 M
	C.12	FOOTBRIDGE OVER CANAL DE ISABEL II INSTALLATIONS	1,900,000 €	40 M
	C.13	RESTORATION PUENTE DE BOLAS	400,000 €	40 M
	C.14	REHABILITATION OF DAM 8	350,624 €	40 M
2010	D.1	LANDSCAPING THE ROOF OF M-30 TUNNEL. SAN POL - PUENTE REY	5,767,753 €	0.94 HA
	D.2	LANDSCAPING THE SIDE LANE OF C/ ANICETO MARINAS	3,573,689 €	1.09 HA
	D.3	SURROUNDINGS OF THE CASA DE VARGAS	2,497,915 €	1.20 HA
	D.4	PLATAFORMA DEL REY (RIGHT BANK OF THE MANZANARES)	4,399,999 €	1.52 HA
	D.5	TOPOGRAPHY AND CLADDING OF NORTHWESTERN RIVERWALL PUENTE SEGOVIA	3,935,463 €	2.40 HA
	D.6	GARDENS NORTHERN PUENTE DE SEGOVIA	3,904,857 €	1.13 HA
	D.7	FLUVIAL PONDS IN THE MIDDLE COURSE OF THE MANZANARES RIVER	3,430,294 €	0.60 HA
	D.8	REMODELING OF THE HISTORICAL PUENTE DE SEGOVIA AND PUENTE DE TOLEDO	3,862,800 €	465 M
	D.9	LOW GARDENS, PUENTE DE SEGOVIA (LEFT BANK)	3,333,666 €	0.85 HA
	D.10	GARDENS SOUTHERN PUENTE DE SEGOVIA	3,467,564 €	1.20 HA
	D.11	LANDSCAPING AROUND THE CEDEX (LEFT BANK)	6,369,818 €	2.29 HA
	D.12	LANDSCAPING ROAD LINKS TO C/ SAN AMBROSIO	3,381,980 €	1.18 HA
	D.13	ADAPTATION OF PUENTE DE SAN ISIDRO	789,025 €	0.25 HA
	D.14	LINEAR PARK NORTH OF PUENTE DE TOLEDO (RIGHT BANK)	4,987,385 €	3.08 HA
	D.15	REHABILITATATION NORTH PONTOON PUENTE DE TOLEDO	1,580,000 €	80 M
	D.16	ADAPTATION OF PUENTE DE TOLEDO	4,987,385 €	3.95 HA
	D.17	REMODELING THE GLORIETA DEL MARQUÉS DE VADILLO	4,899,039 €	1.13 HA
	D.18	REHABILITATION Pº YESERÍAS SIDEWALK ALONG PARK	4,769,282 €	1.55 HA
	D.19	LANDSCAPING AROUND COLEGIO CONCEPCIÓN ARENAL	4,875,572 €	2.98 HA
	D.20	MONUMENTAL ARGANZUELA BRIDGE	13,600,000 €	278 M
	D.21	PLANTING BETWEEN C/ ORGAZ AND C/ SAN DAVID	4,983,244 €	3.04 HA
	D.22	IMPROVE ACCESS TO ARGANZUELA PARK FROM Pº YESERÍAS	4,403,478 €	1.06 HA
	D.23	ARGANZUELA FOOTBRIDGE	1,700,000 €	40 M
	D.24	SPORTS COURTS AT PUENTE DE PRAGA	3,987,975 €	2.40 HA
	D.25	EXTENSION OF AV. MANZANARES BETWEEN SAN DAVID AND SAN GRACIANO	5,799,710 €	4.60 HA
	D.26	ADAPTATION OF PUENTE DE PRAGA	762,320 €	0.22 HA
	D.27	PUENTE DE PRAGA FOOTBRIDGE	1,790,000 €	40 M
	D.28	NEW MUNICIPAL POLICE CENTER	5,753,600 €	920 M²
	D.29	GARDENING SIDE LANE BETWEEN C/SAN GRACIANO AND C/SAN ZACARÍAS	4,985,000 €	3.11 HA
	D.30	TWIN FOOTBRIDGES FACING MATADERO	5,055,441 €	80 M
	D.31	REMODELING AREA UNDER PUENTE DE LA PRINCESA	5,368,547 €	4.30 HA
	D.32	PUENTE DE LA PRINCESA FOOTBRIDGE	1,770,000 €	40 M
	D.33	REHABILITATION OF DAM 9	380,000 €	40 M
	D.34	INSTALLATIONS FOR BMX CYCLING	3,662,932 €	4.29 HA
2011	E.1	"PUENTE DE LOS FRANCESES" FOOTBRIDGE	3,863,727 €	70 M
	E.2	ALMUÑECAR FOOTBRIDGE	3,525,318 €	45 M
	E.3	SALÓN DE PINOS BETWEEN SAN POL DE MAR AND RIBERA DEL MANZANARES	7,439,918 €	1.88 HA
	E.4	PEDESTRIAN AND CYCLING CONNECTION CAMPO DEL MORO - PUENTE DEL REY	4,750,156 €	1.39 HA
	E.5	PEDESTRIAN AND CYCLING PATH ON MANZANARES' LEFT BANK	5,103,650 €	2.73 HA
	E.6	RECOVERY OF VIRGEN DEL PUERTO GARDEN SLOPE	3,900,347 €	1.91 HA
	E.7	RECOVERY OF LANDSCAPE AREA AROUND ERMITA VIRGEN DEL PUERTO	3,801,612 €	0.47 HA
	E.8	RECOVERY OF LANDSCAPE AREA AROUND NORTH PUENTE DE TOLEDO	5,032,907 €	1.81 HA
	E.9	RECOVERY OF GREEN AREA GARDENS SOUTH OF PUENTE DE TOLEDO	5,200,000 €	2.15 HA
	E.10	REHABILITATION OF SPORTS FACILITIES AT PASAJE DE MONSERRAT	1,902,123 €	0.90 HA
	E.11	ARGANZUELA PARK	39,826,540 €	20.85 HA
	E.12	ARGANZUELA PARK SPORTS COURTS	2,899,858 €	1.00 HA
	E.13	ARGANZUELA PARK SKATING PATHS	3,799,820 €	0.87 HA
	E.14	SENIOR CITIZEN SPORTS CIRCUITS		1.07 HA
	E.15	MANZANARES RIVER INTERPRETATION CENTER	2,130,000 €	676 M²
	E.16	MATADERO	21,219,981 €	13.90 HA
	E.17	PEDESTRIAN AND CYCLE CONNECTIONS AT PUENTE DE LA PRINCESA	1,899,724 €	360 M
	E.18	PEDESTRIAN AND CYCLE CONNECTIONS PLAZA LEGAZPI - SOUTH JUNCTION	4,200,269 €	1.33 HA
	E.19	REHABILITATION OF EL VADO SPORTS FACILITIES	2,901,047 €	1.66 HA
	E.20	PEDESTRIAN AND CYCLING BRIDGE BARRIO LEGAZPI - SOUTH JUNCTION	5,618,482 €	160 M
	E.21	RECOVERY OF SOUTH MANZANARES PARK FOREST		7,67 HA
2011 ELECTIONS	E.22	FOOTBRIDGE SOUTH MANZANARES PARK	2,233,803 €	300 M

CATALOGS AND RULES

Beyond the thematic and stylistic references in a proposal narrated as the sum of six landscapes dialoging with the existing city, the design took shape through the establishment of generic rules and systems, automatically applicable methods that depend on the diverse physical situations the project encountered in its interaction with the context. The technical solutions were as simple as possible but in every area, social, patrimonial, and symbolic requirements were extremely complex. In that sense, the work was approached as a paradoxical balance between the extraordinary quantity of data (intellectual, geographic, sociological, political, and infrastructural) that had to be dealt with, and the maximum simplification of stylistic and technological resources with which to approach them. The fundamental problems, those tangible problems whose resolution was one of the operation's goals, had to be addressed in the project's two primary sections: below ground and above ground. Those two sections were approached as basic formulae that, once obtained, would offer solutions to particular problems through the local application of general laws.

The section below ground had to address three main questions: the limited load-bearing capacity of the slabs covering the tunnel, the management of irrigation, and runoff waters — their reuse, drainage, and channeling — and finally, the survival of plant species, which had to be approached both biologically and structurally. The solution had to be unified in order to solve all three problems in a mutually compatible manner, notwithstanding their apparently opposing requirements. A single section — consisting of layers whose nature and order were constant but whose thickness varied in response to each situation — resolved the behavior of the substratum for plants throughout the park. That section included the following systems in successive layers: waterproofing, drainage, structure (capable of bearing the trees), weight reduction (necessary to protect the slabs), and soils (with a triple function: plant nutrition, oxygenation of their root structures, and high filtering capacity).

The section above ground addressed an essential requirement: to establish the borders between different kinds of spaces. In the project, this fundamental question of defining the limits between contiguous areas of opposite categories (safe or unsafe, soft or hard, pedestrian or vehicular, wet or dry, active or inactive, vegetable or mineral, horizontal or inclined, raised or sunken, etc.) had to be addressed as primary concern. Once formulae were found to rationalize these separations, the inclusion of other contents to define the park's different zones would follow naturally and inexorably. That way, the design team's efforts focused on developing a border system based primarily on mechanically carved granite. Beyond its symbolic quality as the predominant rock in Madrid's geography, granite offered the optimum conditions as an extremely durable material that could be easily handled and offered a very competitive ratio of cost to quality.

Through research, the team developed a reduced catalog of pieces capable of establishing functional limits without compromising access to different settings where necessary. This handbook of border pieces furnished a systematic and unified manner of generating a topography that would allow planting over deep strata while integrating the multiple tunnel service elements that jutted up above ground. Moreover, the establishment of rules as a work system insured uniformity in the application of granite for various formats of pavement and installation cladding.

In a second approach to systematizing the compendium of border pieces, the latter were designed to serve other purposes as well: urban furnishing, protective structures, lighting supports, and water fountains. The generic criteria employed in the design of those pieces of granite were analogously applied to metal elements used in certain spaces requiring transparent limits and protectors.

Thanks to the different catalogs they developed, the design team was able to draw on a unique building vocabulary and syntax, an elementary grammar that allowed them to embody the narrative construction of the extensive and varied public space with a unified discourse.

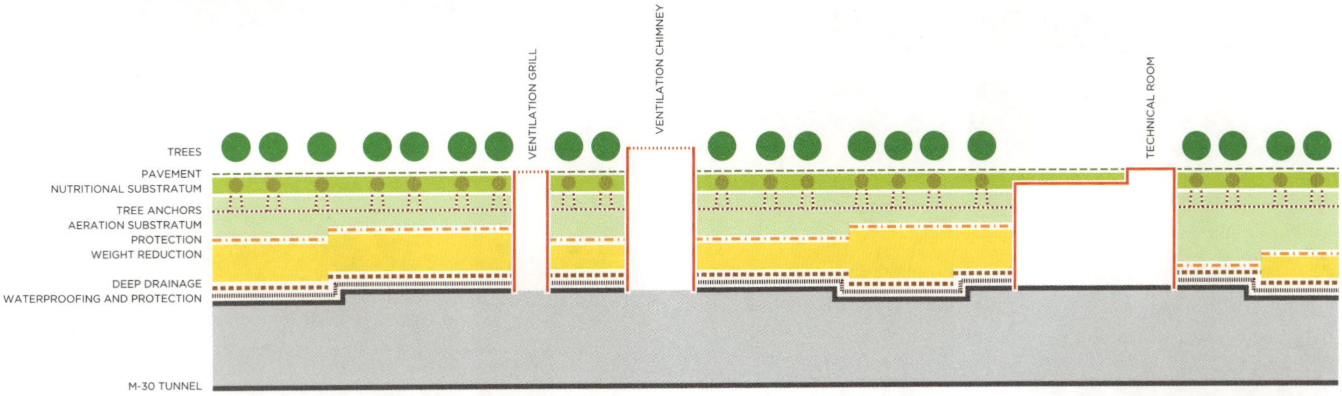

STANDARD LONGITUDINAL SECTION

KP 340 / KP 325 / KP 330

KP 510 / KP 335 / KP 590

KP 600 / KP 700 / KP 650

K.P. 3.90 / K.P. 4.10 / K.P. 4.20

K.P. 2.30 / K.P. 4.15 / K.P. 7.00

K.P. 5.05 / K.P. 4.60 / K.P. 4.70

K.P. 2.40 / K.P. 4.85 / K.P. 2.40

K.P. 2.45 / K.P. 4.75 / K.P. 5.40

K.P. 6.40 / K.P. 5.20 / K.P. 2.30

K.P. 0.90 / K.P. 3.75 / K.P. 6.40

K.P. 6.20 / K.P. 6.25 / K.P. 6.45

K.P. 4.95 / K.P. 7.05 / K.P. 5.85

K.P. 2.30 / K.P. 2.30

K.P. 2.30 / K.P. 2.40

PAVING

MATERIAL	PIECE	DIMENSIONS (CM)	FINISHES TOP	BOTTOM	SIDES	LOCATION	INSTALLATION RULES
GRANITE	COBBLESTONE	6x6x6	FLAMED / BUSHHAMMERED / SHEARED	SAWED / SHEARED	SHEARED	RIVERSIDE PATH NON-ACCESIBLE PATHS	R1 - CHECKERED R2A - CONTINUOUS LENGTHWISE JOINT (LARGER SIDE) AND PERPENDICULAR TO THE DIRECTION OF TRAFFIC. STAGGERED TRANSVERSE JOINT R3 - IRREGULAR
		9x9x9	FLAMED / BUSHHAMMERED	SAWED / SHEARED	SAWED / SHEARED	MAIN ACCESSIBLE PATHS	R2A - CONTINUOUS LENGTHWISE JOINT (LARGER SIDE) AND PERPENDICULAR TO THE DIRECTION OF TRAFFIC. STAGGERED TRANSVERSE JOINT
		15x15x8	FLAMED / SHEARED	SAWED / SHEARED	SAWED / SHEARED	SIDEWALKS / ACCESSIBLE PATHS	R2A - CONTINUOUS LENGTHWISE JOINT (LARGER SIDE) AND PERPENDICULAR TO THE DIRECTION OF TRAFFIC. STAGGERED TRANSVERSE JOINT
	NEW AND REUSED COBBLESTONES	20x10x8	SHEARED	SAWED	SAWED	REST AREA IN MONUMENTAL SURROUNDINGS	R2B - CONTINUOUS LENGTHWISE JOINT (SMALLER SIDE) AND PERPENDICULAR TO THE DIRECTION OF TRAFFIC. STAGGERED TRANSVERSE JOINT
	SLAB	30-90x15x6/8	FLAMED / BUSHHAMMERED	SAWED	SAWED	ACCESS RAMPS	R2A - CONTINUOUS LENGTHWISE JOINT (LARGER SIDE) AND PERPENDICULAR TO THE DIRECTION OF TRAFFIC. STAGGERED TRANSVERSE JOINT
		90/120/180x60x10	FLAMED	SAWED	SAWED	SIDEWALKS AROUND PUENTE DE SEGOVIA AND ERMITA VIRGEN DEL PUERTO	R2A - CONTINUOUS LENGTHWISE JOINT (LARGER SIDE) AND PERPENDICULAR TO THE DIRECTION OF TRAFFIC. STAGGERED TRANSVERSE JOINT
		90x120/180x75	BUSHHAMMERED	SAWED	SAWED / BUSHHAMMERED / SHEARED	BRIDGES OVER STREAM	R2A - CONTINUOUS LENGTHWISE JOINT (LARGER SIDE) AND PERPENDICULAR TO THE DIRECTION OF TRAFFIC. STAGGERED TRANSVERSE JOINT
	REUSABLE SLAB	50-80x80x10	BUSHHAMMERED	SHEARED	SHEARED	ACCESSES TO MONUMENTAL SURROUNDINGS	R2A - CONTINUOUS LENGTHWISE JOINT (LARGER SIDE) AND PERPENDICULAR TO THE DIRECTION OF TRAFFIC. STAGGERED TRANSVERSE JOINT
LIMESTONE (BLACK AND WHITE)	COBBLESTONE	6x6x6	SHEARED	SHEARED	SHEARED	ZEBRA CROSSINGS, BULEVAR AV. PORTUGAL, EXPLANADA DEL REY	R1 - CHECKERED R3 - IRREGULAR
		9x9x3	FLAMED	SHEARED	SHEARED	BEACH	R2A - CONTINUOUS LENGTHWISE JOINT (LARGER SIDE) AND PERPENDICULAR TO THE DIRECTION OF TRAFFIC. STAGGERED TRANSVERSE JOINT
IPE WOOD PLANKS	PLANK	150/200x15x5	AUTOCLAVE PROTECTION TREATMENT			HUERTA DE LA PARTIDA VIEWPOINT	R2A - CONTINUOUS LENGTHWISE JOINT (LARGER SIDE) AND PERPENDICULAR TO THE DIRECTION OF TRAFFIC. STAGGERED TRANSVERSE JOINT
STEEL	CAST PLATE	180x60x8	RELIEF ON VISIBLE SIDE, SAND-BLASTED FINISH			ARGANZUELA PARK ENTRANCE	R1 - CHECKERED
DECOMPOSED GRANITE		0-5 MM	EARTHEN PAVING MADE WITH NATURAL-FINISH GRANITE AGGREGATES			FORESTED ZONES	R4 - CONTINUOUS EXTENDED AND COMPACTED
GRAVEL		2-8 MM	RIVER STONES WITH NATURAL FINISH			PLAYGROUNDS	R4 - CONTINUOUS EXTENDED
ASPHALT MICROSURFACING			MICROSURFACE WITH SYNTHETIC TAR			YELLOW OCHRE: CYCLE PATHS, VIRGEN DEL PUERTO SLOPE PATHS AND ARGANZUELA PARK SLOW PATH BLACK: ARGANZUELA PARK FAST PATH AND SIDEWALKS	R4 - CONTINUOUS

EDGING

MATERIAL	PIECE	DIMENSIONS (CM)	GUIDELINES	FINISHES	APPLICATIONS	PLACEMENT RULES
GRANITE	BC21	21/12x15x60	STRAIGHT AND CURVED	FLAMED ON VISIBLE SIDES, SAWN ON THE REST	CURBSTONE TO DELIMIT GARDENED ZONES	CONTINUOUS PIECE, BUTT JOINT SET INTO PAVEMENT 7 CM VISIBLE ROUNDED EDGE WITH 15 MM RADIUS
	BC36	36/24x15x60	STRAIGHT AND CURVED	FLAMED ON VISIBLE SIDES, SAWN ON THE REST	CURBSTONE TO DELIMIT GARDENED ZONES AND SLOPE FOOTING	CONTINUOUS PIECE, BUTT JOINT SET INTO PAVEMENT 7 CM VISIBLE ROUNDED EDGE WITH 15 MM RADIUS
	BC45	45/36x21x60	STRAIGHT AND CURVED	FLAMED ON VISIBLE SIDES, SAWN ON THE REST	SLOPE FOOTING CURBSTONE	CONTINUOUS PIECE, BUTT JOINT SET INTO PAVEMENT 8 CM VISIBLE ROUNDED EDGE WITH 20 MM RADIUS
	EC	60x15x90	STRAIGHT	BUSH-HAMMERED ON VISIBLE SIDES, SAWN ON THE REST	CYCLE PATH CURBSTONE	CONTINUOUS PIECE, BUTT JOINT SET INTO PAVEMENT 75 CM
	A	30x12x60	STRAIGHT AND CURVED	FLAMED ON VISIBLE SIDES, SAWN ON THE REST	CHANNEL SLAB ROAD EDGING	CONTINUOUS PIECE, BUTT JOINT FLUSH WITH PAVEMENT
	B	30x26x60	STRAIGHT AND CURVED	FLAMED ON VISIBLE SIDES, SAWN ON THE REST	RAMP AND SIDEWALK CURBSTONE	CONTINUOUS PIECE, BUTT JOINT SET INTO PAVEMENT 12 CM
	C	10x12x60/100	STRAIGHT AND CURVED	FLAMED ON VISIBLE SIDES, SAWN ON THE REST	TRANSVERSE PARKING-STRIP EDGING	CONTINUOUS PIECE, BUTT JOINT FLUSH WITH PAVEMENT
	C'	10x26x60	STRAIGHT AND CURVED	FLAMED ON VISIBLE SIDES, SAWN ON THE REST	CURBSTONE FOR PARKING STRIPS AND SIDEWALKS	CONTINUOUS PIECE, BUTT JOINT SET INTO PAVEMENT 12 CM
	N	30x26/22.5x60	STRAIGHT	FLAMED ON VISIBLE SIDES, SAWN ON THE REST	BARBACAN IN CROSSWALKS AND CURBCUTS	CONTINUOUS PIECE, BUTT JOINT SET INTO PAVEMENT 12 CM
	QC	36x81x21/13.2	STRAIGHT AND CURVED	BUSH-HAMMERED ON VISIBLE SIDES, SAWN ON THE REST	FAST-PATH EDGING AT ARGANZUELA PARK	CONTINUOUS PIECE, BUTT JOINT FLUSH WITH PAVEMENT. VISIBLE ROUNDED EDGE WITH 15 MM RADIUS
	PYR	45x15/11x150	CURVED	FLAMED ON VISIBLE SIDES, SAWN ON THE REST	BEACH-SHELL EDGING	CONTINUOUS PIECE, SEALED BUTT JOINT FLUSH WITH PAVEMENT. VISIBLE ROUNDED EDGE WITH 15 MM RADIUS
	E/SC	45x12x60	STRAIGHT	FLAMED ON VISIBLE SIDES, SAWN ON THE REST	EDGING FOR GRILLS AND VENTILATION TOWER COPING	CONTINUOUS PIECE, BUTT JOINT SET IN 9 CM WITH REGARD TO VENTILATION TOWER CLADDING
IPE WOOD	CURB	8,5/6x15x150	STRAIGHT	AUTOCLAVE PROTECTION TREATMENT	CURB FOR PLAYGROUNDS NEXT TO CYCLE PATH	CONTINUOUS PIECE, BUTT JOINT SET INTO PAVEMENT
STEEL	PLATEN	0,8x10/27x300	STRAIGHT AND CURVED	GALVANIZED STEEL	SEPARATOR FOR PAVING,TREE WELLS, AND DECOMPOSED GRANITE PAVING	CONTINUOUS PIECE, BUTT JOINT FLUSH WITH PAVEMENT

GRANITE COBBLESTONE PAVING

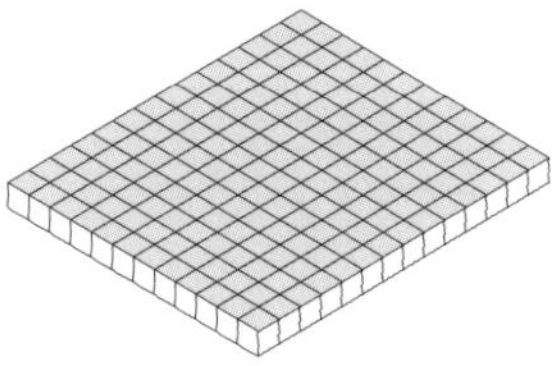

GRANITE COBBLESTONE 6x6x6 CM
POSITIONING REQUIREMENT R1 - E: 1/30

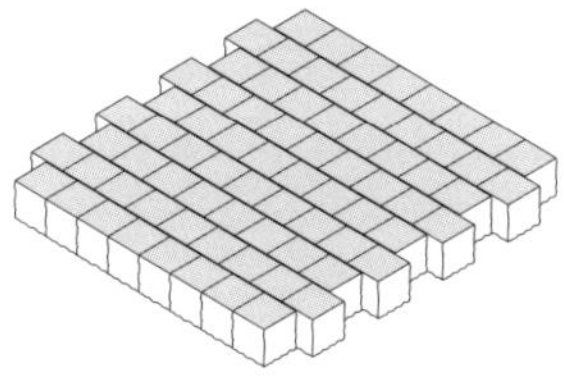

GRANITE COBBLESTONE 9x9x9 CM
POSITIONING REQUIREMENT R2A - E: 1/30

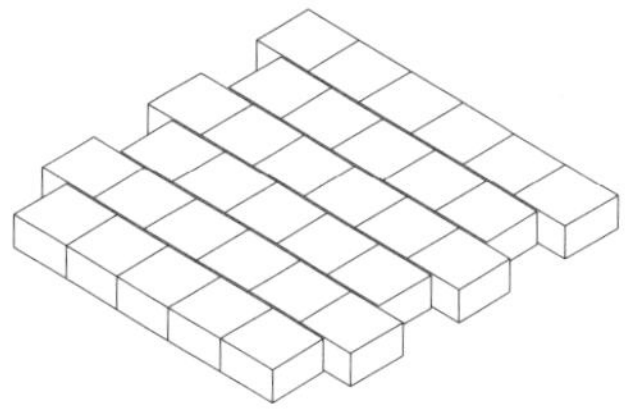

GRANITE COBBLESTONE 15x15x8 CM
POSITIONING REQUIREMENT R2A - E: 1/30

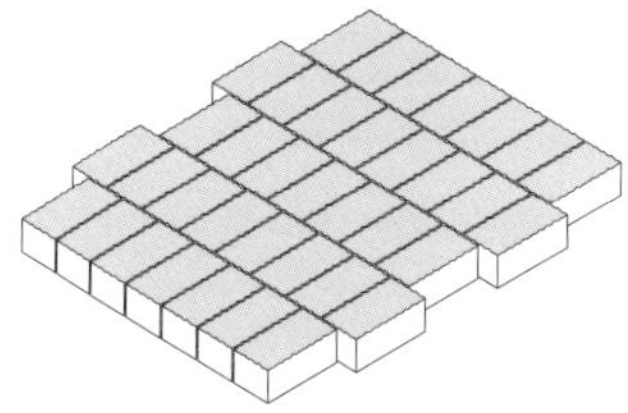

GRANITE COBBLESTONE 20x10x8 CM
POSITIONING REQUIREMENT R2B - E: 1/30

GRANITE SLAB PAVING

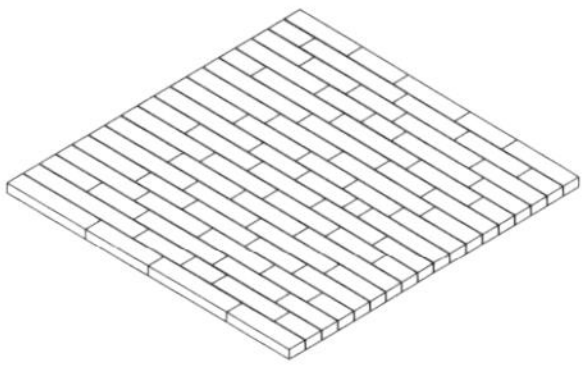

GRANITE SLABS 30-90x15x6/8 CM
POSITIONING REQUIREMENT R2A - E: 1/100

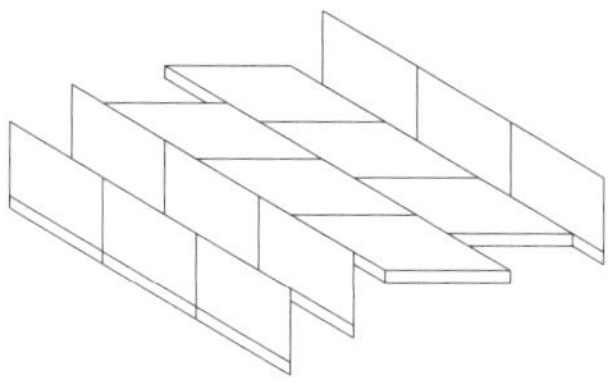

GRANITE SLABS 90/120/180x60x10 CM
POSITIONING REQUIREMENT R2A - E: 1/100

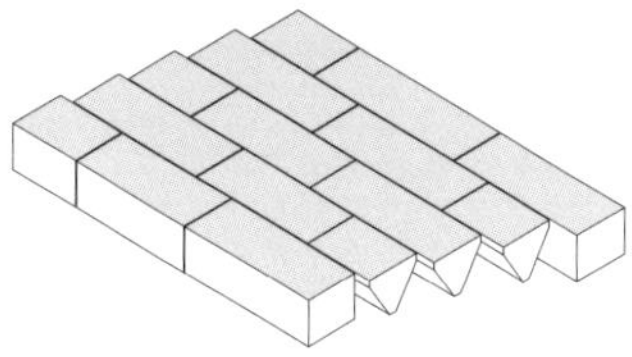

GRANITE SLABS 90x120/180x75 CM
POSITIONING REQUIREMENT R2A - E: 1/200

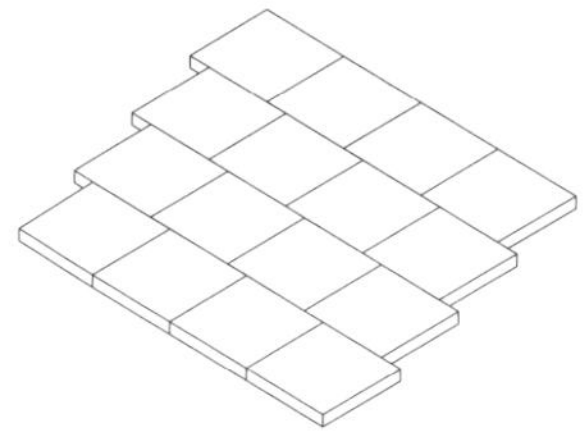

GRANITE SLABS 50-80x80x10 CM
POSITIONING REQUIREMENT R2A - E: 1/100

PAVEMENT OF OTHER MATERIALS

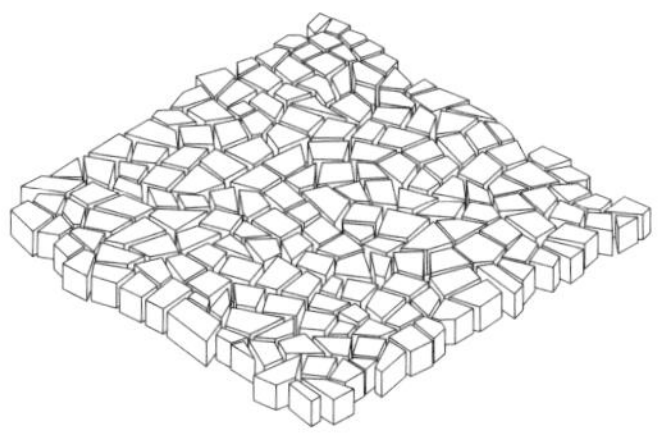

LIMESTONE COBBLESTONE 6x6x6 CM
POSITIONING REQUIREMENT R3 - E: 1/30

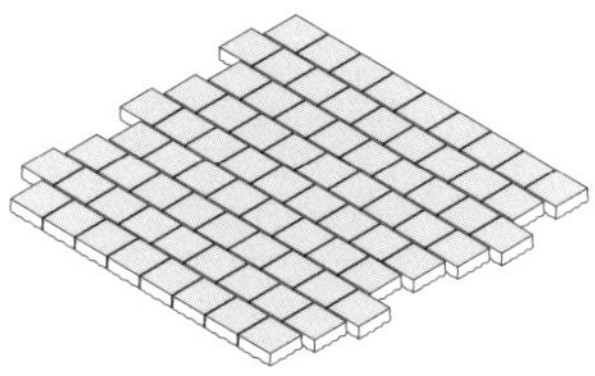

LIMESTONE COBBLESTONE 9x9x3 CM
POSITIONING REQUIREMENT R2A - E: 1/30

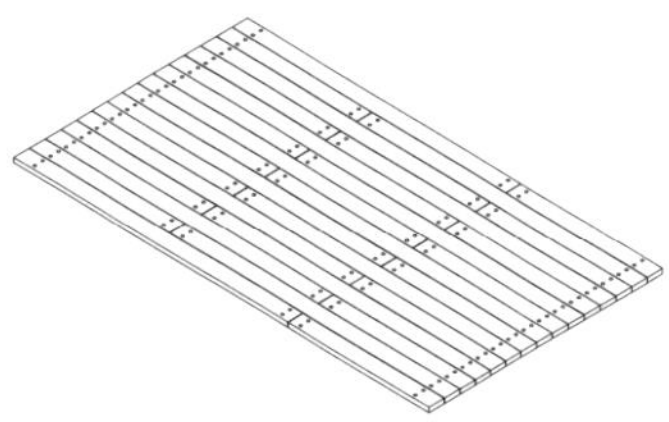

IPE WOOD PLANKS
POSITIONING REQUIREMENT R2A - E: 1/100

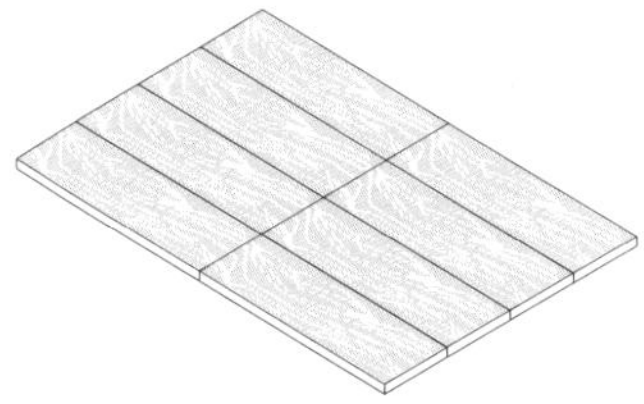

CAST PLATES
POSITIONING REQUIREMENT R1 - E: 1/100

GRANITE EDGING ON PATHS AND CYCLE PATHS

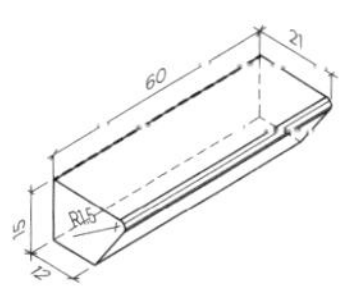

BC21

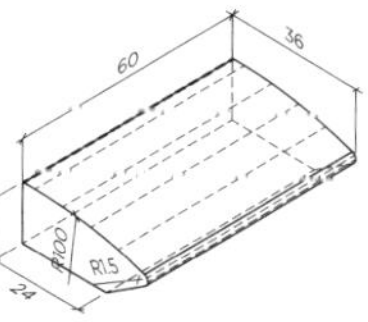

BC36

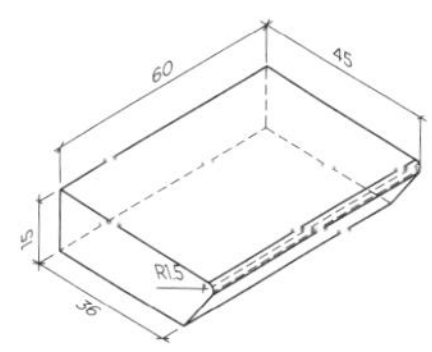

BC45

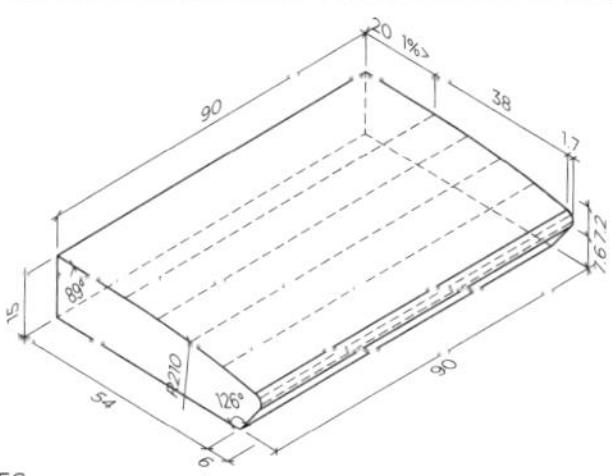

EC

GRANITE EDGING ON SIDEWALKS

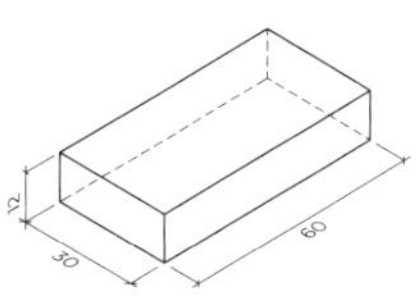

A

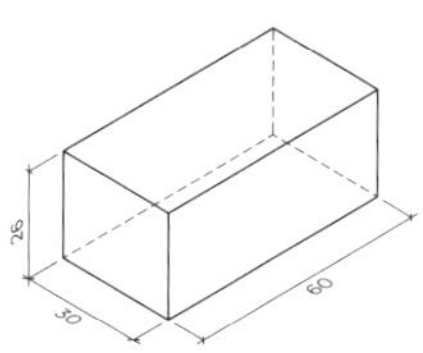

B

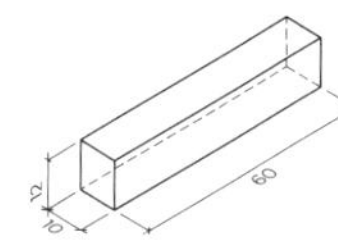

C

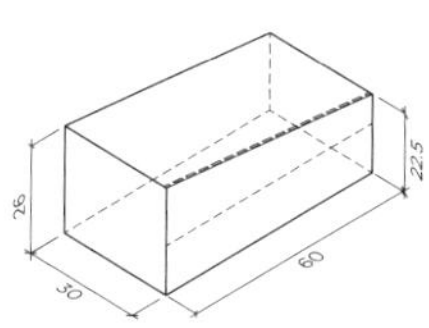

N

SPECIAL GRANITE EDGING

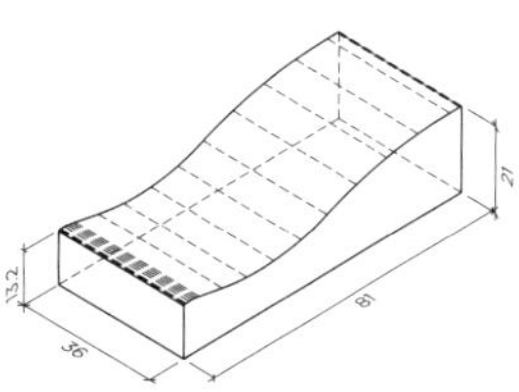

QC

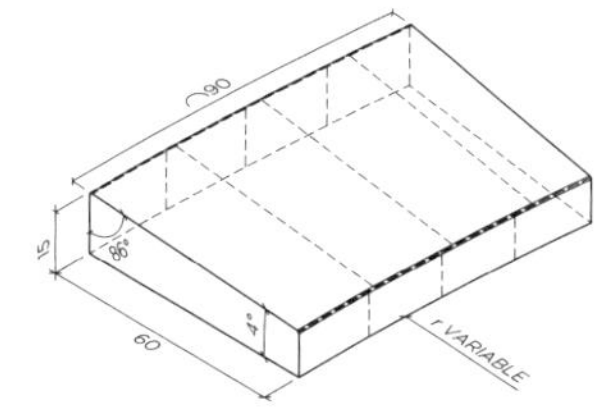

PYR

EDGING OF OTHER MATERIALS

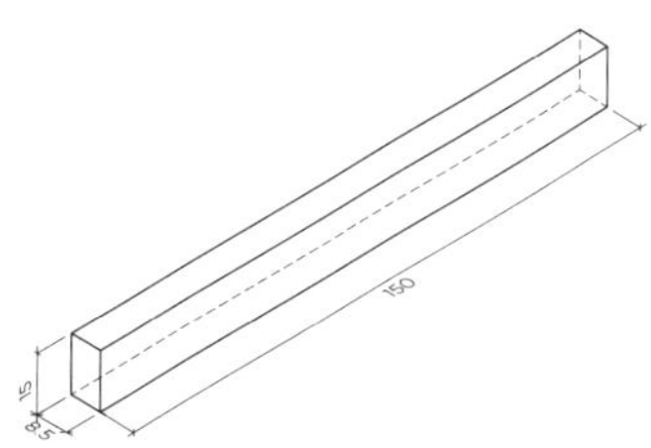

IPE WOOD EDGING

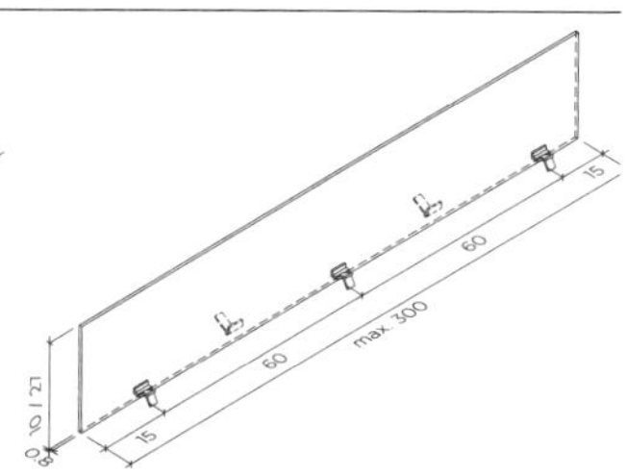

STEEL PLATEN

1/30 10 20 50 CM

COPING

MATERIAL	PIECE	DIMENSIONS (CM)	GUIDELINE	FINISH	LOCATION	PLACEMENT RULES
GRANITE	MC30	66x30x60	STRAIGHT	FLAMED ON VISIBLE SIDES, SAWED ON THE REST	WALL CROWN ON SLOPE TOWARDS THE RIVER	CONTINUOUS PIECE, BUTT JOINT SET INTO PAVEMENT VISIBLE ROUNDED EDGE WITH 6 MM RADIUS
	MC36	60/54x36x90	STRAIGHT	FLAMED ON VISIBLE SIDES, SAWED ON THE REST	SLOPE BORDER	CONTINUOUS PIECE, BUTT JOINT SET INTO PAVEMENT 6 CM VISIBLE ROUNDED EDGE WITH 6 MM RADIUS
	MC42	66/60x42x60	STRAIGHT AND CURVED	FLAMED ON VISIBLE SIDES, SAWED ON THE REST	SLOPE BORDER	CONTINUOUS PIECE, BUTT JOINT SET INTO PAVEMENT 6 CM VISIBLE ROUNDED EDGE WITH 6 MM RADIUS
	MC60	66x60x60	STRAIGHT AND CURVED	FLAMED ON VISIBLE SIDES, SAWED ON THE REST	SLOPE BORDER	CONTINUOUS PIECE, BUTT JOINT SET INTO PAVEMENT 6 CM VISIBLE ROUNDED EDGE WITH 6 MM RADIUS
	TC12	66x12x60	STRAIGHT AND CURVED	FLAMED ON VISIBLE SIDES, SAWED ON THE REST	WALL TOPS, PAVEMENT SEPARATORS, AND FOUNTAIN EDGES	CONTINUOUS PIECE, BUTT JOINT FLUSH WITH PAVEMENT VISIBLE ROUNDED EDGE WITH 6 MM RADIUS
	TC21	66x21x60	STRAIGHT	FLAMED ON VISIBLE SIDES, SAWED ON THE REST	WALL TOPS	CONTINUOUS PIECE, BUTT JOINT FLUSH WITH PAVEMENT VISIBLE ROUNDED EDGE WITH 6 MM RADIUS
	TC42	60x42x60	STRAIGHT	FLAMED ON VISIBLE SIDES, SAWED ON THE REST	WALL TOPS AND PAVEMENT SEPARATORS	CONTINUOUS PIECE, BUTT JOINT SET INTO PAVEMENT 6 CM VISIBLE ROUNDED EDGE WITH 6 MM RADIUS
	TC57	60x57x60	STRAIGHT	FLAMED ON VISIBLE SIDES, SAWED ON THE REST	WALL TOPS AND PAVEMENT SEPARATORS	CONTINUOUS PIECE, BUTT JOINT SET INTO PAVEMENT 6 CM VISIBLE ROUNDED EDGE WITH 6 MM RADIUS
	GC	75/61x51x60	STRAIGHT	FLAMED ON VISIBLE SIDES, SAWED ON THE REST	CREATION OF PUENTE DE SEGOVIA TIERS	CONTINUOUS PIECE, BUTT JOINT SET INTO PAVEMENT 6 CM VISIBLE ROUNDED EDGE WITH 5 MM RADIUS
	BIB BETWEEN CANALS	60x12/9x60	STRAIGHT	FLAMED ON VISIBLE SIDES, SAWED ON THE REST	DRAINAGE PIECE FOR RIVER CONTAINMENT WALL CANAL	VISIBLE ROUNDED EDGE WITH 6 MM RADIUS
	CC	84x42x60	STRAIGHT	FLAMED ON VISIBLE SIDES, SAWED ON THE REST	TOP OF RIVER CONTAINMENT WALL BIB	CONTINUOUS PIECE, BUTT JOINT VISIBLE ROUNDED EDGE WITH 6 MM RADIUS
	CF	66x81x81	STRAIGHT	FLAMED ON VISIBLE SIDES, SAWED ON THE REST	END-PIECE OF RIVER CONTAINMENT WALL BIB	VISIBLE ROUNDED EDGE WITH 6 MM RADIUS
	U-SHAPED PIECE	70x24/12x60	STRAIGHT	FLAMED ON VISIBLE SIDES, SAWED ON THE REST	CROWN OF PUENTE DE SEGOVIA PIER WALL	CONTINUOUS PIECE, BUTT JOINT FLUSH WITH PAVEMENT VISIBLE ROUNDED EDGE WITH 3 MM RADIUS
	L-SHAPED PIECE	70x24/12x60	STRAIGHT	FLAMED ON VISIBLE SIDES, SAWED ON THE REST	REPARATION PIECES FOR PUENTE DE SEGOVIA PIERS	CONTINUOUS PIECE, BUTT JOINT FLUSH WITH PAVEMENT VISIBLE ROUNDED EDGE WITH 3 MM RADIUS
	BC60E	75/60x51x60	STRAIGHT	FLAMED ON VISIBLE SIDES, SAWED ON THE REST	TOP OF POOL BIBS IN VIRGEN DEL PUERTO GARDENS	CONTINUOUS PIECE, BUTT JOINT VISIBLE ROUNDED EDGE WITH 6 MM RADIUS
	MTC	33x43x60	STRAIGHT	BUSHHAMMERED ON VISIBLE SIDES, SAWED ON THE REST	CREATION OF SIDEWALK PLANT BOXES	CONTINUOUS PIECE, BUTT JOINT FLUSH WITH PAVEMENT VISIBLE ROUNDED EDGE WITH 12 MM RADIUS
COLMENAR LIMESTONE	COPING FOR OLD RIVER CONTAINMENT WALL	33x40x100	STRAIGHT	SAWED ON ALL SIDES	REPLACEMENT PIECE FOR RIVER CONTAINMENT WALL	CONTINUOUS PIECE, BUTT JOINT ARCHED TOP
	FASCIA FOR OLD RIVER CONTAINMENT WALL	40x30x85	STRAIGHT	SAWED ON ALL SIDES	REPLACEMENT PIECE FOR RIVER CONTAINMENT WALL	CONTINUOUS PIECE, BUTT JOINT
CONCRETE	PREFABRICATED BENCH	75/48x64	STRAIGHT AND CURVED	REINFORCED CONCRETE WITH SMOOTH ETCHED TEXTURE	CREATION OF PLANT BOXES AND BENCHES ON AV PORTUGAL	CONTINUOUS PIECE, BUTT JOINT SET INTO PAVEMENT 10 CM VISIBLE ROUNDED EDGE WITH 15 MM RADIUS
STEEL	SHEET	66x0.15	STRAIGHT AND CURVED	PRIMED AND PAINTED RAL 9007	CROWN OF WALL BIB PUENTE DE SEGOVIA GARDENS	CONTINUOUS PIECE, BUTT JOINT CURVED DIRECTION PARALLEL TO WALL AXIS EDGES SLIGHTLY ROUNDED

MC-TYPE GRANITE COPING

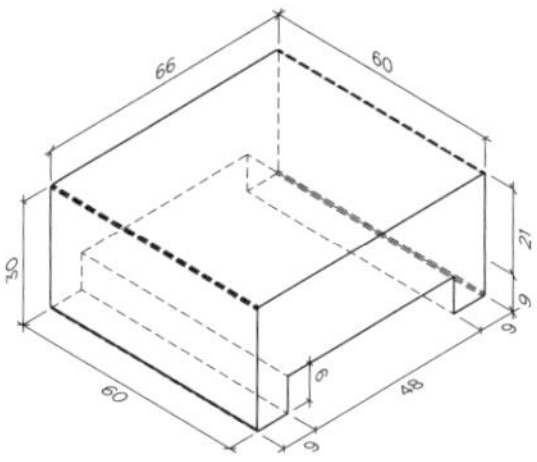

MC30

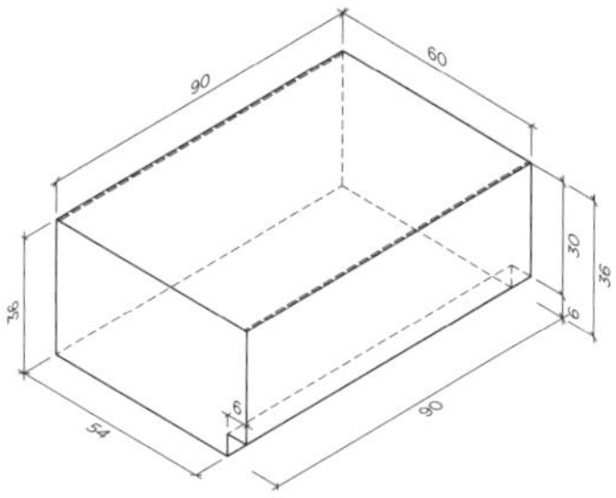

MC36

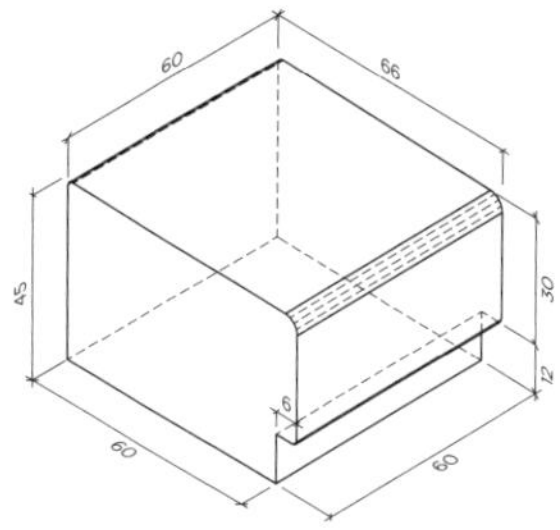

MC42

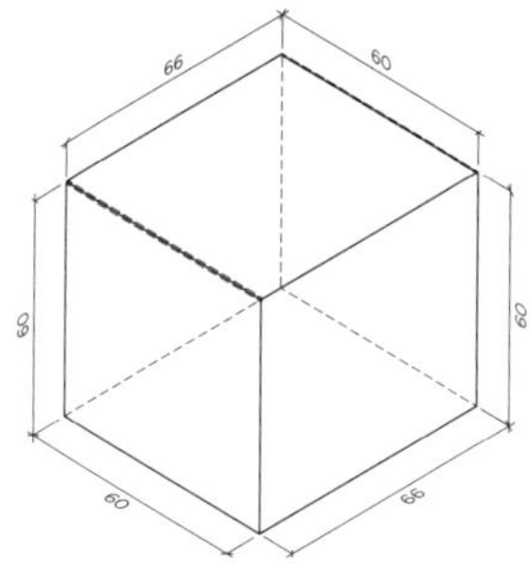

MC60

TC-TYPE GRANITE COPING

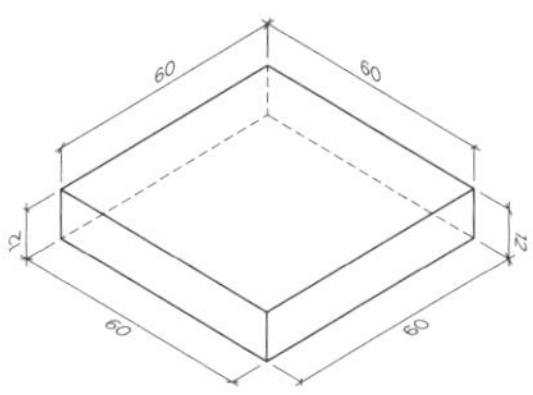

TC12

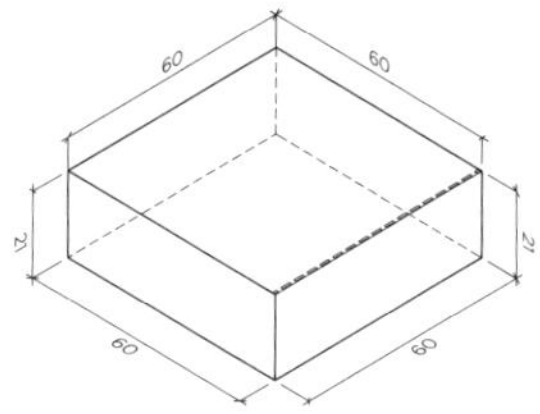

TC21

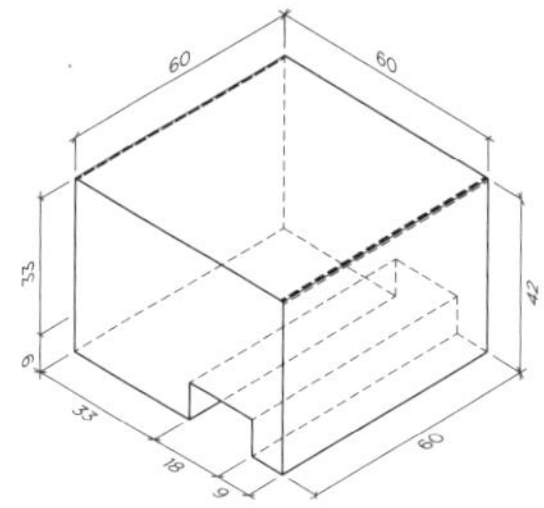

TC42

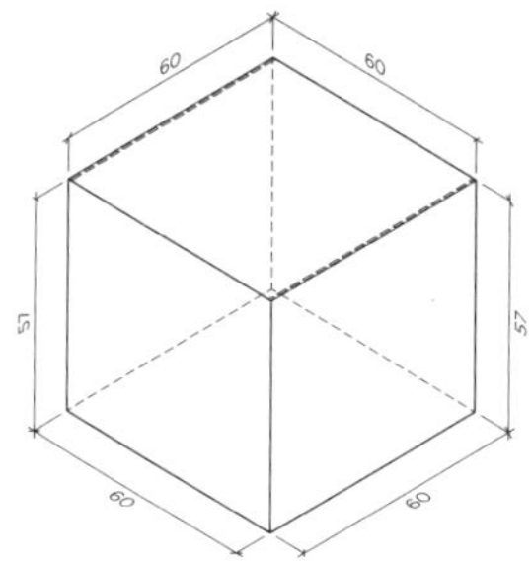

TC57

GRANITE COPING ON RIVER SEATING AND CONTAINMENT WALLS

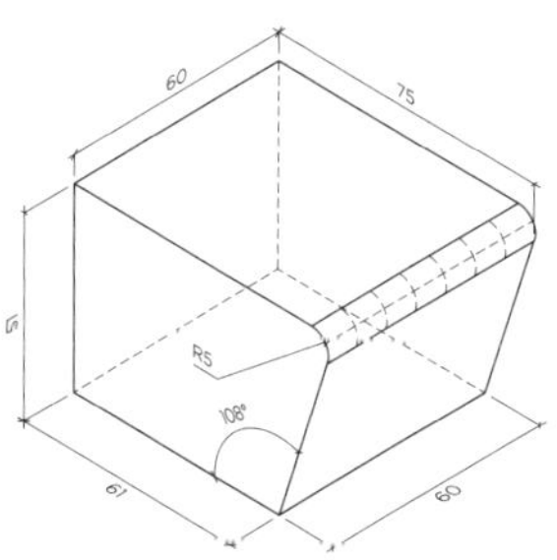

GC

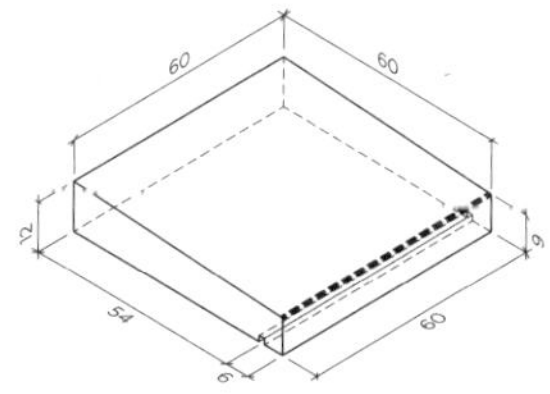

BIB BETWEEN CANALS

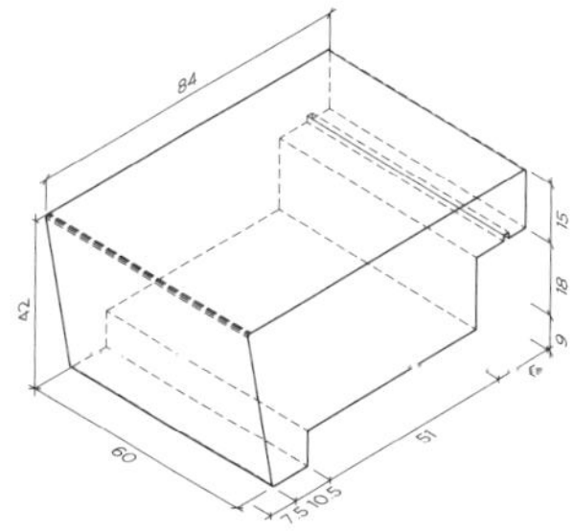

CC

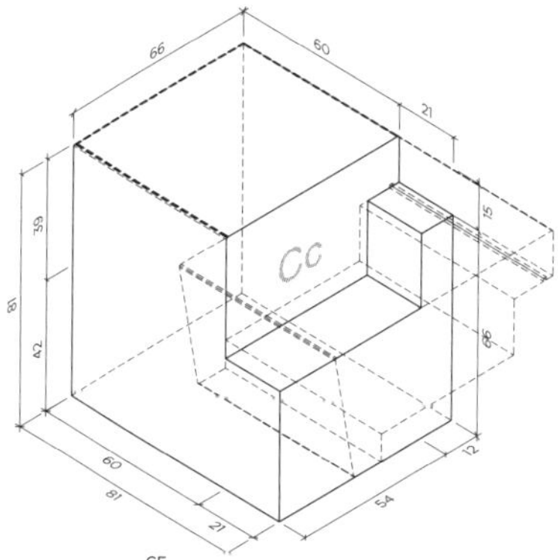

CF

GRANITE COPING ON PUENTE DE SEGOVIA PIERS, FOUNTAINS, AND GARDENS

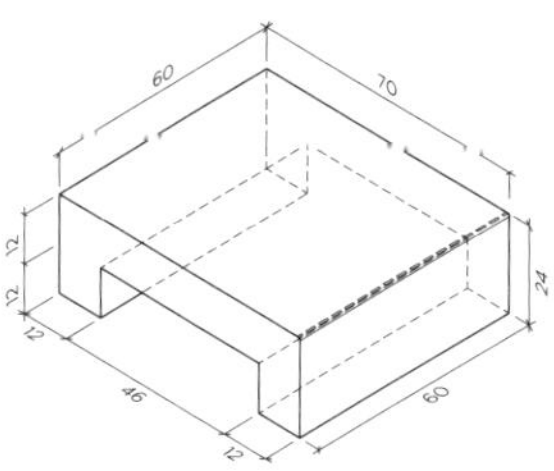

U-SHAPED PIECE

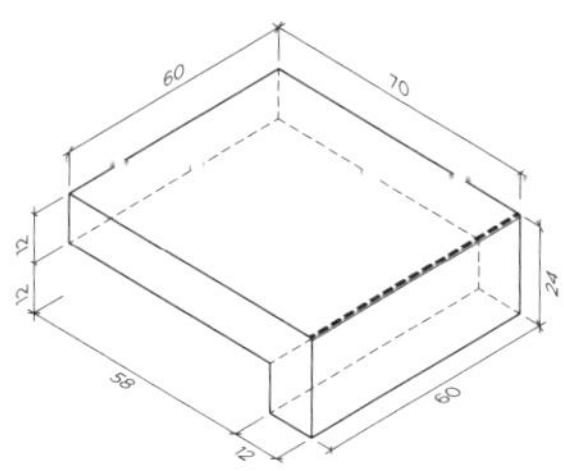

L-SHAPED PIECE

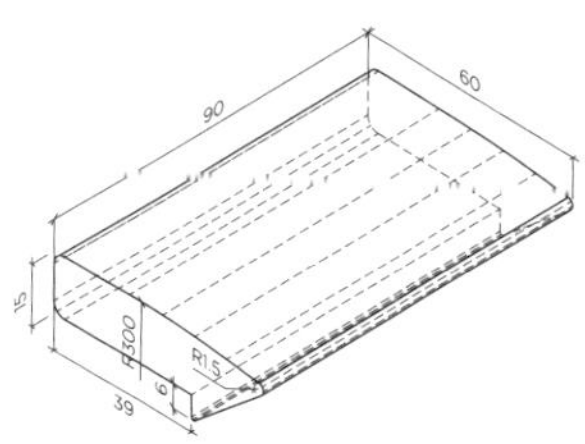

BC60E

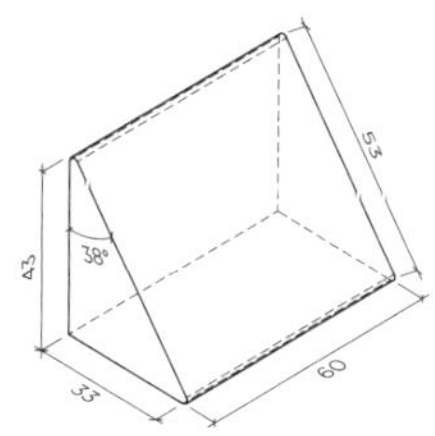

MTC

COPING OF OTHER MATERIALS

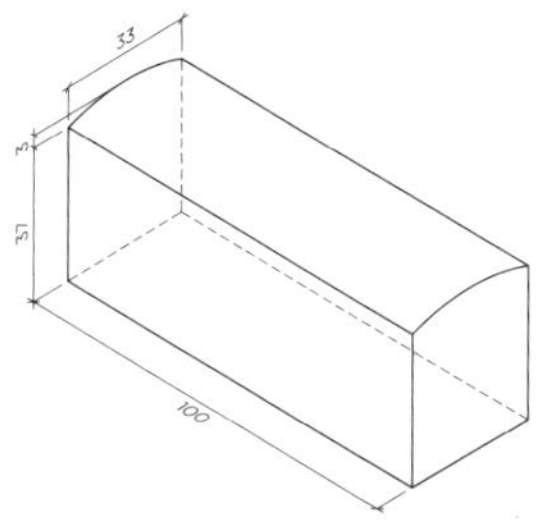

LIMESTONE REPLACEMENT COPING
FOR RIVER CONTAINMENT WALL

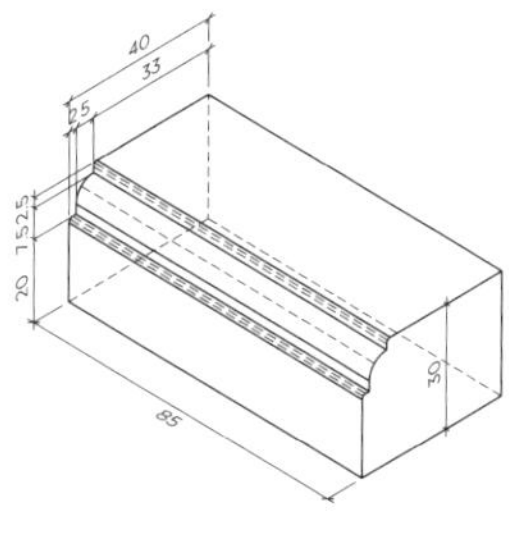

LIMESTONE REPLACEMENT FASCIA
FOR RIVER CONTAINMENT WALL

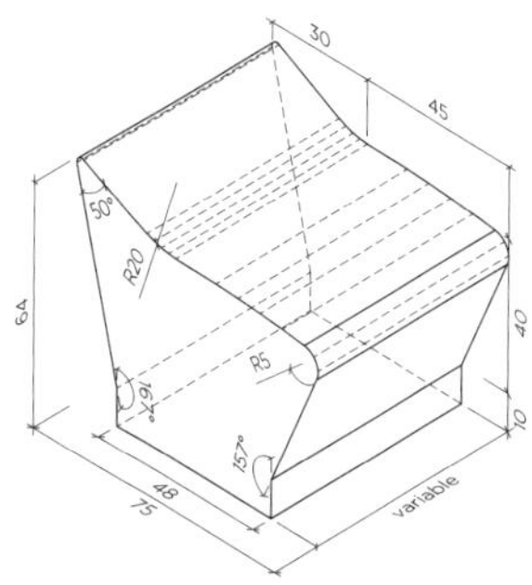

CONCRETE BENCH

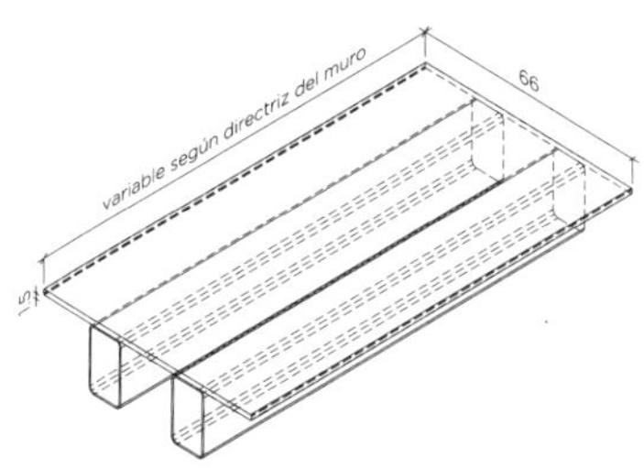

SHEET STEEL

------ ROUNDED SURFACE RIDGES

1/30 10 20 50 CM

CLADDING

MATERIAL	PIECE	DIMENSIONS (CM)	FINISHES	LOCATION	PLACEMENT RULES
GRANITE	RAW SLAB	12x10x60-180	VERY ROUGH SHEARED ON VISIBLE SIDES, SAWED ON THE REST	SIDEWALK WALLS EMERGENCY EXIT WALLS ON SLOPE	9 MM JOINT BETWEEN PIECES
		18x10x95/160	VERY ROUGH SHEARED ON VISIBLE SIDES, SAWED ON THE REST	VENTILATION TOWERS	6 MM JOINT BETWEEN PIECES
		18-45x10-12x45-210	VERY ROUGH SHEARED ON VISIBLE SIDES, SAWED ON THE REST	OUTER CLADDING OF RIVER CONTAINMENT WALL ALONG SALÓN DE PINOS	SIZE OF PIECES AND JOINTS FOLLOWS SCHEME FOR RIVER CONTAINMENT WALL
		21-93x12x45-240	VERY ROUGH SHEARED ON VISIBLE SIDES, SAWED ON THE REST	WALLS LOW GARDENS AT PUENTE DE SEGOVIA, STAIRS AT ERMITA VIRGEN DEL PUERTO AND BONAPARTE PAVILION	SCHEME FOR LARGE WALLS 3 CM JOINT BETWEEN PIECES
		21x12x45-240	FLAMED ON VISIBLE SIDES, SAWED ON THE REST		
		86x10x40-105	VERY ROUGH SHEARED ON VISIBLE SIDES, SAWED ON THE REST	WALLS VIRGEN DEL PUERTO TIERS	9 MM JOINT BETWEEN PIECES
		15x15x60-210	VERY ROUGH SHEARED ON VISIBLE SIDES, SAWED ON THE REST	FERN FOUNTAIN ARGANZUELA	CONTINUOUS HORIZONTAL JOINT OF 4-7 CM STAGGERED VERTICAL BUTT JOINTS
		15x15x120-150	FLAMED ON VISIBLE SIDES, SAWED ON THE REST		
		45x8x90	VERY ROUGH SHEARED ON VISIBLE SIDES, SAWED ON THE REST		
	SLAB	59x8x40-150	FLAMED ON VISIBLE SIDES, SAWED ON THE REST	OUTER CLADDING OF RIVER CONTAINMENT WALL ALONG VIRGEN DEL PUERTO GARDENS	9 MM JOINT BETWEEN PIECES
		94.8x8x180	FLAMED ON VISIBLE SIDES, SAWED ON THE REST	FOUNTAINS ON WALLS AND VENTILATION TOWERS	12 MM JOINT BETWEEN PIECES
STEEL	STRUCTURAL TEES	80.9 40.5	PRIMED AND PAINTED RAL 9007	CLADDING OF WALLS, VENTILATION TOWERS, CABINETS AND RIVER CONTAINMENT WALL	VERTICAL JOINT BETWEEN PROFILES: 2-3 CM
	CAST PLATE	117x54x8	RELIEF ON VISIBLE SIDE SAND-BLASTED FINISH	INTERIOR OF RIVER CONTAINMENT WALL BIB	JOINT BETWEEN PIECES: 37-40 MM
STONEWARE	CERAMIC PIECES	9x20.75/42x4.5	LOW POROSITY STONEWARE FIRED AT HIGH TEMPERATURE WITH ENAMEL FINISH (150G/M²)	VENTILATION TOWERS AND ELEVATORS AT AV DE PORTUGAL	VERTICAL JOINT BETWEEN PIECES > 5 MM

SCHEME FOR LARGE WALLS CLADDED WITH RAW GRANITE SLABS

BASE PIECE SERIES: PIECES 21 CM WIDE, SHEARED, 3 CM JOINTS

A-PIECE SERIES: PIECES 21 CM WIDE, FLAMED, EVERY 13 AND 34 BASE PIECES

B-PIECE SERIES: PIECES 45 CM WIDE (DOUBLE), SHEARED, EVERY 34 BASE PIECES

C-PIECE SERIES: PIECES 69 CM WIDE (TRIPLE), SHEARED, EVERY 55 BASE PIECES

D-PIECE SERIES: PIECES 93 CM WIDE (QUADRUPLE), SHEARED, EVERY 89 BASE PIECES

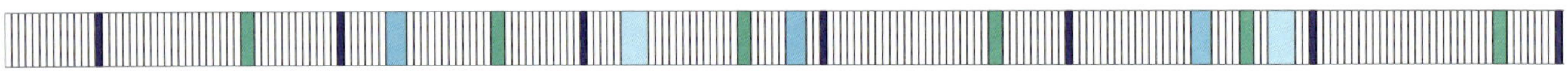

COMPOSITE SERIES

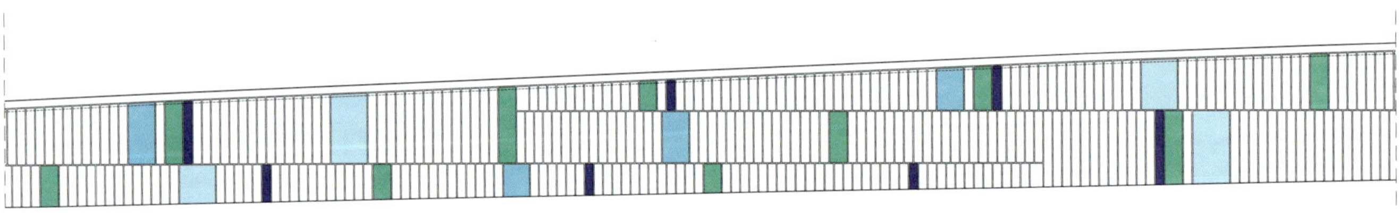

APPLICATION OF SCHEME FOR LARGE WALLS IN THE PUENTE DE SEGOVIA GARDENS

1/200 1 2 5

SCHEME FOR RIVER CONTAINMENT WALLS CLADDED WITH RAW GRANITE SLABS

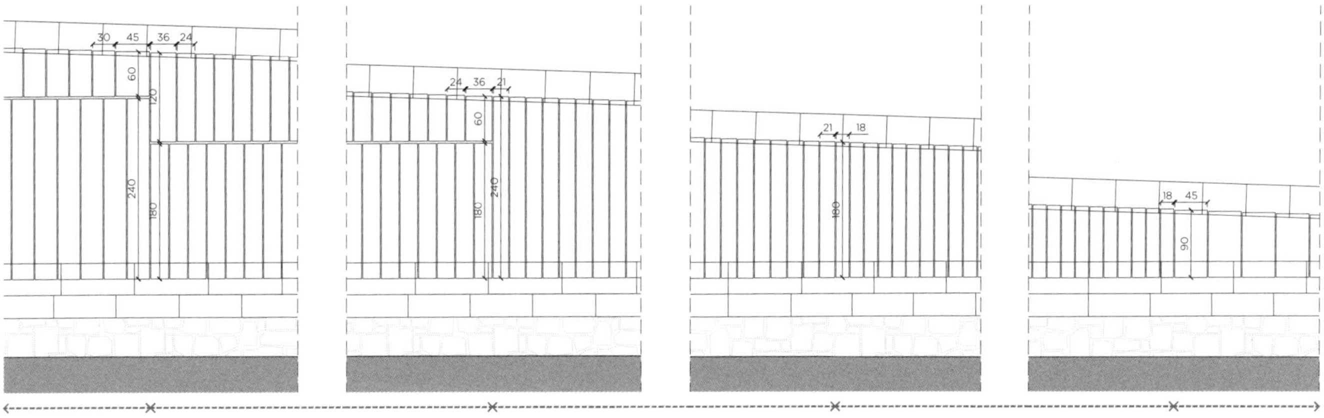

CASE A1: H>300 CM
PIECE WIDTH: 30 CM
PIECE THICKNESS:
10 CM (PIECES H<180 CM)
12 CM (PIECES H>180 CM)
JOINT BETWEEN PIECES: 45 MM

CASE A2: 240<H<300 CM
PIECE WIDTH: 24 CM
PIECE THICKNESS:
10 CM (PIECES H<180 CM)
12 CM (PIECES H>180 CM)
JOINT BETWEEN PIECES: 36 MM

CASE A3: 180<H<240 CM
PIECE WIDTH: 21 CM
PIECE THICKNESS: 12 CM
JOINT BETWEEN PIECES: 21 MM

CASE A4: 90<H<180 CM
PIECE WIDTH: 18 CM
PIECE THICKNESS: 10 CM
JOINT BETWEEN PIECES: 12 MM

CASE A5: H<90 CM
PIECE WIDTH: 45 CM
PIECE THICKNESS: 10 CM
JOINT BETWEEN PIECES: 6 MM

SCHEME FOR CLADDING WITH STRUCTURAL TEES

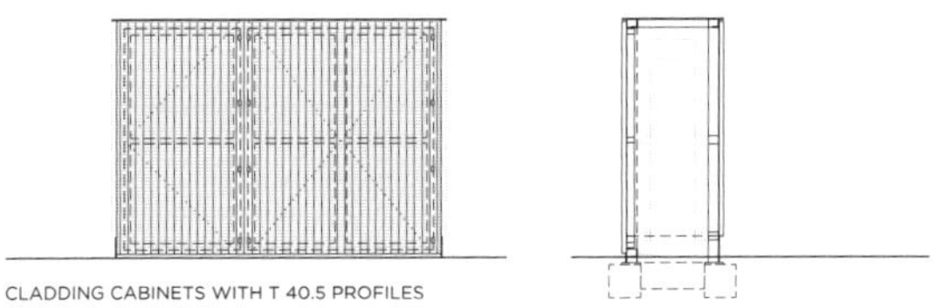

CLADDING CABINETS WITH T 40.5 PROFILES

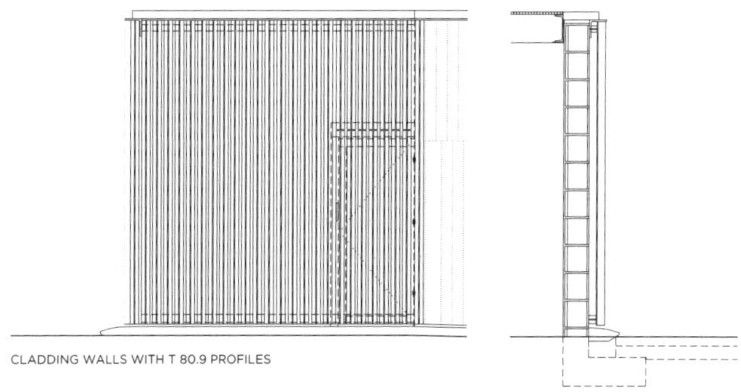

CLADDING WALLS WITH T 80.9 PROFILES

1/100 0,5 1 3

SCHEME FOR CLADDING WITH CAST PLATES

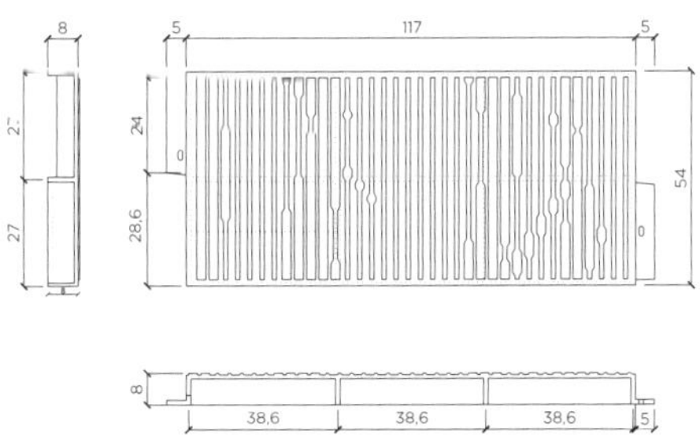

CENTRAL CAST PIECE

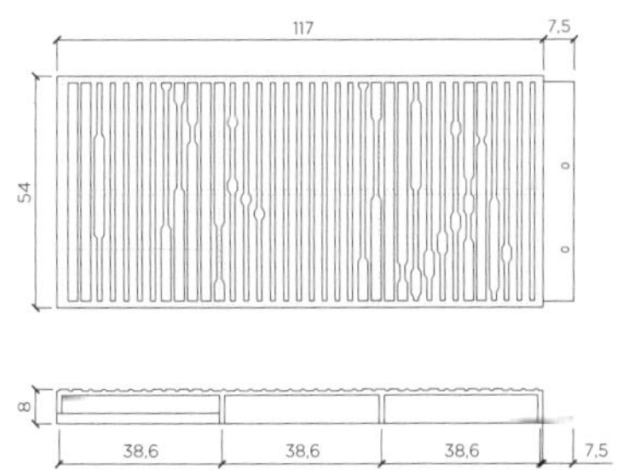

TERMINAL CAST PIECE

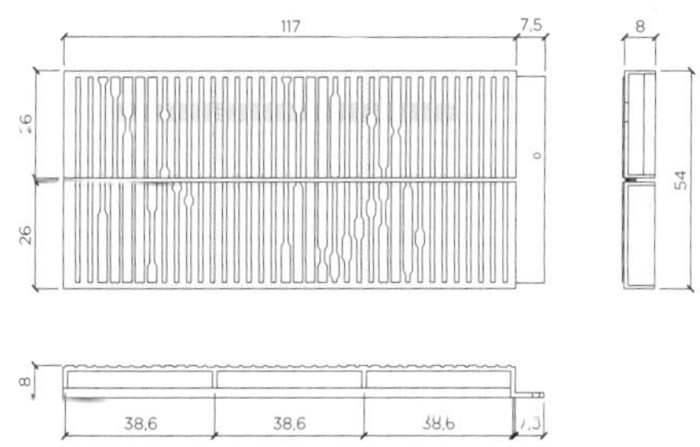

SEARCHABLE CAST PIECE

1/50 20 40 100 CM

SCHEME FOR CERAMIC CLADDING OF AV. DE PORTUGAL VENTILATION TOWERS

A.01-1
COLORS ATP-7-80, 2440-40, 3C

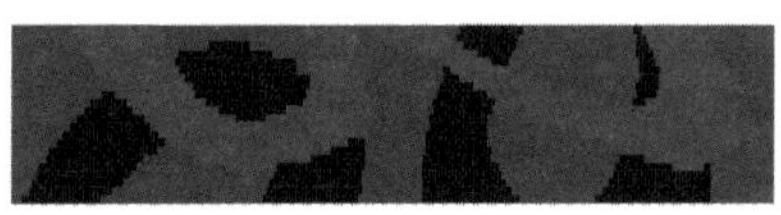

V.01-6
COLORS 3C, 770-10, 1967-14

COLOR LEGEND
- ATP-7-80
- 2440-40
- 3C
- 1945-96
- 2421-14
- 770-10
- 1967-14
- 2421-1

V.02-A-2
COLORS 1945-96, 770-10, 3C

V.01-2
COLORS ATP-7-80, 3C, 2421-14

V.04-A-1
COLORS 1967-14, 2440-40, 3C

V.02-A-4
COLORS ATP-7-80, 3C, 2421-1

1/400 1 2 3 4 5 10

RAILINGS

MATERIAL	TYPE	DIMENSIONS (CM)	ANCHORING	FINISHES	LOCATION	PLACEMENT RULES
STEEL	LIGHT WITH MESH	90x120. PLATEN 80.8	SET INTO THE PAVEMENT	PRIMED AND PAINTED COLOR RAL 9007 STAINLESS-STEEL MESH, 1.5 CM DIAMETER, REGULAR GRID OF 100x12 MM	WALL TOPS AND DIFFERENCES IN PLANE LEADING TO SOFT SURFACES, SUCH AS GARDEN ZONES OR SLOPES	SCREWED JOINTS WITHOUT RAW EDGES VERTICAL PLATENS EVERY 90 CM, SET 30 CM INTO THE PAVEMENT HORIZONTAL ONES AT 15, 60 AND 90 CM FROM THE PAVEMENT
		90x90. PLATEN 80.8	ANCHORED TO THE COPING			SCREWED JOINTS WITHOUT RAW EDGES VERTICAL PLATENS EVERY 90 CM HORIZONTAL ONES AT 15, 60 AND 90 CM FROM THE PAVEMENT
		90x120. PLATEN 80.8	HANGING		RIVER CONTAINMENT WALLS	SCREWED JOINTS WITHOUT RAW EDGES VERTICAL PLATENS EVERY 90 CM HORIZONTAL ONES AT 30 AND 90 CM ABOVE THE PAVEMENT AND 30 CM BELOW
	DENSE	90x120. PLATEN 80.8	SET INTO THE PAVEMENT	PRIMED AND PAINTED RAL 9007 OR GREEN	WALL TOPS AND DIFFERENCES IN PLANE LEADING TO HARD SURFACES, SUCH AS COBBLESTONES OR EARTH DAMS	SCREWED JOINTS WITHOUT RAW EDGES VERTICAL PLATENS EVERY 10 CM, SET 30 CM INTO THE PAVEMENT HORIZONTAL ONES AT 15 AND 90 CM FROM THE PAVEMENT
			HANGING			SCREWED JOINTS WITHOUT RAW EDGES VERTICAL PLATENS EVERY 10 CM ANCHORED EVERY 90 CM HORIZONTAL ONES 90 CM ABOVE THE PAVEMENT AND 30 CM BELOW
	BARS	BARS DE 16 MM IN DIAMETER	SET INTO PREVIOUSLY PERFORATED COPING	PAINTED WITH MATTE BLACK SYNTHETIC ENAMEL, WITH INDUSTRIAL WAX FINISH, WITH SYNTHETIC IRON-OXIDE RED PIGMENT	ARGANZUELA PARK ENTRANCES	BARS SET IN ZIG-ZAG PATTERN WITH 12 CM SEPARATION IPE WOOD HANDRAIL, 5 CM THICK
	TUBE	TUBE 45.4	SET INTO THE STAIRS	PAINTED IRON-OXIDE BLACK	ANICETO MARINAS SLOPE STAIRS	HANDRAIL AND MAIN SUPPORTS CONTINUOUS WITH WELDED JOINTS INTERMEDIATE SUPPORTS OF 25 MM DIAMETER STEEL ROD, SCREWED TO THE HANDRAIL
		TUBE 90.8	ANCHORED TO THE COPING OR SET INTO THE PAVEMENT	PRIMED AND PAINTED RAL 9007	SALÓN DE PINOS ACCESS RAMPS AND STAIRS	HANDRAIL OF 908 TUBING, 608 VERTICAL PLATENS EVERY 120 CM WELDED JOINTS
	L-PROFILE	L 60.8	ANCHORED TO THE EDGE OF THE PLANK	PRIMED AND PAINTED RAL 9007	OBLIQUE BRIDGE	ZIG-ZAG L PROFILES EVERY 90 CM 60 MM DIAMETER TUBULAR HANDRAIL 3 MM DIAMETER STRANDED STAINLESS-STEEL CABLE RUNNING HORIZONTALLY
WOOD	TREE-TRUNK RAILING	TREE TRUNKS 30 CM IN DIAMETER	SCREWED ONTO SLABS	UNTREATED WOOD	BRIDGES OVER DRY STREAM IN ARGANZUELA PARK'S SLOW PATH	WHOLE, STRIPPED TREE TRUNKS WITH CUT-OUTS FOR ANCHORING PLATES AND FIXING SCREWS

FENCE AND GATE

MATERIAL	TYPE	DIMENSIONS (CM)	ANCHORING	FINISHES	LOCATION	PLACEMENT RULES
STEEL	MESH-OVER-TUBE FENCE	MESH 4M HIGH TUBES 60606 AND 1201006	SET INTO THE PAVEMENT WITH STRIP FOOTING	TUBES PRIMED AND PAINTED WITH RAL 9007 GALVANIZED STEEL DIAMOND MESH	PADDLEBALL COURTS, NORTHERN SALÓN DE PINOS	DIAMOND MESH FACING COURT, TIGHTENED EACH METER HIGH WITH TRIPLE-STRAND STAINLESS-STEEL CABLE, 3 MM IN DIAMETER UPRIGHTS EVERY 2 TO 244 M
	MESH-OVER-TEE-PROFILE FENCE	MESH 15 M HIGH PROFILES T 809	SET INTO THE PAVEMENT WITH BASE NUTS	TEE PROFILES PRIMED AND PAINTED WITH RAL 9007 GALVANIZED STEEL DIAMOND MESH	SPORTS COURTS SAN ISIDRO GARDENS	DIAMOND MESH FACING COURT, TIGHTENED AT TOP AND BOTTOM WITH TRIPLE-STRAND STAINLESS-STEEL CABLE, 3 MM IN DIAMETER UPRIGHTS EVERY 18 M
	PLATEN-AND-TUBE FENCE AND DOORS	FENCING 257 M HIGH TUBES 20602 AND 401203 PLATENS 1207	SET INTO GRANITE SLAB	PRIMED AND PAINTED WITH RAL 9007	CASA DE CAMPO ENTRANCES FROM AVENIDA DE PORTUGAL	WELDED JOINTS VERTICAL TUBES EVERY 19 CM, HORIZONTAL TUBES AT 24 AND 247 CM ABOVE PAVEMENT CURVED PLATENS TO GENERATE A PATTERN FOLDING DOORS WITH PNEUMATIC WHEELS
	BAR FENCE AND DOORS	BARS 20MM IN DIAMETER	SET INTO PREVIOUSLY PERFORATED GRANITE COPING	PAINTED WITH MATTE BLACK SYNTHETIC ENAMEL, WITH INDUSTRIAL WAX FINISH, WITH SYNTHETIC IRON-OXIDE RED PIGMENT	PERIMETER FENCES AND ENTRY GATES TO THE HUERTA DE LA PARTIDA	BARS SET IN ZIG-ZAG PATTERN, 12 CM APART, JOINTED AT THE TOP WITH AN 8 MM STEEL PLATEN
	PLATEN FENCE AND DOORS	PLATENS 20010	SET INTO PREVIOUSLY PERFORATED GRANITE COPING	SET INTO THE PAVEMENT AND WELDED TO FOUNDATION PROFILE	PERIMETER FENCES AND ENTRY GATES TO MATADERO	SCREWED JOINTS WITHOUT RAW EDGES VERTICAL PLATENS EVERY 11 CM ANCHORED EVERY 66 CM HORIZONTAL PLATENS AT 10 AND 222 CM ABOVE THE PAVEMENT CABLE-OPERATED FOLDING DOORS
WOOD AND STEEL	WOOD-PLANK DOORS	WOOD SLATS 210x30 CM, 222 M HIGH	SLIDING DOOR WITH PNEUMATIC WHEELS	UNPLANED IPE WOOD	ENTRY GATES TO MATADERO	SLATS FACING THE OUTSIDE OF THE ENCLOSURE, HELD AT THE TOP AND BOTTOM WITH 9MM-THICK SHEET METAL METAL SUBSTRUCTURE INNER SIDE OF 3 MM-THICK FOLDED SHEET STEEL THE DOORS SLIDE BEHIND EXISTING WALLS OR INTO SOCKETS IN BENT SHEET-METAL WALLS
	MESH-OVER-TRUNK FENCE AND DOORS	MESH 210 M HIGH TRUNKS BETWEEN 3 AND 5 M HIGH AND 12 TO 16 CM IN DIAMETER	SET INTO THE PAVEMENT WITH FOUNDATION WELL	UNTREATED WILD PINE GALVANIZED STEEL MESH	PERIMETER FENCE AND GATES TO ARGANZUELA SPORTS COURTS	TREE TRUNKS OF DIFFERENT HEIGHTS SEPARATED BY DISTANCES BETWEEN 45 AND 180 CM, WITH DIAMOND MESH TIGHTED WITH GALVANIZED CABLE 6 MM IN DIAMETER, FACING THE COURT

LIGHT PLATEN RAILINGS WITH MESH

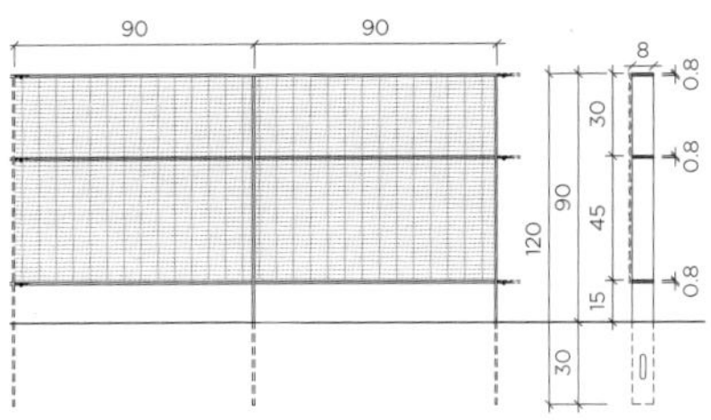

BUILT IN

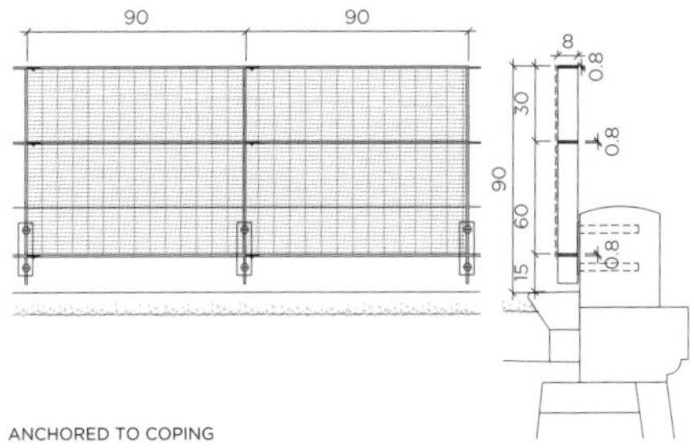

ANCHORED TO COPING

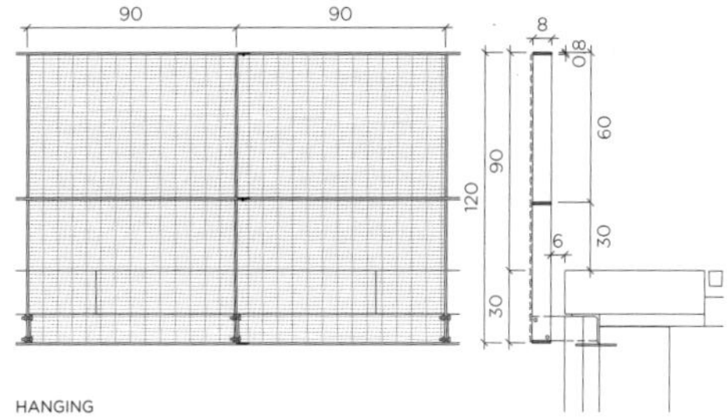

HANGING

DENSE PLATEN RAILINGS AND BARS

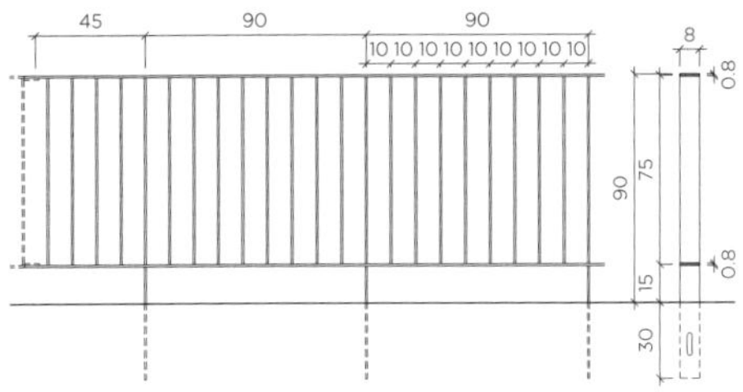

PLATEN RAILINGS - BUILT IN

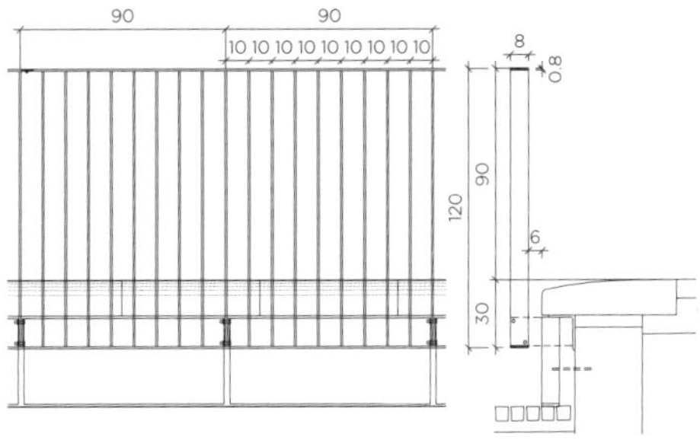

PLATEN RAILINGS - HANGING

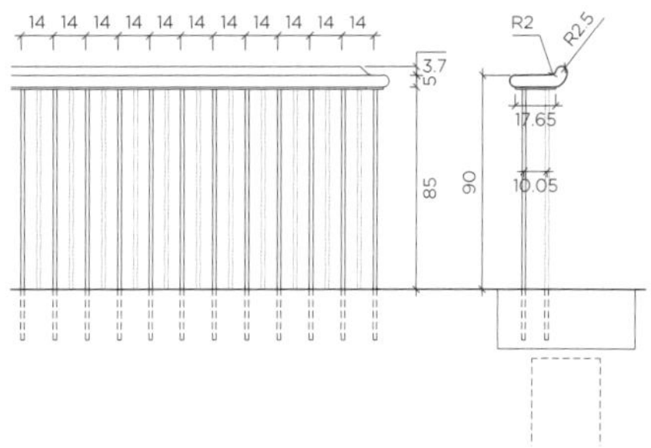

BAR RAILINGS - BUILT IN

PROFILE AND TUBE RAILINGS

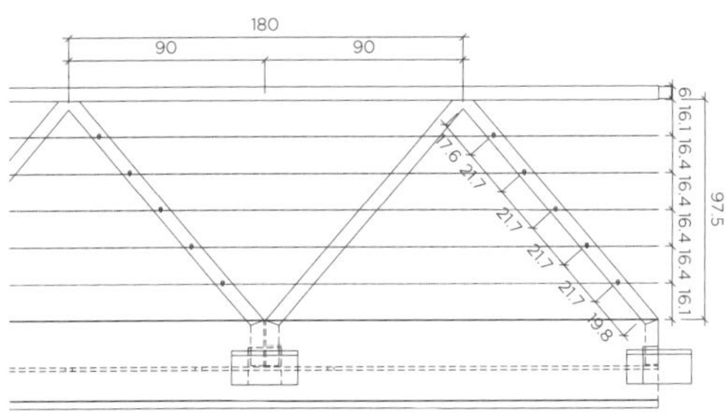

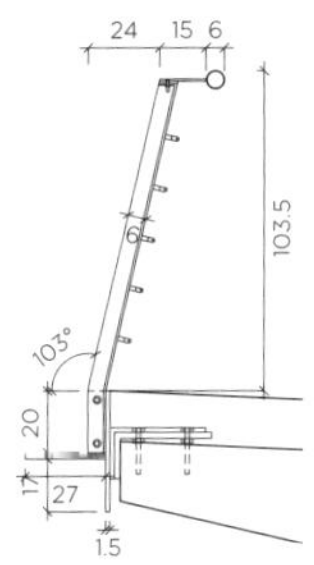

WITH ZIG-ZAG PROFILES

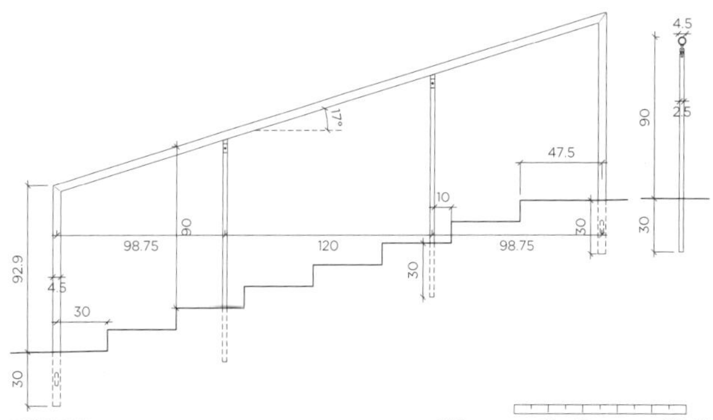

WITH TUBES

1/50 20 40 100 CM

PLATEN AND BAR FENCES AND GATES

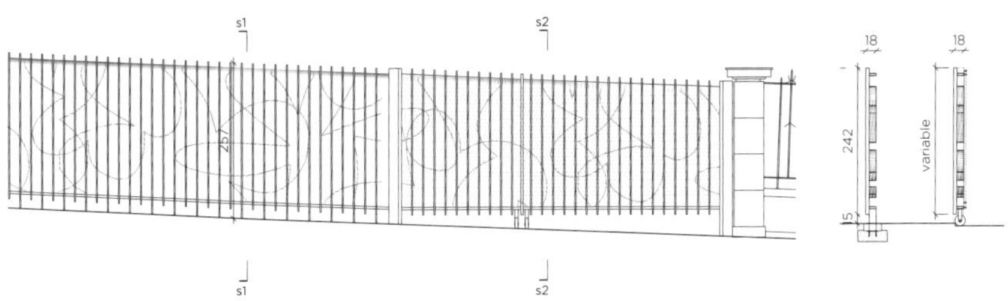

PLATENS AND TUBES

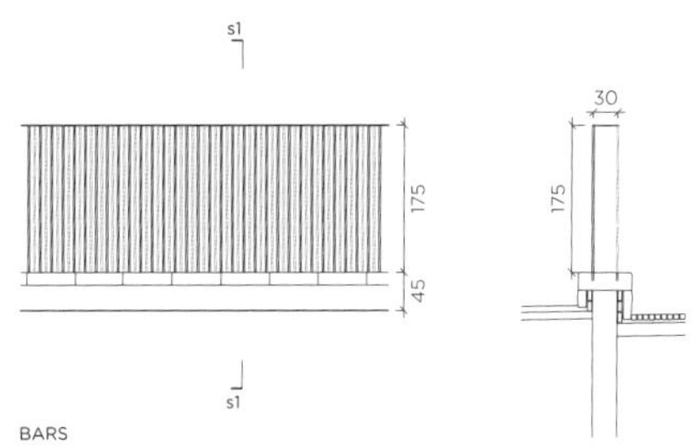

BARS

WOOD AND STEEL FENCES AND GATES

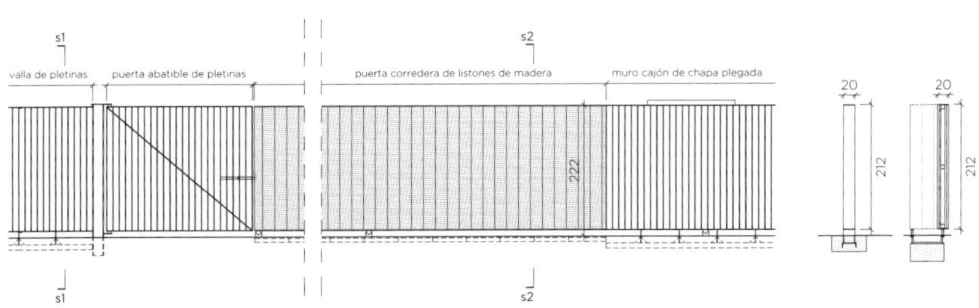

PLATENS AND WOODEN PLANKS

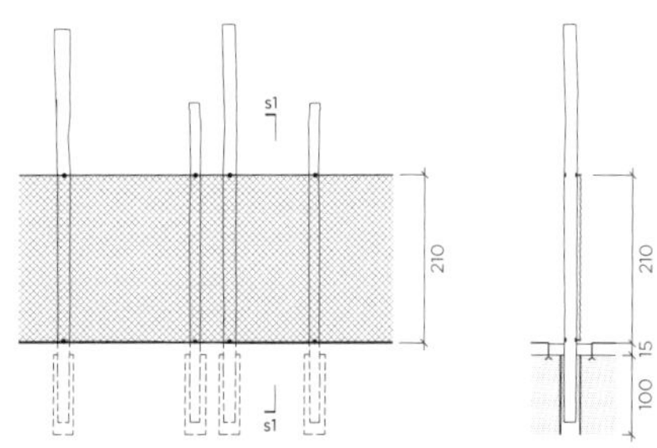

MESH OVER TREE TRUNKS

1/150 1 2 5

URBAN FURNISHING

FAMILY	TYPE/MODEL	DIMENSIONS (CM)	MATERIAL AND FINISH	ANCHORING	LOCATION	PLACEMENT RULES
LAMPOSTS AND LIGHTING	A3 LIRIO COLUMN BY SELUX*	5,40 M HIGH	HEAT-GALVANIZED STEEL COLUMN PAINTED WITH COLOR RAL 9007 PREPARED FOR ANCHORING 1, 2, OR 3 PROJECTORS LIGHTS ARE SELUX MODEL SX A3	INSTALLED UNDER THE PAVEMENT WITH FOUNDATION	CYCLE PATH AND INSIDE PARKS AND GARDENS	COLUMNS EVERY 18-21 M, WITH 1 OR 2 PROJECTORS ON PATHS AND CYCLE PATHS. 3 PROJECTORS WHERE PATHS CROSS AND AT ENTRANCES
	LIRIO OLIVIO MEDIO LIGHTING BY SELUX*	VARIABLE HEIGHT	SELUX MODEL SX A3 LIGHTS	SIDE-MOUNTED PROJECTOR	AREAS UNDER BRIDGES, PUERTA DEL REY AND BUILDINGS	WALL-MOUNTED PROJECTORS EVERY 5 M
	MECA COLUMN MODEL MCP 10002 BY ETM	16 M HIGH	COLUMN COMPOSED OF TWO SEGMENTS OF DIFFERENT LENGTH AND SECTION, MADE OF GALVANIZED SHEET STEEL, PAINTED RAL 9007. PYROS MODEL LIGHTS WITH LONG ARM BY TARGETTI	INSTALLED UNDER THE PAVEMENT WITH FOUNDATION	LIGHTING OF BRIDGES, FOOTBRIDGES AND DAMS. ENTRIES AND BEACH. AREA AROUND ERMITA VIRGEN DEL PUERTO	THE UPPER PART OF THE COLUMNS INCLUDE 3 TRACKS SET AT 120º TO SET THE PROJECTORS
TREE GUIDES	METAL	METAL TUBE Ø 603 MM, 2,5 M LONG	ENAMELED STEEL, COLOR RAL 3016	DRIVEN INTO THE TERRAIN	PUENTE DE SAN ISIDRO GARDENS AND PUENTE OBLIQUO	AT AN ANGLE, STRAPPED TO TREES WITH NYLON TAPE 5 CM WIDE AND 3.8 CM BLACK RUBBER TAPE
	WOOD	ROUND PINE SHAFT, 2.5 M LONG AND 6 CM IN DIAMETER	WOOD UNPAINTED OR BRIGHTLY PAINTED: RAL 1403, 2001, 3007, AND 3016	DRIVEN INTO THE TERRAIN	THROUGHOUT THE PARK	VERTICALLY OR AT AN ANGLE, STRAPPED TO TREES WITH NYLON TAPE 5 CM WIDE AND 3.8 CM BLACK RUBBER TAPE
BENCHES	CAST-METAL BENCH WITH WOOD SLATS	79x105 CM MODULES 1,20 M LONG	CAST-IRON STRUCTURE AND IPE WOOD SLATS	SET INTO THE FOUNDATIONS	GARDENS AT PUENTE DE TOLEDO AND ARGANZUELA PARK	CONTINUOUSLY IN RUNS OF VARIOUS LENGTHS DEPENDING ON THE PATH'S LAYOUT
	"BAN" MODEL BENCH BY DAE, NO BACK	73x43x337 CM	ELONDO WOOD TREATED WITH TEAK OIL OVER 6 MM-THICK GALVANIZED SHEET-STEEL STRUCTURE	SET INTO THE FOUNDATIONS	GARDENS AT VIRGEN DEL PUERTO, SALÓN DE PINOS AND SIDEWALKS	INSTALLED IN GROUPS OF 2 OR 3, COMBINING BENCHES WITH AND WITHOUT BACKS
	"BAN" MODEL BENCH BY DAE, WITH BACK	73x82x337 CM	ELONDO WOOD TREATED WITH TEAK OIL OVER 6 MM-THICK GALVANIZED SHEET-STEEL STRUCTURE BACK OF SAME MATERIAL	SET INTO THE FOUNDATIONS	GARDENS AT VIRGEN DEL PUERTO, SALÓN DE PINOS AND SIDEWALKS	INSTALLED IN GROUPS OF 2 OR 3, COMBINING BENCHES WITH AND WITHOUT BACKS
	WOODEN BACK AND SEAT OVER COPING	66x77 CM TWO BACK MODULES, 178 CM SEAT MODULE, 480 CM	LAMINATED WOOD SEAT. ONE PIECE WOOD BACK. BOTH OF IPE WOOD	THE BACK IS ANCHORED A GALVANAIZED STEEL BAR PAINTED TO RAL 9007. THE SEATING MODULE IS SCREWED TO THE GRANITE	GARDENS AT VIRGEN DEL PUERTO	AT THE END OF A GROUP OF MC42 COPINGS. EACH UNIT CONSISTS OF TWO BACK MODULES AND ONE SEAT MODULE
	GRANITE BENCH	72/60x42x90CM	GRANITE BENCH WITH BUSHHAMMERED FINISH ON VISIBLE SIDES AND VISIBLE EDGES ROUNDED	SET INTO THE PAVEMENT	GLORIETA DE SAN VICENTE	CONTINUOUSLY, WITH SPECIAL END PIECES WITH BUSHHAMMERED SIDES AND ROUNDED EDGES
		60/36x42 CM. RHOMBOIDAL SHAPE WITH SIDES MEASURING 90 AND 85 CM, AND ANGLE OF 45º	GRANITE BENCH WITH BUSHHAMMERED FINISH ON VISIBLE SIDES AND VISIBLE EDGES ROUNDED	SET INTO THE PAVEMENT	PUENTE DE SEGOVIA	CONTINUOUSLY, WITH SPECIAL END PIECES WITH BUSHHAMMERED SIDES AND ROUNDED EDGES
	GRANITE BENCH WITH IPE WOOD BACK	90/70x40x240 CM	GRANITE BENCH WITH SHEARED FINISH. SEAT WITH FLAMED SAWED FINISH. BACK OF IPE WOOD CONSISTING OF THREE GLUED PIECES	BENCH SET INTO THE PAVEMENT. BACK ANCHORED WITH A GALVANIZED STEEL TUBE FACTORY PAINTED TO RAL 9007	SALÓN DE PINOS	IN GROUPS THAT COMBINE BENCHES WITH SINGLE AND DOUBLE BACKS
		120/100x40x280 CM	GRANITE BENCH WITH SHEARED FINISH SEAT WITH FLAMED SAWED FINISH. BACK OF IPE WOOD CONSISTING OF THREE GLUED PIECES	BENCH SET INTO THE PAVEMENT. BACK ANCHORED WITH A GAVANIZE STEEL TUBEFACTORY PAINTED TO RAL 9007	SALÓN DE PINOS	PLACED IN GROUPS THAT COMBINE BENCHES WITH SINGLE AND DOUBLE BACKS
BOLLARDS	HIGH CAST-METAL BOLLARD	HEIGHT 99 CM DIAMETER 75 MM	CAST-IRON IN ONE PIECE.CASTING WITH CHEMICAL MOLDING	SET INTO THE CONCRETE SLAB	THROUGHOUT THE PARK	AT A DISTANCE OF 1.8 M FROM EACH OTHER
	LOW CAST-METAL BOLLARD	HEIGHT 18.6 CM DIAMETER 30 CM	CAST-IRON IN ONE PIECE. CASTING WITH CHEMICAL MOLDING	SET INTO THE CONCRETE SLAB	THROUGHOUT THE PARK	AT A DISTANCE OF 1.2-1.8 M FROM EACH OTHER
	GRANITE BOLLARD	48x26x30 CM	PIECE OF GRANITE SAWED ON ALL SIDES AND FLAMED ON VISIBLE SIDES. VISIBLE EDGES ROUNDED	SET INTO THE CONCRETE SLAB	AVENIDA DE PORTUGAL	AT A DISTANCE OF 1.8 M FROM EACH OTHER
WASTE BASKETS	ON LAMPPOST	122 CM HIGH AND 33 CM IN DIAMETER	CAST-ALUMINUM WASTEBASKET, 9 MM THICK ON POST. EXTRACTABLE METAL-GRILL BASKET WITH HANDLES AND FOLDING CIRCULAR TOP PAINTED WITH OXIRON BLACK COLOUR	SCREWED TO THE LAMPPOST	THROUGHOUT THE PARK	EVERY THREE LAMPPOSTS
	ON POST	108 CM HIGH AND 33 CM IN DIAMETER	CAST-ALUMINUM WASTEBASKET, 9 MM THICK ON POST. EXTRACTABLE METAL-GRILL BASKET WITH HANDLES AND FOLDING CIRCULAR TOP PAINTED WITH OXIRON BLACK COLOUR	SET INTO THE CONCRETE SLAB	THROUGHOUT THE PARK	EVERY 50-60 M
BICYCLE STANDS	STEEL STAND	60.3 TUBING. STAND MEASURES 75x75 CM	GALVANIZED STEEL TUBING	SET INTO THE CONCRETE SLAB	THROUGHOUT THE PARK IN SPORTS, REST AND CULTURAL ZONES	PARALLEL, 80 CM. APART
SIGNAGE	VERTICAL SIGN WITH MAP	75x172x12/40 CM	STRUCTURE WITH OPENWORK STEEL AND ALUMINUM PANELS. COLORS: RAL 9007, RAL 1021, RAL 2000 AND RAL 3016	INSTALLED UNDER THE PAVEMENT WITH FOUNDATION	PARK ENTRANCES	AT MAIN ENTRANCES FROM THE CITY AND AT ALL ENTRANCES TO GROUND LEVEL, RAMPS OR STAIRS. LEFT BANK IN COLOR RAL 1021 AND RIGHT BANK IN COLOR RAL 2000
	VERTICAL SIGN WITHOUT MAP	75x172x12 CM	STRUCTURE WITH OPENWORK STEEL AND ALUMINUM PANELS. COLORS: RAL 1021 AND RAL 3016	INSTALLED UNDER THE PAVEMENT WITH FOUNDATION	CHILDREN'S AND ADULT PLAYGROUNDS, VIEW POINTS, BEACH AND SPORTS COURTS	ALONGSIDE DIFFERENT PARK ACTIVITIES. IN CHILDREN'S PLAYGROUNDS, THEY INDICATE THE RECOMENDED AGES FOR EACH GAME. LEFT BANK IN COLOR RAL 1021 AND RIGHT BANK IN COLOR RAL 2000
	SHEET-STEEL SIGN	WIDTH 60 CM, VARIABLE HEIGHT THICKNESS 8 MM	UNPAINTED SHEET STEEL WITH OPENWORK TEXT	WELDED TO A LAMINATED STEEL PROFILE SCREWED TO THE RIVER RETAINING WALL	RIVER RETAINING WALLS, RIGHT BANK	ACCORDING TO THE LOCATION OF THE RIVER RETAINING WALL PILASTERS, AT A QUARTER OF THE DISTASNCE BETWEEN THEM
	HORIZONTAL MEDALION	Ø 54CM	STAINLESS STEEL PLATE, WITH OPENWORK TEXT	SET INTO THE ASPHALT MICROSURFACING	CYCLE PATH AND RAPID AND SLOW PATHS AT ARGANZUELA PARK	AT THE SIDE OF THE CYCLE PATH, EVERY 50 M. THE REFERENCE POINT WILL BE THE K.P. LOCATED AT THE PUENTE DE LOS FRANCESES ON THE RIGHT BANK. THEY INDICATE THE DISTANCE FROM THE RIVER'S SOURCE AND ON THE LEFT BANK, THE DISTANCE TO ITS MOUTH
WATER FOUNTAINS	WALL FOUNTAIN	3 TAPS AT A HEIGHT OF 110 M	OPERATED BRASS FAUCETS BY SANTA&COLE. POLISHED BRASS SHIELD OVER GRANITE PIECE 12 CM THICK WITH FLAMED FINISH ON VISIBLE SIDE	FAUCETS SET INTO THE GRANITE CLADDING	WALLS AND CHIMNEYS AT SALÓN DE PINOS AND ARGANZUELA PARK	IN GROUPS OF 3 AT THE END OF A WALL OR CHIMNEY, 1.10 M ABOVE GROUND

WOODEN AND GRANITE BENCHES

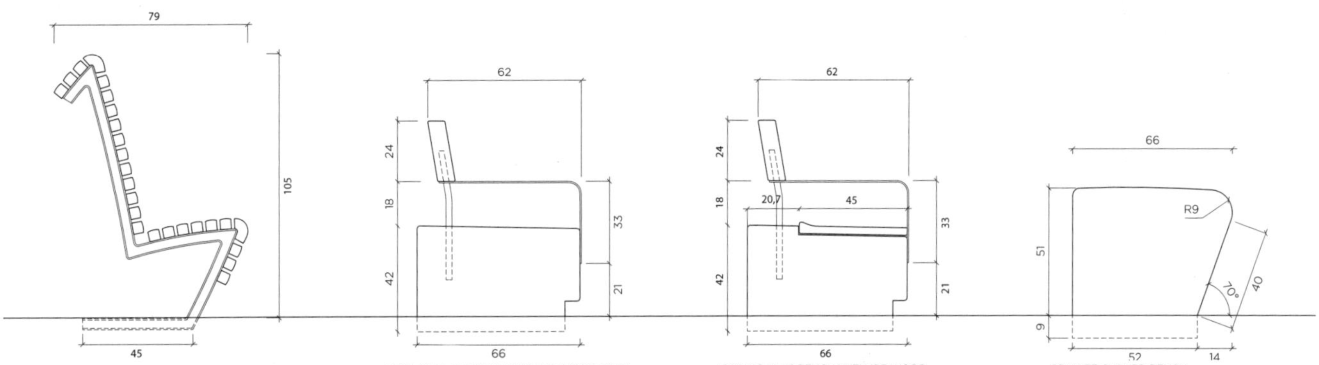

CAST-METAL BENCH WITH IPE WOOD SLATS AND BACK

COPING Mc42 BENCH WITH IPE WOOD BACK

COPING Mc42 BENCH WITH IPE WOOD BACK AND SEAT

GRANITE CURVED BENCH

GRANITE BENCHES

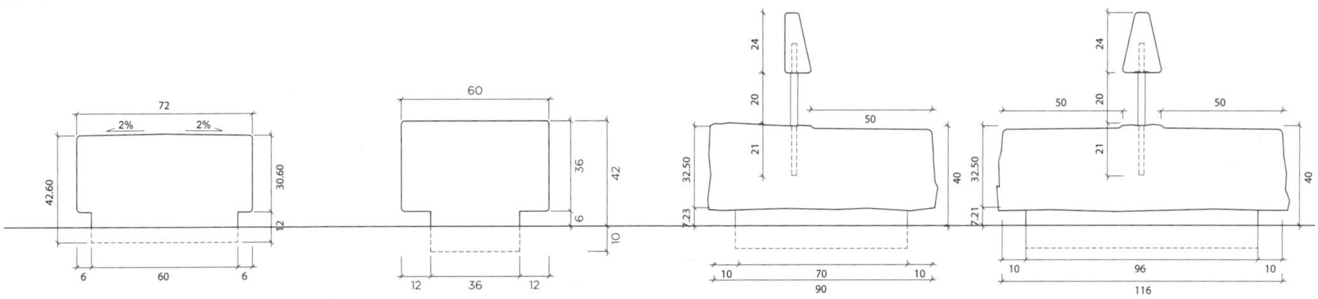

GRANITE BENCH, 90 CM LONG

GRANITE BENCH WITH RHOMBOIDAL SHAPE

SHEARED-GRANITE BENCH WITH IPE WOOD BACK

SHEARED-GRANITE BENCH WITH DOUBLE IPE WOOD BACK

1/30 10 20 50 CM

SIGNAGE

BOLLARDS AND WASTEBASKETS

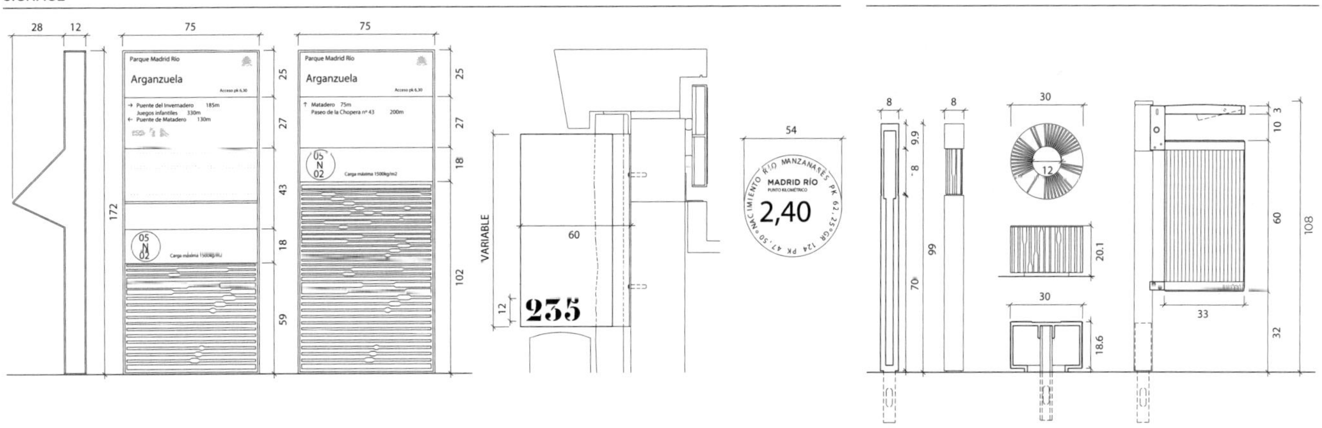

VERTICAL SIGN TYPES 1, 2, AND 3

STEEL SIGNPOST

STEEL-PLATE MEDALLION

1/40 10 20 50 CM

CYLINDRICAL CAST-IRON BOLLARDS

CAST-METAL WASTEBASKET

1/30 10 20 50 CM

STREETLAMPS AND TREE GUIDES

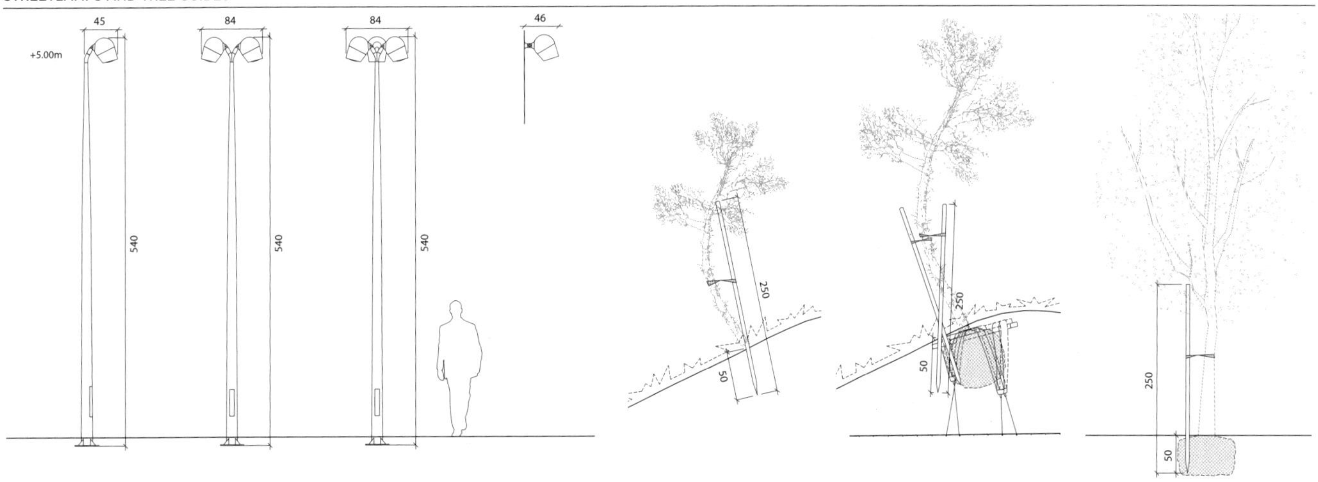

SELUX* COLUMN WITH 1 PROJECTOR

SELUX* COLUMN WITH 2 PROJECTORS

SELUX* COLUMN WITH 3 PROJECTORS

SELUX* WALL-MOUNTED LIRIO OLIVIO MEDIO STREETLIGHT

INCLINED TREE GUIDE

DOUBLE INCLINED TREE GUIDE

VERTICAL TREE GUIDE

1/40 10 20 50 CM

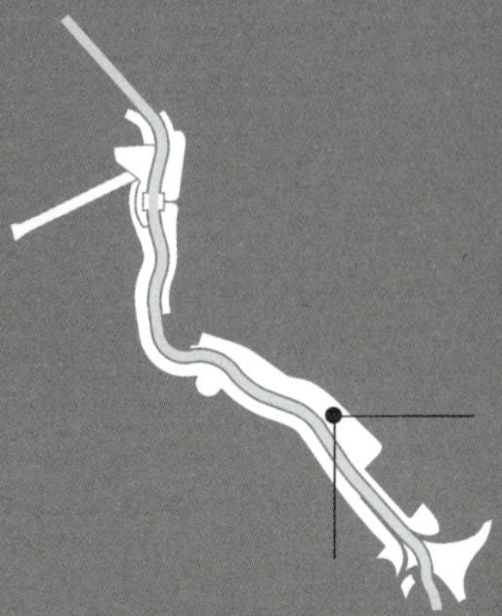

BOOK CREDITS

Editors
Francisco Burgos
Ginés Garrido
Fernando Porras-Isla

Associate editor and text writing
Irene Álvarez de Miranda

Editor of drawings and diagrams
Ana Palancarejo

Photography
Ana Muller

Graphic design
gráfica futura

Additional photography
Ayuntamiento de Madrid, pp. 14, 44-49, 52-59, 96, 112, 296, 304
Comunidad de Madrid, pp. 1-7
Burgos & Garrido Arquitectos and Porras La Casta Arquitectos, pp. 306-309
Twelve buildings at Matadero: Ensamble Studio, p. 249. Carlos Fernández Piñar, pp. 251 and 260. Carlos Roca, p. 253. FG+SG fotografia de arquitectura, p. 255. Miguel de Guzmán, pp. 257 and 261. Vías y construcciones SA, p. 261. Justo Benito, p. 263. Ana Muller, pp. 263 and 269. Luis Díaz Díaz, p. 265. Roland Halbe, p. 267. Javier Callejas, p. 271.

Translation
Wade Matthews

Image processing
Irene Álvarez de Miranda, pp. 1-7, 14, 46, 50, 92, 108, 292, and 320

Photocomposition
Núria Saban

Printing
Brizzolis

Binding
Ramos

Publishing, production, and distribution
Turner
www.turnerlibros.com

ISBN: 978-84-15832-41-6
D.L.: M-22442-2014

Distributed in United States by:
DAP
orders@dapinc.com
www.artbook.com

Distributed in Europe by:
IDEA BOOKS
webform@ideabooks.nl
www.ideabooks.nl

Distributed in United Kingdom by:
ART DATA
orders@artdata.co.uk
www.artdata.co.uk

Spanish edition available

Distributed in Spain by:
Machado Grupo de Distribución
machadolibros@machadolibros.com

Les Punxes Distribuidora
punxes@punxes.es
www.punxes.es

Distributed in Latin America by:
Océano
info@oceano.com
www.oceano.com

We thank the help in the making of this book to:
Pedro Álvarez de Miranda de la Gándara
Sergio Barral García
Yago Bouzada Biurrun
Diego Capellari Dos Santos
Laura Domingo Vera
Juan García-Aráez Martín-Montalvo
Ignacio Gómez de Escauriaza
Diana González Díaz
Belén Hermida Rodríguez
José Luis Infanzón Priore
Javier Malo de Molina Bodelón
Pedro Martín Rivera
Pablo Martínez Muñiz
Luis Mayor Sanz
Sara Medialdea Veiga
Ignacio Núñez Montero
José María Ortega Antón
Santiago Porras Álvarez
Juan Porras-Isla La Casta
Pura Silgo Martínez
Manuel Silgo Martínez
Nieves Vicente Mangas

BASIC PROJECT INFORMATION

Date of the master plan 2006-08
Date of the urban development projects 2006-11
Number of urban development projects drawn up 93

Planned surface area (master plan) 680 hectares

Surface area with urban development projects drawn up 146 hectares

Districts affected 6

Surface area affected by urban development 138 hectares
(50 hectares built over the M-30 tunnels)
Parks and gardens 118 hectares
Sidewalks 13 hectares
Roadways 5 hectares
Other uses 2 hectares

Length of pedestrian and cycle paths 10 km

Number of newly built bridges and walkways 12
Number of renovated dams 7
Number of recycled bridges 1
Number of restored bridges 5
Number of widened bridges 2

Number of trees planted 33,500
Number of bushes planted 460,000

Number of new sports installations 8

Number of restored sports installations 2

Number of children's playgrounds 15
Number of number of bio-health circuits 2

Number of new ornamental fountains 24
Number of restored ornamental fountains 1

Number of buildings constructed 12

PROJECT CREDITS

Architects

Burgos & Garrido Arquitectos
Francisco Burgos, Ginés Garrido

Porras La Casta Arquitectos
Fernando Porras-Isla, Arantxa La Casta

Rubio & Álvarez-Sala Arquitectos
Carlos Rubio, Enrique Álvarez-Sala

with
WEST 8
Adriaan Geuze, Edzo Bindels

[Team director Ginés Garrido]

Coordinating architect

Javier Malo de Molina Bodelón

Architects and landscape architects

Jaime Álvarez Santana, Irene Álvarez de Miranda Silgo, Silvia AydilloZuazo, María Bandrés de Lucas, Rocío Caro Cámara, Sergio del Castillo Tello, Alicia Colmenarejo Navalmoral, Isabel Cuellas Aguilera, Mª Ángeles Fernández García, Carlos Fernández Salgado, Gabriela Galíndez Pisarello, Pablo García Neila, Elena Garicano Fernández, Ignacio Gómez de Escauriaza, Eduardo González Corrales, Gabriela Hombravella López-Dóriga, Miguel ÁngelLópez-Mir, Raquel Lozano Gutiérrez, Marina del Mármol Peces, Rocío Martín Ruiz-Jarabo, Raquel Marugán Burgos, Samir M'hamdi Alaoui, Gemma Montañez Sánchez, Eleucidio Moreno Sanz, Víctor Muñoz Sanz, Matías Nieto Tolosa, Ana Palancarejo Méndez, Susana Paz Rodríguez, Nerea del Pozo Palomo, Jonás Prieto Vivanco, Xosé Ramiro Sánchez Carro, Marco de Simone, Emma Simonsson, Juan Tur McGlone, Alfonso Urbano López de Carrizosa, Elena Verdú Riaza

Christian Dobrick, Enrique Ibáñez González, Joost Koningen,Freek Boerwinkel, Karsten Buchholz, Lennart van Dijk, Juan Figueroa, Michael Gersbasch, Madalén González, Sander Lap, Silvia Lupini, Perry Maas, Ricardo Minghini, Eva Recio, Marta Roy, Carlos Saldarriaga, Alexander Sverdlov, Mariana Siqueira, ShacharZur

Enrique Álvarez-Sala Gómez-Morán, Beatriz Amann Vargas, PierreBanchet, Araceli Barrero González, Jimena Campillo González, Carlos Carnicer Guzmán, Almudena Carro Rejas, Rebeca Caso Donadei, Cristina Cordero Mora, Mateo Fernández Muro, Estela Fernández Rocafull, Juan Galvís Urrecha, Maya González González, Irene Gonzalo Sánchez, Myriam López Rodero, Alberto Martín Hernández, Agustín Martín Salas, Juan José Mateos Bermejo, Mª Ángeles Navarro Arrate, María Ortega Losada, María Perales Vargas, Marina Pereda López-Garma, Bosco Pita Acha, Pedro Pitarch Alonso, Lucía Prado Benayas, Mª Pilar Recio Cámara, Marta Rogado Albert, Javier Rubio Donzé, Beatriz Rubio Montiel, Eduardo Ruiz de Assín, Ricardo Saldías Barreneche , Marta Villamor Blanco

Artist for Greenhouse and Matadero Footbridges
Daniel Canogar

Delegate for Urban Planning and Housing from the Ayuntamiento de Madrid
Pilar Martínez López

Technicians from the Ayuntamiento de Madrid responsible for public works
General Coordinators
Manuel Arnaiz Ronda, Beatriz Lobón Cerviá, Carlos Baztán Lacasa
General Directors
Cristina Conde de Beroldingen, Javier Hernández Morales, Ana Perpiñá Carrera, José María Ortega Antón
General Subdirectors
José Luis Infanzón Priore, Carlos Lasheras Merino, Federico Manzarbeitia Arambarri, Emilio Martínez Vidal, Jorge Presa Matilla
Technical Specialists
Camino Álvarez Muñoz, Rafael Castejón León, Guillermo de la Calzada Rodríguez-Porrero, Emilio Esteras Martín, Mercedes Jack Páramo, Rosa Olivé Barrau, Federico Rodríguez Rodríguez,Teresa Riestra Rodriguez-Losada
Technicians
Ángel Arias Sánchez, Lucio Lorenzo Benito, Enrique Montilla Seguín, Ramón Suso Rodríguez, Cristina Pérez Sánchez, Juan Ortigosa Zamorano, Javier Viñas Sánchez

Consultants
General engineering, installations, and structures
TYPSA

Special structures
Fhecor (tunnel slab testing)
Gestión de Proyectos (testing of extant elements and bridges)

Bridge structures
Fhecor (Almuñécar footbridge, puente Oblícuo, Matadero, and Greenhouse footbridges)
Gestión de Proyectos (puente del Rey, rehabilitation of dams, North Pontoon, Canal footbridge, puente de Bolas)
Cesma Ingenieros (Y-shaped footbridge)
NB 35 (Princesa footbridge)

Hydraulic calculations
Pilar Jaén

Environmental evaluation
Tecnoma

Lighting
ALS, Architectural Lighting Solutions

Soil science and forestry
Fundación Conde Valle Salazar [ETS. Ingenieros de Montes de Madrid]

Botany
SC Paisajismo, Maria Jesús Franco, Fundación Conde Valle Salazar [ETS. Ingenieros de Montes de Madrid]

Aquatic biology
Grupo de Enxeñaría da Auga e do Medio Ambiente, E.T.S.I.C.C.P. Universidade de A Coruña

Historical cartography
Departamento de Ideación Gráfica y Arquitectónica [ETS. Arquitectura de Madrid]

Playgrounds
Richter Spielgeräte, BDU

Onamental fountain technology
Imes Api, Somhidros

Rowing Installations
Federación Madirleña de Remo, Astilleros Amilibia S.L.

Climbing Installations
Federación Madrileña de Montañismo

Legal advice and urban affairs
Bufete Barrilero

Graphic design
gráfica futura

Digital technology advisor
Manuel Capón Mouriz

Additional computer graphics
Hpal

Additional models
Blanca Pérez, Gilberto Ruiz , Nivel+Maquetas, Gregorio Manzano, Miguel Calabuch

Fountain technology
Lumiartecnia Internacional, IMESAPI and Somhidros

Metal Technology
Belén Jack Sanz-Cruzado, Alberto Iglesias García

The architects responsible for the Madrid Río project offer special thanks for the inestimable cooperation, drive, and support, without which this work would not have been possible, to Pilar Martínez López, and also to Cristina Conde de Beroldingen, Juan Manuel Fernández Alonso, Luis Fernández-Galiano, Rosa García Colmenero, Javier Hernández Morales, José Luis Infanzón Priore, Alicia Moreno Espert, José María Ortega Antón, and Ana Perpiñá Carrera.

This book was written and illustrated between May 2011 and April 2014.

It was printed on 150g. Magno Satin and 150g. offset Pioneer papers.
The cover is made with 300g. Invercote G SBS board.
The texts were printed in fonts from the Gotham and Mercury families.

Each copy includes a bookmark with a key that allows readers to correctly interpret the drawings.

There are two editions in two languages, with 2,400 copies in Spanish and 1,380 copies in English.